Sight Readings

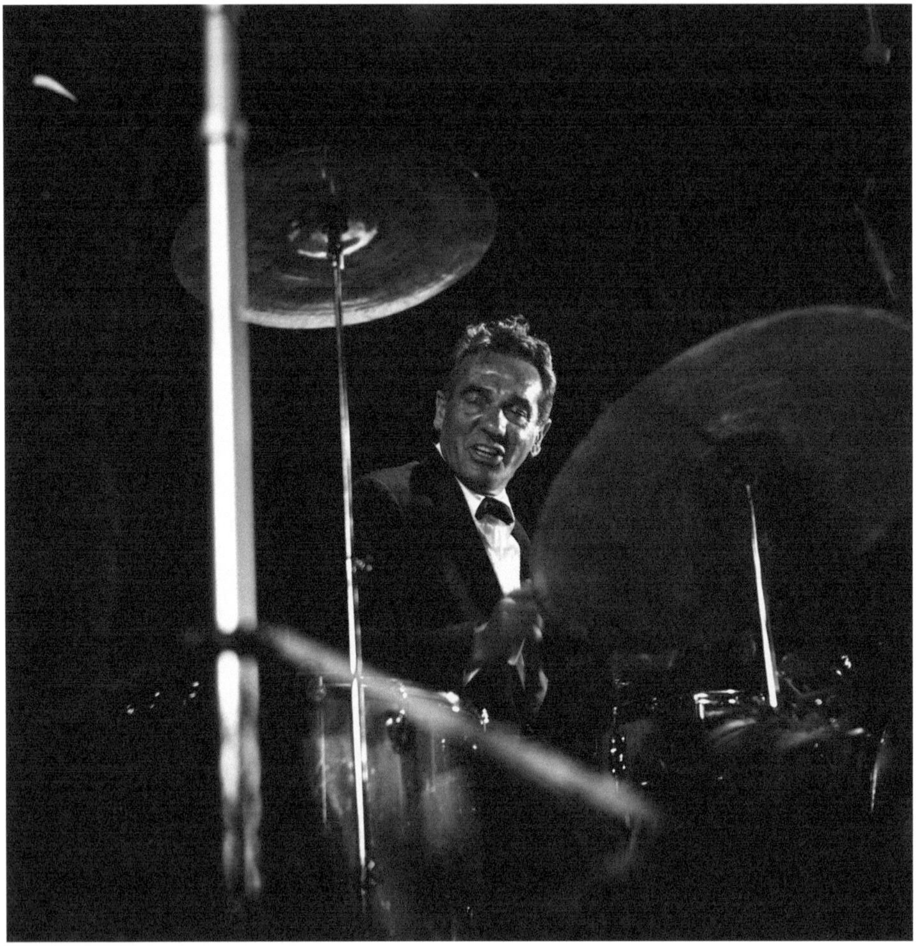

Sight Readings
Photographers and American Jazz, 1900–60

Alan John Ainsworth

Foreword by
Darius Brubeck

intellect
Bristol, UK / Chicago, USA

First published in the UK in 2022 by
Intellect, The Mill, Parnall Road, Fishponds, Bristol, BS16 3JG, UK

First published in the USA in 2022 by
Intellect, The University of Chicago Press, 1427 E. 60th Street, Chicago, IL 60637, USA

A catalogue record for this book is available from the British Library

Copy editor: Newgen Knowledge Works
Cover designer: Holly Rose
Cover photo: Ted Williams. *Gene Krupa.* Newport Jazz Festival. 1958. Iconic Images.
Managing editor: Tim Mitchell
Layout Designer: Aleksandra Szumlas
Typesetting: Newgen Knowledge Works

Hardback ISBN 978-1-78938-421-5
Paperback ISBN 978-1-83595-056-2
ePDF ISBN 978-1-78938-422-2
ePUB ISBN 978-1-78938-423-9

This is a peer-reviewed publication

In memory of my father,
Eric Ainsworth (1926–2019)
and for my mother,
Irene Ainsworth

Contents

Illustrations

Foreword

Darius Brubeck

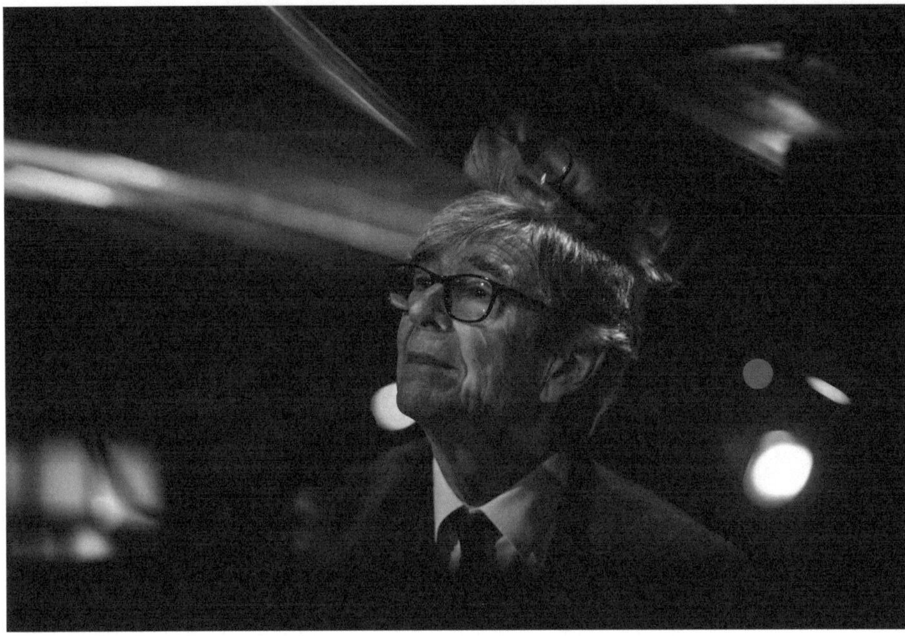

Photo: Darius Brubeck. Monika S. Jakubowska, @msj_photos.

The Kodak Song

The usual preconcert conversation about stage photography goes: "Do you mind flash?" Answer: "I don't, but please ask them to keep it to the first or last number and no shooting during ballads." Imagine exploring the darker shadings of unrequited love in a song like "Body and Soul"; you are unconsciously holding your breath in deep concentration and—claff! As a pro, all you can do is pretend not to notice so that maybe the audience won't, but you've been yanked back into performing the music rather than living it. Conversely, a volley of flashes near the end of a concert has a galvanizing effect on players and audience alike, marking the concert as an *event*. The photographer, and only the photographer, has the power to create an image *outside of time* that can be printed in newspapers and posted on the internet and stay there forever.

Taking pictures isn't as easy as it looks. In my experience it is rare indeed that all four members of my quartet are identifiable in a concert shot. (From stage left, my back is to the camera; from out front, the cymbal is in front of the drummer's face; from stage right, the bass player is blocking me or I'm just too far away—and so on.) Needing an album cover, a poster, a printed program, an agency brochure means organizing a photo shoot. In times past the inevitable result was a dignified but boring 8½ × 11 "glossy" to pack into a publicity kit or mail directly to fans. Thanks to digital images this convention is obsolete, but we still need to have our pictures taken—not by people wanting selfies—but by professionals like those whose work is exhaustively contextualized, analyzed, and in some cases rescued from obscurity as in this comprehensive book.

A merely transactional account belies the collaborative and symbiotic relationship of jazz musicians and photographers, but I wanted to reveal the unpromising, even adversarial, ways that musicians encounter photographers in their professional milieu. It is to the credit of photographers that so much information, human interaction, and sheer beauty has been captured in their work. Frankly, I've lived with jazz photography my whole life but never *thought* about it until reading Alan John Ainsworth's eye and mind-opening critique of photographic history.

I made a casual audit of the photography books I own and the pictures on my walls. At this moment I have ten jazz photography books (by the way, that's not very many) including staples such as *Black Beauty, White Heat* (Driggs & Lewine), and *A Pictorial History of Jazz* (Keepnews & Grauer), which are compilations of photos by many photographers presented as history, biography, and visual archives of jazz in general. Also books by individual photographers like *Jazz Street* (Stock & Hentoff), *Jazz Photographs of the Masters* by Jacques Lowe, and Polish photographers Andrzej Dabrowski and Ryszard Horowitz highlight the photographer-as-artist. Two collections by South African photographers, Jurgen Schadeberg's *Jazz, Blues & Swing* and Chris Albertyn's *Keeping Time: 1964–1974, The Photographs and Cape Town Jazz Recordings of Ian Bruce Huntley*, are crucial for reconstructing neglected biographies and histories. These and other South African photographers show us who played where and with whom—knowledge that would otherwise vanish with living memory.

On my studio walls, I have Gjon Mili's black-and-white photo of my father at the piano as a student watched over by his mentor, French composer Darius Milhaud, who is surrounded by members of the Dave Brubeck Octet playing their instruments. On the opposite wall is a color photo of Dave and Wynton Marsalis taken at the Newport Jazz Festival by John Abbott in 2005. Dave is seated, and Wynton stands with one elbow on the piano, trumpet in hand. The background is a sea of people receding to the actual sea stretching to the sky. Mili's picture (although smokeless) *looks like* jazz photography; black-and-white, high-contrast, dramatically lit, tightly composed, and carefully processed. Abbott looks quite natural—what you would have seen had you been there, but this too is jazz photography.

Of course, *Sight Readings* is not a picture book like the ones I've collected over the years. Alan John Ainsworth not only commands the historical breadth and analytical depth of his own subject, but he also makes effective use of up-to-date jazz criticism and critical theory.

Which leads one to ask whether a photo of a boy of about 10 leaning against a tree counts as jazz photography. What if the photographer was Paul Desmond, and the boy was me? As a keen amateur photographer and celebrated wit, "Uncle Paul" always referred to "Someday My Prince Will Come" as the Kodak song.

Acknowledgments

I am grateful to the archivists and librarians who have patiently guided me through their collections and made reproductions available: Kira Kikla (Louisiana State Museum), Ann Sindelar (Western Reserve Historical Society), Tad Hershorn and Elizabeth Surles (Institute of Jazz Studies, Rutgers University), Richard Boursy (Gilmore Music Library, Yale University), Ricky Riccardi (Louis Armstrong House Museum), Keith Rice (Tom & Ethel Bradley Centre, California State University, Northridge), Larry Applebaum (Library of Congress), Adam Lyon (Museum of History and Industry Seattle), David Nathan (National Jazz Archive, Loughton, Essex), Molly Haigh (UCLA Library Special Collections), Jessica L. Wood and Tom Lisanti (New York Public Library), Steven Galbraith (Rochester Institute of Technology), Carl Fuldner (Yale University Art Museum), Crystal Willer (Oberlin Conservatory Library), Brigitte Billeaudeaux (University of Memphis Library), Laurel Mitchell (Carnegie Museum of Art), and the staff at the Schomberg Centre, New York Public Library.

As an independent writer I have been extremely fortunate in that friends working in academic institutions have been willing to devote time to my questions as well as commenting on early drafts. I owe a debt to Benjamin Cawthra, whose pioneering book *Blue Notes in Black and White: Photography and Jazz* was an inspiration as well as setting me on the road that eventually led to *Sight Readings*. Professor Cawthra's often penetrating analysis addressed the work of the key names in jazz photography and carefully analyzed the impact of their powerful images in national media, jazz magazines, and as album cover artwork. Building on this work necessitated that I look beyond his choices of photographers and explore jazz images from a perspective that complemented this important book—an ambition which he generously encouraged.

Other scholars who have been generous with their time and advice include Michael Berkowitz, Krin Gabbard, Heather Pinson, Tom Perchard, Alyn Shipton, Larry Ray, John Gennari, and Chuck Hersch. Tim Wall, Nick Gebhardt, Tony Whyton, and Nic Pillai at Birmingham City University offered ideas and advice, as well as being hospitable to an interloper. After his initial surprise at being asked about jazz, Professor Charles Spence generously shared ideas arising from his cross-modal research in the Department of Experimental Psychology at the University of Oxford. Ramsey Castaneda and Amanda Quinlan were kind enough to share their research findings on the use of photographs in jazz educational texts. At a low point during the preparation of this book, my doctoral supervisor Simon Frith rescued me with some extremely helpful suggestions. I am extremely grateful to Simon for his help and assistance this second time around.

Several other researchers provided me with ideas and advice, and I would like to acknowledge in particular Maxine Gordon, Robert Lawson-Peebles, Paul Archibald, Isaac Maupin, Catherine Tackley, Paul von Blum, Fernando Ortez de Urbina, Dr Michael Pritchard FRPS, Fernando Ortiz de Urbina, and

John March. Peter Blecha, Earnestine Lovell Jenkins, Janis Bultman, and Jessica Ferber were very generous in sharing information from their research into the work of Al Smith, Hooks Brothers, James J. Kriegsmann, and Bob Campbell, respectively. Hank O'Neal provided me with ideas, information, and lines of enquiry sufficient for a follow-up book and was as hospitable to me as I subsequently learned he is to all visitors to his New York apartment.

I have benefited from discussing my ideas with the family and friends of a number of the photographers about whom I have written in this book: Patricia Willard (for information about Howard Morehead and Bob Douglas), Michael Randolph ("PoPsie" Randolph), Rosalind Withers (Ernest Withers), Diane Lara and Lorraine Adams (Harry Adams), Tanya Kalischer (Clemens Kalischer), Clyde Adams (Murray Korman), Gene Kimball and Dan Mortesen (Fred Plaut), Deborah Charles (Roland Charles), Michael Cuscuna (Francis Wolff), Adrienne Williams (Ted Williams), Steve Gottlieb (Bill Gottlieb), David Berger (Milt Hinton), Christopher Willoughby (Bob Willoughby), and James J. Kriegsmann Jr. (James J. Kriegsmann). Joan Bertin was most kind in helping to identify ownership of photographs by George Maillard Kesslère. Donald Bernard spoke to me about his involvement with Roland Charles and the photographers associated with the Black Gallery in Los Angeles. Among the active photographers with whom I have discussed this project the following were more than generous: Herb Snitzer, Veryl Oakland, Jimmy Katz, Enid Farber, John Loengard, Lourdes Delgardo, Gerald Cyrus, David Williams, Jay Maisel, Chuck Fishman, and Leo Howard Lubow.

I am grateful to Susannah Straughan for her editorial input and thoughtful observations. For a while I was assisted by Lucy Brown who was an able and enthusiastic research assistant.

There remain a few special thanks to make. I was delighted when Darius Brubeck accepted an offer to contribute a foreword to this book. Darius's comments remind us that the musician's perspective on photography can provide new insights and is all too often overlooked. I am also particularly grateful to Peter Vacher who was unstinting in his encouragement of this project. Peter gave up an enormous amount of time to listen to my ideas and guide me through his collection of jazz photographs toward the images that helped to tell my story. Along the way he took every opportunity to share his deep knowledge of jazz and to recount his encounters with many of the great musicians he himself interviewed.

Susan Sontag warned that "to interpret is to impoverish, to deplete the world." If I have managed to sidestep this danger it is because these friends and acquaintances encouraged me to look beyond interpretation by keeping at the forefront of my mind the remarkable experience of engaging with jazz as music.

Reproduction of photographs

Every effort has been made to secure approval for reproduction of all the photographs in this book from copyright owners and archives. I would be grateful if any errors of miscrediting could be drawn to the attention of the publisher so that they can be corrected in future editions.

Previous publications

Early versions of parts of this book have been previously published as shown below:

Ainsworth, Alan John. "Early New Orleans Band Photography." *Jazz Research Journal* 11, no. 1 (2017): 28–61.

Ainsworth, Alan John. "Herb Snitzer-American Photography." *Jazz Journal* 70, no. 9 (2017): 12–13.

Ainsworth, Alan John. "Photographic Representations of Jazz: Testimonial Advertising in Down Beat, 1938–48." *Jazz Research Journal* 11, no. 2 (2018): 111–52.

Ainsworth, Alan John. " 'A Private Passion': The Jazz Photography of Bob Douglas." *Southern California Quarterly,* 101, no. 3 (2019): 317–38.

A Note on Language

"Photographer" does not connote gender assumptions and so I have been able to avoid the ungainly neologisms sometimes introduced to avoid gendered generics. Avoiding gendered pronouns is more challenging: most jazz photographers we currently know about were men but there were women involved, so both "he" and "she" are in their own ways inaccurate. I have opted for plural nouns and pronouns, using an article instead of a pronoun, using the relative pronoun "who" and recasting the sentence to avoid the need for a pronoun (the *Chicago Manual of Style*'s recommended "invisible gender neutrality"). These forms are preferred to repeating pronouns ("s/he", "his or her", "he or she") or nouns ("slash constructions" he/she) and the use of "they" as a universal singular pronoun.

Perhaps there are more women jazz photographers whose work is yet to be explored. Several researchers have spotted a female photographer emerging from one of the 52nd Street clubs as captured around 1948 by William Gottlieb (Figure 1). There have been suggestions that the photographer was Dickie Chapelle (Georgette Louise Meyer), the renowned war photographer and the first female war correspondent to be killed in Vietnam. Is this Dickie Chapelle? And was she photographing jazz? It is a fascinating thought and perhaps her work in this field might surface at some future date—as might that of other women photographers.

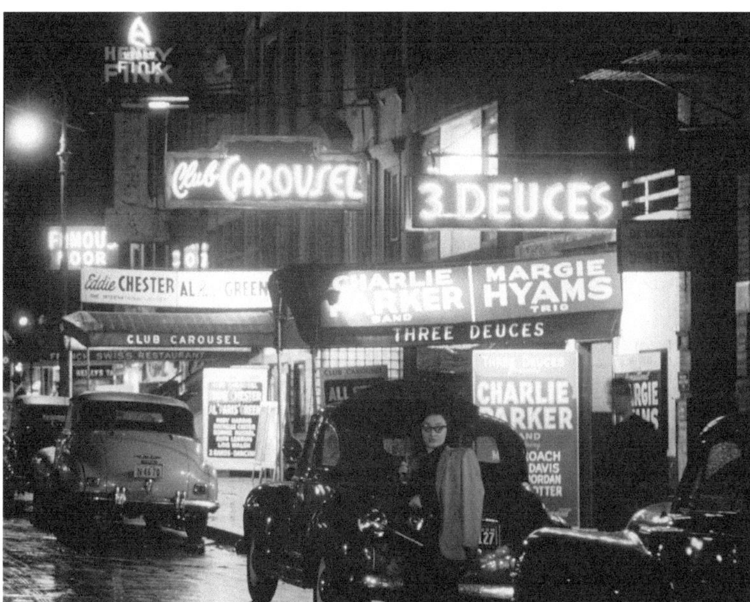

Figure 1: William Gottlieb. *52nd Street*. New York. *c.*1948.
Ed Gottlieb/Library of Congress.

Introduction
Approaching Jazz Photography

It is now almost ten years since I embarked on the research that eventually led to this book. My interest in the history of jazz photography grew out of my work as a practicing music photographer, an activity that brought me into close contact with players and afforded valuable insight into the world of the professional jazz musician. As a practitioner I naturally turned to the masters of the genre for ideas and inspiration. What started as a search for ideas quickly developed into a quest to understand the work of these photographers—why they made the images they did, what the photographs meant to them, and what they tell us about the music and musicians. Over the course of my research these lines of enquiry have been the subject of many twists and turns. Throughout the period however I found myself returning to a small number of concerns that eventually coalesced to form the central problematic of this book.

Among the earliest of these concerns was my steadily growing unease about the way in which the jazz photography "tradition" appeared to resolve into the work of a small number of mainly white art photographers. There appeared to be little critical scrutiny of photography in the jazz literature and the images made by these photographers are widely accepted as "iconic" representations. As my research progressed I increasingly became aware of jazz imagery from photographers rarely acknowledged and, on occasions, almost completely absent from the jazz literature: African American photojournalist on the west coast, in New York and the Midwest, studio portraitists, early twentieth-century émigré photographers, and the modernist exiles of the 1930s, not to mention the collections of amateur photographers I call in this book the "jazz family album." Coming from a wide range of social and racial backgrounds and bringing very different life experiences to jazz from those of the white photographers, I was struck by how eclectic "jazz photographers" in reality were.

That jazz writers should canonize a cohort of photographers is surprising. Scholars are now well aware that jazz, to use John Gennari's phrase, is a very big story, a hugely diverse musical form whose history of almost unbroken evolution and change is now seen less as a linear evolution of stylistic developments and more as a fractured and contested terrain involving the tensions of ethnic, racial, regional, social, and economic differences.[1] Like any big story, no one telling seems able to capture the totality of the narrative, raising the question as to whether we are entitled to speak of a unified jazz photography tradition.

Two photographs illustrate this diversity. The first (Figure 2), taken by Charles Peterson around 1946 in the New York club Eddie Condon had opened the previous year, shows the guitarist with Gene Krupa, Lou McGarity, and Wild Bill Davidson, members of that coterie of musicians attracted to the freedoms of jazz and a lifestyle offering escape from the confines of their conventional white American backgrounds. This image, like much of Peterson's work, vividly

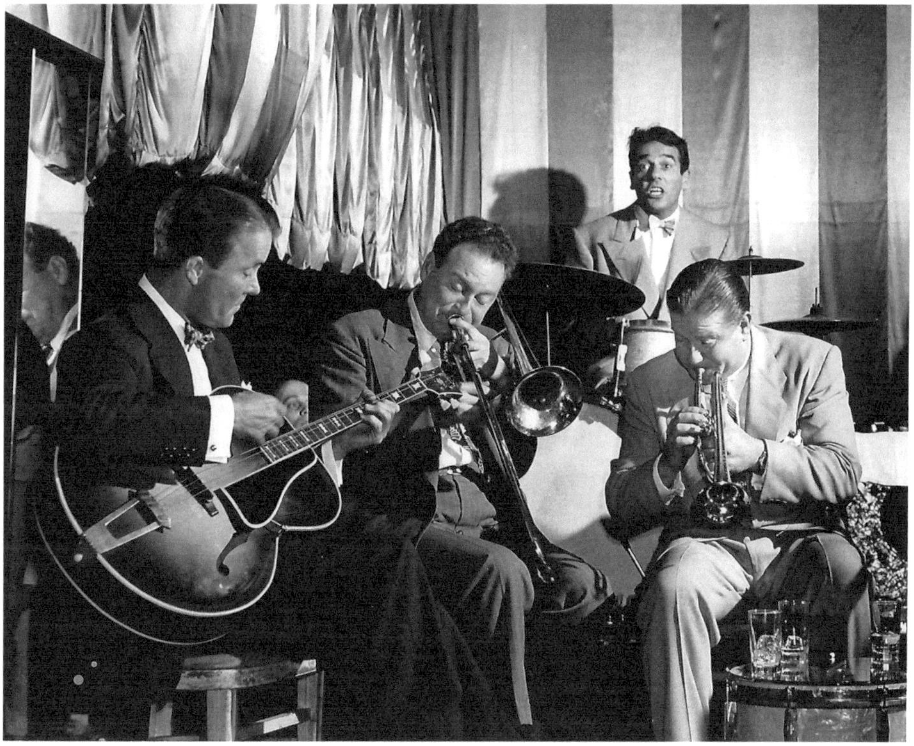

Figure 2: Charles Peterson. *Eddie Condon, Gene Krupa, Lou McGarity, and Wild Bill Davidson.* New York. *c.*1946.
Don Peterson.

conveys a sense of the bohemian community inhabited by freewheeling, hard-drinking white jazz musicians in east coast clubs in the 1930s and 1940s: informal, even chaotic, backstage socializing or jam sessions where musicians, in shirt sleeves and with ties undone, are squeezed into dark spaces, drink flows freely, and cigarette smoke fills the rooms. Peterson's crowded scenes are replete with expressions, gestures, and dress styles signifying "hot jazz" and the life that goes with it, an assertive white male world in which players strived to outdo each other with explosions of hard-blowing technical virtuosity in unrestrained cutting sessions. Jazz for these musicians offered a sense of liberation and camaraderie even if, as Patrick Burke observes, "it was constructed in an environment of exclusion and misrepresentation in which women and African American men were virtually absent."[2]

On the other side of the country Charles Williams, the official photographer for the black-owned *California Eagle* and the *Los Angeles Sentinel,* captured a scene that could not be more different (Figure 3). Close up to the stage at the 1948 Cavalcade of Jazz in Los Angeles he made a photograph of the International Sweethearts of Rhythm, the first integrated all-female band in the United

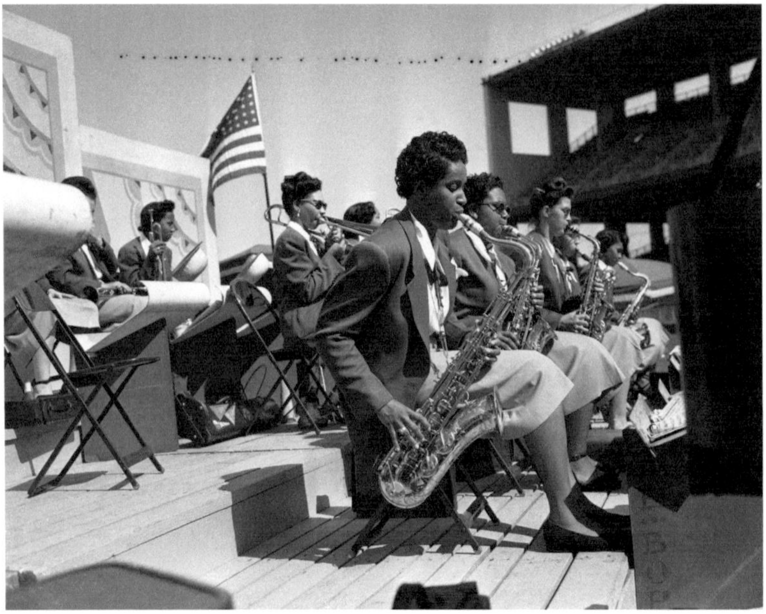

Figure 3: Charles Williams. *Cavalcade of Jazz*. Los Angeles. 1948.
Tom and Ethel Bradley Centre for African American Arts, California State University, Northridge/ Charles Williams Collection.

States. The original members of this band had met at Piney Woods Country Life School, an institution for poor African American orphans established in Mississippi by Carl van Vechen's father. Featuring some of the best performers of the day, the Sweethearts played predominantly swing jazz on the national circuit. As female musicians in a male world, they were frequently dismissed as a novelty, although with arrangements by Eddie Durham and Jesse Stone the Sweethearts attracted large crowds as they toured coast to coast, often sleeping and rehearsing in their bus when southern discrimination prohibited the use of hotels and restaurants. During the 1939–45 war, the band attracted a large following among African American servicemen, and at the end of the conflict they embarked on a six-month tour of Germany and France, the first such tour to be undertaken by black women. Recalling the Sweethearts, Leonard Feather emphasized how diverse, if occasionally mutually uncomprehending, the world of jazz could sometimes be: "if you are white, whatever your age, chances are that you have never heard of the Sweethearts."[3]

What are we to make of the contrasts between these two almost contemporaneous photographs? In terms of generation, race, location, presentation, style, and repertoire, the players seem as far removed from each other as it is possible to be. It is hardly surprising that there is little agreement among jazz scholars about the definition of the jazz tradition; some even question whether there is such a tradition.

Similar questions might be raised about a jazz *photography* tradition, a term encountered frequently in jazz texts but whose freighted construction is rarely questioned.[4] Whereas Peterson's photographs appear regularly in jazz writing Williams's work is rarely mentioned. Omissions of this nature are found so frequently that it is difficult to avoid the conclusion that for most enthusiasts, commentators, and scholars the jazz photography tradition comprises white art photographers who followed Peterson's "lead"—Gjon Mili, Marvin Koner, Burt Glinn, Art Kane, Bob Willoughby, Robert Parent, Don Hunstein, Dennis Stock, Lee Tanner, and Herb Snitzer—while most consider William Gottlieb, Herman Leonard, William Claxton, and Francis Wolff to be the core of the tradition. Joe Maita provides an example from the enthusiast community:[5]

> *For many of us who revere jazz music—especially those fortunate enough to have grown up during the era of the 12 x 12 record album jacket and coffee table photography books—the images of great musicians taken by photographers like William Gottlieb, Herman Leonard, William Claxton and Lee Tanner provided ample inspiration to explore the music and culture they so passionately chronicled.*

Among jazz scholars Benjamin Cawthra credits Charles Peterson and Gjon Mili with the "launch of a jazz photographic tradition" while Tony Whyton's account of the power of the photographic image to construct the media image of jazz references only Francis Wolff and omits mention of those practitioners whose work might reasonably be argued *not* to conform to this description.[6] If, as Henry Louis Gates has observed, "a canon is often represented as the 'essence' of the tradition, indeed as the marrow of the tradition,"[7] the canonization of white photographers in this way seems hard to justify when so many others appeared to have made a contribution.

Yet whatever the background or practice of these photographers, a careful reading of their notes, memoirs, and biographies, or interviews and contemporary accounts of their practices, reveals that a common affinity with jazz spanned the differences. This affinity, which often developed at an early stage and remained with these photographers as their careers took them in other directions, made jazz a meaningful and continual form of engagement rooted in what was believed to be the cultural significance of the music; and it is clear that many of these photographers found meaning in the work absent from the general run of photographic assignments. In his sweeping history of photography, André Rouillé identified the dialectic between what he termed "photographie-document" and "photographie-expression" as the key to understanding the developmental trajectory of the medium while simultaneously confirming the "vitality," "force," and agency of the photographic act.[8] Adapting this thesis, a fundamental pillar of the argument developed in this book is that the history of photography is marked not so much by the transcendence of one mode but by the continuing tension between the two; and that it is precisely here that license for the exercise of agency in the photographic act emerges. Whatever their different voices, these photographers held onto a shared belief in the need to record and interpret—to *document* and *express*—the practitioners and culture of a musical form that they believed said something of personal significance about the country and their place within it.

It became clear then that differences between photographers' approaches to jazz were rooted not so much in the formal qualities of photographs but rather in the *nature of the affinity* between photographer and subject. I realized that I wanted to not only embrace the diversity of jazz photography but also explain a common affinity impelling photographers toward the jazz subject that emerges as a deeply personal choice intimately related to questions of personal self-understanding and identity. If the work of individual photographers was to be understood, it seemed necessary to address the nature of the subjective in photographic production, an enquiry that opens up questions about photographic agency. Understanding the photographers' own objectives and how they were shaped and expressed visually became a key objective of my research. I approach this by making the case for photographic agency.

I. Agency and jazz photography

Human agency does not unfold in a vacuum. This book therefore proceeds from the idea that the images these photographers made stood at the intersection between artistic subjectivity and the broader context of a changing world. The relationship between subjectivity and context—between agency and structure—has been the subject of extensive theoretical enquiry in social and cultural studies and I have drawn on this body of work to develop the conceptual approach that underpins the argument in *Sight Readings*. This approach is set out in the appendix, "Photographic Agency and Jazz Photography." For the benefit of readers less concerned with theoretical questions of this nature, and for whom the account of jazz photography in the following chapters is of primary interest, the main lines of this theoretical argument are summarized below. This brief account should provide sufficient context for these chapters without recourse to the detailed appendix. Readers approaching the subject from the perspective of cultural and/or photography studies and anxious for greater detail may find it helpful to turn to the appendix immediately after this introductory chapter and before tackling the main body of text.

The study of photography has moved decisively away from the traditional formal conventions of art historians locating meaning within an image itself by stressing factors such as the location of a photograph on a printed page and its intertextual relation to other visual material, surrounding text and captioning, the narrative structure of a photo essay or album, the siting of a photograph in an exhibition or other form of display, and the role of personal and collective memory. A photograph, it is now argued, is coded to communicate messages beyond the immediate control or consciousness of the photographer. The material material conditions of production, distribution, and presentation and the analysis of ideological differences that undergird these functions rather than the agency of the photographer have become a central concern of contemporary photographic theory. While most theorists today take pains not to excise completely the agency engaged in photographic production by stressing various formulations of mutual interdependency between social agency and social structure, the empirical modalities through which agency operates are rarely spelled out. The result is that the photographer is all too frequently excised by default. Whatever advances photography theorists have made in recent years, we lack a convincing theory of photographic action.

"New" photography studies was born out of a reaction against the art historical model with its insistence on formal surfaces and authorial primacy. Photography however presents its own modalities of production and tropes of expression. If the ontology of the photograph is defined above all by the index – those signs asserting the presence of the photographer at a point in time in a given situation—there is a necessary relationship between the embodied subjectivity of the photographic act and the image that remains encoded whatever the subsequent life cycle experience of the image. Following an idea introduced in Michel Foucault's late writings, I describe photography as a "technology of the self," a term encapsulating the complex technological modalities that photographic framing necessarily entails. Framing is implemented by photographers both at a conceptual level, involving primarily the selection and/or exclusion of specific subjects, and through visual composition, a series of necessary and contingent decisions concerning exposure, light and shadow, focus, movement, viewpoints and relational hierarchies, and the boundaries of the frame. These decisions interact in myriad ways to bring to fruition the vision of the photographer. Conceptualizing a subject and creating a visual frame are modalities that both constrain and liberate the exercise of agency in production, and their interactions are key to understanding the nature of photographic agency.

This is not to suggest that the agency of the photographer should be the sole or even primary focus of attention. Photographic agency may of course rest with both photographers and their subjects; indeed, many photographs discussed in this book point to circumstances in which modalities of "coproduction" were at work. Nor can photographic agency replace the complex of questions arising once a photograph moves into use. Rather, I make the case for photographic agency not only as the prerequisite for a nuanced understanding of photographic action but also as the essential baseline against which competing interpretations of the photograph once "in use" might be weighed and judged. Understanding a photograph requires cognizance of the *relationships* between the sites at which interpretation of photography occurs—the sites of production, the image, and audiencing.[9] However much, and for what purposes, photographs might be deployed in circulation, identifying the agency at the point of production is essential if our understanding of that image is not to be reduced to a form of radical relativism or hegemonic co-option. Even as the accretions of contingency may seductively lead us to believe otherwise, the agency of the photographer is as firmly encoded in the photographic image as the messages to which the "pictorial turn" has drawn our attention.

The guiding theoretical framework I employ to support this argument is that developed over many years by the British scholar Margaret Archer. For Archer "reflexivity" is the conscious human process through which we make sense of the world and our identity within it without losing that which is essentially our own, essentially human. The fundamental premise of this book is that photography is a form of practical engagement in the real world and the photograph a site of reflexivity. Photographic "sight reading" engages the photographer in an act of human agency—interpretation through the inscription of subjective meaning perceived in what is often a transitory moment. The promise of jazz photography calls above all for an understanding of the *sui generis* nature of the jazz image and a methodology through which these images can be better understood by relating them to the ultimate concerns of their creators – the photographers' own *Sight Readings*.

II. Scope of the study

This book covers the period between 1900 and 1960. Historians are now much less inclined to structure their work around "decades" or "eras" that once made sense to the profession but which flatten out the contingencies of the moment and would no doubt have baffled people at the time. Within my chosen time frame I am therefore particularly concerned to account for those events such as wars that punctuate and disrupt discretely boxed time frames as well as the generational movements that inevitably span those periods. As to the time frame as a whole, I justify the choice of start and end point period by reference to my subject matter and the approach I adopt. There is little identifiably "jazz" prior to the turn of the nineteenth century, but there is clear evidence of proto-jazz bands emerging in the decade that followed such that by 1913 the first mention of the word "jazz" in the *San Francisco Bulletin* would not have been entirely foreign to its readers. So far as 1960 is concerned, the momentous social, racial, and economic upheavals prefigured in the 1950s and stretching well into the 1970s and beyond found expression in radical cultural changes that argue for a recalibration in the relationship between the generation of photographers coming to prominence in the period and the jazz tradition. This could hardly be otherwise: the shifting place of jazz within America's cultural mainstream, the fragmentation of jazz styles and the opening up of entirely new trajectories of musical explorations by musicians like Miles Davis, Ornette Coleman, Charles Mingus and Dave Brubeck were matched by the metaphorical explorations of American culture by Robert Frank, whose book *The Americans* first published in 1958 profoundly redefined the terrain of subsequent American photographic practice. Post-1960s jazz photography is the subject of a book yet to be written, one whose central features are prefigured by Herb Snitzer and Bert Stern's portraits of Louis Armstrong with which the final chapter closes this book.

III. Methodology

In the course of preparing this book I have reviewed thousands of many previously unpublished images. The majority are more or less formal portraits or performance shots; a significant number comprise studio portraits commissioned as publicity material while others are informal, backstage, or social images. Considered from a technical or aesthetic point of view many of these images are routine at best: poor lighting and the hastily grabbed nature of these images make them artistically suspect and the strikingly expressive nature of well-known photographs casts a long shadow over images of this kind. The approach I take in this book is to regard *all* these photographs as being of significance. The value of a photograph is not a function of its aesthetic appeal but rests in the objectives of the photographer, the context of production, the uses to which it was put and the impact on viewers.

I have used archives to examine a sufficiently wide selection of photographs to support a book whose thesis rests on a broadly based conception of jazz photography; and, where possible, I have presented reproductions of the original images even though some may now be in relatively poor condition. This has involved examining photographs often overlooked by jazz writers—commercial photography, environmental photographs, publicity shots, theatrical and artistic studios, and family albums as well as turning to the work of photographers not known primarily for their jazz images. I pay particular attention to the work of those African American photographers whose output has gone by default and the exiled photographers of the 1930s and 1940s. Readers may therefore be surprised then to find photographers they might not have thought of as jazz photographers discussed here and those that they might automatically associate with jazz only briefly considered. For similar reasons, I pay little attention to analysis of photography in album cover art from the late-1950s onward. Several excellent collections of this artwork are now available and a number of scholarly articles explore the images that accompanied 12″LPs, particularly those produced by the smaller independent labels.

All these photographs have been subjected to careful scrutiny. I have taken into account details embedded in the images, the dates and location of production, the conditions of material circulation, the technology and constraints involved in its production, and its relationship to other aspects of that photographers practice. I adopt content and semiotic analysis as necessary and I pay attention to those aspects (composition, use of light, monochromatic tonalities, perspective, and pose) that I believe have enhanced the affective and emotional nature of the subject matter and speak particularly to the objectives of their creator. Above all, I have tried to read these photographs against what we know of the photographer's biography and practice in order more clearly to situate their images within the reflexive agency that is key to their understanding. With its emphasis on the relationship between photographers and the specific sociocultural context(s) of their work, *Sight Readings* is concerned exclusively with American photographers.

Notes

1. John Gennari, *Blowin' Hot and Cool: Jazz and Its Critics* (Chicago: University of Chicago Press, 2006), 17.
2. Patrick Burke, *Come In and Hear the Truth: Jazz and Race on 52nd Street* (Chicago: University of Chicago Press, 2008), 14; William H. Kenney, *Chicago Jazz: A Cultural History, 1904–1930* (New York: Oxford University Press, 1993), 102, offers a more nuanced account describing how white Chicago musicians initially knew little of black jazz but came to understand it visiting South Side clubs. Robert Sylvester, *No Cover Charge: A Backwards Look at the Night Clubs of New York* (London: Peter Davis, 1936), 54–56, provides anecdotes about the male antics of the Condon gang and their attitudes to women.
3. Leonard Feather, "The Memories of Sweethearts," *Los Angeles Times* (April 13, 1980): 64. Antoinette D. Handy, *The International Sweethearts of Rhythm: Ladies' Jazz Band from Piney Woods Country Life School* (Lanham, MD: Scarecrow Press, 1998), recounts the history of the Sweethearts. By the 1940s there were "hundreds of all-woman bands": Sherrie Tucker, *Swing Shift: "All-Girl" Bands of the 1940s* (Durham, NC: Duke University Press, 2000), 29.
4. Raymond Williams, *Keywords* (Croon Helm: Fontana, 1976), 269; and Eugenia Shanklin, "Two Meanings and Uses of Tradition," *Journal of Anthropological Research* 37, no. 1 (1981): 71–89, explore the different meanings of "tradition" and the assumptions often made as a result of ambiguous definition.
5. Joe Maita, "The Jazz Photography Issue," Jerry Jazz Musician (2019), https://jerryjazzmusician.com/2019/08/the-jazz-photography-issue/.
6. Benjamin Cawthra, *Blue Notes in Black and White: Photography and Jazz* (Chicago: University of Chicago Press, 2011), 36, 39–40, 68; and Tony Whyton, *Jazz Icons: Heroes, Myths and the Jazz Tradition* (Cambridge: Cambridge University Press, 2010), 6–8.
7. Henry Louis Gates Jr., "The Master's Pieces: On Canon Formation and the African-American Tradition," in *Loose Canons: Notes on the Culture Wars* (New York: Oxford University Press, 1992), 32.
8. André Rouillé, *La Photographie. Entre document et art contemporain* (Paris: Gallimard, 2005).
9. Gillian Rose, *Visual Methodologies: An Introduction to the Interpretation of Visual Materials* (Los Angeles: Sage, 2007), 13–26.

1

Jazz Photography and Photographers, 1900–60

During the course of the twentieth century a wide range of American photographers made images of jazz musicians. Like many of their predecessors, these photographers were preoccupied with the reality of the American experience, the land, culture, and the myths that defined America.[1] Jazz was central to their experience.

Their photographs show the leading players on the bandstand creating moments of musical history, but the contribution of these images to our understanding of the music goes beyond performance portraiture. Jazz photographs document the wide variety of musical practices embraced by jazz musicians; the development of instruments and playing techniques; and provide insights into musicians' lifestyles, working conditions, social, communal, and familial activities, and professional practices and associations. The use of photography in publicity material tells us how musicians wished to present themselves and indicates changes in the place of jazz in American entertainment and visual culture. Photographs show the variety of and evolutions in the spaces in which jazz was performed, the nature of audiences and dancers, and provide pointers to the relationships between musicians and spectators. Musicians often inscribed messages on the face of photographs, which tells us about their relationships with mentors and colleagues, professional associates, friends, family, and fans. In short, these photographs reflect the hopes and concerns of a period when the country was undergoing cultural upheaval on a scale never previously experienced and speak of personal, social, and racial struggles and achievements as much as the strivings of men and women toward a new form of artistic expression.

The relationship between photographers and jazz dates back to the earliest days of the music and is uniquely comprehensive. Anthologies such as Al Rose and Edmond Souchon's *New Orleans Jazz*, Orrin Keepnews and Bill Grauer's *Pictorial History of Jazz*, and Frank Driggs and Harris Lewine's *Black Beauty, White Heat* present images of jazz pioneers from the early-1890s: "Cracked and faded with age," as Rudi Blesh affectionately explained, "they are documentary relics of a bygone era from the tooting of Fate Marable's calliope on the Mississippi River to the polished notes of Bix Beiderbecke's green gold cornet."[2]

As the number of photographers interested in the field grew in the decades that followed, images of virtually every jazz musicians of any stature were made and many are now available to researchers in private or public archives, published anthologies, and websites. These archives range from the enormous collection assembled by Frank Driggs and now held by Jazz at Lincoln Centre, around 3,500 photographs by Francis Wolff recently made available online from the Mosaic Records website, some 2,500 items in the William Gottlieb collection in the Library of Congress, and around 2,250 photographs of the writer, editor, critic, and producer Dave E. Dexter at the University of Missouri. Smaller collections, such as the 200 images at the Oberlin Conservatory of Music made by the photographer Frank Kuchirchuk in the early-1950s and the jazz photography of James Arkatov, a Russian-born cellist with the Pittsburgh Symphony Orchestra now held by UCLA Library Special Collections, contain important images although they are almost entirely overlooked by jazz scholars. While the photograph of Buddy Bolden reminds us that the authenticity of some of the earliest images in these collections might be problematic,[3] the fact remains that the entire history of jazz as an art form has been extensively documented in images of its most important practitioners in publicity portraits, in studio or live performance, in informal jam sessions, traveling between venues, or in social settings.

Jazz photographs stand as both documentary records and artifacts of enormous expressive potency. As documents they are of inestimable value to critics, historians and musicologists, discographers and biographers, enthusiasts and collectors. They provide evidence about the nature and compositions of jazz bands, changes in instruments, and the ways they were combined; they offer clues to the backgrounds of individual musicians, locate itinerant musicians in a particular place at a particular time, and show how their identities as artists developed; recording studio photography has helped identify players on particular records and provides an understanding about how recording techniques developed over time; and we can sense changing social trends and the halting progress toward integration in photographs of musicians at work, leisure, or traveling. The affective potency of jazz photography is however just as important as their evidential status. Jazz critics and enthusiasts alike find that these expressive images often stimulate memories of performances and experiences that often hold deeply personal meanings. In describing their evocative power, these images are frequently described as "atmospheric," a term used to foreground the ability of photographs to rekindle the experiential impact of live performance and the personal memory of these experiences.

In short, jazz is an art form whose entire existence has been both documented and expressed through photography and it is this combination that situates these photographs among the most valuable visual records in modern American history. That such an archive exists is due to the enthusiasm of photographers to what for significant periods was a minority—and always racially charged—music. Some made a commitment to documenting jazz at particular stages in their careers, including those to whom the label "jazz photographers" is most often applied: Charles Peterson, Herman Leonard, William Claxton, Francis Wolff, Charles Stewart, Dennis Stock, Herb Snitzer—to name but a few. Rarely, or at best insufficiently, remunerated for occasional illustrations for magazine articles, album covers, or publicity shoots; operating under difficult conditions; and usually struggling to find exhibition opportunities at the time, they are now celebrated as key contributors to the jazz photography tradition. These photographers have attracted considerable attention, but they were by no means the only ones with an interest in the subject. Studio portraitists, art photographers, fashion photographers, documentarians, and photojournalists also made photographs of jazz musicians in the course of their professional practices and as personal projects. These photographers were a diverse group including among their ranks African American as well as white studio workers and the émigrés and exiles who arrived in the United States in the first half of the twentieth century.

I. The significance of jazz photographs

First published in *Life* in 1938, Charles Peterson's portrayal of a "typical" swing fan collages a variety of media as collectively they facilitated the experience of jazz (Figure 4). The fan sits beside his radio, his left ear close to the speaker; his body is moving with the beat of a swing band, feet jerked off the floor in excitement.

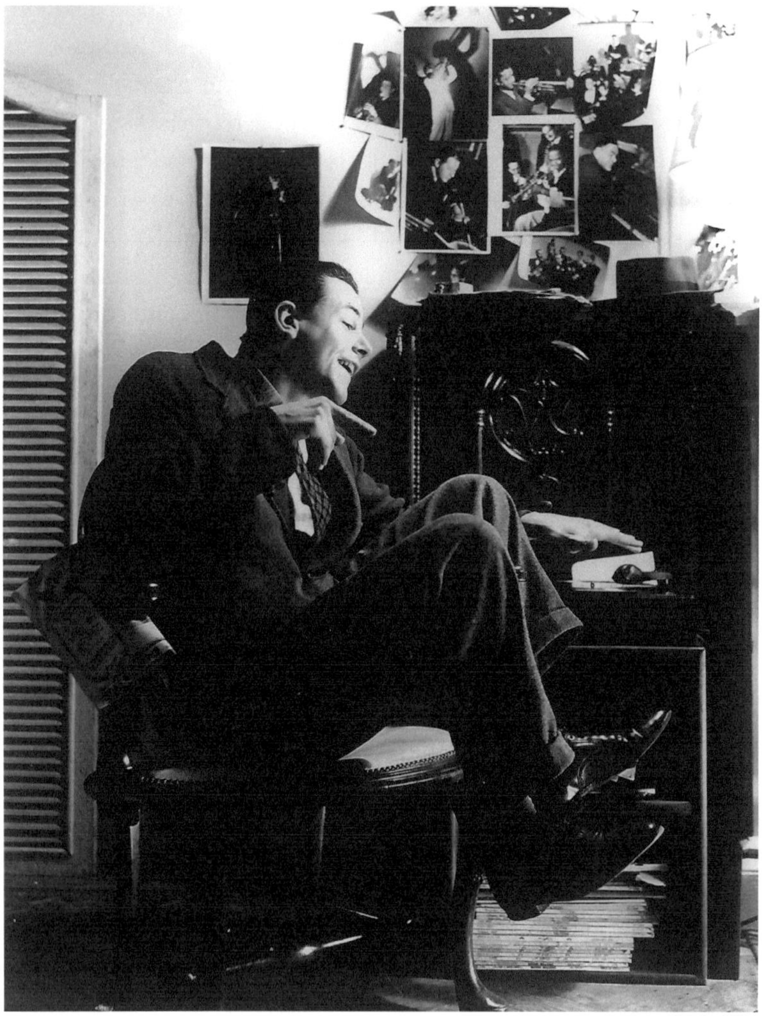

Figure 4: Charles Peterson. *The Swing Fan*. New York. 1938.
Don Peterson.

A record is turning on the turntable, a record store bag hangs over the back of the chair, and a pile of magazines illustrates the place of the jazz press. Photographs are pinned to the wall. Peterson's image is a contrived *tableau vivant*, but his portrayal appears accurately to represent the social and demographic characteristics of a typical swing fan of the period and effectively directs attention toward the role of photography as part of an immersive process through which many aficionados of the period consumed their music.[4]

Jazz photographs have always been important to fans, enthusiasts, and collectors. By the late-1920s photography was firmly enmeshed in a network of technologies that included recorded music, radio, and illustrated print media. These technologies changed the ways in which the music was consumed and enjoyed, creating "circles of resonance" in which "listeners shared, debated, analyzed, and fought, often passionately, over their personal patterns of empathy and appreciation for what they heard in the grooves of 78 rpm recordings."[5] Young white collectors and enthusiasts like Peterson's swing fan went to considerable lengths to acquire signed photographs of their jazz idols. Bob Inman's swing era diary recounts how as a teenager in the mid-1930s he toured New York streets to call on magazines and management offices, visiting musicians in their hotels, dressing

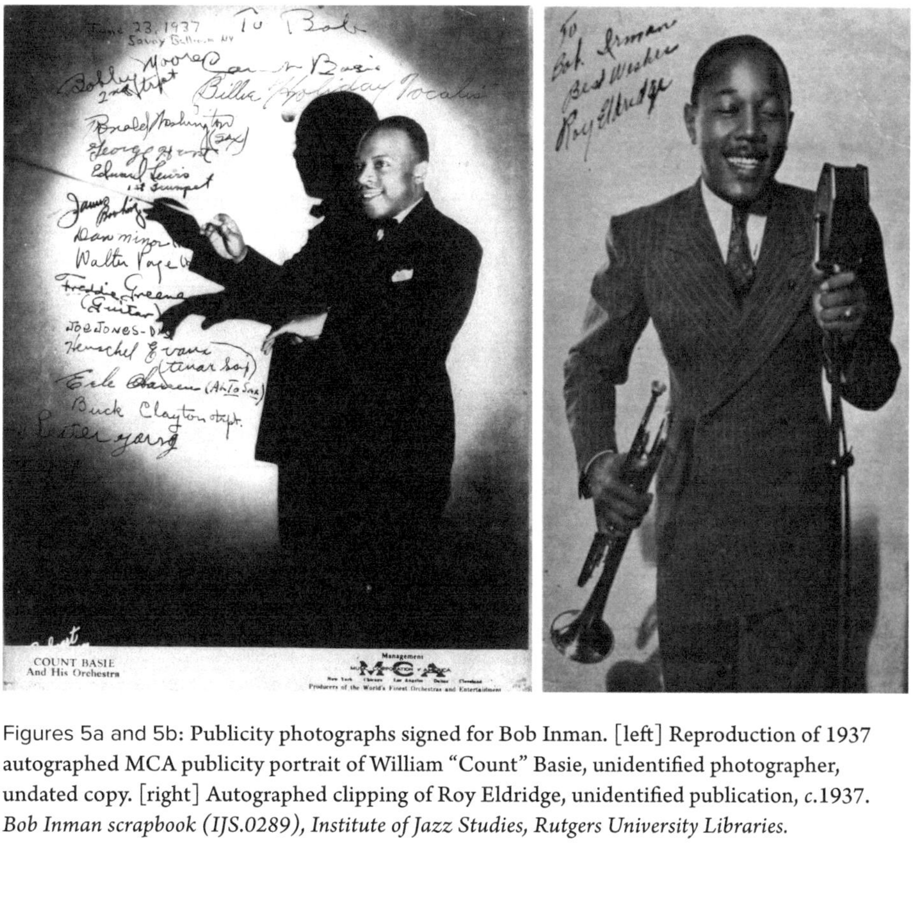

Figures 5a and 5b: Publicity photographs signed for Bob Inman. [left] Reproduction of 1937 autographed MCA publicity portrait of William "Count" Basie, unidentified photographer, undated copy. [right] Autographed clipping of Roy Eldridge, unidentified publication, *c.*1937. *Bob Inman scrapbook (IJS.0289), Institute of Jazz Studies, Rutgers University Libraries.*

rooms, or on stage; or (as in the case of Roy Eldridge) writing directly to the musician's home address to secure signed photographs (Figures 5a and 5b).[6] Letters from the mostly white readers of *Down Beat* confirm that signed photographs were treasured artifacts among fans. One correspondent complained that Charlie Barnet was not a "solid guy" because he refused to sign a photograph while another praised Gene Krupa as "the finest guy there is" because he spoke to the writer behind the stage and gave him five autographed photographs.[7]

For many years *Down Beat* and other music magazines carried advertisements offering photographs of jazz musicians "ready for framing" for as little as 10c. each. Around 55 percent of nearly 1,500 testimonial advertisements appearing in *Down Beat* between 1939 and 1949 included a photography offer as an inducement to enquiry. A total of 175 advertisements in the period (12 percent) offered a free (or nominal charge) 10 × 8-inch photograph of the musician(s) featured in the advertisement (Figures 6a and 6b). Advertisers used photography to extend the reach and life span of the sales dialogue initiated by advertisements with a range of visual material, most commonly photographic brochures

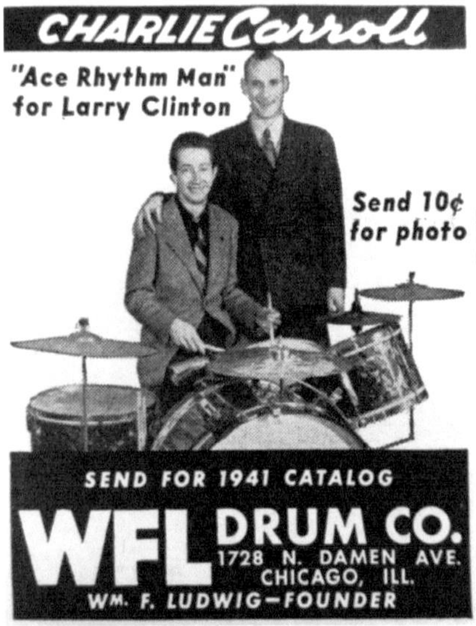

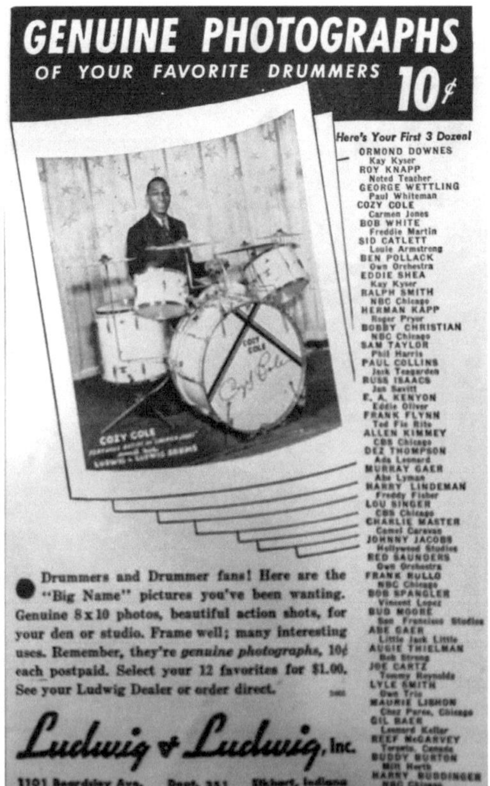

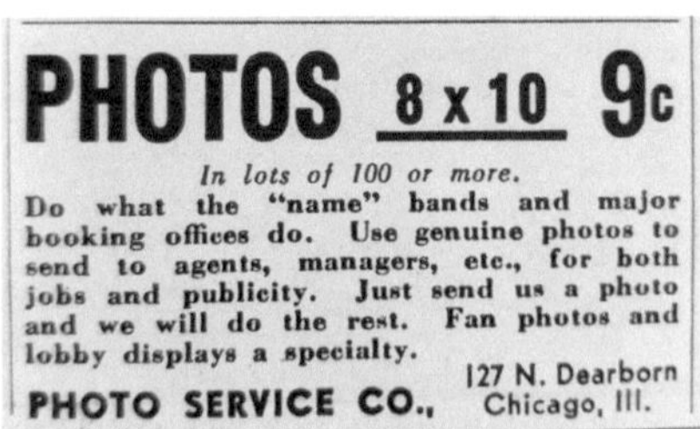

Figures 6a–6c: Photography offers in *Down Beat*.
Down Beat, March 1945 and April 1941.

or "magazines." Always copiously illustrated, advertisers positioned these brochures as packed with helpful information drawn from the life and work of the endorsers by combining detailed product information with personality photographs, discussions about bandleaders' styles and techniques, and tips for success. These brochures elaborated and reinforced the advertisement by drawing on the same visual imagery attracting the enquirer initially (Figure 7).[8]

In the pretelevision age photographs filled a gap in the demand for visual information for black as much as white enthusiasts. African American families had a long tradition of pinning photographs cut from magazines and newspapers to the walls of their homes, a practice originally born of necessity among the rural poor but one that migrated with people to the urban setting. Zora Neale Hurston described the walls of a cabin in Alabama adorned with calendars, scarves, and colorful advertisements and spoke of how "Decorating a decoration . . . did not seem out of place . . . Whatever the Negro does of his own volition he embellishes."[9] Collected, exchanged, and pinned to walls and doors in African American homes and clubs (Figure 8), photographs were vested with a permanence that has now all but vanished.

At Harlem's Apollo Theatre Gordon "Doc," "El Fabuloso," "Candid Camera King," or "The World's Greatest" Anderson, as he variously styled himself, spotted the opportunity to make a living by selling photographs taken in

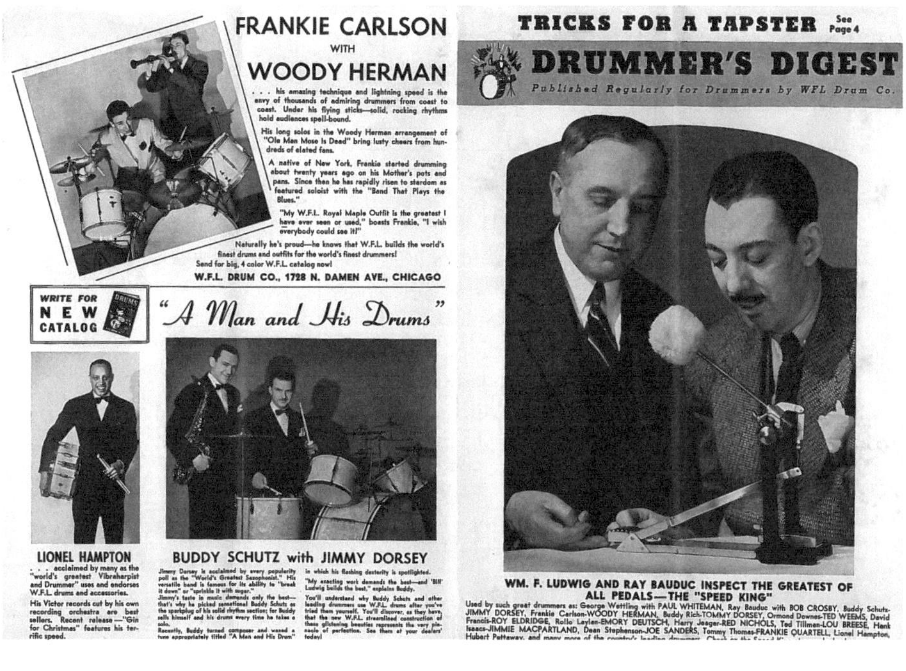

Figure 7: *Drummer's Digest*. WFL Drum Co. n.d.
Ray Bauduc Collection, Hogan Jazz Archive, Tulane University.

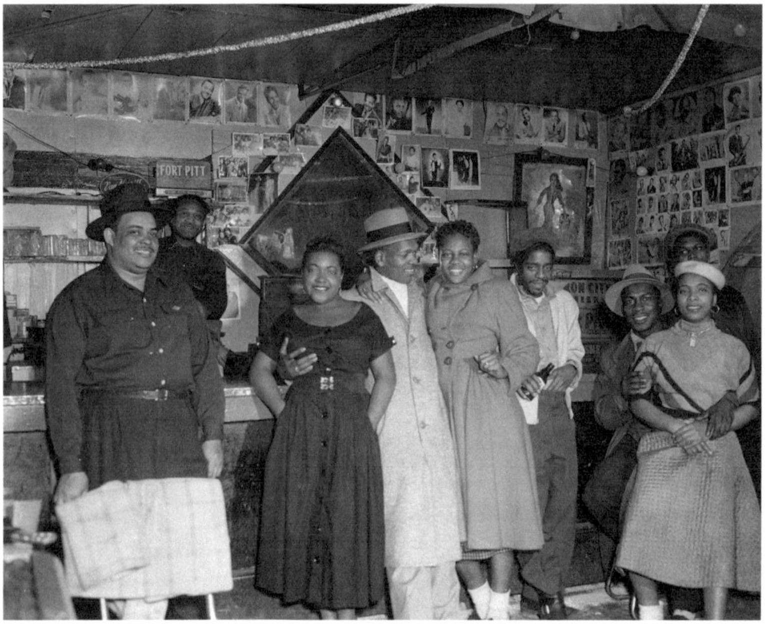

Figure 8: Charles "Teenie" Harris. *Photographs on wall of club*. n.d. *Carnegie Museum of Art.*

performance and backstage to the large and increasingly sophisticated black population of Harlem.[10] Born in 1916 in Baltimore, Anderson started as a photographer at the city's Royal Theatre immediately after his military service before moving to the Apollo. In New York he made candid shots of artists both on- and offstage, greeting friends and fans, and as they arrived or left the theatre. His subjects included all the great names from the late-1940s to the mid-1970s (including a rare shot of a teenage Billie Holiday). Anderson usually photographed the first show and then printed his montaged shots in order to sell them to the artists and fans (Figure 9) while the memory of the performance was still fresh. His ability to earn a living in this way for over twenty years underlines the importance of visual imagery to both artists and audiences at the time.

This demand for photography underlines what John Raeburn has called "Americans' picture hunger" in the 1930s. Rooted in the belief that photographs offered a permanent and inner-directed pleasure in an age of uncertainty and material absence, "What is certain is that the extraordinary expansion of photography's art world [. . .] meant that larger, more varied audiences had unprecedented access to pictures." This shift toward the consumption of visual media had profound effects as the growing hegemony of photography in the 1930s increased Americans' self-awareness of culture and community while at the same time stimulating interest in the power of symbol, myth, and rhetoric.[11]

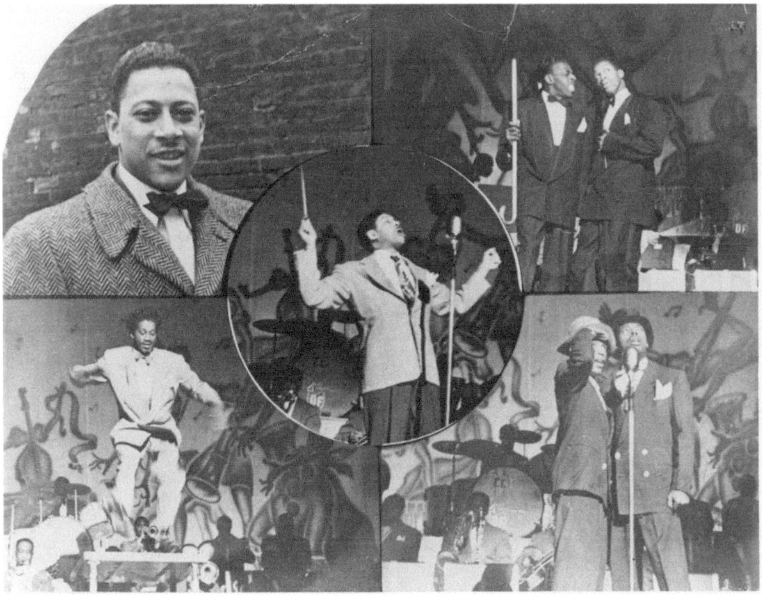

Figure 9: Gordon Anderson. *Cab Calloway*. Apollo Theatre. 1947.
Cab Calloway. Clockwise from top left: trombonist Jimmy Buxton, Berry Brother tap dance team, dancer Count Leroy and comedy-dance duo Moke and Pole. Peter Vacher Collection.

Jazz and photography came of age as popular art forms at a moment when cultural assessments of jazz were not yet settled, allowing the visual image to play a critical role in shaping perceptions by complementing the aural experience of jazz. Recent research has confirmed that interactions between technologies—or, more correctly, the interactions between their sensory effects on users—can underpin new forms of social meaning and have helped to clarify the processes involved in these exchanges. What have come to be known as cross-modal correspondences between the senses suggest that sound can enliven sight, sight can enliven sound, and that both in combination enhance memory recall of an event through their apparent mimetic fidelity; and the greater the congruence between cross-modal sensory exchanges, the greater the mutual influence. W. J. T. Mitchell, for instance, has questioned whether *any* medium can be described as purely as visual, tactile or auditory. He concludes that all visual media turn out to involve the other senses.[12] Barry E. Stein and M. Alex Meredith consolidated much of this research in the following terms:[13]

> *The integration of inputs from different sensory modalities not only transforms some of their individual characteristics, but does so in ways that can enhance the quality of life. Integrated sensory inputs produce far richer experiences than would be predicted from their simple co-existence or the linear sum of their individual products . . . the*

use of one sensory system can influence (i.e. enhance, degrade, change) perception via. another sensory system, and that information can be transferred across modalities so that they may substitute for one another.

Generally, "the visual modality predominates," although "co-operative interactions" among sensory modalities are most evident when the individual sensory systems carry "concordant information."[14] We can be sure then that for jazz enthusiasts and listeners of all types, photography not only deepened the experience of jazz by complementing its sounds, whether consumed on record or in live performance, but also helped to shape the meaning of the music.

Photographs and the "Golden Age" of jazz

The significance that viewers attached to the jazz photograph stretched well beyond the period of youthful enthusiasm. In 1989 Sara Robbin of Los Angeles wrote to Benny Goodman's daughter, Rachel Goodman Edelson, enclosing a small snapshot of the musician and his orchestra taken over 50 years earlier at the San Francisco World Fair in July 1939. The photograph (Figure 10), a simple snapshot pasted onto card by the local drugstore processing Sara's film, held deeply personal meanings:[15]

My late husband and I with our two sons (ages-12–16 years) were visiting the World's Fair in San Francisco (1939) where your father was playing. We were all fans of his and enjoyed his music very much. I thought you would like to have these pictures, as

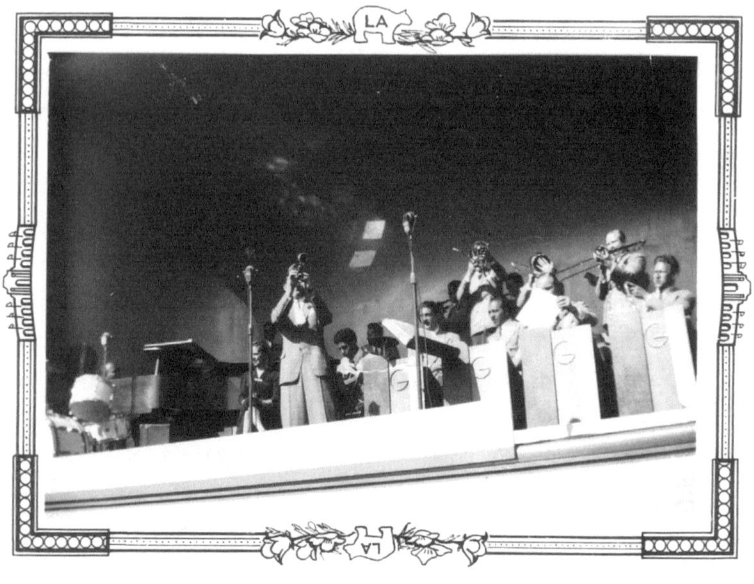

Figure 10: Sara Robbin. *Benny Goodman Orchestra*. World's Fair. San Francisco. 1939. *Gilmore Music Library/Benny Goodman Collection.*

I know it would give you pleasure to see them. It also gives me pleasure for being able to bring a little remembrance of him to you. He was a great musician.

The following year Goodman's daughter received another photograph of the band taken in Atlantic City in 1939 by Buck Schaub, whose accompanying letter explained that

during a break in a performance I went backstage and passed the picture around to the various members of the band. Some said, "I'm not in the picture." I replied, "Please sign it anyway." I was a great admirer of your Dad and his music.

The Benny Goodman archive at Yale's Gilmore Music Library contains many other examples of snapshots sent to the musician by admirers stirred by the memories the images evoked.

An extensive body of research concerned with family albums and vernacular photography has revealed the potency of photographs in creating and shaping both personal and social memory in the manner described above. Perhaps more than any other domestic object photographs assist in preserving the memory of personal ties and rekindling the emotions associated with them.[16] Photographs communicate tangible and enduring signs of relationships, experiences, and values, confirming and enlarging personal identity through symbols that provide a broader perspective on present-day life. As material objects, photographs can form what Pierre Nora has termed *lieux de mémoire* "where memory crystallizes and secretes itself [. . .] at a particular historical moment [. . .] the embodiment of memory in certain sites where a sense of historical continuity persists."[17]

The relationship between personal and collective memory and the visual image is however complex, and scholars have stressed the mediating power of the photograph as a constructed object.[18] A photograph conveys reminiscences and memories and the moods associated with them, but the interaction between the viewer and the object has its own permeating quality. As the photograph ages, signs contained with it "spread" from indexical to iconic; metaphor replaces mimesis as the image acquires its own autonomy to stand on its own in constituting a sign. The reception of visual sensations is intricately tied to context and biography as the information in the photograph is transformed into a memory-image by the pervasive and quite possibly involuntary power of imaginative recreation. Indeed, the photograph can indicate intention that a memory should be brought into being in which absences can be as revealing as the recall of specific event.[19]

Often consumed by viewers (including, it should be stressed, jazz writers and critics) highly motivated to nostalgize the image, jazz photographs appear to be particularly potent in this respect, creating links with the past that transcend personal experience, evoking recollections and moods which do not depend on the viewer having experienced those events or times. Acting as a prompt to vicarious recollection, jazz photographs bring back to life the experience of jazz performance in some past golden age, a glimpse inside a long-lost world of jazz.

Yet every viewer has their own "golden age." One of Vilém Flusser's key insights was the observation that the photograph's location in time and place is undermined by the very form of its material presentation. As the eye wanders over the surface of an image, the viewer takes in one element after another, producing new temporal relationships between them: the eye "can return to an element of the image it has already seen, and 'before' can become 'after.'" Geoff Dyer developed this theme when he proposed that the best jazz photographs have an achronological character, inviting the viewer to speculate as to what preceded and immediately followed the action represented in the image.[20] This lack of temporal fixity further mediates the relationship between image and memory. Once detached from the origins and practice of the music and embodied in sites of memory, photographs can assume the status of myth as they appear and reappear in motion pictures, advertisements, and popular literature.

Jazz photography has developed then not simply as an adjunct to memory recall but has played an active role in constructing a narrative and aesthetic for jazz, framing the way the music has come to be understood. For Tony Whyton, visual representations of jazz are seductive, "artistic" monochromatic images that turn musicians into icons and make the subject "look more real whilst signifying honesty, nostalgia and sentimentality;" and, for Peter Townsend, photography has been central to the changing meaning of jazz through "the ensemble of visual signs [. . .] iconic personalities and cool composition that comprises the myth of jazz." Mourning the passing of the renowned jazz photographer Paul Hoeffler, Len Dobbin proposed that each of his images "helped shape our collective view of the jazz musician as sophisticated artist." Perhaps more than any other, Herman Leonard's photographs have emerged as the exemplar of the visual expression of jazz, evoking a sound as much as a look.[21]

Interest in jazz photography

For much of their careers, the work of the photographers surveyed in this book went largely unacknowledged; the images of many of even the most storied of these practitioners were made in the course of personal projects and generally went unremunerated. Few, if any, self-identified as "jazz" photographers—at least at the time. William Claxton's 1955 *Jazz West Coast*—arguably the first single-author jazz photobook of significance—sold well on first publication but was soon out of print; within a few years Claxton had moved away from jazz toward Hollywood portraiture and fashion photography.

Recent decades have however seen a marked increase in the awareness and appreciation of jazz imagery. This resurgence is related to the growth of scholarly research in visual culture and the development of jazz studies programs in universities around the world. Increasing interest in jazz photographs must also be situated alongside changing perceptions of the music. Benjamin Cawthra believes that jazz photography began to aspire to the status of art as artistic validation of the music itself moved to the mainstream of the American cultural establishment and Heather Pinson has linked the rising status of photography with the sway of neoclassicism in jazz associated with Wynton Marsalis and Jazz at Lincoln Centre. To be sure, jazz photography began to gain traction just at a point when jazz became "Jazz on Jazz [. . .] attempting to energize the present by mining the past."[22] What seems to have been renewed interest in a "Golden Age" of jazz perhaps accounts for the enthusiasm with which Robert Parent's touring photographic exhibitions of classic jazz imagery in 1978 were greeted and which encouraged William Gottlieb, after having quit the jazz scene some 30 years previously, to publish a selection of his negatives in 1979 as *The Golden Age of Jazz*. The success of the book launched Gottlieb on a late career shift involving lectures and exhibitions, personal appearances at galleries and museums, and "a cottage industry of postcards, T-shirts and posters."[23]

In other signs of emerging interest, Roy DeCarava's show "The sound I saw" at the Studio Museum in Harlem opened on January 18, 1983; Milt Hinton's memoir, lavishly illustrated with his own photographs, was published in 1988 following dedicated conservation efforts by David G. Berger and Holly Maxson; and a few years later W. Royal Stokes published an anthology of photographs by the jazz musician turned photographer Charles Peterson.[24] Following Lee Tanner's group showings of jazz photography at Kimballs East in Emeryville, California, in 1990 and curation of jazz photography in *Jazz Times* and other writings, exhibitions of jazz photography have become more frequent and photobooks by other jazz photographers began to emerge with some regularity. These publications in turn drew renewed attention to a series of older jazz photobooks, especially those by Keepnews and Grauer, Driggs and Lewine, and Rose and Souchon.[25]

The decisive moment however came with the rediscovery of the work of Herman Leonard. Leonard had produced memorable photographs of musicians between 1948 and 1956, many of which appeared in promotional material and on the covers of album from RCA Victor, Decca, Capitol, Mercury, and Verve. After several lean years he left the music scene and pursued a career in fashion, advertising, and film work. "Rediscovering" his negatives some 30 years later, Leonard published his first book, *The Eye of Jazz,* in 1985. An exhibition at the Special Photographers' Company in London generated considerable interest and led to exhibitions in the United States, including an important showing in New Orleans in 1992. Exhibitions of his work continued and in 1995 his second book, *Jazz Memories,* appeared. Renewed attention began to be directed toward other photographers: William Claxton's photographs of west coast musicians, particularly the highly photogenic trumpeter Chet Baker, were reappraised as indicative of a practice at the intersection of film, fashion, and music, and Dennis Stocks's jazz portraits have been resituated within a practice devoted (at least at the time) to avant-garde and counterculture trends.

II. Key names in jazz photography

While the work of many photographers will be addressed throughout this book, constraints of space mean that not all can be discussed in detail. The following section therefore provides an overview of the key names in jazz photography, the context in which they worked, and the nature of their affinity with the music. Many points raised here will be picked up and developed in later chapters.

Studio photographers

Studio portraiture in jazz is often considered by jazz scholars as publicity, a commercial practice telling us little about photographers and sitters.[26] Chapter 5 takes a more critical view of this practice. Many of the studio photographers whose sitters regularly included jazz musicians were émigrés arriving in the United States in the first decades of the twentieth century: James J. Kriegsmann, who arrived from Vienna in 1929 to launch a 40-year career as a portraitist of black musical talent; Murray Korman; the Russian-born brothers Maurice and Seymour Zeldman who formed the Maurice Seymour studio for theatrical and celebrity portraiture; and Bruno Bernard, another German exile. While Murray Korman occasionally worked on location his portrait of Billie Holiday is more typical of the studio approach of these photographers (Figure 11). Overwhelmingly Jewish and often fleeing persecution in their native countries of central and eastern Europe, émigré photographers forged an identity with black musicians rooted in their own experiences of discrimination, flight, and assimilation.

By mid-century a wide range of studio photographers around the country were making portraits of jazz musicians and bands. The Bert Studio in Kansas City; Sussman in Minneapolis; the Bloom, Daguerre and Gibson Studios in Chicago; and Hollywood and New York celebrity portraitists such as Anton Bruehl, George Maillard Kesslère, Lansing Brown, W. G. Harris, Bert Parry, John E. Reed, A. L. "Whitey" Schaeffer, Lee of Hollywood, and Clarence Bull all made stylish studio portraits of jazz musicians. Working at a point in time when leading jazz musicians were beginning to move away from the early ensemble tradition, these portraitists help raise the cultural capital of jazz by imbuing the presentation of black artists with production values previously reserved for white sitters. Their engagement with jazz might not have been as personal as that of the émigré photographers, but in their use of lighting, pose, setting, and techniques—the "play of gestures" unique to studio portraiture—the contribution of their output in raising the cultural capital of jazz was no less significant.

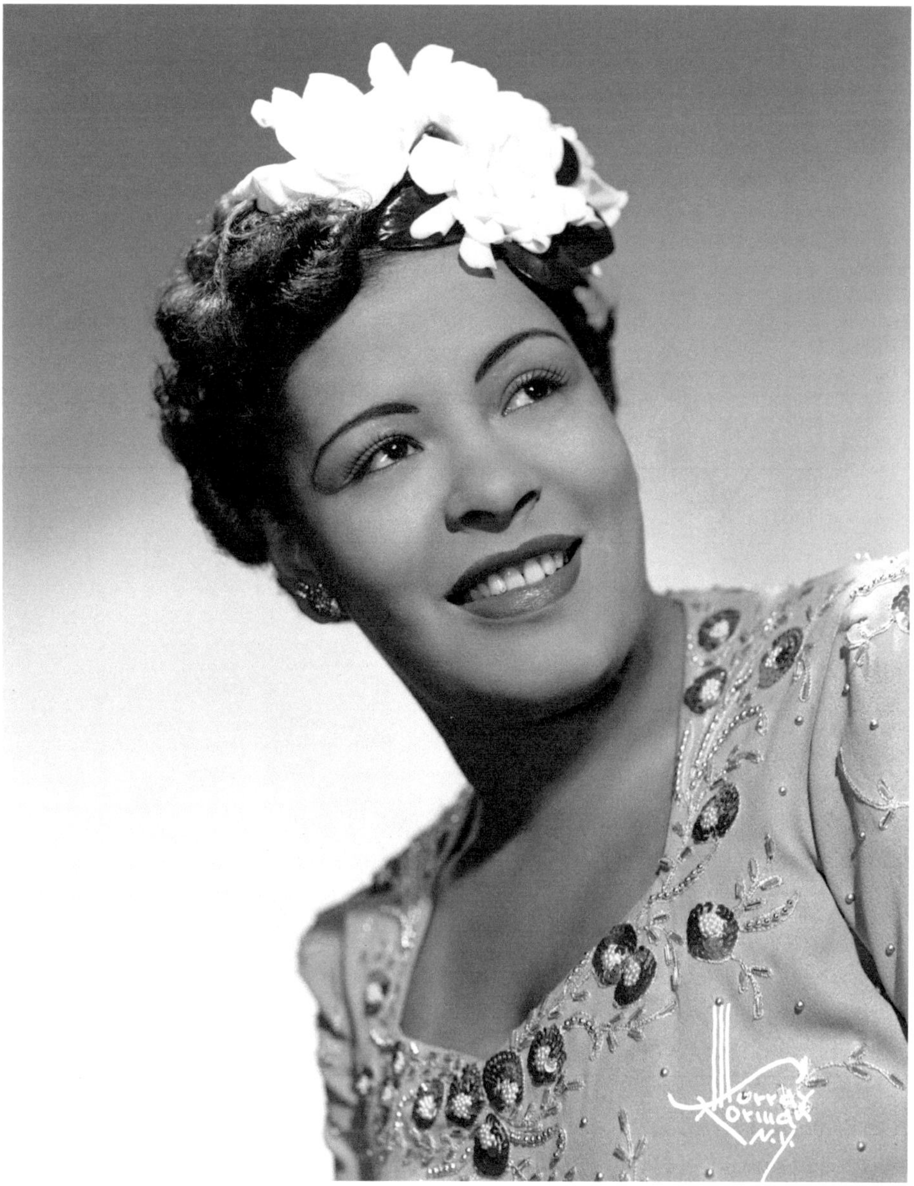

Figure 11: Murray Korman. *Billie Holiday*. n.d.
Clyde Adams Collection/permission of Leslie Greaves.

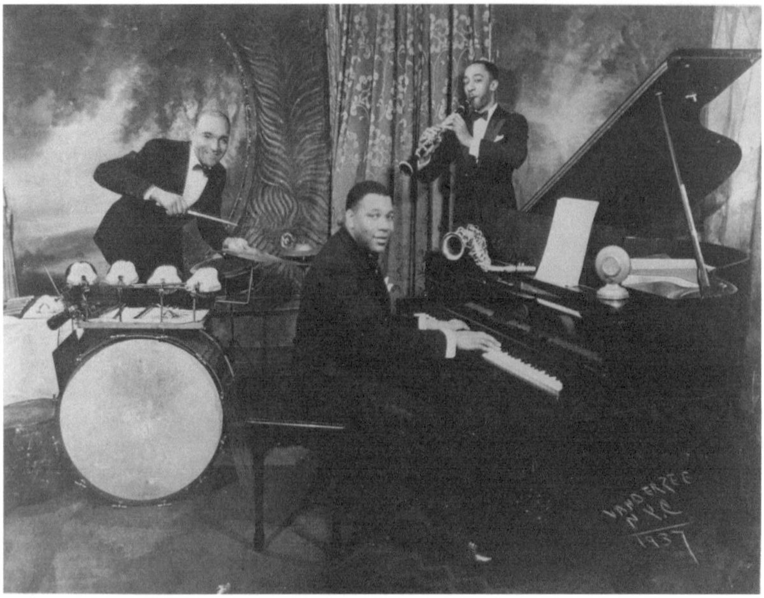

Figure 12: James Van Der Zee. *Don Frye Trio*. New York. 1937. *Peter Vacher Collection.*

African American jazz photography

Other than Charles ("Chuck") Stewart and Milt Hinton, few black photographers are recognized specifically for jazz imagery. Hugh Bell's early jazz photographs are only occasionally reproduced in jazz texts even though many consider these to have been central to his practice. Roy DeCarava's photographs, with their deep blacks, spare but sensitive composition and subtle use of lighting, do not conform to what is generally thought of as the "jazz image," and it falls to writers outside jazz scholarship to offer insightful interpretative essays on his photographs of musicians.[27] Nevertheless, a wide range of African American photographers were involved in documenting jazz musicians and their activities. Their work is discussed in Chapters 6 and 7.

As African American photography advanced in the decades following the turn of the century, New York photographers like R. E. Mercer, William Edward Elcha, the leading African American chronicler of "Jazz Age" Manhattan and the Harlem studio portraitist James Van Der Zee (Figure 12), Arthur Bedou and Villard Paddio in New Orleans, Caroll Maynard, William Edward Woodard's Studios in Chicago, Kansas City, and New York City, and Hooks Brothers in Memphis were acutely conscious of the ways in which they represented black identity. Evidence of this concern can be located in their portraits of jazz musicians and bands just as much as in individual and family portraiture.

Roy DeCarava and Gordon Parks were pivotal figures in the development of African American photography during the 1940s. Parks has only occasional involvement with jazz subjects but was influential in shaping black photography's representation of race. If Parks was postural, Roy DeCarava was quietly experiential. Born in 1919 to a single mother in Harlem, DeCarava became one of the most important photographers of his generation in his portrayals of Harlem's people and jazz giants. Milt Hinton, a working bass player and talented amateur photographer, made a point of documenting the people and events of his long career as a jazz musician. After studies at Ohio University and an apprenticeship with Herman Leonard, Chuck Stewart made jazz one of his specialties. During a career of over 50 years, Stewart captured images of virtually every well-known musician and vocalist as well as taking on advertising and other commercial assignments. Other black photographers engaged with jazz included the record producer and designer Esmond Edwards and the theatre photographers Gordon Anderson and Bert Andrews. Andrews apprenticed with Chuck Stewart and assumed Elcha's mantle in the 1950s as photographers of black theatrical and musical talent including many jazz musicians of the period.

Many African American photographers training their cameras on jazz subjects did so as one aspect of their varied work as photojournalists with black newspapers and magazines and/or studio portraitists. For some, like Marion J. Porter in New Orleans, Austen Hansen and Morgan and Marvin Smith in New York City, Allen Edward Cole in Cleveland, Ohio, R. C. Hickman in Dallas, and John W. Moseley in Philadelphia, jazz musicians were an occasional part of the daily routine documenting the lives and events of local African American communities. Others concentrated rather more on jazz subjects: Charles "Teenie" Harris, who opened a portrait studio in Pittsburgh in 1931, became the main photographer for the *Pittsburgh Courier*; Benny Joseph in Houston and Ernest C. Withers in Memphis combined journalistic activities with operating a local portrait studio; and in Seattle, Al Smith captured images of African Americans in the many jazz clubs and bars of his city, creating an impactful sense of participation in his images. Ted Williams carried out assignments in the United States, Europe, Latin America, and the Far East for publications such as *The Saturday Evening Post*, *Time*, *Newsweek*, *Ebony*, and *Look*. His involvement with jazz was much more than an occasional requirement of the job and his extraordinarily accomplished images represent an archive of the highest artistic quality.

On the west coast Charles Williams and Harry Adams were news photographer for the *California Eagle* and the *Los Angeles Sentinel*. Even more committed to jazz were Bob Douglas, Bob Moore, and Howard Morehead. Douglas began his career in the early-1940s as a nightclub photographer in Detroit and later moved to Los Angeles (Figure 13), while Morehead combined jazz photography with black glamour photography in freelance activities

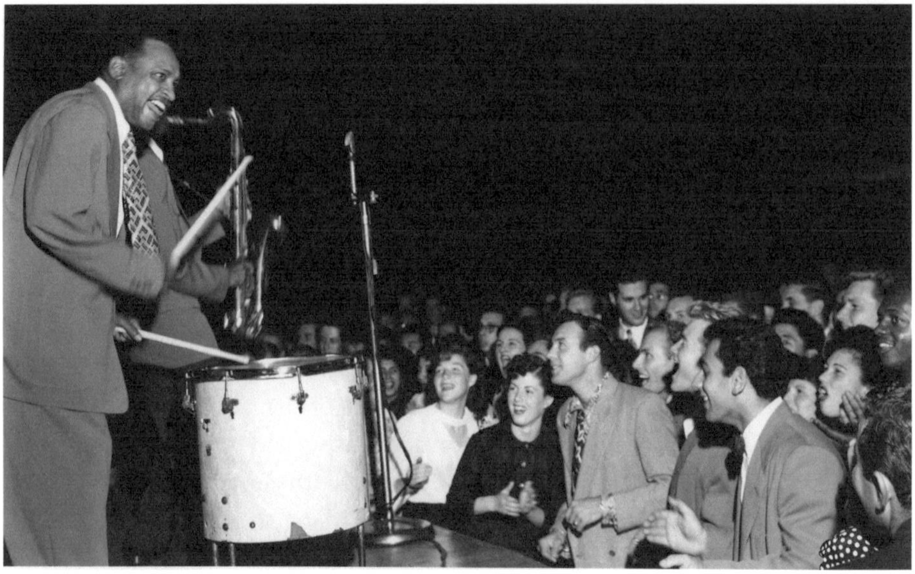

Figure 13: Bob Douglas. *Lionel Hampton*. Los Angeles. 1950.
Tom and Ethel Bradley Centre for African American Arts, California State University.

and work for the *Herald Dispatch*. Jack Davis chronicled the African American community and its music in Los Angeles. San Francisco in the 1940s and 1950s was another city with an active jazz scene with a wealth of documentary images left by photographers such as Wesley Johnson Jr., Red Powell, Steve Jackson Jr., and J. B. Coleman. Born in Florida in 1926 David Johnson, Ansel Adams's first African American student, made images of jazz as part of his work as a community photographer and photojournalist in the Bay area for over five decades.

White photographers of the interwar period

Another group comprises the young white Americans who moved into photography as the medium extended its reach during the interwar period. This cohort includes those most widely recognized as contributors to jazz photography: Charles Peterson, Burt Goldblatt, Marvin Koner, Herman Leonard, Robert Parent, Burt Glinn, Art Kane, William Claxton, Bob Willoughby, Don Hunstein, Dennis Stock, and Bert Stern. Their work is discussed in Chapter 8.

Early documentarians such as Berenice Abbott, Genevieve Naylor, and Lucy Ashjian took an interest in jazz and black culture while Jack Delano and Russel Lee made images of Chicago jazz clubs for the Photographic Section of the Farm Security Administration in the 1930s. Few photographers were closer to the world of 1930s and 1940s jazz than Charles Peterson and Skippy Adelman. For two years Peterson lived with his family above the Onyx Club; on hand to photograph in the 52nd Street clubs, his images reflect his friendships with the players he knew best, the coterie of musicians around Eddie Condon and his hard-drinking "gang of Chicago ruffians." Adelman, a Greenwich Village resident and one of the new generation of hard-bitten photojournalists, was as close as Peterson had been in midtown Manhattan to the swirl of activities around Condon.

Most of these photographers combined an interest in jazz with commercial practices based on art, fashion, documentary, photojournalism, portraiture, and advertising commissions. William Gottlieb's photography was made as an adjunct to his journalism; Phil Stern, Bert Stern, and Duncan P. Schiedt built successful careers as advertising photographers. Among fashion photographers, Arthur Elgort and Doug Quackenbusch saw a natural affinity between style and jazz. Ed Feingersch, a student of Alexey Brodovitch and assistant to Gjon Mili, was a photojournalist known for his images of Marilyn Monroe but who memorably documented Thelonious Monk's daily life and performances. Both Herman Leonard and William Claxton were attracted to fashion and the look of jazz: after his early jazz period Leonard moved toward fashion photography and reportage while William Claxton was always attracted to jazz personalities like Chet Baker at the intersection of glamour, celebrity, and cultural change. Dennis Stock's jazz work mainly dates to the years between 1957 and the early-1960s, when he completed the photography for what would become *Jazz Street*. "PoPsie" Randolph was encouraged to take photography seriously by Benny Goodman and returned frequently to making jazz portraits.

Bob Willoughby and Don Hunstein at Columbia; Bob Parent, a freelancer with Prestige and other labels; Don Bronstein at Columbia and Chess; David B. Hecht at RCA Victor and Carnegie Hall; and Charlie Mihn and Ray Whitten, the first photographers hired by Capitol Records, were all successful commercial photographers. Hecht headed RCA Victor's photo department and was primarily responsible for producing record covers. Influenced by Hans Kaden, Sid Grossman, and Alexey Brodovitch, he photographed several thousand record covers over a period of more than twenty years (Figure 14). Esther Bubley's images from Norman Granz's "Funky Blues" session in 1952 brought a documentary photographer's eye to a music with which she was previously unfamiliar. Eliot Elisofon took on a number of jazz-related assignments and W. Eugene Smith's involvement with the jazz loft movement was an unusually sustained and intensive documentary project. The photojournalist Frank Kuchirchuk made a series of glorious monochrome images at Lindsay's Sky Bar in Cleveland in the early-1950s while moonlighting from his day job as a photographer with the International News Service. Reid Miles, Bob Cato, Burt Goldblatt, Victor Kalin, and Ralston Crawford all trained as artists or designers and linked their aesthetic aspirations with jazz. Burt Glinn's photographs in *The Beat Scene* taken between 1957 and 1960 framed Thelonious Monk and

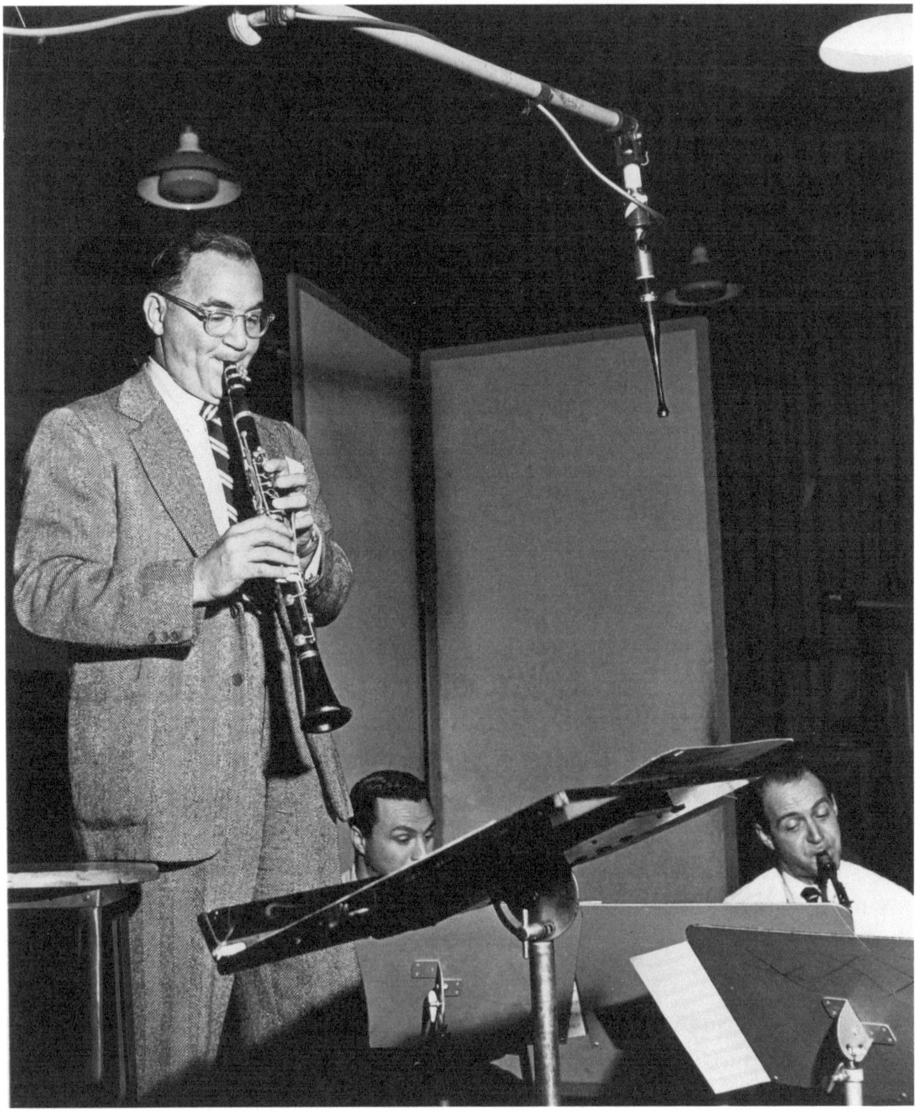

Figure 14: David B. Hecht. *Benny Goodman. Recording session.* Carnegie Hall. 1953. *Gilmore Music Library/Goodman Papers, Yale University.*

other jazz musicians as members of the artistic avant-garde. The renowned film director Stanley Kubrick was a jazz enthusiast and accomplished photographer who carried out a number of assignments for the illustrated press among traditional musicians in New Orleans.

Amateur photography was for a long time a white pursuit. The writer, historian, and revivalist William Russell was a keen amateur photographer with a profound affinity with the early New Orleans scene. John Steiner, the respected historian of Chicago jazz and founder of the City's Jazz Institute, used his camera to document the lives of the many musicians he befriended, many of which were published in the anthology *Destination Chicago Jazz* written with Sandor Demlinger, another photographer. Enthusiasts such as Harry Perkins Tate Jr. in Los Angeles and Bernie Moss in Boston were also assiduous in documenting local jazz people and activities. Stanley Dance, the British-born writer, business manager, record producer, and historian, photographed many of his encounters and his "family albums" at Yale University are a treasure trove of jazz memory. New Orleans has benefited from a large number of talented amateurs and participant observers with a passion for the city's culture and music, notably Grauman Marks and Dr. Bernard "Bernie" Steinau.

The European exiles

The exiles who arrived in Americas after fleeing Nazi terror between the mid- to late-1930s and the early-1940s included many accomplished photographers. More invested in European modernism than were many American photographers, this group made a major contribution to the development of American visual culture in documentary, photojournalistic, and art practices and were extremely important contributors to the new illustrated press. Almost all Jewish in heritage if not belief, an affinity with African Americans and their music found expression in the photography of a number in this cohort as they sought to evolve personal and social identities in their new country. Their work is discussed in Chapter 9.

Zinn Arthur, whose work as a band leader has overshadowed his contribution as a photographer, arrived from the Ukraine in 1921. While Weegee (born Usher Fellig in Hungary) is known for his uninhibited street photography, his humane and sympathetic images of black culture and musicians lack the acerbic vision of his better known work. Gjon Mili was a pioneer in stroboscopic photography and accomplished portraitist. Mili made a series of well-known photographs of a staged jazz jam session in his New York studio in the early-1940s as well as making stopped motion photographs of Lindy Hoppers and other dancers.

Jazz was seen by many of the exiles as a powerful form of cultural expression by another minority group offering scope for an exploration of their own place in the United States. Drawing on modernist ideas developed in Europe prior to their flight, the work of exiles such as Rose Mandel, John Guttmann, Alexander Alland, and Lisette Model is imbued with unsettling, exploratory, and enquiring signs. Francis Wolff, the cofounder with Alfred Lion of Blue Note Records, who arrived in 1939, had been a commercial photographer in Berlin and brought with him a deep sense of German Jewish *kultur*. Fred Plaut, a German electrical engineer who became a sound engineer with Columbia as well as being an accomplished photographer, also took a special interest in jazz. Lisl Steiner was a portraitist who found an affinity with musicians and other artistic personalities. The work of other exiles showed the signs of the documentary ethic: Roman

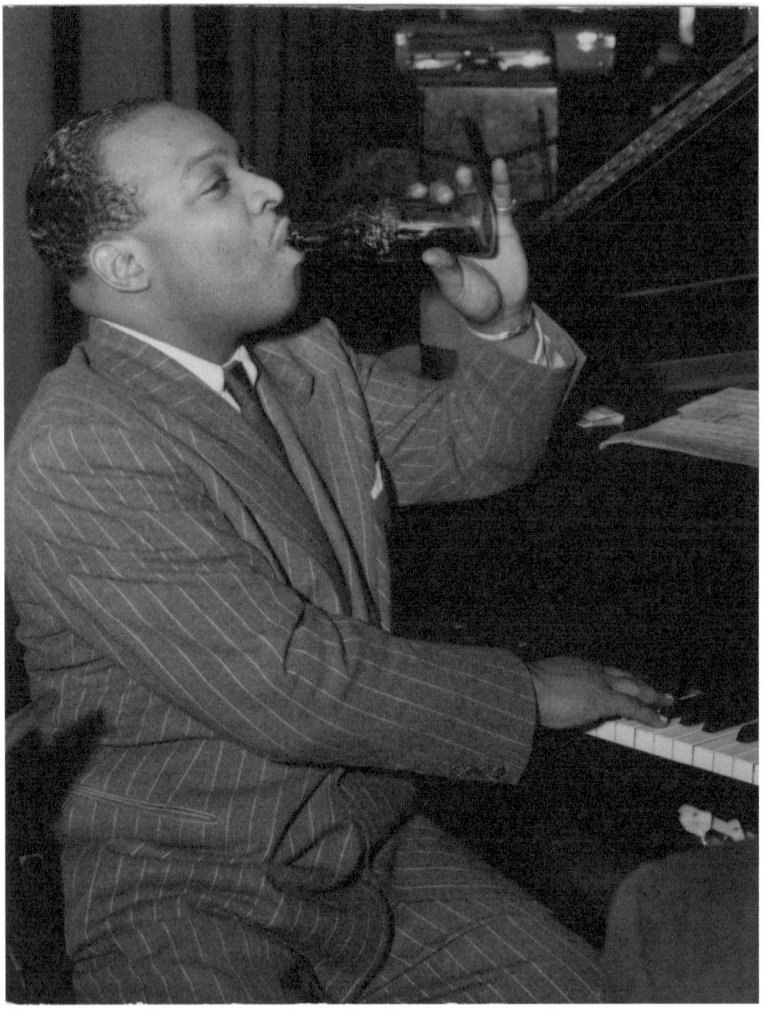

Figure 15: Otto Hess. *Count Basie and the Coca Cola Bottle*. New York. n.d. *New York Public Library, Otto Hess Collection.*

Vishniac's photographs of the guitarist and activist Josh White performing at Café Society; Otto Hess (Figure 15) and Henry Ries's documentation of the midtown Manhattan jazz scene of the 1930s and festivals on Randall's Island; and Clemens Kalischer and Joe Petrovec's candid portrayals of the personalities around the jazz roundtable meetings at Lenox and Tanglewood.

Notes

1. Jonathan Green, *American Photography: A Critical History 1945 to Present* (New York: Harry N. Abrams, 1984), 1.
2. Rudi Blesh, "Old Photographs: They Document the Legendary Days of Jazz," in *Jazzways*, ed. George S. Rosenthal and Frank Zachary (London: Musicians Press, 1946), 19.
3. The only known photograph of Buddy Bolden is perhaps the most famous example of the difficulties surrounding early jazz imagery. Taken around 1905 it has been reproduced many times; although the date was once stated as "before 1895," it may have been printed in reverse and the personnel are in doubt. There has even been a suggestion that the photograph in fact is a montage of two separate square negatives. Neither an original print nor negative exists so none of these contentions can be verified. See Donald M. Marquis, *In Search of Buddy Bolden: First Man of Jazz* (New York: Da Capo Press, 1978), 76–77; and Gerhardt Kubik, Justin Winston, and Clive Wilson, "The Buddy Bolden Band Photograph," *Jazz Archivist* 22 (2009): 1–24.
4. Bruce Boyd Raeburn, *New Orleans Style and the Writing of American Jazz History* (Ann Arbor: University of Michigan Press, 2009), 152–53, presents survey evidence compiled in 1942 by William C. Love and his collaborators suggesting that the average collector of the period was a 26-year-old white male: "Broadly speaking, the middle-class composition of the collector community is indisputable, as is the preponderance of males compared to females (a ratio of 15 to 1)."
5. William Kenney, *Recorded Music in American Life: The Phonograph and Popular Memory 1890–1945* (New York: Oxford University Press, 1999), xv. Ken Prouty, "The Problem with Community," in *Knowing Jazz: Community, Pedagogy, and Canon in the Information Age* (Jackson: University Press of Mississippi, 2012), 41, makes the point that to assume that recordings are poor substitutes for performances misconstrues how relationships in jazz are constructed. Susan J. Douglas, *Inventing American Broadcasting 1899–1922* (Baltimore, MD: John Hopkins University Press, 1987), 302, notes that radio broadcasts also brought about new associations of like-minded amateurs.
6. Ken Vail, *Swing Era Scrapbook: The Teenage Diaries and Radio Logs of Bob Inman 1936–38* (Lanham, MD: Scarecrow Press, 2005), 2.
7. "Ella Fitzgerald Mobbed by Crowd," *Down Beat*, July 15, 1940 and "Chords and Dischords," *Down Beat*, September 15, 1940.
8. Alan John Ainsworth, "Photographic Representations of Jazz: Testimonial Advertising in Down Beat, 1938–48," *Jazz Research Journal* 11, no. 2 (2018): 111–52, presents the results of an analysis of over 1,500 testomonial advertisements over a ten-year period from which the data in this paragraph are drawn.
9. Patricia Hills, *Cultural Legacies and the Transformation of the Cubist Collage Aesthetic* (Washington, DC: National Gallery of Art, 2011), 229–32; Hurston quoted by Thomas Brothers, *Louis Armstrong: Master of Modernism* (New York: W. W. Norton, 2014), 84.
10. "Apollo Threater's Gordon 'Doc' Anderson and Billie Holiday, 1950s," *Harlem World*, 2014. https://www.harlemworld.com There is a collection of Gordon Anderson's photographs at the New York Public Library's Schomberg Centre.
11. John Raeburn, *A Staggering Revolution: A Cultural History of Thirties Photography* (Chicago: University of Illinois Press, 2006), 7; Warren Susman, *Culture as History: The Transformation of American Society in the Twentieth Century* (New York: Pantheon Books, 1984), 160.
12. For cross-modal interactions, see Charles Spence and others, "Store Atmospherics: A Multisensory Perspective," *Psychology and Marketing* 31, no. 7 (2014): 472–88 and (with Massimillano Zampini), "The Role of Auditory Clues in Modulating the Perceived Crispness and Staleness of Potato Chips," *Journal of Sensory Studies* 19, no. 5 (n.d.): 347–63. Emily Keightley and Michael Pickering, "For the Record: Popular Music and Photography as Technologies of Memory," *European Journal of Cultural Studies* 9, no. 2 (2006): 149–65, propose that "the mutual compatibility and interaction" between recorded sound and photography is what viewers and listeners generally believe to be the mimetic fidelity of both media. In combination the "apparently uncoded actuality" of recorded music and photography is the source of their "symbolic potency, the indexical connection with flesh-and-blood referents that makes the experience so moving." W. J. T. Mitchell, "There Are No Visual Media," *Journal of Visual Culture* 4, no. 2 (2005): 257.
13. B. E. Stein and M. A. Meredith, *The Merging of the Senses* (Cambridge, MA: MIT Press, 1993), xi, 1.

14. Stein and Meredith, *The Merging of the Senses*, 7.
15. Benny Goodman Papers, Box 28, Folders 66 and 67A, Gilmore Music Library, Yale University.
16. Mihaly Csikszentmihalyi and Eugene Rochberg-Halton, *The Meaning of Things: Domestic Symbols and the Self* (Cambridge: Cambridge University Press, 1981), 69.
17. Pierre Nora, "Between Memory and History: *Les Lieux de Mémoire*," *Representations* no. 26 (Spring 1989): 7. For family snapshots and albums, see R. Chalfen, *Snapshot Versions of Life* (Bowling Green, OH: Bowling Green State University Press, 1987); Marianne Hirsch, *Family Frames: Photography, Narrative and Postmemory* (Cambridge, MA: Harvard University Press, 1997); Patricia Holland, "Introduction: Memory and the Family Album," in *Family Snaps: The Meanings of Domestic Photography*, ed. Jo Spence and Patricia Holland (London: Virago Press, 1991), 1–14; and Gillian Rose, "Family Photographs and Domestic Spacings: A Case Study," *Transactions of the Institute of British Geographers* 28, no. 1 (2003): 5–18.
18. Emily Keightley and Michael Pickering, *Photography, Music and Memory: Pieces of the Past in Everyday Life* (London: Palgrave Macmillan, 2015); Emily Keightley and Michael Pickering, "Echoes and Reverberations: Photography and Phonography as Historical Forms," *Media History* 13, nos. 2–3 (2007): 273–88. A special edition of *photographies* in 2010 was also devoted to the subject of memory and included Karen Cross and Julia Pec, "Editorial: Special Issue on Photography, Archive and Memory," *Photographies* 3, no. 2 (2010): 127–38; and David Bate, "The Memory of Photograph," *Photographies* 3, no. 2 (2010): 243–57. Hannah Arendt, *The Human Condition* (Chicago: University of Chicago Press, 1958), 174–75 and 224, has described the "reification which resemblance needs for its own fulfillment."
19. Clive Scott, *The Spoken Image: Photography and Language* (London: Reaktion Books, 1999), 34.
20. Vilém Flusser, *Towards a Philosophy of Photography* (London: Reaktion Books, 2000–2006), 9; Geoff Dyer, *But Beautiful: A Book about Jazz* (London: Jonathan Cape, 1991), xi–xii.
21. Tony Whyton, *Jazz Icons: Heroes, Myths and the Jazz Tradition* (Cambridge: Cambridge University Press, 2010), 7; Peter Townsend, *Jazz in American Culture* (Edinburgh: Edinburgh University Press, 2000), 166; Len Dobbin, "Legendary Jazz Photographer Paul Hoeffler Passed Away," AllAboutJazz.com, 2005, https://archive.is/20120722154154/http:/www.allaboutjazz.com/php/news.php?id=6823#selection-1057.0-1057.53; K. Heather Pinson, *The Jazz Image: Seeing Music through Herman Leonard's Photography* (Jackson: University of Mississippi Press, 2010), 1. John F. Szwed describes how jazz musicians have "become models of a lifestyle, popping up in chic ads or flavoring the walls of apartments of hip characters in films." The jazz musicians in turn become "one of the first truly nonmechanical metaphors for the twentieth century [. . .] Not since the English Gentleman, with his modality of poise, authority and how-one-should-be, has such an image dominated the world." John F. Szwed, *Jazz 101: A Complete Guide to Learning and Loving Jazz* (New York: Hyperion, 2000), 7–9.
22. Benjamin Cawthra, *Blue Notes in Black and White: Photography and Jazz* (Chicago: University of Chicago Press, 2011), 263; K. Heather Pinson, *The Jazz Image: Seeing Music through Herman Leonard's Photography* (Jackson: University of Mississippi Press, 2010), 127; and Gary Giddins and Scott DeVeaux, *Jazz* (New York: W. W. Norton, 2009), 575.
23. Library of Congress, "The Faces of Jazz," Online Text. Retrieved from the Library of Congress, accessed September 3, 2015, https://www.loc.gov/item/ihas.200185530/.
24. Milt Hinton and David G. Berger, *Bass Line: The Stories and Photographs of Milt Hinton* (Philadelphia: Temple University Press, 1988); and W. Royal Stokes, *Swing Era New York: The Jazz Photographs of Charles Peterson* (Philadelphia: Temple University Press, 1994).
25. Orin Keepnews and Bill Grauer Jr., *A Pictorial History of Jazz: People and Places from New Orleans to Modern Jazz* (Feltham, Middlesex: Spring Books, 1968); Frank Driggs and Harris Lewine, *Black Beauty, White Heat: A Pictorial History of Jazz 1920–1950* (New York: Da Capo, 1995); and Al Rose and Edmond Souchon, *New Orleans Jazz: A Family Album* (Baton Rouge: Louisiana State University Press, 1978).
26. Hank O'Neal, "Interview with the Author," 2018. O'Neal argues that much excellent jazz photography has been overlooked because it is considered commercial. He cites the example of the Polish-born photographer Ryszard Horowitz who relocated to America in 1959 to study under Alexey Brodovitch. Horowitz worked for a number of film and design companies and as an art director in advertising. He is recognized as a pioneer of special effects photography

predating digital imaging, often employing fictitious and surrealist imagery and was a pioneer of the photocomposition style that found expression in dream-like images. All the time he continued making jazz photographs of leading players. Horowitz's photos of jazz musicians have been collected in a book, *All That Jazz* (2014).

27. Qiana Mestrich, "RIP Photographer Hugh Bell," Dodge and Burn: Decolonizing Photography, 2012, https://dodgeburnphoto.com/2012/11/rip-photographer-hugh-bell/, considers Bell to be best known for jazz imagery. Geoff Dyer's perceptive analysis of DeCarava's photograph of Elvin Jones, "On Portraits," *Aperture*, no. 224 (2016): 23–24, is an example from outside jazz scholarship of a critical assessment. Saul Scott is one jazz writer who has taken a close interest in DeCarava's work: see Scott Saul, *Freedom Is, Freedom Ain't: Jazz and the Making of the Sixties* (Cambridge, MA: Harvard University Press, 2005), 248–53.

2

Jazz Writing and the Photographic Image

Scholars have tended to view photographs in the light of their own specialties and are often uncomfortable with the broader skills or methodologies necessary for the interpretation of visual evidence. Historians have been especially slow to accept visual evidence, preferring to rely on texts rather than the deeper levels of experience that images convey. The result, according to Roy Porter writing in 1988, is that historians have neglected the "socio-cultural 'voice' " of visual evidence:[1]

> *Our training encourages us to assume the primacy of written records [. . .] our most serious monographs are rarely "illustrated" (the very term suggests mere decorativeness). And when we do resort to pictures, publishers help by keeping the illustrations at a safe, non-contaminating distance from the chaste body of the text.*

Attitudes began to change toward the end of the last century. The interrogative stance introduced by literary and cultural studies has illuminated the role of photography in the construction of consciousness and raised lines of enquiry that demanded source material beyond conventional documentary texts and the development of methodologies new to the historian.[2] Nevertheless, when historians do use photography it is still too often for the strictly limited purpose of describing the subject of the image or to support conclusions previously reached; and the choice of material often underscores an affective stance. Peter Burke asserts that relatively few historians work in photographic as opposed to documentary archives and, when they do use images,[3]

> *... they tend to treat them as mere illustrations, reproducing them in their books without comment. In cases where the images are discussed in the text, this evidence is often used to illustrate conclusions that the author has already reached by other means.*

Martha A. Sandweiss adds the observation that few historians refer back to individual photographers and their intentions. Treating photographs as illustrations, historians have largely avoided any engagement with photographers and photography as a social activity or with the historicity of the photograph itself—an engagement that requires an altogether different interpretive act.[4] Music historians have been less resistant to the use of visual evidence, although they have tended to favor painting, etching, drawings, and sculpture over photography. The Research Center for Music Iconography has traditionally focused on artworks before the twentieth century with only occasional forays into the world of still or cinematic photography at its conferences, symposia, and annual monograph, *Art in Music.*[5] Any mention of photographs is absent from the entry "Iconology" in the Grove Encyclopedia of Music.

I. Jazz studies and visual evidence

Jazz texts frequently use photographs. In what ways, and how well, this material is used requires establishing the status of photography within jazz studies and, more specifically, the extent to which the "new" jazz studies movement changed attitudes toward visual evidence. Krin Gabbard's 1995 anthology *Jazz among the Discourses* was a seminal moment, initiating a critical interdisciplinary perspective toward previously unchallenged assumptions in the history of jazz. Pointing to the limitations of traditional musicology, jazz's "objects of study" expanded to embrace race, gender, class, nationality, and the diaspora and the movement raised contested claims to origination and ownership, technology, distribution and consumption, the impact of social and cultural currents, identities, and hegemonic and competing discourses.[6]

To this end documents traditionally considered to have claims to veracity have been rigorously interrogated. Recordings have attracted critical attention as constituting a primary document of jazz while being cultural artifacts with their own agency and subjected to their own forces of production. This fundamental duality resolves into a series of consequential problems concerning the relationship between live and recorded music, the location and attribution of authorship, aura and control, the experience of listening, and the place of technology. The consequences are serious for what earlier generations of jazz scholars regarded as unassailable evidential media.[7] Oral histories, memoirs, biographies and autobiographies, journalism and jazz criticism, radio and motion pictures, and the texts of jazz pedagogy have also been called into question.[8] Brent Edwards has recently tested the boundaries of "sayable" evidence by exposing even "ancillary texts" to critical scrutiny—letters, dairies, interviews, oral reminiscences and memoirs, poetry and other writings, and jottings by musicians. Mary Lou William's gas receipts and Duke Ellington's Bible reading notes are exposed to Edwards's archival hermeneutics, which draws connections through the "interplay and self-reflexivity" between these "texts" and the practice of jazz itself.[9]

It is curious that the status of the photograph and its place in jazz historiography has been only intermittently addressed by writers at the forefront of this turn in scholarship. The absence of a critical stance toward photography within new jazz studies becomes even more surprising when we recall the extensive body of "new" photography scholarship that in parallel has highlighted the mediated ontology of the photograph. Theorizing the photograph as an object and elucidating its ideological implications, this work calls into question the referential status of the photograph and suggests that the evidential veracity of the visual image is no less vexatious than that of records or the other documents of jazz. It seems extraordinary then that photography—at once the most obviously evidential of sources and ambiguous of media—should have been excluded from challenge by jazz scholars.

There was a point when it seemed that a more critical view of jazz photography might emerge. The reemergence of Herman Leonard's work in the 1980s and the publication of several reissued photobooks and memoirs had begun to stimulate new interest in the subject. Following a round table session in 1990 on representations of jazz in film, literature, and photography, Gabbard noted the importance of photography in his introduction to *Representing Jazz.* Among contributors to his anthology, Arthur Knight foregrounded the critical question of "control of the visible" while Michael Jarrett offered an informed and imaginative reading of William Claxton's cover photography for Sonny Rollins's album *Way Out West.*[10] Around the same time the subject of photography was treated in an extended interview between Gary Carner and the photographer Herb Snitzer.[11] The low profile of jazz photography was however underlined by Ingrid Monson in her influential book *Sayin' Something* when she observed that "the image we have of musicians is constructed through the activities of many types of agents" but conspicuously omitted photographers.[12] Nevertheless, the symposium on jazz and the art of photography curated by C. Daniel Dawson for the Centre for Jazz Studies at Columbia University in late 2000 seemed to be a positive sign.

Yet the paucity of published research into jazz photography over the following decade was noticeable. Describing photography as "the best place to find compelling images of jazz," Gabbard was obliged in 2002 to concede that no extended treatment of the subject was currently available.[13] In their extensive surveys of jazz scholarship and pedagogy, neither Gary Carner nor Eddie Meadows mentioned a single critical book about jazz photography.[14] Unsurprisingly, jazz photography is never mentioned within the broader practice of photographic and cultural studies. The *Oxford Companion to the Photograph* includes an entry for Roy DeCarava that couches his "extended study of Harlem" in formal artistic terms while making no mention of the centrality of jazz culture. The book completely omits Herman Leonard, William Claxton, William Gottlieb, Chuck Stewart, and other key names while Lee Friedlander's entry recounts that he "found work photographing jazz musicians for album covers"—hardly an accurate explanation of the importance of the music to Friedlander's practice.[15]

Although little new on the subject was published in the 2000s, research activity was going on behind the scenes. K. Heather Pinson's *The Jazz Image: Seeing Music through Herman Leonard's Photography* (2010) explored the rediscovery of Leonard's work in the 1980s, the conditions that facilitated an enthusiastic reception for these images, and the impact on Leonard's images in creating broad perceptions of the look of jazz. Inspired by the 2000 Columbia Seminar, Benjamin Cawthra became aware of the lack of scholarship and embarked on research for a dissertation on jazz photography eventually published in 2011 as *Blue Notes in Black and White: Photography and Jazz*. Cawthra offered a broader view than had Pinson, with discussions of William Gottlieb, Dennis Stock, Marvin Koner, Roy DeCarava, Chuck Stewart, Gjon Mili and, particularly, Herman Leonard and William Claxton. His book explored the relationships between photographers and jazz subjects, the effects of photography in the validation of jazz, and the importance of album artwork, and he was particularly incisive in his analysis of the relationship between the work of Herman Leonard and bebop, William Claxton and west coast jazz, and Roy DeCarava and John Coltrane. As the first extended treatment of jazz and photography this book was an extremely important achievement; and although Cawthra offered little analysis of African American photographers he took care to explore the relationships between black musicians and white photographers in collaboratively producing jazz photographs.

Cawthra and Pinson's work might have stimulated further research into jazz photography, but the impetus faded. Peter Townsend and Tony Whyton have briefly approached the subject in the context of wider cultural surveys and Mark Laver addressed photographs in his survey of jazz and marketing. A potentially fruitful approach to photography was suggested by Daniel Stein in his approach to jazz autobiography. Stressing the multimedial nature of Armstrong's autobiographical sketches, Stein argues that "photographs are visual reminders of the autobiographical past [. . .] They open up a space for visual modes of self-performance" as text and image complement each other. Stein failed to take full advantage of the possibilities of photographic meanings by focusing on Armstrong's own photomontages while the intertextual interventions of the photograph in his account become confirmatory or contradictory of *other texts* rather than meaningful at the level of *sui generis* properties.[16]

How can this absence of critical attention to photographs by jazz writers be explained? One factor might be the lack of exchange between photographic theorists and jazz scholars although at first glance this seems strange. Contemporary jazz and photography writers have generally been alive to the mainstream of critical and historical writings. Drawing on the same theories of language, discourse, and power from literary and art criticism, on social history, psychoanalysis, and ideological critique, both have produced new works that move well beyond traditional jazz or photography historiography. So why have jazz scholars not capitalized on the insights of photography theory to a greater extent? Perhaps it is because jazz writers face a considerable challenge posed by a heterogeneous and often conflicting body of work, the confident manner of which gives the impression that the major questions hanging over the medium have been resolved. Yet for much of its existence photography has been riven by disagreements about the nature, function, and effect of the medium. Contestations around photography's central problematic—whether a photograph is defined by the person who took it or what it represents—remain vigorous: as Richard

Bolton points out, "It seems that wherever we look in photography we find contradictory impulses and opposing aims. The wide range of photographic applications raises the possibility that photography has no governing characteristics at all save adaptability."[17] The lack of consensus within photographic theory has undoubtedly encouraged jazz writers to remain within the relatively safe harbor of the photograph as a straightforwardly transcriptive medium—after all, it is difficult enough to interpret visual evidence if photography theorists cannot themselves agree whether photographs are or are not coded.[18]

Another factor is the tendency on the part of jazz writers to be daunted by the large number of frankly dull and routine jazz images that lack the immediacy of meaning of well-known "iconic" images. As Gary Carner put it in 1991,[19]

> *Thumbing through jazz photography books can be a uniquely soporific experience [. . .] the few evocative, truly expressive photographs there may be are usually so overwhelmed by page upon page of numbing documentary shots that the significant work is leeched of its visceral impact.*

As an editor Eugene Lees was also well aware of the limitations of many jazz photographs:[20]

> *Remarkably few photographers get good pictures from jazz. Too many are satisfied with routine shots-head-on pictures of the star [. . .] Or they are hindered by the mike booms and other paraphernalia, instead of taking advantage of them. And, evidently not enough photographers are yet sufficiently adept at available light shooting to get all the mood possibilities out of dim rooms and spotlights, or concert hall lighting.*

Recognizing that *all* photographs can offer valuable information beyond their aesthetic or affective appeal requires distinctive methodological skills and a mindset attuned to visual nuance. Generally unaccustomed to handling and assessing material in photographic archives, jazz writers have gravitated toward the well-known photographs from a small group of photographers whose work is immediately recognizable and whose appeal is congruent with the myths around jazz—many of which, of course, photography itself has helped to create and sustain.

II. Perception and surface interpretation

Although photography is widely employed by jazz writers it has mostly been as illustrative material rather than a historical source requiring critical interpretation. When jazz writers attempt to interpret or read visual material their comments tend to fall into or across two types.

Picture perception. Photographs in jazz texts are generally used for the identification of players, locations, and dates, for which purpose the identity of the photographer is at best a secondary consideration and mostly omitted. Examples of typical captions drawn from six leading jazz texts are shown below:

> *(Photo of Freeman and Ellington)*
> *Bud Freeman and Duke Ellington at a Private Party, August 1939*
> *(Gillespie greeting fans)*
> *Dizzy Gillespie greeted by fans upon his March 1948 return from a two-month tour of Europe*
> *(Audience shot)*
> *A segregated audience enjoys a Duke Ellington concert at Fort Dix, New Jersey*
> *(Orchestra shot)*
> *McKinney's Cotton Pickers, 1933, Directed by Billie Bowen, featuring Roy Eldridge and Joe Eldridge, Cuba Austin (drums), and Prince Robinson (Tenor/clarinet). Photo Courtesy of Frank Driggs Collection*
> *(Photo of Davis)*
> *Miles Davis During a Live Concert in 1969*
> *(Studio scene)*
> *Tenor saxophonist Don Byas (with hat) on a 1945 recording session with trumpeter Benny Harris*

Krin Gabbard used nine images of musicians in his 2016 biography of Charles Mingus in which captions are limited to identifying personnel and location.[21] Alyn Shipton's acclaimed biography of Cab Callaway included twenty photographs sourced from the Frank Driggs Collection (eleven), the musician Danny Barker (four), and the Calloway family (three). Eleven photographs are band portraits and/or performance shots used to identify sidemen playing with Calloway at the time; four are informal scenes with friends and family. Captions are confined to dates and personnel while the photographers, agencies, publications, or other institutional affiliations are not identified. There is little if any cross-reference between the main body text and the photographs, which are presented separately within the volume.[22] In *Jazz Style in Kansas City and the Southwest* Ross Russell presents no fewer than 80 photographs, many of which are extensively captioned although none offers any information beyond personnel, location, and date.[23]

Writers such as Sherry Tucker, Sally Placksin, and Linda Dahl have actively sought out archival photography to help identify women musicians and bring to light their contribution to jazz.[24] Here again photographs have been used mainly for illustration or identification purposes. This is surprising in view of the ambitions of feminist jazz historiography to stretch beyond that of simply *recognizing* the "lost women" of jazz history toward a contextually sensitive gender analysis explaining the social construction of masculinity and femininity.[25] This requires interpreting the position of women in jazz so as to challenge the dominant interpretation of jazz as a masculine preserve—an objective in which photography might have been more imaginatively used to evoke the deeper levels of experience of women players.

While in many cases these images are presented without identifying the photographer, one might imagine that jazz photobooks designed to showcase the work of specific photographers might allow the author's voice to emerge. Even here illustrations are nearly always accompanied by brief text describing the scene or the recollections of musicians or other writers. Edited by W. Royal Stokes in collaboration with Charles Peterson's son Don, *Swing Era New York* presents several hundred of Peterson's photographs drawn from his entire career. The book is attractively produced, the landscape format does justice to the visual material, the images are well reproduced, and all are accompanied by (occasionally lengthy) explanatory text. Yet nowhere in the text is there any analysis or interpretation of Peterson's photographs. Much the same can be said of other jazz photobooks.

Surface perception. It would be misleading to suggest that jazz texts never go beyond identification captioning. Curators and critics frequently pick up on the surface motifs of jazz photographs as the basis for atmospheric, evocative, or affective interpretations. Surface perception therefore moves beyond that which is immediately perceivable to attribute meaning to those perceptions. Ryan Smith's comments on exhibits in an exhibition of jazz portraits by Herman Leonard at Washington's National Portrait Gallery in 2017 are typical:[26]

> *The artists in Leonard's photographs are caught in moments of splendid isolation, their focus locked unshakably on their music, their every muscle fully engaged. In one shot, Billie Holiday's reverent gaze is lost in the middle distance, the supple curved fingers of her dark-nailed hands caressing the air on either side of her mic stand. In another, Charlie Parker plays, his brow knitted, his lips pursed tightly about the mouthpiece of his alto sax, his eyes closed, captivated in a dream of his own making.*

The exhibition curator, Ann Schumard, pointed to "[t]he vitality of these performers [. . .] the excitement their music generated [which] made them ideal subjects for photography [. . .] There's almost a three-dimensionality to the images [. . .] There's an atmospheric effect."[27] A cottage industry of introductions to jazz photobooks, anthologies, and collections relies on observations such as the following:[28]

> *Look again at the photograph of Duke Ellington lifting his band and his sidemen, and that thrust of life may enter your own being as well.*
> (Nat Hentoff)

> *[Larry Fink's photograph] stand as aesthetically complex and socially insightful records of musicians (famous and not) and those for whom music—especially jazz—is often life-defining.*
> (George E. Panichas)

> *Herman Leonard's work comes close to pure art: in the beauty of the image, for the emption and feeling that it radiates.*
> (Francis Paudras)

In their use of photography, it seems then that jazz writers move between the immediacy of perceptual description, in which evidential detail is insulated from the more ambiguous metaphorical signs and read as more or less unmediated transcription of "what actually happened," and the allure of surfaces in which interpretation flows seamlessly from appearances to nostalgic or affective statements that are often difficult to disentangle from personal memory.

Few jazz writers have deployed critical perspectives that might guide readings toward a deeper level of interpretation. Picture perception is a level of interpretation that relies on an assumption of mimesis as adequate to denotation and in which the apparent referential fidelity of the photograph makes it difficult to move beyond the simple description of what appears in the image. Even surface interpretation, which is a higher level of understanding, is nonetheless "routine," appearing natural without relying on cultural assumptions. As Arthur C. Danto puts it, "surface interpretation undertakes to characterize the external behavior of an agent with reference to the internal representation of it presumed to be the agents"; for this reason, "surface interpretation must be distinguished from the sort of [. . .] hermeneutic or what I shall designate *deep* interpretation."[29]

The lure of photographic surfaces: Four bebop pioneers

William Gottlieb's famous photograph of Thelonious Monk, Howard McGee, Roy Eldridge, and Teddy Hill outside Minton's (Figure 16) provides an example of the seductive quality of surface perception. Described by Robin D. G. Kelley as "one of the most widely circulated and iconic photographs in jazz history [. . .] Four pioneers of modern jazz standing abreast [. . .] a Mount Rushmore of modern jazz,"[30] Gottlieb's photograph has regularly been interpreted as

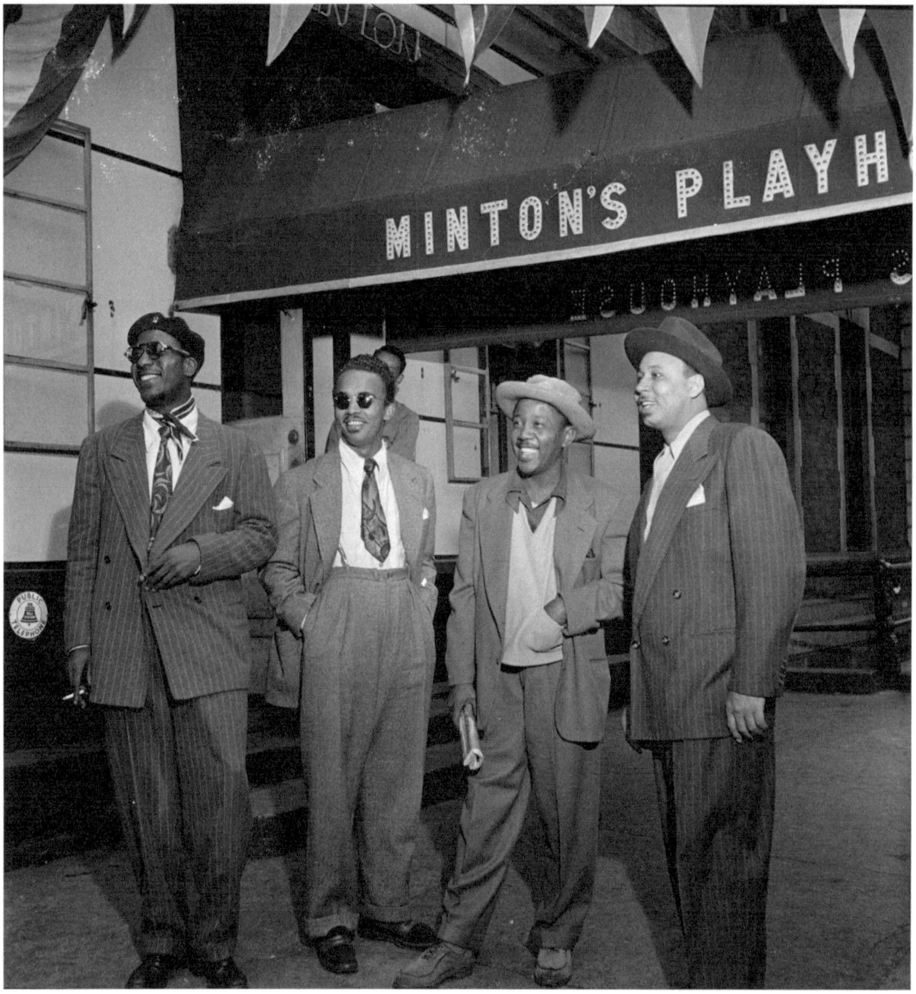

Figure 16: William P. Gottlieb. *Portrait of Thelonious Monk, Howard McGhee, Roy Eldridge, and Teddy Hill, Minton's Playhouse*. New York. 1947.
Ed Gottlieb/Library of Congress.

showing a group of equal style partners in the new bebop music. James Lincoln Collier for instance provides the following caption: "Minton's, the club where bebop first found acceptance, with some of the heroes of the time" and he includes Eldridge in his list of names of those who dropped in on the jam sessions that incubated bebop.[31] Careful observation suggests that Eldridge's dress—an important signifying practice of the new music—is out of kilter with that of Monk and McGhee and hardly the distinctive cut associated with advanced bebop musicians of the period. This should not be surprising: John Chilton recounts that Eldridge "fairly bristled" when anyone linked him with the jazz developments at Minton's: "I hardly went there. It wasn't my scene, but because there was a photo of me, Monk, Howard McGhee and Teddy Hill outside

Minton's, people thought I was always there."[32] On one level then the photograph misleads about the engagement of particular individuals in the creation of bebop, especially when we remember the grouping was engineered by Gottlieb who had probably tipped off McGee, Eldridge, and Hill to be around Minton's when he was planning to take the photograph in connection with an article on Monk that subsequently appeared in *Down Beat* in September 1947.

This is the least of the problems. Gottlieb's photograph has been distributed and reprinted so many times that it has taken on what Cawthra calls "a visual memory of its own," standing in for other events and contingencies.[33] This has led to a broad acceptance of the veracity of the image that appears to link the musicians with a specific location and a collection of cultural values embodied in the term "bebop." As a statement of the constellation of behaviors, presentation, and claims that set the public context and material culture of modernist artistic production the photograph cannot be bettered. The musicians' stylish yet informal suits, fancy shirts and ties, dark shades and headwear are matched by their expressions of nonchalant confidence, signs that play into the attribution of race confidence, defiance, and even arrogance of the bebop pioneers. The visual memory that the photograph has helped bring into being acts as a sweeping visual shorthand: "The lettering on the awning, Monk's attire, McGhee's sunglasses, all seem to spell 'bebop.' "[34] The players form a united cultural front separate from the wider world, "sealed," as it were, by location, posture, gestures, style, and material culture.

It is precisely the affective and nostalgic expressive immediacy of such surface readings that skews the claims of many contemporary interpretations of Gottlieb's photograph. By far the most problematic aspect thus becomes the way in which interpretations of the photograph dissolve the development of bebop to a small subculture apart from conventional life, casting the music as hermetically sealed art in opposition to commercial music. Contemporary readings ironically chime with older accounts of bebop, the "world of dreamers" described by Alun Morgan and Raymond Horricks, in which the participants "had no thought of a cohesive modern jazz form [. . .] merely an exploration for their personal satisfaction, a relief, a form of relaxation":[35]

> *The public had no say over policy or style, and each man was allowed to improvise for the satisfaction of his own artistic standards. Amidst a listening audience chiefly composed of fellow musicians the soloists found an atmosphere most conducive to the fanciful roaming of their inspiration. No brows were puckered with annoyance if a more progressive thinker began to introduce his theories. Into the sessions; theories were presented, examined and judged.*

This reading finds support in Gottlieb's *Down Beat* article, which positioned Monk as the founder of the new music, and the subsequent iconization of Monk in Blue Note photography and recollections by writers like Paul Bacon.[36] Yet, as Scott DeVeaux has demonstrated, bebop cannot be understood simply as the development of a new art form, the product of a cadre of musical revolutionaries who upended the music, nor can that art form be universalized as the product of gifted individuals. Bebop was the response of a wide range of enquiring musicians (some, like Coleman Hawkins, predating the bebop explosion proper) to specific social, economic, and cultural factors, including the quest to reach an accommodation with commercial entertainment.

When it comes to photography, it is as if DeVeaux's strictures against the "transcendent universality" of bebop have been lost by many jazz scholars. "Once a photograph ages, the immediate reference to the original is no longer possible," as Siegfried Kracauer observed: "The truth content of the original is left behind in its history; the photograph captures only the residuum that history has discharged."[37] This has surely been the fate of Gottlieb's famous image.

III. Conclusion: The new jazz photography canon

If photography is seen as having little to "say" beyond picture perception and surface expression, it is not surprising that jazz writers have found little reason to seek out competing voices beyond a small cohort at the core of the jazz photography tradition. Gravitating toward the most impactful images at the level of surfaces, jazz writers have engaged in a canonical practice similar to that found in other areas of photographic scholarship. Exploring the work of the FSA photographers, Hank O'Neal was disturbed[38]

> *. . . seeing the same photographs over and over; for example, in every book I examined Dorothea Lange's "Migrant Mother" was reproduced. Virtually every book [. . .] used the famous images over and over. It was almost as if someone had once said, "Here are a hundred representative photographs and they alone will be available for publication."*

Jazz texts are remarkably similar. In his book on race and jazz, Patrick Burke stresses that among his "eclectic range of colorful [source] material" photography "will shed new light on 52nd Street's racial dynamic."[39] It is surprising then to find that 23 of the 25 images in the book are by well-known white photographers (14 by Charles Peterson and 9 by William Gottlieb) and two are unidentified. Burke's captions on his photographs are confined to identification and are little other than illustrative. The 1998 edition of Ted Gioia's *West Coast Jazz* includes no less than 30 of William Claxton's photographs with no other photographer represented; apart from a frontispiece, the images are grouped separately with no cross-references from the main body of text and captions are confined to naming personnel.[40]

In a study of three key jazz educational texts, Ramsey Castaneda and Amanda Quinlan have analyzed the authors' selections of some 402 images representing the work of 57 photographers. Of 211 credited photographs, nearly half (47.8 percent) are the work of just four photographers (Gottlieb, Leonard, Stewart, and Schiedt). All the photographers used in these texts are white commercial practitioners with the exception of Chuck Stewart.[41] Comments by the authors on their selection of photographs in one of Castaneda and Quinlan's texts, Garry Giddins and Scott DeVeaux's seminal *Jazz,* are particularly instructive. These authors do not seek to hide their affective stance toward visual material:[42]

> *We are privileged to have the participation of the brilliant Herman Leonard, considered by many the greatest photographer ever to focus his camera on jazz [. . .] Leonard is distinguished in his work by his total control of light. In the late 1940s, the peak of his jazz period, Leonard brought his equipment to clubs, blocked out the natural light, and created his own chiaroscuro effects, emphasizing the excitement of the music through reflected highlights and his signature use of cigarette smoke.*

Most of the photographs chosen by DeVeaux and Giddins were taken in club or other performance settings and demonstrate Leonard's trademark lighting, composition, and visual language. The work of a superb technician, these portraits are nevertheless decontextualized statements of artistic transcendence, figures in an idealized realm as removed from current events as it is possible to be. With little reading across text and images, it is clear that these images have been selected purely for their impact as illustration. The power of Leonard's photographs to convey statements of artistic achievement has only gained in force through their frequent reproduction in texts such as *Jazz,* retrospectively encouraging categorial rather than particularizing explanations.[43] The process naturally became self-sustaining as Leonard eventually cast himself along with Gottlieb and Claxton as "inventors" of jazz photography—an unsupportable claim but one generally accepted in jazz writing even if usually shorn of Leonard's bombastic rhetoric:[44]

> *In my estimation, there are three photographers who recorded the history of modern jazz: William Gottlieb, who worked primarily in the late-1930s and early-1940s; William Claxton, who worked from the early-1950s to now and myself, who started in the mid-1940s. Between us, we visually recorded for eternity the modern jazz movement. Thankfully for future generations, our work hangs in many museums, including the Smithsonian Institution in Washington D.C [. . .] Bill Gottlieb, William Claxton and I documented jazz, America's only original art form, in an artistic and dynamic way, virtually inventing jazz photography.*

The consequence of choices like these by jazz writers has been to privilege a jazz photography tradition comprising almost exclusively white art photographers, effectively establishing an archive that defines and delimits that tradition. Archives condition knowledge and understanding by imposing an order on materials through which interpretative meaning is opaquely constructed, an abstraction from both their use and the contingencies of usage. The photographic archive, as Allan Sekula describes it, is particularly potent in providing the "paradigm or iconic system from which photographic 'statements' are constructed."[45] Care is however required not to elide variations between the different uses to which the photographic document can be put.[46] If this style of jazz photography is far removed from the standardized techniques (subdued lighting, consistent orthogonal composition, even tones, etc.) of photographs specifically created for official or institutional archives through what Sekula calls their "abstracted visual equivalence," the subsequent *selection* of photographs created for other purposes to represent jazz from the many thousands available has established a construct—a nostalgic or affective assembly—with many of the conditioning features characterizing an archive. The style of photography established by the white photographers of the classic period have come to represent the core cultural symbols of the tradition and the benchmark for the visual representation of jazz. As DeVeaux and Giddin's comments show, these photographs form a hugely affective composite myth of a heroic past in which elements of fact are combined with less well-founded beliefs in a process that serves to reduce the historical complexity and specificity of jazz into manageable—but potentially value-laden—form.[47]

One effect of this archive has been to remove from consideration many of the competing photographic voices examined throughout this book. The most profound effect of the new jazz photographic canon however is not simply to exclude *some* photographers from consideration but rather to bring about the effective excision of *all* photographers as historical witness. If photographs have no more to say than to confirm the presence of their referents or as artifacts of affective or nostalgic affect, *any* interpretation or meaning consciously invested by a photographer is effectively dismissed as a valid object of historical enquiry. So why bother going to the lengths of finding out about the photographers, their own aims, objectives, and aspirations? In Castaneda and Quinlan's survey, no fewer than 191 (47.5 percent of the sample) of jazz images were uncredited or credited to archives. It is this lack of recognition that led Marc Myers to describe the environment in which New York jazz photographers worked in the 1960s as "miserable": "Unlike painters, dancers, musicians and writers [. . .] photographers were largely anonymous. If their names appeared at all [. . .] it was in the smallest font possible [. . .] Unless you cared, you never knew."[48]

Ultimately, jazz photography is defined tautologically in the overwhelming majority of jazz texts as the work of selected jazz photographers. Building on the affinity between photographers of different kinds and jazz, and seeking to identify the key lines of photographic agency inscribed in the image, the approach developed throughout this book has been crafted to allow for a more pluralistic and culturally rooted definition. As Larry Viskochil reminds us, it is only by examining the medium (the photograph), the sender (the photographer), and by asking of the image "Why?", "How?," "When?," and "Where?" that we are able to move beyond the readings based on simple perception and surface expression.[49]

Notes

1. Roy Porter, "Review Article: Seeing the Past," *Past & Present* 118 (1988): 188. See also Hans Belting, *Likeness and Presence: A History of the Image before the Era of Art* (Chicago: University of Chicago Press, 1994), 2–3.
2. Jennifer Tucker, "Entwined Practices: Engagements with Photography in Historical Inquiry," *History and Theory* 48, no. 4 (2009): 1–8; Jens Jäger, "Elective Affinities? History and Photography," in *Global Photographies: Memory–History–Archives*, ed. Sissy Helf and Stephanie Michels (Bielefeld: Transcript-Verlag, 2018), 39–43; Joshua Brown, "Historians and Photography," *American Art* 21, no. 3 (2007): 9–13. Leigh Raiford, "Photography and the Practices of Critical Black Memory," *History and Theory* 48, no. 4 (2009): 112–29; and bell hooks, *Outlaw Culture: Resisting Representations* (London: Routledge, 1994), esp. 165–72, are examples of the use of photographic evidence as a means of excavating the experience of subaltern groups.
3. Peter Burke, *Eyewitnessing: The Uses of Images as Historical Evidence* (London: Reaktion Books, 2001), 10; Brown, "Historians and Photography," 10; Julia Adeney Thomas, "The Evidence of Sight," *History and Theory* 48, no. 4 (2009): 151–68. Gordon Fyfe and John Law, "On the Invisibility of the Visual," in *Picturing Power*, ed. Gordon Fyfe and John Law (London: Routledge, 1988), 1–14.
4. Martha A. Sandsweiss, "Photography in Nineteenth Century America," in *Photography in Nineteenth Century America*, ed. Martha A. Sandweiss (New York: Harry N. Abrams, 1991), xiii; Shirley Teresa Wajda, "History Writing, with Light," *Reviews in American History* 26, no. 3 (1998): 567.
5. It is, however, planned that the 2021 edition of *Music in Art* will be devoted to photography.
6. Eric Porter, "Incorporation and Distinction in Jazz History and Jazz Historiography," in *Jazz/Not Jazz: The Music and Its Boundaries*, ed. David Ake, Charles Hiroshi Garrett, and Daniel Goldmark (Berkeley: University of California Press, 2012), 13–15. See further Sherrie Tucker, "Deconstructing the Jazz Tradition: The 'Subjectless Subject' of New Jazz Studies," in *Jazz/Not Jazz: The Music and Its Boundaries*, ed. David Ake, Charles Hiroshi Garrett, and Daniel Goldmark (Berkeley: University of California Press, 2012), 264–68.
7. Catherine Tackley, "Recording as Social Text," in *Recorded Music: Performance, Culture and Technology*, ed. Amanda Bayley (Cambridge: Cambridge University Press, 2010), 167–86; Jed Rasula, "The Media of Memory: The Seductive Menace of Records in Jazz History," in *Jazz Among the Discourses*, ed. Krin Gabbard (Durham, NC: Duke University Press, 1995), 134–62; Tony Whyton, "Jazz and the Disembodied Voice," in *Jazz Icons: Heros, Myths and the Jazz Tradition* (Cambridge: Cambridge University Press, 2010), 38–56 and Mark Katz, *Capturing Sound: How Technology Has Changed Music* (Berkeley: University of California Press, 2004), 72–84.
8. For critical assessments of oral histories see Sherrie Tucker, "Telling Performances: Jazz History Remembered and Remade by the Women in the Band," *Oral History Review* 26, no. 1 (1999): 67–84, and Burton W. Peretti, "Speaking in the Groove: Oral History and Jazz," *Journal of American History* 88, no. 2 (2001): 582–95; and "Oral Histories of Jazz Musicians: The NEA Transcripts as Texts in Context," in *Jazz Among the Discourses*, ed. Krin Gabbard (Durham, NC: Duke University Press, 1995), 117–33. For memoires, autobiographies, and biography see William H. Kenney, "Negotiating the Color Line: Louis Armstrong's Autobiographies," in *Jazz in Mind: Essays on the History and Meanings of Jazz*, ed. Reginald T. Buckner and Steven Weiland (Detroit, MI: Wayne State University Press, 1991), 38–59; Kathy Ogren, "'Jazz Isn't Just Me': Jazz Autobiographies as Public Personas," in *Jazz in Mind: Essays on the History and Meaning of Jazz*, ed. Reginald T. Buckner and Steven Weiland (Detroit, MI: Wayne State University Press, 1991), 112–27; Daniel Stein, *Music Is My Life: Louis Armstrong, Autobiography and American Jazz* (Ann Arbor: University of Michigan Press, 2012), 12–26, 33–47; and Thomas Brothers, "'Swing a Lot of Type Writing' An Introduction to Louis Armstrong's Writings," in *Louis Armstrong in His Own Words: Selected Writings* (Oxford: Oxford University Press, 1999), vii–xxiii. For jazz journalism and criticism see Ron Welburn, "Jazz Magazines of the 1930s: An Overview of Their Provocative Journalism," *American Music* 5, no. 3 (1987): 255–70; John Gennari, *Blowin' Hot and Cool: Jazz and Its Critics* (Chicago: University of Chicago

Press, 2006); and Bruce Boyd Raeburn, *New Orleans Style and the Writing of American Jazz History* (Ann Arbor: University of Michigan Press, 2009). For radio see James P. Kraft, *Stage to Studio: Musicians and the Sound Revolution, 1890–1950* (Baltimore, MD: John Hopkins University Press, 1996), 59–87. For jazz in motion pictures see Krin Gabbard, *Jammin' at the Margins: Jazz and the American Cinema* (Chicago: University of Chicago Press, 1996). For the materials of jazz education see Prouty, "Toward Jazz's 'official' History: The Debates and Discourses of Jazz History Textbooks."

9. Brent Hayes Edwards, *Epistrophies: Jazz and the Literary Imagination* (Cambridge, MA: Harvard University Press, 2017), 20.
10. Krin Gabbard, "Introduction: Writing the Other Jazz History," in *Representing Jazz*, ed. Krin Gabbard (Durham, NC: Duke University Press, 1995), 1–8; Arthur Knight, "'Jammin the Blues, or the Sight of Jazz," in *Representing Jazz*, ed. Krin Gabbard (Durham, NC: Duke University Press, 1995), 11–53; Michael Jarrett, "The Tenor's Vehicle: Reading Way Out West," in *Representing Jazz*, ed. Krin Gabbard (Durham, NC: Duke University Press, 1995), 260–82.
11. Gary Carner, "Jazz Photography: A Conversation with Herb Snitzer," *Black American Literature Forum* 25, no. 3 (1991): 560–92.
12. Ingrid Monson, *Saying Something: Jazz Improvisation and Interaction* (Chicago: University of Chicago Press, 1996), 14.
13. Krin Gabbard, "Images of Jazz," in *The Cambridge Companion to Jazz*, ed. Mervyn Cooke and David Horn (Cambridge: Cambridge University Press, 2002), 336–40, 356, fn.4. At the time of writing Gabbard suggested that Mona Hadler's 1983 article "Jazz and the Visual Arts" was the best treatment of the subject although its emphasis is overwhelmingly on the influence of jazz on painting—Mona Hadley, "Jazz and the Visual Arts," *Arts Magazine* (1983): 91–101 and "Jazz and the New York School," in *Representing Jazz*, ed. Krin Gabbard (Durham, NC: Duke University Press, 1995), 247–59.
14. Gary Carner, *Jazz Performers: An Annotated Bibliography of Biographical Materials* (New York: Greenwood Press, 1990), 339–42; Eddie S. Meadows, *Jazz Scholarship and Pedagogy: A Research and Information Guide* (New York: Routledge, 2006): 47–51.
15. Camara Dia Holloway, "'DeCarava, Roy' and Molly Rogers, 'Friedlander, Lee'," in *The Oxford Companion to the Photography*, ed. Robin Lenman (Oxford: Oxford University Press, 2005), 160, 239. See Mary Warner Marien, *Photography: A Cultural History*, 3rd ed. (London: Laurence King, 2002–20), for an example of a broad cultural treatment of photography in which there is no mention of jazz photography.
16. Peter Townsend, *Jazz in American Culture* (Edinburgh: Edinburgh University Press, 2000), 163–66; Whyton, *Jazz Icons: Heroes, Myths and the Jazz Tradition*, 6–8; Mark Laver, *Jazz Sells: Music Marketing and Meaning* (New York: Routledge, 2015); and Daniel Stein, *Music Is My Life: Louis Armstrong, Autobiography and American Jazz* (Ann Arbor: University of Michigan Press, 2012), 16–17.
17. Richard Bolton, "Introduction," in *The Contest of Meaning: Critical Histories of Photography*, ed. Richard Bolton (Cambridge, MA: MIT Press, 1989), ix, xi. See also Carol Squiers, "Introduction," in *The Critical Image: Essays on Contemporary Photography*, ed. Carol Squiers (Seattle: Bay Press, 1990), xx.
18. A pivotal debate in photographic theory. See Roland Barthes's essays "The Photographic Message," in *Photography in Print*, ed. Vicki Goldberg (Albuquerque: University of New Mexico, 1961), 521–33 and "The Third Meaning: Research Notes on Some Eisenstein Stills," in *Image-Music-Text*, ed. S. Heath (London: Fontana, 1977), 61. John Berger shifted from the idea that the photograph was coded toward the opposite view in John Berger and Jean Mohr, *Another Way of Telling* (New York: Pantheon, 1982), 96. For others the photograph is inevitably coded—see John Tagg, *The Burden of Representation: Essays on Photographies and Histories* (London: Macmillan, 1988), 3.
19. Gary Carner, "Literature of Jazz Issue: Introduction," *Black American Literature Forum* 25, no. 3 (1991): 445.
20. Gene Lees, "A Cool Appraisal," in *The Iconic Images of Ted Williams*, ed. Ted Williams (London: ACC Editions, 2016), 8.
21. Krin Gabbard, *Better Git It in Your Soul: An Interpretive Biography of Charles Mingus* (Oakland: University of California Press, 2016), 39, 79, 95, 108, 162–63, 204, 211, 221.
22. Alyn Shipton, *Hi-De-Ho: The Life of Cab Calloway* (Oxford: Oxford University Press, 2010).
23. Ross Russell, *Jazz Style in Kansas City and the Southwest* (Berkeley: University of California Press, 1971). viii–xv.
24. Sherrie Tucker, "A Feminist Perspective on New Orleans Jazz Women," New

Orleans Jazz National Historical Park (Lawrence, KS: University of Kansas, 2004) and Sally Placksin, *American Women in Jazz 1900 to the Present: Their Worlds, Lives and Music* (New York: Wideview Books, 1982) both use archival photographs to help identify women players and participants in jazz.

25. Tucker, "A Feminist Perspective on New Orleans Jazz Women," 7.
26. Ryan P. Smith, "Jazz Has Never Looked Cooler Than It Does in This New Exhibition," Smithsonian.com, 2016. www.smithsonianmag.com/smithsonian-institution/jazz-has-never-looked-cooler-than-it-does-new-exhibition-180960191/.
27. Shumard cited by Smith, "Jazz Has Never Looked Cooler Than It Does in This New Exhibition."
28. Nat Hentoff, "Introduction," in *The Jazz Image: Masters of Jazz Photography*, ed. Lee Tanner (New York: Abrams, 2006), 7; George E. Panichas, "Somewhere There's Music," in *Larry Fink: Somewhere There's Music* (Bologna: Damiani Editore, 2006), xx; and Francis Paudras, "Introduction," in *Herman Leonard: The Eye of Jazz*, ed. Herman Leonard (London: Viking, 1985), 15.
29. Arthur C. Danto, *The Philosophical Disenfranchisement of Art* (New York: Colombia University Press, 1986), 48, 50–51; Allan Sekula, "On the Invention of Photographic Meaning," in *Thinking Photography*, ed. Victor Burgin (London: Macmillan, 1982), 453–55. In his analysis of art perception, Pierre Bourdieu describes the lack of appreciation that images might be coded at a level below that of surface marks in a similar way as that "one unconsciously applies the code which is good for everyday perception": "Outline of a Theory of Art Perception," *International Social Science Journal* 20, no. 4 (1968): 590.
30. Robin D. G. Kelley, *Thelonious Monk: The Life and Times of an American Original* (New York: Free Press, 2009), 124.
31. James Lincoln Collier, *The Making of Jazz: A Comprehensive History* (London: Macmillan, 1978), 348–49.
32. John Chilton, *Roy Eldridge: Little Jazz Giant* (London: Continuum, 2002), 113.
33. Cawthra, *Blue Notes in Black and White: Photography and Jazz*, 102.
34. Cawthra, *Blue Notes in Black and White: Photography and Jazz*, 100.
35. Alun Morgan and Raymond Horricks, *Modern Jazz: A Survey of Developments since 1939* (London: Victor Gollancz, 1956), 34, 31.
36. William Gottlieb, "Thelonious Monk-Genius of Bop," *Down Beat*, September 24, 1947; Paul Bacon, "The High Priest of Bebop: The Inimitable Mr. Monk," in *The Thelonious Monk Reader*, ed. Rob van der Bliek (Oxford: Oxford University Press, 2001), 56–62.
37. Siegfried Kracauer, "Photography," in *The Mass Ornament: Weimar Essays*, ed. and trans. Thomas Y. Levin (Cambridge, MA: Harvard University Press, 1995), 54–55; Alan Trachtenberg, "Signifying the Real: Documentary Photography in the 1930s," in *The Social and the Real: Political Art of the 1930s in the Western Hemisphere*, ed. Alejandro Anreus, Diana L. Linden, and Jonathan Weinberg (University Park: Pennsylvania State University Press, 2006), 4, makes a similar point about documentary photography which "may even intefere with historical knowledge, distracting us from a quest for underlying causes, from tracing visible clues to invisible meanings."
38. Hank O'Neal, *A Vision Shared: A Classic Portrait of America and Its People 1935–1943* (New York: St. Martin's Press, 1976), 10. Another example of canonization in photographic history can be seen in Colin Westerbeck and Joel Meyerowitz, *Bystander: A HIstory of Street Photography* (Boston, MA: Little, Brown, 1994), where the "street photography" canon is established as leading up to and following on from Cartier-Bresson.
39. Patrick Burke, *Come In and Hear the Truth: Jazz and Race on 52nd. Street* (Chicago: University of Chicago Press, 2008), 9.
40. Ted Gioia, *West Coast Jazz: Modern Jazz in California 1945–1960* (Berkeley: University of California Press, 1998).
41. Ramsey Castaneda and Amanda Quinlan, "Through the Lens: How Photography in Jazz History and Appreciation Textbooks Shapes Our Understanding of the Music," unpublished paper presented to the *Documenting Jazz Conference* (Birmingham, 2020). I am grateful to the authors of this study for providing the underlying data on which this section is based. The texts analyzed by Castaneda and Quinlan are Gary Giddins and Scott DeVeaux, *Jazz* (New York: W. W. Norton, 2009); Mark Gridley, *Jazz Styles: History and Analysis*, 11th ed. (Boston, MA: Pearson, 2012); and Benjamin Bierman, *Listening to Jazz*, 1st ed. (New York: Oxford University Press, 2016).
42. Giddins and DeVeaux, *Jazz*, xii.
43. Gennari, *Blowin' Hot and Cool: Jazz and Its Critics*, 161.

44. Herman Leonard, "William Claxton," *Jazz Times*, 2008, https://jazztimes.com/archives/william-claxton/.
45. Jacques Derrida, *Archive Fever: A Freudian Impression* (Chicago: University of Chicago Press, 1996), 3; Allan Sekula, "Reading An Archive: Photography Between Labor and Capital," in *The Photography Reader*, ed. Liz Wells (London: Routledge, 2003), 445. See further Friedrich A. Kittler, *Discourse Networks 1800/1900*, ed. Michael Meteer and Chris Cullens (Cambridge, MA: MIT Press, 1990), 369.
46. Molly Nesbit, *Atget's Seven Albums* (New Haven, CT: Yale University Press, 1992), 16.
47. A full account of the personal, professional, and contextual factors leading jazz writers to favor certain types of jazz imagery and make these selections must be held over for reasons of space.
48. Marc Myers, "The Photographer Who Never Was But Now Is," in *Rebirth of the Cool: Discovering the Art of Robert James Campbell*, ed. Jessica Ferber (Brooklyn, NY: Powerhouse Books, 2015), 8.
49. Larry A. Viskochil, "The Elephant That Never Forgets," in *Chicago at the Turn of the Century in Photographs*, ed. Larry A. Viskochil (New York: Dover, 1984), xi.

3

The Jazz Image as Document

The ideal [jazz photograph] is both artistic and documentary. If you have to have one or the other, documentary is what I would go for. Some people can combine the two but they are rare. This photograph is one of the few known photographs of Billie Holiday with Artie Shaw in 1938—and that's just a wonderful thing.[1]

I. Introduction

A "presumption of veracity" underpinned the claims of American documentary photography in the 1930s. Shorn of the "sterility" and "technical '*capricci*' " of art photography, the documentary image offered, in Elizabeth McCausland's words, "an application of photography direct and realistic, dedicated to the profound and sober chronicling of the external world."[2] William Gottlieb's portrait of Charlie Parker and Red Rodney in Morris Levy's Downbeat Club at 66 W. 52nd Street in 1947 (Figure 17) can be interpreted in this way. The image clearly presents the two musicians, their dress, demeanor, and (as has occasionally been noted) the relatively healthy and smart appearance of two notoriously enthusiastic exponents of the jazz life; and it details the furnishings, decoration, and material surroundings in a notable 52nd Street club while confirming the presence of players onstage as reflected in the mirrored walls. We know that Gillespie's big band played the Downbeat from July 10 to August 28, 1947, with Barbara Carroll's trio as the opening act. A close inspection of the reflections in the mirrored wall behind Parker confirms Carroll (usually misidentified by jazz scholars as Margie Hyams following the photograph's incorrect description at the Library of Congress) on piano with Clyde Lombardi, Chuck Wayne, and Gillespie sitting in. At the time, Parker was playing next door at the Three Deuces (between August 7 and 20) while Rodney was with George Auld at the nearby Troubadour on August 14. The photographs can therefore be dated to the week of August 14, 1947, which ties in with Carroll's own account of her first appearance in New York City, and corrects the often repeated misidentification of the personnel.

After a few moments the photograph moves the viewer beyond the apparent facticity of surface detail toward a deeper realm of expressive meanings. The decoration recalls the ambience and material fittings of clubs like the Downbeat where the drapes and play of glass reflections appear like "Foucault's mirror," an imaginary doubling that prompts us to explore real and imagined spaces and the relationship between the photographer, subjects, and the viewer. Details of material culture encourage the viewer to reflect on cultural change and performative practices. Objects too assume a performative quality: the tablecloths, plates, glasses, and ash trays bring to mind the sounds and sensations of the small, smoke-filled jazz clubs on 52nd Street in that affinity that prompted Geoff Dyer to hear in Carol Reiff's photograph of Chet Baker at Birdland "not just the sound of the musicians as they are crowded into the small stage of the frame but the

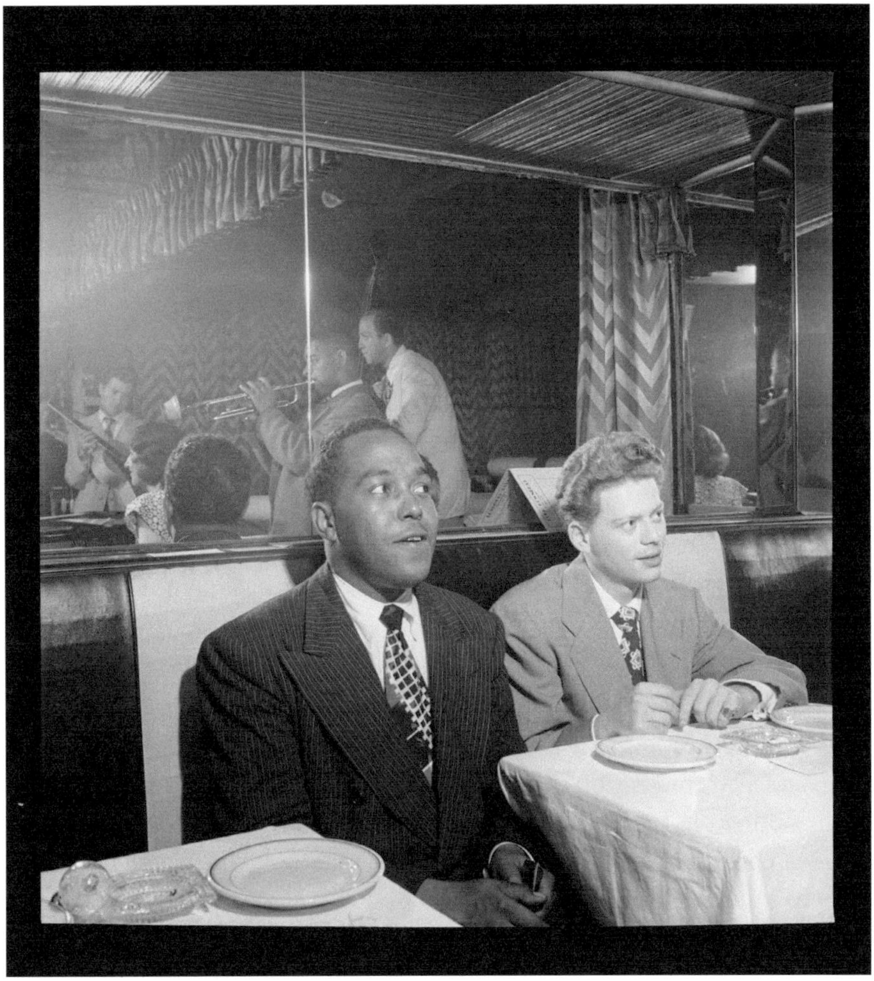

Figure 17: William P. Gottlieb. *Portrait of Charlie Parker, Red Rodney, Dizzy Gillespie, Margie Hyams and Chuck Wayne.* Downbeat. New York. 1947.
Ed Gottlieb/ Library of Congress.

background chat and clinking glasses of the nightclub."[3] Over time, interpretations like these permeate the memory of similar experiences as associations become increasingly distanced from the immediate context.

Rich in mimetic detail yet shot through with expressive signs, jazz photography inherently conjoins its documentary function with cultural meanings emanating from the combined effect of the subject matter and the specific modalities of the medium. This dual function mirrors the ontology of the photograph in which documentary and expressive signs are composed and counterposed within the frame: "Photography copies the world and invents the world at the same time," according to Alan Trachtenberg—"together and in the same act."[4] It is however important to draw an analytical distinction between different elements of the image in order to avoid conflating what the image shows with what we believe it to say. This chapter therefore explores the jazz image as document and describes the more important ways in which photographs yield information to jazz scholars and researchers. Maintaining the same analytical dualism, the following chapter explores the ways in which photographers have strived to capture the musical and cultural expressions of jazz. In later chapters the work of photographers whose work reunites these elements of the photographic image in a variety of ways will be discussed.

II. Reading documents

Many scholars and critics would agree with the archivist and photographer Tad Hershorn cited above when he says that the value of jazz photographs is located above all in the documentary information they contain. A clear understanding of the nature of the medium is however critical if photography is to be used as an evidential source. Jazz photographs can be misleading, and care is required in reading them. Prints were often carelessly labeled and annotated at the time and mistakes have been repeated over years as these images are unquestioningly reproduced. In his discography *Jazz and Ragtime Records, 1897–1942,* Brian Rust shows how a published 1921 photograph is presented as showing Mamie Smith recording *Sax-o-phoney Blues* with a black group although the racial composition and instrumentation of the group suggest this was from a quite separate session; another photograph, announcing recordings by Byron Warner's Seven Aces is not consistent with the evidence of the recording itself, which appears to point to a quite different lineup.[5] Hollywood movie stills can be particularly unreliable. Harold Young's 1937 film *52nd Street* was billed as featuring musical acts connected with "Swing Street" clubs. Production stills tell a different story (Figure 18). Although the African American pianist Maurice Rocco plays himself the band includes alto saxophonist Elmer Fain, the business agent for the black Local 767 and Winslow "Winnow" Allen, a trumpeter well-known on Los Angeles' Central Avenue.[6]

These problems ought not to detract from the value of jazz photographs as documents so long as they are recognized and addressed. Photographs can be incomplete, even misleading, and may need to be supplemented by other forms of historical evidence, but in this they differ little from other documentary sources: "What differs is less the uniqueness of historical materials than our tendency to see photographs as more 'real' than other sources and our relative inexperience in using them historically."[7] There are indications that as familiarity with the medium grows scholars are beginning to use photographs for documentary purposes more imaginatively and in ways that address these issues. In his recent study of early drumming, Paul Archibald has demonstrated how the greater availability of early photography and the use

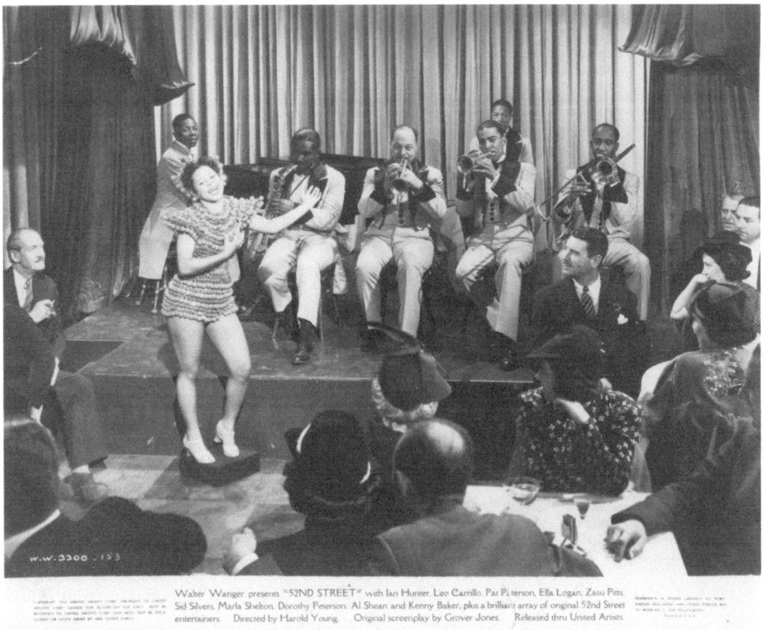

Figure 18: Production still from United Artists' motion picture 52nd Street.
Peter Vacher Collection.

of digital search functionality can facilitate comparisons across photographs and between textual sources. This has enhanced the value of photography in cross-evidential research methods as well as helping to correct errors in mislabeling and misidentification. Drawing on John Collier's pioneering use of photography in ethnographic research, Colter Harper has explored the possibilities of "photo-elicitation" by using photographs as interview stimulus material in connection with his study of Pittsburgh jazz during the interwar years. Daniel Stein has also used photography intertextually in his critical account of Louis Armstrong's autobiographical interventions. For Stein, Armstrong's autobiography must be read across texts, images, and sound (including musical sounds)—what he calls Armstrong's "trans-medial" impulse to communicate ideas and sentiments across different media.[8]

Musicians and their activities

Biographers, historians, enthusiasts, and collectors have traditionally relied on photographic evidence to place players at a particular point and to trace careers, band associations, and locations over time. The historian and collector Peter Vacher explains:[9]

> *I want to know about the players, who played the trumpet solo [. . .] In many cases the photographer has helped me to put a face to the name. With more obscure*

players it's been invaluable to have that documentation [. . .] the photo records that the band was put together at a specific time, in a specific location, for a specific purpose [. . .] Equally [photographs] help us to document the career progress of certain players and bands. For example, the important Les Hite black LA orchestra is said to have appeared in some 60 feature films. Having spotted them in many of these films, it's possible to document their personnel and to see how an important band changed personnel over a period.

Photographs are often the only source available to researchers seeking to place early jazz musicians and understand the makeup of jazz bands. Reviewing early jazz source material, Richard Wang for example relies on photographs to place Manuel Perez and his five-piece band in Chicago in 1915.[10] Researchers find information of this kind in incidental details captured by the camera. During his period as Fats Waller's manager between 1938 and 1943, Ed Kirkeby assiduously documented the musician's travels with his camera. Many of Kirkeby's photographs show street scenes, theatre frontages, billboards, and hoardings, which vividly convey the nature of the out-of-the-way venues played by African American artists and which had come as such a "rude awakening" to Kirkeby, who was used to handling white artists.[11] The hoardings in Kirkeby's photograph taken at Old Orchard Beach, Maine, in 1941 (Figures 19a and 19b) tell us much about the nature of these venues and help to contextualize his music in showing the types of popular entertainment that framed performances by musicians like Waller.

Photographs may at certain points in time be the only available documentation about particular musicians or bands. After quitting Billy Eckstein's band in late-1944 Charlie Parker drifted back to New York to work on various band jobs and all but disappeared from view for several months. We would know little of his activities during this period had not the black-owned trade magazine *Music Dial* published rare photographs of Parker in jam sessions at a club called Heat Wave on West 145th Street.[12] A few years later when Parker sat in with Thelonious Monk's trio with Roy Haynes and Charles Mingus at the Open Door, Bob Parent's photograph taken with his Speed Graphic provides the only record of this unique moment, leading some to speak of the image as one of the most significant jazz photographs ever taken.[13] A similar event occurred during the extended Thelonious Monk-John Coltrane residency at New York's Five Spot Café in July 1957—a magnetic draw for devoted listeners and musicians but only one photographer, Don Schlitten. One of the most remarkable documents of a jazz recording session came about when the photojournalist Esther Bubley was asked in a chance meeting with the artist and graphic designer David Stone Martin in 1952 to photograph Norman Granz's *Funky Blues* recording session. This date boasted the remarkable lineup of Ray Brown, Benny Carter, J. C. Heard, Johnny Hodges, Barney Kessel, Charlie Parker, Oscar Peterson, Flip Phillips, Charlie

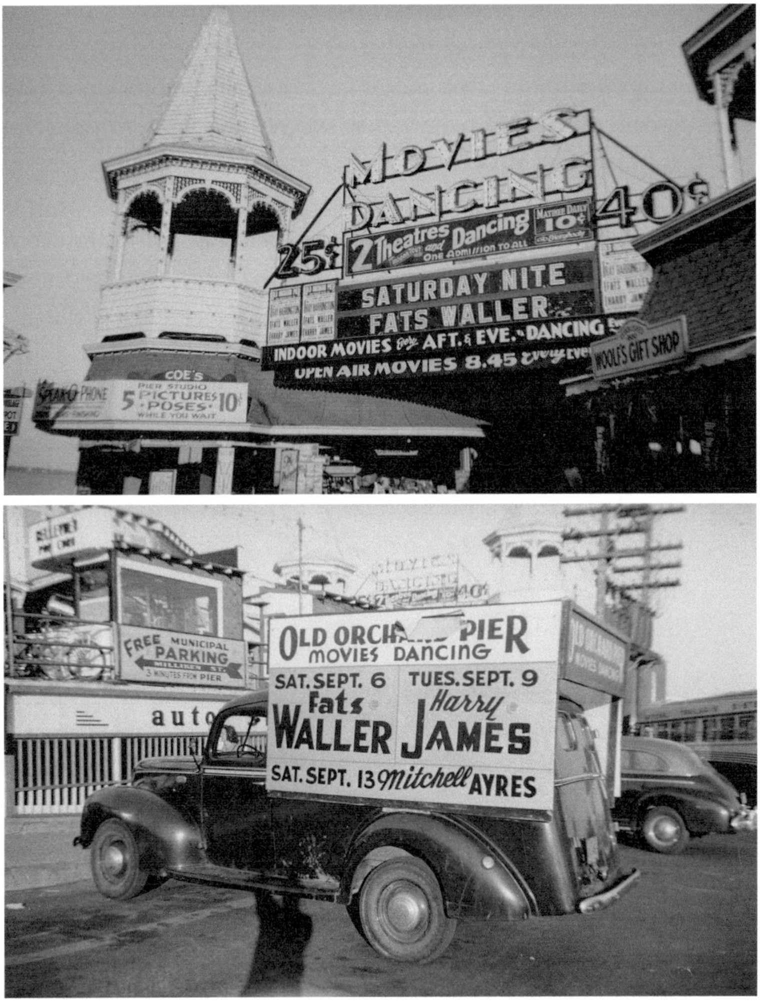

Figure 19a and 19b: Ed Kirkeby. *Old Orchard Pier, Maine—Marquee and advertisement.* September 1941.
Ed Kirkeby papers (IJS.0016), Institute of Jazz Studies, Rutgers University Libraries. With permission of Marc Kirkeby and Keith Aronowitz.

Shavers, and Ben Webster. The photographs from the session—the only occasion on which these top-flight musicians had played together, offer "an extended portrait of something which is extremely difficult to achieve, let alone photograph: a joint creative act, being accomplished in real time."[14]

Musical relationships

Photographs can guide us toward a better understanding of the relationships between musicians and the modalities of influence and/or mentoring. Musicians help construct the jazz "tradition" by deciding who is worthy of emulation and these claims are generally well-documented; "horizontal" interactions between musicians who perform together have proved more difficult to pin down.[15] One way in which photographs help to throw light on these relationships is through the greetings, advice, and *aperçues* often inscribed on the face of the image (Figure 20). We find that musicians often wrote messages for fellow musicians on photographs and passed them on as a keepsake. For itinerant musicians this was a way of keeping in touch and some like Louis Armstrong inscribed hundreds of photographs during his career. There are also many examples of photographs inscribed for *current* band members—a practice that directs attention to the importance of the photograph as a keepsake or record of fleeting moments in performance, venues, or recording sessions and the relationships that these events engendered.[16] Signed photographs were particularly valued as a marker of significant events. After Jean Goldkette's orchestra finally succumbed to economic pressures in September 1927, an emotional final appearance took place at the Roseland Ballroom: as Bix Beiderbecke's biographers recall, "[a]t the end, when the last note had been played, there was nothing left to do but sign and exchange copies of the latest band photograph."[17]

Instrumental techniques

Photographs have proved extremely valuable in documenting the evolution of instrumental techniques. In the study of drumming history mentioned above, Paul Archibald has collated photographic evidence pointing to the shift to cymbals suspended by wire and the emergence after the turn of the century of "double drumming" and the subsequent introduction of the bass drum pedal. Photographs challenge the popular theory that Tony Sbarbaro did not use the bass drum in the ODJB's famous 1917 recordings and confirm his use of the snare drum (with stand), two different size cowbells, a woodblock, a Chinese tom-tom, and Chinese cymbal (with bass drum mount). Archibald demonstrates the value of this sort of evidence by reference to a photograph from the early-1930s of Chick Webb using the short-lived handheld Gladstone cymbals. The photograph helps to account for the particular sound Webb achieved on recordings such as Brunswick's 1928 *Dog Bottom* and allows Archibald to identify the use of this device by Zutty Singleton on Louis Armstrong's famous *West End Blues.*[18]

The gradual decline in the string bass played *arco* is another example of changing techniques that have been documented with the aid of photographs. Bertram Turetzky has used photographs of the New Orleans–born bass player George "Pops" Foster to show how the jazzman's left-hand grip facilitated greater clarity, strength, and prolonged the note. By adding power and sustain to the string bass notes, the instrument was able to ease the tuba aside in the lineup of jazz bands during the 1920s.[19] Charlie Christian is often described as the pioneer of the amplified guitar, but photographs demonstrate that players such as Leon

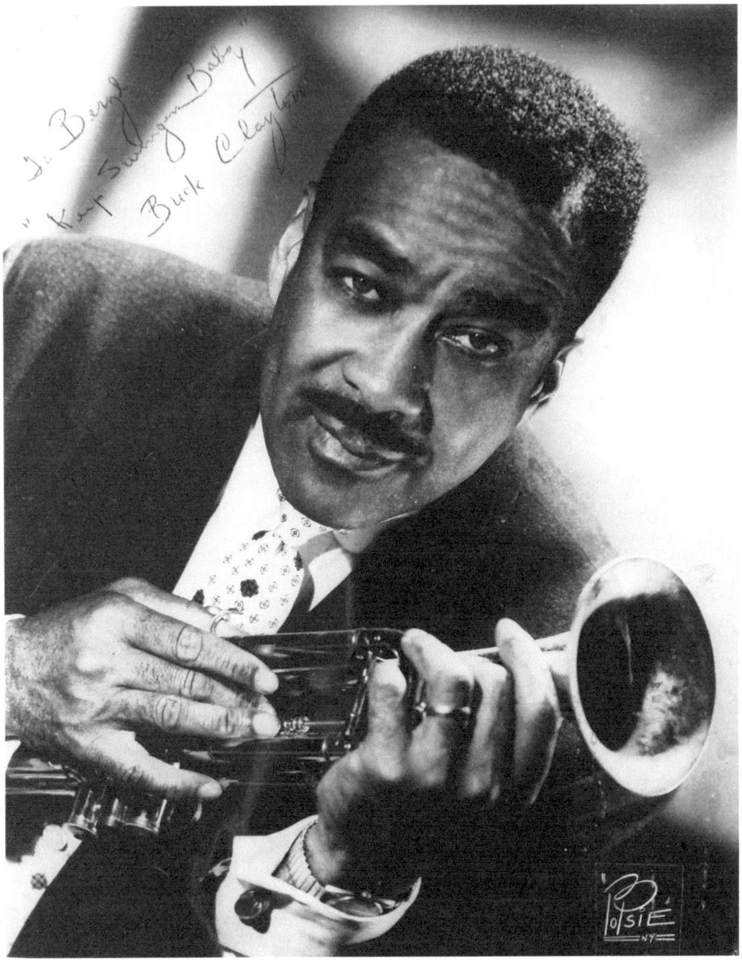

Figure 20: "PoPsie." *Buck Clayton*. n.d.
Peter Vacher Collection/Permission of Michael Randolph, Executive to the Estate of William "PoPsie" Randolph.

McAuliffe, George Barnes, and Muryel "Zeke" Campbell were as early in adopting amplification while the first public appearance of an amplified instrument can be attributed to Gage Brewer in 1932.[20]

Evolution of jazz bands

Photographs are particularly important in providing information about instrumentation and the evolving composition of bands. A late 1890s photograph of the John Robichaux orchestra shows how the small "tin" band had expanded into an eight-piece orchestra—two violins from the string band, a trombone, and two cornets from the brass band plus bass fiddle, clarinet, and drums. By 1910 the seven-piece orchestra had become standard, and photographs confirm how the violin fell out of the lineup, leaving six-piece bands of three rhythm instruments and the cornet, clarinet, and trombone. This change was partly the result of pressure from the smaller white Dixieland bands, which were forceful but cheaper to hire.[21]

Further changes occurred in the 1920s, when the saxophone began to appear in dance bands, increasing the volume of sound and leading to greater use of the banjo and bass horn. Photographs from 1915 onward confirm that both uptown and downtown New Orleans bands expanded beyond the three-man front line and regularly added saxophones. A 1919 photograph of King Oliver playing at a Liberty Bond drive in Chicago boasts a saxophone section and the Albert Nichols Band was photographed with saxophones at Tom Anderson's Café in 1923.[22] Villard Paddio's photograph of the Sam Morgan Jazz Band from about 1928 has led jazz historians to conclude that the New Orleans area led the way in replacing tubas with the double bass and reshaping the rhythm section to become the staple of jazz bands from that point onward.[23] These changes occurred over time and transition periods are often illuminatingly captured by photographs such as that of Carroll Dickerson's Orchestra in 1929 demonstrating the persistence of the tuba and banjo in larger orchestral formations (Figure 21).

Discographies

The first jazz discographies appeared in the 1930s with Charles Delauney's *Hot Discography* in Paris, Hilton R. Schleman's *Rhythm on Record* published in the

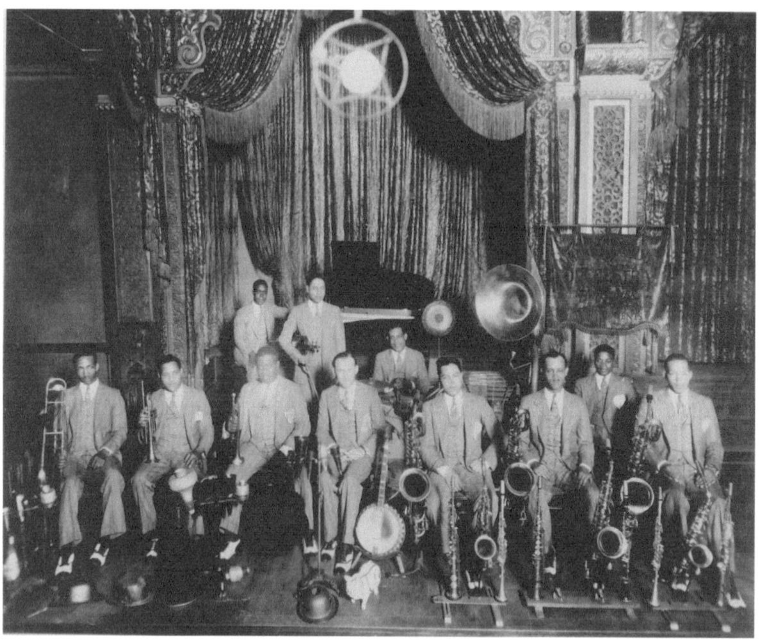

Figure 21: Unknown photographer. *Caroll Dickerson's Orchestra*. New York. 1929–30. *Peter Vacher Collection.*

British weekly *Melody Maker*, and Hughes Pannassié's *Hot Jazz* in the United States. The format of discographies was gradually standardized during the 1940s and 1950s and their contents became both more comprehensive and accurate. Photography can be an indispensable resource to discographers providing confirmation of the musicians in the studio or correcting mislabeling by the recording company. Evidence is often provided by what might otherwise be thought of as insignificant details in the photograph. Bruce Boyd Raeburn provides an example of this when he recounts how the initials on the bass drum shown in a photograph of the Original Creole Stompers in a 1949 recording session resolved discographical misunderstandings over one band member.[24]

Studio recording techniques

Photography has proved to be especially useful in documenting evolving studio recording techniques. Photographs are now the only extant record of the famous Gennett Studio in Richmond, IN, on the basis of which an exact recreation of this famous location has recently been presented by the Indiana Historical Society.[25] Before electrical recording, careful studio positionings were vital to achieve anything approaching a balanced sound, although some instruments were simply never forceful enough to be captured. Images of Gennett's New York studio published in the early-1920s show specially constructed double-decker chairs designed to balance the sound being collected by five recording horns. Some players face backward and sheet music hangs from rods in the ceiling. The disposition was quite different from performance arrangements, and the positioning of players affected both the volume and timbre of the recordings of the instruments; difficulties with the bass drum in particular often resulted in its omission from the studio.[26] Photographs also show how the instrumental lineup of early jazz bands started to adapt to the demands of recording as instruments less suited to the studio were replaced by those better able to be heard and recorded by pre-electric recording methods. Banjos were substituted for keyboards, bass drums were often dropped while difficulties in registering the frequencies of the double bass sometimes led to its substitution by the tuba. Recorded jazz may also have led to new playing techniques, such as the slap bass; much as classical violinists began to exaggerate vibrato in the recording studio, jazz techniques also adapted to the recorded environment.[27]

Over twenty years later in the age of electrical recordings, Conrad Eiger, one of Black Star Picture's mostly German émigré photojournalists working in the New York area, captured Count Basie's musicians in an RCA recording session in May 1947 (Figure 22). Positioning himself in the middle of the players, Eiger's photograph takes us right into the heart of the action and draws attention to the careful positioning of the players such that each has a clear line of sight to Basie—even if the bass player had to stand on a stool to allow other players a line of sight! In the age of electrical

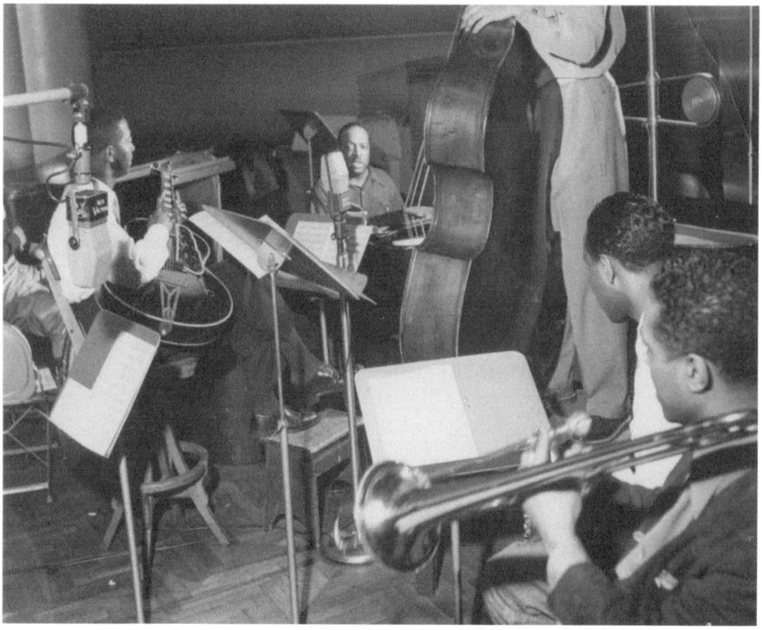

Figure 22: Conrad Eiger. *Count Basie and His Orchestra*. RCA Victor Recording, RCA Studios. New York. 1947.
Peter Vacher Collection.

recording sight lines rather than acoustic power took precedence and brought the sound of the recording closer to that of the performance.

Gender and race in jazz

Photographs make manifest the race and gender of the musicians involved and the documentary value of photographs in these areas is significant but has to be treated with care. Partly because so few jazz images showing women players were published in their day, and those that did appear were so frequently skewed by their context of presentation, the use of published photographs has tended to support the "normative definitions of gender and labor in the societies in which jazz discourse has circulated."[28] On the other hand the existence of a large archive of previously unpublished photography has provided source material for historians looking to locate and identify women participants and to understand better the formal and informal dynamics of race relations in jazz.

Few photographs of female jazz musicians were published before 1960. While this was often an omission reflecting the prevailing assumption that jazz was a male occupation, there were occasions when women were consciously excised from photographs. Claude Thornhill made strenuous efforts to dissuade his protégée Maxine Sullivan from being photographed fearing that visual images would make her race obvious and might undermine his attempts to present her as a swing interpreter of folk songs such as *Loch Lomond*. Whatever the motivation, the emphasis in print media was to present women as singers often in poses expressly designed for the male gaze with camera viewpoints chosen in such a way as to sexualize their appearance. This was particularly true of advertising: many female players appeared in the context of testimonial advertising in which endorsers were glamourized or even overtly sexualized, as a means of attracting attention to the product (Figures 23 and 24).[29] However, the large number of unpublished jazz photographs in libraries and archives has provided opportunities for reassessing the contribution made by female musicians. As previously noted, writers writers such as Sherrie Tucker and Linda Dahl have Dahl have used archival archival photography to help identify women identify woman players in a music regarded as a male preserve.[30]

Turning to photographic representations of race, there is overwhelming evidence that white-owned mass market and specialist media such as *Down Beat* and *Metronome* favored the presentation of white players. At least until the mid-1940s when the participation of black servicemen prompted mainstream publications to relax strict segregation, photographs of black players and integrated scenes were largely avoided, with the result that editorial copy and advertisements were

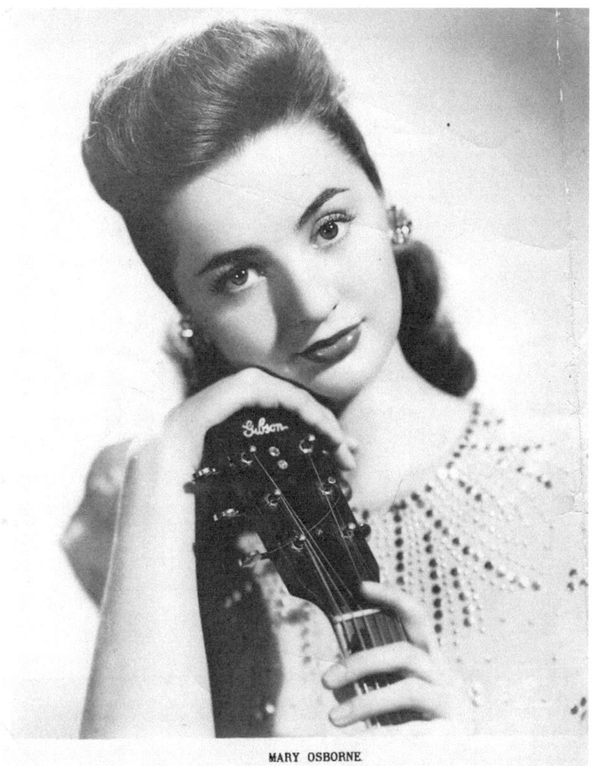

Figure 23: Mary Osborne Gibson promotional photograph. 1946.
Vintage Guitar magazine.

significantly skewed toward the representation of whites.[31] Many unpublished photographs however capture different forms of racial interactions between musicians in a wide range of locations and provide evidence for a more nuanced assessment. In his autobiography Andy Kirk recalled how his band's residency at Billy Craig's Blossom Heath, an Oklahoma City club with a Columbia wire, opened up southern audiences for his band: "Since they only came to know us by radio, they didn't know whether we were white or black."[32] Photographs of studios and radio broadcasts, in which a greater degree of integration was possible, provide a corrective to those taken in performance where segregation was more rigorously enforced (Figure 25). Interracial recording sessions dated back to at least July 1923 when Jelly Roll Morton recorded with the New Orleans Rhythm Kings. These photographs help historians track relationships between musicians of different races who might only rarely have appeared in public together. "PoPsie" Randolph's photographs from Miles Davis's *Birth of the Cool* sessions provide a visible reminder of the contribution of white musicians to these sessions and help contextualize Davis's insistence that the music came from Duke Ellington via Claud Thornhill.[33]

It cannot be assumed that photographs like these mitigate the overwhelming fact of segregation. Rather, they provide pointers to the subtle and often hidden

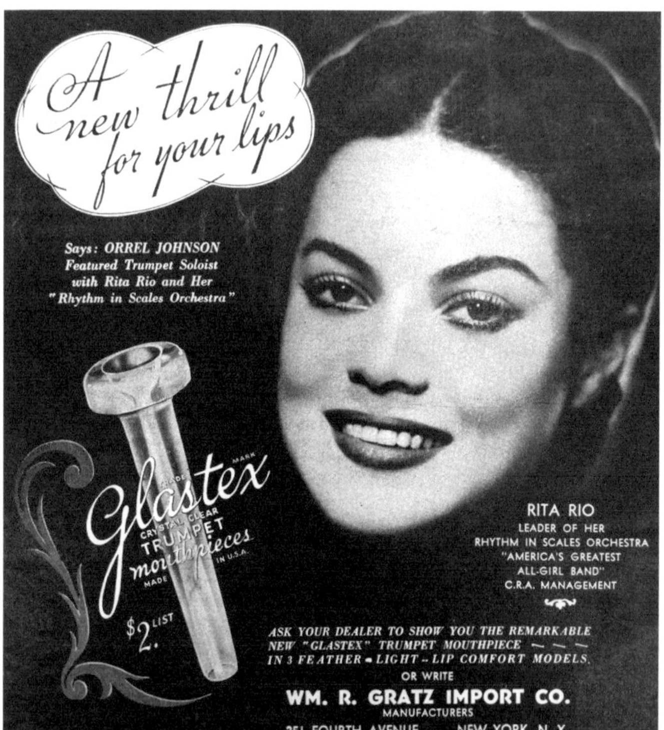

Figure 24: "A New Thrill for Your Lips"—Rita Rio testimonial advertisement. 1939. *Down Beat, August 1, 1939.*

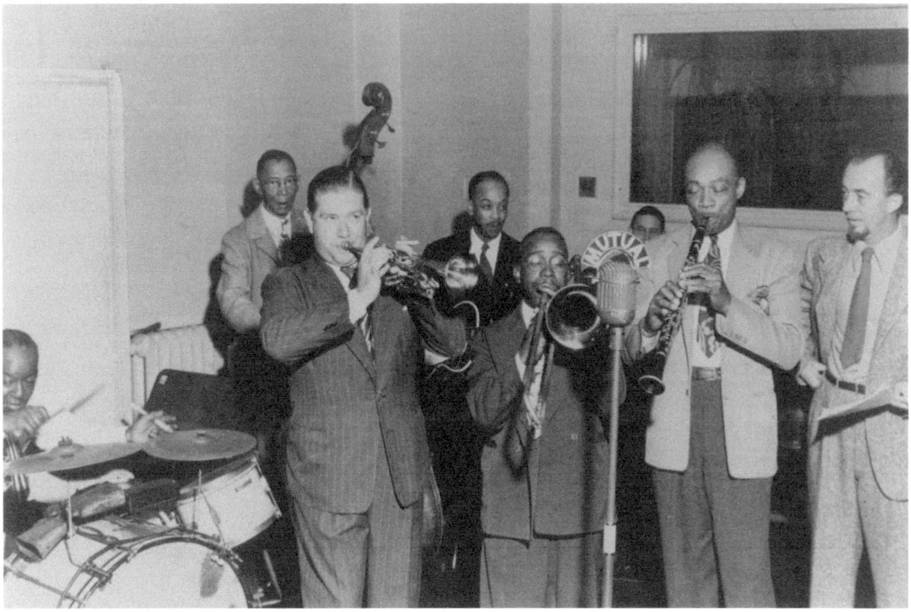

Figure 25: Unknown photographer. *This Is Jazz*. Mutual Network Radio Broadcast. New York. September 1947.
Peter Vacher Collection.

forms of resistance to racial discrimination that musicians practiced away from the eye of official sanction. Robin D. G. Kelley makes the point in his study of black working-class "infrapolitics"—those covert forms of resistance often confined to spaces away from the white gaze—that the very nature of these spaces means that few records were kept.[34] It seems reasonable to regard the integration of musicians in studios, jam sessions, and other less public places as a form of infrapolitics and the camera as one of the few ways in which these behaviors were documented.

Performance spaces and audiences

Jazz performance spaces and audiences varied considerably over time and from location to location, crucially affecting the ways in which musicians present the drama that is improvised music. Photographs provide detailed records of the bewildering array of venues in which jazz was performed during the twentieth century, allowing us to explore the dimensions, layout, architectural divisions, separations, proximities, and the spatial relationships between audiences and musicians in different jazz spaces. Music plays a spatial role through its unique embodiment in individual and collective movement, gestures, expressions, and interchanges, all of which visually signify emotional and affective states. Photographs can be invaluable in pointing out the varying "competences" of audiences such as their uniformity or heterogeneity and the degrees and qualities of spectator attention; and they provide insights into demographic characteristics, material culture and presentation, racial mix, and relationships between audiences and musicians.[35] Guided by a substantial body of research highlighting the links between musical performance and space, there is a tangibility and immediacy about photographic evidence of this kind that cannot be replicated in words and discourse.[36]

A long section in Paul Berliner's *Thinking in Jazz* describes the important effects that different spaces and audiences can have on jazz performance and interactions between musicians and audiences. Recalling his time as a jazz pianist, Howard Becker has described how the social and racial character of the jazz venues in the 1940s and 1950s defined the nature of the space, framing the attitudes of musicians and their performance; among other factors, the nature of accompanying acts—which, in Becker's case, included dancers, magicians, jugglers, comedians, and striptease artists—forced the musicians to respond in very different ways. The "extraordinary" interactions between performers and the audience at Harlem's Apollo Theatre which Dan Morgenstern recalled as being "entirely different" from the responses in 52nd Street clubs where blacks were admitted but often segregated are confirmed by photographers such as Morgan and Marvin Smith, Lucy Ashjian, Berenice Abbott, and many others. An entirely different form of jazz space is vividly illustrated in Burt Goldblatt's portrait of the Newport Jazz Festival in which audiences are seen standing, lying on the grass, or lounging on the bleachers, chatting and smoking.[37]

Dicky Wells was one of many musicians who believed that interactions between dancers and musicians shaped the music in performance:[38]

> *There was more soul when jazz and dancing went together [. . .] It was always inspiring to have people dancing in front of you [. . .] We wouldn't have played that music the way we did if we hadn't got the spirit of things from watching those girls dance.*

As venues changed players responded in different ways. Stanley Dance claimed that with the move toward concert halls, Count Basie's style mutated:

> *Playing in concert halls [. . .] required a far greater degree of instrumental polish and precision, and this has often resulted in a reduction of that remarkable feeling of spontaneity the early bands conjured up when riffing as an ensemble or behind soloists.*

Before 1950 Basie band retained many of its original characteristics despite personnel changes—looser, with more emphasis on the contributions of the soloists as opposed to the ensemble. From around 1952, with new personnel and a greater frequency of playing in concert halls, there came more emphasis on ensemble precision. As Basie himself said, "Everybody has converted over to jazz concerts, and there's a different atmosphere altogether."[39]

A series of photographs of the Basie Orchestra taken over a period of nearly 30 years allows us to trace some of these changing dynamics. Strict formality reigns in Carnegie Hall in 1948 (Figure 26), where a conservatively dressed and seated white audience is positioned at a respectful distance from the players. There is a clear line of demarcation between musicians and audience members who sit upright and maintain an appropriate distance from their neighbors. "PoPsie" Randolph's photograph portrays a music environment largely sealed off from outside influences with its "buffer zones" of silence to distinguish music from "other" sounds.[40] The setting is quite different from that of the club shown in Dudley Stouch's 1970 photograph (Figure 27) in which an older and smartly dressed audience is positioned much closer to the musicians and to each other. Their movements are less constrained but their attitudes suggest that they are paying close attention to the music. We might reach quite different conclusions about the competence of this audience from that shown in Alexander Marshall's photograph of an upscale ballroom (Figure 28) in which a formally attired middle-aged white dancing audience appears more concerned with their partners than the music on offer. The photograph confirms how the swing era inherited the racial segregation of the 1920s big city dance halls, distancing self-absorbed social dancers from the musicians. There seems to be little scope here for the kind of interaction between dancers and musicians that players like Wells and Young believed to be so important to their performance. These three venues display varying degrees of formality and the audiences are exclusively white. In a much less formal venue, a predominantly young and clearly attentive audience is so close to the musicians that several are breaching the divide between players and audience

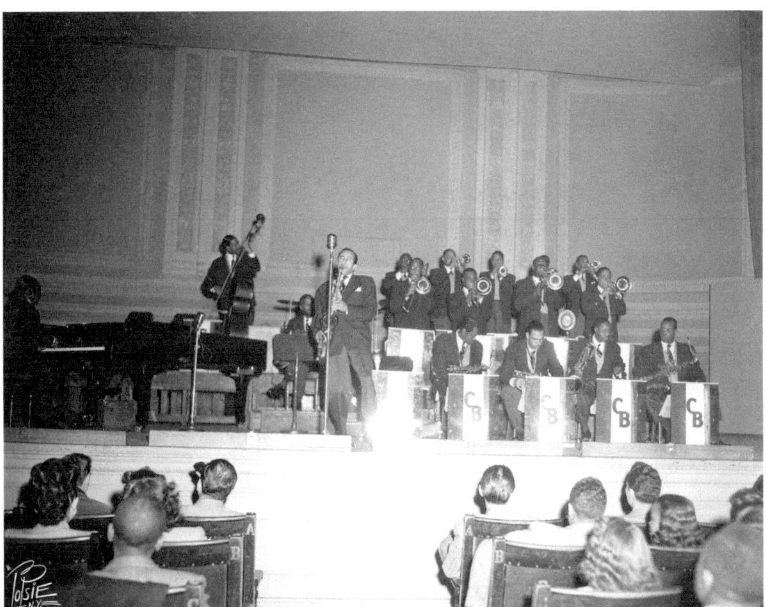

Figure 26: "PoPsie." *Count Basie Orchestra*. Carnegie Hall. 1948.
Permission of Michael Randolph, Executive to the Estate of William "PoPsie" Randolph.

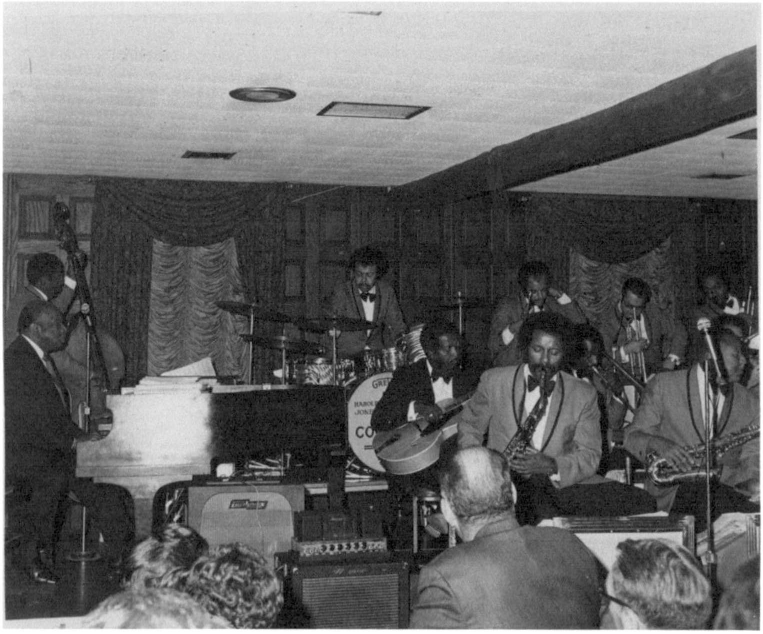

Figure 27: Dudley L. Stouch. *Count Basie Orchestra*. poss. Dover PA. 1970. *Peter Vacher Collection.*

by putting their feet on the stage (Figure 29). Here the physical distinction between performers and an integrated audience has all but broken down.

Life on the road

The trials and tribulations of the jazz life were never more present than when a band was on the road—particularly, of course, if it was an African American band. All sorts of problems could arise as the *Pittsburgh Courier* reporter Floyd Snelson discovered when he traveled with the Don Albert Band on their bus in the late-1930s (Figure 30) and arranged to send back photographs of his experiences. One of Snelson's reports speaks of "a great deal of union trouble" forcing Albert to take the band south: "Then management by unscrupulous agents caused the band to lose money and prestige through cancelled appointments."[41] Like Snelson, photographers have documented different aspects of the traveling life of jazz musicians and their images bring life to accounts of the encounters and activities of a life on the road described in the memoirs of musicians. For most musicians the tour bus became an important space of social and professional interaction. Buck Clayton remembered how musicians used their time on the Basie tour bus to sleep and relax, socialize, hold discussions on all manner of topics, play dice, drink whiskey, smoke pot, and run through charts. It was on the bus that friendships were formed, cemented, and dissolved, where rituals developed around seating hierarchies, and individuals assumed distinctive positions

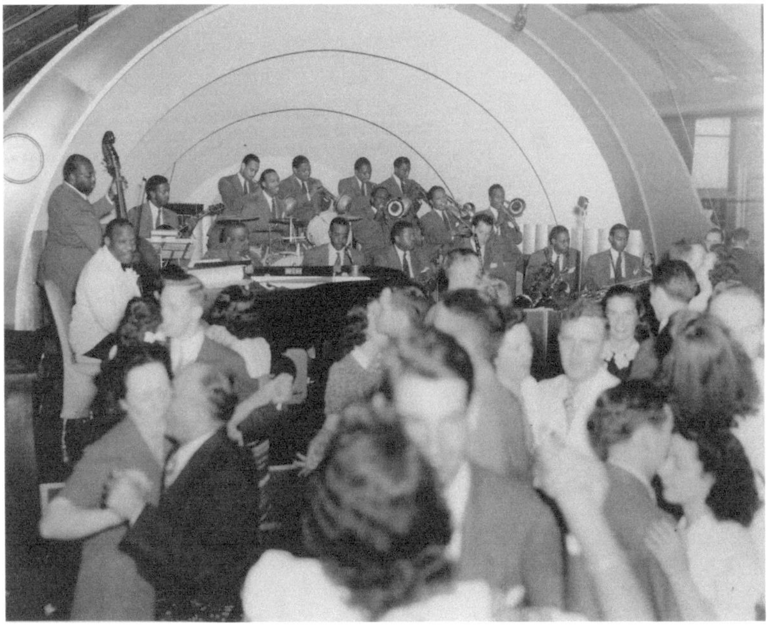

Figure 28: Alexander Marshall. *Count Basie Orchestra*. Unknown location. 1941. *Peter Vacher Collection.*

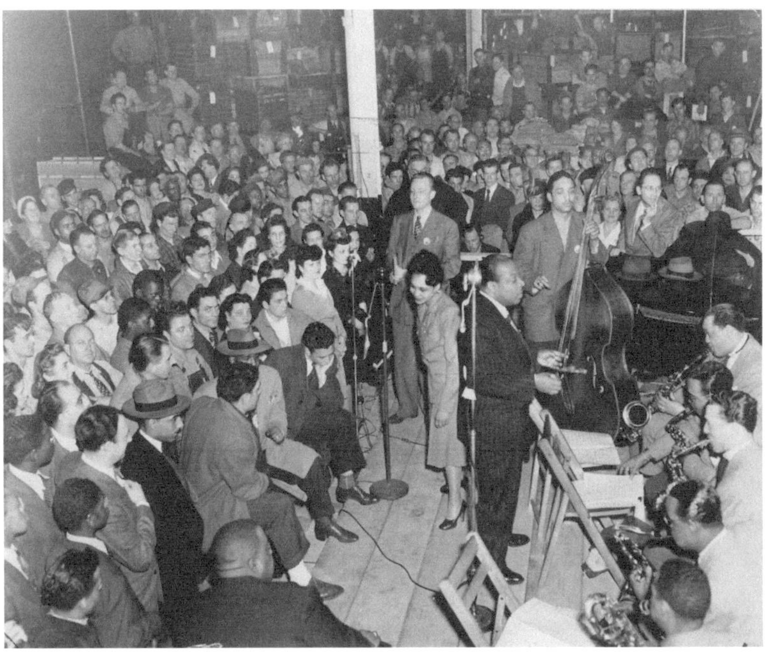

Figure 29: Unknown photographer. *Count Basie and His Orchestra*. 1944. *Peter Vacher Collection.*

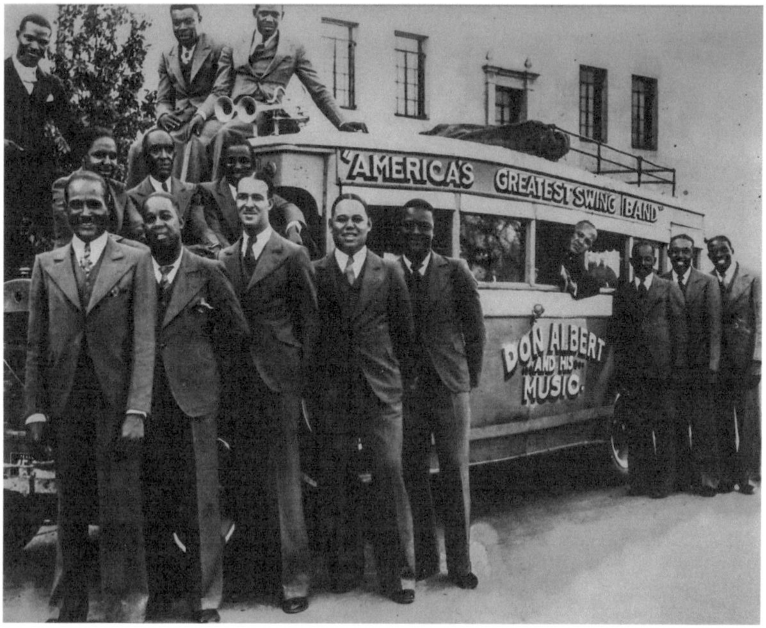

Figure 30: Unknown photographer. *Don Albertson and His Music.* San Antonio, TX. 1934. *Author's Collection.*

in the band's social structure. Lester Young was known for his comic warfare and hilarious commentaries on long bus journeys.[42] As a musician himself, Milt Hinton was acutely aware of the importance of the bus and his photographs recording scenes such as that portraying Danny Barker and Dizzy Gillespie illustrate the conditions musicians had to endure (Figure 31). Hinton was also concerned to document the constant difficulties faced by black musicians in finding suitable washrooms, restaurants, and accommodation. His photograph of a colored lodging house showing members of the Calloway Orchestra brazenly pointing to the signs of segregation is typical of his understated portrayals of touring in the Jim Crow south (Figure 103).

W. T. "Ed" Kirkeby's account of his years between 1938 and 1943 with Fats Waller tells of arduous 500–600 mile overnight journeys between venues in sweltering and unreliable buses; as he laconically noted, "Incessant road travel can do strange things to people." Kirkeby's photographs provide an invaluable insight into the ways in which Waller's insecurity found expression in a compulsion to engage with complete strangers when on tour.[43] Photographs show Waller joking with fellow travelers and playing up to female traveling companions, engaging in mock boxing matches, eating ice creams while talking to passersby, local shopkeepers, train porters, and with people on blacks-only beaches. It seems that Waller would go just about anywhere where he could chat to someone (Figure 32). Tad Herschorn emphasizes the extraordinary value of Kirkeby's documentary archive:[44]

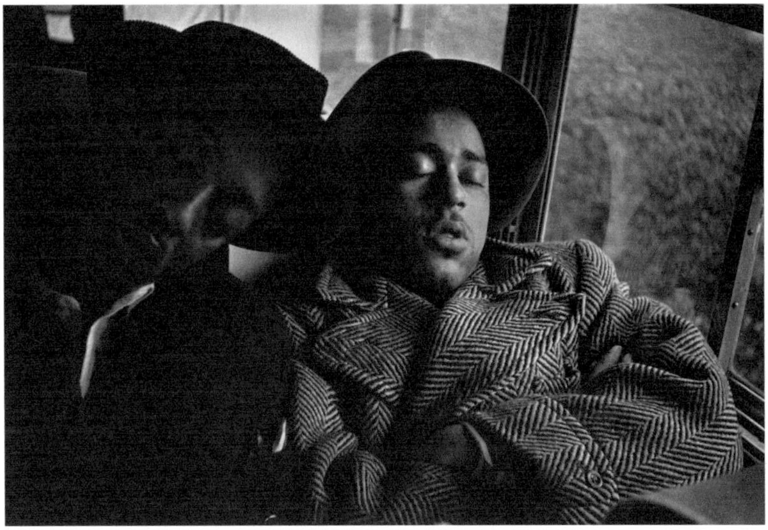

Figure 31: Milt Hinton. *Danny Barker and Dizzy Gillespie on the road with Cab Calloway. c.1940. © Milton J. Hinton Photographic Collection. Permission of David G. Berger and Holly Maxson.*

> *The detail in the Kirkeby collection is remarkable [. . .] He photographed as a photojournalist would. All the sleeves are annotated with the names and details of cities. Musicians, locations, trains, theatres and interiors, interaction with fans [. . .] a wealth of marvelous detail which you can extrapolate to the life of a travelling musician in the period.*

The jazz family album

Vernacular photography like Kirkeby's is increasingly appreciated by photographic historians as a spontaneous and honest form of documentary aesthetic. Emphasizing communicative rather than "artistic" qualities, photographs of this kind offer what Shawn Michelle Smith has described as "counter-archive" insights; frequently overlooked by scholars, albums carefully assembled by musicians, their families, friends, acquaintances, and associates can provide a less mediated record outside the circumscribing meanings imposed by official archives.[45] Repetition turns the snapshot into the visual equivalent of a verbal cliché, a mnemonic device which goes beyond instrumentality to influence consciousness and perceptions. As such, photographs in the "jazz family album" tell us much about the personalities away from the performance stage: they point to the role played by participants such as wives and girlfriends, whose contribution is frequently passed over, illustrate the broader family and communal relationships and support networks that helped bind various circles within the community of musicians, present the private lives of musicians away from the bandstand, and help explain shifting social relationships between players.

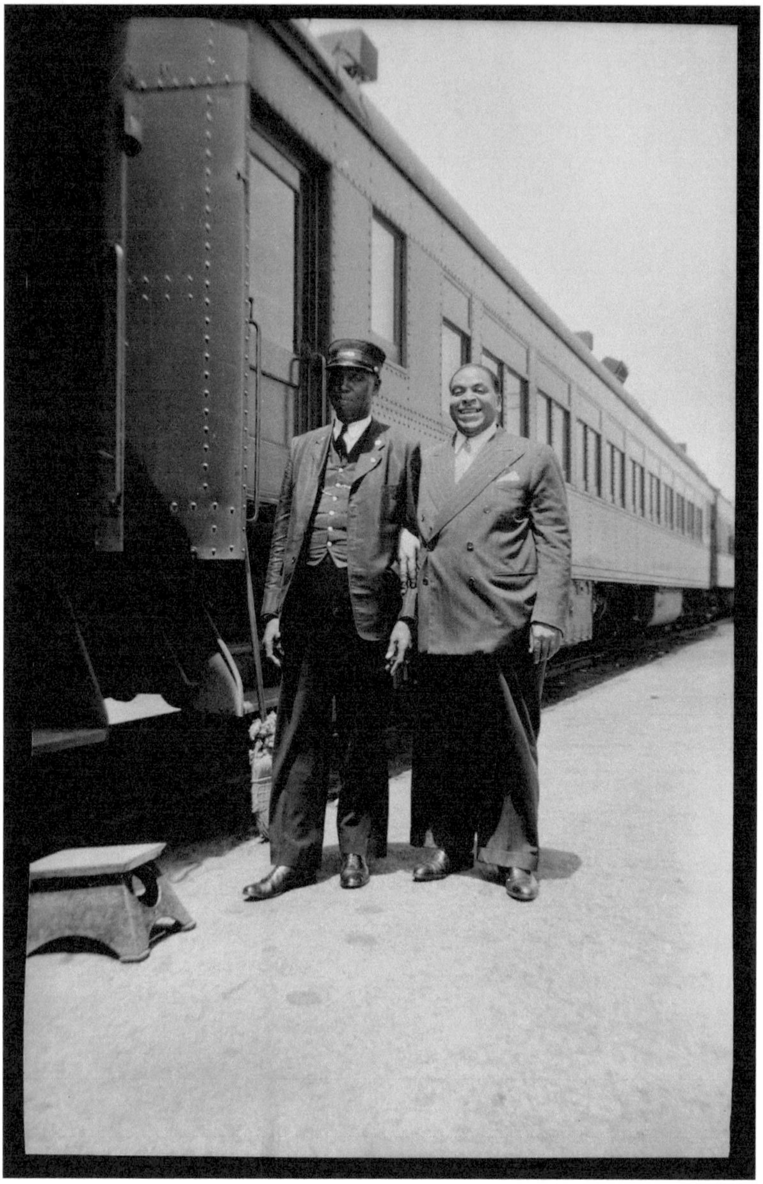

Figure 32: W. T. "Ed" Kirkeby. *Fats Waller with railroad porter*. June 1941.
Ed Kirkeby papers (IJS.0016), Institute of Jazz Studies, Rutgers University Libraries/Permission of Marc Kirkeby and Keith Aronowitz.

Several important jazz family albums illustrate the wealth of information in collections of this nature. A photograph in the family's collection of Lester Young aged about 2 with his mother Lizetta departs from pictorial convention in placing the subject's heads on the same level, pointing to the particularly close relationship between the two; and, in a similar vein, Val Wilmer's image of the clarinetist Paul "Polo" Barnes on his verandah with his granddaughter is a touching example of the way in which snapshots can provide a rare glimpse of the private life of a musician's life beyond the band stand.[46] Stanley Dance's photograph albums now housed in the Gilmore Music Library at Yale University demonstrate the care and attention often devoted to collections of this nature; with personnel and locations carefully noted, Dance's albums provide an invaluable record of musicians in social as well as performance settings (Figures 33a and 33b). Pannonica de Koenigswäter certainly made no claims to be a photographer. As musicians came and went from her homes in the early-1960s the "Baroness" took Polaroid photographs that over the years built up into a remarkable archive posthumously published in 2008 as *Three Wishes: An Intimate Look at Jazz Greats.* Many among this collection of after-hours snapshots are out of focus, blurred, or damaged, yet it is their very informality that makes the images so engaging. As Nadine de Koenigswäter writes in her introduction, the images are unusual and rare "due to the truly candid, private situations in which Nica captured her subjects [. . .] in the intimate surroundings of [her home] rather than in public."[47]

A striking example of the power of the jazz family archive to offer insights about a musician's life as well as providing a new perspective on what might otherwise be considered established biography is provided by Jeremy Marre's 2018 film "Count Basie Through His Own Eyes." Marre drew on a range of previously little-noticed sources in the Basie family archive including film reels, photograph

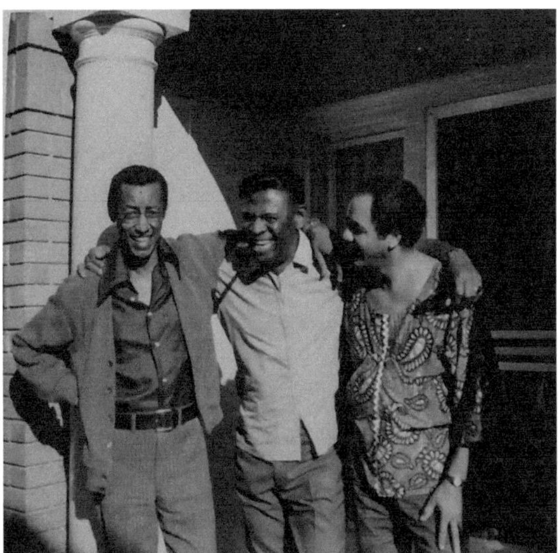

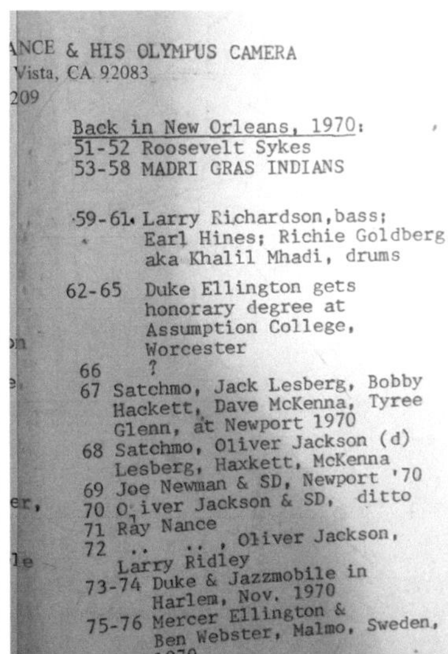

NCE & HIS OLYMPUS CAMERA
Vista, CA 92083
209

Back in New Orleans, 1970:
51-52 Roosevelt Sykes
53-58 MADRI GRAS INDIANS

59-61 Larry Richardson, bass; Earl Hines; Richie Goldberg, aka Khalil Mhadi, drums
62-65 Duke Ellington gets honorary degree at Assumption College, Worcester
66 ?
67 Satchmo, Jack Lesberg, Bobby Hackett, Dave McKenna, Tyree Glenn, at Newport 1970
68 Satchmo, Oliver Jackson (d) Lesberg, Haxkett, McKenna
69 Joe Newman & SD, Newport '70
70 Oliver Jackson & SD, ditto
71 Ray Nance
72 " " , Oliver Jackson, Larry Ridley
73-74 Duke & Jazzmobile in Harlem, Nov. 1970
75-76 Mercer Ellington & Ben Webster, Malmo, Sweden, 1970

Figures 33a and 33b: Stanley Dance. *Larry Richardson, bass; Earl Hines; Richie Goldberg and Khalil Mhadi.* New Orleans. 1970
Stanley Dance Collection, Gilmore Music Library, Yale University.

albums, diaries, and other handwritten material. In his autobiography, Basie was notoriously guarded about his family and home life. Marre's film cast light on the bandleader's stable and mutually supportive relationship with his wife, Catherine, and demonstrated how behind the scenes he supported her efforts in the civil rights struggle of the 1960s, an area in which the official biography is particularly terse. His love and continuing concern for his disabled daughter Diane, who "was never out of his heart and mind: the hidden core of his creative life," is another aspect of the musician's life vividly captured in photograph albums carefully assembled over the years by Catherine.[48]

As a young jazz enthusiast, Bob Inman kept detailed records and artifacts from many broadcasts and concerts in the mid-1930s and the photographs he acquired added value by being accompanied by ticket stubs, programs, meticulously detailed performance notes, and other materials.[49] Among other treasures in this collection is the extremely rare photograph of Billie Holiday with Artie Shaw to which Tad Hershorn referred in the quotation that opened this chapter. The photograph is an important document but equally, as Hershorn notes, "a wonderful thing," an assessment that draws on the expressive depths this image is capable of revealing beyond its "factual" significance. However important as documents, jazz photographs are inevitably imbued with expressive potential as will be seen in the next chapter.

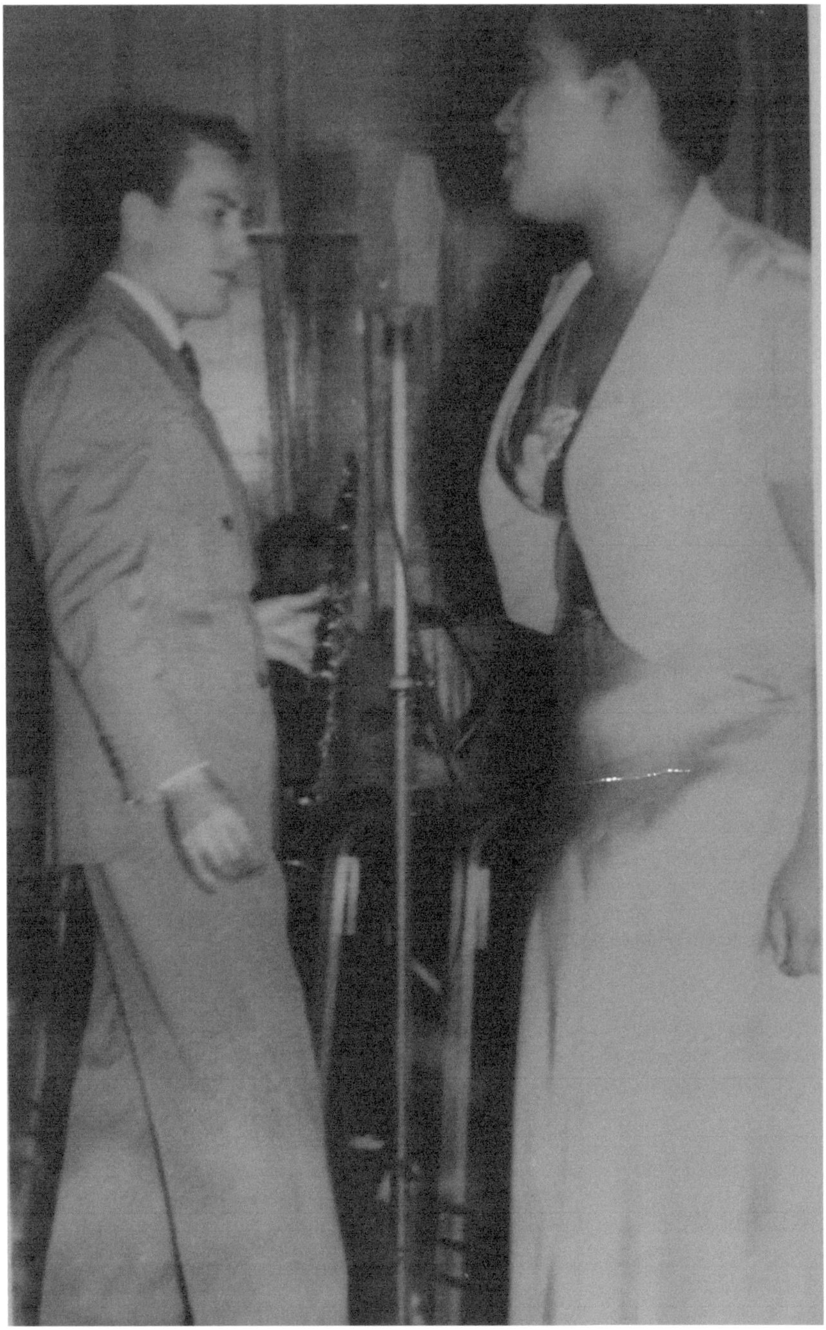

Figure 34: Unknown photographer. *Billie Holiday and Artie Shaw onstage at the Roseland-State Ballroom*. 1938.
Bob Inman scrapbook (IJS.0289), Institute of Jazz Studies. Rutgers University Libraries.

Notes

1. Tad Hershorn, Interview with the Author, 2018.
2. Allan Sekula, "The Body and The Archive," in *The Contest of Meaning: Critical Histories of Photography*, ed. Richard Bolton (Cambridge, MA: MIT Press, 1989), 342, speaks of the "evidentary promise" of the photograph supporting its claims to veracity; Elizabeth McCausland, "Documentary Photography," *Photo Notes*, 1939, n.pag.
3. Dyer, *But Beautiful: A Book About Jazz*, xi–xii.
4. Alan Trachtenberg, "Photography and Social Knowledge," *American Art* 29, no. 1 (2015): 7. Joshua C. Taylor, *Learning to Look: A Handbook for the Visual Arts* (Chicago: University of Chicago Press, 1957), 43–44.
5. Brian Rust, *Jazz and Ragtime Records, 1897–1942*, 6th ed. (Littleton, CO: Mainspring Press, 2002), 1585, 1782.
6. I am grateful to Peter Vacher for drawing this to my attention and providing background information. Correspondence with the author, June 27, 2019.
7. Lawrence W Levine, "The Historian and the Icon: Photography and the History of the American People in the 1930s and 1940s," in *Documenting America, 1935–1943*, ed. Carl Fleischhauer and Beverly W. Brannan (Berkeley: University of California Press, 1988), 24.
8. Paul Archibald, "Construction of, and Performance on, the Early Drum Kit" (Ph.D. Thesis, The University of Edinburgh, 2017); Colter Harper, " 'The Crossroads of the World' " A Social and Cultural HIstory of Jazz in Pittsburgh's Hill District, 1920–1970" (Ph.D. Thesis, University of Pittsburgh, 2011) 12–17; Daniel Stein, *Music Is My Life: Louis Armstrong, Autobiography and American Jazz* (Ann Arbor: University of Michigan Press, 2012), 16–19 *et passim*.
9. Interview and correspondence with the author, June 23, 2018, and June 29, 2019.
10. Richard Wang, "Researching the New Orleans-Chicago Jazz Connection: Tools and Methods," *Black Music Research Journal* 8, no. 1 (1988): 107–8.
11. Ed Kirkeby, Duncan P. Schiedt, and Sinclair Traill, *Ain't Misbehavin': The Story of Fats Waller* (New York: Da Capo, 1975), 187.
12. *Music Dial* 2, October 1944: 2, 32 and November 1944: 2 cited by Scott DeVeaux, *BeBop: A Social and Musical History* (Berkeley: University of California Press, 1997), 369; Ross Russell, *Jazz Style in Kansas City and the Southwest* (Berkeley: University of California Press, 1971), 198.
13. Peter Facini describes the making of Parent's image in "Four Titans of Bebop, and 'the Greatest Photo in Jazz'," *New York Times*, 2019, p. MB5. Robert George Reisner, *Bird: The Legend of Charlie Parker* (London: McGibbon and Kee, 1962), 24, reproduces the photograph alongside his description of Parker as the "amoral, anarchistic, gentle, and overcivilized" hipster.
14. Unpublished translation (with permission of the author) in manuscript of Hank O'Neal, "Introduction," in *Charlie Parker* (Filipacchi, 1995).
15. Mentoring in jazz has been extensively documented especially by Paul Berliner in *Thinking in Jazz: The Infinite Art of Improvisation* (Chicago: University of Chicago Press, 1994). On the distinction between vertical and horizontal relationships in jazz, see Frank Kofsky, "Elvin Jones Part I: Rhythmic Innovator," *Journal of Jazz Studies* 4, no. 1 (1976): 8–9.
16. The British jazz musician and composer Ben Crosland initially expressed surprise when I told him about this practice. On reflection, he realized that passing on a suitably inscribed photograph might be a meaningful way of marking relationships or as a keepsake of a particularly memorable performance. "I think we should resurrect the practice," he said—Interview with the Author, 2019.
17. Richard M. Sudhalter, Philip R. Evans, and William Dean-Myatt, *Bix: Man & Legend* (London: Quartet Books, 1974), 212.
18. Archibald, "Construction of, and Performance on, the Early Drum Kit." 20–28, 60, 81–82.
19. Bertram Turezky, "Introduction," in *Pops Foster: The Autobiography of a New Orleans Jazzman*, ed. Tom Stoddard (Berkeley: University of California Press, 1971), xiii–xvi. In this matter photographs have provided a useful supplement to Gunther Schuller's view that the long "melodic" notes that a player like Ray Brown was capable of producing were the product of a changed right-hand position and raising of the bridge. Gunther Schuller, *Early Jazz: Its Roots and Musical Development* (New York: Oxford University Press, 1968), 159 n.39. Brian Wood, *The Song for Me: A Glossary of New Orleans Musicians (and Others of That Ilk)* (Walmer, Kent: Brian Wood, 1999) 20, has argued that photographs establish that the bass was probably bowed until

about 1920—a claim that rests on the mistaken assumption that the camera could not stop action in 1920.

20. Barry Kernfeld, ed., *The New Grove Dictionary of Jazz* (London: Macmillan, 1998), 209–10; Martin Williams, *The Art of Jazz: Ragtime to BeBop* (New York: Da Capo, 1981), 182. Fernando Ortiz de Urbina, "Electric Guitar-Who's on First?," The Sounds of Surprise, 2016, http://jazzontherecord.blogspot.com/2016/09/electric-guitarwhos-on-first.html, summarizes the evidence about early electric guitar use.
21. R. Collins, *New Orleans Jazz: A Revised History* (New York: Vantage Press, 1996). 259.
22. Alyn Shipton, *A New History of Jazz* (London: Continuum, 2002), 127; Martin Williams, *Jazz Masters of New Orleans* (New York: Macmillan, 1967), 101; Frank Driggs and Harris Lewine, *Black Beauty, White Heat: A Pictorial History of Jazz 1920–1950* (New York: Da Capo, 1995): 25.
23. Shipton, *A New History of Jazz*, 248–49.
24. Jerry Atkins, "Magnificent Obsession: The Discographers," reprinted at JazzDiscography.com at https://jazzdiscography.com/magnificent-obsession-the-discographers/; Bruce Boyd Raeburn, "Appreciating Jazz Discography," *The Jazz Archivist* 3, nos. 1–2 (1988): 3.
25. Domenica Bongiovanni, "How a Quirky Indiana Studio Was the First to Record Many of America's Famous Musicians," *Indianapolis Star*, 2020, available at https://eu.indystar.com/story/entertainment/music/2020/07/27/richmonds-gennett-records-first-record-louis-armstrong/3215616001/.
26. The photographs appeared in T. Giddings, W. Earhart, R. Baldwin, and E. Newton, *Music Appreciation in the Schoolroom* (Boston, MA: Ginn, 1926) and are reproduced in Archibald, "Construction of, and Performance on, the Early Drum Kit," 106–27.
27. Mark Katz, *Capturing Sound: How Technology Has Changed Music* (Berkeley: University of California Press, 2004), 83–93.
28. Sherrie Tucker, "Bordering on Community: Improving Women, Improvising Women in Jazz," in *The Other Side of Nowhere: Jazz Improvisation and Communities in Dialogue*, ed. Daniel Fischlin and Ajay Heble (Middletown, CT: Wesleyan University Press, 2004), 255.
29. Burke, *Come In and Hear the Truth: Jazz and Race on 52nd. Street*, 98 provides an account of Thornhill's strategy; Vicky Willis, "Be-in-Tween the Spa[]Ces: The Location of Women and the Subverion in Jazz," *Journal of American Culture* 31, no. 3 (2008): 296; Ainsworth, "Photographic Representations of Jazz: Testimonial Advertising in Down Beat, 1938-49," 138.
30. Sherrie Tucker, "A Feminist Perspective on New Orleans Jazz Women," New Orleans Jazz National Historical Park (Lawrence, KS: University of Kansas, 2004) and Sally Placksin, *American Women in Jazz 1900 to the Present: Their Worlds, Lives and Music* (New York: Wideview Books, 1982) both use archival photographs to help identify women players.
31. Gennari, *Blowin' Hot and Cool: Jazz and Its Critics*, 9, 103–4, *et passim*. Ron Welburn, "Jazz Magazines of the 1930s: An Overview of Their Provocative Journalism," *American Music* 5, no. 3 (1987): 261, discusses the racial basis of the jazz press; Ainsworth, "Photographic Representations of Jazz" demonstrates the preponderance of white endorsers in testimonial advertising in *Down Beat* in the 1930s and 1940s.
32. Andy Kirk, *Twenty Years on Wheels* (Oxford: Bayou Press, 1989), 82–83.
33. Ian Carr, *Miles Davis: The Definitive Biography* (London: HarperCollins, 1999), 56.
34. Robin D. G. Kelley, *Race Rebels: Culture, Politics and the Black Working Class* (New York: Free Press, 1996), 35–53.
35. Dana Gooley, "The Outside of 'Sitting In': Jam Sessions and the Politics of Participation," *Performance Research* 16, no. 3 (2011): 43–44, for a discussion of audience competencies.
36. Andy Bennet, "Music, Space and Place," in *Music, Space and Place: Popular Music and Cultural Identity*, ed. Sheila Whiteley, Andy Bennet, and Stan Hawkins (Aldershot: Ashgate, 2004), 2–8; Holly Watkins, "Musical Ecologies of Place and Placelessness," *Journal of the American Musicological Society* 64, no. 2 (2011): 404–8; and Susan J. Smith, "Performing the (Sound) World," *Environment and Planning D: Society and Space* 18 (2000): 615–37.
37. Paul Berliner, "Vibes and Venues: Interacting with Different Audiences in Different Settings," in *Thinking in Jazz: The Infinite Art of Improvisation* (Chicago: University of Chicago Press, 1994), 449–84; Howard Becker, "Jazz Places," in *Music Scenes: Local, Translocal, and Virtual*, ed. Andy Andy Bennett and Richard A. Peterson (Nashville, TN: Vanderbilt University Press, 2004), 17–27; Dan Morgenstern, "Jazz-The Jewish Black Connection," in *Creators and Disturbers: Reminiscences by Jewish Intellectuals of New York*, ed. Bernard Rosenberg and

Ernest Goldstein (New York: Columbia University Press, 1982), 98–99; and Burt Goldblatt, *Newport Jazz Festival: The Illustrated History* (New York: Dial Press, 1977).

38. Wells cited by Jeffrey Magee, *Fletcher Henderson: The Uncrowned King of Swing* (Oxford: Oxford University Press, 2005), 111. Lester Young made a number of similar comments on the relationship between jazz performance and dancers—see Douglas Henry Daniels, *Lester Leaps In: The Life and Times of Lester "Pres" Young* (Boston: Beacon Press, 2002), 158–59. See further Christopher J. Wells, "You Can't Dance to It," *Daedalus*, 148, No. 2: 36–51 for a fascinating discussion of "jazz choreographies."
39. Stanley Dance, *The World of Count Basie* (London: Sidgick & Jackson, 1980), 6, 15.
40. Holly Watkins, "Musical Ecologies of Place and Placelessness," *Journal of the American Musicological Society* 64, no. 2 (2011): 407; and DeVeaux, "The Emergence of the Jazz Concert 1935–1945."
41. Floyd Snelson, "Don Albert Tries for 'Comeback,'" *Pittsburgh Courier*, 1937.
42. Buck Clayton and Nancy Miller Elliott, *Buck Clayton's Jazz World* (Oxford: Bayou Press, 1989). 93–94; Douglas Henry Daniels, *Lester Leaps In: The Life and Times of Lester "Pres" Young* (Boston: Beacon Press, 2002), 37.
43. Kirkeby, *Ain't Misbehavin'*, 185–87, 210; Shipton, *Fats Waller*, 72–73. See also Joel Vance, *Fats Waller: His Life and Times* (London: Robson Books, 1979), 118. Maurice Waller and Anthony Calabrese, *Fats Waller* (Minneapolis: University of Minnesota Press, 1977), 128–60; Martin Williams, *Jazz Heritage* (New York: Oxford University Press, 1985), 14–17; and James Lincoln Collier, *The Making of Jazz: A Comprehensive History* (London: Macmillan, 1978), 202–3, describe Waller's insecurities.
44. Hershorn, "Interview with the Author."
45. Shawn Michelle Smith, *Photography on the Color Line: W. E. B. DuBois, Race and Visual Culture* (Durham, NC: Duke University Press, 2004), 8; Lynn Berger, "Snapshots, or: Visual Culture's Clichés," *Photographies* 4, no. 2 (2011): 180. On vernacular photography and the family album see further Rosy Martin, "Family History and Photography," in *Oxford Companion to the Photograph*, ed. Robin Lenman (Oxford: Oxford University Press, 2005), 212–13; Geoffrey Batchen, "Vernacular Photographies: Responses to a Questionnaire," *History of Photography Journal* 24, no. 3 (2000): 229–31; Chalfen, *Snapshot Versions of Life*; Holland, "Introduction: Memory and the Family Album"; and Catherine Zuromskis, *Snapshot Photography: The Lives of Images* (Cambridge, MA: MIT Press, 2013).
46. Douglas Henry Daniels, *Lester Leaps In: The Life and Times of Lester "Pres" Young* (Boston, MA: Beacon Press, 2002), 28, discusses the photograph of Young and his mother, which is reproduced in pages 264–65. I am grateful to Peter Vacher for drawing the photograph of Paul Barnes to my attention: Interview with the author, June 23, 2018.
47. Pannonica de Koenigswäter, *Three Wishes: An Intimate Look at Jazz Greats* (New York: Abrams Image, 2008), 22, 25.
48. I am grateful to Melissa Morton Hicks of Eagle Rock Films for information about the photographic records on which the film drew.
49. Vail, *Swing Era Scrapbook: The Teenage Diaries and Radio Logs of Bob Inman 1936–38.*

4

Expression in the Jazz Image

Introducing an anthology of jazz images, Nat Hentoff remarked, "There isn't a page in this book that doesn't evoke the distinctiveness of each of these shapers of the universal language that is jazz." Commenting on Jim Marshall's photograph of Paul Gonsalves's seminal performance with Duke Ellington at the Newport Jazz Festival in 1956—a performance that revived Ellington's career, transformed assessments of Gonsalves, and provoked a near riot among the audience—the San Francisco journalist and broadcaster Philip Elwood thought the image "tells the whole story in a single frame." Jazz scholar Peter Townsend remarked that jazz photography at its best can "open up a sense of reality outside the frame of the image itself [. . .] carried back into a mythologized past, into the same visual realm as images made in the 1930s and 1940s." According to Jimmy Katz, a leading contemporary New York jazz photographer, Herman Leonard's image of Dexter Gordon is "an image which almost singularly represents the history and totality of jazz."[1]

As these observations confirm, the allure of jazz images lies as much in their expressive potency as in documentary significance—the ability to evoke the atmosphere of the spaces and sounds of jazz performance; to stimulate, confirm, and even reconfigure personal and social memories; and to provide visual confirmation of the myths around these personalities. The previous chapter considered ways in which jazz photographs provide information to researchers, historians, discographers, and collectors. In this chapter the expressive and imaginative possibilities incited by jazz imagery are considered through the work of photographers who have strived to visualize the sounds of jazz and its cultural associations.

I. Visualizing the sounds of jazz

Sight and sound

An apparently unbridgeable gap between music, the most abstract of art forms, and the representational nature of photography has discouraged many from discussing cross-modal commonalities. Yet it is possible to identify similar artistic concepts across these media.[2] In the 1950s Adrian Siegal, a classical musician and accomplished photographer, explained that initially a photograph "powerfully indicates the effort of making music" but with longer looking "the sense of effort is replaced with a sense of music [. . .] Once it takes place, the pictures evoke musicians with integrity passionately creating music."[3] The idea that photographs can evoke the sounds of jazz has been advanced by many observers. Leonard Feather proposed that "the sight of jazz, or more specifically of jazz performers, sometimes seems virtually inseparable from the sound of the music," an argument that found support from Herman Leonard:[4]

> *I wanted to capture the atmosphere of the club. I wanted to capture the feeling of a particular musician if it could be done in a graphic form rather than an audio form*

[. . .] I wanted to capture the music, but I had to interpret it with black and white, with light, with shades and shadows.

For Sherry Turner DeCarava, Roy DeCarava's photography evoked "Life sounds [. . .] in singing tones" while Gordon Parks was struck by "the sounds emerging—a trumpet screaming, a saxophone moaning, a melodious voice crying" in the jazz portraits of Carol Friedman. John Leland has spoken in similar terms of "hearing music in photos":[5]

Charlie Parker's photograph erupts from the frame with the kinetic restlessness of his blowing; Dizzy Gillespie's disarming studiousness over the chessboard hums like his geometric solos. Count Basie is all smoke and rhythm, and Billie Holiday doesn't need sound to sing the blues. The camera says it all for her [. . .] You can almost fill in the sounds of the bass and drums, the temperature in the room, the suspended breath of the audience, wondering what will come next.

When the photographer Lee Tanner proposed a "magnificent synergism" between jazz and photography deriving from the ability of the visual to make an "emotional connection" with the sounds of the music, he was describing what some have suggested as a synesthetic response.[6] For Roland Barthes human vision is perpetually searching for signs, combining optical, linguistic, and haptic functions: all the senses thus have the capacity to "look" and, conversely, "the look has the capacity to smell, to listen, to touch, etc."[7] In its fusion of representational precision and expressive potency, the jazz photograph is arguably the perfect site for the release of synesthetic responses. This appears consistent with Jay Maisel's description of his own jazz work: "It's like trying to capture lightening in a bottle because once you've finished there's no sound. You have to distil all five senses in to the visual."[8]

Visualizing musical embodiment

What is it about the visual that might summon the sounds of music? Charles Seeger's observation made almost a century ago that music functions to express ideas that cannot be communicated in language seems particularly appropriate in the case of jazz. Tracing a line from the "shared conceptual approaches" of African American musical practices, jazz has often been described as a *uniquely* embodied music, a music "played with the body, the entire body, by a musician who is so totally involved in what he is doing that one should not only hear his performance, one should also see it, in order better to understand what he is trying to express." Bebop intensified this trend, decentering dancers in order to recenter the music in the bodies of performers.[9] It is in the very nature of a spontaneous and improvisatory music that the meaning of jazz is relocated from the object of art to the individual artist and performance and it is in the performative embodiment of jazz that many photographers have identified unique moments of visualization.[10]

The physicality of jazz performance has often been described. Alfred Appel recalled how Louis Armstrong "played the trumpet with his entire body," his legs vibrating rapidly against his trousers in time with the music. Seeking to replicate the famous cadenza with which Armstrong opens "West End Blues," Robert Walser found his own body stance shifting to accomplish the power and authority of Armstrong's musical statement. David Ake has described the bodily and facial gestures of the pianist Bill Evans as reinforcing an impression of a "jazz intellectual" and player of "sensitive male interiority" while Tom Perchard pays particular attention to Lee Morgan's gestural practices as a statement of racial identity. Jazz musicians are just as aware of this aspect of their music. Oscar Petersen said that playing jazz "draws on everything about you [. . .] It requires you to collect all your senses, emotions, physical strength and mental power, and focus them totally on the performance." It might not be surprising that the more physically animated activity of drumming should, as Geoffrey Curran explains, be consciously employed by musicians to create an immediate visual link between bodily playing style and genre, but similar features attend to other less kinetic instruments. In his account of learning to be a jazz improviser, David Sudnow recounts how he was driven by an awareness of bodily engagement in improvisation, particularly through his hands. His self-tuition advanced primarily through manual, visual, and kinesthetic means heightened by feeling sounds through his body. A significant moment in his self-education was observing the body movements of the pianist Jimmy Rowles; imitating Rowles's bodily actions Sudnow felt new sensations and heard "well-spoken" improvisations.[11]

Jazz writers have seized on embodied expressions as captured in photographs to interpret the mood and atmosphere surrounding performances. When Miles Davis took his nonet into Capitol Records' studio in 1949 and 1950 to record the three *Birth of the Cool* 78s, "PoPsie" Randolph was on hand to capture the sessions. Randolph's glowing black-and-white photographs show Davis relaxed and in control. At the second recording session of Davis's *Kind of Blue* on April 22, 1959, both Fred Plaut and Don Hunstein took photographs. According to Ashley Kahn, the loose confidence of the band is apparent from their images: "If a camera can be trusted to catch the essence of a moment, Miles and his sidemen were on common, comfortable ground that day." Chuck Stewart was called in to photograph the second day of the recording of John Coltrane's seminal album *A Love Supreme* in December 1964 and the six rolls of film he shot are the only record of that memorable session. Using a bounced strobe to create the effect of natural lighting, Stewart's images convey the relaxed atmosphere in the studio that evening: "For one reputed to be so tight-lipped, he appears quite conversational. The session tapes may have recorded little of his leadership role, but Stewart's images show him in charge and comfortably so."[12]

These corporeal associations constitute what Nat Hentoff called the "insistent visibility" of jazz performance, in which "the players *are* their music" and through which jazz *as* music becomes available to photographic representation:[13]

> *The major instrumentalists and singers communicate with physical as well as musical impact [. . .] the urgency that possesses Roy Eldridge as he lifts his horn; the go-for-broke immersion of Charles Mingus in his bass; the waves of humor and let's-enjoy-being-now that radiate from Jimmy Rushing. The bitter poignancy, the strangely cynical hopefulness, the shocking tenderness of Billie Holiday were most affecting when you saw her as well as heard her [. . .]. This is where the camera can help supply the important visual dimension of jazz.*

It is above all else in bodily posture and movement, facial signs, hand signals, instrumental address, and a range of other corporeal expressions that embodied meanings of musical embodiment assume visual form. Bob Douglas's extraordinarily visceral photograph of Stanley Turrentine playing at a jazz festival offers an intense expression of jazz as a music through gesture, expression, and posture (Figure 35). It is for this reason that jazz photographers have stressed "the moment"—the precise point at which these expressions are at their most intense, forcefully conveying the meaning of the music to the player. Seizing these opportunities means that photographers must be constantly alert to the ebb and flow of the music, a form of creative awareness that suggests parallels between photography and the processes of jazz improvisation.

Spontaneity and improvisation

The embodiment of jazz performance must be translated into a visual language. It has been suggested that photographers are able to capture powerful visual statements by mirroring the improvisation and spontaneity of the music in a kind of processual symbiosis; much as improvisation takes the form of an "inner dialogue," so too are photographers continually reading the scene, improvising in order spontaneously to seize the moment. Photographic improvisation has been described as being akin to the jazz musician improvising without preestablished goals, engaging control over the process but "relaxing cognitive control over the *direction* of the music."[14] However, the parallels between photography and jazz improvisation go further in that the outcome of both processes is the realization of a *unique* work of art. Gerard Genette makes the case that a jazz piece on which a musician repeatedly improvises should be considered "singular, in the full sense [. . .] unique." In the same way, the photographer's

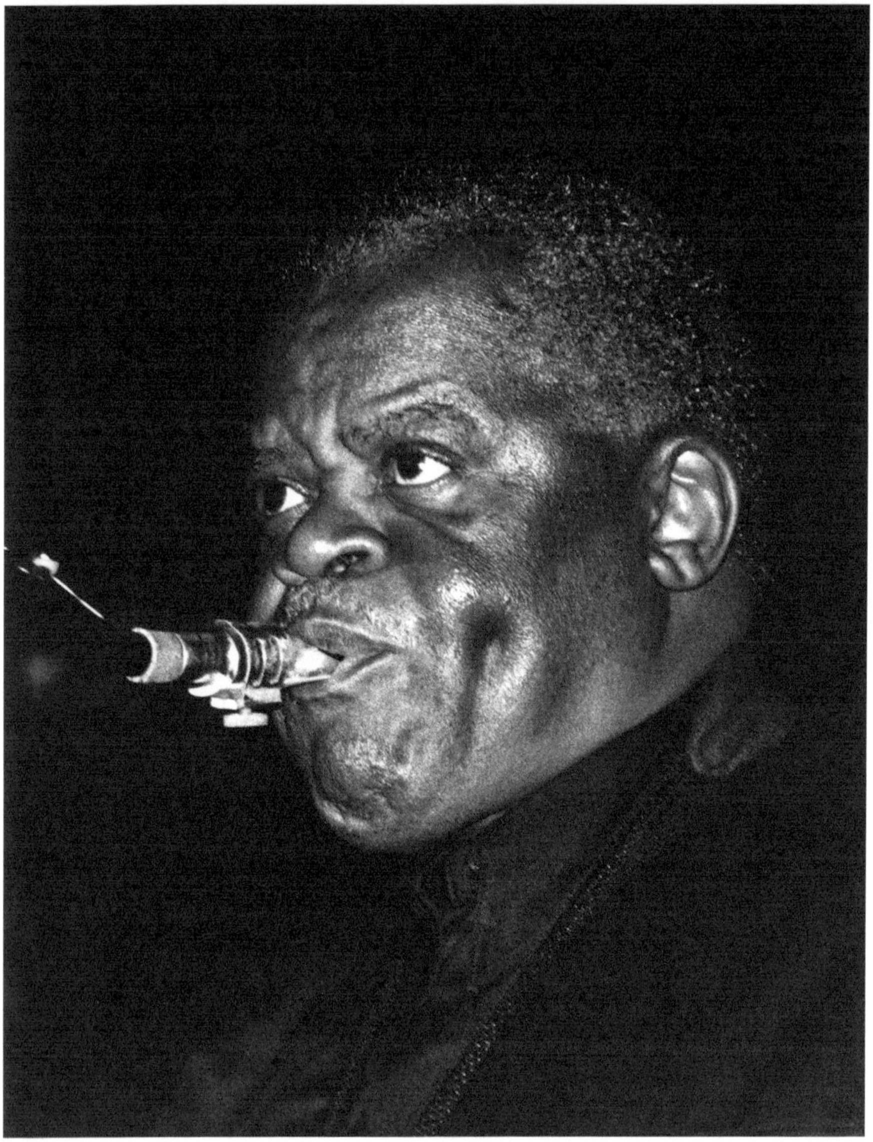

Figure 35: Bob Douglas. *Stanley Turrentine*. Long Beach. 1993.
Tom and Ethel Bradley Centre for African American Arts, California State University, Northridge.

improvisation on a recurring subject (the performance) is at least capable of uniqueness on every occasion, although the degree to which this is achieved lies with the photographer.[15]

Critics and musicians alike have been drawn to the common ground between jazz improvisation and photography. Sherry Turner DeCarava proposes improvisatory exchanges between musicians as a model for photographic visualization: jazz "exists as a moment to moment interchange between expressive voices, much like the individual pictorial voices of light, shape, shadow and plane in the print."[16] Nat Hentoff described jazz photographs as capturing the "spontaneity and individuality that are the essence of the music and those who make it," and Barry Singer has spoken of "improvised moments" that have "infatuated photographers for nearly a century now, inspiring viewfinder variations as eloquent as the most transcendent jazz solos."[17] Musicians have also suggested that photographic and musical improvisation work effectively in tandem:[18]

> *The attraction that jazz musicians have for photographers is understandable when one considers that both are concerned with the moment. For the musician it is the fleeting moment that involves the creation of some kind of valid music and for the photographer the attempt to express in pictorial terms [. . .] This affinity seems specifically confined to jazz music—most portraits of classical musicians could just as well be of politicians or bank managers.*

Among the photographers, Dennis Stock was insistent that the form of his book *Jazz Street* had emerged from the same improvisatory process that governed the art of the musicians he captured; and Roy DeCarava believed that the immediacy of photography found its equivalent in improvisation, "because jazz music is based on the improvisation of the individual who at one time brings all of his talents to bear at the precise moment he's playing. So you have the same kind of immediacy." DeCarava's photographs, charged with the emotional *Gestalt* of the moment, bring to mind Cartier-Bresson's famous notion of the "decisive moment" and it is no surprise to discover that the French photographer was highly influential on DeCarava's own development. The result, according to A. D. Coleman referring to DeCarava's images of John Coltrane, is that "Coltrane is alive. The music, as well as the man, can be felt in them."[19]

When Don Heckman observed that William Claxton "works with an instrument" he was proposing that the photographers use the camera much as the jazz musicians use an instrument as an improvisatory tool. The New York photographer Enid Farber also speaks of the camera as "her instrument":

> *I always wanted to play an instrument and I really feel camera is another form of instrument. Like any musical instrument it provides a means of personal expression—a kind of "call and response" where the photographer responds to the music as the instrumentalists do with each other.*

Veryl Oakland makes a similar observation of his own work as a jazz photographer:

I had substituted photography for playing an instrument. There was nothing conscious on my part, but I found that the instrument I used for "improvising"—for creating some of those special jazz moments—wasn't my cornet. It was the camera.

From the musician's point of view, Wynton Marsalis describes the Jazz at Lincoln Centre photographer Frank Stewart as "a jazzman with a camera. Improvisational, empathetic, and accurate" and Billy Taylor reiterates the comparison:[20]

The photographer often uses his camera the way a jazz musician uses his instrument. It becomes his medium of personal expression, and, like the jazz musician, he sometimes creates a theme of his own and uses a variety of subjects to define and explore it [. . .] he also seeks to capture a moment in time, saying something personal and spontaneous.

Less charitably perhaps, Jay Maisel likes to tell people that photographers are drawn to jazz as a result of their unfulfilled—or unattainable—goal of being themselves musicians![21]

Photography and interiority

If the musical essence of jazz can find visual expression in this way, we should not be surprised to encounter the argument that images are capable of probing and expressing the "inner state" of the jazz musician. This is an interpretation that rests on the contention that an intangible inner life is manifested in musical performance, what Robert Walser has called the "deep jazz" conception. Walser expresses serious concerns about this notion. He argues that ideas of psychological interiority elevate an artistic "essence" above the social grounding of musical practices and experiences and historical circumstance. This is, he continues, a trap into which white critics, inclined to explain jazz in terms of precultural, or instinctual interiority, tend to fall. The end result is the universalization of jazz as an autonomous art form divorced from contextual forces.[22]

There is evidence to support the racial orientation of Walser's thesis although (as he accepts) it does not apply without exception. To be sure, Nat Hentoff's suggestion that individual subjectivity in jazz cannot but reveal itself in photographs appears to align with the deep jazz thesis: "Because jazz musicians are less likely than most people to wear masks, their faces make for marvelous portraits of the person within," Hentoff observed, describing how Jimmy Rushing "smiles with the look of someone who has seen it all but isn't in the least jaded" while "Cecil Taylor [. . .] smiles here with the immense satisfaction of knowing that he is now of worldwide renown, and he hasn't compromised one note of his music to get there."[23] Photographers have been particularly attracted to the idea that their images can reveal some form of personal interiority. William Gottlieb was insistent on the need to look beneath the surface appearances of his jazz subjects: "Ideally, I tried to capture a person's personality or inner qualities," he recalled, referring to a photograph of Billie Holiday "that clearly shows the anguish in her voice." Lourdes Delgardo has confirmed that revealing the "inner state" of the jazz musicians she photographed was one of her primary concerns:[24]

> *I'm fascinated by relating specific, concrete facts with the feelings and emotions they arouse. For example, between a hand holding another hand and the tenderness, security, happiness or whatever you get from it. And in the case of music, between the physicality of a musician playing an instrument and the music itself. Perhaps my jazz pictures, which I call my notes, gives me a gleam of what I feel as a magical and undefined path that connects both worlds.*

On the other hand, this cannot be said to be a purely white conceptualization of jazz. Dizzy Gillespie spoke about jazz photographs in similar terms to Hentoff and Gottlieb when he suggested that the most important thing about a jazz musician is that the music is a reflection of his true self and, "like his music, a fine photograph of a musician reflects his soul."[25]

II. Visualizing jazz culture

John Gennari tells us that "Jazz, like all music, is an invisible art form. And yet jazz culture is intensely visual, its history not just one of dazzling sound but also of imagery replete with beauty, cultural meaning, and social importance."[26] Moving beyond interpretations of jazz as a musical form, photographers have strived to capture signs that signify "jazz" in a broader cultural sense. The notion of "jazz culture" has attracted a range of definitions and is frequently used interchangeably with that of the "jazz community"—itself, as Ken Prouty reminds us, a heterogeneous term comprising a range of constituencies separated by race, age, gender, style, tradition, and location. Scholars have discussed the jazz community and/or culture in terms of occupational identity, particular types of participants or behavioral and psychological traits, gender, musical styles, race, locations, and spaces; some have attempted to embrace listeners and audiences in the definition of jazz culture while others employ concepts such as imagined communities and the art world.[27] Alan P. Merriman and Raymond W. Mack's 1960 article on the jazz community was a foundational text in this debate and it is interesting that photographers have followed the three broad lines they describe: the jazz community as a subculture based around work, education, and lifestyle, as deriving from the social and artistic requirements of distinctive art form and as a manifestation of racial difference.[28]

Jazz as subculture

Photographers have been captivated by the visual possibilities of jazz as a distinctive subculture. Exploiting the participants' embodied behavior, expression, and gestures and the spaces in which they are situated, photographers have mobilized visual signs to create tableaux which reinforce sociological distance from conventional society. Set in Tony's Tavern in Chicago, in 1935, an unknown photographer captured a party thrown for Duke Ellington and Louis Armstrong in a jazz world social landscape. The image is redolent of depression-era joints in which jazz might typically be heard with its associations of night-time entertainment, music, and alcohol. The participants (including six members of Ellington's Orchestra, family members, and Isidore Langlois with guitar) are well dressed but the gathering is informal, even unstructured, and there is obviously some impromptu musical accompaniment going on.[29] In another cramped dark space, a remarkable 1937 photograph by Robert H. Lehman of a jam session involving Duke Ellington, Chick Webb, and Artie Shaw (Figure 36) again presents an informal unstructured scene apparently sealed off from the wider society; and an even less inhibited backstage scene captured by Art Weismann (Figure 37) shows a group of musicians (including Benny Goodman and Roy Eldridge) and onlookers enjoying a spontaneous blowing session.

Charles Peterson's photographs of the musicians around Eddie Condon are classic depictions of the behind-the-scenes world of the jazz subculture. Peterson's photographs captured informal moments in which musicians are shown

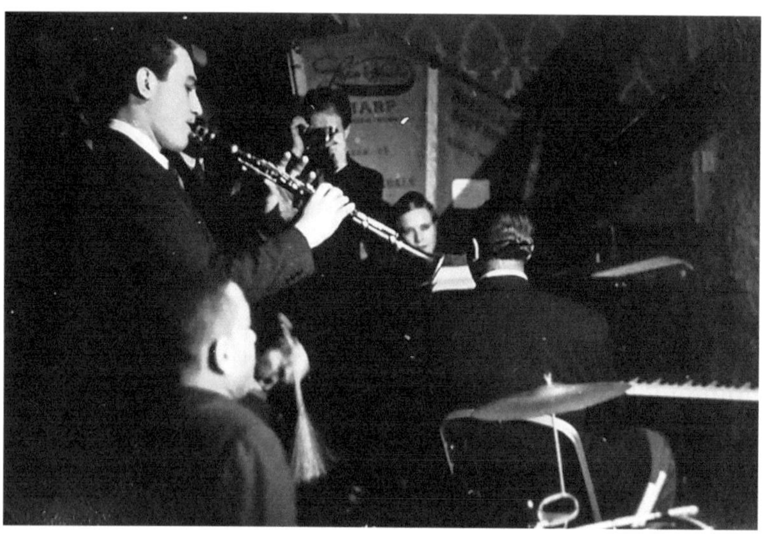

Figure 36: Robert H. Lehman. *Artie Shaw, Chick Webb, Irving Mills, and Duke Ellington—jam session*. 1937.
Gilmore Music Library-Stanley Dance Collection.

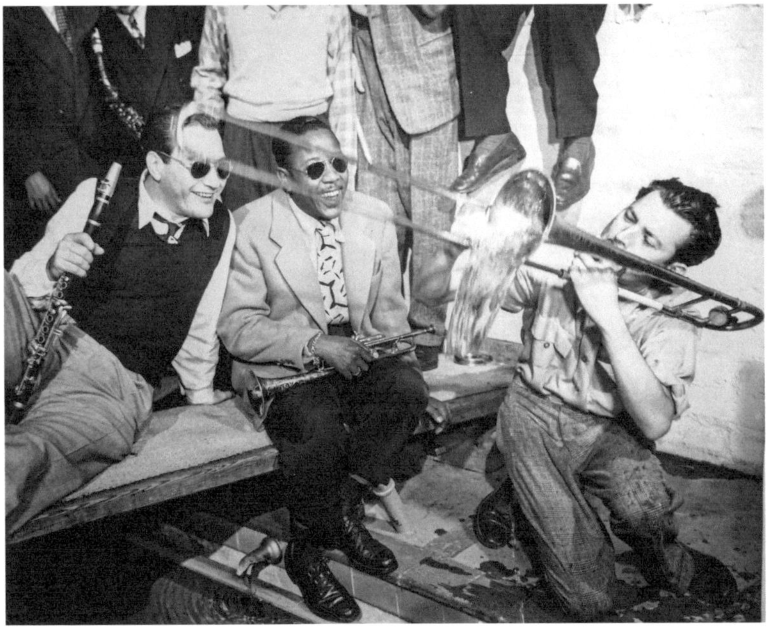

Figure 37: Art Weismann. *Benny Goodman and Roy Eldridge.* n.d. *Author's collection.*

eating, drinking, laughing and joking, playing instruments backstage, in bars and restaurants or in hotel rooms, and jam sessions. Peterson was himself part of this world and was observing from the inside. For a time the house guitarist at Columbia Records, his regular appearances at Harlem night spots led him to strike up friendships with many musicians of the time and his images reflect his friendships with the players he knew best and the access to intimate scenes that this provided (Figure 2).[30] As the 1940s turned into the 1950s, the music press used innumerable photographs of Gillespie and Monk with their dark glasses and fashionable styling to support a narrative of the romantic outsiders living in a world governed by norms in some sense outside those of conventional society.[31] With its prominent use of instruments, sharp suits, and the trappings of the night club setting, "PoPsie" Randolph's photograph of an integrated group comprising Fats Navarro, Miles Davis, Kai Winding identifies the scene as signifying the separate world of "jazz" (Figure 38).

An artistic subculture

A second approach visualizes the subculture of jazz primarily in artistic terms often by drawing on its modernist overtones. There was of course an element of symbiosis in this endeavor. Early twentieth-century American photography was deeply engaged with the quest for "common icons of modernity," the iconic signifiers that linked the pictorialists of Stieglitz's circle and modernist pioneers

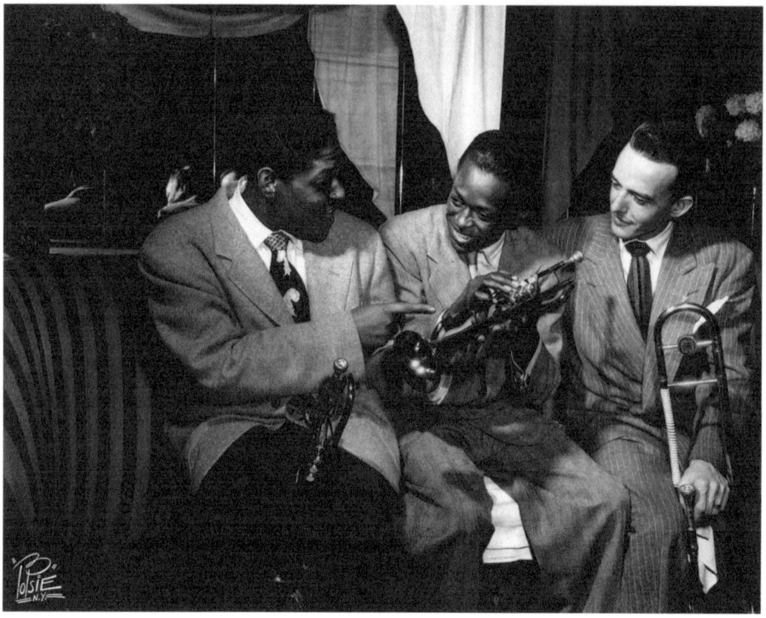

Figure 38: "PoPsie." *Fats Navarro, Miles Davis, Kai Winding.* Clique Club (later Birdland). New York. December–January 1948–49.
Permission of Michael Randolph, Executive to the Estate of William "PoPsie" Randolph.

with documentarians and amateur photographers in a shared interpretation of a forward-looking age. Jazz, which by the 1920s had come to stand for almost anything modern, was one such sign. Painters such as Aaron Douglas, Romare Bearden, Arthur Dove, Stuart Davis, Jackson Pollock, and Franz Kline drew on jazz for inspiration and as a source of visual motifs while graphic designers were quick to adopt "jazz style" as an aesthetic in book and magazine design, posters, and record sleeves.[32] Visualizing jazz in this way appealed to white photographers like Herb Snitzer who situated their work at the nexus of jazz and modernist art forms:

> *The painters of the fifties, including Jackson Pollock and Stuart Davis, were drawn to the clubs of Greenwich Village where bebop, the new jazz, was being played, where blacks and whites came together in racial harmony [. . .] The musicians were doing in their way what the painters were doing on canvass [. . .] Each tried new techniques coming out of a time when America was transforming.*

Having recently accepted Bill Coss's offer of the job of photography editor and circulation director at *Metronome,* Snitzer was convinced that photography was the appropriate medium in which to record these cultural shifts. Alongside images of musicians,[33] *we also published the work of American photographers, because we as a staff took the view that we were publishing a cultural magazine, not a music magazine per se, and photography was an American art form [. . .] we brought into the magazine stories about these and other photographers: Mathew Brady, Alfred Stieglitz, Roy DeCarava, Berenice Abbott, Aaron Siskind.*

Burt Glinn's readings of the affinity between jazz and the artistic avant-garde were captured between 1957 and 1960 in photographs from beat venues in New York City and San Francisco.[34] Glinn helped establish this profile for jazz with a photo-spread feature in *Esquire* magazine when David Amram's band were in residence. His shots of Amram's band playing to leading avant-garde artists such as Jack Kerouac, the poet Kenneth Koch, painters Joan Mitchell, Helen Frankenthaler, Larry Rivers, Franz Kline, and Grace Hartigan, dancer and sculptors Anita Huffington and David Smith, Charles Mingus, and other leading jazz musicians help evoke the atmosphere of literary-artistic jazz venues in the late-1950s. No image better displays Glinn's reading of the cultural affinity between jazz and the avant-garde as that of Earl Bostic playing chess, both player and a trumpet silhouetted in deep reds and blacks by the rising sun.[35] It is noticeable Burt Glinn's photographs of the supposedly integrated avant-garde scene of the late-1950s overwhelmingly show young white people.

Thelonious Monk's reappearance at the Five Spot in 1957 after the six-year hiatus caused by the loss of his cabaret card captured in Burt Glinn's photographs has been taken as marking the start of his association with leading artistic modernists. Although in reality Monk was never able fully to identify with the avant-garde, photographers were attracted to this associational trope.[36] In a photograph taken at New York's Five Spot, Raymond Ross also linked jazz with the avant-garde. The image shows Pharaoh Sanders, Henry Grimes, Ed Blackwell, and Don Cherry closely grouped together on a small stage; the players form a half-circle and behind them the wall is plastered with posters that immediately locate the image as the 1960s New York art scene. A poster to the right of Grimes announces poetry and jazz sessions held at the Five Spot every Thursday and brings to mind the "poetry to jazz" recitals that Langston Hughes had staged with musicians like Charles Mingus at the Village Vanguard. Ross's photograph is redolent of the beat haunts and jazz lofts that emerged in the 1950s and 1960s and which, as we shall later see, were extensively documented by W. Eugene Smith.[37]

The association between white jazz and avant-garde modernism is especially noticeable in the populist and filmic portrayal of jazz as mid-century modernism, the aesthetic that found expression in French-inspired "existential cool" and came to embrace furniture, fabrics, plastics, modern domestic architecture as well as music and the visual arts.[38] As the shockwaves of bebop subsided the classical European-infected jazz of white bandleaders like Stan Kenton, Woody

Herman, Boyd Raeburn, and Claud Thornhill, musicians such as Lennie Tristano, Lee Konitz, and Dave Brubeck's Quartet gained in ascendance. Among these musicians, Gerry Mulligan emerged as the exemplar of a "cult of the white jazz artist."[39] A production still from Ranald MacDougall's 1960 MGM movie *The Subterraneans* shows Mulligan's quintet in a coffee bar scene and collages a range of mid-century modernist tropes to convey a visual impression of jazz as congruent with a predominantly white cultural *zeitgeist* (Figure 39).[40] The musicians' casual but fashionable dress and integrated band are immediate signs: the louche and self-consciously unconventional pose of the trombone player Bob Enevoldsen; the two female figures whose dress and hairstyles immediately connote "student"; the coffee bar setting (and even the small Italian expresso cup) and its bare brick walls. To make the point, contemporary art works have been deployed around the scene.

Just like the stereotyped "Beat" photograph with its jazz associations that accompanied a dismissive 1959 *Life* article by Paul O'Neil, the coffee bar scene is of course a media contrivance.[41] But the idea that jazz and photography might be conjoined as modernist art forms appealed to many photographers. With his images of Shorty Rogers, Art Pepper, and Chet Baker, William Claxton has often been linked with the west coast cool movement and modernist culture.[42]

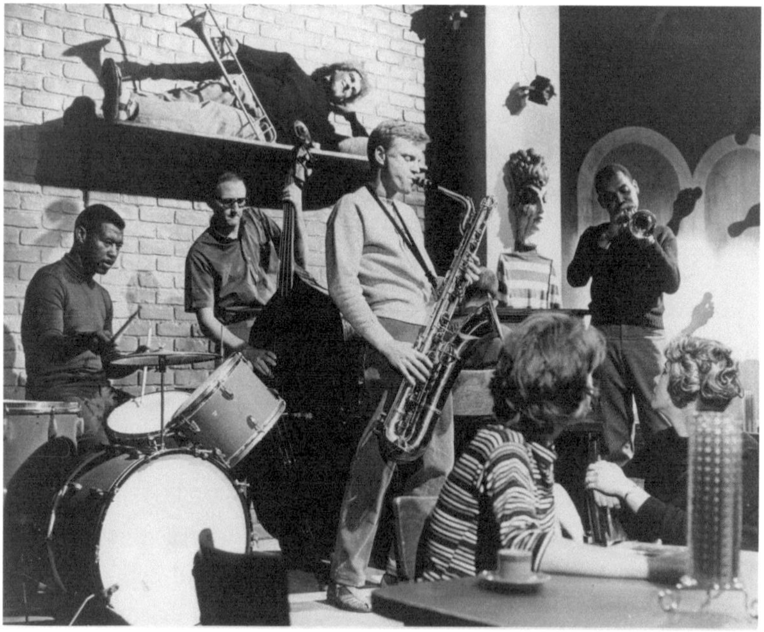

Figure 39: Unknown photographer. *Gerry Mulligan Quintet in a scene from the Subterraneans.* MGM. 1960.
Peter Vacher Collection.

Black culture

The idea that jazz images might express the nature of black American culture is common. George E. Panichas speaks of Larry Fink's photographs as embodying "a deep understanding of, and special insights regarding, the social, political and economic circumstances of their time" and Peter Fetterman described jazz imagery as "stories of lives lived [. . .] of hopes and dreams and struggles and triumphs. I see the spirit and energy of a great art form and the American people who created it." Both Duncan P. Schiedt and Herb Snitzer linked their own jazz work firmly to black concerns. At *Metronome* in the late-1950s Snitzer and his colleagues saw their role as representing African American culture alongside artistic modernism: "We proselytized, telling our readers how creative these individual black performers were."[43] Snitzer proclaimed his commitment to "the expressiveness of the people and the expressiveness of the culture [. . .] captured on film":

> *For me, personally [. . .] jazz is a metaphor for freedom, spirit, spontaneity, and also for culture, because jazz is an expression of the development of black culture in America. It's not music made in a vacuum, nor is photography made in a vacuum, so when I put the two together, I want to get more than a description.*

Snitzer's nuanced understanding of the ways in which black culture might be presented contrasts with the tendency among other white photographers to express their empathy with the African American experience by focusing on what Barry Singer described as "the sweetness and the pain of African-American experience" by focusing on cultural marginalization or on the tropes of "coolness" styled by black jazz musicians.[44]

As we shall see in Chapters 6 and 7, jazz for African American photographers on the other hand was frequently conceived in terms of its place among the rituals of communal life, situated as much in expressions of musically inflected behaviors than as a specific and discrete form of musical activity. Just as Aaron Douglas's paintings of musical events moved beyond merely descriptive scenes of local color to express sites of a larger ritual drama, jazz for many black photographers was essentially an expression of social and communal relations "saturated," to use Stephen Henderson's term, by the music as one expression of the "black experience."[45] Less enmeshed in artistic modernism, the form and content of relationships, gesture, and behavior of audiences increasingly emerged in the hands of black photographers after the 1920s as realist expressions of individuality and community-wide ritual celebrations of the black group. Viewed in this way it becomes possible to understand why deeper meanings of jazz for Charles "Teenie" Harris were to be found less in an expression of music as in the responses of the young, elegantly dressed African American women crowding around Duke Ellington (Figure 40).

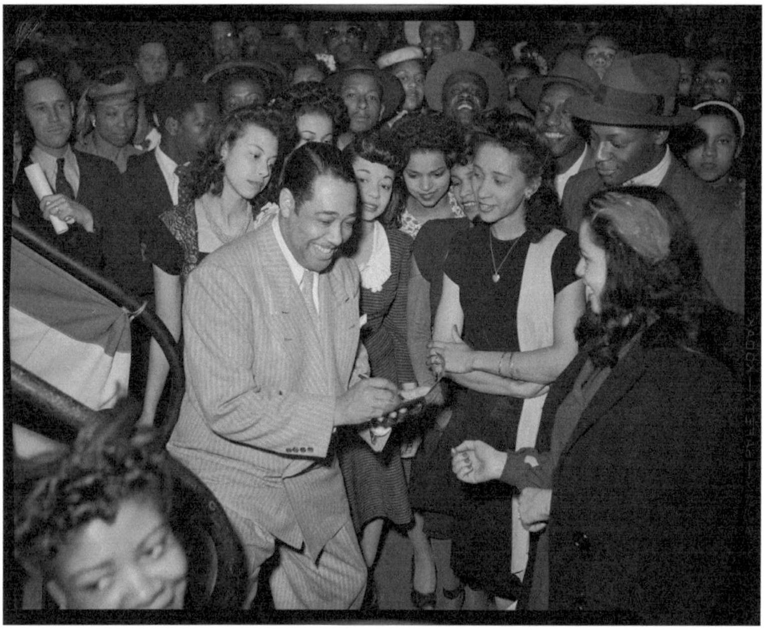

Figure 40: Charles "Teenie" Harris. *Duke Ellington signing autographs in a crowd.* 1946–47. *Carnegie Museum of Art.*

Few photographers have linked jazz to African American culture in both formal and conceptual terms quite as explicitly as Roy DeCarava and his contribution was pivotal for many African American photographers following him. What makes DeCarava's contribution special is the way in which he synthesizes these ideas with his portrayal of the context of black life. The carefully sequenced images in DeCarava's *the sound i saw: improvisations on a jazz theme* juxtapose jazz portraits with the material realities of Harlem life. Black becomes a metaphor for the relationship between the players and the African American community. While many white photographers used the dark backgrounds in low-light club environments to isolate the player, in DeCarava's hands black tones *link* the player with his background. These are jazz photographs made "through black eyes [. . .] an attempt [. . .] to say things about ourselves as black people that only we could say."[46] We will return to the realist black aesthetic as it found expression in the jazz photography of photographers such as Harris and DeCarava in Chapter 8.

The "jazz life"

The visual expression of jazz culture has been interpreted more broadly by several photographers who have tried to capture the essence of the "jazz life." None is more panoramic in scope than William Claxton's *Jazz Life,* a remarkable visual and written description of the journey across the United States made by

Claxton and the German musicologist Joachim Berendt in 1960. *Jazz Life* was a journey *for* jazz, more a homage to jazz culture in all its manifold aspects than simply photographs of musicians; it was, as Claxton described it, a "jazz odyssey [. . .] a chance to photograph many of my jazz heroes, in addition to the many unknown and yet-to-be-discovered jazz musicians all round America."[47] Dennis Stock's own odyssey into the jazz life began three years earlier in 1957, a journey that took him across the country exploring the variety and vitality of jazz. The result, published in 1959 as *Jazz Street,* mirrors the music with the first and last images providing a statement and recapitulation and, across some 130 monochrome images in between, a carefully structured presentation of themes and variation.[48] Although his focus was largely on the music's storied names and more consciously art photographic than Claxton, Stock's achievement lay in his creative treatment of the peripheral and the commonplace which he brought center stage into the mainstream of jazz reportage.

Lee Friedlander's *Playing for the Benefit of the Band* is an anthology comprising photographs made between 1958 and 1992.[49] Friedlander probed the jazz life through the relationship between individual players and the ensemble, metaphorically invoking the collective nature of early jazz. The photographs, many of which are set in the homes of elderly New Orleans musicians, segue into the streets as an environment for music making. These veterans didn't enjoy the success of Armstrong or Bechet. Friedlander places them in sparsely furnished rooms in their homes where they play or hold passively the instruments they once commanded: Chester Zardis' euphonium is stored on top of a wardrobe, gathering dust; a wire trumpet hangs on the wall of "Kid" Thomas Valentine's house, the only link with the world of the jazz musician; and George Lewis's band play in a dive whose ceiling is so low that Lewis cannot stand upright and the single audience member seems unaware of the players' pedigree. Friedlander's subjects stare out of the frame while family photographs and, in a few cases, portraits of the players in their younger days heighten the poignancy of the images. There is a sad irony in noticing that the Young Tuxedo Brass Band now comprises old men.

III. The expressivity of material objects

The capacity of material objects to embody social and cultural values has been highlighted by the turn toward the "materiality and thingness of the trace."[50] Scholars like Pierre Bourdieu, Ajun Appadurai, Daniel Miller, Janet Hoskins, Mihaly Csikszentmihalyi, and Eugene Rochberg-Halton have elaborated ideas first advanced in the 1980s by Violette Morin, who drew attention to the temporal, spatial, and individual relationships between people and what she termed biographical (*biographique*) objects. Hoskins for example has found that objects and possessions reveal more introspective, intimate, and "personal" accounts of many people's lives and that ordinary household possessions are often granted extraordinary significance as they become sufficiently enmeshed in a person's life to express a sense of selfhood.[51] It is in the *relationships* with, rather than *possession* of, objects that personal identities and biographies are frequently shaped around those objects. This turn signals a move away from how things signify to how they *matter* and makes possible the identification of "the more subtle connections with cultural lives and values that are objectified through these forms."[52] Photographers have made considerable use of material objects to represent cultural lives in the world of jazz.

Certain instruments have developed an intimate iconographic association with jazz. The saxophone becomes the main point of focus in Sulaiman Imara Ellison's moody composition *Jazz Is* in which the recognizable shape and glints of light bring meaning to the indistinct figures in the frame (Figure 41). A member of the New York City-based Fifth Art Collective, Ellison documented notable figures in the black community, black intellectuals, and religious themes in Ethiopia and other African countries as well as recording of the City's jazz loft scene. His jazz portraits were mostly shot in or around performance sites in the city in the 1970s and 1980s and show a particularly acute sense of composition.[53] Jacques Lowe used instruments as both signifier and compositional device when he framed Joe Henderson's face with the curve of the saxophone neck and Louis Bellson's face by the V-shape of his drumsticks in two well-constructed images; and his portrait of the trombonist Wycliffe Gordon draws attention to the musician's eyes by framing them within the parallel line of the instruments' slide. In these photographs instruments take on enhanced iconic force as essential compositional elements.[54] Perhaps the most effective element in Herman Leonard's famous portrait of Dexter Gordon is not cigarette smoke but the integration of the player's saxophone into the composition by using it to frame the musician's face—a frame within the larger frame. Employing the lines and shapes of musical instruments as a graphical device, Lee Tanner used the parallel lines of Sonny Rollins and Coleman Hawkins's saxophones to evoke a sense of both individuality and musical interplay in his photograph of the musicians at the 1963 Newport Jazz Festival.[55]

Photographers have been quick to pick up on the metaphorical possibilities of idiosyncratic uses of instruments. Dizzy Gillespie's upturned trumpet is a visual favorite as was the angle of Lester Young's saxophone, a unusual stance which for several photographers offered a form of visualization of the inner state of a confirmed individualist. By the late-1940s Young had started to hold his instrument nearer to the conventional position which some have questionably interpreted as a sign of waning creativity.[56] Jim Marshall's famous portrait of Bill Evans is another notable example: the musician's head is bowed so low over the piano that it is framed by the strings, hammers, and architecture of the piano in the foreground, a viewpoint that creates a powerful series of lines leading back to

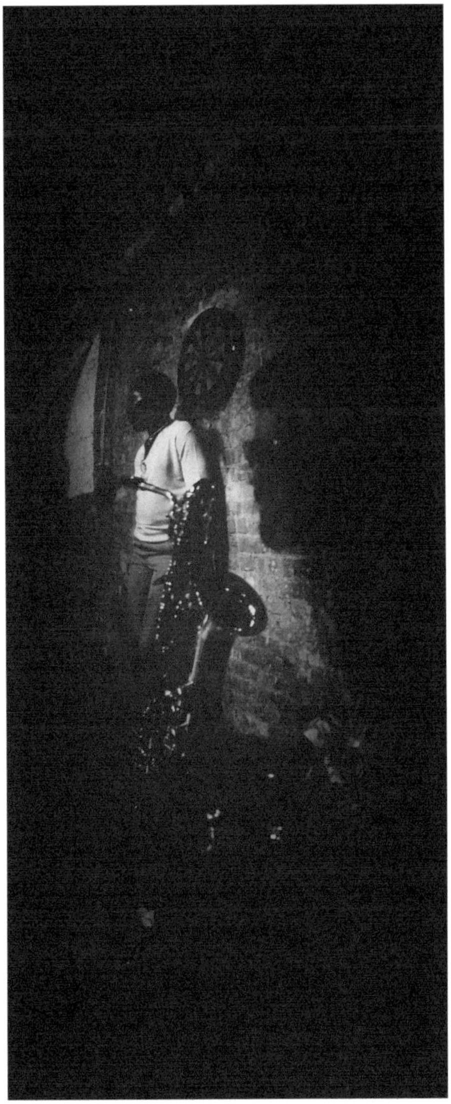

Figure 41: Sulaiman Ellison. *Jazz Is*. New York. n.d.
Permission of Sulaiman Ellison.

Evans. Recalling David Ake's discussion of Evans's performative gestures, Marshall's image creates a metaphorical vision of "sensitive interiority" as the musician almost literally disappears into the body of the instrument.[57] Francis Wolff used the piano lid as an architectural divide in his portrait of Oscar Pettiford, Miles Davis, and Gil Coggins, and Herman Leonard's low viewpoint 1949 photograph of Lennie Tristano rakes the keyboard so as to form a right angle with the players' tilted body, turning a static instrument into a dynamic composition which evokes the pianist's groundbreaking style.[58]

Many other material objects assume iconic effectivity in jazz imagery. Chuck Stewart rarely failed to make effective use of stage properties to form shapes and leading lines within the frame. His 1956 photograph of Lester Young used microphone stands to create a lattice work frame around the musician and on another occasion positioned Johnny Griffin's face within the space created by the curved neck of Lockjaw Davis's instrument.[59] Don Hunstein prominently featured a music stand and score in front of Miles Davis taken during the recording of *Porgy and Bess.* Framed by stark backlighting making it to glow incandescently, cigarette smoke has become perhaps *the* standard jazz motif that associates the music with "a particular set of postures, from movies and fashion photography, and sustains the underworld exoticism jazz has been coupled with ever since the 1920s."[60] Smoke took on more particular associations when Herman Leonard incorporated the idea into a still life evoking (but not including) Lester Young through his saxophone case, pork pie hat, and gently ascending cigarette smoke. When Fred Plaut photographed Julian "Cannonball" Adderley's music stand during the *Kind of Blue* studio sessions (Figure 42) he also created a still-life tableau in which objects stood as iconic representations of music and musician: a scrap of manuscript paper with modal scales, a packet of saxophone reeds, cigarettes, sugar substitute, aspirin, and other medications (Adderley was a diabetic and suffered from migraines).

Objects can become "biographical" in Morin's sense by virtue of close personal relationships with the musician. Maxine Gordon has persuasively argued that Dexter Gordon's life and career cannot be fully understood unless the meaning of his extended period in Europe between 1962 and 1976 is taken into account. Sometimes considered a "lost" period in Gordon's career, his biographer shows how, like his friend James Baldwin, the musician was forced to reflect on the ambiguities and meanings of "expatriate" status: "Baldwin yelled across the room, 'Hey Dex, I read in the paper that we were expatriates. I thought we were just

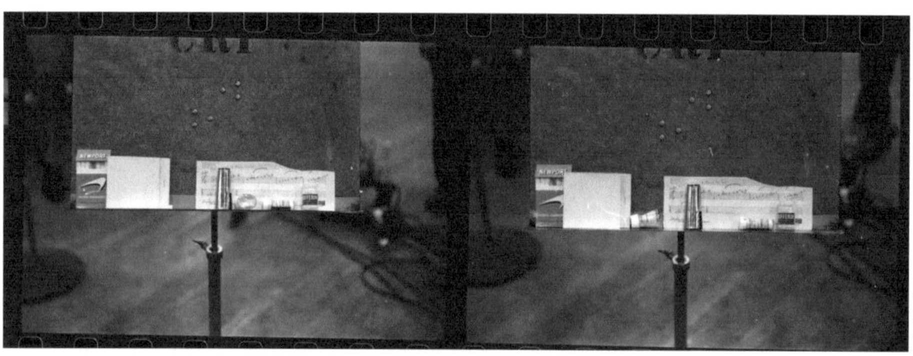

Figure 42: Fred Plaut. *Cannonball Adderley music stand.* n.d. *Gilmore Library, Yale University-Fred Plaut Collection.*

living in Europe.' Dexter roared, then strolled over and bent down and hugged Baldwin, who seemed to disappear in his embrace. 'I thought we were just living in Europe.' "[61] It is not difficult to see how a still life assembly of Gordon's passport and other travel objects (Figure 43) might represent an extremely significant period in the musician's life.

Perhaps more than other material objects, jazz clothes and styling have "participated quite significantly in determining the public reception of the 'primary' modernist products, and hence in the constitution of their public meanings."[62] Dress styles and deportment express conscious choices in the formation and projection of self-identity and photography captures the use of material culture to express something deeper about their artistic personae.[63] The "look of jazz"—most obviously expressed in what Joel Dinerstein has termed "African American cool," the repudiation of racial accommodation through the conscious adoption of jazz art, style, and slang—has seized the imagination of a wide range of commentators. The reviewer of a recently published anthology of jazz photographs for instance tells us that the book "just oozes cool. It's more than 300 pages documenting the era of zoot suits and skinny ties. This was a time when the magnitude of a great singer jumped off the pages of the weekly magazines." Observers as far apart as the jazz scholar Krin Gabbard and *Playboy* magazine have been equally seduced by the "cool."[64]

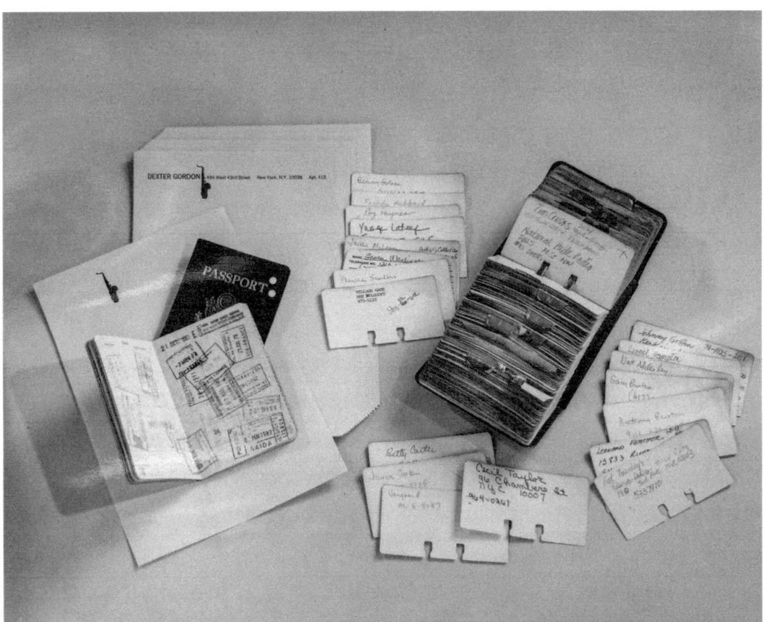

Figure 43: Unknown photographer. *Dexter Gordon travel documents*. n.d. *Dexter Gordon Collection, Library of Congress/Maxine Gordon, www.dextergordon.com.*

As one biographer has noted, "For Miles [Davis], looks and playing were so closely allied that after gigs, he often asked not 'How'd I play' (because he knew) but 'How'd I look?'. Clothes, especially shoes, competed with music for his attention." While a member of Parker's band in the mid-1940s, Miles Davis, who was wearing "three-piece Brooks Brothers suits that I thought were super-hip" was told by Dexter Gordon to get something more fashionable. Davis saved 47 dollars for a gray, big-shouldered suit. Adopting an open-necked green Oxford shirt for Dennis Stock's cover photograph on the late-1950s album *Milestones*, Miles Davis consciously sought to project an image of the cool jazz musician, appropriating and subverting what previously had been a quintessentially white college fashion statement. For Richard Williams,

> *the green shirt, with the perfect button-down collar, was as good an emblem as any of Miles Davis's inextinguishable need to be the coolest man on the planet. But it symbolized more than just an aesthetic: it spoke of an entire set of values.*

Throughout his life Miles Davis used clothes to indicate the twists and turns of his musical career from his early sharp-suited styling on record covers from Prestige, Blue Note, and Columbia to Anthony Barboza's photograph taken around 1970 of the musician standing proudly as the rock fashions *du jour* pour out of his closet.[65]

Photographs show that as early as 1937 Lester Young had started wearing sunglasses on stage, perhaps as a mask or to create an air of mystery; along with his porkpie hat (which Gjon Mili turned into a graphical statement in his short motion picture *Jammin' the Blues*), "his shoes were particularly important stylewise [. . .] he used to buy pairs of suede shoes in different colors to match his suits."[66] Billy Eckstein favored the rolled collar and Thelonious Monk's hats and dark shades (which, according to Mary Lou Williams, he had made to his precise specification) became visual trademarks. Dizzy Gillespie's goatee, beret, and horn-rimmed glasses, the adoption of which was a conscious attempt to fix a distinctive visual aesthetic, were soon copied by audiences, but all the bop players wore the best and most fashionable suits that stressed elegance over extravagance, racial pride over consumption. Contemporary photographs demonstrate that Benny Carter was equally aware of the way appearance shaped identity. His style sense helped create a generalized refined identity, occasionally leading press reports to comment on his sophisticated tastes in other areas of life, including choice of foods and leisure pursuits.[67]

Photographs not only convey the meanings of material presentation but allow us to trace the development of musical identities over time. Cab Calloway's adoption of the zoot suit—an emblem of ethnicity and identity for black Harlem youth of the 1940s—was a conscious effort to imbue his stage shows with the subcultural overtones implied by the lyrics of his songs; equally calculated was his switch after 1940 captured in many photographs to a more contemporary style of dress in order to broaden his appeal.[68] Billie Holiday progressed through a variety of identities that were expressed by marked shifts in visual image. Photographs from the early-1930s show her wearing relatively simple, homespun clothes with her hair pulled back and cut short. As she grew more confident in her career, she adopted elaborate dresses and accessories. Photographs taken a few years later at the integrated Café Society in the late-1930s show Holiday growing in sophistication and elegance, a transition which found expression in long silk, velvet, or crepe gowns more often than not accompanied by jewelry and other accessories. All this appears to be a prelude to her emergence as a chanteuse in the 1940s when her appearance become even more dynamic and varied. Her choice of wardrobe included printed floral gowns, knotted turbans, and pompadour bags. It was also during this period that she took to wearing the gardenia in her hair as can be seen in Robin Carson's 1944 portraits. By the 1950s photographs by Burt Goldblatt, Herman Leonard, and George Simon show how her gowns became more structured and decorative, often voluminously cut with ornate embroideries, lace, jewelry, tulle shells, and crinoline supports.[69] The battle between white music business insiders and intellectuals, jazz critics and writers for possession of Billie Holliday's legacy is at least partially—but certainly vividly—signed in these photographs.[70]

Photographs confirm that Duke Ellington adopted the elegant dress for which he became famous very early in his career and show how this style evolved over time. Whether on stage with white tie and tuxedo, or away from the bandstand with his cashmere coats and houndstooth jackets, Ellington's renowned collection of over 120 suits demonstrated confidence through the appearance of conspicuous consumption. A photograph of the Washingtonians at New York's Orchard Beach in August 1926 shows the band smartly dressed in evening suits and black bow ties. From the start the band "paid a lot of attention" to appearances, but the impact is offset by hints of informality of the poses: Rudy Jackson, an overcoat slung on his right arm which rests on his hip, leans on Percy Glascoe's right shoulder while Edgar Sampson has his arm round Joe Nanton's shoulder. Nearly ten years later, a similar posed photograph shows a marked change in the band's presentation: suits with satin collars now seem extravagantly elegant and the players stand erect with their arms at their sides.[71]

Photographs situate material objects within the public context which jazz musicians sought to create through displays of both personal style and material objects. Ornette Coleman's challenge to the dominant culture of jazz was signaled in the cover photo of his 1959 album *The Shape of Jazz to Come*. Eschewing many of the visual norms of jazz, Coleman traded the characteristically slick bebop-style suit for a shirt and tie under a dark sweater. Looking more like a bank clerk than a jazz musician, the image contrasts markedly with the "hip" male sexuality and styling of the bebop players and was a conscious attempt by the musician to distance himself and his music from the bebop crowd: as Michael Agovino recalled of Coleman, "if he wasn't wearing a purple suit, he wore something that called attention to itself—he usually did." Indeed, Coleman's subsequent albums from Atlantic (*Change of the Century* (1960) and *This Is Our Music* (*1961*)) were also notable for the way in which their cover photography presented the musician and band members conservatively dressed in relatively conventional compositions. With Coleman's white Grafton 10265 plastic sax and Don Cherry's pocket trumpet, it should be no surprise that the reaction to the Coleman quartet was to a considerable extent based on the way they looked.[72]

IV. Conclusion: Reuniting document and expression

Barnaby Haran has explained how Walker Evans's "archival mode" created "excessive" documents which "stretched to capacity" their documentary function and invited aesthetic consideration.[73] Much the same effect can be seen in the world of jazz photography. Commenting on Paul Nodler's photographic record of the filming of Gjon Mili's and Norman Granz's film *Sitting In*, Tad Hershorn noticed that Nodler's contact sheets have "undeniable documentary value, for like *Jammin' the Blues* it is one of the few examples of moving images to convey a sense of at the Jazz at the Philharmonic series."[74] Much as Evans sought to cloak the conscious agency of observation within documentary banality, Hershorn's observation points to possibility that the jazz image as document is equally capable of exciting imaginative recreation.

Analytically separating the documentary and expressive components of jazz imagery, this and the previous chapter have discussed ways in which photographers have created documentary records of jazz musicians, events, and spaces and strived to express the meanings of those subjects. The separation cannot be maintained in practice but a process of analytical dualism is necessary if we are to understand the nature of that interaction. To understand this interaction we need to situate photography in the context of the distinction conventionally drawn between music, which exists by definition in time, and the spatial existence of the visual arts. Unlike painting and the plastic arts, photography is capable of *stopping time*, a momentary halt in what is theoretically the infinite time continuum of music but a frozen moment of such authoritative mimesis that we are prepared to accept it as the *representation of time*. It is then a small step to the representation of *a* time. It appears then that the mimesis of the photograph, so fundamental to its documentary purpose discussed in the previous chapter, is simultaneously the locus of its interpretative latitude.[75] This is close to the position adopted by Siegfried Kracauer when he observed that photographs may be essentially realist but this does not conflict with their expressive role: realism is the starting point of photographic meaning but cannot be completely achieved without imaginative presentation and response. Patrick Maynard credits Kracauer with undermining a "harmful false dichotomy" by showing that photography's "realist recording powers are fully consistent with its being highly interpretative, even self-expressive."[76]

The photograph therefore ineluctably comingles "reality" with its expressive representation, mirroring the world and creating a discourse with its object; the relative importance of documentary and expressive signs shifts over time as connotation infiltrates denotation, subtly underlining the *coexistence* of the iconic and the indexical. The different signs may be complementary, supplementary, or even contradictory.[77] Understanding these signs and the relationships between them can only be fully realized by returning to the agency of photographic production. It is in the self-reflexively directed activities of photographic framing—the choices and decisions made at the point of capture—that the dialectic of document and expression is initiated. It is now therefore necessary to devote attention to the photographers behind the camera, to questions of personal and social identity and the contingencies of the contexts of production. These questions are addressed throughout the remainder of this book.

Notes

1. Nat Hentoff, "Introduction," in K. Abé, *Jazz Giants: A Visual Retrospective Compiled by K. Abé* (New York: Billboard, 1986), n.pag; Philip Elwood, "Introduction," in Jim Marshall, *Jim Marshall/Jazz* (SanFrancisco, CA: Chronicle Books, 2005), 9; Peter Townsend, *Jazz in American Culture* (Edinburgh: Edinburgh University Press, 2000), 164; Jimmy Katz, "Interview with the Author" (2018).
2. Lindsey Macchiarella, "Early French Modernism across Modalities: Erik Satie and Eugène Atget," *Music in Art*, no. 42, 1–2 (2017): 309.
3. Adrian Siegel, "Photographs of Musicians," *Image* 2, no. 9 (1953): 21. Hajo Düchting, *Paul Klee: Painting Music* (Munich: Prestel Verlag, 2004), provides an account of one artist directly inspired to make visual representations of music.
4. Leonard Feather, "The Sight of Jazz," in *Jazz*, ed. William Claxton and Terry Southern (San Francisco, CA: Chronicle Books, 1966), 5; Leonard quoted by Kaluma Ya Salaam, "Herman Leonard: Making Music with Light," *African American Review* 29, no. 2 (1995): 242.
5. Sherry Turner DeCarava, "Celebration," in *Roy DeCarava Photographs*, ed. James Alinder (Carmel, CA: Friends of Photography, 1981), 7; Gordon Parks, "Foreword," in *Carol Friedman, The Jazz Pictures* (Santa Fe, NM: Arena Editions, 2001), 9; John Leland, "Hearing Music in Photos of Jazz Giants," *New York Times*, August 16, 2016.
6. Lee Tanner, *The Jazz Image: Masters of Jazz Photography* (New York: Abrams, 2006), x.
7. Roland Barthes, "Droit Dans Les Yeux," in *L'obvie et l'obtus: Essais Critiques III* (Paris: Editions du Seuil, 1982), 279–83.
8. Jay Maisel, "Interview with the Author" (2018).
9. Andre Hodier cited by Terry Southern, "Grand Guy Clax," in *Jazz*, ed. William Claxton and Terry Southern (San Francisco, CA: Chronicle Books, 1966), 121. Among the "shared conceptual approaches" in African American music making is "[t]he tendency to incorporate physical body motion as an integral part of the music making process": Olly Wilson, "The Heterogeneous Sound Ideal in African American Music," in *Signifyin(g), Sanctifyin' and Slam Dunking: A Reader in African American Expressive Culture*, ed. Gena Dagel Caponi (Amherst: University of Massachusetts Press, 1999), 159; Charles Seeger, "On the Principles of Musicology," *Musical Quarterly* 10, no. 2 (1924): 244–50; See also Paul Gilroy, "Black Music, Ethnicity, and the Challenge of a 'Changing' Same," *Black Music Research Journal* 11, no. 2 (1991), 113; and Christopher Small, *Music of the Common Tongue: Survival and Celebration in Afro-American Music* (New Haven, CT: John Calder, 1987).
10. Ted Gioia, *The Imperfect Art: Reflections on Jazz and Modern Culture* (New York: Oxford University Press, 1990), 67. Gavin Bryars, an English composer and double bassist, set out his objections to improvisation as follows: "One of the main reasons I am against improvisation is that [...] the person creating the music is identified with the music. The creator is there making the music and is identified with the music and the music with the person [...] And because of that the music, in improvisation, doesn't stand alone. It's corporeal". Bryars cited in Derek Bailey, *Improvisation: Its Nature and Practices in Music* (Ashbourne: Moorland, 1980), 115.
11. Alfred Appel, *Jazz Modernism: From Ellington and Armstrong to Matisse and Joyce* (New York: Alfred A Knopf, 2005), 193; Robert Walser, "Valuing Jazz," in *The Cambridge Companion to Jazz*, ed. Mervyn Cooke and David Horn (Cambridge: Cambridge University Press, 2002), 314; David Ake, "Jazz Cultures" (Berkeley: University of California Press, 2002), 87–101; Paul Allen Anderson, "'My Foolish Heart:' Bill Evans and the Public Life of Feelings," *Jazz Perspectives* 7, no. 3 (2013): 205–49; Tom Perchard, *Lee Morgan: His Life, Music and Culture* (London: Equinox, 2006), 25. Oscar Peterson quoted by Nat Hentoff, "Introduction," in *The Jazz Image: Masters of Jazz Photography*, ed. Lee Tanner (New York: Abrams, 2006), 6; Geoffrey M. Curran, "From 'Swinging Hard' to 'Rocking Out': Classification of Style and the Creation of Identity in the World of Drumming Author(S)," *Symbolic Interaction* 19, no. 1 (1996): 37–60; David Sudnow, *Ways of the Hand: A Rewritten Account* (Cambridge, MA: MIT Press, 2001), 73–77.
12. Ashley Kahn, *Kind of Blue: The Making of the Miles Davis Masterpiece*, 2nd ed. (London: Granta Books, 2002), 133; Ashley Kahn, *A Love Supreme: The Creation of John Coltrane's Classic Album* (London: Granta Books, 2002), 132. See also Nelson George, "New Photos of John Coltrane Rediscovered 50 Years

After They Were Shot," *Smithsonian Magazine*, 2014, https://www.smithsonianmag.com/smithsonian-institution/new-photos-john-coltrane-rediscovered-50-years-after-they-were-shot-180950260/.

13. Nat Hentoff, "Introduction," in *Jazz Street: Photographs by Dennis Stock* (London: Andre Deutsch, 1960), 12. Joachim-Ernst Berendt echoed Hentoff's sentiment when he said of jazz performance that "one should not only hear his performance; one should also see it, in order to understand what he is trying to express [. . .] Jazz people [. . .] have always known about the visual component of the music" J.-E. Berendt, *Jazz: A Photo History*, trans. William Odom (London: Andre Deutsch, 1979), 5.
14. Davide Sparti, "Images of a Sound: Portraits and Pictures of Jazz," *Imaginations: Journal of Cross-Cultural Image Studies* 1, no. 1 (2014): n. pag.; Nat Hentoff, "Introduction," in *Jazz Street*, 13. A similar point has of course been made about the "spontaneous prose" of Jack Kerouac, who often relied on jazz metaphors to describe his own writing: "sketching language is undisturbed flow from the mind of personal secret idea-words blowing (as per the jazz musician) on the subject of the image [. . .] vigorous space dash separating rhetorical breathing (as jazz musician drawing breath between outblown phrases." Jack Kerouac, "Essentials of Spontaneous Prose," in *A Casebook on the Beat*, ed. Thomas Parkinson (New York: Thomas Y. Crowell, 1961), 65–66. Regina Weinreich, *The Spontaneous Poetics of Jack Kerouac: A Study of the Fiction* (New York: Paragon House, 1990), 8–9, argues that in building "associations" between the "spontaneous flow of images" Kerouac successfully approaches the essence of jazz improvisation in prose at the technical level.
15. Genette, *The Work of Art: Immanence and Transcendence*, 40–41, 69, 200–201.
16. Sherry Turner DeCarava, "Celebration," in *Roy DeCarava Photographs*, ed. James Alinder (Carmel, CA: Friends of Photography, 1981), 15.
17. Nat Hentoff, "Introduction" in *Jazz Giants* n.pag.; Barry Singer, "Eloquent Images of a Smoky, Sultry World," *New York Times*, 1997, https://www.nytimes.com/1997/04/27/books/eloquent-images-of-a-smoky-sultry-world.html.
18. Ronnie Scott, "Foreword," in *Jazz Portraits: An Eye for the Sound: Images of Jazz and Jazz Musicians*, ed. Tim Motion (New York: Salamander, 1995), 7.
19. Dennis Stock, "Preface," in *Jazz Street*, n.pag.; Richard Ing, "And You Slip into the Breaks and Look Around": Jazz and Everyday Life in the Photographs of Roy Decarava," in *Hearing Eye: Jazz and Blues Influences in African American Visual Art*, ed. Graham Lock and David Murray (New York: Oxford University Press, 2009), 318–19, 323–27; Peter Galassi, "Introduction," in *Roy DeCarava: A Retrospective* (New York: Museum of Modern Art, 1996), 17, 26–27; A. D. Coleman, "Roy DeCarava: 'Thru Black Eyes,'" in *Light Readings: A Photography Critics Writings 1968–1978* (New York: Oxford University Press, 1979), 18, 23.
20. Don Heckman, "Introduction," in *Jazz Seen by William Claxton* (Cologne: Taschen, 1999), 10–11; Enid Farber, "Interview with the Author," 2018; Veryl Oakland, *Jazz in Available Light: Illuminating the Jazz Greats from the 1960s, '70s and '80s* (Atglen, PA: Schiffer, 2018) 16 and Veryl Oakland, "Interview with the Author," 2018; Colleen Walsah, "The Soul of a Jazz Man," *Harvard Gazette*, 2019, https://news.harvard.edu/gazette/story/2019/10/the-sound-of-my-soul-brings-frank-stewarts-photos-into-focus-at-cooper-gallery/; Billy Taylor, "Foreword," in *Chuck Stewart's Jazz Files* (London: Quartet Books, 1986), 7.
21. Maisel, "Interview with the Author."
22. Robert Walser, "Deep Jazz: Notes of Interiority, Race, and Criticism," in *Inventing the Psychological: Toward a Cultural History of Emotional Life in America*, ed. Joel Pfister and Nancy Schnog (New Haven, CT: Yale University Press, 1997), 271–96.
23. Hentoff, "Introduction," in *Jazz Giants*, n.pag.
24. Lourdes Delgardo, "The Photography of Lourdes Delgardo," accessed May 20, 2019, http://www.jazzhouse.org/jpg/delgado/.
25. Dizzy Gillespie, 'Foreword,' in *Jazz People: Photographs by Ole Brask*, ed. Dan Morgenstern (New York: Da Capo, 1993), 10.
26. "The Jazz Salon: Photographer Clemens Kalischer and Music Inn:" unpublished research paper kindly provided by the author.
27. The literature on the subject of the "jazz community" is extensive. Ken Prouty, "The Problem with Community," in *Knowing Jazz: Community, Pedagogy, and Canon in the Information Age* (Jackson: University Press of Mississippi, 2012), 13–45, provides a guide to the central lines of the debate around the jazz community, and Ken Gelder, *Subcultures: Cultural Histories and Social Practice* (London: Routledge, 2007),

107–114, assess contributions from a sociological perspective.

28. Alan P. Merriam and Raymond W. Mack, "A Theory of Jazz Community," *Social Forces* 7, no. 2 (1960): 211–22.
29. The image is available at Tulane University's Digital Library at https://digitallibrary.tulane.edu/islandora/object/tulane%3A15509.
30. W. Royal Stokes, "Introduction," in *Swing Era New York: The Jazz Photographs of Charles Peterson* (Philadelphia: Temple University Press, 1994), 1–5; and Bo Lindstrom, "Charles Peterson and the Life Magazine Photo Story on Panassie," n.d., http://www.jazzresearch.se/upl/website/charles-peterson/Photographer-CharlesPeterson.pdf.
31. Thomas Turner, "Being Bop: How the Press Shaped the Cult of Bebop," *Jazz Research Journal* 1, no. 2 (2007): 205–24, shows how *Metronome* helped to foster the image of the jazz musician as outsider. See also Neil Leonard, "Some Further Thoughts on Jazzmen as Romantic Outsiders," *Journal of Jazz Studies* 2, no. 2 (1975): 42–52.
32. Luc Sante, "A Nation of Pictures," in *American Photography, 1890–1965: From the Museum of Modern Art, New York*, ed. P. Galassi (New York: Museum of Modern Art, 1995), 45; Elizabeth Armstrong, *Birth of the Cool: California Art, Design and Culture at Midcentury* (Newport Beach, CA: Orange County Museum of Art, Prestel Publishing, 2007); and R. Roger Remmington, *American Modernism: Graphic Design 1920 to 1960* (London: Laurence King, 2003) survey modernist jazz graphic design; and Driggs and Lewine, *Black Beauty, White Heat: A Pictorial History of Jazz 1920–1950*, 123–24, present a variety of early book and magazine graphics that clearly show the influence of modernist visual motifs.
33. Herb Snitzer, *Glorious Days and Nights: A Jazz Memoire* (Jackson: University of Mississippi Press, n.d.), 33.
34. Burt Glinn, *The Beat Scene* (New York: Real Art Press, 2018).
35. David Amram, "David Amram: Ringing the Bells of Freedom in 1950s East Village," The Local East Village, n.d., http://localeastvillage.com/2012/01/23/david-amram-ringing-the-bells-of-freedom-in-1950s-east-village/. Glinn's photograph of Earl Bostic is displayed on the Magnum Photos website at https://www.magnumphotos.com/arts-culture/art/burt-glinns-beat-scene/.
36. Robin D. G. Kelley, "New Monastery: Monk and the Jazz Avant-Garde," *Black Music Research Journal* 19, no. 2 (1999): 135–69; Ingrid Monson, *Freedom Sounds: Civil Rights Call Out to Jazz and Africa* (Oxford: Oxford University Press, 2007), 17, discusses the relationship between African American and white artists and modernism.
37. Val Wilmer, *As Serious as Your Life, John Coltrane and Beyond* (London: Allison & Busby, 1992), 160–61, reproduces Ross's photograph. Arnold Rampersad, *The Life of Langston Hughes* (New York: Oxford University Press, 1988), 279–80, 285, 288, describes Langston Hughes "poetry to jazz" events.
38. Joel Dinerstein, *The Origins of Cool in Postwar America* (Chicago: University of Chicago Press, 2017); and Tom Perchard, "Mid-Century Modern Jazz: Music and Design in the Postwar Home," *Popular Music* 36, no. 1 (2017): 55.
39. Krin Gabbard, *Jammin' at the Margins: Jazz and the American Cinema* (Chicago: University of Chicago Press, 1996), 130–32; James Lincoln Collier, *The Making of Jazz: A Comprehensive History* (London: Macmillan, 1978), 408–20, summarizes this development in jazz.
40. *The Sunterraneans* was based on a short novel of the same name by Jack Kerouac that attracted much criticism for its portrayal of African Americans. Gerald Nicosia, *Memory Babe: A Critical Biography of Jack* Kerouac (Berkeley: University of California Press, 1994). 568, cites Kenneth Rexroth's opinion that Kerouac "knows nothing about [. . .] Jazz and negroes." Jon Panish, "The Subterraneans: A Study of 'Romantic Primitivism,'" *Melus* 1, 2809, no. 3 (1994): 107–23, levels charges of "romantic racialism" against Kerouac.
41. Paul O'Neil, "The Only Rebellion Around," *Life*, November 30, 1959, 230
42. Dave Hickey, "Cool on Cool: William Claxton and the Way Music Looked," in *Birth of the Cool: California Art, Design and Culture at Mid-Century* ed. Elizabeth Armstrong (Newport Beach, CA: Orange County Museum of Art, Prestel Publishing, 2007), 134–49, examines the relationship between Claxton and the cool.
43. Duncan P. Schiedt , *Twelve Lives in Jazz* (Parma, Italy: Delta, 1996), 5. Gary Carner, "Jazz Photography: A Conversation with Herb Snitzer," *Black American Literature Forum* 25, no. 3 (1991): 560–61; and Herb Snitzer, "Interview with the Author" (St. Petersburg, FL, 2016).

44. Singer, "Eloquent Images of a Smoky, Sultry World"; Dinerstein, *The Origins of Cool in Postwar America.*

45. Robert G. O'Meally, "The Flat Plane, the Jagged Edge: Aaron Douglas's Musical Art," *American Studies* 49, nos. 1/2 (2008): 21–35, discusses Douglas's paintings and their relationship to music; Stephen Henderson, "Saturation: Progress Report on a Theory of Black Poetry," in *African American Literary Theory: A Reader*, ed. Winston Napier (New York: New York University Press, 2000), 104.

46. DeCarava cited by A. D. Coleman, "Roy DeCarava: 'Thru Black Eyes,'" in *Light Readings: A Photography Critics Writings 1968–1978* (New York: Oxford University Press, 1979), 22.

47. William Claxton and Joachim E. Berendt, *Jazz Life* (Cologne: Taschen, 2003), 25.

48. Dennis Stock, *Jazz Street* (New York: Doubleday, 1960).

49. Lee Friedlander, *Playing for the Benefit of the Band: New Orleans Music Culture* (New Haven, CT: Yale University Press, 2013). This book was an expanded version of Lee Friedlander's earlier *The Jazz People of New Orleans* (London: Jonathan Cape, 1992).

50. Ewa Domanska, "The Material Presence of the Past," *History and Theory* 45, no. 3 (2006): 337.

51. Violette Morin, "L'Object Biographique," *Communications* 13 (1969): 131–39. Morin speaks of the way in which the biographical object "imposes itself as the witness of the functional unity of its user, his or her everyday experience made into a thing." Janet Hoskins, *Biographical Objects: How Things Tell the Stories of Peoples' Lives* (New York: Routledge, 1998), 190–98.

52. Bruno Latour, "Why Has Critique Run Out of Steam? From Matters of Fact to Matters of Concern," *Critical Inquiry* 30, no. 2 (2004): 225–48; Daniel Miller, "Why Some Things Matter," in *Material Cultures: Why Some Things Matter*, ed. Daniel Miller (London: UCL Press, 1998), 11. As Miller points out (pages 12–13), ascertaining what "matters" is problematic. Steering a course between positivism (reporting what subjects themselves believe matters) and the formal application of schema of analysis is possible through the rigorous use of ethnographic research, "the careful observation of what people actually do and in particular do with things." Photographs should be considered an evidential source in this second sense.

53. Ellison's photographs can be viewed at https://fith-artcollective.jimdo.com/sulaiman-ellison/.

54. These images are reproduced in Jacques Lowe, Bob Blumenthal, and Cliff Preiss, *Jazz: Photographs of the Masters* (New York: Artisan, 1995), 95, 142, and 231.

55. This image is reproduced in Tanner, *The Jazz Image: Masters of Jazz Photography*, 114.

56. Dave Gelly, *Being Prez: The Life and Music of Lester Young*, 2nd ed. (London: Equinox, 2009), 106; see the photograph of Young's band at Birdland in 1949 reproduced on page 115. Young's waning powers are hotly disputed—see also Douglas Henry Daniels, *Lester Leaps In: The Life and Times of Lester "Pres" Young* (Boston, MA: Beacon Press, 2002), 7.

57. The image is reproduced in Jim Marshall, *Jazz* (San Francisco, CA: Chroncile Books, 2005), 93; Ake, "Jazz Cultures," 87.

58. These images are reproduced in Tanner, *The Jazz Image: Masters of Jazz Photography*, 53; and Herman Leonard, *The Eye of Jazz: The Jazz Photographs of Herman Leonard* (London: Viking, 1989), 105.

59. These images are reproduced in Chuck Stewart and Paul Carter Harrison, *Chuck Stewart's Jazz Files* (London: Quartet Books, 1985), 58; and Tanner, *The Jazz Image: Masters of Jazz Photography*, 77.

60. Townsend, *Jazz in American Culture*, 165.

61. Maxine Gordon, *Sophisticated Giant: The Life and Legacy of Dexter Gordon* (Oakland: University of California Press, 2018), 2.

62. Bernard Gendron, *Between Montmartre and the Mudd Club: Popular Music and the Avant-Garde* (Chicago: University of Chicago Press, 2002), 31.

63. Elizabeth Wilson, *Adorned in Dreams: Fashion and Modernity* (Berkeley: University of California Press, 1987), 52; Dick Hebdige, *Subculture: The Meaning of Style* (London: Methuen, 1979): 117–27, discusses style as a signifying practice among subcultural groups; Nelson George, *Elevating the Game: Black Men and Basketball* (New York: Fireside, 1992), 62, shows how "cool came to define a certain sartorial elegance, smooth charm and self-possession" for young urban African Americans in the 1940s. Jazz style is treated by Alphonso D. McClendon, *Fashion and Jazz: Dress, Identity and Subcultural Improvisation* (London: Bloomsbury, 2015).

64. Joel Dinerstein, "Lester Young and the Birth of the Cool, " in *Signifyin(g), sanctifyin' and slam dunking: A Reader in African American Expressive Culturea* (Amherst, MA: University of Massachusetts Press, 1999), 239–79; "Photography: An Iconic Representative for the Jazz

Age," *Manual*, October 11, 2016, at https://www.themanual.com/living/ted-williams-jazz-photography/. For Gabbard Francis Wolff's photographs of black artists "with their dark glasses, their cigarettes and their streamlined cars [. . .] represent a standard of 'cool' to which subsequent generations still aspire": Krin Gabbard, "Images of Jazz," in *The Cambridge Companion to Jazz*, ed. Mervyn Cooke and David Horn (Cambridge: Cambridge University Press, 2002), 337. For Playboy "jazz meant sophistication, cosmopolitanism [. . .] fusing art, lifestyle, and aspiration:" Patty Farmer, *Playboy Swings: How Hugh Hefner and Playboy Changed the Face of Music* (New York: Beaufort Books, 2015), 64.

65. John Szwed, *So What: The Life of Miles Davis* (London: Arrow Books, 2003), 27; Carr, *Miles: The Autobiography*, 110–11; Richard Williams, *Miles Davis: The Man in the Green Shirt* (London: Bloomsbury, 1993), 8. Barboza's photograph is reproduced in Deborah Willis, *Posing Beauty: African American Images from the 1890s to the Present* (New York: W. W. Norton, 2000), 170.
66. Daniels, *Lester Leaps In: The Life and Times of Lester "Pres" Young*, 155–56; Joel Dinerstein, "Lester Young and the Birth of the Cool," in *Signifyin(g), Sanctifyin' and Slam Dunking: A*, ed. Gena Dagekl Caponi (Amherst University of Massachusetts Press, 1999), 250, 271 fn.64.
67. Mary Lou Williams in *Thelonious Monk Reader*, ed. Rob van der Bliek (Oxford: Oxford University Press, 2001), 14; Cawthra, *Blue Notes in Black and White: Photography and Jazz*, 125–68; McClendon, *Fashion and Jazz: Dress, Identity and Subcultural Improvisation*, 135–37.
68. Steve Cosgrove, "The Zoot Suit and Style Warfare," in *Zoot Suits and Second-Hand Dresses: An Anthology of Fashion and Music*, ed. Angela McRobbie (Basingstoke: Macmillan, 1989), 3–4; and Alyn Shipton, *Hi-De-Ho: The Life of Cab Calloway* (Oxford: Oxford University Press, 2010), 173–74.
69. McClendon, *Fashion and Jazz: Dress, Identity and Subcultural Improvisation*, 115–28; Carol Tulloch, *The Birth of Cool: Style Narratives of the African Diaspora* (London: Bloomsbury, 2016), 87–126. Early photographs of Holiday appear in R. O'Meally, *Lady Day: The Many Faces of Billie Holiday* (New York: Arcade, 1991): see especially pp. 10 and 57. Carson's photographs can be found on page 8 of O'Meally's book and in David Margolick, *Strange Fruit: Billie Holiday, Café Society and an Early Cry for Civil Rights* (Philadelphia: Running Press Books, 2000) between pp. 72 and 73. The photographs by Goldblatt and Leonard are reproduced on pp. 124–25 of McLendon's book. George Simon's photograph of Holiday preparing to go onstage is reproduced as the frontispiece in Julian Blackburn, *With Billie,* Jonathan Cape, London, 2005.
70. Margolick, *Strange Fruit: Billie Holiday, Café Society and an Early Cry for Civil Rights*, 76, 80, cites John Hammond's sneering critique ("I think she began taking herself seriously and thinking of herself as very important") and Michael Davis's claim that she "was a born actress and as she performed [Strange Fruit] night after night before an enthralled audience of white intellectuals, so she began to live the part and see herself as the living symbol of injustice and oppression." Mathew Sutton, "Bitter Crop: The Aftermath of 'Lady Sings the Blues,'" *a/b: Auto/Biography Studies* 27, no. 2 (2012): 294–315, speaks of the "identity theft" that Holiday suffered after the publication of her autobiography.
71. Edward Kennedy Ellington, *Music Is My Mistress* (New York: Da Capo, 1973), 70, 74, 133.
72. Muchael J. Agovino, "Ornette Coleman, the Saxophonist Who Transformed Jazz," *New Republic* (2015), https://newrepublic.com/article/122051/ornette-coleman-saxophonist-who-transformed-jazz; Stephen Cottrell, "Charlie Parker, Massey Hall and Grafton 10265: An Object Biography," paper presented to the *Documenting Jazz Conference* (Birmingham, 2020), charts the history of the plastic Grafton 10265 saxophone together with its various photographic representations. Cottrell attributes racial significance to Coleman's display of the instrument in photographs and album cover art.
73. Barnaby Haran, "Homeless Houses: Classifying Walker Evans's Photographs of Victorian Architecture," *Oxford Art Journal* 33, no. 2 (2010): 193.
74. Tad Herschorn, *Norman Granz: The Man Who Used Jazz for Justice* (Berkeley: University of California Press, 2011), 152–53.
75. Susanne K. Langer, *Feeling and Form: A Theory of Art* (New York: Charles Scribner, 1953), esp. chs. 5–8. The photographer Leo Howard Lubow explained to me that photographing jazz musicians feels for him "like entering another time zone, where everything slows down and feels heightened, like a peak experience." Jazz photography for Lubow is all about capturing the ecstatic moment: Leo Lubow, "Interview

with the Author" (2018). See also Leo Howard Lubow, *Blue Note Moments and Other Points in Time* (Baltimore, MD: Private Publication, 2009), 7, where he speaks of seizing a "slide in time that captures the individual separated from the mainstream of life."

76. Siegfried Kracauer, *Theory of Film: The Redemption of Physical Reality* (New York: Oxford University Press, 1965), 11–13; Patrick Maynard, *The Engine of Visualization: Thinking through Photography* (Ithaca, NY: Cornell University Press, 1997), 11.
77. Clive Scott, *The Spoken Image: Photography and Language* (London: Reaktion Books, 1999), 34; Clive Scott, *Street Photography: From Atget to Cartier-Bresson* (London: I. B. Tauris, 2007), 156, points that "Documentary photography would become nonsensical if its indexicality were to become a-chronological, free to move through time and space."

5

Jazz in the Portrait Studio

After Samuel French Morse introduced the daguerreotype to America in 1839, pioneer photographic entrepreneurs such as Mathew B. Brady, John Draper, and Albert Sands Southworth quickly responded to what Peter Bacon Hales has termed "the American obsession with individual identity." Opening elegantly designed and furnished "galleries" in which photographers and "posers" offered artistically constructed portraits, these businessmen scrambled to meet surging demand. By the 1850s daguerreotype studios in New York and other major cities offered to a wide cross-section the chance to establish a visible self-image, an affirming statement for Americans obsessed with the question of identity at a time of nation- and city-building.[1] The awareness that photography replaced rhetorical description by directing attention above all else to the "play of gestures" of physical and psychic poses was recognized by portraitists and their sitters from the start.[2]

Jazz photographs from the early decades of the twentieth century also point to an emerging sense of self-consciousness among sitters and studio photographers. Musicians became increasingly aware of the publicity potential of visual imagery as leading players started to redefine their relationship with commercial entertainment and, by the mid-1920s, were demanding finished studio portraiture of a kind not previously seen. For their part, photographers started to appreciate the potential of jazz as a visual subject through the expressive control of lighting, focus, pose, and studio props. Both parties were aware of the emergence of new styles in theatrical, artistic, and celebrity portraiture and that the photographic image was gaining currency within a rapidly emerging visual culture. It was in the studio then that the first experiments in making the jazz body photogenic took place, with the result that a new form of representation began gradually to emerge.

A photograph taken around 1915 of the New Orleans trumpeter Lee Collins shows him slumped in a chair in an ungainly pose. A second portrait taken eight years later is more considered and shows the musician formally dressed holding his trumpet prominently in his left hand (Figure 44). The composition is stilted, the musician stares straight at the camera, there is little modeling light, and the background is basic. Even so this is a more carefully composed image taken by a portrait photographer concerned with the way in which the sitter was presented.[3] By the early-1940s the jazz portrait had changed beyond recognition. Formerly the head of stills at MGM and Warner Bros, but by this time a freelance portraitist, Clarence Bull's portrait of Tommy Dorsey (Figure 45) presents an altogether more polished impression. The musician's dress connotes sophistication, the pose is relaxed, skin tones have been rendered with finesse, lighting is subtly modulated, and the faintly graduated backdrop is less intrusive. The portrait demonstrates how ideas from celebrity and Hollywood portraiture had been absorbed by the world of jazz and provides evidence of the emergence of a studio aesthetic in jazz during the 1920s and 1930s.

None of the studio photographers discussed in this chapter could be described as "jazz photographers" and their work has often been overlooked by

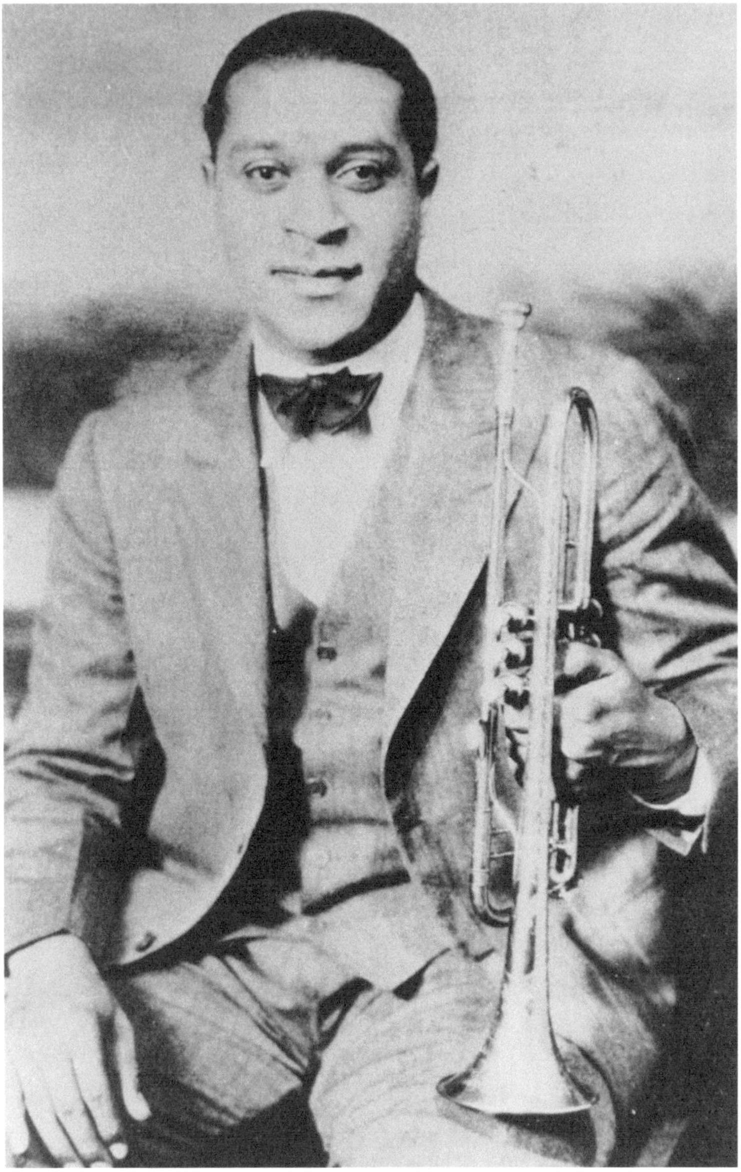

Figure 44: Unknown photographer. *Lee Collins*. New Orleans. 1923.
Peter Vacher Collection.

scholars as commercial product with little to contribute to our understanding of the music. Yet studio portraits are among the first conscious representations of jazz and tell us much about the emerging self-identity of jazz musicians. As leading players emerged as soloists, increasingly conscious that music was a full-time professional activity with attendant presentational and promotional demands, the need for publicity portraiture became apparent. For black musicians, these

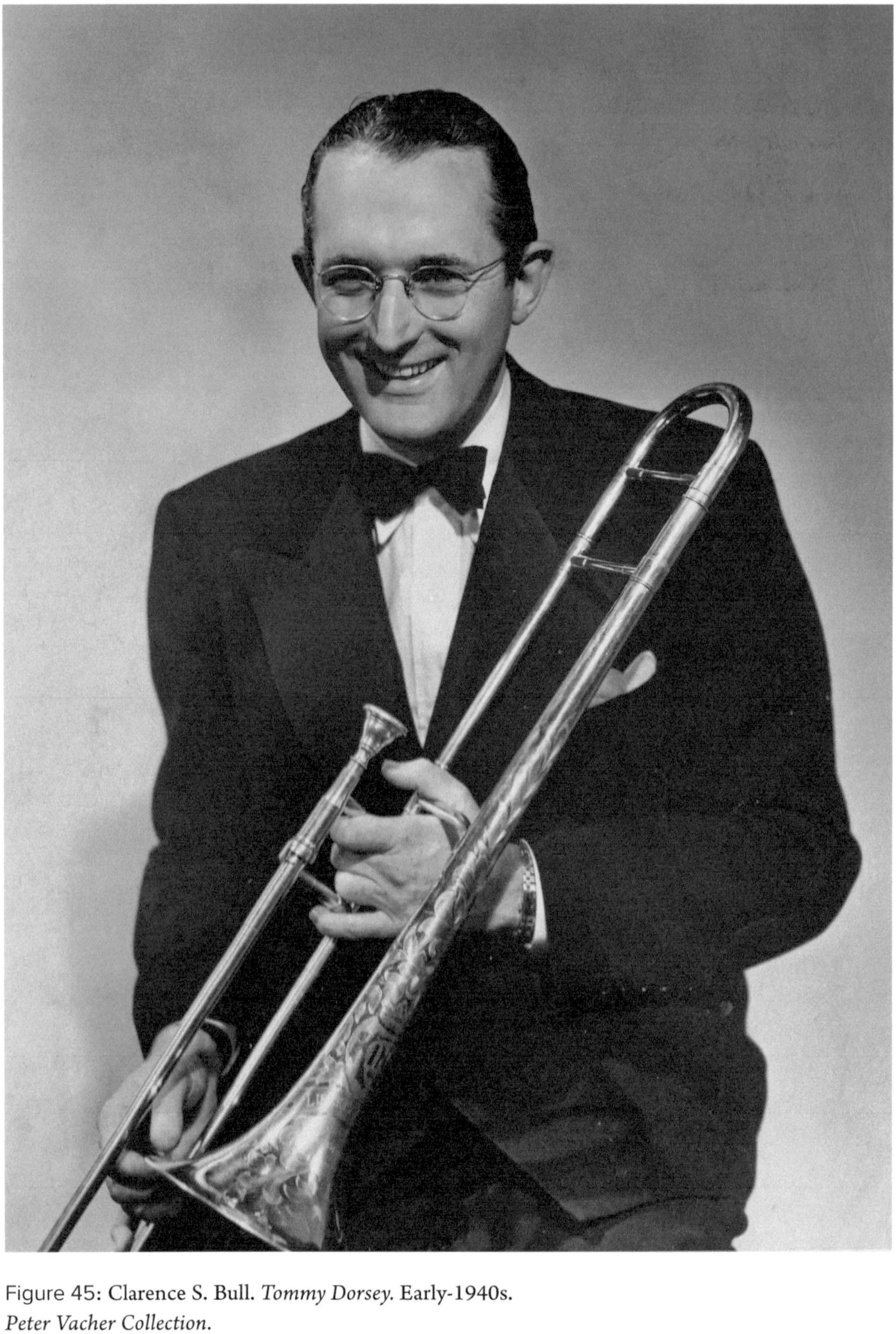

Figure 45: Clarence S. Bull. *Tommy Dorsey.* Early-1940s.
Peter Vacher Collection.

portraits formed part of the delicate but unavoidable negotiations with the white world of commercial entertainment and studio portraits show how photographers and sitters responded to this requirement. Even the earliest studio portraiture has proved enduring: with his "seriousness, earnestness, white middle-class good manners, youth and romanticism," the portrait of Bix Beiderbecke taken in a studio in Davenport, Iowa, in August 1921 as he was about to join Ralph Miedke's Society Orchestra has shaped the perception of the musician ever since.[4]

I. Artistic and theatrical portrait studios

After 1920 increasing numbers of jazz musicians started to enter commercial portrait studios. With few African American studios from which to choose, black jazz musicians were often obliged to turn to white theatrical and artistic studios in New York, Chicago, and other cities for publicity portraits. These photographers were not afraid to innovate when directing their sitters and the stilted poses of the early days of silent movies gradually faded away to be replaced by a more modern presentation characteristic of theatrical and Hollywood portraiture.

Theatrical portrait studios

By 1900 a wide range of specialist portrait studios serving vaudeville artists, actors, and singers as well as celebrities and society personalities had been established.[5] Like Napoleon Sarony, one of the earliest to establish a studio in Manhattan in 1867, many of these photographers were émigrés to the United States: the DeHaven Studio of David and Samuel Bloom, Herman Mishkin at the Metropolitan Opera, and the Hungarians Nikolas Murray and Herbert Mitchell; Irving Chidnoff made portraits of the Jewish elite, Mortimer Offner specialized in theatrical portrait between 1925 and 1934, and Nasib was a photographer of vaudeville and dancers. James J. Kriegsmann, Murray Korman, and the Russian-born Maurice and Seymour Zeldman created studio businesses in the late-1920s.

These émigrés joined the ranks of established society and theatrical photographers like James Abbé, Tony Bruno, George Hoyningen-Heune, British expatriates Cecil Beaton and Florence Vandamm, John De Mirijan, George Maillard Kesslère, Hal Phyfe, Ralph Oggiano, and Alfred Cheney Johnson. Large diversified studios were also important on the New York theatrical scene. DeBarron Studio, formed in 1927 by the "camera artist" Paul Barron, grew to be a major force in theatrical and glamour photography. Jack Freulich built Underwood & Underwood's New York studio and provided still photography for Universal Pictures. Operating between 1903 and 1939, the White Studio was Broadway's foremost photographer of stage productions through the work of Edward Thayer Monroe and Ralph Shaklee. Apeda, Byron & Co., and Brown Brothers were diversified studios that carried out theatrical and celebrity portraiture when required.

Theatrical portraiture was not confined to New York. Kansas City developed as a center of theatrical studio portraiture as performers passed through one of the vaudeville circuits that followed the rail lines into the midwest hub.[6] Benjamin Strauss, Orval Hixon, and James Hargis Connelly, and David Baker's Cornish-Baker studio established their businesses after 1910 providing publicity portraits and lobby photographs for the Kansas City Theatres.[7] Two of Hixon's later collaborators,

H Kenyon Newman and James A. Wiese, established the Bert Studio in the city in the late-1920s. The photographer Bernard Guttenstein set up a studio in the 3000-seat Alhambra Theatre in Milwaukee to make portraits of artists as they passed through and employed around fifteen staff; and, in Minneapolis, Joseph I. Sussman established a theatrical portraiture business between 1902 and 1915, notably portraying Charlie Chaplin in vaudeville in 1911, and the studio photographed a number of black musicians and bands in the 1920s and 1930s.[8] W.C. Fields regularly used a Blackface photograph taken in 1899 by the Baker Art Gallery in Columbus, Ohio. There were many high-quality photography operations in downtown Chicago premises. Some were founded on the promise of the flow of work from the Sears & Roebuck, Spiegel and Montgomery Ward catalog businesses while others, such as Barnes-Crosby (1897), Kauffman & Fabry (1910), and Raymond Trowbridge (1923), exploited the boom in real estate. Theatrical photographers included George Moffett of the Moffett Studio, Daguerre, Bloom, and Gibson.[9]

Through the conscious use of pose, costume, and setting, theatrical photographers developed innovative styles of representation that contrasted with the artificiality of early motion pictures. Pioneers like Jose Maria More and Antonio Moreno and the actor-photographers Burr McIntosh and Frank C. Bangs had begun manipulating photographs, laying the groundwork for the distinctive style of artist portraiture that developed in Kansas City between 1900 and 1926. The Strauss Studio perfected background painting on the negative and their style was copied by Cornish-Baker and Hixon and Connelly soon followed suit. Newman and Wiese took the style to the newly formed Bert Studio and it subsequently spread as Connelly took it to Chicago where it was also adopted by the rival Daguerre Studio while Wilson Todd used the approach in St. Louis.[10] Connelly and Hixon made prints more modern by doing away with painted landscape or classical architectural backdrops in favor of scraping the negative, high-key chiaroscuro electric lighting and abstract backgrounds.

Hollywood modernism

Film production studios started to employ their own photographers in the early-1920s and by the end of the decade most had created their own stills and portraiture departments. This led to a remarkable flowering of photographic creativity and innovation. The classic Hollywood glamour portrait was widely regarded as the epitome of modernism, "the physical appearances that are presented in these photographs were images of a type that had never existed before, either in painting or photography [. . .] a breed of celebrity with the extraordinary power to transfix."[11] Abandoning pre-1914 pictorialism, the hallmarks of the new portraiture included sharper focus, sculpted lighting creating a direct personal appeal, a subtle blend of glamour and elusiveness, and the head shot, a composition previously reserved for statesmen and men of science or letters. The impact of Hollywood photography on American visual culture of the 1930s was enormous and it was not long before the jazz portrait felt its impact.[12]

MGM's stills department dates from 1924 and was headed by Clarence Sinclair Bull. Bull was joined by the legendary George Hurrell in 1929 although he soon left to join Warner Brothers. Ted Allan replaced Hurrell and brought a controlled approach to lighting and superb retouching skills to the presentation of MGM's stars. Ernest Bachrach established RKO's stills department assisted by John Miehle and Eugene Robert Richee, who introduced the use of contemporary clothing and art nouveau and deco designs. Paramount's roster of portrait photographers included Donald Biddle Keyes, William Walling, Jr., Otto Dyer, and John Engstead while A. L. "Whitey" Schafer made portraits of Columbia's stars. Jack Freulich had been Universal's photographer since the silent days; Bert "Buddy" Longworth took the bulk of the stills for Warner Brothers' musicals in the early to mid-1930s and Fred Archer, Elmer Fryer, Madison Lacey, Bert Six, and Scotty Welbourne were the principal portraitists at Warners.

By the late-1920s the major studios had almost completely replaced orthochromatic with panchromatic film, significantly altering the tonality of prints and stills. With new film stock such as Pan Speed Portrait the relationship between tonal values became much more realistic; skin tones took on a creamy look, and increased film sensitivity (particularly Eastman's fast pan films introduced in the late-1930s). allowed faster shutter speeds, reducing motion blur significantly. The soft-focus style of early portraiture began to look outdated. These developments enhanced the perceived verisimilitude of still portraiture and were important in the move toward the idealization and glamorization of star personalities.

Advances in lighting were probably the most significant contributor to the development of the Hollywood style. Lightweight spots encouraged photographers toward more adventurous uses of light and shadow to emphasize character and establish a mood. George Hurrell is often credited with leading innovations with a moveable boom light that allowed him to create dramatic "Rembrandt" and "butterfly" effects. "I always had an understanding about lighting," Hurrell recalled, "That's all I thought about when I was working with a person [. . .] until I was ready to shoot."[13] Rejecting the sentimental diffused style of portraiture, Hurrell drew on his fine art training in Chicago to develop a style that was modern yet rooted in traditional photographic values by relying on carefully deployed spots to create a more flattering and natural effect. His dramatic lighting, which filled the frame in numerous variations, created forms and shapes accenting or highlighting facial features while background shapes were often arranged to throw the star presence into high relief. It wasn't long before photographers across America were imitating the "Hurrell look" with its use of sharp lenses and spots first seen in his portraits of Norma Shearer. Ted Allan, Clarence Bull (Figure 46), and Joseph von Sternberg were equally innovative with their own lighting styles.

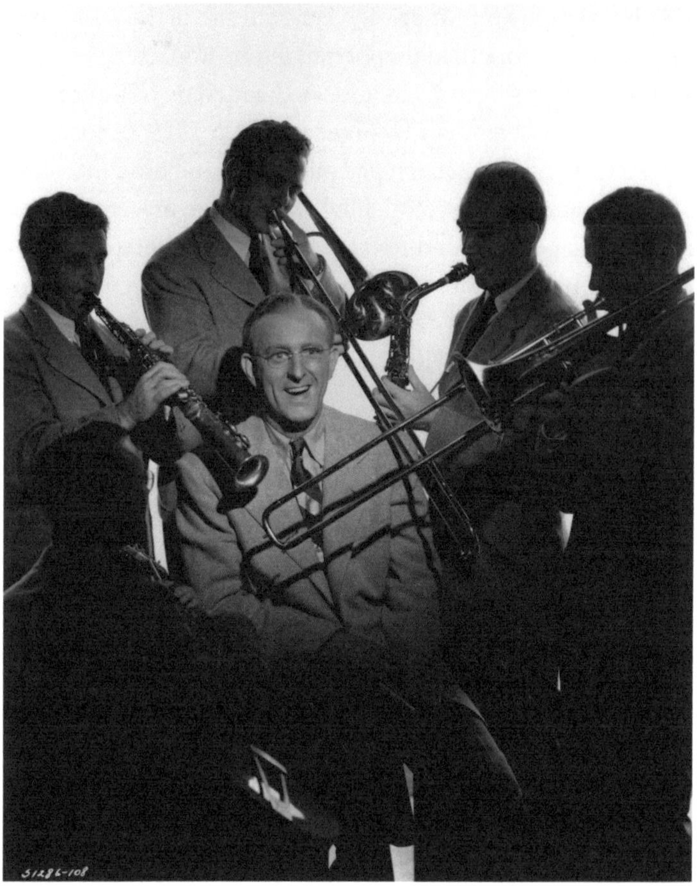

Figure 46: Clarence S. Bull. *Kay Keyser in a publicity still from MGM's "Right About Face."* 1939. *Fernando Ortiz de Urbina.*

Publicity portraits made by these photographers had enormous currency. Bull remembered that "Sam [Goldwyn] believed in publicity photographs by the thousand [. . .] the emphasis was on getting still photographs of his people and his films in the newspapers and the magazines."[14] Publicity portraits were distributed in vast numbers to fashion and fan magazines, several of which carried a richly printed and tinted rotogravure section showcasing the latest studio "portrait art." Virtually unprotected by copyright law, these photographs were distributed free of charge while thousands more were signed and mailed directly to fans.[15] By 1930, MGM's studio was turning out 25,000 negatives and 14,000 prints each week and quantity printing machines made single-weight 10 × 8 gloss prints in batches of 1000. Seventeen hundred different photographs of Carole Lombard were distributed by Paramount in an eight-year period and on one shoot Robert Coburn made portraits of Rita Hayworth for nineteen magazines in a single day.

In 1931 the *Los Angeles Times* noted that still photography was now "Abreast of Talkies":[16]

> *The use of the new super-sensitive type of panchromatic film, the development of angles, new methods of lighting and numerous other results of constant effort on the part of stills photographers in the various studios have little by little eliminated the orthodox rules which sprang up in the early days.*

Most notably with the glamorous close-up, the impact and currency of the Hollywood image-makers was perhaps the single most important contributor to the "age of personality."[17] Glamour was hardly a new idea in the 1920s and 1930s, but Hollywood photographers added cultural resonance with a sharper and internally coherent visual language—a precursor to the harnessing of aesthetic sensibilities to commercial ends that Nigel Thrift has termed "technologies of public intimacy," the creations of "new and alluring imaginative territories." As László Willinger recalled, "Glamour was one of the few English words I'd never heard before I went to America."[18] Aware that still photography directs the eye toward

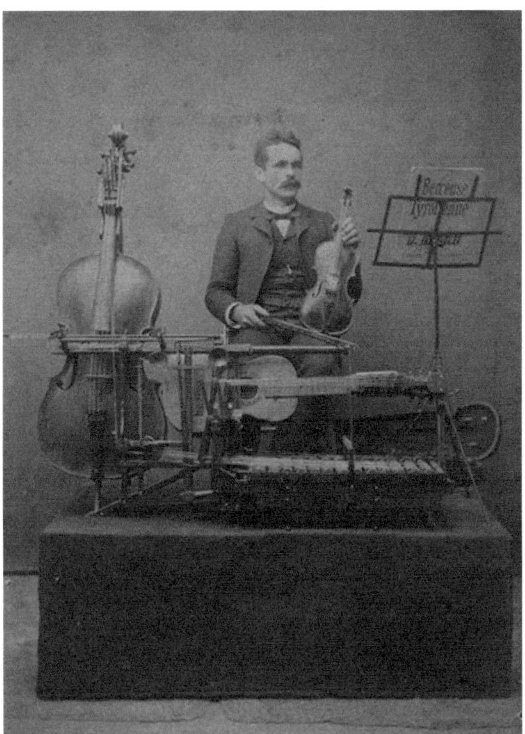

Figure 47: An "occupational" musician tintype *c.*1860. *Author's collection.*

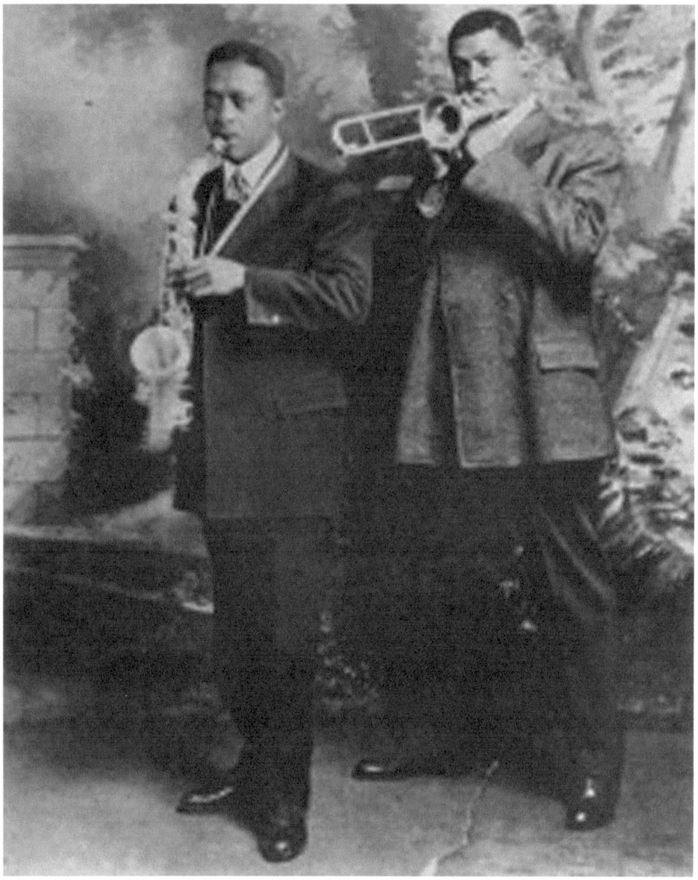

Figure 48: Unknown photographer. *"Big Eye" Louis Nelson and Freddie Keppard.* Kansas City. 1916. *Author's collection.*

a close study of shapes, textures, line, and details, celebrity photographers strived to make surfaces, objects, and people congruent with the legitimating discourse of "entertainment" and "celebrity" through meticulous control and selection of detail.[19] Facial expressions were painstakingly framed with supportive makeup, costume, poses, lighting, and a wide range of studio properties were deployed to create internally consistent *gesamtwerken* from which discordant details were removed. By the 1930s photographers were increasingly taking the stock glamour photography of the motion picture industry as their model.[20]

II. Jazz enters the studio

Early jazz studio portraiture

Many early studio photographers emerged from the pictorialist era. Preoccupated with "artistic" effects and artifice, their work with newly arriving jazz sitters shows clear evidence of these retentions. A portrait of "Big Eye" Louis Nelson Delisle and Freddie Keppard made in Kansas City in 1916 has obvious antecedents in

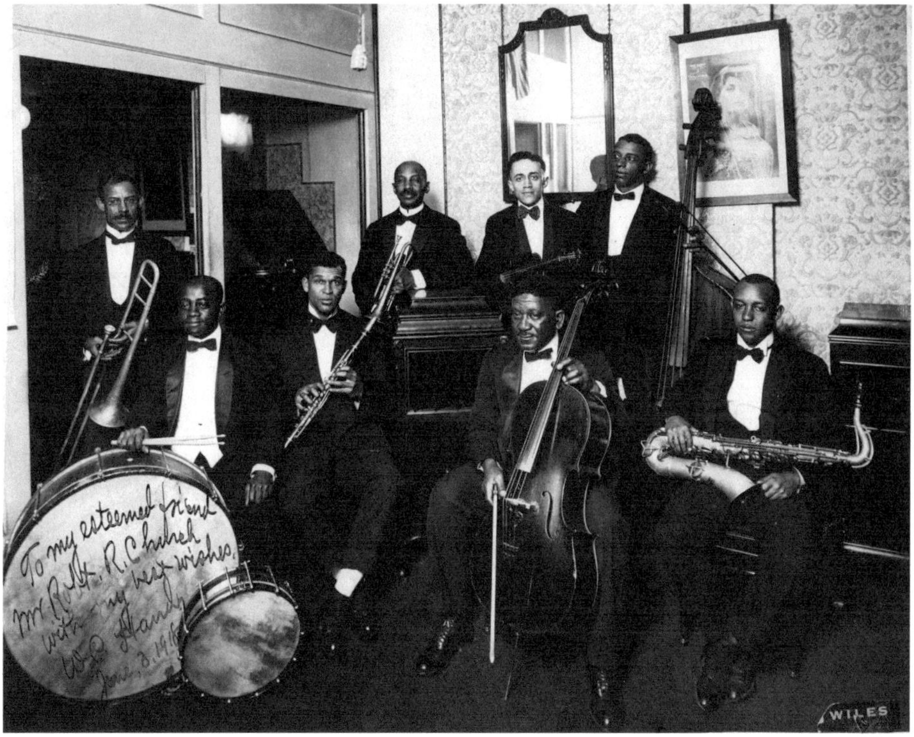

Figure 49: Marvin Willard Wiles. *W. C. Handy ensemble.* 1918.
University of Memphis/Church Collection.

the 1850s and 1860s when the photograph as a signifier of occupation skill and expertise developed (Figures 47 and 48). Often produced in the form of cheap tintypes, these occupational portraits captured subjects in their work clothes with the tools and other signifiers of their work and proved extremely popular among African American families.[21] In other respects, the elaborate and contrived props, background, and static poses resemble late-Victorian portraiture conventions. Further evidence that a distinctive jazz style had yet to emerge is evident in Marvin Willard Wiles's portrait of W. C. Handy's ensemble made in 1918 (Figure 49). Born in Hagerstown, MD, in 1895, Wiles had established his first studio in Nashville in 1910 by covering major local events such as the breach of the city's reservoir and the inauguration of Woodrow Wilson in 1913. Jazz bands were simply one aspect of his daily round as an African American community photographer. Wiles continued in business until the early-1950s.[22]

By the 1920s musicians were becoming more conscious of the messaging power of visual imagery. Armand J. Piron succeeded Keppard as leader of the Olympia Orchestra in 1912 but his presentation could not have been more different. When the classically trained Piron took his "sweet" society dance band featuring Peter Bocage and Lorenzo Tio to the New York's Cotton Club in 1923 the leader employed

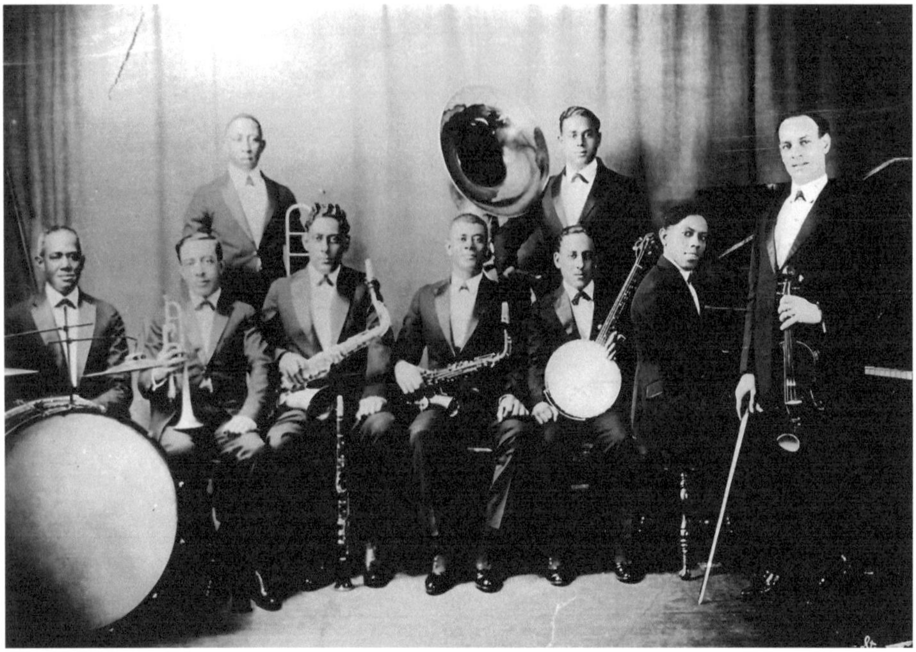

Figure 50: Strand Studios. *Armand J. Piron's Society Orchestra*. New York. 1923. *Peter Vacher Collection.*

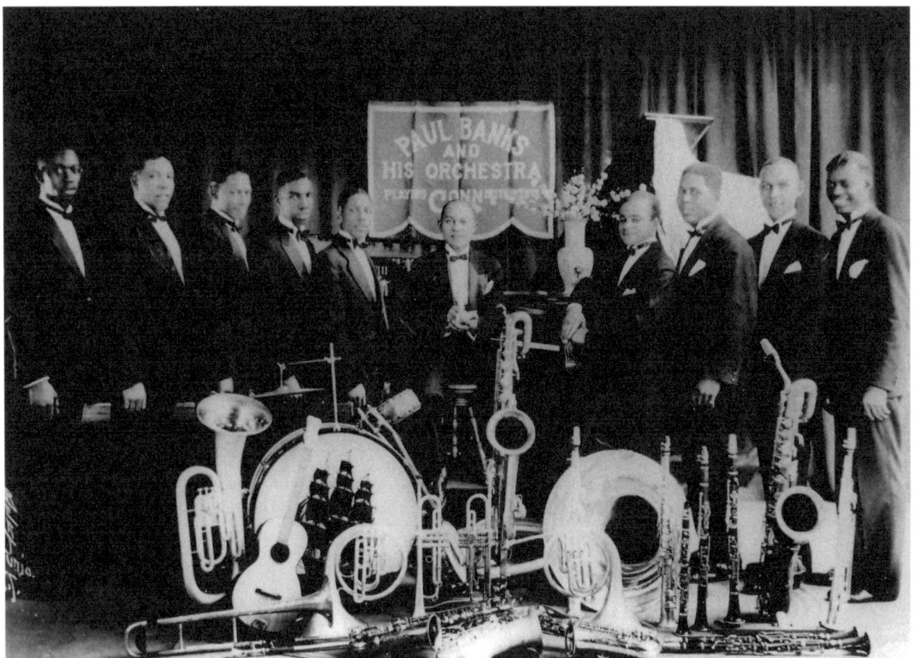

Figure 51: Bert Studio, Kansas City. *The Paul Banks Orchestra*. Kansas City. 1926 *Peter Vacher Collection.*

Strand Studio to make a number of band portraits (Figure 50). Strand was known for its portraits of vaudevillians and raunchy burlesque dancers but the Creole Piron needed photographs that emphasized the orchestra's refinement as well as conveying his policy of employing only colored players who might pass as white. Photographs such as these helped establish Piron and Fletcher Henderson's Orchestras with white patrons in midtown Manhattan hotels and ballrooms in the early-1920s.[23]

Kansas City's Bert Studio photographed the local band leader Paul Banks on location in 1926 (Figure 51). Banks toured the Midwest with minstrel and road shows on the vaudeville circuits but as a part-time band leader he was never able to develop a personal profile and was soon being left behind by jazz musicians emerging as accomplished soloists and entertainment personalities. Louis Armstrong's recordings with King Oliver and the Hot Fives and Sevens in the mid-1920s have often been described as the start of this development although as early as 1921–22 Bernard "Doc" Berendsohn's recordings with Bailey's Lucky Sevens displayed more clarinet soloing than was common in the New Orleans style. "Pops" Foster confirmed this timing when he recalled that "About 1920 or '21, guys started taking down their horns after they'd blown a chorus," suggesting that the music comprised a series of solos accompanied by the rhythm section.[24] By 1923 the NORK's pioneering Gennett sides featured solos while Jimmy Noone with the Apex Club Orchestra, Sidney Bechet, Red Nichols, Miff Mole, Jack Teagarden, and Earl Hines were advancing solo instrumental techniques. Tommy Ladnier, Joe Oliver, Freddie Keppard, and Reuben Reeves soon followed Armstrong as cornet and trumpet "kings" and additions to Fletcher Henderson's Orchestra like Coleman Hawkins in August 1923 meant that "hot" players were beginning to dominate the brass and reed sections by the mid-1920s.

Jazz "stars" and the portrait

It is not difficult to identify the relationship between the rising status of the soloist in jazz and the shift away from the ensemble toward individual "star"—and even glamour—portraiture. As leading jazz musicians sought accommodation with commercial entertainment, the generic band names common in early New Orleans jazz were replaced with those of the principals. Technical playing standard began to improve, the difference between the improvising soloist and background accompaniment became more marked, and jazz developed a "star system" that came to replace the "folk anonymity" of the New Orleans musicians. Recordings sharpened further the focus on instrumental techniques and the accomplishment of the leading soloists made leaders conscious of being outshone by their sidemen.[25] Although the cooperative "commonwealth" practiced by Walter Page's Blue Devils into the age of the soloist went against the grain of these developments, their business principles were almost certainly a key factor in changes of leadership and the eventual demise of the band in the early-1930s.[26]

At the same time professional management of black musicians became more common. Starting with the dance band market, whose potential the vaudeville booking agencies had been slow to exploit, Ernie Young and Jules C. Stein's Music Corporation of America organized in 1922 typified the new breed of band bookers. Although Jelly Roll Morton's was the first band to sign with MCA and other African American musicians followed suit, MCA focused rather more on the "sweet" jazz bands led by the likes of Guy Lombardo and Bernie Cummings. Nevertheless, MCA set the promotional standards with which black musicians and managers were required to compete. Between 1929 and 1935 white managers created and consolidated the management practices to emerge as the gatekeepers controlling access to both black and white audiences.[27] Count Basie's first recording contract, arranged with Dave Kapp of Decca in 1936, was highly disadvantageous and illustrated Noble Sissle's observation at the time that white backing and the publicity that went along with it had become essential if black bands were to find success.[28] These changes provided further impetus to the development of the individual publicity photograph in jazz although the professionalization of the dance band booking system solidified the power of whites over the marketing of African American musicians, including that of their visual representation.

Promotional jazz portraits were used in a variety of ways in the 1920s. Booking agencies, managers, and promoters introduced new styles of marketing and the artists they represented were promoted in music stores "where windows were decorated with special publicity streamers, hangers, folders, catalogues and cardboard cut-outs" and MCA's national booking system even involved an elaborate experimental ballroom.[29] Race records put out by Okey, Brunswick, and other companies began to carry small photographic images of the artists, publicity posters featured both band and individual portraits, and playbills and sheet music were illustrated with photographs. Between 1925 and 1927 Vocalion Records incorporated photographs from Chicago studios of King Oliver in advertisements that ran in black newspapers like the *Defender*. As early as 1904 the sheet music of Scott Joplin rags carried the composer's image in imitation of the conventions of classical scores and the New York publisher Leo Feist used a portrait of the Original Dixieland Jazz Band on the sheet music for "Bluin' the Blues." By 1923 the Melrose Brothers Music Company had started to focus on jazz-based players and their sheet music for "Wolverine Blues" carried a band portrait of the New Orleans Rhythm Kings taken by the Bloom studio in Chicago.[30] Bloom of Chicago made a number of studio portraits of Benny Goodman with the Ben Pollack Orchestra in 1927. Many of these were formal band photographs but a portrait by Maillard Kesslère of the musician, with its soft focus and three quarters pose, is much closer to the celebrity style emerging at that point in time from the theatrical studios.[31]

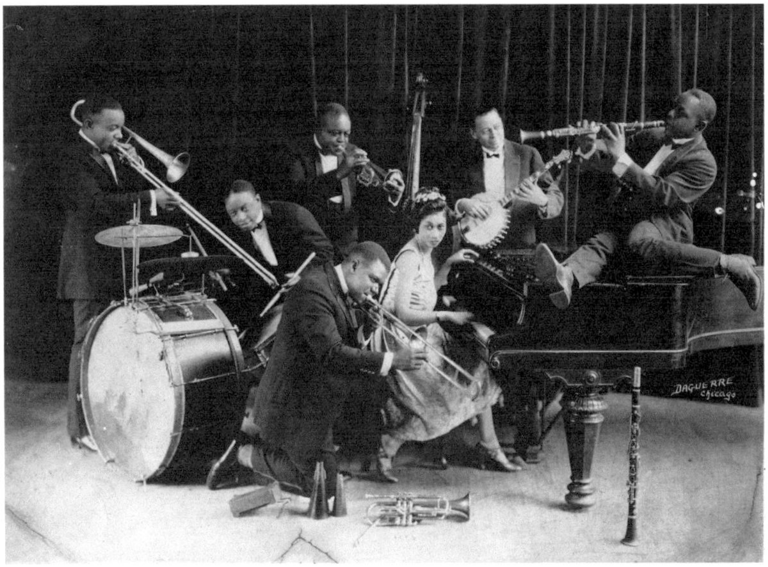

Figure 52: Daguerre (Chicago). *Louis Armstrong's Hot Five.* Okeh recording studio. Chicago. 1922–23.
Credit: Al Rose's New Orleans Jazz: A Family Album Collection, Hogan Jazz Archive, Tulane University.

Few, if any, publicity photographs of Louis Armstrong were taken before he left New Orleans to join King Oliver in Chicago in 1922. As his reputation grew Okeh arranged for publicity photographs to be taken by the Daguerre Studio in Chicago (Figure 52). These images were sent to stores around the country inscribed "Exclusive Okeh Record Artists" and reproduced in advertisements and other print material from Gennett, Columbia, Paramount, as well as Okeh. "One thing that helped the sales was the fact for a while the Okeh people gave away a picture of Louis to everyone that bought one of the records," Kid Ory recalled. "When they did that, the sales went way up, because Louis was so popular."[32] Daguerre's photograph has often been reproduced and illustrates the hesitant evolution of the pose in jazz with the continued emphasis on the exaggerated ensemble compositions. Other photographs from the same session were used regularly throughout the 1920s in record company advertisements.

As the 1920s advanced Louis Armstrong had portraits made by a variety of studios including Bloom, Gibson, Apeda, Mart, Theatrical, and Perry-Atlas. Located in the State-Lake Theatre Building, Bloom Studio was active in Chicago in the 1920s and 1930s. With a focus on theatrical and vaudeville performers, their promotional material claimed to offer clients "the Largest and Best Equipped Posing Rooms in the Country." John Jefferson Gibson had moved to Michigan in 1870 and opened a studio in Bay City. In 1881 he established a presence in Detroit followed by Ann Arbor where aggressive advertising helped secure a steady flow of business. The Chicago studio was opened in 1892 and Gibson

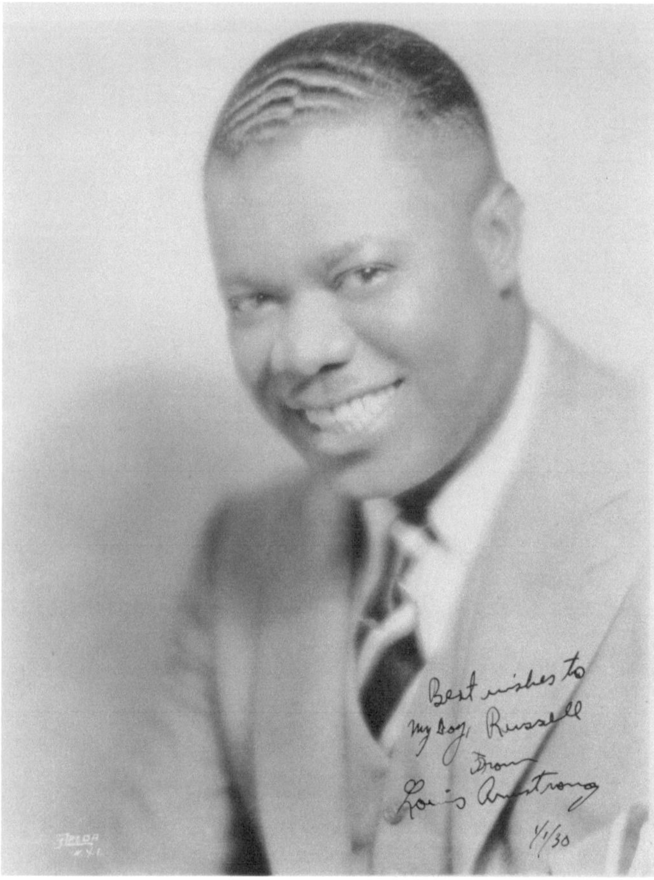

Figure 53: Apeda. *Louis Armstrong*. New York. 1930.
Peter Vacher Collection.

became the official photographer for the 1893 World's Columbian Exposition. Following his death in 1892, the studio was run by his widow Mary May Gibson and eventually became part of the Montgomery Ward photography studio.[33]

By the 1930s Armstrong was regularly appearing in individual rather than ensemble photography. Portraits by Theatrical, Apeda, and Gibson (Figures 53 and 54) show studios evolving a presentational style appropriate for the emerging jazz soloists. Theatrical's portrait shows Armstrong rather self-consciously examining his trumpet against a faintly-patterned backdrop; the eye is distracted by the intrusion of an ungainly pedestal, probably a general use studio prop.[34] Apeda's work is difficult to attribute: the studio was a broadly based New York business established in 1906 by Alexander W. Dreyfoos and Henry Obstfeld. While making original portraiture (Dreyfoos was the head photographer) the studio also reproduced uncopyrighted images by other photographers rebranding the new image with the Apeda name. The practice was deemed legal in a landmark

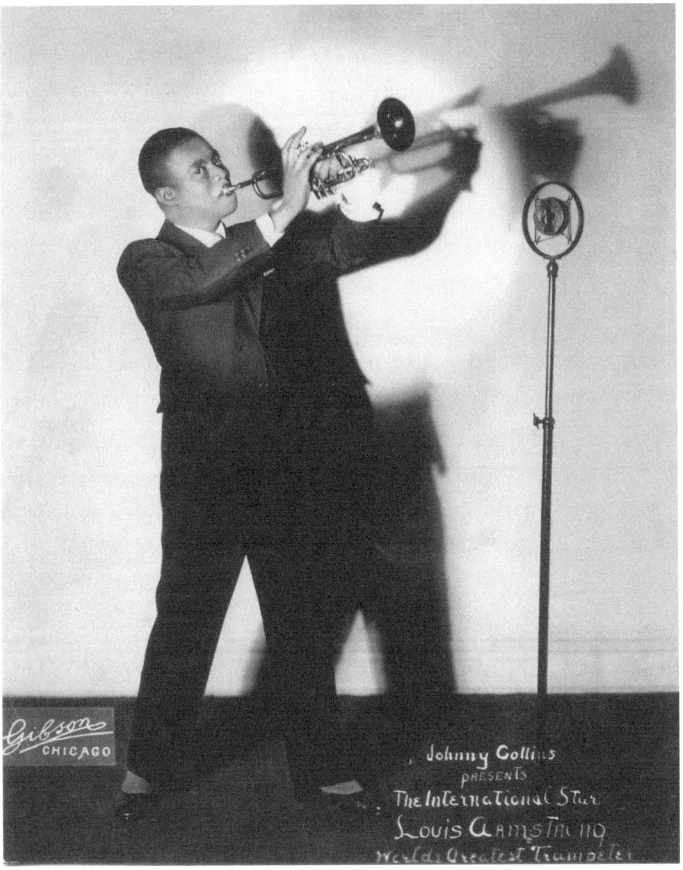

Figure 54: Gibson Studio. *Louis Armstrong*. Chicago. 1933.
Peter Vacher collection.

copyright case involving Apeda and the White Studio in 1913 with the result that "in the theatrical trade [. . .] 'Apeda' has become almost synonymous with photographic reproduction."[35] Like Underwood & Underwood, Apeda would buy up the entire production archive of photographers who had business difficulties or were moving to other parts of the country. The 1930 portrait of Armstrong incorporates many of the theatrical studio tropes with the head and shoulders profile, plain back drop, and use of shadow but the shallow depth of field might have been a hangover from the soft focus favored by pictorialists. Gibson's portrait shows the deep crisp shadows of Kansas City style that was also popular among Hollywood studio photographers.

In all there are 33 known images of Jelly Roll Morton. The earliest images, taken between 1906 and 1921, are mostly informal snapshots by unidentified photographers; two show Morton in vaudeville performance, one was taken with the performers in the Cadillac Café in Los Angeles and one, the only studio photograph, was a formal portrait with the woman Morton referred to as his wife, Anita

Gonzales. The first studio portrait of Morton made specifically for publicity purposes accompanied an article in *The Music Trade* on June 21, 1924, announcing that the Vocalstyle Music Co. had recently completed a series of recordings. Several more studio photographs made for publicity purposes were taken in September 1926, two with the first Red Hot Peppers and one showing a pensive Morton sitting at a grand piano. These photographs were probably taken in the ballroom of the Webster Hotel, Chicago, where Morton's first Victor recordings took place. Further publicity photographs were taken in 1927, one showing Morton posing as if conducting his band. This photograph was first published in August 1927 in *The Milwaukee Journal* in a pictorial advertisement for Morton and his Red Hot Peppers who were performing at the Alhambra Theatre, Wisconsin. The concert was promoted by MCA, who might have arranged the studio photograph. Several later photographs taken between 1929 and 1939 were located in recording studios, including shots by Charles Peterson and Otto F. Hess. Unlike Armstrong, whose publicity shots moved toward individual portraiture, Alyn Shipton makes the point that by the late-1930s Morton came increasingly to be represented as a working musician in shirt-sleeves, often directing from the piano. This may have been an attempt to bolster his credentials after fluctuations in his career.[36]

Hitting Chicago in 1925 after leaving his native Pittsburgh, pianist Earl Hines quickly made an impression and was soon being photographed in various stylish poses by Chicago studios such as Maurice Seymour, Bloom, as well as the black-owned Woodard's Studio, whose work is discussed in the next chapter. Bloom's portrait of the pianist and arranger Gene Rodgers taken in early-1930s (Figure 55) is a classic example of this phase in the development of the jazz studio portrait. Within a few years James J. Kriegsmann, Maurice Seymour, and Murray Korman would be producing portraits that consciously drew on the Hollywood style for the jazz subject. It was at this point that jazz entered the émigré studio.

III. Jazz in the émigré studio

Early emigrants and strategies of assimilation

Between 1880 and 1920 some 23 million immigrants swelled the foreign-born population of the United States to around one in seven. The influx included more than 3 million Jews mainly from Germany and eastern Europe. Overwhelmingly concentrated in New York and the cities of the northeast and the Midwest, Jewish emigrants showed a propensity to settle quickly, often improving their lot by moving quicker from the "ghetto" to better residential areas; and most possessed the tangible and intangible skills to succeed in the metropolis—and had white skins.

All these émigrés moved to secure a better life and this often meant continuing the trades and professions they knew best. This is particularly true of Jewish photographers.[37] The business of photography in western and central Europe (excluding perhaps France and Belgium) was overwhelmingly a Jewish

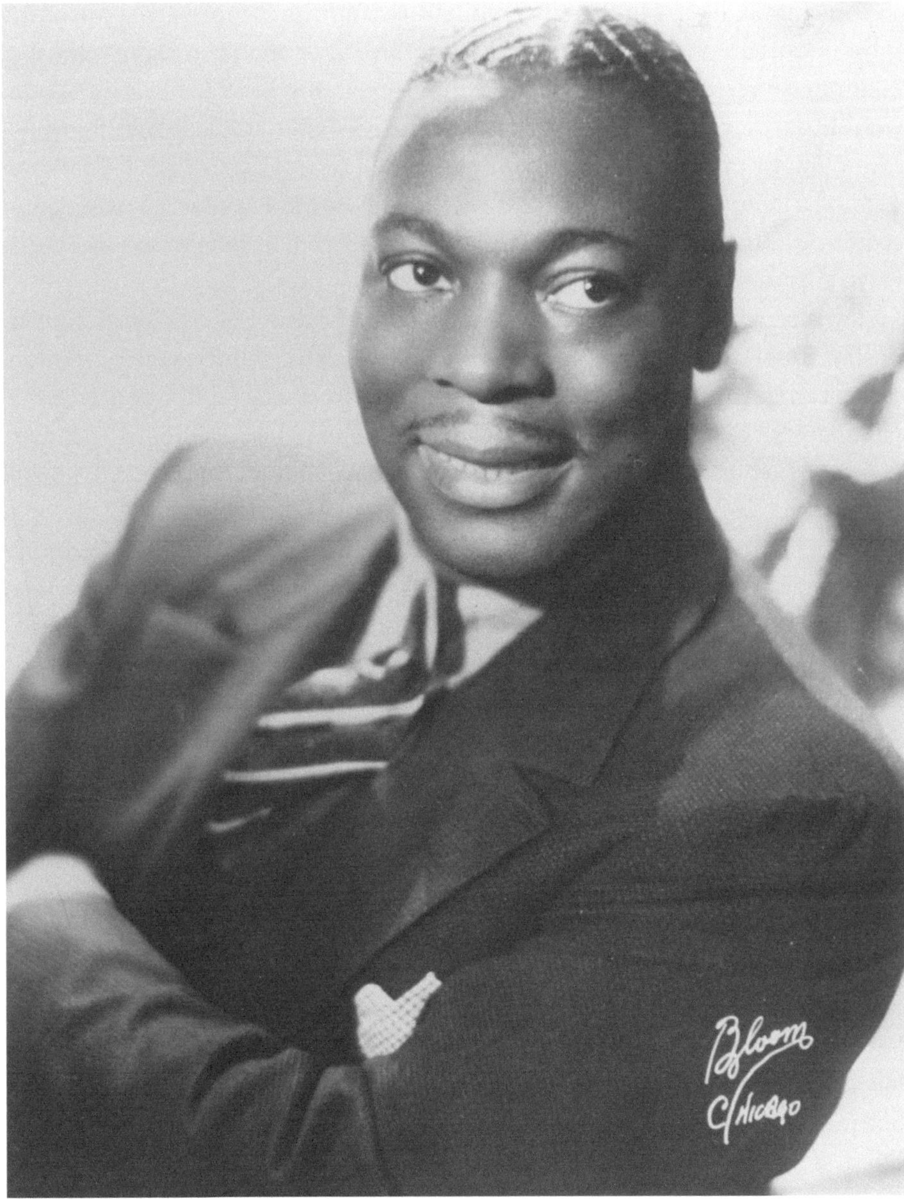

Figure 55: Bloom Studio. *Gene Rodgers*. Chicago. Early-1930s.
Peter Vacher collection.

occupation. Stricter interpretations of the Mosaic prohibitions appeared not to trouble photographers; indeed, far from perpetuating aniconism, the twentieth century saw a remarkable penetration of visual culture into Jewish life.[38] From humble portrait studios in Germany, in small towns throughout the Pale of Settlement in Russia to the great courts in Central Europe, Jewish photographers dominated image-making. Photography was a vocation that "seemed to come naturally to Hungarians" while Russian Jews comprised "some of the most important photographers working at the center of power," a presence that continued forcefully into the Soviet cultural apparatus. In 1920s Berlin the fashionable portrait studios clustered near Kufürstendamm were all Jewish owned. Photography offered Jews, frequently excluded from other activities, a way of earning a living and a degree of self-respect; it was attractive as a new medium requiring both creativity and an entrepreneurial spirit, lacking traditional barriers to entry and was one in which Jewish women were also keen to participate.[39]

Jewish émigré talent quickly made its mark in the fledgling motion picture industry[40] but just as influential were immigrant Jewish celebrity, society, fashion, theatrical, and artistic portraiture studios in New York and Hollywood. Maurice Goldberg (in 1905) and Baron Adolf De Meyer (1913) were among the earliest of the studio portraitists to arrive. David and Samuel Bloom, who arrived in 1908 from Russia, ran the DeHaven photo studio from 1915 to around 1930. Herman Mishkin left Russia in 1885 and became the official portraitist at the Metropolitan Opera between 1908 and 1932 and the German émigré Arnold Genthe, who would make notable portraits of Greta Garbo, moved to New York in 1911. Nikolas Murray, born in Hungary in 1892, established a studio in Greenwich Village in 1920 while Herbert Mitchell (born Daniel Epstein) established the Mitchell-Strand Studios in 1922 after fleeing the pogroms in his native Poland. Zinn Arthur arrived from the Ukraine in 1921 and Irving Chidnoff was a successful theatrical and celebrity portraitist particularly among the Jewish elite. Mortimer Offner specialized in theatrical portrait between 1925 and 1934. Although his practice servicing vaudeville and the burlesque circuits had less cachet than the movie portrait specialists, Nasib made portraits of several well-known jazz musicians (Figure 56). James J. Kriegsmann and Murray Korman established studios in 1929 and two Russian-born brothers, Maurice and Seymour Zeldman, formed the Maurice Seymour studio. Bruno Bernard ("Bruno of Hollywood") was another German Jewish exile from Nazi Germany, and the Bulgarian art-trained M. I. Boris set up business in the late-1930s before moving to Paramount to make art portraiture. Many of these studios were called on to make portraits of jazz musicians.

While many of these émigré photographers had fled to escape religious and ethnic intolerance and persecution, they were also economic migrants anxious to assimilate. Most Jewish defense organizations and the Jewish press in the early decades of the twentieth century were firmly assimilationist and there was considerable pressure on Jewish émigrés from established German Jews and others within their own community to adopt American habits and modes of life. The People's Art Guild (1915) pressed to "Americanize" Jews through art while the Educational Alliance founded in 1893 was active over several decades in Americanizing new immigrants "in spite of themselves, in the mode prescribed by their friends and benefactors."[41] Neal Gabler speaks of the "ferocious, even

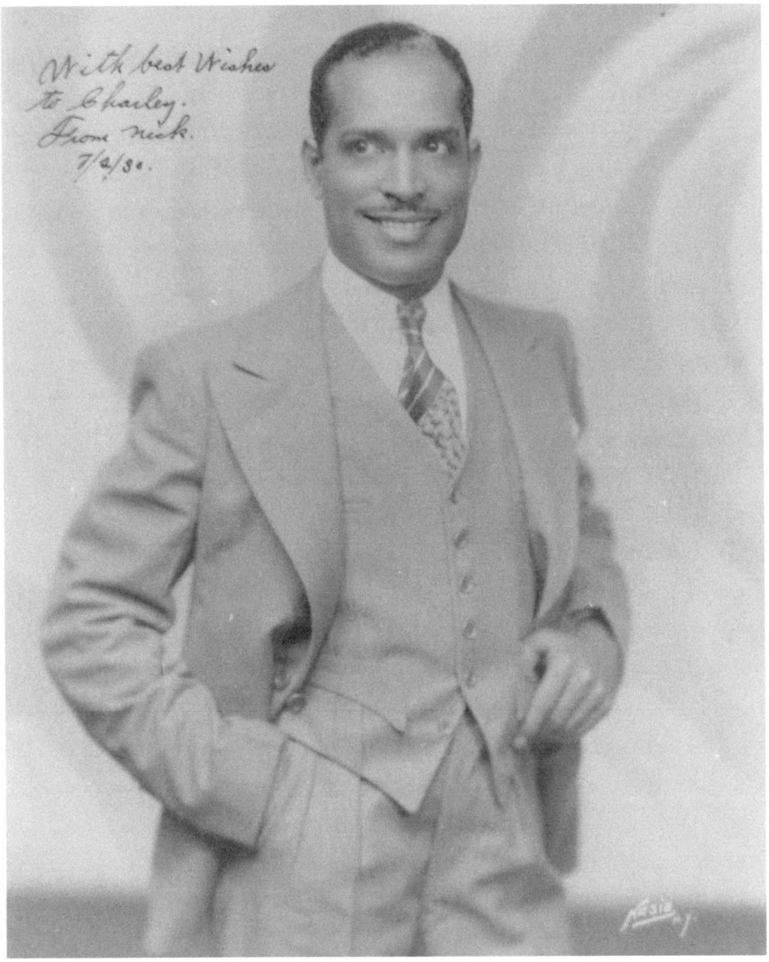

Figure 56: Nasib. *Albert Nicholas*. New York. July 2, 1930.
Peter Vacher Collection.

pathological, embrace of America" by Jews in Hollywood and it has been argued that émigré photographers expressed the desire for assimilation by enthusiastic adoption of the American "band box" style.[42]

There is much truth in this characterization but it underestimates the pluralism of assimilation strategies. Deborah Dash Moore has described how New York's social structure encouraged ethnic diversity and sustained the vitality of a pluralist Jewish ethnicity: "In New York there were many ways to be a Jew."[43] Comprising a remarkable diversity of ethnic and religious traditions, many had relocated to escape anti-Semitism but their adherence to Jewish religious tenets can be overestimated. Eastern European Jews transformed American Orthodoxy while others arrived from less religious and even secularized traditions, further complicating patterns of religious observance. Many Jews soon adopted an acculturated style of observance that embraced modernity with its commitment to individual rights and pluralism. Secularizing and universalizing tendencies were most evident within the new Reform movement. In spite of the pressure on artists from assimilating Jewish arts organizations, their approach was sufficiently open-minded to embrace the progressivism of the Ashcan School while Louise Nevelson's sculptures and Abraham Walkovitz's abstractions were among the earliest modernist works by American artists. Émigrés artists of the period such as Weegee, Walkowitz, Ben Shahn, and Jacob Epstein were secularized Jews but they retained close cultural ties with their heritage and integrated Jewish themes into their work. These artists substituted the high modernism of Stieglitz, the streamlined forms of the machine age and fractured distortions of Dada for a modernist subjectivity that grappled with issues of representation rooted in questions about personal and national identity. The specificity of photography was a perfect tool to capture the aesthetic and political tensions that lie between group identification and self-representation. Certainly, Weegee was particularly interested in cultural traditions and his photographs of Jewish life show a respectful concern with *Yiddishkeit*, the cultural icons of immigrant culture and Jewish identity.[44]

Political opinions were also diverse, but these arrivals were certainly less conservative than the older-established German Jews in Manhattan and other cities. Some brought a tradition of social activism evidenced by their embrace of labor organization, commitment to socialist and social reform movements by prominent Jewish leaders, and the political line of leading newspapers such as the *Jewish Daily Forward*. By the 1920s American Jews had developed a political ideology of American Jewish ethnicity that embraced liberalism, civil rights, civil liberties, and support for others. This last usually included African Americans although there was always more than an element of self-interest in professed fellow-feelings.[45] Taken as a whole, the immigrant generation initiated a cultural explosion that helped to shape a moral community and a feeling of involvement.[46]

Secular Jewishness made itself felt in the studios of the émigré photographers as much as assimilationism. While émigré portraitists broadly accepted the conventions of celebrity and Hollywood portraiture many were tolerant and open-minded. In welcoming black entertainers and musicians into their studios they provided a bridge between the all-white world of Hollywood glamour and the African American world of jazz just as its leading soloists were developing their own artistic profiles.

Maurice Seymour Studio

Maurice Zeldman and Seymour Zeldman came to Chicago from Russia in 1920 and established their studio in 1929.[47] Inspired by the Russian theatre and dance photographer Maurice Goldberg, the brothers worked collaboratively photographing ballet dancers, celebrities, musicians, and entertainers. Studio portraits were taken with a large accordion 8×10 camera; images were brightly lighted

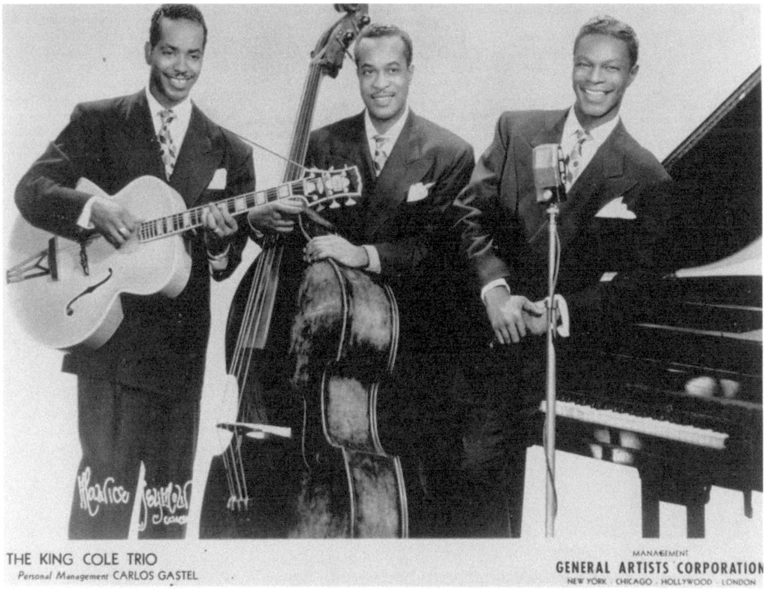

Figure 57: Maurice Seymour Studio. *Nat King Cole Trio.* Los Angeles. Late-1940s. *Peter Vacher Collection.*

with neutral background and printed on high gloss stock after skillfully executed retouching (Figure 57). When Seymour moved to run the New York City studio, both legally changed their name to "Maurice Seymour." The New York brother expanded his clientele from dancers and actors to singers, jazz musicians, and burlesque stars and often placed advertisements in *Down Beat* promoting his services (Figure 58). Both Zeldman bothers worked into the 1970s.

Murray Korman

Born Moritz Korman in the Ukrainian city of Kamenets Podolsk in 1902, Murray Korman came to the United States sometime after 1912. He studied at Cooper Union and worked in the 1920s as a newspaper illustrator as well as making nightclub sketches. He established a studio in the Mayfair Theatre Building on 47th Street and Seventh Avenue New York City and, in 1940, a second studio at 324 Madison Avenue for society portraits. At its peak, the business employed twelve staff. His reputation for Hollywood-style high-key glamour relied on pose and lighting rather than extensive retouching as found in the portraits of Herbert Mitchell, M.I. Boris, Irving Chidnoff, and Alfred Cheney Johnston. He later turned to glamour photography.[48]

Working with jazz musicians, Korman occasionally carried out location commissions (Figure 59) but mostly made Hollywood-style portraits in the studio such as that of the pianist Teddy Wilson (Figures 60a and 60b). He was in his element making portraits of female artists like Billie Holiday (Figure 11) and Lena

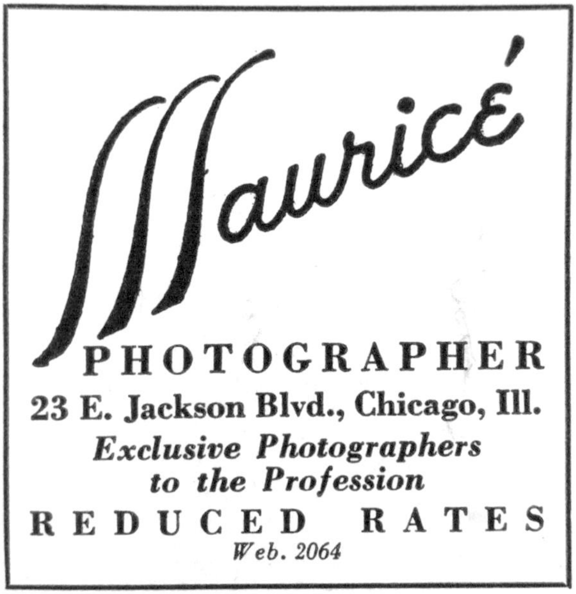

Figure 58: Maurice Seymour Studio. Advertisement in *Down Beat*.

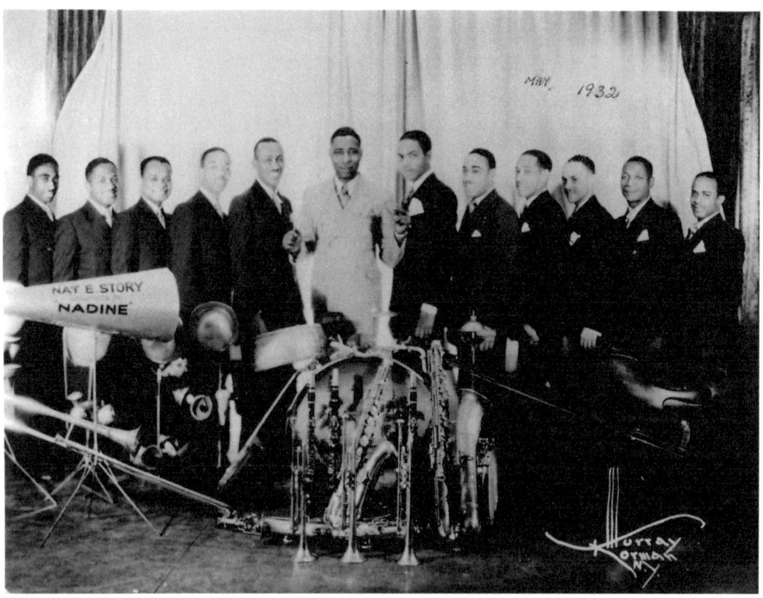

Figure 59: Murray Korman. *The Bud Harris Rhythm Rascals*. RKO Tour. May 1932. *Peter Vacher Collection/permission of Leslie Greaves.*

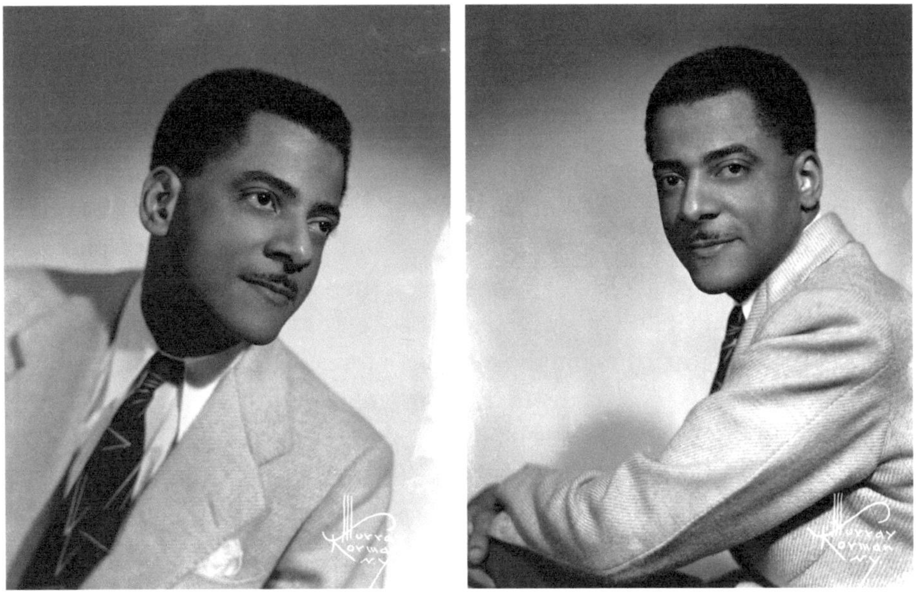

Figures 60a and 60b: Murray Korman. *Teddy Wilson*. New York. n.d.
Clyde Adams Collection/Permission of Leslie Greaves.

Horne. Clyde Adams, who has spent many years researching Korman's life and work, is convinced of the photographer's inclusiveness when it came to working with black artists and relates this to his émigré status and Jewish heritage:[49]

> *He had no prejudices [. . .] some of the most intriguing and beautiful works of his were of African American entertainers [. . .] my assumption is that coming from very humble roots, being Jewish, he had an aversion to bigotry and prejudices. He was a very kind, personable and warm individual to anyone who wanted to use his services.*

Bruno of Hollywood

Bruno Bernard once defined his "ultimate photograph" as a "biography of the physical and mental makeup of the sitter—and, at the same time, an autobiography of the photographer."[50] Bernard's life story is indeed the key to understanding the man and his work, the thread that weaves through photographs as seemingly diverse as those depicting glamorous movie stars, blond pinup girls, and—on occasions—black jazz musicians.

Bernard was born in Berlin in 1912. He started photographing early and continued while studying criminal psychology at Kiel University: "An innate sense of social justice more than anything tipped the scale of my professional choices. My goal was to become the advocate of the poor and the downtrodden." As a Jewish activist he was forced to flee to the United States in 1937, enduring a traumatic journey whose outcome was far from certain. Haunted by his past and the fate of the family he was forced to leave behind in Germany, he continued his work to help fellow Jews escape to freedom once in America. Bernard tried to find work in motion pictures and the theatre but soon focused on photography. In 1938 he set up a darkroom in his Los Angeles apartment and started making "posed candid" glamour shots inspired by the Peruvian painter of pin-up girls Alberto Vargas. Bernard favored natural light, occasionally adding flash. He opened a studio on Sunset Boulevard and built a practice photographing actresses including a young Marilyn Monroe. By the 1950s he was one of the most well-known glamour and theatrical photographers of the age. In the early-1960s he returned to Germany to build a career as a foreign photojournalist. Among his assignments was the Eichmann trial for *Der Spiegel.*

Photography for Bernard was more than a way of making a living; it was the key to a form of assimilation that embraced the new but refused to disavow an ethnic and artistic heritage of which he was proud. Photography also countered his personal nightmares and gave his life balance. The curator Carole Kismaric observed that Bernard did not make standard Hollywood glamour photos: "When you see his pictures, you want to stop and look at them, because of the obvious connection between the subject and the camera." Bernard's daughter said that her father's insights were rooted in "his astonishing courage in facing the huge challenges of his early life. It gave him the ability to reflect both the inner and outer character of his subjects." While it was Bernard's reputation that attracted many of the leading jazz musicians of the 1930s and 1940s, there can be little doubt that his sensitivity to his sitter's own life stories created a bond that allowed him to create images treating sitters with respect as artists (Figure 61).

James J. Kriegsmann

In 1938 when Moe Gale needed a publicity portrait of Sister Rosetta Tharpe he turned to the New York portrait photographer James J. Kriegsmann. Kriegsmann's portrait showed the singer with her steel National guitar and established an image that would follow her throughout her career. In February 1963 Dinah Washington celebrated twenty years in the business by going to Kriegsmann's studio to have a portrait made, "a choice both sentimental and symbolic, since James Kriegsmann had taken her first formal publicity shot." Ten years later, Sonny Rollins decided to have a "glossy" made to give to his hero, Coleman Hawkins: "There was a great photographer named James J. Kriegsman," he remembered, "who used to make these pictures of musicians, and he made a beautiful picture of Coleman. So I had my eight-by-ten."[51]

Rosetta Tharpe, Dinah Washington, and Rollins were among thousands of black musicians and artists to sit for Kriegsmann. Although a wide range of movie stars, singers, entertainers, personalities, and politicians visited his Broadway studio, jazz musicians were particularly important to his practice.[52] Subtly adapting

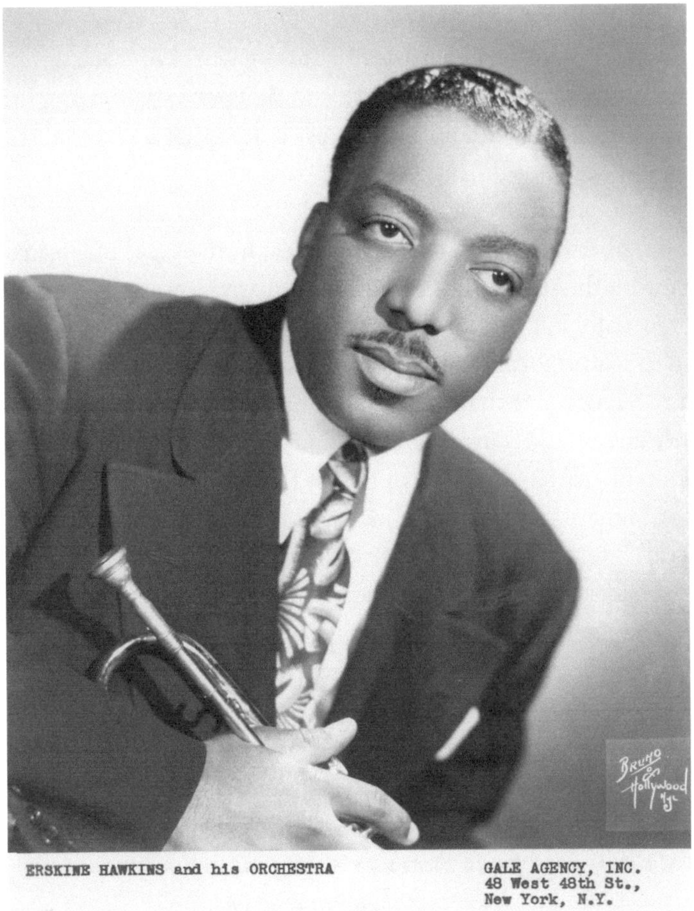

Figure 61: Bruno Bernard ("Bruno of Hollywood"). *Erskine Hawkins*. Late-1930s. *Peter Vacher Collection.*

Hollywood-style portraiture just as leading jazz musicians were entering the world of commercial entertainment, Kriegsmann offered a valuable space for black musicians whose relationship with white-dominated American entertainment was ambiguous. As his son, James J. Kriegsmann Jr., recalled, "No matter how famous these [black] people were, many photographers wanted nothing to do with them, but they knew that the door to my father's studio was always open."[53] In spite of his importance, Kriegsmann has unfortunately been overlooked in jazz histories.

James J. Kriegsmann was born in 1909 in Vienna and learned his craft as an apprentice with a local studio. In 1929 Kriegsmann left Vienna for New York where he joined the new breed of émigré theatrical, society, and celebrity portraitists. He opened his own studio and within a few years became the official photographer for the newly opened Cotton Club Review where he was plugged on menu cards as the "famous Viennese photographer."[54] With access to names like Duke Ellington, Cab Calloway (his first black sitter), and Chick Webb, Kriegsmann began to build his reputation as a portraitist in the world of black entertainment. By 1944 he was obliged to place a notice in *Billboard* apologizing for delays in accepting appointments, and it has been estimated that he conducted over 20,000 photography sessions during a 42-year career.[55]

Kriegsmann's identity once in America was conditioned by his experience as a Jew in Austria: "I'm sure he experienced discrimination at home [. . .] In Germany it may have been under the surface but in Catholic Austria it was more open. The whole family eventually left directly because of discrimination."[56] Kriegsmann had converted to Catholicism before leaving for America: "He felt like a second-class citizen in Vienna. He made a decision he didn't want anything to do with Jewish culture and would reinvent himself in America." The family originally lived in Brooklyn but in 1948 moved to Forest Hill Gardens, "a very anti-Semitic neighborhood" where Kriegsmann joined a Protestant church and eventually became a deacon. "He felt that being Jewish was a curse—and I'm quoting him—the rest of his family were hurt by that decision. He kept them away from [his sons] because of the Jewish issue." Yet he was always conscious of his heritage and this helps to explain his affinity with the world of black entertainers:[57]

> *[He] could probably feel the same kind of pain suffered by his black clients [. . .] His relationship with the black community was based on discrimination he had experienced in Austria. He also appreciated their talent—a tremendous appreciation for the talent—he loved them—and found them very photogenic. But above all he empathized very much with how they were treated and that's a fact.*

Kriegsmann himself brusquely dismissed criticisms of his openness to black clients: "Don't tell me that! They're human beings like you and me. Sure, their skin may be different. But the talent they have, most of the white people haven't got. That's the truth."[58] He might have renounced his Jewish faith but his relationship with black entertainers was integral to the way he "reinvented" himself. Searching for a photographic language in which to express a new identity for a new life, he turned to the style of portraiture emerging from the Hollywood movie studios in the 1930s and 1940s. "I very seldom missed a new motion picture. I used to sit down and just look at the lighting. Then I copied it."[59]

Kriegsmann became a favored portraitist among jazz musicians not only because of his lack of discrimination but also because he made them look good. Avoiding location work, his portraits of jazz musicians were taken in the studio where he could control the look and project the stylized aesthetic he brought into the world of black entertainment. He took over certain elements of Hollywood-style portraiture and adapted others. He rarely made head shots, preferring the full or three-quarter composition, and steered away from the suggestive props, flowing costumes, and soft materials with which the Hollywood photographers adorned the movie stars. Kriegsmann favored a "harder" aesthetic based on stage clothing, occupational signifiers, and the props available in his studio. His poses reflected the world of the working musicians; his sitters were posed directly *en face*, as if playing to an audience, in a conscious rejection of the languid poses adopted by many movie stills photographers. These adaptations shifted the emphasis toward the sitter as an individual and away from Hollywood's merging of individual and type (Clara Bow as the "It Girl," Lillian Gish as adorable waif, Jean Harlow as blond bombshell, etc.). Kriegsmann also subverted the gendered nature of Hollywood portraiture, which had created entrancing fiction for a mostly female audience, paving the way for jazz portraiture to enter the predominantly young male world of the swing era.

In other ways Kriegsmann was more open to Hollywood styling. He realized that low-key tones could be gently turned to create an atmosphere of brooding

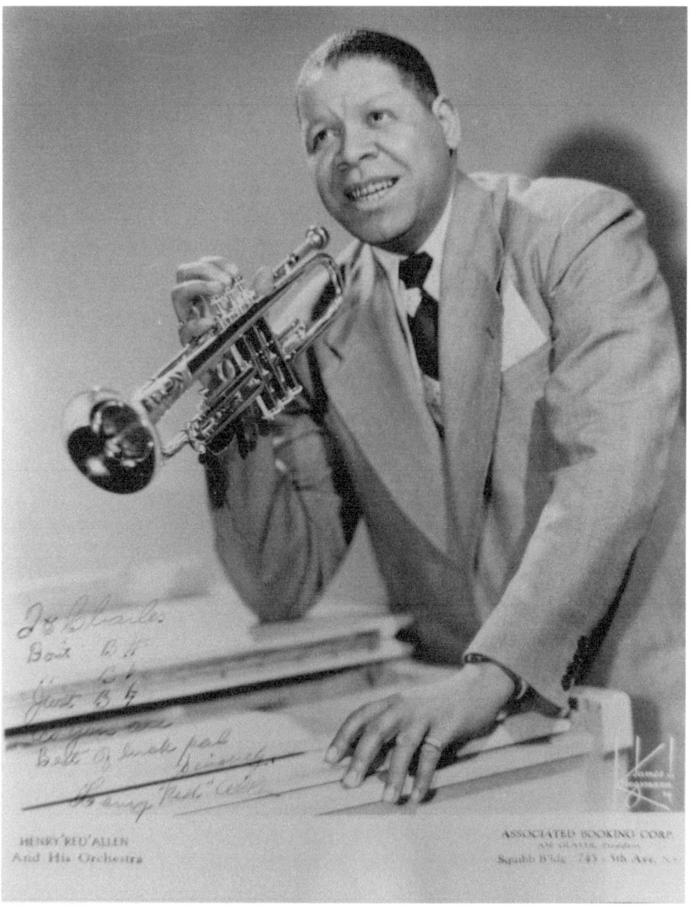

Figure 62: James J. Kriegsmann. *Henry "Red" Allen*. New York. n.d.

intensity appropriate to the portrayal of jazz musicians. African American sitters generally were often wary that white photographers might be inexperienced with darker complexions and fail to render skin tones to their liking. Kriegsmann used oils on the skin and hair of his sitters and was adept as a full negative retoucher and printer.[60] Tending toward low-key, Henry "Red" Allen and Mary Lou Williams (Figures 62 and 63) are framed by a subtly graduated backdrop while Jimmie Lunceford's background is underexposed to light gray (Figure 64); the original version of the Allen portrait was marked "flop" and the final version reversed as shown here. In these shots Kriegsmann has positioned the key light to the right, creating a shadow over the left side of his sitter's face; skin textures have been smoothed and highlights carefully modulated. In a portrait of Sarah Vaughan Kriegsmann followed his common practice of shadowing the left side of the face but variegated the plain the plain background with a latticed shadow effect (a technique he had previously used when he photographed a young Miles Davis in the early-1940s).

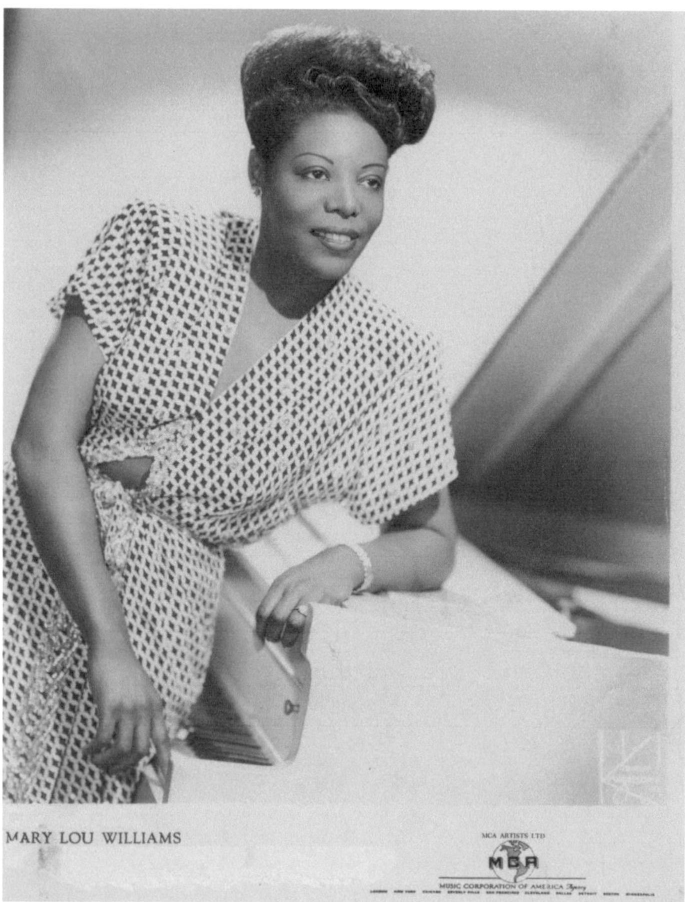

Figure 63: James J. Kriegsmann. *Mary Lou Williams*. New York. n.d. *Peter Vacher Collection.*

Kriegsmann used sharply defined and dramatic shadow effects to a much greater extent than the movie studios photographers. His mid-1940s portraits, such as that of Illinois Jacquet (Figure 65), with its mid- to dark-gray tones and stark shadows, refer back to early vaudeville photographs from Connelly and Hixon. The shadow on the musician's face is particularly deep and the crisp silhouette of the player and instrument on the backdrop create a second plane of interest. Kriegsmann would employ this technique with portraits of Clora Bryant (Figure 66) in contrast to the more usual softening techniques employed with female artists.

With its low-key shadows, muted highlights, and restricted depth of field there is an atmosphere of intensity about Kriegsmann's portrait of Ben Webster (Figure 67) that captures this most committed of jazz musicians. Unsmiling and looking away from the camera this is a dramatic portrait of the jazz musician as artist.

Kriegsmann met the growing need for commercial portraiture among African American musicians by adapting, shaping, and subtly inverting prevailing glamour

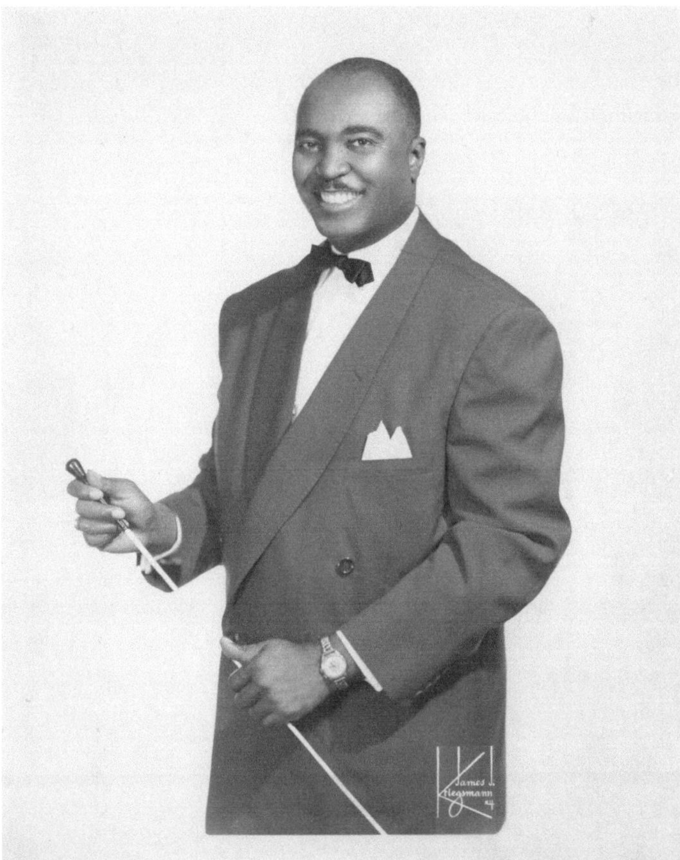

Figure 64: James J. Kriegsmann. *Jimmie Lunceford*. New York. Late-1930s. *Peter Vacher Collection.*

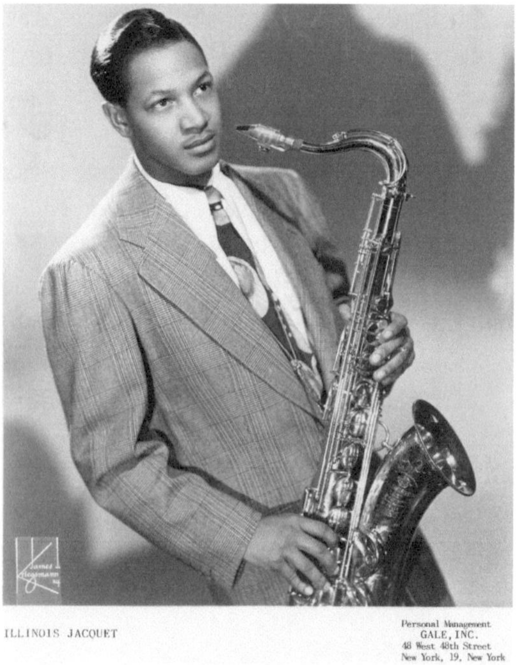

Figure 65: James J. Kriegsmann. *Illinois Jacquet.* New York. *c.*1948. *Peter Vacher Collection.*

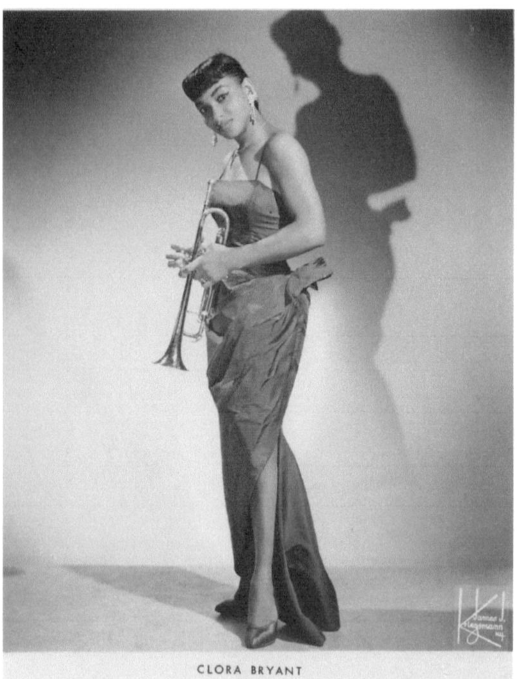

Figure 66: James J. Kriegsmann. *Clora Bryant.* New York. n.d. *Peter Vacher Collection.*

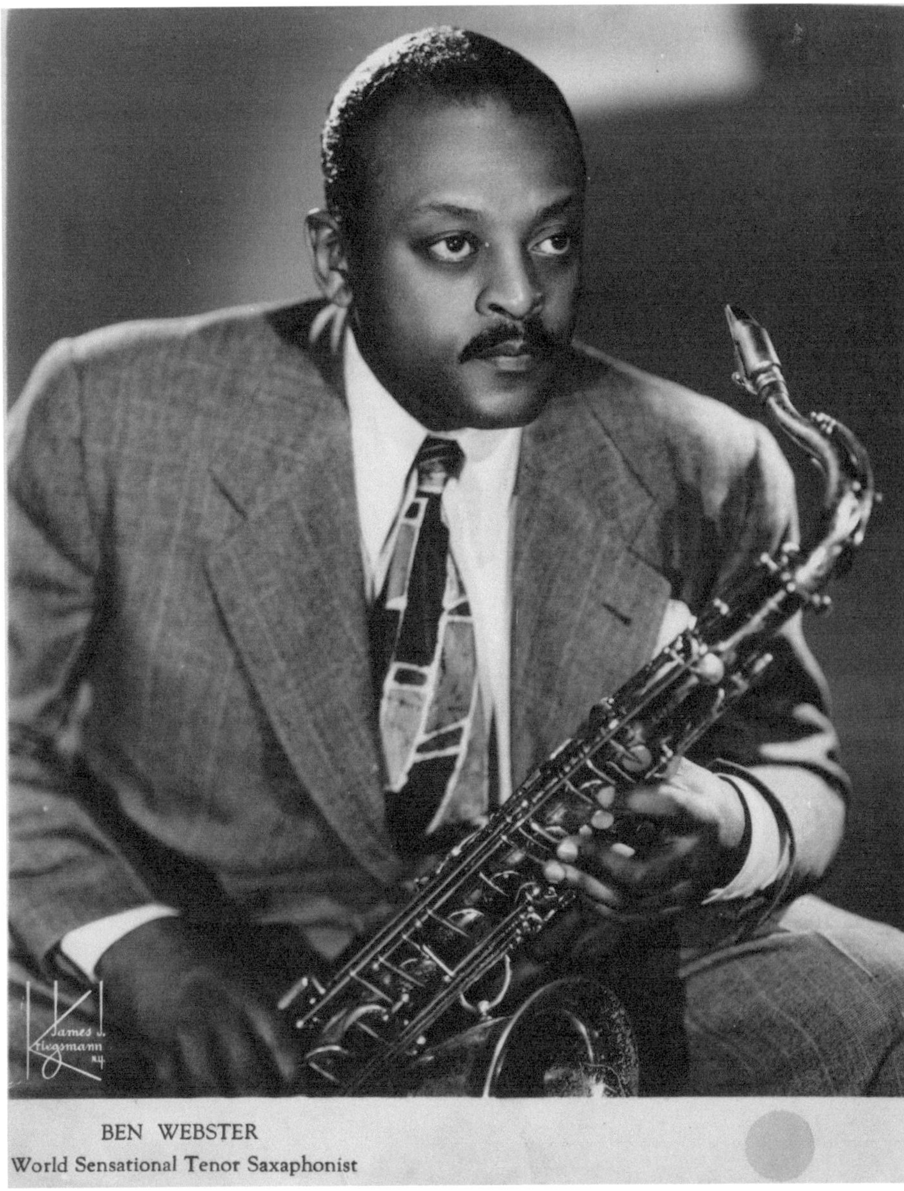

Figure 67: James J. Kriegsmann. *Ben Webster*. New York. 1950s. *Peter Vacher Collection.*

portraiture conventions. In representing African American musicians with all the values usually accorded to white artists, Kriegsmann contributed to the growing cultural capital of jazz during the 1930s and 1940s and allowed black musicians to engage with commercial publicity photography on their own terms. Illinois Jacquet first went to Kriegsmann in 1947 and was still returning to his studio in the mid-1980s.[61] The trombonist Slide Hampton, who had his picture taken in

Kriegsmann's Times Square studio, remembered: "What he did for black entertainers was very noble. After all these years, the fact that some black stars are still working with his son as a way of paying homage to his father is just as noble."[62]

IV. Mid-century studio photography

From the 1930s onward an ever-widening range of studio photographers around the country found themselves in demand by jazz musicians. Few among these photographers and studios are well-known today: in New York the Volpe Studio and Hiners (often used by Irving Mills), National Studios, Bert Black, Michael Caputo, and James Kollar (whose studio was located in Radio City) were located in Manhattan; Harry Rossner and the Kenby Studio operated in Brooklyn and Duncan Butler was in Ridgewood, New Jersey. Other businesses included the Standard Standard Art Studio and Brown Photo Studio in Philadelphia; Electric Studio, Gushiniere, Magic Karpet, and Ray Rising in Chicago; Etudes Studio in St. Louis; Kuhli Studio in Milwaukee; Cresswell and Stiger Studios of Kansas City; the Ohio photographers at Lowe's Studio in Akron; and the Gordon Connor Studio at 1935 Euclid Avenue in Cleveland—an especially enthusiastic enthusiastic exponent of the Hollywood lighting style (Figures 68 and 69).

In the southern states Jones-Puroy in Memphis and Jimmy Wilson in Birmingham, Alabama, were occasional choices. Wilson opened a portrait studio in the

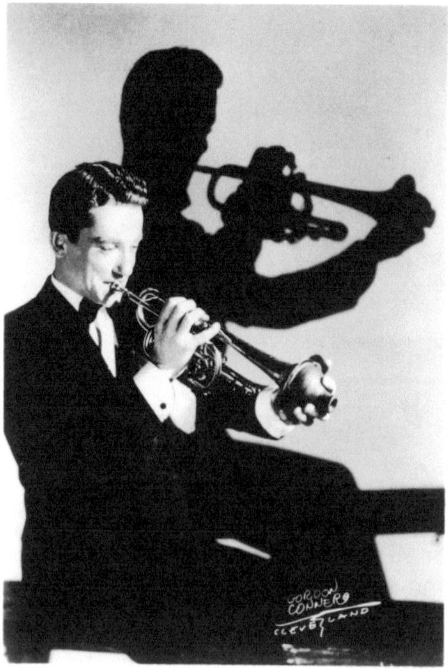

Figure 68: Gordon Connor. *Red Nichols*. Cleveland. n.d.
Bob Inman scrapbook (IJS.0289), Institute of Jazz Studies, Rutgers University Libraries.

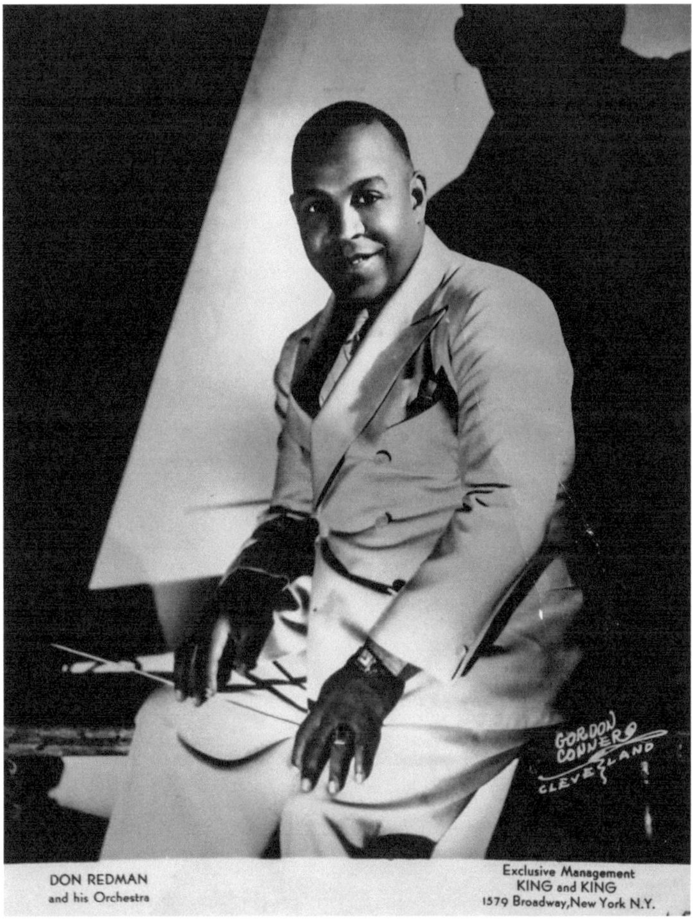

Figure 69: Gordon Connor. *Don Redman*. Cleveland. 1935.
Peter Vacher Collection.

Southside suburb of Birmingham in the early-1930s and the business survived the depression into the 1940s helped by income from band portraits of visiting and local musicians such as Fess Whatley.[63] In the Midwest Youngs of St. Louis (a studio that produced montaged images of band members) and, on the west coast, Jimmy Dale and the Coleman and Sheffield Studio in Los Angeles were regularly called upon. Walters Studio of Seattle recorded many of Benny Goodman's live performances in the city. Little is known about these studios and almost nothing about others whose jazz images can be found in archives and private collections: Avair, Stewart's Art Studio, Fedor, Don Johnson, and Paraltra.

These photographers were often required to visit the theatres or dance halls in which the musicians were playing and make individual and band portraits between performances using the stage, backdrops, and other props available in the location to recreate a studio aesthetic. Others preferred the studio setting. Bill Bennett of

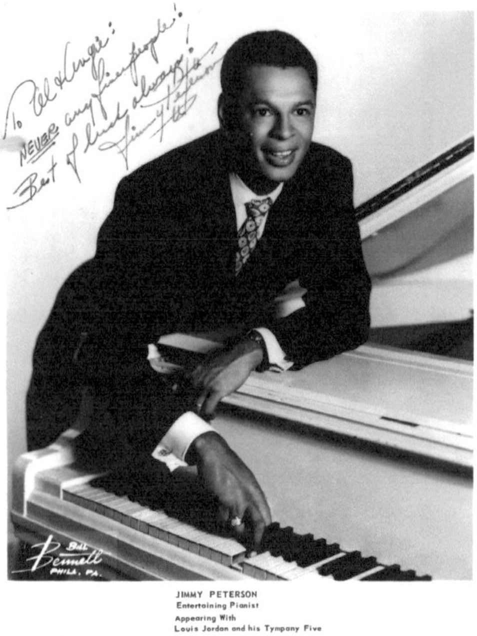

Figure 70: Bill Bennett. *Jimmy Peterson*. Philadelphia. n.d.
Peter Vacher Collection.

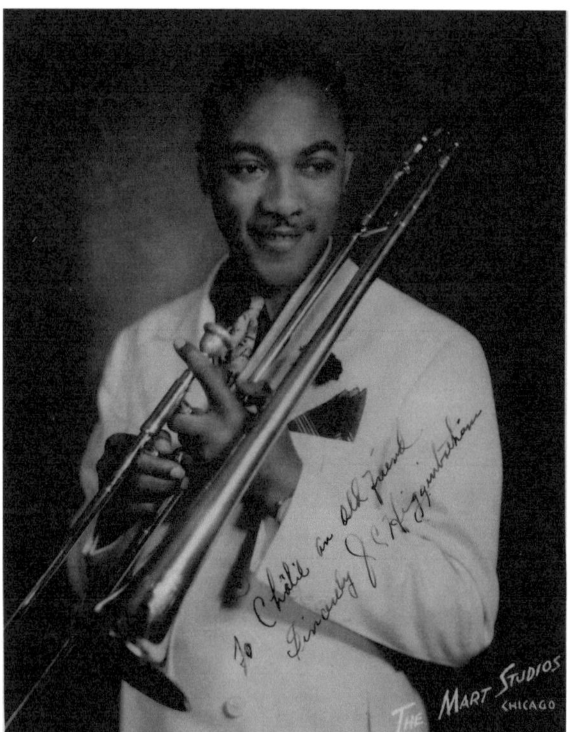

Figure 71: Mart Studio. Chicago. *J. C. Higginbotham*. Chicago. n.d.
Peter Vacher Collection.

Philadelphia was known for his portraits of dancers and gained something of a reputation for his Burlesque Historical Company postcard set. His portrait of the "Entertaining Pianist" Jimmy Peterson (Figure 70) is straight out of the Kriegsmann playbook with its compositional lines and even a Kriegsmann-signature white piano. The Mart Studio of Chicago posed J. C. Higginbotham conventionally displaying his instrument but the hint of a smile, coy off-center glance and unusual lighting was a low-key variant on the Hollywood style (Figure 71).

George Maillard Kesslère on the other hand cast W. C. Handy as a venerable man of letters in his 1940 portrait (Figure 72). Moving easily in New York's high society between the wars, Maillard Kesslère's diaphanously clad dancers had attracted much attention. In 1935, Kesslère exhibited 500 of his photographs, paintings, and drawings in the Patricia Lounge of the Loew's Ziegfeld Theater in Manhattan

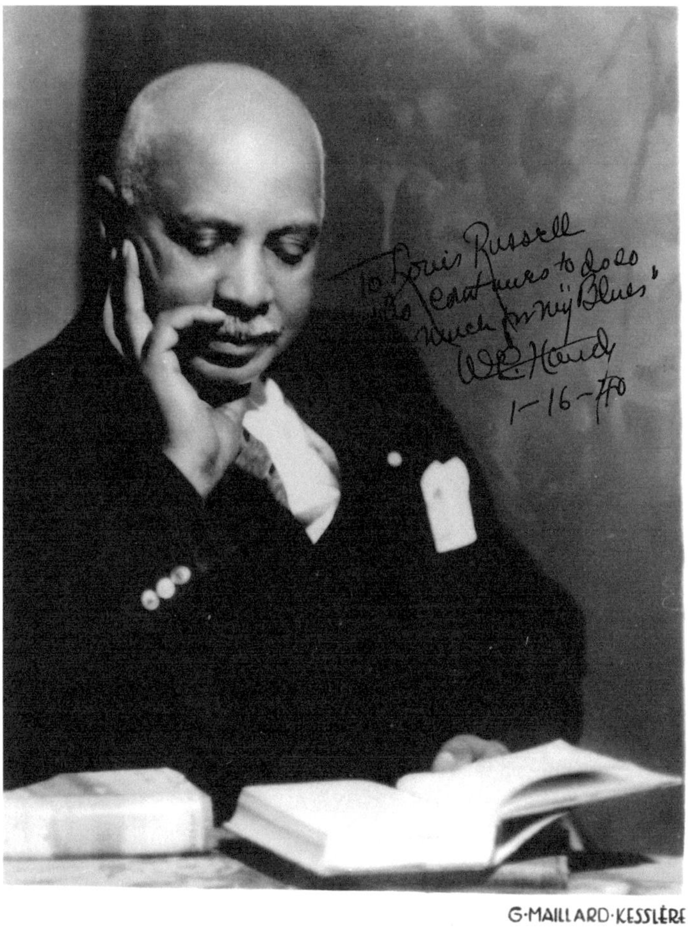

Figure 72: George Maillard Kesslère. *W. C. Handy*. New York. 1940. *Peter Vacher Collection/with permission of Joan Bertin.*

and his subjects included people involved in almost every aspect of the entertainment arts. As a theatrical portraitist he was known as the best of the bust format photographers as well as creating modernist displays for Helena Rubenstein.[64]

By mid-century the leading Hollywood portrait photographers were regularly accepting jazz sitters. Edward Thayer Monroe styled himself "Monroe Hollywood" but worked in Manhattan with Luther White's studio between 1915 and 1919 after which he established himself as an independent artist. In 1923 *Vanity Fair* listed him among the ten most significant portraitists of the day. Following the Depression he teamed up with another former White colleague George W. Lucas to form Lucas-Monroe, an important production studio that operated until 1952. His experience at White gave him a mastery of natural lighting and photographic printing. The typical Monroe portrait shows a sitter in a natural relaxed position, well-lighted with moderate depth of

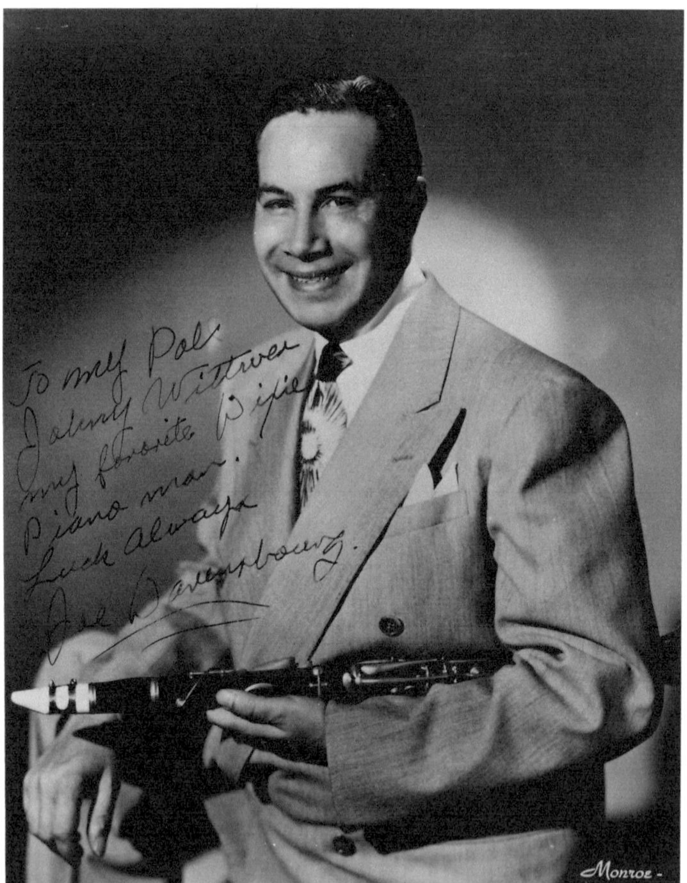

Figure 73: Monroe Hollywood. *Joe Darensbourg*. New York. n.d.
Peter Vacher Collection.

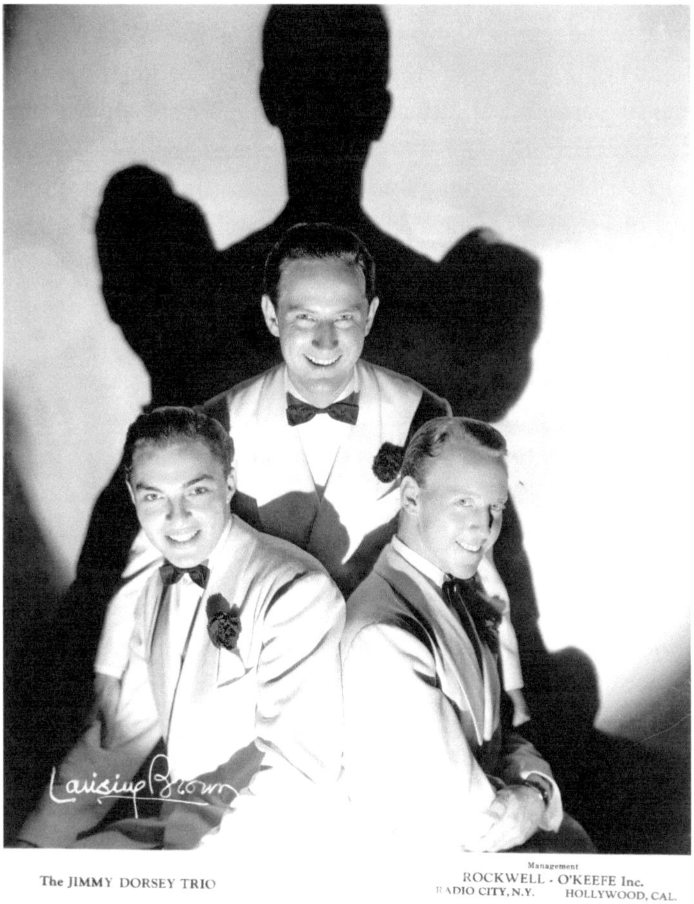

Figure 74: Lansing Brown. *Rockwell O'Keefe publicity photo of The Jimmy Dorsey Trio.* 1938. *Bob Inman scrapbook (IJS.0289), Institute of Jazz Studies, Rutgers University Libraries.*

field (Figure 73). The Hollywood style is equally evident in portraits of white jazz musicians in this period by W. G. Harris, Bert Parry at Warner Brothers and *Modern Screen Magazine*, A.L. "Whitey" Schaeffer, John E. Reed, Lansing Brown (Figure 74), and Lee of Hollywood. Clarence Bull's early-1940s portrait of Tommy Dorsey shown at the beginning of this chapter exemplifies the style (Figure 45).

V. Conclusion

The development of the jazz studio portrait between 1900 and mid-century is testament to changing perceptions of jazz. Most noticeable was the emergence by the mid- to late-1920s of individual artist portraits. Band and orchestral photographs remained in demand but the growing demand for individual portraiture emphasizes the extent to which the "play of gestures" available to studio workers came to assume a signifying role in the representation of individual players. With innovations in style, props, and lighting and increasing use of theatrical and Hollywood portraiture techniques to glamourize musicians, the studio portrait represented a marked break in the way jazz musicians had previously been portrayed. Drawing on their own life experiences and often finding a bond with black jazz musicians, émigré studio photographers made a particularly significant contribution.

In an era when music was explicitly racialized, it is significant however that this development was largely a product of white-owned studios. Other than in their use of iconic musical instruments as an "occupational" signifier, photographers deployed stylistic tropes and techniques drawn from the general run of their portraiture practices. Framing black musicians with production values commonly found in the presentation of white artists, actors, and film stars, these portraits confirmed the rising status of the leading players and their engagement with commercial popular entertainment; and, while this did much to raise the cultural capital of individual musicians, it also reflects the delicate racial negotiations faced by many African American musicians and band leaders from the mid-1920s onward. Louis Armstrong's solo portraits demonstrate his rising status as a musician, but his ascent created a dilemma for other black jazz players after around 1926 as to how they might build on his advances yet appeal to white audiences. Publicity portraiture was a key element in this process of identification.[65]

Ted Allen's 1948 photograph *Benny Carter Wearing White Suit* is perhaps an appropriate end point for this discussion. Ted Allan, who began his career in Los Angeles creating drawings, paintings, and pastels from still photographs for Metropolitan Theatre lobbies, was one of the most accomplished of the Hollywood portraitists and by the 1960s was under personal contract to Frank Sinatra. Known as "Rembrandt" for his lighting skills, Allen "adhered to the portrait photographer's mandate, to make mere men and women into objects of fantasy [. . .] with poses and dramatic lighting [. . .] and retouching." Allen's portrait identifies Carter through the discrete incorporation of the saxophone; but with his polished "tailored suits and tuxedos, likewise well-groomed coif and upright posture with serious demeanor," the portrait is most notable for the manner in which he represents the jazz musician in the form of a "traditional dandy."[66] The 1948 portrait is one of a series of the musician made by Allen in the 1940s as Carter gave up the life of a touring bandleader and began working extensively in the Hollywood studios, composing, directing, and arranging. It is fitting that Carter's determination and superb musical skills played an important role in breaking down racial barriers in Hollywood and in creating a merger between the black and white sections of the AFM in Los Angeles.

It would fall to the "new generation" of white art photographers from the 1930s onward to elaborate a more pointed and specifically jazz aesthetic centered on notions of authenticity and artistry; the work of these photographers will be explored in Chapter 8. At the same time as jazz musicians entered the portrait studio, photography was being taken up by increasing numbers of African Americans. Their approach, which is the subject of the next two chapters, suggests many points of contrast with the studio workers discussed in this chapter.

Notes

1. Peter Bacon Hales, *Silver Cities: Photographing American Urbanization, 1839–1939* (Albuquerque: University of New Mexico Press, 2005), 16, 216; Miles Orvell, *American Photography* (Oxford: Oxford University Press, 2003), 21–29, 58–70.
2. Gottfried Boehm, "Es Zeight Sich: Geste-Deixis-Bild," in *Hold It!: Zur Pose Zwischen Bild Und Performance, Theater Der Zeit*, ed. John Hoberman (Berlin: Theater der Zeit-Recherchen 89, 2012), 22–40; Marshall McLuhan, *Understanding Media* (Cambridge, MA: MIT Press, 1994), 197; Kelley E. Wilder, "Disdéri, André-Adolphe-Eugène," in *Oxford Companion to the Photograph*, ed. Robin Lenham (Oxford: Oxford University Press, 2005), 173; Susanne Holschbach, "The Pose: Its Troubles and Pleasures," in *Street & Studio: An Urban History of Photography*, ed. U. Eskildsen, F. Ebner, and B. Kaufmann (London: Tate Modern, 2008), 171–77.
3. The two photographs can be compared in Mary Collins, *Oh, Didn't He Ramble: The Life Story of Lee Collins*, ed. Frank J. Gillis and John W. Miner (Oxford: Bayou Press, 1989), 70.
4. Richard M. Sudhalter, Philip R. Evans, and William Dean-Myatt, *Bix: Man & Legend* (London: Quartet Books, 1974), 59. The photograph was used on the cover of David R. Collins's 1998 biography of Beiderbecke.
5. David S. Shields, *Still: American Silent Motion Picture Photography* (Chicago: University of Chicago Press, 2013), esp. 1–50, and the same author's "Photography & the American Stage," Broadway Photographs, 2019, https://broadway.cas.sc.edu/.Broadway Photographs website at www.broadway.cas.ec.edu; Barbara McCandless, "The Portrait Studio and the Celebrity," in *Photography in Nineteenth Century America*, ed. Martha A. Sandsweiss (New York: Harry N. Abrams, 1991), 48–75.
6. Arthur Frank Wertheim, *Vaudeville Wars: How the Keith-Albee and the Orpheum Circuits Controlled the Big-Time and Its Performers* (New York: Palgrave Macmillan, 2006), 95–96.
7. David S. Shields, "Kansas City Style: The Artist's Hand and the Vaudeville Portrait 1912–1930," Broadway Photographs, https://www.broadway.cas.sc.edu/content/kansas-city-style-artists-hand-and-vaudeville-portrait-1912-1930; Strauss Peyton, "Strauss Peyton:Exceptional Portraiture," Strauss Peyton website, n.d., http://www.strausspeytonkc.com/blog/history-strauss-peyton/.; Minnesota Historical Society, "Directory of Minnesota Photographers," accessed November 10, 2017, https://www.mnhs.org/people/photographers/S.php.
8. Scott W. Raether, *Wisconsin Family Albums & Photographer's Imprints and Biographies 1800s to Early 1900s* (Xlibris, 2013), 238.
9. Shields, "Kansas City Style: The Artist's Hand and the Vaudeville Portrait 1912–1930"; Sandor Demlinger and John Steiner, *Destination Chicago Jazz* (New York: Arcadia, 2003), 7–8; Larry Vishochil, "Photography," Encyclopedia of Chicago, n.d., http://www.encyclopedia.chicagohistory.org/pages/967.html.
10. Shields, "Kansas City Style: The Artist's Hand and the Vaudeville Portrait 1912–1930."
11. John Kobal, *The Art of the Great Hollywood Portrait Photographers 1925–1940* (London: Allen Lane, 1980), 23, 16.
12. To avoid repetitious references, sources consulted for this section are listed here: Robert Dance, "The Hollywood Studio Photographers," in *Glamour of the Gods: Photographs from the John Kobal Foundation*, ed. Robert Dance and John Taylor (Göttingen: Steidl, 2008), 20–35; and Robert Dance and Bruce Robertsdon, *Ruth Harriet Louise and Hollywood Glamour Photography* (Berkeley: University of California Press, 2002); John Kobal, ed., *Hollywood Glamour Portraits: 145 Photos of Stars 1926–1949* (New York: Dover, 1976); and *The Art of the Great Hollywood Portrait Photographers 1925–1940*; Roman Freulich and Joan Abramson, *Forty Years in Hollywood: Portraits of a Golden Age* (South Brunswick, NJ: A.S. Barnes, 1971); Terence Pepper and John Kobal, *The Man Who Shot Garbo: The Hollywood Photographs of Clarence Sinclair Bull* (London: National Portrait Gallery, 1989); Fahey and Rich, *Masters of Starlight: Photographers in Hollywood*. Clarence Sinclair Bull and Raymond Lee, *The Faces of Hollywood* (South Brunswick, NJ: A.S. Barnes, 1968); John Engstead, *Star Shots: Fifty Years of Pictures and Stories by One of Hollywood's Greatest Photographers* (London: Columbus Books, 1978); and Joel W. Finler, *Hollywood Movie Stills: Art and Technique in the Golden Age of the Studios* (London: Titan Books, 2012).
13. Hurrell quoted by Fahey and Rich, *Masters of Starlight: Photographers in Hollywood*, 19.

14. Bull quoted by Pepper and John Kobal, *The Man Who Shot Garbo*, 16.
15. John Raeburn, *A Staggering Revolution: A Cultural History of Thirties Photography* (Urbana: University of Illinois Press, 2006), 12.
16. *Los Angeles Times*, May 31, 1931: 33.
17. Warren Susman, *Culture as History: The Transformation of American Society in the Twentieth Century* (New York: Pantheon Books, 1984), 271–85.
18. Willinger quoted by Kobal, *The Art of the Great Hollywood Portrait Photographers 1925–1940*, 258; Steve Ditlea, "American Glamour," *Esquire*, July 1, 1980, 40; Nigel Thrift, "Understanding the Material Practices of Glamour," in *The Affect Theory Reader*, ed. Melissa Gregg and Gregory J. Seigworth (Durham, NC: Duke University Press, 2010), 296–97. See also Anne H. Hoy, "'I'm Ready for My Close-Up': Hollywood's Glamour Photographs," in *Silver Screen Silver Prints: Hollywood Glamour Portraits from the Robert Dance Collection* (New York: Grolier Club, 2011), 11.
19. Astrid Huopalainen, "Manipulating Surface and Producing 'Effortless' Elegance-Analysing the Social Organisation of Glamour," *Culture and Organization* (2016): 4.
20. Helen Wilkinson, "'The New Heraldry': Stock Photography, Visual Literacy and Advertising in 1930s Britain," *Journal of Design History* 10, no. 1 (1997): 23–38.
21. See further Michael Carlebach, *Working Stiffs: Occupational Portraits in the Age of Tintypes.* (Washington, DC: Smithsonian Institution Press, 2002); Steven Kasher, "Democratic Visages: The Tintype and America," in *America and the Tintype*, (Stedl, 2008): 35–39, Janice G. Schimmelman, "The Tintype in America 1856–1880," *Transactions of the American Philosophical Society* 97, no. 2 (2007): 189–200, 202–206. Rose and Suchon made the link between the occupational portrait and later jazz images by reproducing a typical occupational tintype as the frontispiece to their *New Orleans Jazz: A Family Album.*
22. Dixie W. Dittfurth, Wiles Photographic Collection 1896–1910 (Memphis, TN: University of Memphis Special Collections, 1993) http://sostngovbuckets.s3.amazonaws.com/tsla/history/manuscripts/findingaids/WILES_PHOTOGRAPHIC_COLLECTION_1896-1910.pdf.
23. Frank Driggs and Harris Lewine, *Black Beauty, White Heat: A Pictorial History of Jazz 1920–1950* (New York: Da Capo, 1995), 24; Leonard Feather and Ira Gitler, *The Biographical Encyclopaedia of Jazz* (Oxford: Oxford University Press, 1999), 987–88; Jeffrey Magee, *Fletcher Henderson: The Uncrowned King of Swing* (Oxford: Oxford University Press, 2005), 27–37.
24. T. Stoddard, ed., *Pops Foster: The Autobiography of a New Orleans Jazzman* (Berkeley: University of California Press, 1971), 76.
25. Although the practice increased as musicians migrated to Chicago and other northern cities, "Pops" Foster claimed that the use of the leader's name started in New Orleans with Kid Ory: Stoddard, *Pops Foster: The Autobiography of a New Orleans Jazzman*, 51. William H. Kenney, *Chicago Jazz: A Cultural History, 1904–1930* (New York: Oxford University Press, 1993), 40–41, quotes Edmond Suchon's comparison of Oliver in his New Orleans days and as a "star" in Chicago. Rising professional standards came as a shock to "some New Orleans musicians [who] had rarely thought of themselves as professionals, living as manual labourers who also played weekend gigs."
26. Douglas Henry Daniels, *Lester Leaps In: The Life and Times of Lester "Pres" Young* (Boston, MA: Beacon Press, 2002), 129–34, 139.
27. Charles A. Sengstock Jr., *That Toodlin' Town: Chicago's White Dance Bands and Orchestras 1900–1950* (Chicago: University of Chicago Press, 2004), 29; Thomas J. Hennessey, *From Jazz to Swing: African-American Jazz Musicians and Their Music 1890–1935* (Detroit, MI: Wayne State University Press, 1994), 80.
28. Albert Murray, *Good Morning Blues: The Autobiography of Count Basie* (New York: Da Capo, 1995), 166–67, for Basie's own account of this deal; Daniels, *Lester Leaps In: The Life and Times of Lester "Pres" Young*, 208–9, reports Noble Sissle's views.
29. Kenney, *Chicago Jazz: A Cultural History, 1904–1930*, 85–86.
30. For an example of a race record cover see R. Collins, *New Orleans Jazz: A Revised History* (New York: Vantage Press, 1996), 239. Alyn Shipton, *The Art of Jazz: A Visual History* (Watertown, MA: Imagine, 2020), 23, illustrates early sheet music covers. A publicity poster is reproduced in "No Title," *The Jazz Archivist* 3, no. 1 (1988). See also Sandor Demlinger and John Steiner, *Destination Chicago Jazz* (Stroud: Tempus, 2003), 157.
31. The photographs are reproduced in Stanley Baron, *Benny King of Swing: A Pictorial Biography* (London: Thames & Hudson, 1979), n.pag.

32. Nat Shapiro and Nat Hentoff, *Hear Me Talkin' to Ya* (New York: Dover Books, 1955), 109.
33. Ron Seymour, "Photographer to the Celebrities," n.d., https://ronseymour.com/the-maurice-seymour-gallery; Bloom's advertisement is shown in "What's in a Name?," n.d; Bentley Historical Library, "Lens on Gibson," Magazine, https://bentley.umich.edu/news-events/magazine/lens-on-gibson/.
34. Theatrical's photograph is reproduced by Keepnews and Grauer Jr., *A Pictorial of Jazz: People and Places from New Orleans to Modern Jazz*, 53.
35. Shields, "Studio, Apeda"; Casetext, "White Studio, Inc. v Dreyfoos," 1913, https://casetext.com/case/white-studio-inc-v-dreyfoos.
36. Shipton, *The Art of Jazz: A Visual History*, 46.
37. Deborah Dash Moore, "The Urban Vision of East European Jewish Immigrants to New York," in *Proceedings of the World Congress of Jewish Studies* (World Union of Jewish Studies, 1981), 31–38. See further Roger Daniels, *Coming to America: A History of Immigration and Ethnicity in American Life* (New York: Harper Collins, 1990), 230; Caryn Aviv and David Shneer, *New Jews: The End of the Jewish Diaspora* (New York: New York University Press, 2005), 139. Irving Howe, *World of Our Fathers: The Journey of East European Jews to America* (London: Phoenix Press, 1976), 163, notes that mention of photography businesses first appeared in the *Jewish Daily Forward* in the 1900s.
38. Michael Berkowitz, *Jews and Photography in Britain* (Austin: University of Texas Press, 2015), 2–3. On Jewish aniconism see Kalman Bland, *The Artless Jew: Medieval and Modern Affirmations and Denials of the Visual* (Princeton, NJ: Princeton University Press, 2000), 14–33, 39–40 and Anthony Julius *Idolizing Pictures: Idolatry, Iconoclasm and Jewish Art (Walter Neurath Memorial Lectures)* (London: Thames & Hudson, 2001). Growing Jewish engagement with twentieth-century visual culture has been documented by Richard I. Cohen, "The Visual Revolution in Jewish Life," in *Visualizing and Exhibiting Jewish Space and History: Studies in Contemporary Jewry XXVI* (Oxford: Oxford University Press, 2019), 3–24..
39. Nahum (Tim) Gidal, "Jews in Photography," in *Leo Baeck Institute Yearbook* 32, 1987, 437–53; John G. Morris, *Get the Picture: A Personal History of Photojournalism* (Chicago: University of Chicago Press, 1998), 29. William J. Myers, "Jews and Photography," Commentary, 2003, https://www.commentarymagazine.com/articles/jews-and-photography/, emphasizes the attractions of a new technology to Jewish photographers. See also Colin Ford, "Photography: Hungary's Greatest Export," in *Eyewitness: Hungarian Photography in the Twentieth Century*, ed. Peter Baki, Colin Ford, and George Szirtes (London: Royal Academy of Arts, 2011), 13; David Shneer, *Through Soviet Jewish Eyes: Photography, War and the Holocaust* (New Brunswick, NJ: Rutgers University Press, 2011), 15–16 and Olga Gershenson and David Shneer, "Soviet Jewishness and Cultural Studies," *Journal of Jewish Identities* 4, no. 1 (2011): 133. On the participation of Jewish women see Andrea Winklbauer, *Vienna's Shooting Girls – Jüdische Fotografinnen Aus Wien* (Judisches Museum Wien, 2012); John March, "Gerty Simon's Berlin Years, c.1919–1933," in *Berlin-London: The Lost Photographs of Gerty Simon*, ed. Barbara Warnock and John March (London: Wiener Library, 2019), 11–18 and Deborah Dash Moore, *Young Jewish Women with Cameras* (Bloomington: Indiana University Press, 2011).
40. Howe, *World of Our Fathers: The Journey of East European Jews to America*, 164–65. The Jewish involvement in Hollywood extended well beyond famous studio moguls such as Laaemmele, Goldwyn, Meyer, Warner, and Selznick. It has been estimated that in all no fewer than 800 Jews had worked, or were still working, in Hollywood by 1950: Doris Berger, "Illuminated Darkness: Exiles and Émigrés in the Golden Age of Hollywood," *Jewish Culture and History* 17, nos. 1–2 (2016): 81.
41. The words of the *Jewish Messenger*, an uptown weekly favored by German Jews cited by Howe, *World of Our Fathers: The Journey of East European Jews to America*, 230.
42. Neal Gabler, *An Empire of Their Own: How the Jews Invented Hollywood* (New York: Crown, 1988), 4.
43. Deborah Dash Moore, *At Home in America: Second Generation New York Jews* (New York: Columbia University Press, 1981), 6; Cheryl Lynn Greenberg, *Troubling the Waters: Black-Jewish Relations in the American Century* (Princeton: Princeton University Press, 2006), 37–40.
44. Samantha Baskind, "Weegee's Jewishness," *History of Photography Journal* 34, no. 1 (2010): 60–78; David Serlin and Jesse Lerner, "Weegee and the Jewish Question," *Wide Angle* 19, no. 4 (1997): 1–9.
45. Greenberg, *Troubling the Waters: Black-Jewish Relations in the American Century*, 15–47. Nat

Hentoff, *Boston Boy: Growing Up with Jazz and Other Rebellious Passions* (Boston, MA: Faber & Faber, 1986), 4, describes the challenges to established German Jews in Boston posed by the arrival of the *Ostjuden*.

46. Moore, *At Home in America: Second Generation New York Jews*, 9 and "At Home in America?: Revisiting the Second Generation," *Journal of American Ethnic History*, 2006, 156–68. Daniels, *Coming to America: A History of Immigration and Ethnicity* 230; Caryn Aviv and David Shneer, *New Jews: The End of the Jewish Diaspora* (New York: New York University Press, 2005), 139.
47. Obituary, "Maurice Seymour: Photographed Stars," *Chicago Tribune*, October 9, 1993 19; Joseph Haas, "The Saga Behind the Signature, 'Maurice Seymour, Chicago,'" *Chicago Daily News*, May 11, 1968; David Shields, "Maurice Seymour," Broadway Photographs, https://www.broadway.cas.sc.edu/content/maurice-seymour.
48. The most complete and accurate biography of Korman is provided by Clyde Adams, "The One Big Name," Murray Korman Photography, 2017, https://www.murraykorman.com/bio. The author is grateful to Clyde Adams for his comments on this section. See also David Shields, "Murray Korman," *Broadway Photographs*, https://broadway.cas.sc.edu/content/murray-korman, John Ferris, "Dancers or Deb, Korman's Lens Pleases Them All," *Baltimore Sun*, June 1, 1941, p. 10; George Ross, "Showgirls' Favourite Photographer Turns Lens on Debs," *Wausau Daily Record-Herald*, March 14, 1939, p.6.
49. Clyde Adams, Correspondence with the Author, September 2, 2020.
50. All quotations taken from Susan Bernard, "Introduction," in *Bernard of Hollywood* (Koln: Taschen, 2002), 7–14. For the photographer's life and work see also Ann V. Masters, "Behind the Star-Studded Camera: Bruno of Hollywood," *Bridgeport Sunday Post*, September 21, 1969, E1; Kevin Thomas, "When Sex Was Innocent, Sweet and Seductive," *Los Angeles Times-Book Review*, 2002, p. 8; Suzanne Muchnic, "Bernard: He Wanted Out, Is Now In," *Los Angeles Times-Calendar*, January 8, 1984, p. 4; Burt A. Folkart, "Photographer Bruno Bernard Dies at 75," *Los Angeles Times*, June 9, 1987, p.6.
51. Gayle F. Wald, *Shout, Sister, Shout!: The Untold Story of Rock-and-Roll Trailblazer Sister Rosetta Tharpe* (Boston, MA: Beacon Press, 2007), 39; Nadine Cohodas, *Queen: The Life and Music of Dinah Washington* (New York: Knopf Doubleday, 2004), 411; Larry Applebaum, "Before & After: Sonny Rollins" https://larryappelbaum.wordpress.com/2011/09/07/before-after-sonny-rollins-2/, Rollins elaborates on the story in Jean Bach's film *A Great Day in Harlem* at 00:24:00.
52. With more than 160 credits in Michael Och's pictorial history, Kriegsmann captured more singers and musicians in the early days of rock 'n' roll than any other photographer: Michael Ochs, *Rock Archives: A Photographic Journey Through the First Two Decades of Rock & Roll* (Poole, Dorset: Blandford Press, 1985), 396.
53. Quoted by Vincent M. Mallozzi, "Behind the Lens, Continuing a Legacy," *New York Times*, January 11, 2010, https://www.nytimes.com/2010/01/11/nyregion/11photog.html. Benjamin Cawthra's *Blue Notes in Black and White*, to date the only full-length treatment of jazz photography, does not mention Kriegsmann. Beyond the jazz literature, the only extended text on Kriegsmann is Janis Bultman, "James J. Kriegsmann: An Eye for Entertainers," in *Legacies: Interviews with Masters of Photography* (Coralville, IA: Quercus Agrifolia Press, Kindle ed., 2018), n. pag. Otherwise mention of Kriegsmann is confined to the following brief newspaper, magazine, and online articles: Frank V. Chambers, "James J. Kriegsmann," *Camera: A Practical Magazine for Photographers*, January 1944, pp. 60–64; Steve Ditlea, "American Glamour," *Esquire*, July 1, 1980, pp. 40–46; Mallozzi, "Behind the Lens, Continuing a Legacy," Vivien Raynor, "Art; From the Famous to the Nameless," *New York Times*, June 14, 1998, https://www.nytimes.com/1998/06/14/nyregion/art-from-the-famous-to-the-nameless.html, Jennifer Sharpe, "Dumpster of Forgotten Musicians Launches Quest," *NPR*, 2007 https://www.npr.org/templates/story/story.php?storyId=15772871, accessed April 4, 2019; and Anon., "Obituary: James J. Kriegsmann; Theatrical Photographer, 85," *New York Times*, May 1, 1994, 5.1, p. 54.
54. The menu card is now lost although James J. Kriegsmann, Jr. recalls seeing it among his father's papers: Interview with James J. Kriegsmann, Jr. October 2018.
55. Estimate by James J. Kriegsmann Jr.: author interview.
56. All quotations in this paragraph—author interview.
57. James J. Kriegsmann Jr. quoted by Mallozzi and author interview.

58. Kriegsmann quoted by Janis Bultman, n.p. Bultman, who spoke to Kriegsmann in November 1986, confirmed in an interview with the author in July 2018 that the statement was made with considerable feeling.
59. Quoted by Bultman, n.pag.
60. Kriegsmann's retouching practices have led jazz aficionados to question how "realistic" his portraits of musicians really were—see for example "IS THIS WHAT CHARLIE PARKER ACTUALLY LOOKED LIKE?!?!," *Jazz Guitar Online*, 2018, https://www.jazzguitar.be/forum/players/66492-what-charlie-parker-actually-looked-like-print.html.
61. I am grateful to Peter Vacher for pointing this out to me.
62. Mallozzi, "Behind the Lens," A15.
63. Frances Osborn Robb, *Shot in Alabama: A History of Photography 1839–1941* (Birmingham: University of Alabama Press, 2016), 211.
64. David Shields, "George Maillard Kesslère," Broadway Photographs, n.d., https://www.broadway.cas.sc.edu/content/g-maillard-kesslere. Maillard Kesslère's part in Helena Rubenstein's "modernist display" is discussed by Marie J. Clifford, "Helena Rubenstein's Beauty Salons, Fashion and Modernist Display," *Winterthur Portfolio* 38, nos. 2–3 (2003): 83–108.
65. Magee, *Fletcher Henderson: The Uncrowned King of Swing*, 98–99, provides an account of the dilemma Armstrong's "hot" chorus rooted in African American heritage posed for Fletcher Henderson and other black bands following in his wake.
66. Catalogue entry in Edward Maeder (ed.), *Hollywood and History: Costume Design in Film* (Los Angeles: Thames & Hudson/LA County Museum of Art, 1987); Alphonso D. McClendon, *Fashion and Jazz: Dress, Identity and Subcultural Improvisation* (London: Bloomsbury, 2015), 135. Ted Allen's photograph *Benny Cater Wearing White Suit* is in the LaBudde Special Collections—Dave Dexter Collection now at UMKC University Library and can be viewed online at https://dl.mospace.umsystem.edu/umkc/islandora/object/umkc%3A2412.

6

Document and Realism

Early African American Jazz Photography

The photographers responsible for many of the very earliest jazz photographs are frequently unidentified. While it is often assumed that few were taken by black photographers we do know that the early decades of the twentieth century witnessed the rapid growth of African American photography studios and ownership of photographs by black families. Henry A. and Robert B. Hooks, who established their Memphis studio in 1900, typify this new breed of photographers. Continuing in business until 1984, it has been claimed that every black family in Memphis has a Hooks Bros. photograph.[1] The studio's archive comprises a remarkable record of a community outside mainstream America, an alternate black city with its own doctors, lawyers, bankers, businessmen, ministers, schoolteachers, laborers, shopkeepers, musicians, restaurateurs, hoteliers, and barbers. Earnestine Lovell Jenkins considers Hooks Bros. to have been "the equivalent of James Van Der Zee and Addison Scurlock," photographers who "made discernible the aspirations, hopes and dreams of a people" in Memphis much as Van Der Zee had done in Manhattan and Scurlock from his practice at Howard. Hooks Bros. photographs provide an early example of the insertion of black imagery into the emerging black print culture of books, magazines, and newspapers, providing what Jenkins elsewhere describes as "a hidden transcript, the world of segregated Memphis."[2]

Music was firmly part of the black community's activities and the Hooks brothers left a valuable record of black entertainment personalities from the worlds of cinema, gospel, jazz, and blues music. The studio is known to have made one of only two surviving photographs of the Delta bluesman Robert Johnson and their portrait of W. C. Handy, taken in Memphis where he had lived since 1909 (Figure 75), typifies the way in which the photographers took care to record middle-class achievements and frame their portraits of prominent race leaders. Adapting the conventions of portraiture to African American subjects, the photographers were careful to capture variations in skin tones through the use of lighting and backdrops and focus on the face and its expression, often experimenting with different poses to achieve the desired effect; sitters were sometimes required to fix their gaze outside the picture's frame of reference, the turned head conveying a sense of refinement and distinction, while on other occasions to pose confidently *en face* in conformity with the "New Negro" aesthetic.[3] The portrait provides a striking visual confirmation of the way in which Handy had shifted the broad understanding of the blues; rearranging and embellishing the "low folk forms" Handy had first heard from Delta bluesmen, the elevated presentation of Handy by the Hooks' brothers underscores Albert Murray's contention that he had moved the blues beyond the realm of folk expression and made the form attractive to more sophisticated musicians.[4]

The Hooks' studio space could accommodate only individual or small group portraits. African American studios of the period were often very basic: props

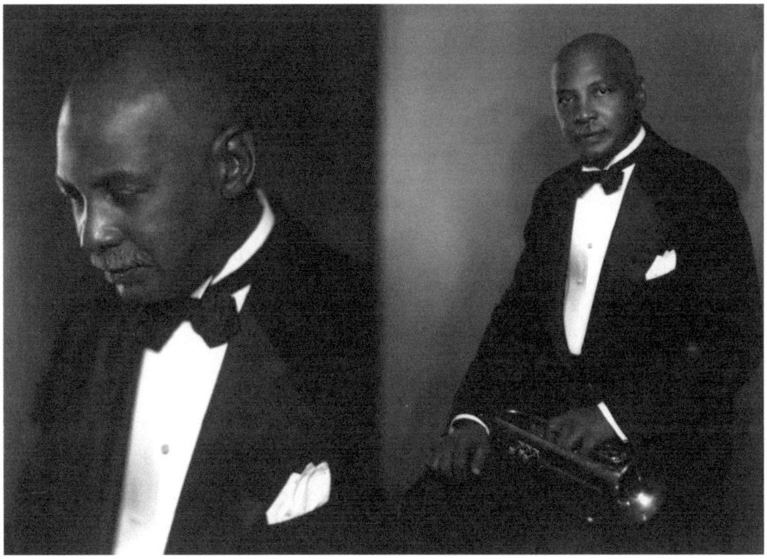

Figure 75: Henry and Robert Hooks. *W. C. Handy*. Memphis. 1920s.
Department of Art, University of Memphis, Charles Church Collection. Courtesy of Earnestine Lovelle Jenkins.

were minimal and bare floorboards, worn carpets or linoleum on the floor were the norm. A small selection of painted backdrops might be changed according to the sitter. One or two lights might have been deployed on a horizontal axis and the prefocused cameras aperture was set to deliver a shallow depth of field. The small space meant that sitters were hard up against the backdrop, flattening the subject within the image plane. The rooms used as studio space by Hooks Bros. had large south-facing windows that allowed natural light to enter, minimizing the need for artificial lighting.[5] It is not surprising therefore to find that many of their band photographs were made on location. Hooks' photograph of a group of musicians led by trumpeter Charlie Williamson, who appeared regularly at the Palace and Daisy Theatres in Memphis, suggests a theatre or backstage setting as the group was probably too large to assemble in the Hooks' studio.

Increasingly aware of the representational power of the camera, a new generation of black photographers like Hooks drew inspiration from inside the black community, laying the foundations for a realist aesthetic that reflected the social position of African Americans. Nourished by deeply rooted communal ties and relationships, their photographs of musicians and musical events must be seen not so much as a separate form of artistic endeavor but as one expression of "the observed and intuitive truth of the black experience."[6] In New Orleans the Creole photographers Arthur Bedou and Villard Paddio made images that speak back to us about the place of musicians and bands in early New Orleans jazz, the relationships between musicians and the ensemble, and the role played by race in the complex racial and ethnic patterning of New Orleans. Equally concerned with black self-image, photographers like James Van Der Zee, Edward Elcha, Caroll T. Maynard, and Woodard's Studio approached their subject as part of a general concern to represent the practices and rituals of black life in a realist and affirmative light.

I. Black photography in the early twentieth century

The development of black photography

Only around fifty black-run photography studios and galleries have been documented as operating by 1850, mostly run by those outside the slave economy such as Jules Lion in New Orleans and Shandy Wesley Jones in Tuscaloosa, Alabama.[7] Black portraiture studios grew slowly in the years following the Reconstruction as men and women of color established themselves as photographic artists or as managers of white-owned studios. Mary E. Warren, the first recorded black woman photographer, Glenalvin Goodridge, Daniel Freeman, James Presley Ball, Augustus Washington, Richard Robert, Herbert Collins, Harry Shepherd, George O. Brown, and Arthur Laidler MacBeth are among the better documented of these early photographers. By the turn of the century, Addison Scurlock, Howard University's official photographer, and Cornelius M. Battey, the first director of photography at the Tuskegee Institute in Alabama, had emerged as nationally recognized portrait photographers.[8]

By around 1910 the cost of purchasing a camera, lens, tripod, and film with a supply of developing and printing materials had fallen to around $10 while a ten-day training course might cost about the same again. This was sufficiently low to encourage entrepreneurial blacks (including, as Jeanne Moutoussamy-Ashe reminds us, many women) to set up shop at the heart of black urban communities. Education in photographic skills was encouraged at new African American educational institutions such as the Tuskegee Institute in Alabama while informal training through correspondence courses spread ideas more widely. Patronage and support for black photographers began slowly to become available and by the late-1920s and early-1930s black photographers were coming to be included in the Harmon Foundation competitions and exhibitions. These developments paralleled improvements in the finished appearance of family and studio portraits as sepia tones were replaced by rich blacks and glowing whites and photographers took to mounting their photographs within the mat rather than using glue.[9]

Only 404 African American photographers (against 31,257 whites) were officially registered in 1900, although this is almost certainly an underestimate. The accelerating growth of black-owned photographic studios in the first decades of the new century points to emerging demand for portraits on the part of urban African American families. Historians have often linked this growth with the development of the northern "black Metropolises," in which large and increasingly self-conscious African American families were demanding familial portraiture, but there is evidence that black photography was just as strongly represented in southern urban areas.[10] By the 1920s this demand was being met by professional portraitists such as Lucy Calloway, Walter Baker, the Vernon & King studio, Herbert Collins, Perry A. Keith, the pictorialist King Daniel Ganaway in Chicago, James Conway Fraley in Richmond, VA, Edgar Eugene Phipps, James Van Der Zee, and James Lattimer Allen. Allen Edward Cole in Cleveland and Prentice Herman Polk, Battey's student at Tuskegee and a noted educator, also established important reputations. The work of Herbert Collins and Hamilton Smith (Boston), Frank Harris (Philadelphia), William E. Woodard (Chicago), Frank Cloud (Birmingham, Alabama, and later Los Angeles), Edwin and Elise Harleston and Frank G Smith (Los Angeles) and Walter J Stephens (Syracuse NJ) is also now well documented. James P. Newton, the Hooks Bros., the Rev. Lonzie Odie Taylor, Mark Stansbury, and R. Earl Williams were leading portraitist in Memphis. In smaller neighborhoods, such as North Webster, a black community in a middle-class suburb of St. Louis, Missouri, where Craig Studios established a central position, and Orange Mound, Tennessee, where Charles Williams operated a successful studio business for many years, black photographers put down deep roots.[11]

"First-generation" concerns

In a seminal essay, Allan Sekula has argued that "photography came to establish and delimit the terrain of the other."[12] Empirical research confirms Sekula's judgment that photographic representations nourished racial ideologies and the creation of racial typologies. Paradoxically, when placed in the hands of those who suffered most, photography also proved itself to be an effective mode of challenging these representations.

Cowed by mob rule and lynch law, the position of the black population between the end of Reconstruction in 1877 and 1918 was as bad as at any time since the end of the Civil War. Yet the legal gains of the Civil War had brought a degree of social improvement for black Americans: "There was a new dignity, a new pride, a new self-respect [. . .] The evidence lay [. . .] in their quiet, undramatic attempts to assume their responsibilities as members of an advanced and changing social order."[13] The ending of the slave economy began to weaken black self-containment but left African Americans culturally marginalized between two worlds. Freedom offered possibilities of acculturation and accommodation but it was limited and uneven and the pull of the black community as a source of security remained strong.[14] It was in this period that first-generation black identity was formed—a proud but still essentially defensive identity nurtured in a separate and segregated world recovering from the cultural trauma of slavery and abolition. Turning inward for succor and solidarity, family life and community with its institutions and rituals became the touchstone of black existence. In education, religion, social welfare, and cultural expression, African Americans built their own institutions separate from those of the whites, a black world with all the trappings of an entirely separate community.[15] It is here that we find the dominant concerns of the first generation of black photographers.

Mid-nineteenth-century photographers like Ball, Shepherd, and Washington were strongly committed to the abolitionist cause; and the potential of photography to counter prejudice and the caricaturing of black people in the scientific and popular media of the period was recognized by Frederick Douglass, Ida B. Wells-Barnett, Paul Laurence Dunbar, and W. E. B. Du Bois.[16] Even so, the dominant response of late-nineteenth and early-twentieth-century black photographers was to turn inward towards black life and its institutions, events, and rituals. The Philadelphia photographer Leon Gardiner, with his "unrelenting determinism" to make known black history and achievements, provides a striking example.[17] Unable to penetrate the worlds of fashion, advertising, or amateur photographic societies, black practitioners searched for realistic and affirmative representations of the world they knew best:[18]

> *The image of the family and community unit: its celebrations [. . .] its grievings [. . .] and its contributions to the workplace [. . .] There is great implicit respect in these works for the camera and its ability to thrust an image or an idea into perpetuity. Exceeding care was taken to show the individual and the culture at its very best, as much a function of the commercial nature of these works as the photographers' personal reluctance to turn the lens on the unfairness of life, black or white.*

African American photographers had little contact with white photographers, new techniques, or modernist experimentation. Standing outside the "two stories" of art and vernacular photography that Peter Galassi identified as the driving dynamic of American photography, black photographers might have been expected to develop a distinctive visual language through which to express these concerns.[19] Several scholars have argued that this was not the case. In Constance Schulz's view African American photographers "mimicked white middle class cultural patterns" at least until the shock of Gordon Park's "American Gothic." Alan Govenar agrees that late-nineteenth century black photographs "do not differ significantly in style from those made of and by their white counterparts" while Nicholas Natanson makes the point that the pressure on black photographers to earn a living forced most to fall in line with market forces rather than pursue "artistic" goals. Marginalized as black Americans might have been it seems to these writers that white acculturating influence could not be completely avoided.[20]

Paul von Blum explains however that a restricted formalist reading of black photography can be misleading, arguing that emphasis should be shifted toward the value standards of groups marginalized by political power and the dominant culture.[21] Assessed in this light, the beginnings of a shift in cultural power cannot be denied: "Once you put a camera in someone's hands, that person is transformed as profoundly as the subjects he or she photographs [. . .] In the hands of such subjects, images can compensate for the lack of material advantages and momentarily create a level playing field."[22] The use of photography by African Americans was a conscious intervention into the space of representation, the beginnings of reclaiming black identity from the normative order. As the lawyer, judge, and civil rights activist D'Army Bailey recalled:[23]

> *We had our portraits made to reinforce our own stereotypes, which were positive. We saw ourselves as sharp. Our shoes were shined, our pants were pressed, and we were very well presented. We had lots of self-pride and pictures provided an affirmation [. . .] We weren't sending messages to white people. We were sending messages to each other, sharing evidence of our vision of ourselves.*

Considerable evidence supports the idea that photography could be used as a positive countervailing force. The critic bell hooks has vividly described how sitting for portraits, collecting photographs of family and friends in parlor books, documenting day-to-day life, or practicing photography helped African Americans to create and sustain a sense of selfhood and resist misrepresentation. For Maurice O. Wallace and Shawn Michelle Smith black photography was "a political tool with which to claim a place in public and private spheres circumscribed by race and racialized sight lines." The act of taking a photograph is symbolic of agency and these writers echo Von Blum's contention that the image should be understood in both literal and figurative terms. Photography was particularly important to black families experiencing the transition to metropolitan life as Douglas Henry Daniels found with black urban settlers in San Francisco; and self-portraiture has been seen as "transformative," an opportunity to face the viewer squarely and proudly in an age when a glance could confirm racial inferiority and even retribution. Perhaps more than any other scholar, Deborah Willis has established that placing a camera in black hands made counterrepresentation possible by celebrating the achievements of black subjects and conveying a sense of self and self-worth.[24]

The modalities through which photography might reveal communal relations have yet to be fully explored. The assumption that photography is capable of indexically capturing the essence of communal relationships is generally unquestioned by historians of black photography. Louis Kaplan has proposed the idea that the relationship between photography and community might be expository—the manner in which photography enables viewers to "expose" themselves to others, to enter into a relationship with the "outside." Communal identity does not reside in a stable core but on the margins, where its limits are set by inclusion and exclusion. Kaplan however accepts that indexical and expository theories can bring photography and community into dialogue with each other and it is worth bearing in mind that black photographers saw confirmation of difference in both signs of communal relations and the limits of those relationships.[25]

II. New Orleans Band Photography

A 1924 photograph of the Original Tuxedo Orchestra (Figure 76) shows the leader, Oscar Philip "Papa" Celestin (seated, second right), surrounded by the members of the band with which he was associated for nearly fifty years.[26] Immaculately turned out, the players emphasize their identity as band members with identical dress and symmetrical display of instruments; their status as an "orchestra" is asserted by the studied formality of the band's presentation while the style and quality of their music is indicated by the range of instruments prominently displayed in front of the players. Band photographs are among the more revealing records of New Orleans jazz in the years between 1900 and the mid-1920s. Shaped by the cultural, racial, and economic environment of early-twentieth-century New Orleans, the conventions of band portraiture point to the evolving

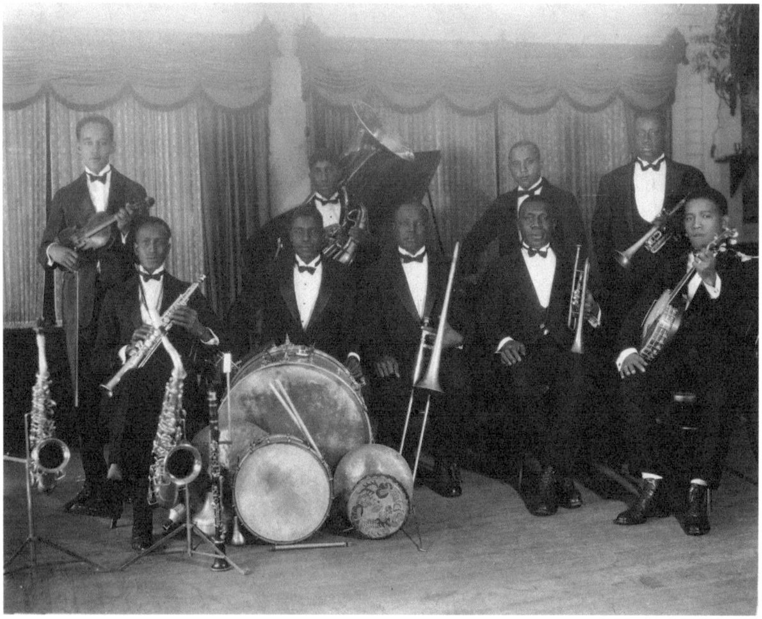

Figure 76: Unknown photographer. *The Original Tuxedo Orchestra*. New Orleans. 1924. *Al Rose's New Orleans Jazz: A Family Album Collection. Hogan Jazz Archive, Tulane University.*

identity of the jazz musician and suggest ways in which band leaders and sidemen confronted the economic pressures of the music business and negotiated racial and social boundaries.

Jules Lion, a Creole portrait painter and lithographer who introduced the daguerreotype to New Orleans in 1839, is the Crescent City's earliest recorded photographer. Here, as elsewhere in the United States, interest in photography spread rapidly although vernacular music appears to have held little attraction for many white photographers in the city. Originally a watchmaker, George Francois Mugnier turned to photography in 1884 with a studio on Exchange Alley and built a substantial reputation as a photographer of views and landscapes but seems to have avoided musicians; and Ernest Bellocq, whose work was brought to attention through Lee Friedlander's painstaking research, had little interest in music as a subject.[27] Florestine Marguerite Perrault, a Creole woman who carved out a successful career in domestic and family portraiture in part through her ability to pass as white, was severely constrained by gender and race: "The most that I ever got to was the [Pythian Temple's] roof garden [dances] on Saturday nights," she remembered, and her portraits reflected middle-class definitions of black femininity, scrupulously avoiding any associations with jazz.[28]

By the turn of the century every black or colored ward in New Orleans had its own photographer and here there was more interest in music.[29] New Orleans' most prominent early photographers of color were Arthur Bedou and his pupil Villard Paddio, both of whom combined studio and location work.[30] Bedou had accompanied Washington on his tours of the American south between 1908 and 1915 and inherited from his mentor a firm belief in the possibilities of black emancipation and advancement through education, entrepreneurship, and citizenship. He took this outlook into his photography, creating images of African American life that spoke of the humanity and achievements of his fellow citizens in New Orleans, devoting as much care and attention to the photographs he made of humble Creole families as to the portraits of prominent figures. Paddio continued Bedou's work in documenting the African American community of New Orleans, including (like Bedou) many jazz musicians. Paddio was born in the New Iberia/Lafayette area of Louisiana in the mid-1890s and later settled in the Treme area of New Orleans, where he opened a photographic studio. Many of Paddio's early photographs documented the city's African American citizens and organizations, including photographs of a young Louis Armstrong. The *Crescent City Pictorial*, a 28-page souvenir booklet dedicated "to the Progress of the Colored Citizens of New Orleans, Louisiana," featured Paddio's photographs of homes of noted African American New Orleanians, businesses, schools, churches, and social organizations and serves as one of the best visual documents of African American middle- and upper-class life in that time.

Bedou and Paddio would certainly have been familiar with the intimate relationship between musicians and the ensemble in early New Orleans jazz.[31] A recurring theme in the memoirs of many early New Orleans jazz musicians, bands were a social as much as cultural institution. The drummer Warren "Baby" Dodds spoke warmly in his autobiography of the "harmony and brotherly love" of New Orleans bands while Sidney Bechet recalled his pride in wearing the uniform of the Eagle Orchestra; for Joe Oliver being a good "band man" was paramount.[32] The status accorded to band musicians by the community reinforced the value of membership and the cohesiveness and longevity of the New Orleans brass bands was a consequence of this outlook. There were strictly speaking no soloists in the New Orleans ensemble style and the notion of a group sound was so dominant that even drummers would try to play "in tune." Bruce Boyd Raeburn explains that the ensemble nature of New Orleans' musical culture had deep social roots:[33]

> *New Orleans-style collective improvisation [. . .] was a way of living [. . .] and the cooperative approach to performance that evolved there reflected not only the distinctive characteristics of the environment and its people but also, more importantly, the coping mechanisms that allowed such diversity to unify, survive, and flourish in a hazardous location.*

The band was the medium through which individual accomplishment and presentational style were developed but economic uncertainty, competition between musicians for work, and exposure to a capricious labor market were ever present and musicians guarded preciously the safeguards of band affiliation as a form of mediation between themselves and the market. Band leaders had considerable status as both mentors and business managers who handled the less salubrious aspects of securing work and negotiating payment.[34]

The question of race could not be avoided. A port city, previously belonging to both France and Spain and almost universally Catholic in the midst of Protestant America, New Orleans' "French, Canadian, German, Spanish, Acadian, American, Irish, Italian, Negro and other ethnic traditions keep it from ever being a typical Southern city."[35] No other city exhibited quite such variety and tolerant attitude toward a mulatto conception of race. This is not to suggest that racial prejudice and discrimination in the city were not widely and harshly experienced. New Orleans was scarred by strict racial exclusion yet important exceptions were everywhere. The bass player Pops Foster was certainly overstating matters when he claimed that "The white and coloured musicians around New Orleans all knew each other and there wasn't any Jim Crow between them" but it seems clear that the complexities of New Orleans' racial and ethnic patterning created a communal culture that overarched racial differences.[36]

Seeking to appeal to as wide an audience as possible, many musicians became adept in negotiating racial and ethnic identities. While few went as far as Jelly Roll

Morton,[37] it was not uncommon for Creole musicians to pass themselves off as white, a strategy adopted by the Afro-French clarinetist Archille Baquet and the trombonist Dave Perkins, a member of Jack Laine's "white" Ragtime Band, and Eddie Cherie, a light-skinned black man who played with Leon Rappolo and the Brunies boys. Musicians with southern European heritage such as Louis Prima found themselves maneuvering between creole, black, and white expectations. King Oliver reportedly introduced the black trumpeter Lee Collins as "my little Creole boy," an approach followed by Freddie Keppard's Original Creole Band, Bill Johnson's original Creole Orchestra, and King Oliver's Creole Jazz Band, whose presentational style and dress as much as their music signaled adherence to the elevated tastes of *créolité*.[38] As Bruce Boyd Raeburn has observed,[39]

> *Creole became a mask that could simultaneously reinforce or subvert racial imaginaries, and jazz musicians were quick to pick up on these implications [. . .] a pragmatic approach to finding work [. . .] their comfort zone was a matrix of masking, racial ambiguity and self-promotion.*

Photography, which made manifest skin tones (or, in the case of passing, obscured them), was a key site of negotiation and representation of these racial concerns. In a city in which divisions generally ensured that bands of specific skin tones could only play before certain audiences, race was key to securing the better-paying and more regular engagements. Photographs assumed particular significance as leaders were acutely aware of the need to manage racial representation and knew the economic consequences attaching to the way photographs were perceived.

As Creoles Bedou and Paddio would have undoubtedly been familiar with the ensemble culture, as well as its subtle racial gradations and dynamics, and conventions apparent in their band portraits convey the complex and shifting affinity between musicians and ensemble. Most of their photographs incorporate elements of the *formal band pose*. In these images the musicians are posed as symmetrically as possible: a (normally) seated front row, usually made up of string or reed players, was placed in front of a row of brass players standing upright while the rhythm instruments were positioned as was usual during performance—drums to the left and rhythm instruments such as the string bass, guitar, or banjo to the right. In Bedou's *Manuel Perez's Garden of Joy Orchestra* the players stand in height order (Figure 77). The instruments figure prominently, often held by musicians who stand stiffly upright, chins projecting forward. Most band leaders required that musicians wore the band uniform or formal clothes and care was taken by the more fastidious leaders to make sure that individual items of clothing were as symmetrically arranged as possible and instruments were held so that all appeared parallel or upright.

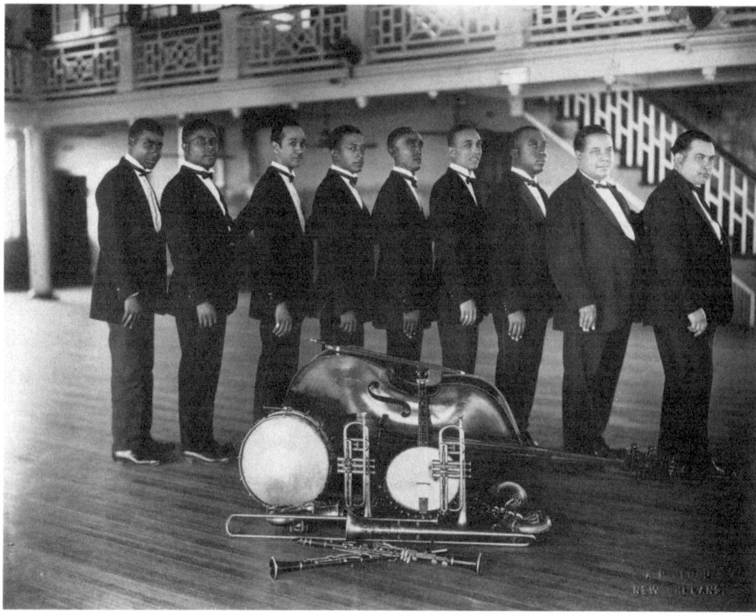

Figure 77: Arthur P. Bedou. *Manuel Perez's Garden of Joy Orchestra*. Knights of Pythian Temple Roof Garden. 1925.
Al Rose's New Orleans Jazz: A Family Album Collection. Hogan Jazz Archive, Tulane University.

The formal band portrait was an opportunity to adopt a considered pose that projected the seriousness and standing of the band musicians and elevated the viewer's assessment of their occupation, a particularly important consideration for musicians in a culture that placed considerable value on musicianship, training, and presentation. The images were also a marketing tool, often passed informally to friends and audiences or used as a relatively cheap supplement to business cards.[40] As a presentation or reinforcement of racial identities, the formal portrait was particularly appropriate context with its connotations of seriousness and disciplined demeanor providing a counter to racial stereotypes.

If the objective of the formal band pose was to convey the organization and discipline of the band and to confirm, meet, or confound racial stereotypes, the *instrumental array* broadened the representation of the band through a more ostentatious demonstration of the band's instrumentation. By the time Bedou came to photograph the Louisiana Shakers in the mid-1920s (Figure 78), the array of instruments had grown considerably. The arrangement of the instruments is a little haphazard and contrasts with the meticulously symmetrical display evident in *Sidney Desvigne's S.S. Capitol Orchestra* photographed by Paddio in 1931 (Figure 79). The instrumental array moved band photography in the direction of foregrounding individual and collective musical accomplishment and versatility. Images like this signified the finer qualities of New Orleans music-making,

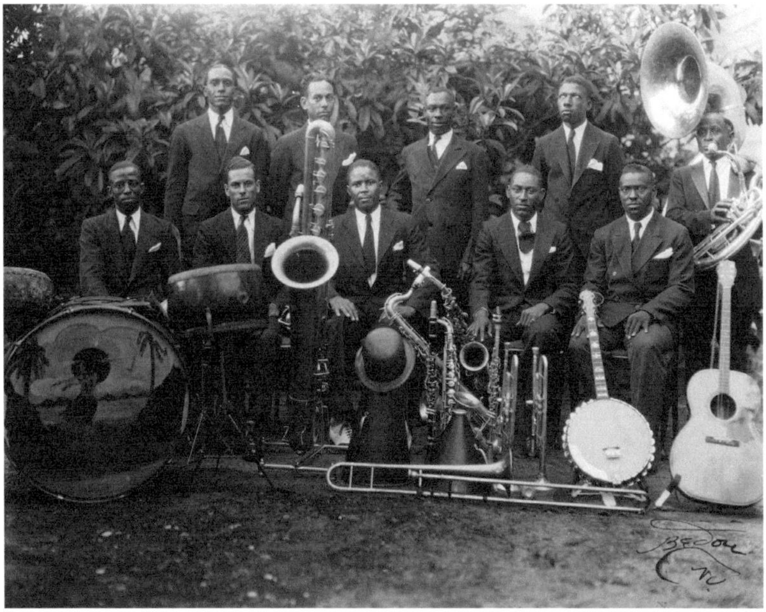

Figure 78: Arthur Bedou, *The Louisiana Shakers.* New Orleans. Mid-1920s.
Al Rose's New Orleans Jazz: A Family Album Collection. Hogan Jazz Archive, Tulane University.

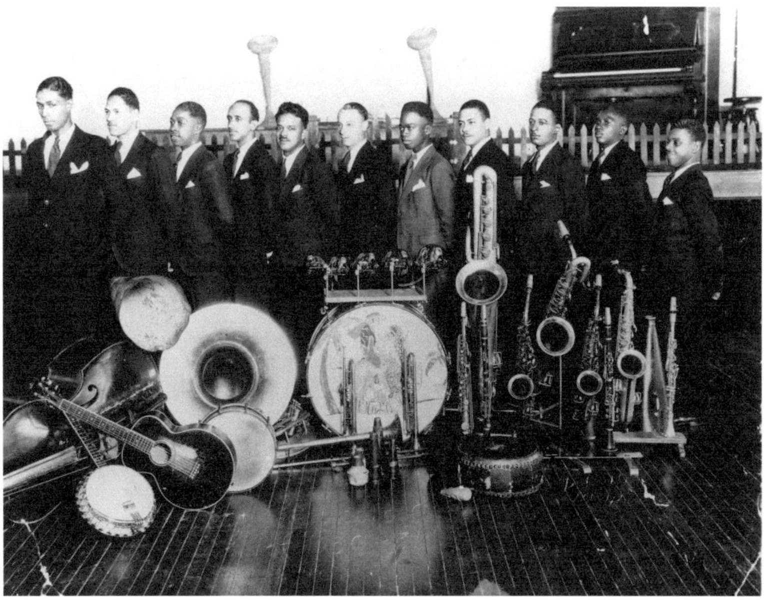

Figure 79: Villard Paddio. *Sidney Desvigne's S.S. Capitol Orchestra.* New Orleans. *c.*1931.
Al Rose's New Orleans Jazz: A Family Album Collection. Hogan Jazz Archive, Tulane University.

proclaiming the pride that musicians took in the instruments they owned and used; the wider the range of instruments on display the more versatile the band might appear to be. The careful alignment of the instruments embodied connotations of musical coordination and discipline and, in an age before recorded music became widespread, the array served to convey an idea of what to expect from the band in performance.

In contrast, the *posed action* band photograph was intended to convey a sense of what audiences might expect from live performance. Inadequate lighting prevented genuine performance photography during this period and so the posed action photograph attempted to recreate the experience of seeing and hearing the band by having the musicians feign performance. This convention can be seen as an extension of the *tableau vivant* favored by daguerreotypists and early portrait photographers. It was however difficult to execute and few of these photographs are particularly realistic. Bedou took pains to make his photograph of Fate Marable's Orchestra taken on board the *S.S. Capitol* in the early-1920s appear more realistic although the viewer is left unconvinced by the composition (Figure 80).

There is clear authorial intent behind all these images. Bedou, as Shawn Michelle Smith has explained, understood his role as "a picture maker within the crowd," a posture that emphasized "African American looking" to disrupt the

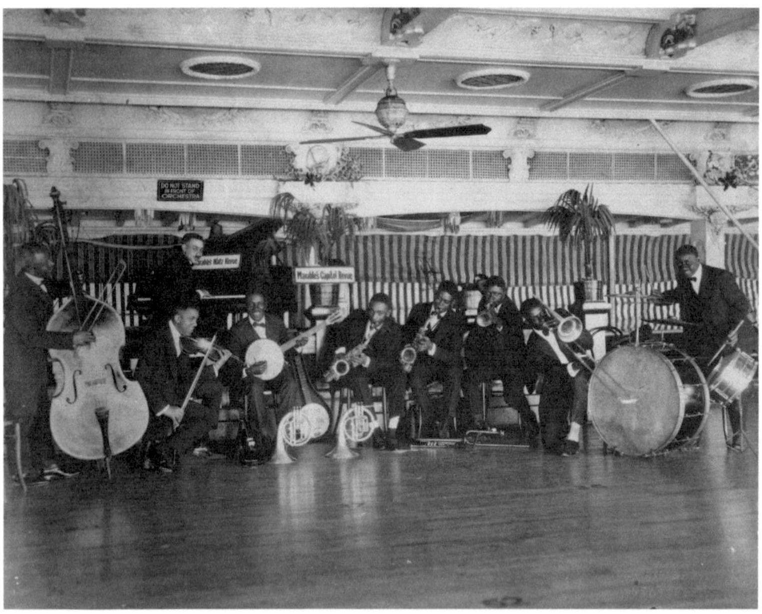

Figure 80: Arthur P. Bedou. *Fate Marable's Orchestra, S.S. Capitol riverboat.* New Orleans. Early-1920s.
Al Rose's New Orleans Jazz: A Family Album Collection. Hogan Jazz Archive, Tulane University

white gaze. Describing Bedou's insider perspective she notes that "The photographer and his camera share the same space as the crowd."[41] In the photographs of Paddio as much as those of Bedou, the ways in which poses were adopted and employed by bandsmen and interpreted by the photographers were far from accidental—an important corrective to those historians who have dismissed them as frivolous, mere vaudeville retentions, or even, as Peter Townsend has suggested, "freakish."[42] The visual conventions of the New Orleans band photography of Bedou and Paddio should be seen as responses by photographers reflexively engaged in the complex patchwork of New Orleans' social, racial, and occupational relationships and whose acculturation sensitized them to the requirements of the musicians they photographed.

III. Black studios, 1900–1930s

James Van Der Zee

As musicians migrated north- and eastward from New Orleans and the southern states, band photographs made in large urban centers like Chicago and New York by black studios began to reflect the emerging metropolitan outlook of urban African American communities. James Van Der Zee's 1931 studio portrait of King Oliver and the Harlem Syncopators appears on the surface similar to the New Orleans band photography of Bedou and Paddio. Instruments prominently displayed, the identically dressed players are carefully aligned and stand stiffly with their hands by their sides. Its constructed *mise-en-scène* is however just one indication of the differences between the New Orleans photographers and Van Der Zee, whose photographs reflect a broader—if distinctly idiosyncratic—concern with black metropolitan identity in the age of the "New Negro." Black musicians in New York in the early- to mid-1920s were often required to tread a fine line: anxious to present themselves as proud representatives of the new, increasingly self-conscious black communities, few could aspire to the same success with white audiences as leaders such as A. J. Piron or Fletcher Henderson had achieved yet all wanted to display their professionalism, expertise, and modernity to a wider public. As the leading black New York photographer of the studio age, James Van Der Zee's photographs responded to a cultural negotiation faced to one degree or another by all black musicians.

Van Der Zee's career began with the emergence of the modern studio and lasted long enough to suffer the decline in formal portraiture in the 1950s and 1960s. He was, as A. D. Coleman reminds us, the only photographer who recorded the whole gamut of Harlem life and rituals throughout the first half of the twentieth century—individual and family portraits, notable black personalities in political and social life, soldiers in uniform, parades and political rallies, street scenes, sporting events, storefronts, wedding and funerals, social clubs and church groups, bridge clubs, fraternities, school groups, A'Lelia Walker's Dark Tower salon, and the parades of Marcus Garvey's UNIA.[43] His career coincided with the entry of jazz musicians into the studio in the 1920s through to late sittings by Miles Davis and Eubie Blake in the 1980s. Jazz was a relatively small part of Van Der Zee's output but was significant enough for him to be regarded as an important source of jazz imagery for the Metropolitan Museum's 1968 exhibition *Harlem on My Mind*.

It was this exhibition that sparked renewed interest in Van Der Zee's work. Almost completely neglected after his studio business went into decline, his inclusion in the show with some 50 out of roughly 700 images has sparked a wide variety of reappraisals.[44] He has been described as the portraitist of the Harlem Renaissance, a chronicler of a new collective post-migration black identity and apologist for individual black success stories. Several writers detect African (and specifically Egyptian) retentions in the use of gothic, even magical, elements in funeral portraits while Louise Siddons has located his work more squarely in the African American tradition of polyvocality. He has been described as a romantic dreamer, a canny entrepreneur, and his style as pictorialist, "vernacular," or "documentary," a striking example of Afro-American modernism with parallels with the avant-garde photomontage of the 1920s, and even as a precursor of postmodernism. Regina Perry makes much of VanDerZee's technical innovations while A. D. Coleman considers him a "naïf" who "did very little exploring and experimenting in the medium [. . .] one whose innocence did not lead him to any technical or aesthetic breakthroughs." What then should we make of Van Der Zee's portraits of jazz musicians? Combining the elaborate props and painted background scenery of late-Victorian portraiture, pictorialist values such as soft focus and elegiac subjects, gothic and magical realism, montages, double exposures, hand-coloring and other retouching techniques, handwritten texts and drawings on the negatives, these images are capable of being read in any number of ways.

Born in 1886 in Lenox, Massachusetts, James Van Der Zee was a product of a relatively comfortable lower middle class family who lived in a small homogeneous black community. He experienced little bigotry in early life although a sense of otherness was ever present, particularly at his white school. Never quite leaving his New England identity behind after migrating to New York City, Van Der Zee was a skilled musician who played at various times at the Lafayette Theatre in Harlem and with Fletcher Henderson. He turned to full-time photography in 1915 when his career as a player faltered although music remained a passion. The tension between tradition and change, the experiences of assimilation and otherness, locality and metropolitan urbanity need to be kept firmly in mind: in Van Der Zee the city, photography, artist, technique, and his subjects are mutually dependent.

With their late-Victorian setting and props, a concern with tradition is obvious in Van Der Zee's portraits. Peter Bacon Hales describes his work as "quaint, antique, appropriate to an older urbanism: to a city, not a metropolis," a style rendered anarchic by the metropolitan modernism of Stieglitz, Coburn, Strand, Steichen and Berenice Abbott's portrayal of New York City.[45] Yet in their ostensibly conventional synthesis of design, objects and composition Van Der Zee was forging his own response to modernism. Much as Alfred Stieglitz argued that pictorialism could be a progressive force, constantly experimenting with chemicals, lenses, light to "elaborate ideas," Van Der Zee portrays the contemporary black image of a people transforming a "usable past" as they embraced the promise of modernity in one of the world's most dynamic cities.[46]

In his use of "traditional" devices, the temporal ambiguity of Van Der Zee's photography provides a mirror to the photographer's own experience of black urban transformation. The creative agency released in backdrops, props, retouching, composition, and print techniques added a performative element to the portrait at a moment of stripped-down modernism, a response to modernism's onslaught on traditional values in photographic reassessments of the American past.[47] Only in this way can we explain Van Der Zee's amalgam of hand-tinting and retouching with the modern visual culture of movies, illustrated magazines, and material culture straight out of the modernist advertising photographer's playbook. It is precisely here, in the shifting ambiguity of tradition and modernity, that Van Der Zee negotiated his path through life by representing African Americans whose own journeys had brought them to New York City. Van Der Zee was above all else a commercial photographer, determined to give his sitters the representations they desired, and the conscious intent behind these images should not be doubted: "I guess it was just a matter of not being satisfied with what the camera was doing," he recalled, "I wanted the camera to take what I thought should be there, too."[48] In directing the pictorial space with such intent he layered reality with artificiality and meaning—and his artistry demands that we recognize their manipulated status.

Van Der Zee's photograph of King Oliver's Syncopators makes obvious this stylistic synthesis of past and present (Figure 81). A clear line can be traced to the New Orleans style through the band uniforms and ostentatious instrumental array, but the image is a constructed amalgam of tradition with modern urbanity and informality. The straight lines and symmetry of earlier band portraits have been replaced by a more fluid formation. Oliver himself stands benignly behind the players as *primus inter pares* rather than dominating leader. Gestures and poses suggest that players are more relaxed, more confident in their own presentation: some lean forward, others backward, hands are held in different positions, and there is no attempt to feign performance or symmetry in posture. If for Bedou and Paddio musicians were identified with the band, the "play of gestures" in Van Der Zee's band portraits point to a group of self-aware and self-assured individuals rather than individuality subsumed within the collectivity, "a potent symbol of [. . .] transformative power which remains connected to a black heritage."[49]

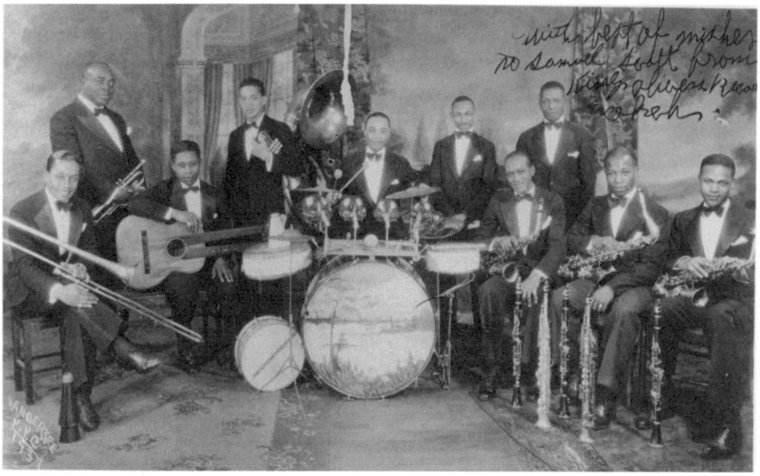

Figure 81: James Van Der Zee. *King Oliver and His Harlem Syncopators.* New York. March 1, 1931. *Peter Vacher Collection.*

Edward Elcha

Another black New York portraitist rising to prominence in the white-dominated entertainment business was William Edward Elcha.[50] A leading chronicler of "Jazz Age" Manhattan, proprietor of the Progress Studio, and a celebrated portraitist of the musical world of Harlem in the 1920s and 1930s, Elcha's premises at 220–25 West 46th Street became a haunt of the African American elite on their visits to New York City. When Jack Goldberg and Joseph J. Myers hired Elcha in 1928 as the exclusive photographer of the Majestic Theatrical Circuit, a national booking agency for black talent, his dominant position as the recorder of the African American entertainment world was beyond doubt. A condition of the contract was that the Circuit should purchase for Elcha's exclusive use new German lenses and cameras and from 1929 until his sudden death in 1939 Progress Studio was a state-of-the-art photographic enterprise. Among the artists and musicians who passed through his studio, Elcha made portraits of Victoria Spivey, Bessie Smith, and other black vaudeville actors and musicians. His photographs of Bessie Smith are impressive examples of portraiture as a performative art. Whether portrayed in long, tasseled robes set off with elaborate headdress and plumes of ostrich feathers or in his close-ups in which the singer is framed by a garland of black ostrich feathers, these images show Smith the height of her powers in the 1920s and capture some of the exuberance of her stage persona.

Many of the bands photographed by Elcha were proto-jazz troupes such as the Siren Syncopators, a band led by the formidable Isabelle Spiller and her husband, William Spiller, shown in Elcha's photograph playing the bass saxophone

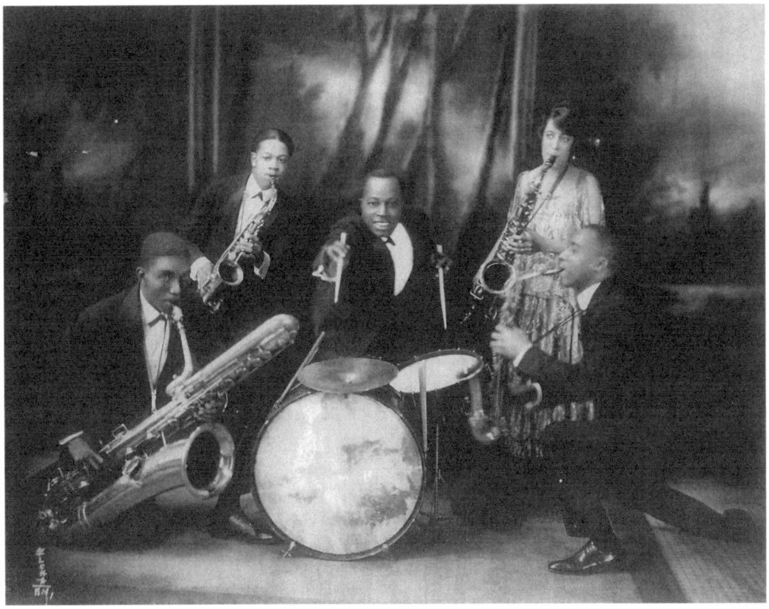

Figure 82: Edward Elcha. *The Siren Syncopators*. New York. February 1922. *Peter Vacher Collection.*

(Figure 82). The Spillers may not be particularly well-known now but their standing at the time should not be underestimated: according to Rex Stewart, who played with the Spillers early in his career, the couple ran "a really thorough organization. [. . .] among the first big-time colored acts in show business. They only played the best show houses in the country."[51] Portraits such as these illustrate the extent to which black culture of the early twentieth century was a continual negotiation between acculturation and traditional African American values. The formal qualities of this image, which on the surface appear derivative of older conventions, are subverted by a bodily display quite unlike the stiff poses of conventional studio portraits. Like Van Der Zee, the tension between past and present is evident in a visual quest for the forms of a modern black metropolitan life made evident in gestural practices associated with a black musical art form.

Carroll T. Maynard

Carroll T. Maynard was born in South Carolina in 1899 and by 1918 was resident in Philadelphia working as a photographer for Bond Bros. He moved to Pittsburgh and in 1925 to Chicago where he reestablished his photography business. Maynard Studios, active between 1930 and 1950, proved popular with black patrons keen to "Get Photos That Please—Downtown Quality at Popular Prices."[52] His images appeared in the *Chicago Defender, Ebony,* and *Bronzeville* magazines and by the late-1940s he had established a photographic school to teach professional techniques.

Maynard's style inclined to the artistic. Graced with an eye for elegant composition and carefully lighted subjects, his stunning photograph of the jazz bassist and composer Johnny Pate is an accomplished study of form. The tightly framed image of Pate and his bass displays subtly modulated light that enhances skin tones; and the strong graphic composition is emphasised by the rounded shape of the player's head and instrument and the dramatic diagonal of the fingerboard and strings of the instrument. These decisions have yielded a portrait that is both sensitive and close to abstract.[53] In his earlier portrait of Earl Hines Grand Terrace Orchestra (Figure 83) Maynard created a location pose that emphasizes the elegance of the subjects and turns the theatre setting to advantage.

Woodard's Studios

William Edward Woodard established his first studio in Chicago in 1920 after an apprenticeship with a city center photographer patronized mainly by white clients. In 1923 he was able to open a studio in Kansas City followed by Cleveland and New York City. Like other early-twentieth century African American photographers, Woodard was a firm believer in the potential of racial pride to counter discrimination in paving the way toward social and economic success; interviewed in 1928, he said that he migrated to Chicago in order to realize "visions of great usefulness and progress." Woodard's Studios became the first choice for black Americans of all classes with subjects ranging from members of the African American elite to female impersonators such as Bonnie Clark and activist Ida B. Wells-Barnett, celebrities, literary figures, theatrical and musical stars to ordinary south side residents. The *Chicago Defender* ventured that "Chicagoans have become so 'Woodardized' that nothing but the most veritable stranger would think of patronizing any other studio."[54] The studio was staffed by family members and photographers Harold E. Young and Lottyle Hale Jacobs.

Amy Mooney's research has demonstrated how Woodard Studios contributed to the development of modern black identity. The studio's portraits were reproduced in the *Chicago Defender* and magazines such as *Reflexus* and *Abbott's Monthly* and their circulation slowly helped shift perceptions toward those which African Americans collectively wished to convey. The "Woodard Way," as the Studio described its portraits, was in effect the way in which African Americans represented themselves to the social group, making a link with their past and the possibilities of the present. African American photographers had an advantage over their white competitors in understanding the meanings associated with skin color. Many black photographers were, like H. M. Brazelton in Tennessee, proud of their ability to render "a variety of colors of faces, ranging from white, brown, black, etc. [and] many of these wearing white costumes which increase

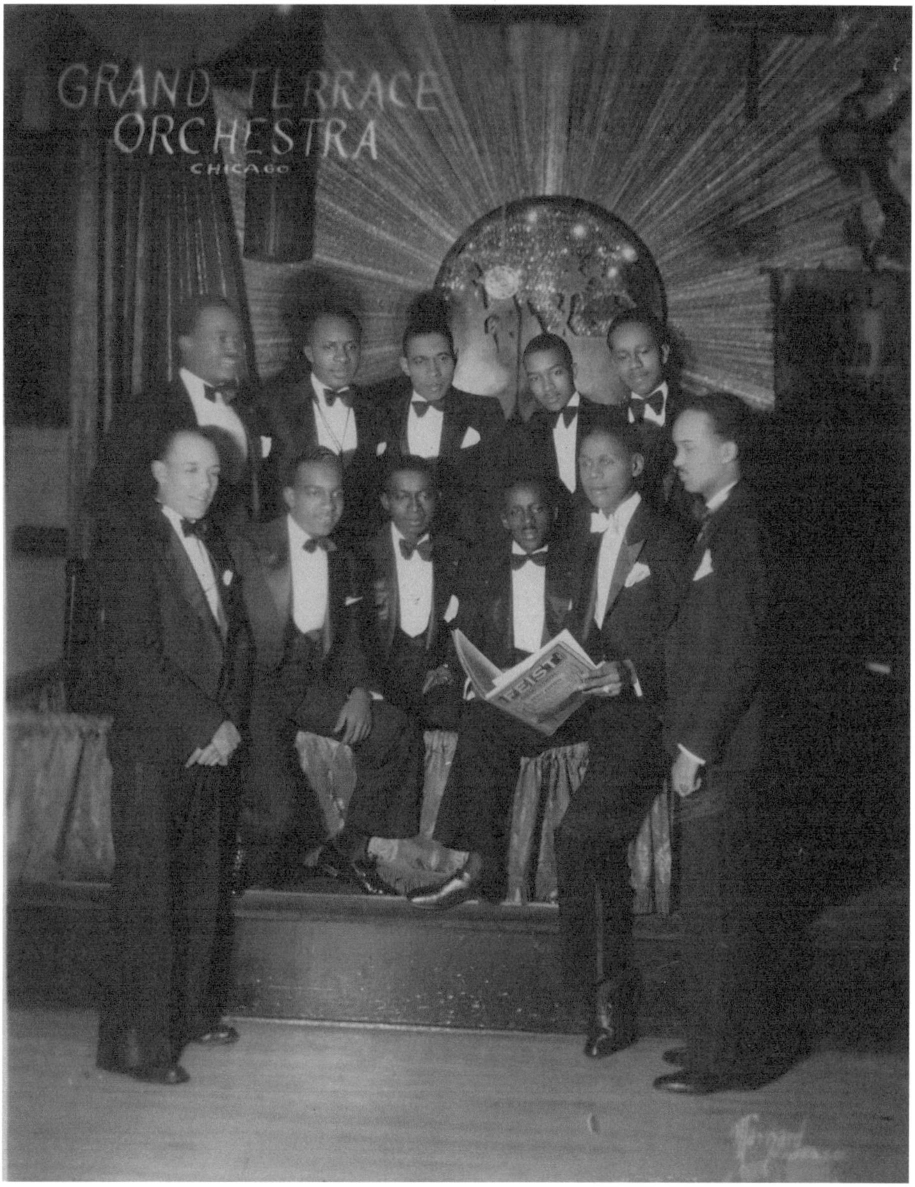

Figure 83: Carroll T. Maynard. *Earl Hines Grand Terrace Orchestra*. Grand Terrace, Chicago. June 1930.
Peter Vacher Collection.

the contrast." Ever sensitive to the politics of skin color, Woodard's photographers knew that their sitters had their own ideas about how they wanted to be represented.[55]

Woodard's Studio in Chicago was a natural choice for Louis Armstrong when a portrait of his 1928 "New" Hot 5 was required (Figure 84). The line-up of Armstrong's musicians continues the formal pose of classic band images although a

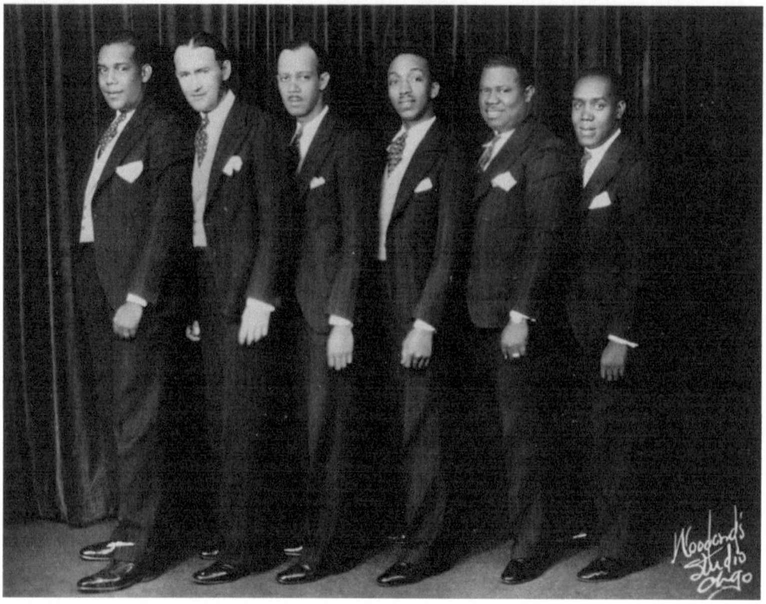

Figure 84: Woodard Studios. *Louis Armstrong's 1928 Hot 5*. Chicago. 1928. *Peter Vacher Collection.*

second image from the same session employs a slightly less contrived arrangement with the musicians standing less stiffly behind Armstrong who is examining his trumpet. An elaborate chair, almost certainly a studio prop pressed into service for the occasion, has found its way into the image in an attempt to add a sense of status. The pianist, arranger, and band leader Sammy Stewart was portrayed by Woodard in "occupational" mode, displaying the tools of his trade (Figure 85). Woodard's portraits of Earl Hines, almost certainly taken on location at Chicago's Grand Terrace Café in the late-1920s, strikes a vaudevillian pose showing the musician with cane and bowler hat in front of carefully arrangement stage curtains. A shot of Hines's big band taken in December 1928 shows the musician at the piano with no fewer than nine players lined up behind him and a large instrumental array.[56] More successful perhaps is Woodard's portrait of the musician and arranger Eddie Mallory probably taken when he was working with The Alabamians between 1927 and 1931.[57] A straightforward upper body portrait with a mid-gray plain background, care has been taken with the modeling lighting on the musician's face and the pose with trumpet seems more natural. The three-quarters pose and slight lean in the body makes the portrait less static than many.

Woodard's Studios took considerable care with the lighting and composition of these images in order to dignify the subjects. A variety of formal and informal poses were adopted, typical of an approach which gave the sitter a measure of agency in shaping their own identity. As Amy Mooney has persuasively

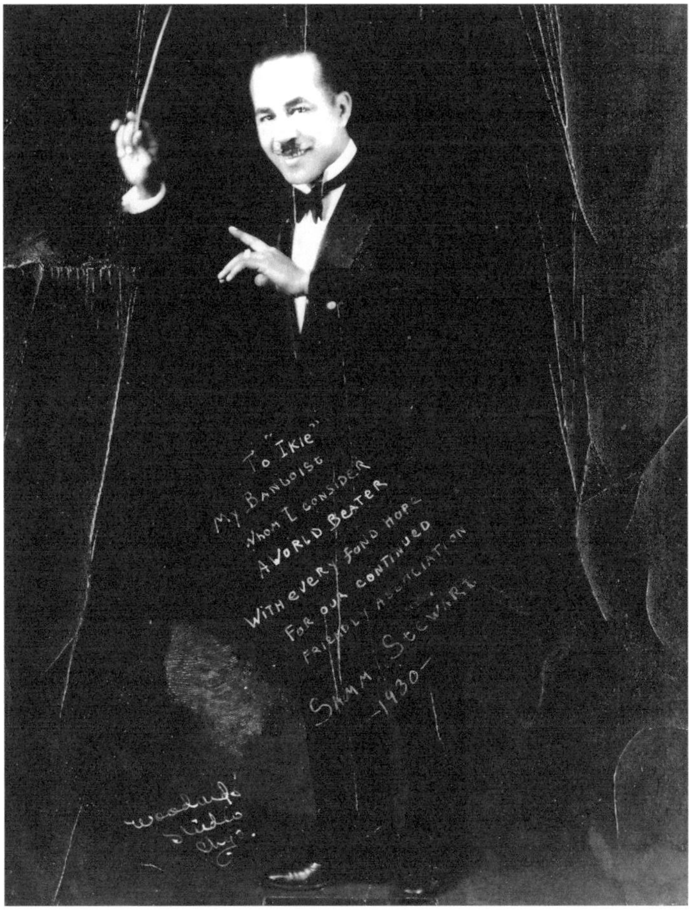

Figure 85: Woodard Studios. *Sammy Stewart*. Chicago. 1930. *Peter Vacher Collection.*

argued, Woodard advanced black representation in the age of the "New Negro." Concerned to capture the character of his sitters in an "artistic" fashion, the studio's portraits not only present their sitters with style and dignity but acted as advocates for the race in their demonstrations of collective social advancement.

IV. Conclusion: Authenticity from the inside

The representational styles employed by the studio photographers discussed in the preceding chapter were largely derived from white commercial portraiture and theatrical practices. The contribution of the black photographers examined in this chapter was of a different order. These photographers understood music as a communal activity, as expressive of the culture in which it was rooted, and their images of musicians and bands can be seen as one element of a broader first-generation concern to counter distortion and reaffirm black self-understanding.

It was here—in the adoption of a distinctive form of realism revealing "the reflexive experiences of both the photographers and their communities"[58]—that the decisive first steps were made toward a black photographic aesthetic.

This aesthetic cannot be reduced to either documentary and modernist formulations. To be sure, black photographers were reluctant to adopt the formal vocabulary of photographic modernism yet subsuming their output into the predominantly white documentary tradition as some critics have suggested is surely an underestimation of the contribution of early black photographers.[59] Their work evidences the beginnings of a realist aesthetic whose expressive qualities move visual representation toward what John Roberts has called the "unveiling."[60] If realism is located in the proximity between the photographer and the represented subject, time, and place, it is equally the case that the bond is sealed between the image and the experience of the viewer. Realism demands not only fidelity but a moral outlook; eschewing generalities, this is an outlook that must be expressive of particulars, the details of life as lived, and "the quest to know and to detail the environment in which ordinary experience unfolds discovers that vision alone is inadequate, that sight triggers the visionary."[61] The significant development was that early black photographers laid the foundations for a photographic aesthetic of authenticity *from the inside*.

Generally devoting little attention to photography, black arts theorists of the 1960s tended to the view that there had been a failure of racial assertiveness until the mid-century civil rights and black nationalist movements. According to Addison Gayle, there were few attempts before 1925 "to express one's dark-skinned self [. . .] [and] to evaluate the myths and stereotypes foisted off on the race by blacks and whites alike;" Hoyt Fuller lamented the failure of black writers to "control their own images" and he was joined in urging an art that "speaks directly to the needs and aspirations of black America" by Larry Neal and Amiri Baraka.[62] Yet failing to recognize the contribution of early black photographers in prefiguring a "black aesthetic" would be unduly harsh. If, as Neal also insisted, the black aesthetic "is radically opposed to any concept of the artist that alienates him from his community,"[63] early black photography demonstrates the location of a black aesthetic in cultural expression if not style. It is in dance, religion, music, and play that societies articulate and transmit the ideas, values, and beliefs that bind people together and express cultural values.[64] Straddling the documentary and modernist traditions (and, hence, largely overlooked by historians of American photography) African American expressive realism in photography was an early black photographic aesthetic *in statu nascendi*. By the 1930s black photographers would more self-consciously develop and exploit the expressive potential of the realist document from the inside as a second generation turned their cameras toward jazz musicians.

Notes

1. For the history of Hooks Brothers see Ernestine Jenkins, "The Hooks Brothers Photographers," Choose 901, https://choose901.com/hooks-brothers-photography-documented-black-memphis/; Anon., "Hooks Brothers Photography Studio–164 Beale Street, Memphis," Mississippi Blues Travellers, http://www.mississippibluestravellers.com/hooks-brothers-photography-beale-street-memphis-tennessee/.; Deborah Willis, "Photographing Memphis: The Memphis World," in *Photographs from the Memphis World 1949–1964*, ed. M. Pacini (Memphis, TN: Memphis Brooks Museum of Art and University Press of Mississippi, 2008), 11–15; Tennessee Historical Commission Markers: 164 Beale Street, Memphis, Tennessee, http://www.mississippibluestravellers.com/tennessee-historical-commission/.
2. Earnestine Lovelle Jenkins, "The Hooks Brothers of Memphis: Artist-Photographers of the 'New Negro' Movement in the Urban South," in *Memphis: 200 Years Together*, ed. Karen B. Golightly and Jonathan Judaken (Memphis, TN: Susan Schadt Press, 2019), 84–99; Andria Lisle, "Black and White: Three photo exhibits," *Memphis Flyer*, Vol. 1 (886) February 17–22, 2006: 20.
3. Lovelle Jenkins, "The Hooks Brothers of Memphis: Artist-Photographers of the 'New Negro' Movement in the Urban South," 89, 91–92, explains how Hooks Brothers' portrait of the prominent Black businessman R. C. Church emphasized his light complexion. This problem would become more acute as color film was introduced. Brian Winston, "A Whole Technology of Dyeing: A Note on Ideology and the Apparatus of the Chromatic Moving Image," *Daedalus* 114, no. 4 (1985): 105–23, shows how color film technology was shaped by cultural considerations in being optimized for white skins.
4. Albert Murray, *Murray Talks Music: Albert Murray on Jazz and Blues*, ed. Paul Devlin (Minneapolis: University of Minnesota Press, 2016), 13.
5. "Hooks Brothers Photography—Where the Only Known Studio Portrait of Robert Johnson Was Taken" shows photographs of the room presumed to have been used as a studio by Hooks Bros. William Brian Piper, *Cameras at Work: African American Studio Photographers and the Business of Everyday Life, 1900–1970*, M.A. Thesis, (Charlottesville: University of Virginia, 2016), presents valuable information about early black photography studios.
6. Stephen Henderson, "Introduction: The Forms of Things Unknown," in *Understanding the New Black Poetry: Black Speech and Black Music as Poetic References* (New York: Morrow, 1973), 62–66; Henderson, "Saturation: Progress Report on a Theory of Black Poetry," 104.
7. Margaret Denton Smith and Mary Louise Tucker, *Photography in New Orleans: The Early Years, 1840–1865* (Baton Rouge: Louisiana State University Press, 1982), 8–23; Robb, *Shot in Alabama: A History of Photography 1839–1941*, 89.
8. For the development of early African American photography see Deborah J. Johnson, "Black Photography: Contexts for Evolution," in *A Century of Black Photographers: 1840–1960*, ed. V. H. Coar (Rhode Island: Rhode Island School of Design, 1983), 15–20; V. Hollins Coar, *A Century of Black Photographers: 1840–1960* (Rhode Island: Rhode Island School of Design, 1983); Alan Govenar, *Portraits of Community: African American Photography in Texas* (Austin: Texas State Historical Association, 1996); George Sullivan, *Black Artists in Photography 1840–1940* (Dutton: Cobblehill Books, 1996) and Deborah Willis, *Reflections in Black: A History of Black Photographers 1840 to the Present* (New York: W. W. Norton, 2000).
9. Jeanne Moutoussamy-Ashe, *Viewfinders: Black Women Photographers* (New York: Readers and Writers, 1993), 29, 18–19. A 1900 photograph by Robert L. Bracklow in the Museum of the City of New York (cat: 93.91.179) shows a hoarding offering "photographic instruction in Ten Days-$10." The growth of Black patronage is described by Mary Schmidt Campbell, "Introduction—The Studio Museum in Harlem," in *Harlem Renaissance: Art of Black America* (New York: Abradale Press Harry N. Abrams, 1987–94), 13; Earnestine Lovelle Jenkins, *Race, Representation and Photography in 19th-Century Memphis* (London: Routledge, 2016), 10.
10. Robert L. Boyd, "The 'Black Metropolis' Revisited: A Comparative Analysis of Northern and Southern Cities in the United States in the Early 20th Century," *Urban Studies* 49, no. 4 (2012): 855.
11. Ann Morris and Henrietta Ambrose, *North Webster: A Photographic History of a Black Community* (Bloomington: Indiana University Press, 1993), 87; Charles Williams, *African American*

Life and Culture in Orange Mound: Case Study of a Black Community in Memphis, Tennessee 1890–1980 (Lanham, MD: Lexington Books, 2013), 98.

12. Allan Sekula, "The Body and The Archive," in *The Contest of Meaning: Critical Histories of Photography*, ed. Richard Bolton (Cambridge, MA: MIT Press, 1989), 345.
13. John Hope Franklin, *Reconstruction after the Civil War*. (Chicago: University of Chicago Press, 2013). 183–84.
14. Lawrence W. Levine, *Black Culture and Black Consciousness: Afro-American Folk Thought from Slavery to Freedom* (Oxford: Oxford University Press, 1978), 77–78, describes black marginal status between an inward-looking communlism and the pressures of white acculturation.
15. Ron Eyerman, "Intellectuals and the Construction of African American Identity: Outline of a Generational Approach," in *Generational Consciousness, Narrative and Politics*, ed. June Edmunds and Bryan S. Turner (Lanham, MD: Rowman & Littlefield, 2002), 51–74.
16. Angela Davis, "Photography and Afro-American History," in *A Century of Black Photographers: 1840–1960*, ed. V. H. Coar (Rhode Island: Rhode Island School of Design, 1983), 25–28; Rayford Logan "The Negro as portrayed in the leading Literary Magazines," in *The Betrayal of the Negro from Rutherford B. Hayes to Woodrow Wilson*, ed. Rayford W. Logan (New York: Da Capo, 1997), 239–74; Ginger Hill, "'Rightly Viewed': Theorisations of Self in Frederick Douglass's Lectures on Pictures," in *Pictures and Progress: Early Photography and the Making of African American Identity*, ed. Maurice O. Wallace and Shawn Michelle Smith (Durham, NC: Duke University Press, 2012), 41–82 and Shawn Michelle Smith, "'Looking at One's Self Through the Eyes of Others': W. E. B. Du Bois's Photographs for the 1900 Paris Exposition," *African American Review* 34, no. 4 (2000): 581–600.
17. James G. Spady, "Gardiner, Leon (1892–1945)," in *Dictionary of African Negro Biography*, ed. Rayford W. Logan and Michael R. Winston (New York: W. W. Norton, 1982).
18. Deborah J. Johnson, "Black Photography: Contexts for Evolution," in *A Century of Black Photographers: 1840–1960*, ed. V. H. Coar (Rhode Island: Rhode Island School of Design, 1983), 16.
19. Peter Galassi, "Two Stories," in *American Photography 1890–1965: From the Museum of Modern Art* (New York: MoMA, New York, 1995), 11–41. Amateur photographic societies, such as the Camerads in New Jersey, were almost completely dominated by white Americans. See "The American Photographic Exchange Club," *Image: Journal of Photography of the Geaorge Eastman House* 1, no. 2 (1952): 4; Clément Chéroux, "The Avant-Garde of Amateurs," in *Photography: A New Vision of the World 1891–1940*, ed. W. Guadagnini (Milan: Skira, 2011), 14–29 and Rune Hassner, "Amateur Photography," in *A History of Photography: Social and Cultural Perspectives*, ed. Jean-Claud Lamagy and André Rouillé, trans. Janet Lloyd (Cambridge: Cambridge University Press, 1987), 80–81. Leading black photographers such as Daniel King Ganaway and James Van Der Zee had no contact with white practitioners. Lilian De Cock and Reginald McGhee, *James Van Der Zee* (New York: Morgan & Morgan, 1973, n. pag, record that James Van Der Zee seemed largely unaware of trends and developments within the medium.
20. Constance B. Schulz, "African American Photography to c.1960," in *The Oxford Companion to the Photography, Ed. Robin Lenman* (Oxford: Oxford University Press, 2005), 17; Govenar, *Portraits of Community: African American Photography in Texas*, 15; Nicholas Natanson, *The Black Image in the New Deal: The Politics of FSA Photography* (Knoxville: University of Tennessee Press, 1992). 30; Levine, *Black Culture and Black Consciousness: Afro-American Folk Thought from Slavery to Freedom*, 138.
21. Paul Von Blum, *Resistance, Dignity and Pride: African American Artists in Los Angeles* (Los Angeles: CAAS Publications, University of California, 2004), xii.
22. Nancy Armstrong, "Realism before and after Photography: The Fantastical Form of a Relation among Things," in *Adventures in Realism*, ed. Matthew Beaumont (Malden, MA: Blackwell, 2007), 100.
23. D'Army Bailey cited by Joerg Colberg, "Spotlight: Photographs from the Memphis World 1949–1964," Conscientious, November 19, 2008, http://jmcolberg.com/weblog/2008/11/spotlight_photographs_from_the_memphis_world_1949-1964/.
24. bell hooks, "In Our Glory: Photography and Black Life," in *Picturing Us: African American Identity in Photography* (New York: New Press, 1994), 43–54; Maurice O. Wallace and Shawn Michelle Smith, "Introduction," in *Pictures and Progress: Early Photography and the Making of African American Identity*, ed. Maurice

O. Wallace and Shawn Michelle Smith (Chapel Hill: Duke University Press, 2012), 4–5; Douglas H. Daniels, *Pioneer Urbanites: A Social and Cultural History of Black San Francisco* (Philadelphia: Temple University Press, 1980), 9–10; James Smalls, "African-American Self-Portraiture: Repair, Reclamation, Redemption," *Third Text* 15, no. 54 (n.d.): 47–62; and Willis, *Reflections in Black: A History of Black Photographers 1840 to the Present*, xvii.

25. Louis Kaplan, *American Exposures: Photography and Community in the Twentieth Century* (Minneapolis: University of Minnesota Press, 2005), xxiv.
26. Leonard Feather and Ira Gitler *The Biographical Encyclopaedia of Jazz* (Oxford: Oxford University Press, 1999), 119; Sally Newhart, *The Original Tuxedo Jazz Band: More Than a Century of a New Orleans Icon* (Charleston, SC: History Press, 2013).
27. Willis, *Reflections in Black: A History of Black Photographers 1840 to the Present*, 4. For Bellocq see Lee Friedlander and John Szarkowski, eds., *E. J. Bellocq: Storyville Portraits* (New York: Museum of Modern Art, 1970).
28. Arthé A. Anthony, "Florestine Perrault Collins and the Gendered Politics of Black Portraiture in 1920s New Orleans," *Louisiana History: The Journal of the Louisiana Historical Association* 43, no. 2 (2002): 171–73.
29. Alma Williams Freeman, "New Orleans Jazz Photography," *Jazz Archivist* 15 (2001): 17–22; and Girard P. III Mouton and Alma D. Williams, "The Eyes of Jazz," *Jazz Archivist* 6, no. 1 (1991): 10–11.
30. For Bedou and Paddio see Nell Irvin Painter, *Creating Black Americans: African-American History and Its Meanings, 1619 to the Present* (New York: Oxford University Press, 2007), 419; J. C. L. H., "The Photographer-Arthur Bedou (1880–1966)," *Creolegen* (2013) www.creolegen.org; Willis, *Reflections in Black: A History of Black Photographers 1840 to the Present*, 40; Michael Bieze, "Ruskin in the Black Belt: Booker T. Washington, Arts and Crafts and the New Negro," *Source: Notes in the History of Art* 24, no. 4 (2005): 24–34.
31. Alan John Ainsworth, "Early New Orleans Band Photography," *Jazz Research Journal* 11, no. 1 (2017): 28–61, https://doi.org/10.1558/jazz.33607, provides an expanded account of the argument developed in this section.
32. Larry Gara, *The Baby Dodds Story* (Baton Rouge: Louisiana State University Press, 1992), 15; Sidney Bechet, *Treat It Gentle* (New York: Hill and Wang, 1960), 88; Frederic Ramsey Jr. and Charles Edward Smith, *Jazzmen* (London: Jazz Book Club, Sidgwick & Jackson, 1958), 68. See also Barney Bigard, *With Louis and the Duke: The Autobiography of a Jazz Clarinetist*, ed. Barry Martyn (London: Macmillan Press, 1985), 12, 29, and 36, which recalls how close New Orleans musicians were even after leaving the city.
33. Bruce Boyd Raeburn, *New Orleans Style and the Writing of American Jazz History* (Ann Arbor: University of Michigan Press, 2009), 213. See also Ben Sidran, *Black Talk* (New York: Da Capo, 1981), 49–50.
34. Danny Barker, *A Life in Jazz*, ed. Alyn Shipton (Basingstoke: Macmillan, 1986), 26, recalls the "lying and conniving" used by musicians to secure work. Barker only felt really secure with bookings after he left New Orelans to join Cab Calloway.
35. Charles L. Dufour, "The People of New Orleans," in *The Past as Prelude: New Orleans 1718–1968* (New Orleans: Tulane University Press, 1968), 41.
36. T. Stoddard, ed., *Pops Foster: The Autobiography of a New Orleans Jazzman* (Berkeley: University of California Press, 1971), 63; Burton W. Peretti, *The Creation of Jazz: Music, Race and Culture in Urban America* (Urbana: University of Illinois Press, 1994), 30–31; Bruce Boyd Raeburn, "Jazz and the Italian Connection," *Jazz Archivist* 6, no. 1 (1991): 3.
37. Morton took full advantage of the scope for negotiation afforded by New Orleans culture. He was taught by his family to believe that non-Creole blacks were inferior and that he was not Black. Changing his name to Jelly Roll Morton cocked a snook at Creole cultural superiority with the sexual innuendo of his forenames; he discarded his French antecedents by anglicizing his surname, frequently used his light-skinned and Spanish appearance to gain engagements in Storyville when black pianists were unacceptable, claimed Latin American heritage when it came to securing rooms in segregated hotels, Cuban lineage when playing with the white New Orleans Rhythm Kings, and, to cap it all, appeared in Blackface. Burton Peretti among others has claimed that Morton adopted racist attitudes as a means of coping with his own victimization: Burton W. Peretti, *Jazz in American Culture* (Chicago: Ivan R. Dee, 1997), 21.
38. Oliver quoted by Martin Williams, *Jazz Masters of New Orleans* (New York: Macmillan, 1967), 100; Gary Boulard, *Louis Prima*

(Urbana: University of Illinois Press, 1989), 9. New Orleans' Creole photographers like Florestine Perrault Collins also took advantage of the ability to pass as white: Willis, *Reflections in Black*, 44. The legal precariousness of Creole *passing* is however stressed by Shirley Thompson, "'Ah Toucoutou, Ye Conin Vous': History and Memory in Creole New Orleans," *American Quarterly* 53, no. 2 (2001): 232–66.

39. Bruce Boyd Raeburn, "'That Ain't No Creole': Masquerade, Marketing and Transgression Against the Color Line in New Orleans," unpublished paper presented to the *Rhythm Changes Conference: Jazz Utopias*, Birmingham, 2017, 4, 7, 11.
40. Big Eye Louis Nelson's business card used a photograph taken from a portrait of the Superior Orchestra taken in 1910 while another use appears to be as an accompaniment to the band's business card, sometimes produced in the form of a post card.
41. Shawn Michelle Smith, "Unfixing the Frame(-up): A. P. Bedou," in *Pictures and Progress: Early Photography and the Making of African American Identity* 269.
42. Peter Townsend, *Jazz in American Culture* (Edinburgh: Edinburgh University Press, 2000), 163.
43. A. D. Coleman, "James Van Der Zee," in *Light Readings: A Photography Critiec's Writings, 1968–1978* (New York: Oxford University Press, 1979), 18.
44. For Van Der Zee's life and work see Regina A. Perry, "Introduction," in *James Van Der Zee*, ed. Liliane De Cock and Reginald McGhee (Dobbs Ferry, NY: Morgan & Morgan, 1973) n.pag. Jim Haskins, *James Van Der Zee: The Picture Takin' Man* (Trenton, NJ: Africa World Press, 1991) and the interviews with Van Der Zee in Camille Billops and Owen Dodson, *The Harlem Book of the Dead* (Dobbs Ferry, NY: Morgan & Morgan, 1978). Other useful sources include Mary Schmidt Campbell, "Introduction," in *Harlem Renaissance: Art of Black America*, 11–56; Deborah Willis-Braithwaite, "They Knew Their Names," in *Van Der Zee Photographer 1886–1983*, ed. Deborah Willis-Braithwaite and C. Birt, Ridger (New York: Harry N. Abrams, 1994), 8–25; Kobena Mercer, *James Van Der Zee* (London: Phaidon Press, 2003); Margaret Ohlin, "Putting Down Photographic Roots in Harlem," in *Touching Photography* (Chicago: University of Chicago Press, 2012), 131–60; Louise Siddons, "African Past or American Present? The Visual Eloquence of James Van Der Zee's 'Identical Twins,'" *African American Review* 46, nos. 2–3 (2013): 439–59; Rodger C. Birt, "A Life in American Photography," in *Van Der Zee Photographer 1886–1983*, ed. Deborah Willis-Braithwaite and Rodger C. Birt (New York: Harry N. Abrams, 1994), 26–74.
45. Peter Bacon Hales, *Silver Cities: Photographing American Urbanization, 1839–1939* (Albuquerque: University of New Mexico Press, 2005), 419.
46. Alfred Stieglitz, "Pictorial Photography," in *Classic Essays on Photography*, ed. Alan Trachtenberg (Leete's Island Books: New Haven, CT, 1980), 118–9; Siddons, "African Past or American Present? The Visual Eloquence of James Van Der Zee 'Identical Twins,'" 449, 451–54, locates Van Der Zee photographs within an American modernism layered over with "Africanizing symbolism" in the search for a "usable past"; Kobena Mercer, *James Van Der Zee* (London: Phaidon Press, 2003), 3.
47. Christopher Phillips, "The United States: American Society," in *A History of Photography: Social and Cultural Perspectives*, ed. Jean-Claude Lemagny and A. Rouillé, trans. J. Lloyd (Cambridge: Cambridge University Press, 1987), 158.
48. Van Der Zee quoted by Mercer, *James Van Der Zee*, 14.
49. Thelma Golden, "James Van Der Zee 'Christmas Morning' 1933," *Aperture*, 2016, 152.
50. As early as 1914 Elcha was being hailed in the Black press for his work as a retoucher at Rembrandt's, a leading New York Studio: "Photographic Retoucher," *New York Age*, September 3, 1914: 1. Elcha was subsequently mentioned on many occasions; see for example Staff Photographer, "Elcha's Work Known from Coast to Coast," *Pittsburgh Courier*, June 7, 1924 and "Courier Reporter Surveys Broadway," *Pittsburgh Courier*, February 4, 1928: 1.
51. Rex Stewart and Claire P. Gordon, *Boy Meets Horn* (Oxford: Bayou Press, 1991), 40.
52. D. Willis-Thomas, *An Illustrated Bio-Bibliography of Black Photographers: 1940–1988* (New York: Garland, 1989), 101.
53. The image is reproduced in V. Hollins Coar, *A Century of Black Photographers: 1840–1960* (Rhode Island: Rhode Island School of Design, 1983), 121.
54. Woodard cited by Amy Mooney, "'Visions of Great Usefulness and Progress': A Chicago Photographer's Studio and Black Modern Subjectivity," Courtauld Institute of Art, 2019;

https://courtauld.ac.uk/event/visions-of-great-usefulness-and-progress-modern-black-subjectivity-through-a-mid-twentieth-century-chicago-photographers-studio; Chicago *Defender* cited by Amy M. Mooney, "Photos of Style and Dignity: Woodard's Studios and the Delivery of Black Modern Subjectivity," in *Beyond the Face: New Perspectives on Portraiture*, ed. Wendy Wick Reaves (Washington, DC: National Portrait Gallery, 2018), 214.

55. Brazelton quoted by Piper, "Cameras at Work: African American Studio Photographers and the Business of Everyday Life, 1900–1970," 34. Piper also quotes the Boston photographer Daniel Freeman who recalls that he was required to photograph not only a wide variety of skin tones but also to render them as the sitters preferred.
56. Three photographs from the series are reproduced in Driggs and Lewine, *Black Beauty, White Heat: A Pictorial History of Jazz 1920–1950*, 72.
57. Driggs and Lewine, *Black Beauty, White Heat: A Pictorial History of Jazz 1920–1950*, 71.
58. James C. Scott, *Domination and the Arts of Resistance: Hidden Transcripts* (New Haven, CT: Yale University Press, 1990), 18–19. In a similar formulation, Robert A. Hill has spoken of the "submerged self"; for black Americans, "the photograph is much more than a complacent mirror of past achievement [and] is constantly examined the submerged self that speaks and performs:" Robert A. Hill, "Making Noises: Marcus Garvey Dada, August 1922," in *Picturing Us: African American Identity in Photography* (New York: New Press, 1994), 181–205.
59. Johnson, "Black Photography: Contexts for Evolution," 15, speaks of the "domination of the document" in the history of black photography, which sets it apart from the history of photography as a whole.
60. John Roberts, "'Realism, Modernism, and Photography: At Last, at Last the Mask Has Been Torn Away," in *Adventures in Realism*, ed. Matthew Beaumont (Malden, MA: Blackwell, 2007), 163.
61. Peter Brooks, *Realist Vision* (New Haven, CT: Yale University Press, 2005), 147. This brings us closer to the realism of Courbet and Cézanne that is the real *as experienced*, the world realized through perception as a form of subjectivity we all have:Brendan Prendeville, *Realism in 20th Century Painting* (London: Thames & Hudson, 2000), 9.
62. Addison Gayle Jr., "The Harlem Renaissance: Towards a Black Aesthetic," in *The Addison Gayle Jr. Reader*, ed. Nathaniel Norment J. (Urbana: University of Illinois Press, 2009), 71 "Hoyt Fuller (1923–1981)—Towards a Black Aesthetic," in *The Norton Anthology of African American Literature*, ed. Henry Louis Gates Jr. and Nellie W. McKay (New York: W. W. Norton, 1997), 1809–16; Richard A. Long, "Fuller, Hoyt," in *The Oxford Companion to African American Literature*, ed. W. A Andrews, F.S. Foster and Trudier Harris (New York: Oxford University Press, 1997), 302–3; Larry Neal, "The Black Arts Movement," in *Visions of a Liberated Future: Black Arts Movement Writings*, ed. Michael Schwartz (New York: Thunder's Mouth Press, 1989), 62.
63. Neal, "The Black Arts Movement," 62.
64. Gena Dagel Caponi, "Introduction: The Case for An African American Aesthetic," in *Signifyin(g), Sanctifyin' and Slam Dunking: A Reader in African American Expressive Culture*, ed. Gena Dagel Caponi (Amherst: University of Massachusetts Press, 1999), 7–8.

7

Expressive Realism
African American Photography

Prowling 1940s Seattle when his full-time job allowed, Albert Joseph Septimus "Al" Smith documented the lives, events, and social activities of the city's ethnic communities. His primary interest was his own black neighborhood as Peter Blecha, a historian of the Seattle music scene, confirmed:[1]

> *African Americans were a minority in Seattle [. . .] this translated into affection for his own community [. . .] weddings, funerals, community festivals or nightlife. He was very aware that this was the black culture in Seattle and probably felt some responsibility to document it.*

The significance of Smith's archive of around 10,000 images was emphasized by former Seattle Mayor Norm Rice, a long-standing friend of the photographer: "There wasn't a major event or happening in the African-American community that Al wasn't chronicling;" Smith, he added, "had that quiet mind's eye who gave us a lens to look at ourselves."[2]

During the 1940s jazz was to be found most nights in the scores of vibrant clubs that lined both sides of Jackson Street from Pioneer Square east into the Central Area. Ignored by most whites, the all-white AFM Local No. 76 and Seattle's local media and recording industry, the jazz scene resembled a self-contained enclave.[3] Smith wasn't an avid music fan but he was acutely sensitive to the relationship between jazz and the social experience of the mostly segregated clubs. A palpable sense of engagement emerges from his photographs that convey through gesture, expression, and movement the interactions between players, audiences, and photographer. His catch line, "Al Smith On The Spot," was well chosen.

Smith's Speed Graphic camera gave him credibility and access that he used to capture remarkably intimate photographs. Most of these images employ the eye-level viewpoint; avoiding acute angles, he chose a viewpoint and sightlines that directly met his subjects *en face*. Smith often positioned himself on the stage with the artists, photographing them close-up as if he were a member of the band. Capturing Lionel Hampton in 1946 in a mid-air jump, Smith was on the stage, as he was when he photographed Al Sears with Duke Ellington at the Civic Auditorium in 1947. Few jazz performance shots are as directly engaging as his photograph of trumpeter Tiny Davis playing with the International Sweethearts of Rhythm (Figure 86). As his son recalled, "He usually didn't ask people's permission [. . .] He would get right on stage to photograph the jazz greats. Though always respectful and courteous, he wasn't in awe of celebrities."[4]

Smith shot from positions chosen to transport the viewer into the heart of the action. The result was a noticeable shift in the relationship between the viewer and the image. His photograph of saxophonist Pete Peterson entertaining soldiers is taken from deep within the group (Figure 87); and, captured at the Senator Ballroom in 1949, our view of Dizzy Gillespie is exactly that seen by a

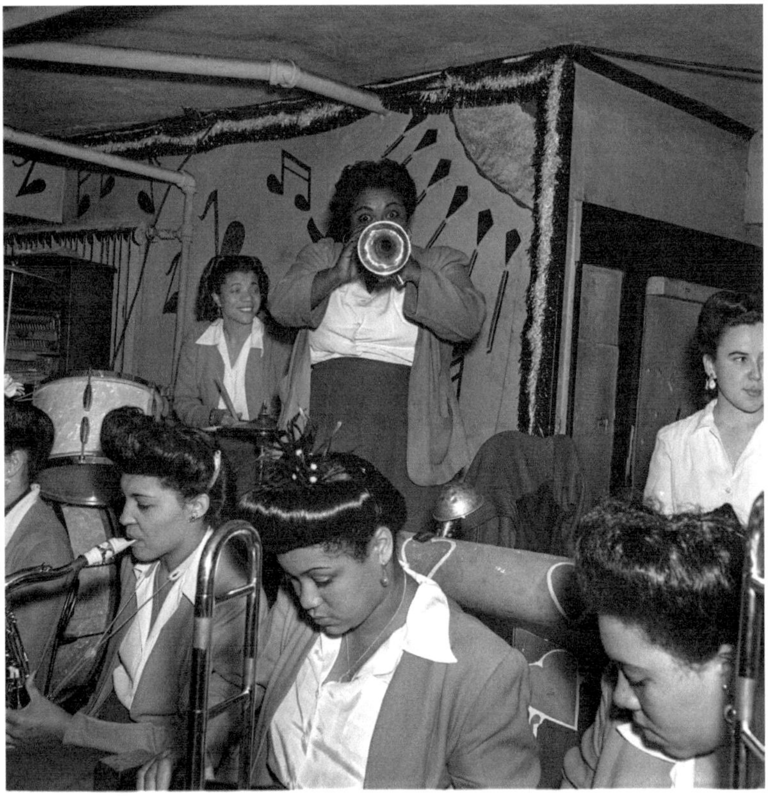

Figure 86: Al Smith. *International Sweethearts of Rhythm at the Black & Tan Speakeasy.* September 24, 1944.
Permission of Museum of History and Industry, Seattle, Al Smith collection.

member of the band. In his photograph of the Leon Vaughan Band at the Basin Street nightclub in 1948 he appears to have been embedded in the band itself (Figure 88). Right up among the players, it is impossible not to feel the spontaneous interaction with the audience which the players' expressions make obvious.

The intimate insights conveyed by these images are those John Collier identified as the possibilities of the "Photographer as Participant Observer"—acute observations of black musical practices from the inside sufficiently attuned to visualize the nonverbal communication that supports discourse. Compared with the work of earlier African American photographers discussed in the previous chapter, Al Smith's photography speaks to a more forceful "second-generation" black identity based on an acute awareness of the "real" as a cultural signifier.[5] Spurred by publication opportunities in the black press, African American photographers from the 1930s onward developed wide-ranging reportage practices that they usually combined with day-to-day studio and portraiture work. Exploiting the greater availability of lightweight cameras and equipment, they began exploring the streets and black spaces beyond their studios looking

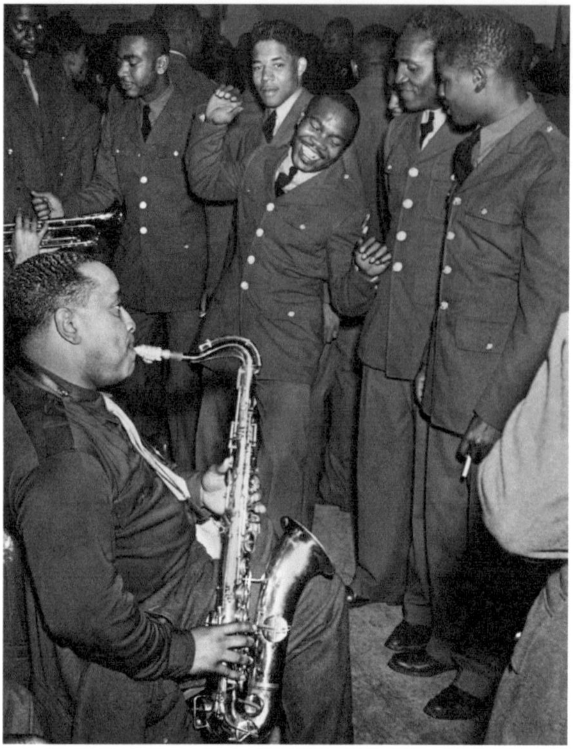

Figure 87: Al Smith. *Pete Peterson.* n.d.
Permission of Museum of History and Industry, Seattle, Al Smith collection.

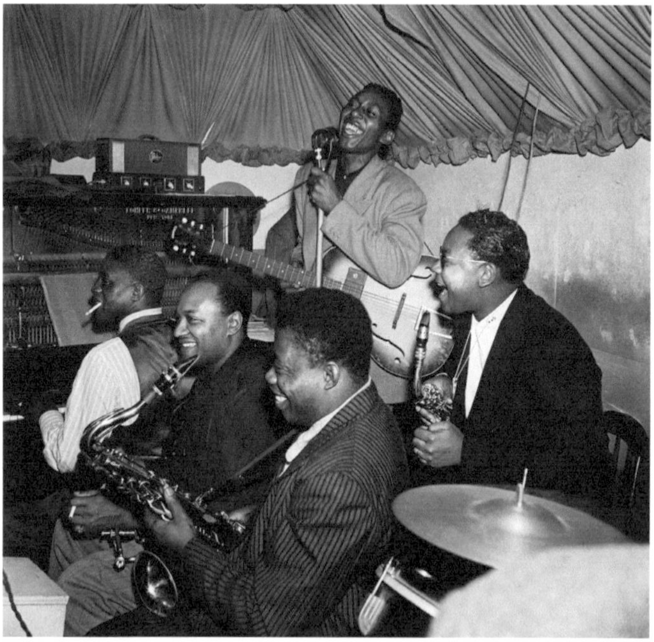

Figure 88: Al Smith. *The Leon Vaughan Band.* n.d.
Permission of Museum of History and Industry, Seattle, Al Smith collection.

to capture life as it was experienced "on the spot" in a more overtly expressive form of the documentary ethos that flourished generally in 1930s America. In gesture, movement, expressions, material culture, and the interactions of race, gender, and class this generation of black photographers began to reveal the inner life of what Robin D. G. Kelley has termed the covert "congregations" of black life—dance halls, juke joints, clubs, and bars.[6] The result was a distinctly demythologizing aesthetic, materially grounded and expressively rendered.

I. "Second-generation" Black identity and photography

Communities and the Black press

Deborah Dash Moore reminds us that the idea of "second-generation" consciousness generally applied to immigrants is just as relevant in the case of internal migrants.[7] There is evidence by the 1930s of a more assertive sense of black identity in the outlook of second-generation black migrants. As early as 1925 Alain Locke had spoken of a "younger generation [. . .] vibrant with a new psychology," a spirit led by Harlem's "talented tenth" and which found expression in music and the arts. This was the beginning of a radical shift that Henry Louis Gates Jr., later described as a "reinvention [. . .] the outcome of the exchange of traditional southern and northern black cultures and the resulting synthesis of the two."[8] The devasting impact of the early Depression years on black lives however initiated what the novelist and associate of Langston Hughes, Arna Bontemps, saw a "second awakening" of African American creative expression, less romantic than that which the 1920s had produced, "but closer to realities." If the Harlem Renaissance of the 1920s had been a period of self-definition the period that followed saw that definition being held to the test. Casting this transformation as an example of generational shift theorized by Karl Mannheim, Ron Eyerman has contextualized second-generation black identity as being nurtured within "a relatively autonomous black public sphere" created by urbanization and economic expansion in the 1920s; the institutions, ideas, and cultural expressions of an increasingly self-conscious and assertive black urban life; and the catalyzing effect of economic necessity.[9]

There was of course a broader context in which second-generation African American identity crystallized. The release of African American initiative, creativity, and self-confidence cannot be divorced from the wider moment of "double empowerment" of the 1920s—the larger (white) cultural American emancipation from its European heritage and the narrower (black) movement toward the celebration of black heritage. These two forces were inextricably linked, resulting in that hybridization which as Ann Douglas has argued accounts for the vitality, iconoclasm, and brash modernity of 1920s "mongrel Manhattan." Yet, in the field of art criticism if not the appreciation of wider cultural phenomena, this interdependence hardly registered among white Americans, effectively forcing black awareness inward toward its own existential realities.[10]

Nor should the effect of war, so often a marker of generational change, be overlooked.[11] The deep-rooted social and cultural changes precipitated by America's engagement in the first world war upended prewar assumptions for all Americans, black and white. Within a short period the prior dominance of Anglo-European high culture had begun to weaken. Innovative forms of cultural expression emerged from the war years to reflect the onset of a new age marked by uncertainty, patriotism, modernism, and the revolt against established artistic, moral, religious and social conventions. Little could hide the disillusion that pervaded black life after 1918: race riots in Washington, Chicago, Longview, and Knoxville (in which 77 African Americans were lynched, some still in uniform) were in part a response to the intense disappointment felt by black Americans in the immediate aftermath of the war. For one black newspaper, recognition for black war service came in the form of the "double cross."[12] In spite of America's remarkable economic advances, African Americans remained severely disadvantaged, sharpening further a sense of racial awareness. Black Americans hardly participated in the economic boom of the 1920s and were largely ignored by Republican administrations during the decade. The depression of the early to mid-1930s worsened their already dire economic situation.[13]

The immediate context in which a critical change in black emotions and attitudes took place were the black urban communities brought into being by the later (and larger) northern and western migration of southern blacks. All Americans were disconcerted by the process of urbanization but none more so that those blacks moving north, for whom the speed of change was incomparably greater. The black writer Charles S. Johnson went so far as to argue that the differences between the old and new modes of life that the migrations brought about in New York's Harlem, Chicago, and other Midwest cities and large conurbations on the west coast was even greater than that between black and white. No other ethnic or racial group was ever subjected to a "seismic sociological shift" of this scale.[14]

Black urban neighborhoods were crowded and unsanitary, working conditions in northern factories harsh and relentless, and many migrants resented the residential segregation and other forms of *de facto* discrimination forced on them when they arrived. Detailed studies have shown however that these communities were socially heterogeneous and many blacks enjoyed a degree of autonomy in their new lives. A black middle class and intellectual stratum emerged to provide cultural, intellectual, and political leadership and an extensive network of black religious, medical, business, educational, legal, professional, and fraternal organizations came into being.[15] New ideas and styles of black life began to develop. In distinctive modes of speech, music, dance, and the visual and plastic arts, a genuinely mass popular culture came into being, insulating blacks from the cultural reorientation that might have been expected to arise from exposure to Hollywood movies, standard brands, and radio. Nowhere was this more evident than in the diversity and vibrancy of black entertainment venues in the South Side of Chicago and the entrepreneurial zeal with which black businessmen managed and promoted their clubs and cabarets.[16]

White ignorance of differences within black communities and residential zoning helped seal the cultural distinctiveness and separation of black communities. Politics exacerbated the divide. Adherents to the progressive movement had been firm believers in racial superiority, motivating black leadership to branch away from the mainstream and focus specifically on local social, political, and economic concerns.[17] Black Americans were equally marginal to mainstream left political and trade union discourse. Philip S. Foner has detailed the "dismal picture" of consistent failure by the American Socialist Party to grasp the problems faced by black Americans in the mid-1930s. The inability of America's craft unions to transcend nativist tendencies and commit to racial equality meant that no viable alternative promoting racial equality existed beyond the wavering attraction of the American Communist Party to black intellectuals in certain urban hot spots and an engagement with jazz during the Popular Front period as an expression of "folk" origins.[18]

The articulation of the emerging black identity found intellectual expression in the Harlem renaissance, a flourishing in arts and letters also evident in Chicago, New Orleans, Los Angeles, and Washington DC.[19] Carrying these ideas to a wider populace was a resurgent and sometimes burningly partisan black press. The history of America's black press, whose roots stretch back to early abolitionist pamphlets and broadsheets, need not be repeated here.[20] Suffice it to say that by 1910 over 275 black newspapers were being published in cities throughout the United States, reaching a cumulative circulation of half a million readers; a decade later, some five hundred black newspapers were in print. Most of these publications sought to instill hope and pride in recently relocated people, although some avoided open social criticism, preferring gossip, crime, and scandal or, like the *Memphis World*, aiming for a balance between black assertion and southern white sensibilities.[21] All however spoke directly to a new era of black concerns. Nothing encapsulates these concerns more vividly than Langston Hughes's Jesse B. Semple (or "Simple") sketches, which began appearing in the *Chicago Defender* in 1943 and ran for almost 23 years. Cast in the form of a dialogue between a sophisticated northern-born narrator and a naïve new arrival from the South, the dialogues illustrate the disruptions of social change and the "inner conversation" through which people make sense of the world and identity: Hughes described these columns as "just myself talking to me. Or else me talking to myself."[22]

The unique role of the black press in conceptualizing blackness cannot be overemphasized; if culture was a critical battleground for African Americans precisely because it was the one area over which they could exert control, it was the black press which anchored that control.[23] Before the creation and consolidation of networks in the 1930s, local radio was important in mediating Americanness and thus central to the efforts of urban, immigrant and working-class Americans in establishing ethnic, racial, and class differentiation. Local non-commercial radio broadcasts in the 1920s did much to reinforce ethnic, class, and religious affiliations. By the mid-1930s, radios had become a staple in working-class homes, and contributed more than any other medium to the establishment of a universal working-class experience. African Americans were almost wholly excluded from participation in this exercise in experiential conceptualization from which they were bracketed by exclusion. Black music might have been broadcast by local stations (it is estimated that some 800 local radio broadcasts showcased black musicians between 1920 and 1930) but it was vastly outplayed by white imitators.[24]

In the absence of a sound medium attuned to their needs, the black press filled the gap in a way that was as much visual as discursive. Black publications markedly increased their use of visual material during the 1930s and there are striking contrasts between their use of illustrations, cartoons, and photography and that of white publications even when sympathetic to the black cause. Unlike the white leftists during the early-1930s, whose visual material mostly sought to dramatize contemporary events such as the trials of the Scottsboro Boys as part of the broader class struggle, the black press:[25]

> [...] *humanized the Scottsboro Boys to a far greater degree in the images they created, effectively asking the predominantly northern black readership to identify with the experience of racial oppression in the South [. . .] Tapping into a wider cultural tendency in the 1930s to draw attention to black mothers, such images worked both to humanize the Scottsboro Boys and lynch victims by presenting them as sons of grieving mothers and to characterize their legal struggle as a universal struggle affecting all African Americans.*

The crucial mediating role played by the black press ensured that visual material played a more important role in the conceptualization of African American identity than was the case with other social and/or racial groups.

The nature of expressive realism

Black photographers could not but be influenced by the growing cohesion and assertiveness within African American communities, the confident visual and discursive tone of the black press, the outpourings of African American advocacy organizations, and new ideas and styles of black life. Cecil J. Williams's memoir of a local portrait and general community photographer in Orangeburg, South Carolina, reveals how his seemingly *quotidienne* work was also "a photographic journey back into the legally segregated world [. . .] entirely shaped by race and color." Transcending transactional necessity his photographs were testimony to the everyday people and their struggles: "My pictures most often salute the unknown people who put their lives on the line to confront and change a system of segregation and racism."[26]

These forces explain the trajectory of black photography toward a more expressive form of realism based on a vision of black communities realized from the inside. Demand for portraiture underpinned the growth of black-owned photographic businesses. Family portraits were to be found in every black household and images of black leaders and role models decorated homes, clubs, and institutes, contributing significantly to the sense of black worth and identity. Studios such as those of R. H. Hicks in Georgia and the Daisy Studio in Memphis "offered a vital medium of self-expression to young blacks during the uncertain interwar period."[27] Alongside portraiture, black photographers made celebratory images by recording social, cultural, and religious events, along with a wide range of club and association activities mostly ignored by the white press. The black press filled the gap by providing a vital outlet at both the national and local level encouraging black photographers to extend the scope and expressiveness of their work in the streets of their communities. Many black photographers found it advantageous to combine portraiture and photojournalist practices, running local studio businesses while acting as a photographic stringer for the local black newspaper or magazine.[28]

The symbiotic relationship between the press and black photographers was especially important at the local level where newspapers fulfilled the demand for news, while photographers supplied images that historicized, celebrated, and documented African American culture. Music was part and parcel of this vision. In Cleveland Ohio Allen Edward Cole was the first black photographer to open a studio in 1922. For the next 40 years he served the local community, supplementing his income as a part-time photojournalist with the *Call & Post*, an African American newspaper founded in 1928. Cole's archive is an enduring chronicle of black life in Cleveland over nearly half a century and his photograph of Evelyn Freeman's musicians illustrates this well (Figure 89). The band comprised aspiring high school players who, in spite of their inexperience, became extremely popular on the local social scene, broadcasted on WHK from the Circle ballroom and several of whose players went on to build national reputations (including "Bull Moose" Jackson).[29]

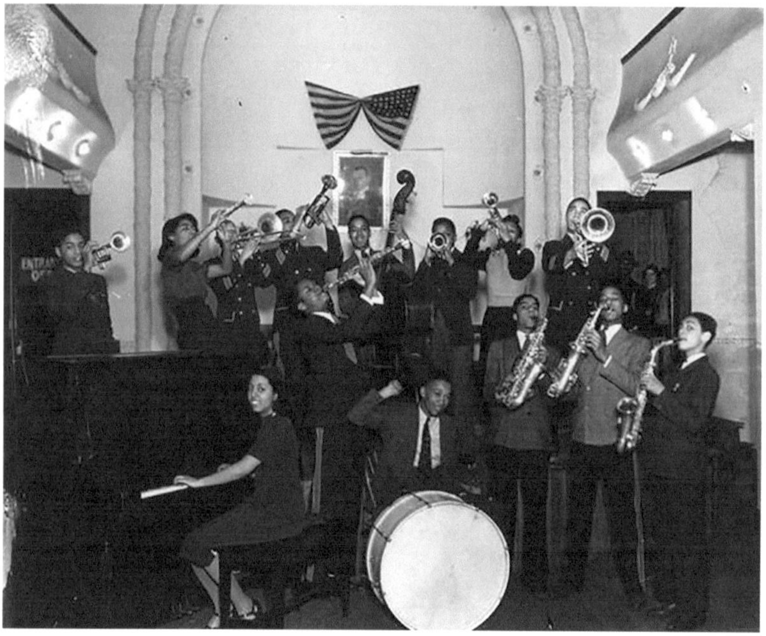

Figure 89: Allen E. Cole. *Freeman Ensemble* (later Evelyn Freeman Swing Band). n.d. *Permission of Western Reserve Historical Society, Cleveland, Ohio.*

Developing reportage practices alongside portraiture deepened the expressive narrative of black photography. Just as early-1930s social realism in American visual arts emerged from a domestic graphic tradition of magazine illustration and poster art, so too black photographic realism was mediated by the aesthetic and narrative demands of the black press.[30] As a photojournalist with the *Pittsburgh Courier*, Bob Douglas recalls his editor Colin Stewart's admonitions when he returned with below-par photographs: "I can't print excuses" and "the picture doesn't say anything—take it back". To be accepted a photograph had to be attractive as a composition and quickly arresting in the story it conveyed.[31] Carefully contextualizing images was one of the photojournalist's methods of enhancing their expressive immediacy. Deborah Willis explains how Harry Adams's photographs went beyond simply recording the event:[32]

> *By including the pastor of the church, stained glass window, the ushers and the people in the balcony, he is documenting a harmonious environment that is highly respectful of the ritual. He invokes the sincerity of the moment [. . .] with a keen understanding of how intimate places are transformed into public space.*

Turning their lenses toward jazz subject, African American photographers after around the 1930s were becoming increasingly aware of jazz as a distinctive form of cultural expression with its own performative practices and rituals. As individual musicians achieved commercial fame, it became clear that the music was a specific achievement of black Americans and these musicians joined sportsmen, entertainers, civic, religious, and political leaders and artists on the pantheon of African American success stories. Yet the context in which photographers worked required that the roots of this success in local communal soil should be made clear and this militated against the natural tendency to mythologize the musicians.

II. Black photographers and jazz

Jacks of all trades

Specialization was a luxury few black photographers could afford. Portraiture yielded only a basic income at best, and most black photographers between 1918 and 1960 found it necessary to balance a range of activities in order to make a decent living.[33] Not all these photographers had a particularly developed interest in jazz but as "jacks of all trades" music was part and parcel of this daily round. Active from the late-1920s onward Marion J. Porter, the proprietor of Porter's Photo News Service in New Orleans, took news photographs and portraits for *Louisiana Weekly*, *Jet*, and *Ebony* magazines. He photographed the civil rights movements and baseball games, prominent public figures, celebrities, and local events. Working well into the 1980s "he recorded the fullness and the rich cultural flavor of New Orleans' black community"[34] including images of Louis Armstrong, Duke Ellington, and Lionel Hampton. Also established in the 1920s, New Orleans' Magnolia Studios was operated by two generations of the McCormick and Abadies families. According to the New Orleans photography historian Girard P. Mouton III, "Their documentation of New Orleans jazz was a normal part of day to day business, with portraits and the like constituting their basic bread and butter."[35]

In Houston Benny Joseph set up his business after discharge from the military in 1945. He knew he had to meet each and every demand:[36]

> *Photography was considered a trade or vocation, not an art form. Like his contemporaries Louise Martin and Herbert Prevost, Joseph had to "do it all" to make a living as a photographer—portraits, snapshots, news, advertising, churches, parades, politicians, dances and musicians.*

Joseph's photographs of jazz and R&B musicians sit alongside his portraits of notable leaders of the civil rights movement. Joseph also offered studio sittings to musicians and his portraits of Sam "Lightin" Hopkins, Clarence "Gatemouth" Brown, "Junior" Parker, Eddie Vinson, Albert Collins, and Lester Williams were generally shot against a plain background with gently modulated lighting and faint shadows.[37]

Ernest Withers's photography business in Memphis followed a similar model. Based around a portrait studio located in downtown Memphis, Withers reported on important moments in the life of the local community for black newspapers including the *Tri-State Defender* which he helped John H. Sengstacke to launch in 1951. If Hooks' Brothers dominated the portraiture market in Memphis and William Eggleston was the leading art photographer, Withers was the foremost photojournalist of the day. A close friend of Dr. Martin Luther King and other civil rights leaders, Withers' documentary record of the racial struggles of the 1950s and 1960s is of particular significance. Music was just as important to Withers as the struggle for racial justice. As well as being the official photographer at Stax Records in Memphis for around 20 years, his daughter Rosalind recalled that "Dad had close relationships with a lot of the musicians. Because of his [studio] location on Beale Street, he interacted with the musical world all the time—Duke Ellington, W. C. Handy, Count Basie, Billy Eckstine—as well as blues musicians like B. B. King."[38] As is so often the case with black photographers, Withers's interest when photographing musicians in performance lay as much in the response of the audiences as with the portrayal of musicians and singers themselves (Figure 90).

In New York City Austin Hansen made his start in business in 1929 by selling a photograph of Charles Lindbergh to the *Amsterdam News*. He offered personal portraiture while supplying newspapers with photographs of the daily life of Harlem and virtually every famous Harlem figure and event until his retirement in the 1960s. Eschewing contrived studio settings, Hansen's location photographs have been described as realist documents, "a map and compass" to Harlem undistorted by race or metaphor.[39] Comparing photographs made at Harlem's Apollo Theatre by Aaron Siskind and Hansen, Richard Ings notes how Siskind's backstage access makes him an invisible observer of "an overwhelmingly 'black' space." Refusing, like Al Smith, to be confined to a prescribed viewpoint, Hansen's photograph depicts the "true audience at the Apollo—black people watching black people [. . .] [and] the theatre's transformation into a cultural landmark."[40]

Morgan and Marvin Smith were photojournalists and studio workers in New York. The twins were among the first black photojournalists to supply black-owned publications such as the *New York Amsterdam News* and *People's Voice* with images ranging from anti-lynching demonstrations to Fats Waller, babies and brides, Jackie Robinson teaching his young son baseball, Nat King Cole's wedding, W. E. B. DuBois recording a speech, the New York black Yankees, Paul Robeson signing autographs, and the dancer Maya Angelou. Morgan Smith made his name with his extended coverage of Joe Louis in a series of remarkable

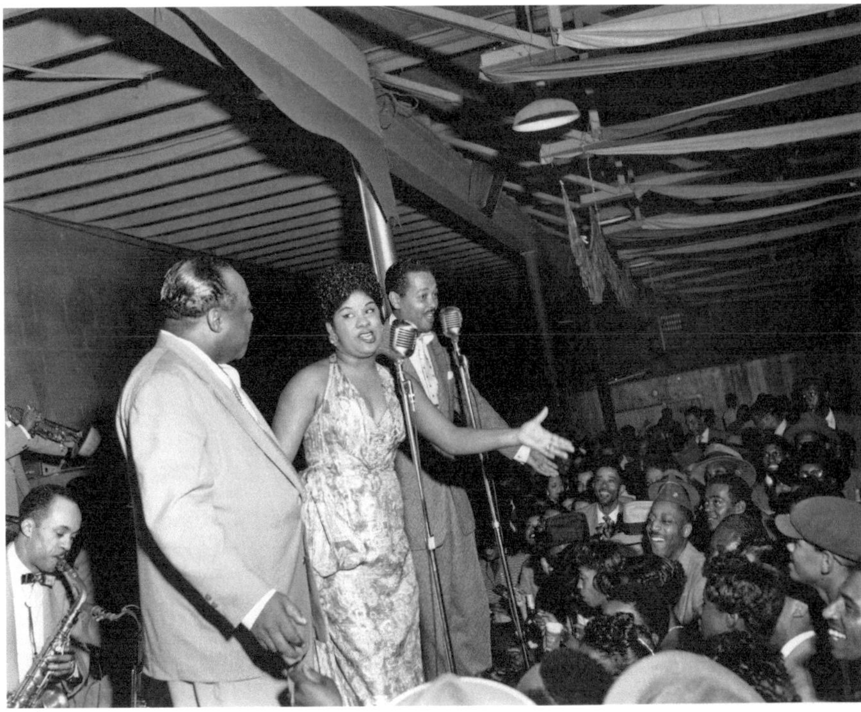

Figure 90: Ernest Withers. *Count Basie, Ruth Brown, Billy Eckstine.* The Hippodrome. Memphis. 1950s.
Ernest Withers Collection/Permission of Rosalind Withers.

photo-essays that ran in the *Amsterdam News* after 1936. The Smiths' studio became an important social hub for glamorous African Americans to have their likeness recorded. According to Gordon Parks, "Harlem spread itself before the cameras of Morgan and Marvin Smith like a great tablecloth, and eagerly they went about devouring what it had to offer."[41]

The Smiths saw jazz musicians and singers as symbols of black achievement and took pains to contextualize their subjects by including interactions between artists and their followers during the performance or before and after the show. Their photograph of "Tiny" Bunch, the legendary Lindy-Hopper, recorded in a memorable shot at the Savoy in 1938, captures perfectly the expressions of an enthusiastic crowd. The composition of the Smiths' 1936 photograph of Ivie Anderson taken during performance carefully interweaves the young singer and her adoring fans. Taken around 1938, their photograph of Ella Fitzgerald with the Chick Webb Orchestra at the Savoy Ballroom portrays the singer smiling and relaxed, surrounded by Webb, Louis Jordan, and other band members. Ella's entry into the Webb Orchestra had not been easy; she found it difficult to establish relations with other band members and struggled with her stage presentation. The Smiths portrayed her smiling and relaxed surrounded by what appear to be supportive colleagues and—whatever her own reservations—presenting herself beautifully.[42]

An important group of African American photojournalists came to prominence in the 1940s and 1950s on the west coast. Assisted in many cases by training under the G.I. Bill, these were "no-nonsense photographers who worked quickly and efficiently because as freelancers they were being paid by the image. They didn't take the time or go to the expense of photographing interesting sites or locations if they didn't have an assignment." For them photography was a job not an avocation; and they faced the same challenge of balancing ideas shaped by the requirements of press publication with the demands of their readers for a tangible and expressive sense of black life.[43]

Several among this group made important images of jazz. Charles Williams was a recognizable figure in black Hollywood as a photographer of actors, models, and musicians for the *California Eagle* and other local publications. Born in Arkansas in 1918, Harry Adams's photographic career began after he completed a tour of duty in World War II and graduated from the California School of Photography and Graphic Design (operated by Charles Williams). With access to the city's inner circle, he became known for his images of politicians, entertainers, society figures, as well as social organizations, churches, schools, civil rights organizations, protests, and cultural events for the *California Eagle* and *Los Angeles Sentinel*. Black photographers like Adams could not afford to indulge in dilettantism as family members recall:[44]

> *Harry was extremely professional [. . .] the African Photographers didn't fool around, meaning Show up, Get the shot, and on to the next assignment, not like today where photographers are part celebrities. This was not a hobby with Harry, he carved out a pretty good living but things were so different then [. . .] once he was in his studio and darkroom, he was strictly a no-nonsense professional, We have over 10,000 images that reflect that. Another important thing: all the black photographers were a tight knit bunch, Guy Crowder, Charles Williams, Murphy Ruffins and a few others seemed to only like each other.*

Adams' image of Count Basie being presented with a box of cigarettes by a local man and Nat "King" Cole with a beauty queen are photographs crafted to pique the interest of readers of the African American media (Figures 91 and 92).[45]

The St. Lucia born photographer Emmanuel Francis (E. F.) Joseph was the first professional African American photographer in the San Francisco Bay Area operating a commercial and studio photography business in his home in Oakland. Other local photographers who, like Joseph, captured images of jazz players

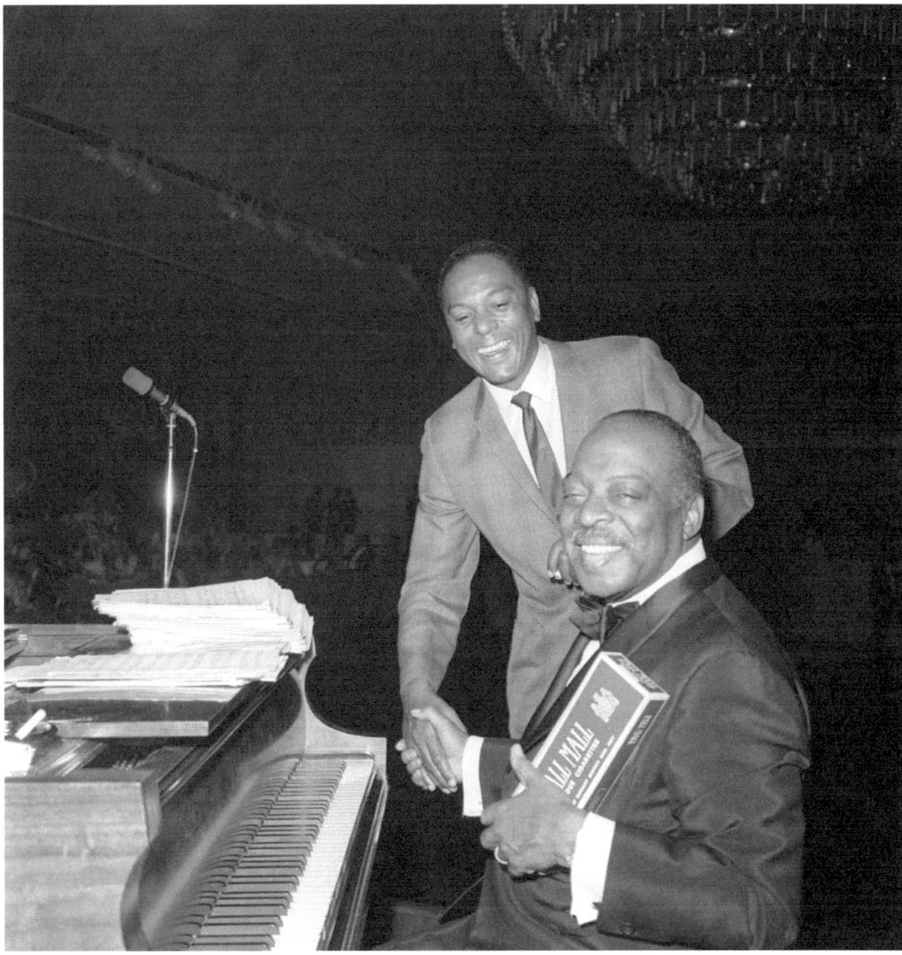

Figure 91: Harry Adams. *Count Basie*. Los Angeles. 1968.
Tom and Ethel Bradley Centre for African American Arts, California State University, Northridge, Harry Adams Collection/Permission of Diane Lara.

when they were in the area included Steve Jackson Jr, J. B. Coleman, Red Powell, and David Johnson.

African American eyes on music

Generalist practitioners such as these visualized jazz as expressive of the arc of the black lives and activities they were recording. Several other black photographers delved more deeply into the world of jazz and their work offers more nuanced insights into the social and cultural practices around the music.

Charles "Teenie" Harris: Celebrating the unidentified

The remarkable archive of Pittsburgh's Hill District conscientiously assembled over nearly half a century by Charles "Teenie" Harris would not have been

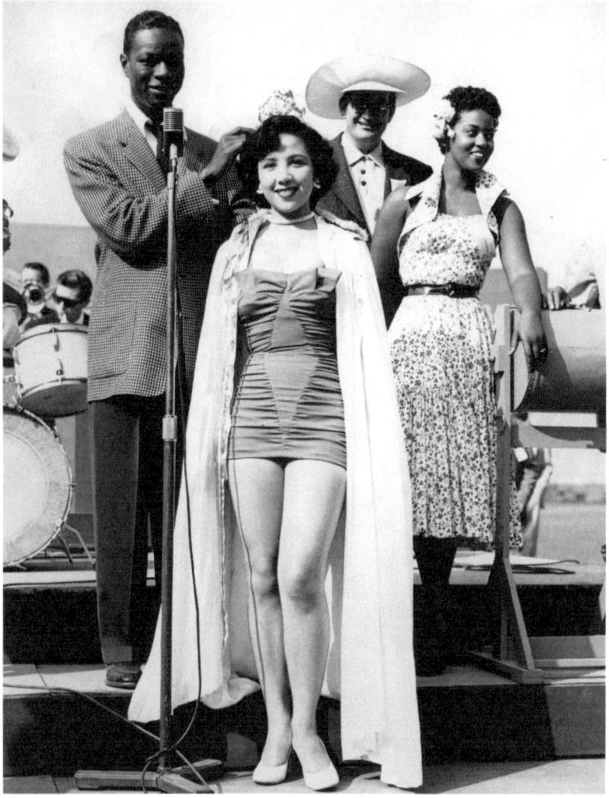

Figure 92: Harry Adams. *Nat King Cole, Hunter Hancock and wife Margie.* Los Angeles. n.d. *Tom and Ethel Bradley Centre for African American Arts, California State University, Northridge, Harry Adams Collection/Permission of Diane Lara.*

possible without the support of the *Pittsburgh Courier.*[46] The paper published over 50 of his photographs in 1939 alone and, like many black photographers, he combined photojournalism with studio portraiture: "I *had* to freelance, take pictures for people, because I couldn't live off what the *Courier* paid me."[47] His studio at 2128 Centre Avenue was listed in the Pittsburgh City directories from 1938 to 1953 and provided Harris's bread and butter income during the lean times when press work was less plentiful.

Writers have stressed the ways in which Harris's photographs presented positive images of the vibrant culture of the Hill: "he did not focus on black poverty. Teenie Harris was not an outsider in the Hill District. His photographs nourish us precisely because they provide a point of view that is familiar, intimate and caring."[48] Harris's portrayals of black success stories—politicians, celebrities, musicians, and sportsmen—are of course integral to the positive ethos that infused his work. Yet his representation of visiting jazz greats like Duke Ellington, Cab Calloway, and Dizzy Gillespie and locally born musicians like Erroll Garner, Earl Hines, Billy Billy Eckstein, Billy Strayhorn, Mary Lou Williams,

Art Blakey, Kenny Clarke, and Roy Eldridge reaches beyond the positive counterstatement. He achieved this partly by capturing these personalities off-guard, backstage in theatres or in restaurants and clubs such as the Loendi, the Crawford Grill, and the Hurricane. The musicians are shown jamming with friends or socializing, immaculately attired yet relaxed and profoundly human. Captured in their dressing rooms, his photographs of Lena Horne and Ethel Fields show the artists without stage personas; and Errol Garner and Leroy Brown lean on a cigarette machine while gossiping, their stage attire incongruously juxtaposed with the backstage setting. In a photograph from around 1942, Billy Strayhorn smiles as Duke Ellington appears to be pulling music from under dancer Charles "Honi" Coles, who is sitting on the upright piano.

The most striking aspect of Harris's photographs however is not the *elevation* of individual success stories but the efforts he made *to ground* this success through inclusion of other members of the community who—as if to emphasize the point—are frequently unidentified (Figure 93). The deportment, dress, poses, and expressions of the unidentified tell us as much about the life of black Pittsburgh as do the obvious material success of the musicians. As Stanley Crouch put it, "As signs of social status and self-respect, nice shoes and clean clothes mattered

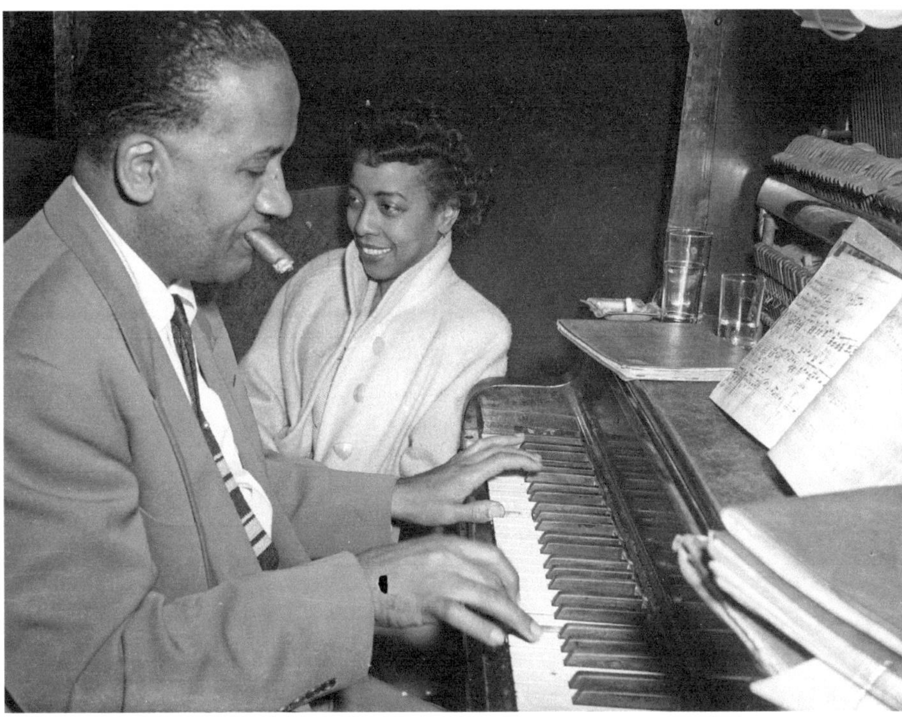

Figure 93: Charles "Teenie" Harris. *Cozy Harris playing sheet music next to an unknown woman.* Pittsburgh. *c.*1950–55.
Carnegie Museum of Art.

in the Hill District and people tried hard to look their best. African Americans in Pittsburgh often shopped in Kaufmann's and Gimbels downtown."[49]

Sitting in a booth at the Crawford Grill, Louis Armstrong slides up close to a unidentified woman who is foregrounded in the frame; Ray Charles is shown behind a group of unidentified women and Ellington was captured by Harris signing autographs in 1940 in the midst of a throng of female fans as poised and elegant as the Duke himself (Figure 40). In these and similar images Harris creates an intimate bond between the musicians and the black community in which their success was rooted by the inclusion of individuals whose presence iconically represents that community. Any mythologizing halo around the musician is immediately dispersed in images that transcend superficial differences, myths "pushed aside by the picture in favor of a range of specifics, and those specifics are as universal."[50]

Howard Morehead and the glamour of jazz

Late in life Howard Morehead circulated a proposal for a book, *Eye on Music,* based on over 50 years' work in the field of jazz. He decided to send to publishers his annual calendar, *Bronze Beauties,* a collection of glamour shots of African American and colored women, rather than the mock-up of the book now in UCLA's special collections or other examples of his jazz photography (Figures 94 and 95). His approaches included testimonials from Ray York, promotional Director, Bronze Beauty Enterprises, who emphasized that "No photographer has such a vast array of jazz greats and celebrities. Morehead has documented jazz since the 1940s."[51] This juxtapositioning of glamour and jazz photography might seem incongruous but provides an important insight into Morehead's photography.

Howard Morehead was born in Topeka, Kansas, and relocated to Los Angeles in the late-1940s.[52] He struggled to make a living as a freelance photographer but was able to secure newspaper and magazine assignments and a weekly newspaper column. He earned a degree in photography at Los Angeles City College, studied journalism at Los Angeles State College, and went on to further studies at UCLA and USC. By the early-1950s he had secured a staff position as the first west coast photojournalist for *Ebony* and *Jet* magazines while freelancing for the *Los Angeles Sentinel.* Within a few years he became the first African American cameraman with a Los Angeles TV station (KABC-TV). He wrote articles and essays to accompany his work or in appreciation of local musicians and produced a number of photojournalistic essays to accompany his extensive archive of travel photography.

It was however as a glamour photographer that Morehead found fame. Proudly describing himself as "the nation's foremost chronicler of beautiful women," he produced and directed the annual Miss Bronze California Beauty Pageant for 12 years. His book of glamour photography, *Gentlemen Prefer Bronze,* was a

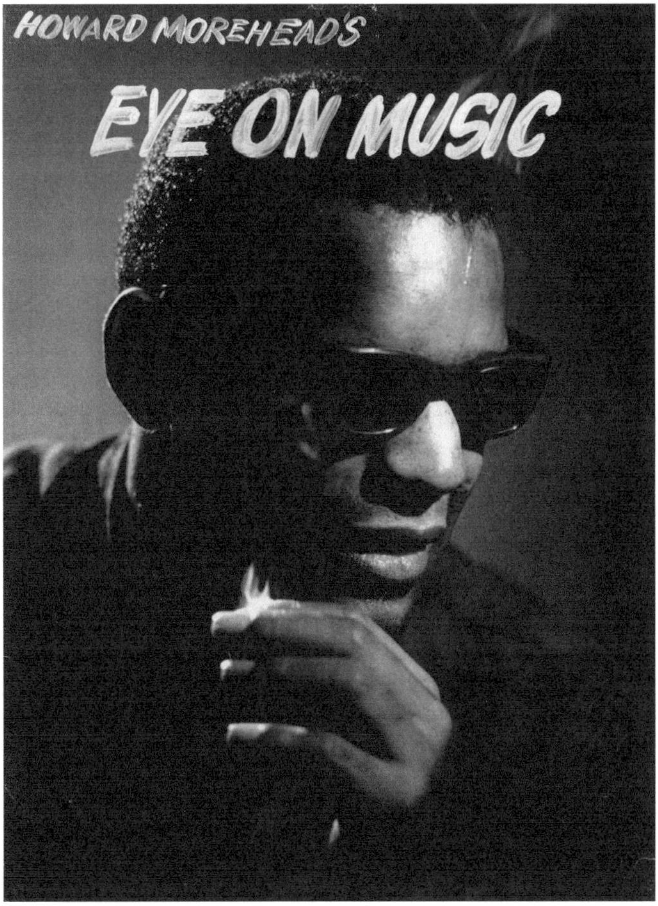

Figure 94: Howard Morehead. Ray Charles on the *Eye for Music* dummy. Los Angeles. n.d. *UCLA Library Special Collections, Charles E. Young Research Library, University of California, Los Angeles.*

big success and was followed by a number of similar publications, most notably the annual *Bronze Beauty Calendar* established in 1986. Sold by mail order and book stores nationwide Morehead's calendar was "savored by many as an annual collector's item [. . .] and has proved a hot item at US Military bases"; his 1994 calendar received the Calendar Marketing Association's Merit Award for Best Glamour Photography.[53]

Beauty pageants were an important element in black popular culture. Blanche Calloway had started her career on the vaudeville circuit appearing in sketches from the "World Famous Bronze Beauties" written by the brothers Salem Tutt Whitney and J. Homer Tutt. At the turn of the century black publications such as the *Colored American* placed alluring shots of women on their front covers in a conscious effort to address questions of beauty, Blackness, and female identity. Other black newspapers promoted beauty contests, inviting readers to submit photographs

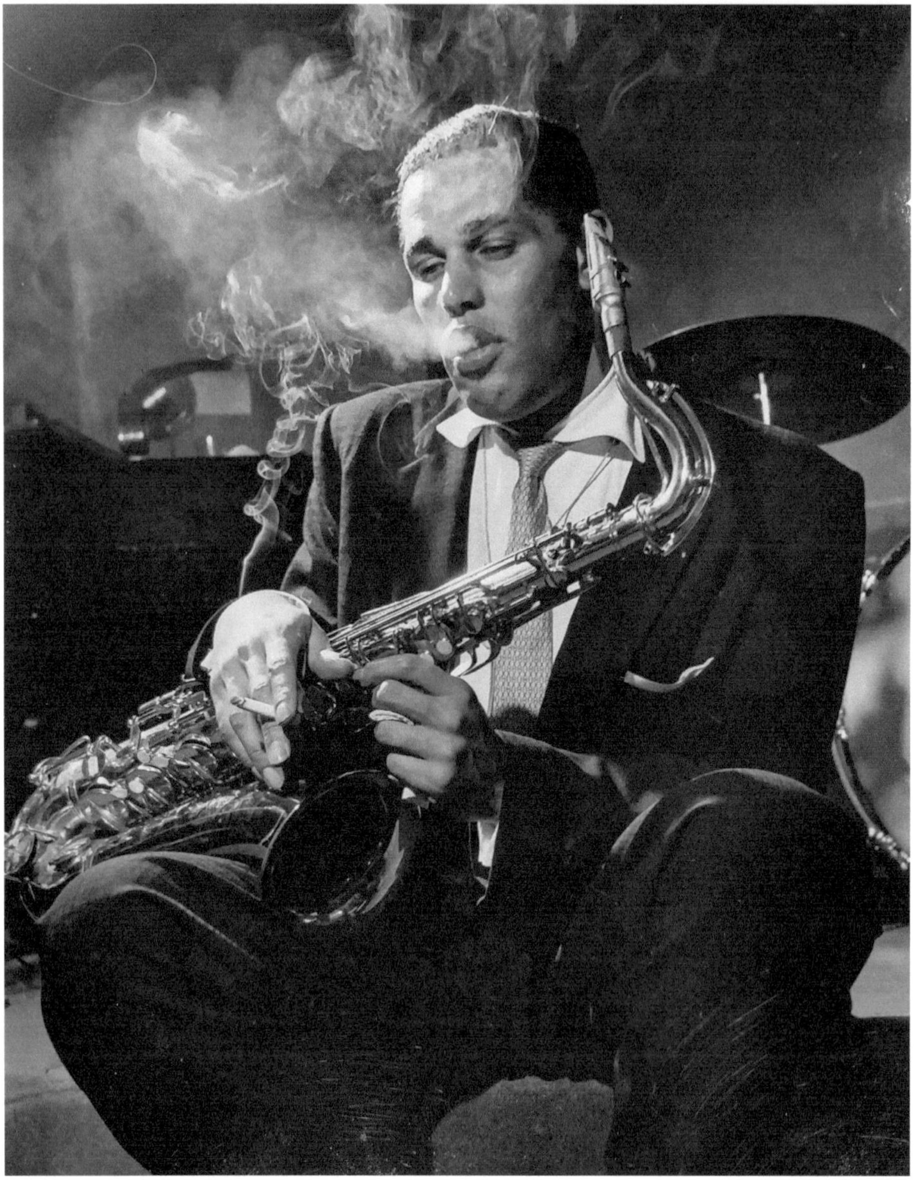

Figure 95: Howard Morehead. *Dexter Gordon at the California Club*. Los Angeles. 1958. *UCLA Library Special Collections, Charles E. Young Research Library, University of California, Los Angeles.*

of glamorous women in social events. The response was generally enthusiastic, evidencing a widespread interest among readers in black beauty.[54]

Glamour work for Morehead was at once a celebration of female beauty and a statement of racial pride much as his commitment to jazz was an equivalent assertion of African American culture. He never attempted to distance one from the other; rather, he took every opportunity to photograph musicians with the winners of his beauty competitions (Figure 96). For Morehead these beautiful women were to be elevated as expressions of black empowerment just as much as jazz musicians; both were deeply rooted in the black community. Morehead was not the only black photographer to make the link and others followed his lead. In the mid-1960s Kwame Brathwaite, who also counted black glamour among his photographic specialisms, formed the artist collective African Jazz Art Society and Studios with his brother Elombe. Very much in the spirit of "Black is Beautiful," Brathwaite photographed Abbey Lincoln and Gradessa models in order to "promote awareness of African-derived black music and dance forms."[55] Working with Reid Miles, Brathwaite provided photographs for Blue Note albums by Horace Parlan and Lou Donaldson among others which elevated black beauty as a central aesthetic statement.

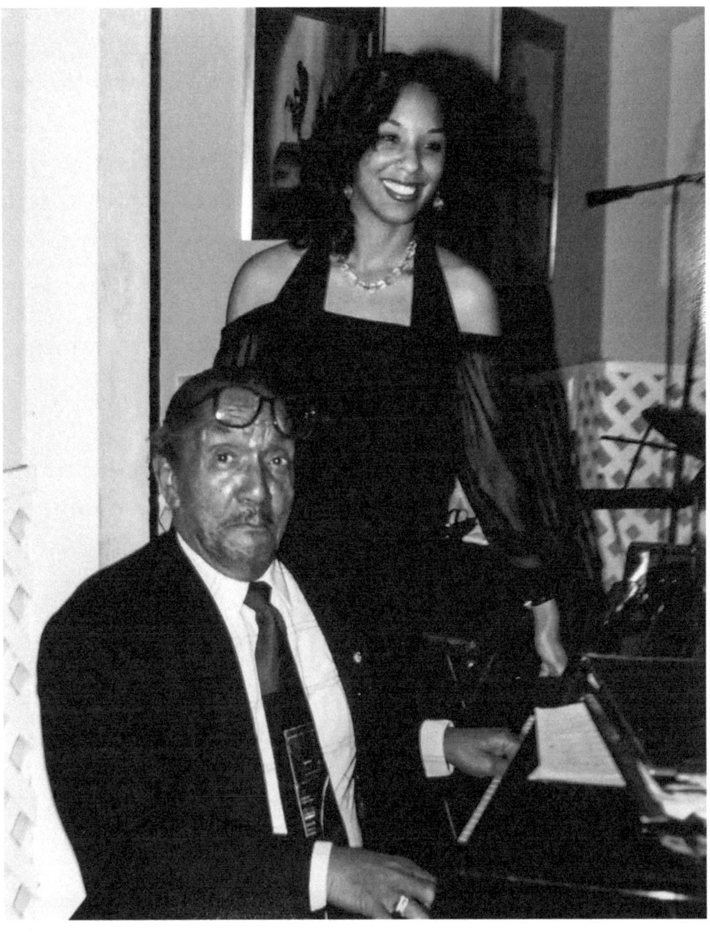

Figure 96: Howard Morehead. *Jazz giant Gerald Wiggins smiles as he plays "Ballad for a Bronze Beauty" for beautiful Bronze Beauty model Monique Gonzaque.* Los Angeles. n.d.
UCLA Library Special Collections, Charles E. Young Research Library, University of California, Los Angeles.

The photojournalist's' credo: Bob Douglas and Ted Williams

John Loengard, one of America's leading photo editors, explained that an effective press photograph need not be "good" but must be interesting, entertaining, or offer a first look at something; it might be emotional, amusing, or intriguing; provide evidence or provoke memories; and it can be posed or candid. The ability of photographers to recognize and marshal these elements in a successful composition is uniquely shaped by their relationship with the subject.[56] Ted Williams and Bob Douglas were African American photojournalists whose approach was deeply imprinted with the ethos and approach of the working photojournalist and animated by their knowledge and love of jazz. Unlike many other African American photographers discussed in this chapter, this affinity to the music led them toward the expressiveness of jazz musicians in performance.

During more than 50 years as a photographer in Detroit and Los Angeles, Bob Douglas worked for national, Midwestern, and west coast black publications, photographed families and children as an itinerant photographer, made nightclub portraits, recruited customers for street portraits, and made corporate headshots.[57] Looking back on his career, however, Douglas was able to say that it was jazz photography that eventually brought him the most recognition although his jazz archive attracted little attention until Roland Charles's black Gallery in the Crenshaw district of Los Angeles included his work in two group exhibitions, *'50s Flashback* (1987) and *Vintage Years* (1988). Late in life Douglas was eventually able to realize his ambition for a solo exhibition, *A Jazz Legend's black and white Photography*, at the Kerckhoff Art Gallery in Los Angeles in 1994.

Born in Detroit in 1921, Douglas had left his job at Ford Motor Company because of discrimination to teach himself the rudiments of photography. He built a darkroom, started developing photographs for the "camera girls" taking snaps in Detroit's nightclubs, and established a nightclub photography business in 1943. In that same year Douglas was offered a job with the *Pittsburgh Courier*, where he covered social occasions, sports, fraternity dances, and a wide range of local events and activities. *Ebony* magazine took on Douglas, who relocated to Los Angeles in 1950, followed by *Sepia* and *Jet*. He also spent time with the *Los Angeles Sentinel*, the black paper founded in 1933 by Col. Leon H. Washington Jr., and with Charlotta Bass's *California Eagle*. He eked out his income in these years by working for a street portraiture business.

Working as a photojournalist had boosted Douglas's self-confidence and it was at the *Courier* that his photographic "credo" as a photojournalist began to take shape. This experience, along with the Courier's commitment to African American civil rights, would have a profound influence on Douglas's professional and personal outlook. The other important influence on Douglas was a period of training at Fred Archer's photography school in California. One of the major names in west coast photography, a central figure in the Southern California

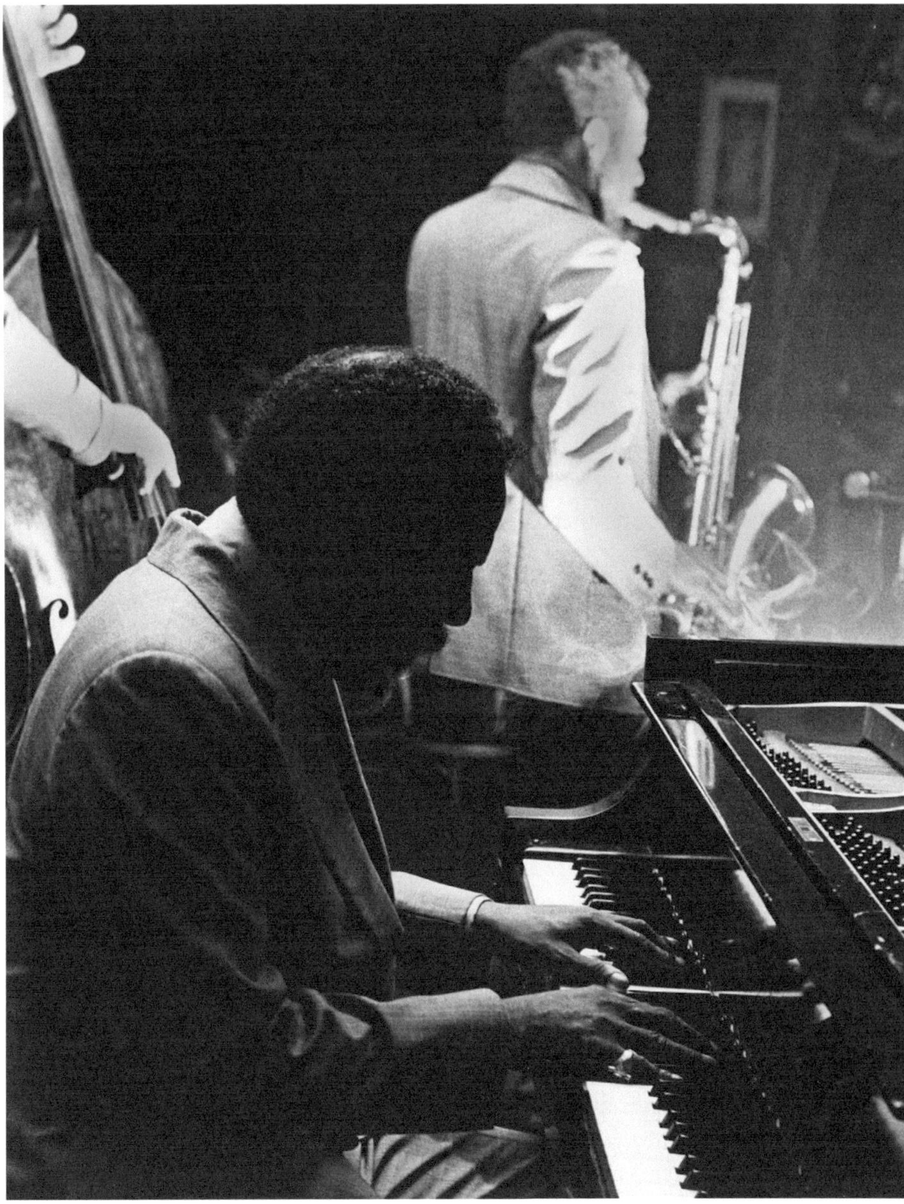

Figure 97: Bob Douglas. *Thelonious Monk.* n.d.
Tom and Ethel Bradley Centre for African American Arts, California State University, Northridge.

Salon Movement, and a collaborator with Ansel Adams, Archer made a number of important contributions to the development of portraiture techniques and fine art photography.[58]

Ted Williams was born in Texas four years after Douglas to an African American father and Mexican mother.[59] After war service he briefly studied art and music before becoming one of the first African American students to attend the Institute of Design at Illinois Institute of Technology in Chicago where he took photography classes with Aaron Siskind, Harry Callahan and Art Siegel and attended lectures by Ansel Adams and Dorothea Lange. Williams carried out assignments in the United States, Europe, Latin America, and the Far East for publications such as *The Saturday Evening Post, Time, Newsweek, Ebony,* and *Look.* He photographed many important moments in the civil rights movement, the Vietnam war, the 1968 Olympics, and participated in a group exhibition in Mexico City. Settling in Los Angeles, Williams worked as a freelancer. His widow Adrienne recalls that he never left home without his camera and would continuously shoot people and scenes that interested him.[60]

Douglas's passion for jazz was sparked when still a teenager listening to radio relays from clubs and hotels. He started making photographs of musicians in the jazz clubs of early-1940s Detroit, where he became adept at deploying his camera in cramped conditions and using low lighting to his advantage (Figure 97). He came to know the musicians and several lifelong friendships developed. Yet photographing jazz musicians was a private passion, and he never imagined that his pictures would one day be exhibited: "I just kept them for myself, I just catalogued them and put them away." Williams's love of jazz was equally deep-rooted but he had much more success in getting his images published. Like Douglas he was inspired by radio broadcasts from Chicago's Grand Terrace Ballroom by Earl Hines and those of Duke Ellington, Cab Calloway, and other jazz greats. His first major magazine article was a 21-page spread for *Down Beat* when he covered the 1958 Newport Jazz Festival (Figures 98a and 98b) and he provided many cover shots subsequently. Covering jazz for *Down Beat, Playboy,* and *Metronome* for over 30 years, his photo library contains images of over 300 jazz artists including all the major names of the period.

There were few restrictions around shooting jazz musicians when Douglas and Williams were active. Douglas described the environment in which jazz photographers worked at the time and the advantages of a press training:

> *There was no problem getting in in those days. There was no cover in the joints and the musicians didn't mind taking pictures [. . .] then again, see when I was working with the paper, one thing I learned is that you go in with a certain amount of authority, so you get in. I mean, I wasn't arrogant in any way [. . .] I guess it was that I belonged there.*

Williams's recollections were similar:[61]

> *In those days you didn't have to go through publicists and managers, so if the guy who owned the club didn't throw you out, you would just start shooting. Sometimes the musicians know me by sight, or I talked to them and some were kind of buddies.*

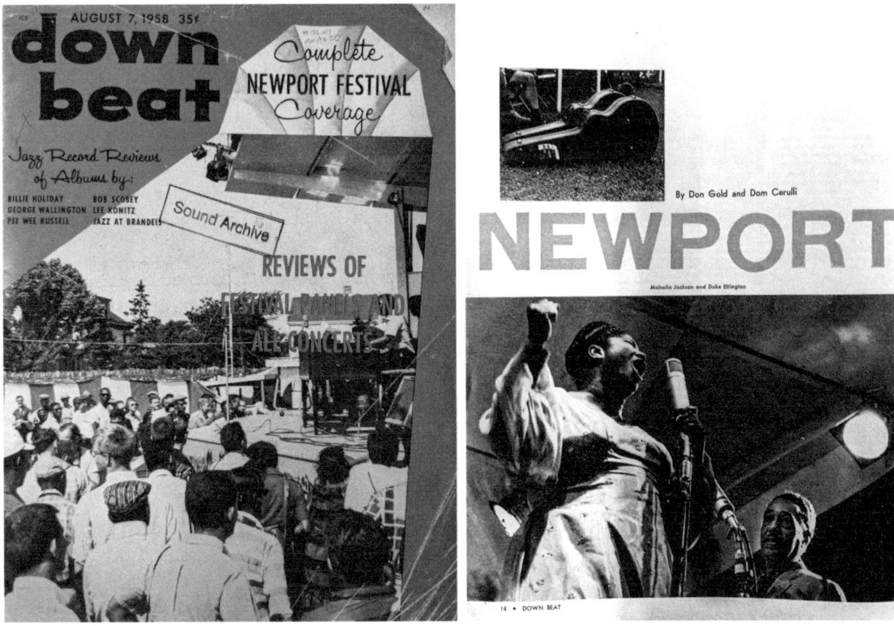

Figure 98a and 98b: Ted Williams. Photographs of the Newport Jazz Festival. 1958. *Down Beat, August 7, 1958.*

> *I was shooting in available light, so a lot of the times the artists didn't even know I was shooting. This is where I got some of my best candid shots.*

Ted's wife, Adrienne, often accompanied her husband to jazz clubs and other venues and remembers that,

> *Ted had a great relationship with the musicians [. . .] he was a big jazz fan and he loved the music. I can picture it when I was with Ted [. . .] When we went to jazz clubs he would never posed a photograph—Ted was spontaneous. He'd walk around the place and take photographs, always looking for the best shot but always spontaneous. He never used flash, always natural light. Not like other photographers whose posed their shots.*

Both photographers took full advantage of these informal shooting conditions to create arresting images, but there were subtle differences between them. Shaped by the portraiture aesthetic instilled by Fred Archer and the photojournalist's eye for composition, Douglas's jazz images evolved to show a strong aesthetic attachment to the music. Speaking about his portraits of Billie Holiday (Figure 99), Douglas appeared to hark back to Archer's portraiture aesthetic:

> *I think they portray her in a very attractive way [. . .] most of the pictures of Billie Holiday are when she's at her worst. The pictures I have of Billie [. . .] she's beautiful [. . .] And I've only seen three or four of her when she looked that good.*

Ted Williams's superb technical abilities and press training led him to create dramatic compositions made with available light. Using cymbals, instruments, microphone stands, cables, and architectural elements to frame the subject, he created leading lines and shadows to make balanced yet dynamic compositions. His use of unusual angles is particularly effective: generally shooting from a low viewpoint Williams's photographs imbue their subjects with a sense of power and authority (Figures 100–102).

Williams's portrait of Gene Krupa frames the drummer between the rounded cymbals and grounds the image with a blurred line along the bottom half of the image. Captured as Krupa looked intensely toward the photographer, the composition brings the focus of attention to a dramatic point. It is impossible to achieve compositions such as this from a static position as the musician's constant movements and their effects on facial lighting, changing gestures, and the movement of fixtures mean that the photographer must be constantly shifting position; and a deep knowledge of the rhythms and cadences of jazz is required so as to be able to anticipate the decisive moments.[62] Williams's ability to move his viewpoint during the performance, reframing the viewpoint through subtle

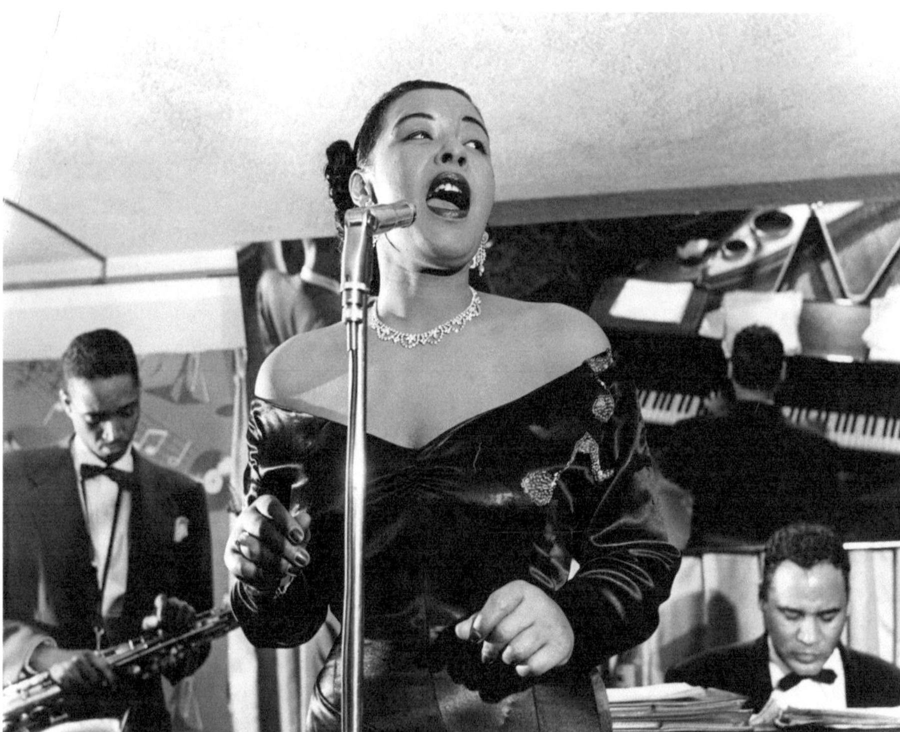

Figure 99: Bob Douglas. *Billie Holiday*. Tiffany Club. Los Angeles. 1950.
Tom and Ethel Bradley Centre for African American Arts, California State University, Northridge, Bob Douglas Collection.

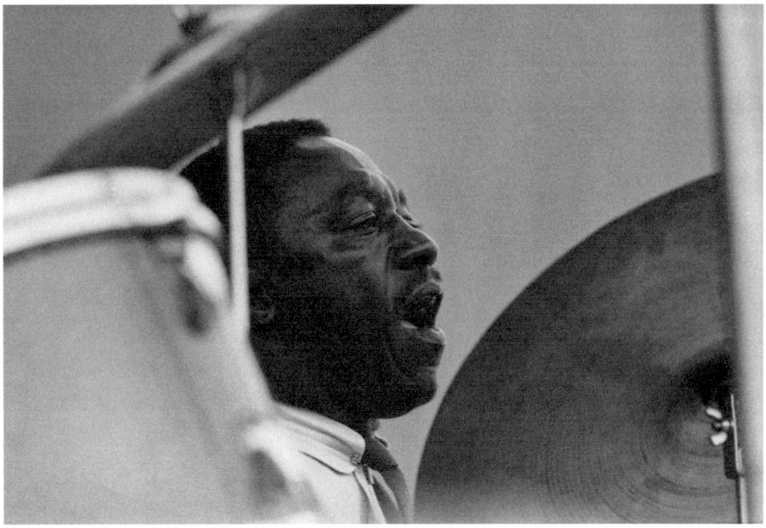

Figure 100: Ted Williams. *Art Blakey*. Newport Jazz Festival. 1965. *Iconic Images.*

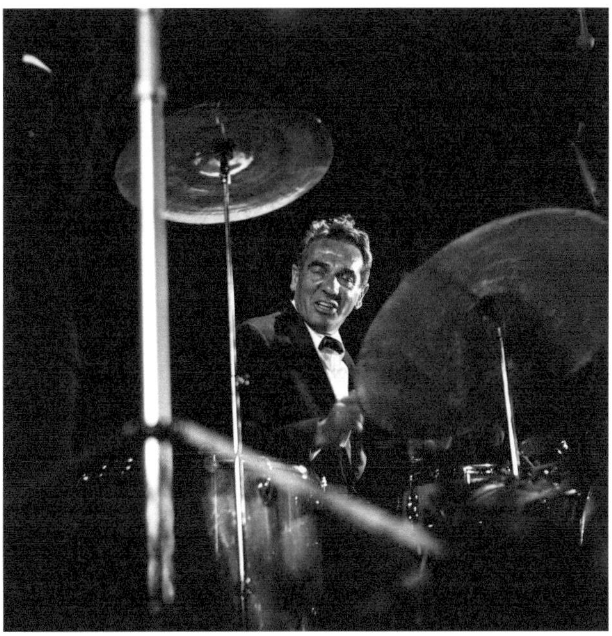

Figure 101: Ted Williams. *Gene Krupa*. Newport Jazz Festival. 1958. *Iconic Images.*

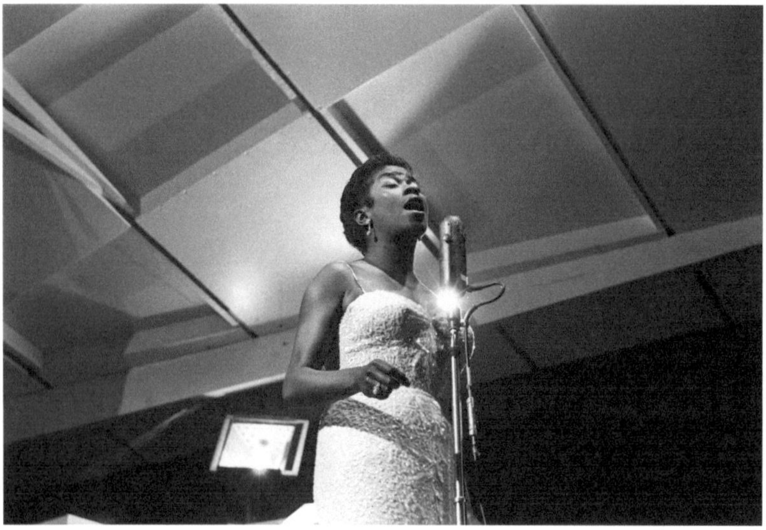

Figure 102: Ted Williams. *Sarah Vaughan*. Newport Jazz Festival. 1958. *Iconic Images.*

shifts in sight lines to capture telling alignments, gestures, and expressions, is apparent. Adrienne Williams recalls that her husband's love of jazz and photography combined to create a different perspective: "Most photographers will find a subject and pose their subject. He always liked to jump around, he never sat still."

III. Expressive realism after mid-century

Agency and expression: Roy DeCarava

Roy DeCarava once explained that

> *The black photographer [. . .] tends to see the world in a more truthful, realistic way [. . .] I do not want a documentary or sociological statement. I want a creative expression, the kind of penetrating insight and understanding of Negroes which I believe only a Negro photographer can interpret.*

This, A. D. Coleman observed, is a conception of the photographer as perceiver that came naturally to black photographers.[63] The quest for black identity was a central concern of the Harlem art community with which Roy DeCarava was closely involved in the 1940s and 1950s.[64] Equipped with hand-held 35mm cameras DeCarava melded a "candid" aesthetic with an expressive formal vocabulary in a detailed exploration of Harlem's African American community. Few photographers have exploited the tones of monochromatic film to quite such expressive and metaphorical effect. The subjects in DeCarava's photographs emerge from "articulate shadows" as if breaking free from a world of darkness into light.[65]

Jazz was central to this concern. Many commentators have focused on DeCarava's seeming privileging of individual jazz musicians and have interpreted his images in terms of artistic subjectivity: Benjamin Cawthra suggests that "DeCarava's photographs visualize Coltrane's spiritual quest" and Scott Saul speaks of DeCarava's depiction of "jazz work" as "religion"; Geoff Dyer argues that DeCarava captures Elvin Jones "in a trance of his own making."[66] DeCarava's involvement with jazz coincided with bebop and many of his greatest photographs do seem to embody individual artistic strivings characteristic of the period. It is also true that DeCarava drew parallels between the individual creativity of jazz improvisation and his own photography and which can be detected in the fluidity of DeCarava's available light photographs with their indistinct, subtle blurs creating a sense of forward movement and spontaneity.[67]

Against the idea that the players' subjectivity *emerges* from black into the individual transcendence of the light, we might perhaps consider his use of deep blacks as a metaphorical device *joining* the players and the people of Harlem within a single material existence. DeCarava and modern jazz shared a common cultural context in Harlem, the district in which DeCarava spent his entire life. Jazz for DeCarava was a cultural expression of black life; reflecting the symmetry with improvisation, the fluidity and shifting characteristics of that life would best be expressed in a continuous photographic presentation, one that mirrored the rhythms and cadences of jazz itself, the back-and-forth of call and response. His long-planned book, *the sound i saw,* an extended and unbroken meditation of Harlem and its culture, comprised photographs of jazz musicians interspersed with shots of daily life, work, and leisure in Harlem—nearly 200 images in total—woven together by a long original poem that wraps itself around the images.

Harlem, in the endless variety of its material life, exists in the minds of the jazz musicians as jazz exists in the minds of Harlemites. As the reader's eye moves between juxtapositions of jazz musicians with people at work, leisure, or simply going about their daily lives, the players emerge as "cultural workers," socially and morally equivalent to the black people who dig the roads or shine shoes. In one spread a street sweeper and guitarist are juxtaposed in almost identical poses, leaning slightly across the fold toward each other, both hunched over the respective tools of their trades; and in another, a guitarist sits on a night bench whose leading lines culminate in the next page with women sitting on a similar bench, "waiting for night benches to release songs of wanting." Architectural lines frame the compositions as the very fabric of Harlem architectonically embraces the musicians and the people on the streets.[68]

This was a radically new realist vocabulary; no one, as Sherry Turner DeCarava remarked, had ever photographed Harlem in this way.[69] In his concern with black life, family and community DeCarava was firmly at one with the traditional concerns of black photographers, but his work left behind the positive counter-statement to propose a new world of expressive possibilities. In certain respects his work points toward the postwar sensitivities of Ben Shahn and Helen Levitt as well as the artistic avant-gardists of the Studio 35 group of abstract artists with their insistence on the universal transcendence of art although it is significant that DeCarava was never able to accept the social disengagement that this implied.[70] DeCarava negotiated a sophisticated form of expressive realism in which photographer, subject, and visual language cohered in a new form of expression carefully steered between the social documentary, with its monumentalizing vantage points and instrumental compositions, and modernist formalism. This was a conscious act of photographic agency: as DeCarava explained, his "uppermost" thought when photographing was "to isolate, capture, some thing, person or time that affects me, that moves me [. . .] I must change it, reshape it into an image which expresses both the object and something of myself."[71]

The insider: Milt Hinton

If Roy DeCarava explored subjectivity through imagistic language, Milt Hinton methodically explored the capacity of the photographic document to infuse personal expression below its surfaces. For Hinton the realist document need only be quietly expressive: simply being an insider was enough.

Hinton combined a career as a professional musician with a life-long commitment to documenting the people he met during his professional life.[72] His interest in photography begun as a hobby but by the late-1940s he realized that he was "experiencing jazz history first hand" and began to take his documentary project seriously. Hinton was very conscious of the significance of the record he was creating:[73]

> *He really saw this as a responsibility, something he would say repeatedly, "I'm making this record [. . .] can you believe these are the people I'm playing with [. . .] he saw this as moving up a level and wanted to document the experiences [. . .] the need to document was always there, like Armstrong's tape recorder."*

Born in Vicksburg, Mississippi, in 1910 Hinton's family had joined the migration north to Chicago. By the late-1920s and early-1930s he was freelancing in and around Chicago. Cab Calloway offered him a place in his orchestra in 1936 and for the next sixteen years Hinton played alongside Chu Berry, Cozy Cole, Dizzy Gillespie, Illinois Jacquet, Jonah Jones, Ike Quebec, and Ben Webster. Hinton worked as a studio musician and became a television staff musician later in life and was one the most-recorded jazz musicians of all time. Initially encouraged and mentored by Keg Johnson while with Calloway, Hinton had acquired a Leica in 1935 and started making candid photographs of his colleagues on tour, backstage and in dressing rooms. For more than 50 years he photographed these encounters and his subjects included all the leading players of the day. In spite of his commitment to his project, photography was a routine aspect of his life, warranting no more than a brief mention in a memoire of his career running to nearly 300 pages.

Hinton was a grounded individual with a refreshingly open artistic ethos. His photographic purposes were equally straightforward and consistently pursued:[74]

> *I always tried to capture something different. Whenever possible, I liked to shoot people when they were off guard or unaware [. . .] I didn't have a flash in the early days and the film speed was slow [. . .] Even so, I did get some unusual shots inside, like pictures of the guys sleeping on the train [. . .] Whenever I wanted a picture of a specific place, I'd always try to include one of the guys in the shot.*

Hinton's shots were invariably balanced compositions in what were frequently cluttered scenes, pensive expressions nicely caught, moments of informal interaction, facial features framed and always well-lighted. He was no less assiduous in recording the people, activities, and scenes encountered on tour, including the signs of segregation encountered by traveling black musicians. While these images have been read as a social comment, Hinton was typically dismissive (Figure 103):[75]

> *When I shot Jim Crow signs in the south I intended to be funny. I wasn't trying to prove anything. We all lived in the north, and one of the only ways we could deal with the stupidity of the segregation laws was to make fun of them.*

Hinton was never malicious but his "candid" portraits could be revealing, and he was occasionally accused of intruding. Herman Leonard criticized Hinton's portrayal of Billie Holiday nursing a whiskey glass in the studio shortly before her sudden death in 1959 (Figure 104)—it was, Leonard said, "despicable to make money from other people's problems—I won't show pictures that are negative."[76] This was surely an overreaction not least because money was the last thing on Hinton's mind. His close friend David G. Berger has responded to Leonard's charges:[77]

> *Whenever [intrusion] came up, he [Hinton] would say something like this, "[Billie Holiday] saw I was taking pictures at the last record date. She didn't care because I wasn't an outsider looking in. I wasn't an intruder, like a photographer who was allowed to come in for a shoot during a ten-minute break. I was there, I was playing with her. I never showed the picture to anyone until long after she had passed. As far as I'm concerned, it was documenting what she was like at the end of her life." If he had left it out it would have been more disturbing.*

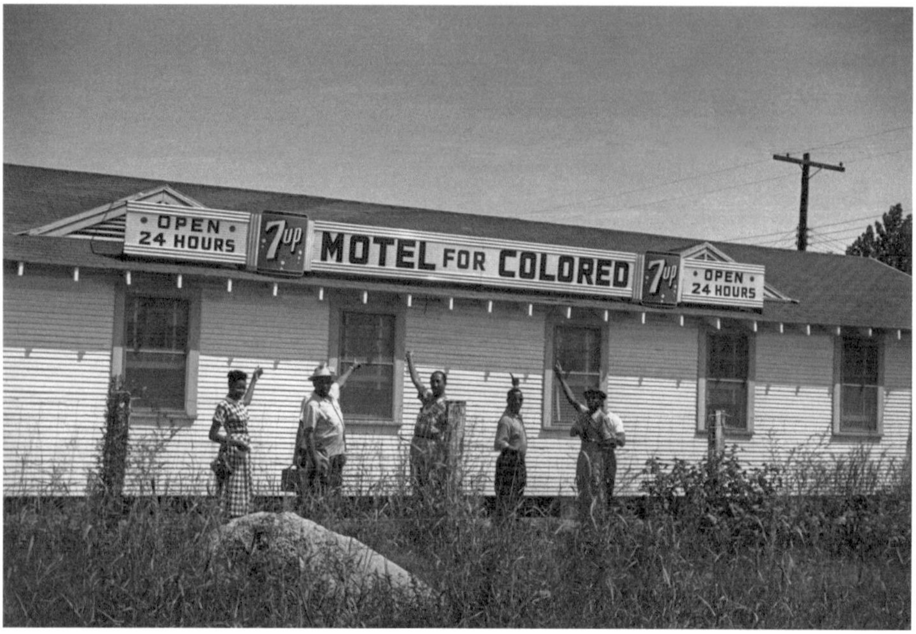

Figure 103: Milt Hinton. *Motel for Colored*. Alabama. *c.*1949.
Milt Hinton Photographic Collection/Permission David G. Berger and Holly Maxson.

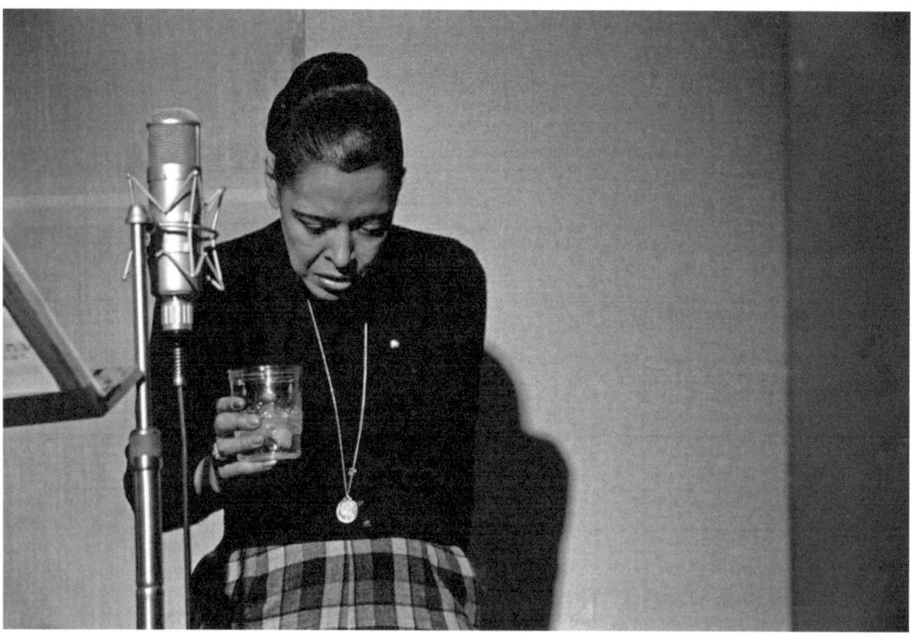

Figure 104: Milt Hinton. *Billie Holiday*. Recording Studio. New York. 1959.
Milt Hinton Photographic Collection/Permission David G. Berger and Holly Maxson.

There is an honesty in Hinton's photography that came from knowing and understanding the musicians he captured, a recognition founded on artistic commonalities. His images take the viewer beyond the public persona of his subjects; and if his quest was to reveal an inner force that animated the artist it was human beings rather than transcendent artists. It would be a mistake to look for a "signature style" in Hinton's images beyond the presence of the photographer himself for it was surely a reflection of his own life than Milt Hinton saw in the people he knew over so many years.

A singular voice: Chuck Stewart

Chuck Stewart, whose career embraced commercial assignments in advertising, travel, fashion, and magazine photography as well as music, imprinted his images with his own identity just as much as DeCarava and Hinton. Stewart captured virtually every musician active between the mid-1950s and his death in 2017, from jazz and blues musicians to pop and salsa artists, and had well over 2,000 record covers to his credit. His early association with Herman Leonard helped him make connections with jazz specialist record companies although things were not always easy. In the 1950s and 1960s he was turned down for lucrative advertising photography because of racial prejudice on the part of clients—a theme to which he returned on several occasions in later interviews.

Born in Texas in 1927, Stewart majored in photography at Ohio University and was Leonard's classmate. Along with Yosuf Karsh Stewart described Leonard as his greatest photographic influence: "I learned a lot from [Leonard] and from Karsh, because when Karsh would come to New York he would take Herman and I as his third and fourth assistants." Yet Stewart was determined that these influential mentors should not overwhelm his own photographic vision,[78]

> *... a picture that Chuck Stewart took of these people, as opposed to just another picture of this famous person. Like, for instance, Count Basie, there must be a million pictures of him. Why is mine distinctive? Well, I'd like to believe it's distinctive because I took it.*

Stewart's thoughtful and unobtrusive approach was the foundation for what emerged as a distinctive vision. "If you look through Chuck's images," Carol Friedman said, "what is immediately apparent is that his subjects have let him into their inner sanctum. They like him and they trust him. Whether he's documenting them at a recording session or capturing them in the privacy of his own studio, he knew how to defer to the moment in time."[79] Dan Morgenstern concurs: "Producers and engineers accepted him. He was not the least bit intrusive. He would never snap a shutter in the middle of a take. He was the extreme opposite of the paparazzi."[80]

Quietly efficient and sensitive to surroundings and people, Stewart was ever alert to the "decisive moment:"[81]

> *When I did a session I would go in and shoot the rehearsal before they did any takes. I couldn't shoot during the take because the recording equipment would pick up the clicks. So what I did was meander around the studio. When I saw a picture I thought worked, I'd take it. One photo shows Coltrane sitting at a piano, lost in thought: "I was looking for a decisive moment."*

Ultimately the "mood creates a fine image." Stewart thrived on the interactions between players in the studio but mastery of the craft was essential if he was to translate what he saw into photographic language:[82]

> *Photography is about a point of view [. . .] You have to learn the techniques of the trade and keep up with the new technology that will help you transmit your point of view into a two-dimensional surface with emotional values that will generate a response from the viewer.*

So Stewart filled the frame with his subjects, composing shots to capture the spirit of performance; he used lighting to good effect and incorporated microphones, instruments, and reflections to create abstract patterns that provided a lyrical tone to his images.

In this way Stewart avoided what might have been the overweening stylistic influences of Karsch and Leonard. Inevitably, some of his images show traces of his mentors: a 1965 portrait of Dizzy Gillespie bathes the trumpeter in a soft light fading to black while a consciously low viewpoint elevates the musician both physically and artistically; Charlie Haden, captured in 1970, shows the musician's starkly lighted face, hand, and bass strings set against deep black; and a 1966 portrait of a seated John Coltrane used the angles, lines, and lighting that Leonard deployed to such effect.[83] Like Leonard, Stewart was driven by the objective of portraying his subjects in the best possible light but unlike his mentor he believed this could never be created: "Most musicians are already energized and full of electricity, so you don't have to prop them up with fake exotic poses." It was a vision that stopped short of imposing visual motifs in favor of allowing the subjectivity of photographer and musician to emerge.

In a photograph of Johnny Hodges taken late in 1961 (Figure 105) Stewart revealed the inner intensity of a taciturn and often tetchy man whose sensitivity usually only became evident in his playing. Embarrassed by his lack of education—particularly when in the company of the grandiloquent Ellington—Hodges rarely spoke and gruffly declined to sign autographs for fear of revealing his poor writing. Stewart however knew a side to the musician rarely on display. At a recording session led by Billy Strayhorn in 1961, Hodges was clearly at ease. In spite of their different characters, Hodges and Strayhorn got on well; previous collaborations were well-received and on the Verve album coming out of this session, "Johnny Hodges with Billy Strayhorn and the Orchestra," Hodges was widely praised for his eloquence, sensitivity, and good humor.[84] Stewart captured the mood beautifully in a photograph that frames Hodges and Jimmy Jones discussing a chart. The photographer portrays the creative bond between two musicians; on the flat surface

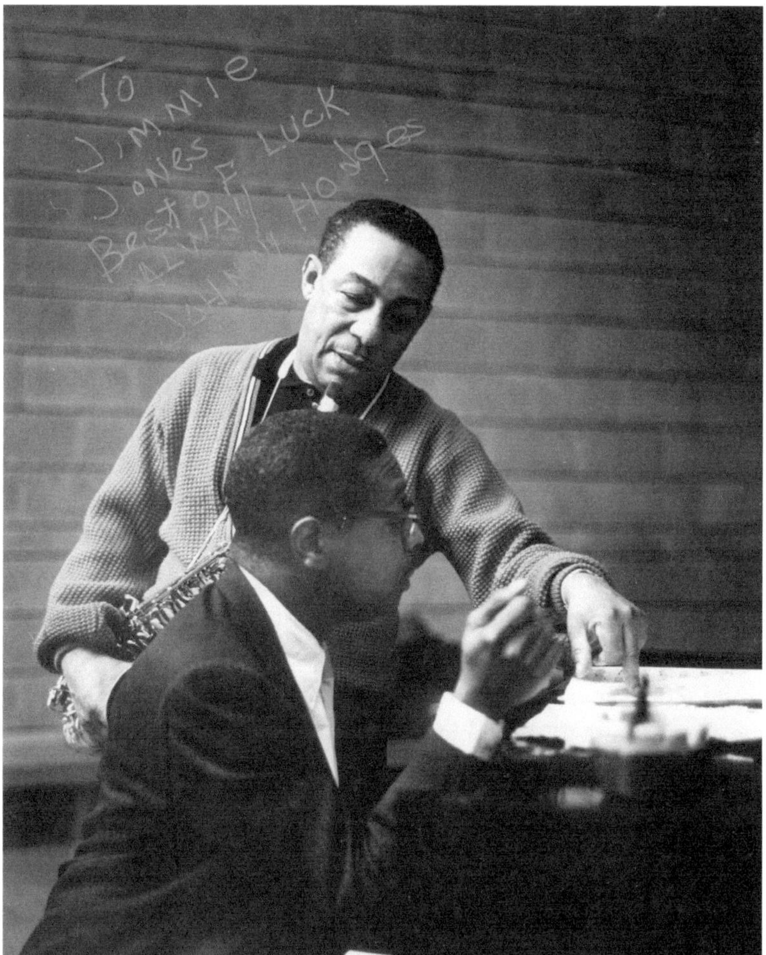

Figure 105: Chuck Stewart. *Johnny Hodges and Jimmy Jones*. Billy Strayhorn and his Orchestra. Verve recording session, Rudy van Gelder studio. Englewood Cliffs, NJ. December 1961. *Peter Vacher Collection/With permission of Kim Stewart and Fireball Entertainment Group.*

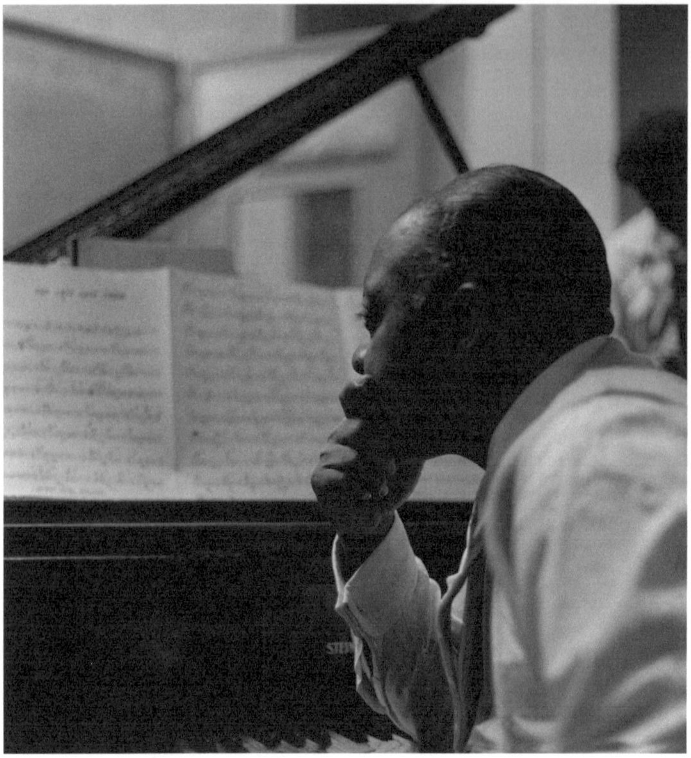

Figure 106: Charles "Chuck" Stewart. *Count Basie at Capitol Studios in New York, October 22, 1957.* Roulette Records recording session for "Atomic Basie."
Institute of Jazz Studies photograph collection (IJS.0048), 1950s/Chuck Stewart's Photography provided by Fireball Entertainment Group/Kim Stewart.

of the photograph their hands appear almost to touch while the alignment of the angle of the musicians' bodies creates a triangular composition through which both subjects lead the eye to the score, signifying its status in the inner world of Hodges. In half-profile, Stewart's portrait of a pensive Count Basie (Figure 106) conveys a similar narrative in foregrounding the bond between musician and the score. These are photographs that could not have been taken without the close access to the subject musicians and deep feeling for the music through which Stewart found a personal voice.

IV. Conclusion

By the late-1920s and early-1930s the urban African American outlook was increasingly shaped by the growing cohesion, rituals, and performative practices of African American urban communities; equally forceful influences included the defiant textual and visual tone of the black press, the political messaging of black African American advocacy organizations, and new ideas and styles of black life enthusiastically adopted by a second generation of migrants. The travails of displacement gave way to a more assertive "second-generation" identity. Socially, economically, and culturally tied into the communities they served, photographers were aware of the new black frame of mind and many were enthusiastic supporters; but they were equally conscious that their work needed to appeal to the readers of the black press on whom they were dependent. Meeting these demands called for an expressive form of photographic realism that narrativized the scenes and activities they recorded from the inside.

These factors help to explain the specific trajectory of black photography during these years. The general practice of African American art for at least two decades after the 1930s was torn between social realist documentary—the form that many Harlem Renaissance intellectuals considered fundamental to the development of an authentic black aesthetic—and modernist experimentation, most notably abstraction. Most found the former to be the stronger force while the latter was seen as a deviation from what ought to have been the overriding concerns of the black artist. Equating "social" realism with an attenuated form of art, the consequence for David Driskell was that "no viable aesthetic was developed among black artists between 1930 and 1950" and this perhaps also explains why Black Arts theorists were skeptical about the extent to which a genuine black aesthetic was evident in these years.[85] Yet the decisive intervention of the black press in the visual culture of African American communities meant that photographers were required to satisfy readers in a way that demanded more than simply "realism"—a requirement for which neither the explicitly ideological and declamatory purposes of the documentary mode nor the affectations of modernist abstraction were adequate.[86] The version of expressive realism that developed among black photographers of the period met this requirement, filling a visual space with affirmative images that spoke to a modern urban future.

It is in this context that the jazz imagery of African American photographers of the classic period should be set. Like Al Smith, with whose work this chapter began, the realism developed by these photographers extended the concern with authenticity from the inside shown by early black photographers into more specific and subtle depictions of the relationships and practices of black communities. Always materially grounded, this was a depiction of jazz that largely steered clear of mythologization; and, if there were universalizing messages to be found, they stemmed from a distinct rooting in the particularities of musical practices. In this respect their work can be contrasted with that of the "new generation" of white photographers active at the same time whose work is discussed in the next chapter.

Notes

1. Pete Blecha, Interview with the Author, 2018.
2. Quoted by Charles E. Brown, "Al Smith Sr., Photographer, Historian," *The Seattle Times*, September 4, 2008. For Smith's life and work see the web posting by Peter Blecha, "Smith, Al (1916–2008)," *HistoryLink.Org*, 2015; Maurice Berger, "Documenting the Dynamic Black Community of 1940s Seattle," *New York Times*, March 27, 2018; Howard Giske, "Meeting Al Smith," in *Seattle on the Spot: The Photographs of Al Smith*, ed. Jacqueline E. A. Lawson (Seattle, WA: Museum of History and Industry, 2017), 11–12. The context of Smith's life and work is described in Quintard Taylor, *The Forging of a Black Community: Seattle's Central District from 1870 through the Civil Rights Era* (Seattle, WA: University of Washington Press, 1999).
3. Peter Blecha, *Music in Washington: Seattle and Beyond* (Charleston, SC: Arcadia, 2007), 49. For the Central Avenue jazz scene in the 1940s see Paul De Barros, *Jackson Street after Hours: The Roots of Jazz in Seattle* (Seattle, WA: Sasquatch Books, 1993), 51; Gary Marmorstein, "Central Avenue Jazz: Los Angeles Black Music of the Forties," *Southern California Quarterly* 70, no. 4 (1988): 415–26; Peter Vacher, *Swingin' on Central Avenue: African American Jazz in Los Angeles* (Lanham, MD: Rowman & Littlefield, 2015); and Taylor, *The Forging of a Black Community*, 147–52.
4. Al "Butch" Smith Jr., "My Father and His Camera," in *Seattle on the Spot: The Photographs of Al Smith* (Seattle, WA: Museum of History & Industry, 2017), 35.
5. John Collier Jr. and Malcolm Collier, *Visual Anthropology: Photography as a Research Method* (Albuquerque: University of New Mexico Press, 1986), 20–23; Scott DeVeaux, *BeBop: A Social and Musical History* (Berkeley: University of California Press, 1997), 61; David Krasner, "The Real Thing," in *Beyond Blackface: African Americans and the Creation of American Popular Culture 1890–1930*, ed. W. Fitzhugh Brundage (Chapel Hill: University of North Carolina Press, 2011), 99.
6. Robin D. G. Kelley, *Race Rebels: Culture, Politics and the Black Working Class* (Free Press: New York, 1994), 36–43.
7. Deborah Dash Moore, "At Home in America?: Revisiting the Second Generation," *Journal of American Ethnic History* 25, no. 2/3 (2006): 159.
8. Alain Locke, "The New Negro," in *The Portable Harlem Renaissance Reader*, ed. David Levering Lewis (New York: Viking, 1994), 46; Henry Louis Gates Jr., "New Negroes, Migration, and Cultural Exchange," in *Jacob Lawrence: The Migration Series*, ed. Elizabeth Hutton Turner (Urbana, VA: Rappahannock Press, 1993), 19.
9. Arna Bontemps cited by Robert Bone and Richard A. Courage, *The Muse in Bronzeville: African American Creative Expression in Chicago, 1932–1950* (New Brunswick, NJ: Rutgers University Press, 2011), 93; Eyerman, "Intellectuals and the Construction of African American Identity: Outline of a Generational Approach," 70.
10. Ann Douglas, *Terrible Honesty: Mongrel Manhattan in the 1920s* (London: Picador, 1996), esp. 73–107; Mary Ann Calo, "African American Art and Critical Discourse between World Wars," *American Quarterly* 51, no. 3 (1999): 580–621.
11. The classic study of the First World War as a marker of generational change is Richard Wohl, *The Generation of 1914* (Cambridge, MA: Harvard University Press, 1980). Lisa R. Williams, "The Furious Battleground: World War 1 and the Development of Jazz in American Popular Culture," *Jazz Perspectives* 8, no. 2 (2014), 117–52; W. Fitzhugh Brundage, "Working in the 'Kingdon of Culture'," in *Beyond Blackface: African Americans and the Creation of American Popular Culture*, 11.
12. William M. Tuttle, *Race Riot: Chicago in the Red Summer of 1919* (New York: Atheneum, 1970); John Higham, *Strangers in the Land: Patterns of American Nativism 1860–1925* (Brunswick, NJ: Rutgers University Press, 2002), 222–33 on the Red Scare. Arthur E. Barbeau and Florette Henri, *The Unknown Soldiers: African American Troops in World War 1* (New York: Da Capo, 1996), 175–89, describes the desperate plight of returning Black soldiers.
13. Cheryl Lynn Greenberg, *To Ask for an Equal Chance: African Americans in the Great Depression* (Lanham, MD: Rowman & Littlefield, 2010); Anthony J. Badger, *The New Deal: The Depression Years 1933–40* (London: Macmillan, 1989), 25, 252–52; Winston C. McDowell, "Keeping Them 'In the Same Boat Together'," in *African Americans and Jews in the Twentieth Century*, ed. V. P. Franklin and others (Columbia: University of Missouri Press,

1998), 217–21; Hugh Brogan, *The Penguin History of the USA*, 2nd ed. (London: Penguin, 2001), 620.

14. Johnson cited by Douglas, 74. The literature on the migrations and life in black urban communities is extensive. Selected texts include: *Chicago*—James R. Grossman, *Land of Hope: Chicago, Black Southerners and the Great Migration* (Chicago: University of Chicago Press, 1989); Christopher Robert Reed, *The Rise of Chicago's Black Metropolis, 1920–1929*, ed. Darlene Clark Hine and Dwight A. McBride (Urbana: University of Illinois Press, 2011); and Allan H. Spear, *The Making of A Negro Ghetto, 1890–1920* (Chicago: University of Chicago Press, 1967). *Harlem*—Jervis Anderson, *Harlem: The Great Black Way, 1900–1950* (London: Orbis, 1982); Claude McKay, *Harlem: Negro Metropolis* (New York: E. P. Dutton, 1940); and Gilbert Osofsky, *Harlem: The Making of a Ghetto, Negro New York 1890–1930*, 2nd ed. (New York: Harper & Row, 1971). *West coast*—Albert S. Broussard, "In Search of the Promised Land: African American Migration to San Francisco, 1900–1945," in *Seeking El Dorado: African Americans in California*, ed. L. B. De Graaf, K. Mulroy, and Q. Taylor (Los Angeles: Autry Museum of Western Heritage, 2001), 181–209; Lonnie G. Bunch, "A Past Not Necessarily Prologue: The Afro-American in Los Angeles," in *20th Century Los Angeles: Power, Promotion and Social Conflict*, ed. Norman M. Klein and Martin J. Schiesl (Claremont, CA: Regina Books, 1990), 101–30; Marne L. Campbell, *Making Black Los Angeles: Class, Gender and Community, 1850–1917* (Chapel Hill: University of North Carolina Press, 2016); Douglas Flamming, *African Americans in the West* (Santa Barbara, CA: ABC-CLIO, 2009); and Lawrence B. De Graaf, Kevin Mulroy, and Quintard Taylor, eds., *Seeking El Dorado: African Americans in California* (Los Angeles: Autry Museum of Western Heritage, 2001).
15. Nell Irvin Painter, *Creating Black Americans: African-American History and Its Meanings, 1619 to the Present* (New York: Oxford University Press, 2007), 166–72. Studies of Black elites include Harold F. Gosnell, *Negro Politicians: The Rise of Negro Politics in Chicago* (Chicago: University of Chicago Press, 1935); Christopher Robert Reed, *The Chicago NAACP and the Rise of Black Professional Leadership, 1910–1966* (Bloomington: Indiana University Press, 1997); and Craig Doughty, "Black Elitism and Cultural Entrepreneurship in 1920s Boston," *European Journal of American Studies* 14, no. 2 (2019): 1–14.
16. Lizabeth Cohen, *Making a New Deal: Industrial Workers in Chicago 1919–1939* (Cambridge: Cambridge University Press, 1990), 99; Davarian L. Baldwin, "Our Newcomers to the City: The Great Migration and the Making of Modern Mass Culture," in *Beyond Blackface: African Americans and the Creation of American Popular Culture 1890–1930* 159–89. Sidran, *Black Talk*, 79, points out that it is at the level of *style* that black Americans were able to remain aloof from the broader society. Kenney, *Chicago Jazz: A Cultural History, 1904–1930*, esp. 3–34, provides an overview of Black entertainment venues in Chicago between 1918 and 1930.
17. Michael McGerr, *A Fierce Discontent: The Rise and Fall of the Progressive Movement in America, 1870–1920* (New York: Free Press, 2003), 199–202. Meeting discrimination with self-help rather than militant protest, this leadership converted the dream of an integrated city into the vision of a "black metropolis" and pursue the dual strategies of fulfilment (progress within society) and transfiguration (prefiguration of alternative social formations) which Paul Gilmore has described as a leading feature of the "black Atlantic" diaspora: Paul Gilroy, *The Black Atlantic: Modernity and Double Consciousness* (Cambridge, MA: Harvard University Press, 1993). 36–37. See also Spear, *The Making of a Negro Ghetto, 1890–1920*, 167, 91.
18. Philip S. Foner, *American Socialism and Black Americans: From the Age of Jackson to World War II* (Westport, CT: Greenwood Press, 1977), 363. Paul D'Amato, "Race and the U.S. Socialist Tradition," *Socialist Worker*, 2010 https://socialistworker.org/2010/11/18/race-and-us-socialist-tradition. James P. Kraft, *Stage to Studio: Musicians and the Sound Revolution, 1890–1950* (Baltimore, MD: John Hopkins University Press, 1996), 30–32, documents the segregationist policies of the Associated Federation of Musicians.
19. Darlene Clark Hine and John McCluskey, *The Black Chicago Renaissance* (Urbana: University of Illinois Press, 2012).
20. For this history of the black press see Roland E. Wolseley, *The Black Press, U.S.A.* (Ames: Iowa State University Press, 1980); Charles A. Simmons, *The African American Press: A History of News Coverage During National Crises* (Jefferson, NC: McFarland, 1998); "The Black Press: Soldiers Without Swords: Press Release,"

PBS, https://www.pbs.org/blackpress/film/pressrelease.html; Nell Painter, "Black Journalism, The First Hundred Years," *Harvard Journal of Afro-American Affairs* 2, no. 2 (1971): 30–42; Gayle K. Berardi and Thomas W. Segady, "The Development of African-American Newspapers in the American West: A Sociohistorical Perspective," *Journal of Negro History* 75, nos. 3/4 (1990): 96–111; Partick S. Washburn, *The African American Newspaper: Voice of Freedom* (Evanston, IL: Northwestern University Press, 2006). Andrew Buni, *Robert L. Vann of the Pittsburgh Courier: Politics and Black Journalism* (Pittsburgh: Universiuty of Pittsburgh Press, 1974); and Regina Freer, "L.A. Race Woman: Charlotta Bass and the Complexities of Black Political Development in Los Angeles," *American Quarterly* 56, no. 3 (2004): 607–32, are studies of individual publications and their editors.

21. Matthew Pratt Guterl, *The Color of Race in America, 1900–1940* (Cambridge, MA: Harvard University Press, 2001), 115–16.
22. Arnold Rampersad, *The Life of Langston Hughes* (New York: Oxford University Press, 1988), 65.
23. Waldo E. Martin Jr., *No Coward Soldiers: Black Cultural Politics in Postwar America* (Cambridge, MA: Harvard University Press, 1988), 3.
24. Cohen, *Making a New Deal: Industrial Workers in Chicago 1919–1939*, 138, 325; William Barlow, "Black Music on Radio During the Jazz Age," *African American Review* 29, no. 2 (1995): 328; Derek W. Vaillant, "Sounds of Whiteness: Local Radio, Racial Formation, and Public Culture in Chicago, 1921–1935," *American Quarterly* 54, no. 1 (2002): 25–66.
25. Erin P. Cohn, *Art Fronts: Visual Culture and Race Politics in Mid-Twentieth Century United States* (Philadelphia: University of Pennsylvania Press, 2010), 55–56. For traditional leftist coverage, see Cristina Doi, "Prentiss Taylor and George Biddle on the Scottsboro Trials," in *The Left Front: Radical Art in the "Red Decade", 1929–1940*, ed. Lisa Graziose Corrin (Evanston, IL, 2014), 15 and Barnaby Haran, "'We Cover New York': Protest, Neighborhood, and Street Photography in the (Workers Film and) Photo League," *Arts*, 2019, open access article, Creative Commons Attribution, 2. Haran shows how the white and mainly Jewish Workers' Film and Photo League, which operated between 1931 and 1936, created "instrumental and incidental representation of the [city] as simply the impetus and locus for mobilized resistance."
26. Cecil J. Williams, *Freedom and Justice: Four Decades of the Civil Rights Struggle as Seen by a Photographer of the Deep South* (Orangeburg, SC: Mercer University Press, 1995), 1.
27. Andria Lisle, "Black and White: Three Photo Exhibits Bring the Long-Hidden World of Segregated Memphis to Life," *Memphis Flyer* 1, no. 886 (2006): 22, https://www.memphisflyer.com/memphis/black-and-white/Content?oid=1124496, accessed February 12, 2018; Nadja Sayej, "Hidden Portraits: Rare Photos of African American Life Get a Spotlight," *The Guardian*, 2018, https://www.theguardian.com/artanddesign/2018/jun/21/metropolitan-museum-art-african-american-portraits-exhibition.
28. James Guimond, *American Photography and the American Dream* (Chapel Hill: University of North Carolina Press, 1991), 170–71; Michael Carlebach, *Photojournalism Comes of Age* (Washington, DC: Smithsonian Institution Press, 1997), 51; Gerry Badger, "To Make the Present Time Come Alive: Magazine Photography 1891–1940," in *Photography: A New Vision of the World 1891–1940*, ed. W. Guadagnini (Milan: Skira, 2011), 176. William Brian Piper, "Cameras at Work: African American Studio Photographers and the Business of Everyday Life, 1900–1970," Dissertation presented to the Graduate Faculty of the University of Virginia, Charlottesville, 2016), esp. ch. 4 confirms that war greatly increased demand for portraiture among African Americans and encouraged black photographers to combine jobs.
29. Deborah Willis, *Reflections in Black: A History of Black Photographers 1840 to the Present* (New York: W. W. Norton, 2000), 85; Joe Mosbrook, "Evelyn Freeman Remembers Her Swing Band," Jazzed in Cleveland, 2001, http://207.170.138.18/wmv_news/jazz67.htm.
30. Barbara Rose, *American Art since 1900* (New York: Holt, Reinhart & Winston, 1967), 107, points out that unlike the realism of Courbet or Daumier based on the painterly tradition of French realism, the early American social realism showed the stylistic origins of their work as illustrators.
31. Bob Douglas, "Interview with Joe Rose" (Oral History Interview 99.01.OH.03.01—04 Oral History Program, Tom & Ethel Bradley Center, California State University, Northridge, 1999).
32. Deborah Willis, "Imagining Themselves: Photography, Race and Representation, 1945–1980," in *Identity and Affirmation: Post War African American Photography*, ed. R. Kent

Kirkton (Los Angeles: California State University, 2011), 6–11.

33. Govenar, *Portraits of Community: African American Photography in Texas*, 100, 196, reports the testimony of black photographers that photography earnings were only just sufficient to keep body and soul together.
34. Carolyn Kolb, "Developing Images," MyNewOrleans.com, 2008, https://www.myneworleans.com/developing-images/.
35. Girard P. III Mouton and Alma D. Williams, "The Eyes of Jazz," *Jazz Archivist* 6, no. 1 (1991): 11.
36. Alan Govenar and Benny Joseph, *The Early Years of Rhythm and Blues: Focus on Houston* (Houston, TX: Rice University Press, 1990), 13; Emanuella Grinberg, "'Photography of Benny Joseph': The Early Years of Rhythm and Blues," *CNN Photos*, 2015.
37. Govenar and Joseph, *The Early Years of Rhythm and Blues: Focus on Houston*. Plates 31–44, 53–66.
38. Rosalind Withers, Interview with the Author, 2020. For Withers's civil rights photography see Ernest C. Withers et al., *Pictures Tell the Story: Ernest C. Withers Reflections in History* (Norfolk, VA: Chrysler Museum of Art, 2000); and Richard Cahan and Michael Williams, *Revolution in Black and White: Photographs of the Civil Rights Era by Ernest Withers* (Chicago: CityFiles Press, 2019). I am grateful to Rosalind Withers for information about her father's music photography, a selection of which appears in Daniel J. Wolff and Ernest C. Withers, *The Memphis Blues Again: Six Decades of Memphis Music Photographs* (New York: Viking Studio, 2001). See further: Deborah Willis, *Reflections in Black: A History of Black Photographers 1840 to the Present* (New York: W. W. Norton, 2000), 117, 137–38, and Preston Lauterbach, *Bluff City: The Secret Life of Photographer Ernest Withers* (New York: W.W. Norton &Co., 2019).
39. Richard Ings, "Making Harlem Visible: Race, Photography and the American City, 1915–1955," unpublished Ph.D. thesis (University of Nottingham, 2004), 25–26.
40. Ings, "Making Harlem Visible: Race, Photography and the American City, 1915–1955," 108.
41. Gordon Parks, "Foreword," in *Harlem: The Vision of Morgan and Marvin Smith*, ed. James A. Miller (Lexington: University Press of Kentucky, 1998), ix. For the life and work of the Smiths, see M. Rachleff, "Photojournalism in Harlem: Morgan and Marvin Smith and the Construction of Power, 1934–1943," in *Visual Journal: Harlem and D.C. in the Thirties and Forties*, ed. D. Willis and J. Lusaka (Washington, DC: Smithsonian Institution Press, 1996), 15–33. Piper, "Cameras at Work: African American Studio Photographers and the Business of Everyday Life, 1900–1970," 98–146, describes the Smiths' studio as "The smartest place for people who like to pose."
42. The Smiths' photograph of Ivie Anderson is reproduced by Willis, *Reflections in Black: A History of Black Photographers 1840 to the Present*, 2000, 93; Stuart Nicholson, *Ella Fitzgerald: A Biography of the First Lady of Jazz* (London: Indigo, 1996), 34–36, 44.
43. "Introduction," *Identity and Affirmation: Post-War African American Photography*, ed. Kent Kirkton (Los Angeles: California State University Northridge, 2011), 2.
44. Diane Lara and Lorraine Adams, Correspondence with the Author, October 9, 2020.
45. "Imagining Themselves: Photography, Race and Representation 1945–80," in Kirkton, *Identity and Affirmation: Post-War African American Photography*, 8–10; R. Kent Kirkton, *Harry Adams: Camera and Community* (Los Angeles: California State University Northridge, 1997), n.pag.
46. For Harris's life and work see Charles A. Harris and others, *Spirit of a Community: The Photographs of Charles "Teenie" Harris* (Greensburg, PA: Westmoreland Museum of American Art, 2001); Stanley Crouch, *One Shot Harris: The Photographs of Charles "Teenie" Harris* (New York: Abrams, 2002); Cheryl Finley, Laurence Glasco, and Joe Trotter, *Teenie Harris Photographer: Image, Memory, History* (Pittsburgh: University of Pittsburgh Press, 2011); Stephen Kinzer, "News Photographer's Quick Eye Revealed an Artist at Heart," *New York Times*, February 7, 2001. The University of Pittsburgh has made a large selection of Harris's photographs available online at https://historicpittsburgh.org/islandora/object/pitt%3Acollection.85.
47. Walter Ray Watson Jr., "Teenie Harris's Life in Pictures," *New Pittsburgh Courier,* December 30, 1944.
48. Linda Benedict-Jones, "A Place in the Pantheon: Teenie Harris in the History of African-American Photography," in *Spirit of a Community: The Photographs of Charles "Teenie" Harris* (Greensburg, PA: Westmoreland Museum of American Art, 2001), 13–15; Deborah Willis, "Introduction," in *Teenie Harris Photographer: Image, Memory, History*, xi–xiv.

49. Crouch, "Steel City Swing," 24–25.
50. Crouch, "Steel City Swing," 14.
51. The mock-up of the book, associated papers, miscellaneous correspondence, and letter from Ray Moore are in Box 9, Howard Morehead Collection, UCLA.
52. For Morehead's life and work, the Howard Morehead Collection, UCLA (Collection PASC-M 142-Howard Morehead Photographs and Papers) is the best source. See also Myrna Oliver, "Howard Morehead, 79; Photographer of Jazz Musicians Broke Color Barrier," *Los Angeles Times*, 2003, http://articles.latimes.com/2003/jul/24/local/me-morehead24.
53. Press releases from Bronze Beauty Enterprises, "1993 Bronze Beauty Calendar Hits Market" and "Bronze Beauty Calendar Acclaimed Worldwide," 1993. Box 9, Howard Morehead Collection, UCLA.
54. Alyn Shipton, *Hi-De-Ho: The Life of Cab Calloway* (Oxford: Oxford University Press, 2010), 6; Earnestine Lovelle Jenkins, *Race, Representation and Photography in 19th-Century Memphis* (London: Routledge, 2016), 275. Deborah Willis, *Posing Beauty: African American Images from the 1890s to the Present* (New York: W. W. Norton, 2000), xvii, argues that "beauty is empowering in black culture."
55. Kwame Brathwaite quoted by Melissa Smith, "The Photos That Lifted Up the Black Is Beautiful Movement," *New York Times*, 2018, https://www.nytimes.com/2018/11/27/lens/kwame-brathwaite-black-is-beautiful.html.
56. John Loehngard, Interview with the Author, 2018. See also Bob Moore, "The Role of the Picture Editor: Interview with John Loengard," ScottKelby website, 2010, https://scottkelby.com/its-guest-blog-wednesday-featuring-john-loengard/.
57. Robert ("Bob") R. Douglas, Résumé of Photographer Robert R. Douglas. Unpublished document, mid-1990s. Bob Douglas Collection, Tom & Ethel Bradley Center, Oviatt Library Special Collections, California State University, Northridge and Douglas, "Interview with Joe Rose." All Douglas quotations are taken from this interview. Douglas's work has been included in exhibitions arranged by the Institute of Arts and Media at California State University, Northridge. See *Identity and Affirmation: Post-War African American Photography*, ed. Kent Kirkton (Los Angeles: California State University Northridge, 2011); and Kent Kirkton (ed.), *Camera and Community: Photographs from the Collection of the Institute for Arts and Media* (Los Angeles: California State University Northridge, 2008). Alan John Ainsworth, "'A Private Passion': The Jazz Photography of Bob Douglas," *Southern California Quarterly* 101, no. 3 (2019): 317–38, offers a detailed assessment of Douglas's work.
58. Michael Dawson, "Photography: South of Point Lobos," in *LA's Early Moderns: Art/Architecture/Photography*, ed. Victoria Dailey, Natalie Shrivers, and Michael Dawson (Los Angeles: Balcony Press, 2003), 264–65; Fred Archer, *Fred Archer on Portraiture* (San Francisco, CA: Camera Craft, 1954).
59. For Ted Williams's work see Ted Williams, *Jazz: The Iconic Images of Ted Williams* (London: Iconic Images, 2016), and John Leland, "Hearing Music in Photos of Jazz Giants," *New York Times*, August 16, 2016. I am grateful to Williams's widow Adrienne for sharing her memories of her husband's life and work.
60. Adrienne Williams, "Interview with the Author," 2018. All quotations taken from the same interview.
61. Lou and Max Modica, "Discovering the Historic Jazz Photography of Ted Williams," Kickstarter, 2012, https://www.kickstarter.com/projects/342833186/discovering-the-historic-jazz-photography-of-ted-w.
62. It is significant that in an account of Charlie Parker at The Bee Hive in Chicago in 1953 Williams speaks only of the music rather than his photographic techniques, suggesting that it is the anticipation of the music's movement that shaped the sight readings.
63. Roy DeCarava quoted by Peter Galassi, "Introduction," in *Roy DeCarava: A Retrospective* (New York: Museum of Modern Art, 1996), 19; Coleman, "Roy DeCarava: 'Thru Black Eyes,'" 22.
64. DeCarava's biography is sufficiently well-known not to require repetition here. Elton C. Fax, "Roy DeCarava," in *Seventeen Black Artists* (New York: Dodd Mead, 1971), 167–87; and Gerald C. Fraser, "For Ray DeCarava, 62, It's Time for Optimism," *New York Times*, 1982, provide succinct summaries. Richard Ings, "'And You Slip into the Breaks and Look Around': Jazz and Everyday Life in the Photographs of Roy DeCarava," in *The Hearing Eye: Jazz and Blues Influences in African American Visual Art* (Oxford: Oxford University Press, 2009), 303–30, Galassi, "Introduction," and Turner "DeCarava," 7–20, all offer detailed commentaries. It was not possible to secure permission from the DeCarava estate to reproduce his photography and the DeCarava

website, which once displayed many images and now no longer operates. Roy DeCarava's photographs can be seen in his books *Photographs* (New York: Friends of Photography, 1981), *Roy DeCarava: A Retrospective*, ed. Peter Galassi and Sherry Turner DeCarava and *The Sound I Saw: Improvisation on a Jazz Theme* (London: Phaidon, 2001). Sherry Turner DeCarava, "Roy DeCarava," *Massachusetts Review* 29, no. 3 (1988): 477–92, presents a selection of photographs.

65. Sherry Turner DeCarava, "Celebration," in *Roy DeCarava: Photographs*, ed. James Alinder, The Friends of Photography, 1981, 15; Stephanie James, "Extraordinary Shades of Gray: The Photographs of Roy DeCarava," *Bulletin of the Detroit Institute of Arts* 80, nos. 1–2 (2006): 58–67, all include discussions of DeCarava's use of black.
66. Benjamin Cawthra, *Blue Notes in Black and White: Photography and Jazz* (Chicago: University of Chicago Press, 2011), xx; Scott Saul, "Jazz as a Religion of Work: Roy DeCarava's John Coltrane," in *Freedon Is, Freedon Ain't: Jazz and the Making of the Sixties* (Cambridge, MA: Harvard University Press, 2003), 248–53. Geoff Dyer, "On Portraits," *Aperture*, no. 224 (2016): 24.
67. Michael Irwin, "Roy DeCarava in New York: A Jazz Photographer in Subject and Technique," Ocula, 2019, https://ocula.com/magazine/insights/roy-decarava-in-new-york/, reports DeCarava's views on the relationship between improvisatory music and photography.
68. These examples are taken from the 2003 unpaginated reprint of the original edition: DeCarava, *The Sound I Saw: Improvisation on a Jazz Theme*.
69. DeCarava, *Roy DeCarava: A Retrospective*, 15.
70. Ann Gibson, "Recasting the Canon: Norman Lewis and Jackson Pollock," *Artforum* March (1992): 66–73, has an interesting account of DeCarava's relationship with the Studio 35 group of abstract artists.
71. Letter to Minor White cited by Maren Stange, "Illusion Complete within Itself: Roy DeCarava's Photography," in *A Modern Mosaic: Art and Modernism in the United States*, ed. Townsend Ludington (Chapel Hill: University of North Carolina Press, 2000), 291.
72. For Milt Hinton's life and career see his memoir Milt Hinton and David G. Berger, *Bass Line: The Stories and Photographs of Milt Hinton* (Philadelphia: Temple University Press, 1988). Hinton's photography is collected in Milt Hinton, David G. Berger, and Holly Maxson, *Overtime: The Jazz Photography of Milt Hinton* (San Francisco, CA: Pomegranate Art Books, 1991). See also David G. Berger, "Milt Hinton's Jazz Legacy," *USA Today* (1998): 66–77; Peter Keepnews, "Milt Hinton, Dean of Jazz Bassists, Is Dead at 90," *New York Times* (2000), available at https://www.nytimes.com/2000/12/21/nyregion/milt-hinton-dean-of-jazz-bassists-is-dead-at-90.html.
73. I am particularly grateful to David Berger for providing information in interviews and correspondence.
74. Milt Hinton, "Milt on Photography" (unpublished paper courtesy David Berger, 2008).
75. Hinton, Berger, and Maxson, *Overtime: The Jazz Photography of Milt Hinton*, 9.
76. Herman Leonard, "Interview with Tad Hershorn" (Institute of Jazz Studies, Rutgers University, n.d.).
77. In correspondence with the author, October 2018.
78. Stewart quoted by Jared T. Miller, "Through Chuck Stewart's Lens, A History of Jazz," *Newsweek*, 2015, https://www.newsweek.com/through-chuck-stewarts-lens-history-jazz-310085.
79. Carol Friedman, "Remembering Chuck Stewart," WGBO Livestream, 2017.
80. Cited by Richard Sandomir, "Chuck Stewart, Jazz Photographer, Dies at 89," *New York Times* (2017), https://www.nytimes.com/2017/01/27/arts/design/chuck-stewart-jazz-photographer-dies-at-89-youve-seen-his-album-covers.html.
81. Stewart cited by George, "New Photos of John Coltrane Rediscovered 50 Years After They Were Shot."
82. Stewart cited by Paul Carter Harrison and Chuck Stewart, "Vampin," in *Chuck Stewart's Jazz Files* (London: Quartet, 1986), 16–18.
83. The photographs are reproduced in Charles Stewart and Paul Carter Harrison, *Chuch Stewart's Jazz Files* (London: Quartet Books, 1986), 25, 49, and 52.
84. Bob Wilber, "The Mysterious Rabbit," *Blue Light: The Journal of the Duke Ellington Society UK* 26, no. 4 (2019): 6; David Hajdu, *Lush LIfe: A Biography of Billy Strayhorn* (London: Granta Books, 1996), 178; Con Chapman, *Rabbit's Blues: The Life and Music of Johnny Hodges* (Oxford: Oxford University Prss, 2019), 81–82. Don DeMichael remarked that Hodges "tosses off phrases buttery in mellowness" and "the honey of imagination:" Don DeMichael, "Johnny Hodges," *Down Beat*, June 7, 1962.

85. Driskell, "Evolution of a Black Aesthetic," 74, 76–78, catalog essay for exhibition "Two Centuries of Black American Art"; David C. Driskell, *Two Centuries of Black American Art* (New York: Alfred A. Knopf, 1976), 74.

86. Maren Stange, *Symbols of Ideal Life: Social Documentary Photography in America 1890–1950* (Cambridge: Cambridge University Press, 1989), 86.

8

Authenticity and Art "New Generation" White Photography

William Gottlieb (1917–2006) was one of the earliest members of a new generation of predominantly white jazz photographers coming to prominence in the interwar years. Gottlieb combined careful framing and composition with an acute sensitivity to expressive gestures in photographs whose technical accomplishments belie his status as self-taught photographer. Creating images that seemed to capture the essence of a "golden age," Gottlieb would influence many of the photographers soon to follow him: "To Bill, my mentor," Herman Leonard acknowledged in a respectful personal dedication in 1996, "Thank God you were there to make those great images!"[1]

According to Barry Singer, Gottlieb's images capture "the essence of jazz—a quality, outside sound, that only a camera can capture. It is the sight of a soul expressing itself." Krin Gabbard speaks of Gottlieb's ability to create multilayered visual meanings while Benjamin Cawthra considers that Gottlieb's photography transcends the powers of biography, an assessment echoed by Walter Schaap:[2]

> *They are such wonderful photographs and so typical of the artist they represented that it stuck in my memory that this is what Coleman Hawkins looked like, and this is what Lester Young looked like, and this is what Louis Armstrong looked like, so that today, when I recall these musicians whom I knew, I think of them in terms of what they look like in Bill's photographs.*

Gottlieb's 1979 collection *The Golden Age of Jazz* earned an American Society of Composers, Authors and Publishers Award and has been continually in print since. In 1997 *Down Beat* honored Gottlieb as the first non-musician to be chosen to receive its Lifetime Achievement Award. His jazz images are still among the most widely reproduced and exhibited not least because the archive entered public domain when acquired in 2010 by the Library of Congress.

Gottlieb's photography career from student journalism to jazz writer-photographer, his move away from jazz in 1948, and late-1970s revival of interest in his "Golden Age" photography between 1938 and 1948 need not be repeated here.[3] The consciously authorial nature of his photographs is however worthy of note. Most of Gottlieb's images were made to illustrate over 160 authored articles for *Down Beat* in the two years prior to his retirement from the jazz scene, an approach he characterized as "purposeful shooting:" "Ideally, I tried to capture a person's personality or inner qualities," Gottlieb recalled, citing as an example his famous photograph of Billie Holiday "that clearly shows the anguish in her voice." Carefully framing Charlie Parker's intense stare (Figure 107), Gottlieb's accompanying text complements the image of a "Weird Wizard" whose transcendent artistic genius can be detected in his "other-world look."[4] Gottlieb's was a conception of jazz as a soaring art form whose realization by accomplished practitioners bore the impress of cultural provenance; and he shot thoughtfully,

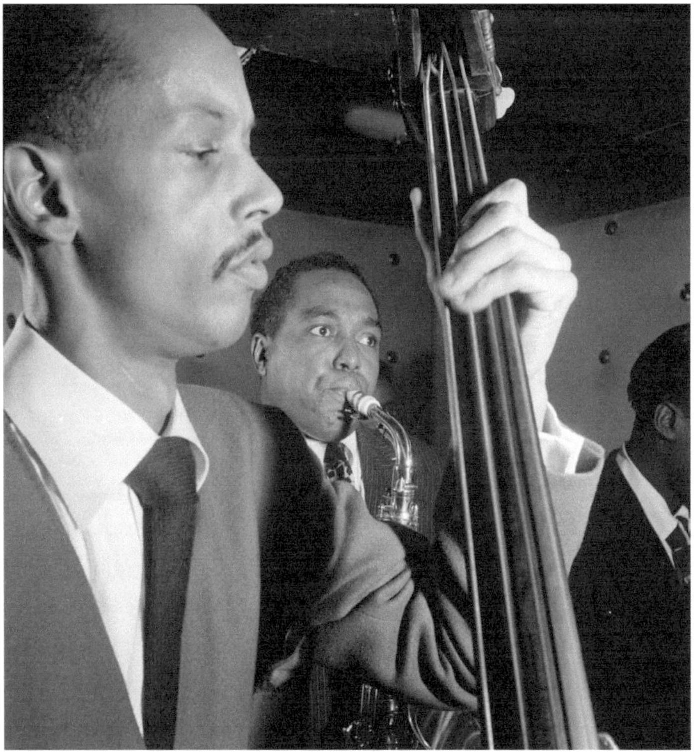

Figure 107: William Gottlieb. *Portrait of Charlie Parker and Tommy Potter*. Three Deuces. New York. 1947.
Ed Gottlieb/Library of Congress.

mastering the creative use of flash and cropping in-camera in order to convey his understanding of the music.

What motivated Gottlieb to make these images? Historians have relied on Gottlieb's own account according to which a family friend brought records and music magazines as he recovered from a nasty illness in 1936, initiating a journey that quickly led from Guy Lombardo to Duke Ellington.[5] There is however a broader context. According to his oldest son Steve, Gottlieb was clever, professional, dedicated, and extremely hard-working, a driven individual always keen to succeed.[6] Gottlieb spoke little about his German-speaking immigrant parents but "was proud of being Jewish [. . .] he spoke on several occasions about Jewish cultural accomplishments and maybe saw himself as part of that legacy." His father had been successful in business and the immigrant virtues of hard work and striving were clearly inherited. Steve Gottlieb argues that jazz presented his father with an opportunity for self-definition and self-expression, an area toward which he could direct his formidable energies, talents, and ambitions:

> *I think he did have some passion for the music, but I always have that sense that this was his chance to stand out—finding a niche that he comfortable in, a niche he knew something about [. . .] There weren't many [jazz] critics and photographers at the time [. . .] when he gave talks in later life I was amazed how people had saved articles he had written and showed them to him.*

Jazz offered Gottlieb an opportunity to express himself and excel. He passionately opposed discrimination and was friendly with jazz musicians, "but he wasn't warm and fuzzy—it was more that he was *the* guy. He would take serious pictures, get them published, write about the musicians and he earned their respect." Even so, while writing about jazz brought peer recognition, the family rarely heard any of his large collection of 78s as Gottlieb preferred classical music: "the day day he left the jazz scene in 1948 was the day when he stopped listening completely."

This is not to suggest that Gottlieb's attraction to jazz was purely instrumental; he could not have produced such subtly layered images without a close affinity with the music, the musicians, and its culture. What it does indicate is Gottlieb's animating conviction that his sense of self could be realized through engagement with jazz and expressed through the medium of photography. The photographers immediately following Gottlieb followed a similar path, mapping their own strategies for making their way in the world. Born mostly in the interwar years, this cohort of art, documentary, and/or commercial photographers comprises what many consider to be the core of the jazz photography tradition: Gottlieb, Gjon Mili, William Claxton, Dennis Stock, Bob Willoughby, Don Hunstein, and Robert Parent are perhaps the most well-known but the group was large and eclectic. Virtually all however were white, young men and (occasionally) women, whose social backgrounds, education, and early experiences positioned them to take advantage of commercial opportunities largely closed to African American photographers discussed in the preceding chapter. Linking these photographers was the role jazz played in a search for personal and cultural meaning, a subject of photographic enquiry that provided—much as it had done for William Gottlieb—"a defining as well as identifying act."[7]

I. A new generation

Photographers and the new middle class

A new middle class emerged numerically and culturally as the chief beneficiary of the economic growth and transformation of occupational structure that followed the wave of technological innovations at the heart of America's second great economic transformation.[8] Defined, in C. Wright Mills's classical formulation, as a mental rather than occupational category, the middle class set about remaking America in a way that testified to the satisfaction which came with this revolution in identity. Estimated at no fewer than 20 percent of the entire population by 1920, the middle class intended "nothing less than to [. . .] remake the nation's feuding, polyglot population in their own middle-class image." For Warren Susman the story of the modern American state is the story of the new middle class.[9]

The new generation of photographers were bound to these changes in the American social structure, belonging to what Wright Mills termed the "new intellectuals," "people who specialize in symbols [. . .] the immediate carriers of art and ideas [. . .] Seeking to cultivate a sense of individual mind."[10] Sociologically, self-made business and professional family backgrounds predominated in the biographies of this cohort of photographers. Many (including Herman Leonard, Don Bronstein, Lida Moser, Sol Libsohn, Stanley Kubrick, Charles B. Nadel, Bert Stern, and Eliot Elisofon) were born to Jewish parents whose success in business or the professions reflected the characteristic striving of first-generation immigrants. The integrationist aspirations of their parents propelled their offspring toward educational attainment and professional success although—as is so often the case with a second generation—many found themselves torn between their parents' inherited culture and that into which they had been born. The overwhelming majority of the new generation photographers benefited from the expansion in higher education and a significant number had an art training.

The middle-class nature of family and educational background sharply distinguishes the new generation photographers attracted to jazz from their African American contemporaries. It is little surprise that Amiri Baraka should scathingly refer to Robert Parent as typifying "a whole group of young university-trained fairly well-to-do white dudes who had come up with the music in their youth, listening and playing or hanging out in the clubs."[11] Just as importantly, the photographers were intimately tied into the new occupational structure as their medium emerged as one of the key components of America's new economy and visual culture: "within a year" of 1936, Roy Stryker recalled, photography became "a national industry [. . .] with a suddenness matched only by the introduction of television twelve years later." Avant-garde, modernist, and art photography became the staple of magazines like *Harper's Bazaar* while advertising, art direction, and graphic design increasingly demanded photographic illustration; the illustrated press fostered a new breed of photojournalists and reportage specialists. In industry generally photography "uses [were] multiplying almost daily as one ingenious mind after another [found] in photography another way in which time and effort [could] be economized or made more effective."[12]

At the very heart of a dynamic occupational structure, these photographers were able to build financially viable diversified commercial practices. When they approached jazz it was often as a personal project or as a relatively small component in a portfolio of commercial activities. Advertising was a major source of revenue for most members of the cohort, often overlapping with art photography, fashion, and celebrity or artistic portraiture. Photojournalists like Elliot Elisofon, John Loengard, Arthur Elgort, Ed Feingersch, and W. Eugene Smith carried out major reportage assignments at home and abroad between which they fitted in jazz-oriented projects; Frank Kuchirchuk combined his day job as a photographer for the International News Service in the early-1950s with jazz work. Commercial work for specialist magazines such as *Down Beat,* the illustrated press and record labels, occupied Herman Leonard, William Claxton, Marvin Koner, Carol Reiff, Bob Parent, and many others in the group. Bob Willoughby and Don Hunstein (at Columbia between 1955 and 1986) worked as motion picture studio photographers. Artist-photographers like Bob Cato, Victor Kalin, and Ralston Crawford regarded their jazz images as part and parcel of broader artistic practices and photographer-designers like Halsman and Burt Goldblatt parlayed their photography skills into record company graphics, illustrations, and portraits. Burt Glinn's range of subjects both before and after capturing jazz musicians as participants of the beat scene in the late-1950s was as wide as that of any photojournalist.

We therefore need to exercise care when speaking of this group as "jazz photographers" as the major part of the careers of even the most storied was outside the world of jazz. Gottlieb left jazz for the best part of 30 years to specialize in writing and producing educational films while Leonard and Claxton made their careers in fashion, film, and celebrity portraits, motion picture stills, and advertising. Leonard's photographs were little appreciated at the time and some 40 years would pass before they saw the light of day and assumed the status of art objects; indeed, Bill Crow recalls that Leonard's photographs hanging on the walls at Birdland were so little valued that they were destroyed during renovation.[13] Robert Parent's work ranged widely to include sporting events, dance, theatre, artists, politicians, civil rights leaders, New York and Boston city life, New England farms and countryside, Japan under US occupation, postwar Havana, and the 1964 World's Fair. During the 1960s Parent turned to social and political photojournalism. Denis Stock's work for Magnum included celebrity and youth culture, reportage, and later moved on to making documentary film, traveling widely and in later life still life and architecture. His jazz photography was confined to the years between 1957 and the early-1960s.

Putting the jazz work of these photographers into perspective provides a corrective to scholars such as Peter Townsend who, in referencing Claxton, Gottlieb, DeCarava, Leonard, Reiff, Tanner, Hilton, and Snitzer, claims these "distinguished photographers have devoted their careers largely to the representation of jazz."[14] It is more accurate to say that their significance as photographers of jazz rests not on the predominance of jazz imagery in their archive or the longevity of their engagement with the music but in the consciously authorial way in which they used their medium to express their affinity with the music.

Authenticity, art, and culture in the 1930s

The social and economic revolution of the first decades of the twentieth century created what many contemporary observers believed to be an irreconcilable divide. "The two generations misunderstand each other as they never did before," Randolf S. Bourne complained in his 1913 book *Youth and Life*; "there is a particularly headstrong and individualistic character among the young people, and a complete bewilderment on the part of the parents."[15] Yet the views of middle-class youth were nowhere near as certain, nor as oppositional, as Bourne implied. While many artists and intellectuals moved to the left, particularly during the early-1930s, a more generalized commitment to culture—both in terms of its antecedents and its potential as a unifying force—had by the late-1930s gained in significance over defined ideological commitment. The concern with defining an American cultural identity made it possible to be both radical and patriotic, and it was the last time that the left focused so single-mindedly on reclaiming the nation's past and present.[16]

Authenticity and art: The "cultural whole"

Intellectuals in the prosperous years before 1929 had reacted with cynicism to stately Victorian traditions, scorning whatever lessons the recent past might have offered. The stock market crash and subsequent economic depression however witnessed a sea change in attitudes, a radically altered mindset manifested particularly in the quest for a "usable" American past. As Alfred Haworth Jones and Warren Sussman have influentially argued, the search for common bonds of genuine identity became the dominant cultural imperative of the 1930s. As intellectuals "turned to the past as a guide to the present, then the landmarks must be accurate and reliable [. . .] Hence, meticulous attention to authenticity became a canon of the decade."[17] This quest was marked by an emphasis on the uniqueness of American ideas and values. Agricultural fairs became a popular theme at upper-class charity balls in the large cities where guests dressed in gingham, calico, and overalls and hotel ballrooms were transformed with sideshows, hired milkmaids, and even lives animals.[18] Alongside a preoccupation with "the people" and their characteristic forms of occupation and amusement, there was a prevailing concern with heroes from the past, "individuals of a special sort [. . .] the spokesmen, the representatives, the symbols finally, of the whole people, the common folk." A renewed sense of heritage became a source of inspiration for a wide range of intellectuals in educational institutions, government programs, popular culture, and the fine arts who turned to black music among other forms of folk expression.[19]

There was an undeniably radical component to these changes in the early to mid-1930s. Michael Denning has used the term "Cultural Front" to describe the totality of cultural expressions generated at the interface between working-class movements and the cultural apparatus of mass entertainment, education, and New Deal cultural policies.[20] Even if they were not actually members of the Communist Party many artists and intellectuals remained firmly radical into the late-1930s. Other scholars however have emphasized the essentially conservative popular and intellectual turn of the 1930s: Alfred Haworth Jones describes as "profoundly conservative" the 1930s reassessment of the past, Alan Brinkley characterizes even that decade's radicalism as "folksy, unthreatening, American," and Warren Susman argues that cultural thinking became "far more conservative than radical."[21]

Despite all efforts a genuinely radical popular culture failed to take root in the 1930s and communalism never overwhelmed traditional American values such as individualism, self-reliance, and private ownership.[22] The renewed search for cultural unity, authenticity, and meaning was evidenced by a variety of distinctly American "cultural nationalisms" that came to overwhelm more fundamentally radical ideas. Although the 1930s have been variously labeled the "Fervent Years," the "Angry Decade," and the "Red Decade," these largely retrospective epithets belie the reality in which solutions premised on fundamental economic change made little headway; as one historian puts it, "proletarian revolution [. . .] repeatedly ran up against the social and economic aspirations of the enormous American middle class."[23] A deep sense of isolationism asserted itself during the 1930s fueled in part by a pervasive fear of anarchism and Bolshevism. By the second half of the 1930s liberals, radicals, and even those once attracted by socialist and communist prescriptions were turning back to old-fashioned American liberties. Support shifted toward the Popular Front whose "American spirit" rhetoric heralded a rapprochement with the New Deal and renewed commitment to American values.

A populist form of celebration of America emerged. The Popular Front cultural left adopted Abraham Lincoln as a working-class hero, romanticized the ethnic diversity of the American "folk" in cultural forms such as Paul Robeson's "Ballad for Americans," and declared, in the words of CPUSA chairman Earl Browder, that "Communism is Twentieth-Century Americanism."[24] Although we cannot ignore Richard Hofstadter's warnings not to draw simple lines of connection between Progressivism and New Deal reforms or underestimate the scale of those reforms when compared with the recent past, it is difficult not to see a reanimated version of the old Progressivist ideals of association and social solidarity emerging in the 1930s—a sense of identification within, and responsibility toward, a social collective as if the general objective of arts and politics, consciousness and society could be made whole. It is in this sense that one historian describes Progressivism as "a rehearsal during which, in sunny times, the Americans learned the techniques they would need in the stormy days to come."[25]

Herbert Croly recognized in 1928 that progressivism had disintegrated but predicted that it had not disappeared. Within a few years he would be proved correct. Although elected as part of a sweeping reaction to the Progressive era of Roosevelt, Taft, and Wilson, the Harding and Coolidge administrations were characterized as much by continuity as change while the 1928 Presidential election contenders, the Republican Hoover and the radical Al Smith, "each represented important sources of pre-war progressivism: the urban working class in Smith's case and enlightened corporate management in Hoover's." With the depression progressivism consequently regained an element of its vitality in the hands of individual reformers whose efforts found expression through New Deal institutions.[26] These bodies—and particularly the work of the cultural agencies within the Federal Arts Project after 1935—played a key role in recasting the cultural components of the Progressivist social whole in the radically changed circumstances of the 1930s.

As head of the Federal Arts Project, Holgar Cahill's ambition was nothing less than a fundamental redefinition of art and its place in American culture. He agitated vigorously to combine high art with craft and design, stressing usefulness as well as aesthetic criteria and democratizing access to all the arts. His was another instance of the search for a "usable past," to capture and save America's artistic heritage for use in the future. The work of the FAP through its programs of Community Arts Centers, the Index of American Design, and other initiatives underpinned the process. Cahill's vision of America's past was tinged with nostalgic longing for small town communality, but the FAP's mantra of "cultural democracy" was profound and widely disseminated. Long after the FAP was wound down in 1943, New Deal cultural leaders "continued to believe in its practical and symbolic value. For them it offered a definition of national cultural identity related intimately to the land and people."[27] The art pavilions at the 1939 New York World Fair each in their own way stressed the need for art to transform life and elevated aesthetic experience as integral to the "democratic" nature of their displays—a mindset that permeated subsequent decades even as the institutional foundations of New Deal cultural democracy were dismantled.[28] A similar revival of Progressivist ideals can be identified in John Steuart Curry's championing of untrained rural art as "artist in residence" at the University of Wisconsin's School of Agriculture, an initiative which in this case drew on the Danish folk school for its model.[29]

The longing for a reanimated cultural whole also permeated the thinking of liberals seeking to overcome the racial lacuna at the heart of the Progressivist legacy. Pro-civil rights, anti-lynch law New Dealers channeled their energies into arts and cultural initiatives in which they found strong support from the NAACP. Black newspapers like the *Defender* were resolute in their coverage and defense of the "cultural democracy" of Chicago's South Side Community Arts Center whose exhibitions, Illinois FAP head Peter Pollack declared, were testimony to the "common heritage and [. . .] common aspirations" of black and white artists.[30] If the idea of cultural unity can again be traced back to the progressivist era, New Deal liberalism helped seal the bond between politics and culture, holding out the prospect that the arts might be the basis for a renewed integrated cultural unity. While some historians have cast doubt on the long-term impact of the FAP's "color blindness," there can be little doubt about:[31]

> *the larger FAP goal of producing a positive vision of the "American scene" through their art, creating work that demonstrated the integral role African Americans played in American history and culture. The FAP's efforts to define the national identity through the production of a distinctly American art built upon a longer tradition of cultural nationalism in the United States [. . .] The impetus to determine the unique contours of American culture was doubly strong in a moment of economic insecurity [. . .] and the FAP attempted to unite the country around a common celebration of the American "folk."*

Certainly, the racial and social integration of the community arts centers was sufficiently noticeable to become a central component of the conservative attack on the FAP.[32]

Cahill's pursuit of "cultural democracy" was shared by the FAP's other cultural leaders—Henry Alsberg, Nikolai Sokoloff, and Haillie Flanagan—each of whom strived in their own way to integrate the artist into the mainstream life, as expressive of the nation and accessible to its people.[33] The objectives of the FAP were however just one expression of a broad concern with the possibilities of culture and art in fostering unity and transforming society. The more experiential definition of culture emerging during a period of Depression led to calls for the desacralization of and broadening participation in the arts and challenges to the auratic Euro-centric model. American vernacular themes were seen as crucial to contemporary expression in what was a broadening of conceptions of art. Among these many sources of inspiration in contemporary culture, the provenance of jazz assured its authenticity and the development of the advanced technical accomplishments of its musicians assured it the status of art. In this decade of cultural reappraisal, "jazzed music," as John Dewey termed it in *Art as Experience*, emerged for many as among the more vital contributions to American culture.[34]

A common artistic discourse

The extent to which an authentic "usable" past linked with the unifying potentialities of art in a common discursive framework has been obscured by the ferocious conflicts over the appropriate form of art for the divisive decade of the 1930s.[35] Seeking a usable past, many artists looked backward to American heritage in arts, crafts, and folk traditions as evidenced by the celebration of early American styles and decorative arts by Charles Sheeler and the regionalism of Thomas Hart Benton, Grant Wood, Marvin Cone, and John Steuart Curry. American scene painting was a quest that found support in a reinvigorated sense of regionalism and valorization of local identities, particularly the rediscovery of African American folk culture.[36]

This turn to a more authentic provenance crossed another debate—that of social realism versus the modernist conception of art as subjectivity and imagination. Modernism had taken deep root in America in the early decades of the twentieth century.[37] By the 1930s, its ideas were being widely adopted in the worlds of architecture, fashion, commercial design and were particularly marked in the visual arts and design: the modernist scenes of Charles Demuth, Marsden Hartley, and John Marin; the landscapes of Georgia O'Keefe; the non-objectivity of George L. K. Morris, Arthur Dove, Ilya Bolotowsky; and the American Abstract Artists group and the surrealist-informed work of O. Louis Guglielmi, Morris Kantore, and Helen Lundeberg. Other artists vigorously disputed the modernist belief in the significance of the aesthetic object and its capacity to address the social and political questions of the day. Although modernists believed that abstraction was a universal language that pushed beyond nationalism, artists like Ben Shahn, Reginald March, Philip Evergood, and Paul Cadmus turned to realism as the basis for an American art. More generally too, in literature, theatre, song and dance, architecture and design, "art for art's sake" now seemed as irrelevant as it was effete. Many artists moved to the left to produce different forms of "social" or "sensational" modernism. While some positioned their work in opposition to commercialized mass culture, others drew on the language, motifs, and techniques of cinema, advertising radio and photography.[38]

Three fracture lines thus divided the American artistic community of the 1930s: social realism versus abstraction, national American themes versus Euro-internationalism, and the integrity of art versus its social utility. Yet at a more fundamental level Sarah Kelly Oehler has argued that all artists—from the American scene painters such as Benton at one extreme to non-objectivists at the other—exploited the flexibility of international modernism to their own stylistic ends. Underlying stylistic differences, most artists seemed enamored of the distinctive visual experiences that distinguished America from Europe. There was more common ground that the heated debates of the period suggested and it is the remarkable body of work produced by Stuart Davis that perhaps best demonstrates the common concern with authenticity and art in the 1930s artistic and cultural mindset.

Throughout his career Davis was remarkably consistent in articulating his philosophy and enumerating his sources of inspiration and from this we are able to see how he spanned the prevailing lines of tension. Davis passionately believed abstraction to be a progressive social force but was insistent on the need to retain recognizably figurative elements in his own work. He drew unabashedly on international modernism (particularly cubism, synthetic cubism, and surrealism), even denying the impossibility of any artist avoiding such influences, yet synthesized the styles and motifs of international modernism with representations of contemporary American culture in all its gaudy variety. Davis laid equal stress on the social leadership role of art while cleaving to the demands of aesthetic integrity, a fundamental belief in the aesthetic quality of great art and its mission to educate the "aesthetically uneducated masses"; far from repudiating a realist heritage, conversion to modernism strengthened his awareness of the autonomous character of the work of art.

Born and raised during the Progressive era, Davis was one of the artists who retained firmly on the left as the 1930s progressed, although his attitudes moderated in the early-1940s. In this commitment he was consistent as he was in citing black jazz as one of the most important sources of vernacular American inspiration. Jazz, he proposed, was the first native expression of modernism and his creation of a unique modernist style drew on its structure, syntax, and practices. Pride of place for Davis went to "Earl Hines hot piano," which, he wrote, "has served me as proof that art can exist." The improvisational lines of players like Hines and Armstrong, the "numerical precision of the Negro piano players," as well as the deep rooting of jazz in urban modernity and its technologies were a model by which the abstract formal and structural problems might be employed in a realist visual aesthetic. If Stuart Davis provides an example of the ways in which many of the artistic tensions of the period might be addressed, it is enormously significant that he chose to work out solutions through the inspiration provided by jazz and its transliteration into plastic form.[39]

Jazz and the new generation

Peter Martin writes that music has[40]

> *an ability to give people a sense of secure identity [. . .] and a sense of belonging at a time when the accelerating pace of economic and technological change is making it increasingly difficult to achieve continuity and stability in social life.*

Clearly modern, yet sufficiently ambiguous in its modernist particulars to suit a range of tastes, jazz offered a vision of that cultural unity that fascinated many in the 1930s, particularly among the new middle class. Jazz, it seemed, might be interpreted as a prefiguring of the cultural whole; as a music that calls for the highest level of individual skill and virtuosity but whose practical realization demands integration into and profound sensitivity with the ensemble, jazz's "inner democracy" embodies civic virtue that "substantiates" the seemingly impossible "ought," that is *e pluribus unum*.[41] The music emerged as a key site of social and personal affirmation for a generation seeking answers to the questions about personal identity raised by social, economic, and cultural change.

The renewed interest in "authentic" folk traditions and black culture explains the fascination in the 1930s with the music's provenance on the part of critics such as Charles Edward Smith, Frederick Ramsey Jr., Bill Russell, E. Simms Campbell, Edward Nichols, Wilder Hobson, Otis Ferguson, Stephen Smith, and Roger Pryor Dodge. In their writings these critics abashedly elevated as a "usable past" the authenticity of folk heroes such as Bunk Johnson over modern forms of the music: "the fine-spun, sometimes abstract, hot choruses of today [1946] have found a more abstruse vocabulary for what New Orleans musicians had said so simply and, to many of us, so beautifully."[42] Yet jazz was also expansive enough to appeal to a range of "modernisms," from Barry Ulanov's advocacy in *Metronome* of Euro-centric modernist jazz to the idea of musical modernism as understood by a broad public. These associations made the music attractive to those among the young middle-class generation looking to distance themselves from their parents' social or assimilating conventions through unorthodox aesthetics, politics, and personal style a range of rebellious postures and practices.[43]

One factor was of particular importance to many: engagement with jazz not only provided a means of energizing the integrationist impetus of New Deal liberalism but also offered a point of identity reference in black culture for young people adrift in a new world or distanced from the old world by immigrant or Jewish heritage (or, as with Mezz Mezzrow, both).[44] Youthful enthusiasm was channeled by the United Hot Clubs of America founded by Marshall Stearns and Milt Gabler in 1934 and numerous other clubs and societies where members indulged their passion. Resembling nothing so much an "Ivy-League cottage industry" in John Gennari's pithy description, the commitment of the almost exclusively white, male, and often well-to-do college students and intellectuals who comprised the bulk of the young fans and enthusiasts found expression in a discourse that marked out the jazz territory from that of commercialized music. Displaying a romantic attachment to individual artists and their latest career moves, disputes over stylistic differences, arguments about what was and what wasn't real jazz were continuous and flared up sharply from time to time.[45]

The job of articulating the different ideas about and meanings of jazz fell to the interlocking network of jazz journalists, writers and researchers, critics, producers, promoters, and managers. Journalism and criticism was yet another of the new middle-class occupations attracting serious-minded middle-class youth. Instilled with a self-consciousness by the colleges and universities established following the emergence of the modern graduate school in the 1870s, these brash and opinionated young graduates formed the core of the journalism that assumed center stage in an emerging jazz art world in the 1930s. These critics initiated a tradition observed almost without exception as "passionately liberal and pro-black on social, political, economic, and aesthetic issues."[46]

These differences exploded in any number of local skirmishes in the decades after 1930—revivalists versus modernists, Dixieland versus swing, "hot" jazz versus swing, authenticity versus commercialism, swing versus bebop, even "west coast" traditional" versus "non-jazz" swing.[47] Bernard Gendron however has made a point of emphasizing the common ground between these "diametrically opposed aesthetic views that nonetheless belonged to the same discursive world." No matter how strongly opposed they might have seemed, critics as much as enthusiasts were united for a righteous cause that found pervading expression in the aestheticized discourse of jazz as an authentic art form.[48] In this respect the jazz world of enthusiasts and critics alike mirrored the general concerns of the 1930s that the authenticity and artistry of jazz might in some sense form a common—and distinctly American—cultural touchstone.

Amiri Baraka and Frank Kofsky would later deride these critics and enthusiasts as "middle-brow" and "middle class" "hobbyists or boyishly brash members of the American petit bourgeoise," who had laid the groundwork for the colonization of black culture by white musicians and advocates.[49] Shorn of bombast, there is merit in Baraka's argument that appropriating jazz into the cultural whole recasts it as "American" rather than "black" music. Critics and enthusiasts however saw in jazz the potential of a revived cultural unity and were more inclined to agree with the Harlem Renaissance writer Joel Roger when he noted the difficulties in deciding whether jazz "is more characteristic of the Negro or of contemporary America."[50]

Photographers and jazz

Like other young middle-class enthusiasts most of the new generation photographers came to jazz as outsiders with little or no background connection with African American life; several recall the opposition of their parents to any involvement with the music. It was often, as William Kenney points out, the "excitement of urban life, their alienation from middle class Victorian moralism and a keen appreciation for the artful way" rather than familiarity of African American culture that formed the basis of the affinity between jazz and young whites.[51] Herman Leonard, William Claxton, Lee Tanner, Ray Avery, Duncan P. Schiedt, Burt Goldblatt, and Arthur Elgort all recall being turned on to jazz at an early age listening to recordings and/or radio broadcasts. Jazz was firmly part of John Vachon's world as Hank O'Neal explains: "he was a serious jazz guy [. . .] he loved the Condon guys, had all those Commodore records." Photographing jazz musicians was frequently a deeply personal activity. As Herman Leonard recalled in a 2009 interview:[52]

> *All of my jazz pictures, I did strictly for myself. After a while I did assignments for record companies, particularly Verve Records with Norman Granz as the producer. But the public didn't know anything about my work in historic terms until 1988.*

Bruce Davidson and Jay Maisel supported their forays into jazz with fees from advertising assignments. Bob Willoughby's love of jazz led him to photograph covers *pro bono* for albums put out by Fantasy Records, an independent label founded by his friends Max and Sol Weiss in 1949. William Claxton agreed to leave his new wife for five months to join Joachim Berendt on the road trip which led to *Jazz Life* without even asking about payment.[53]

The Jewish heritage of many among the new generation photographers was another factor in their relationship with jazz. The involvement of Jews in the world of jazz as musicians, composers, arrangers, club owners and promoters, business managers and booking agents, record label owners and producers, and critics has attracted much scholarly attention in recent years.[54] Several writers have posited a bond between people who have suffered oppression, a natural affinity based on shared suffering between two disadvantaged marginal groups. Although, as will be discussed in the next chapter, a number of questions are raised by the "oppressed brother" thesis, the affective strength of some Jews for black jazz cannot be doubted. Stanley Kubrick developed a love of jazz at an early age, with aspirations to play the drums in a swing band, and he combined this interest with photography; as his biographer explains, "Jazz, photography and chess were extraordinarily Jewish professions or pastimes. The list of Jewish photographers and jazz and chess players is too long to cite here." The affinity was not lost on contemporary observers such as Marshall Chess, who recognized the natural alliance between a Jewish photographer like Don Bronstein and black musicians, an affinity equally evident in the photographs of Sol Libsohn and Charles B. Nadel taken at Café Society. Dan Morgenstern and Nat Hentoff have spoken in similar terms.[55]

William Gottlieb was a racial liberal who had been involved in promoting integrated performances while Bob Willoughby's son recalled that his father was "never aware of him differentiating between black and white artists [. . .]

At the time white photographers were not hanging out with black musicians. Culturally he was comfortable hanging out with black musicians."[56] Leonard was clear about his own views on the subject of race and linked them to his own heritage:[57]

> *I must confess to you that I always felt very comfortable in black society. I never felt that I was out of place or a foreigner. I don't know why I was accepted. I wasn't judgmental when I was in their company as a lot of people are, instinctively, that way. They say "Oh! They're black, they're different." Not me [. . .].They knew that they were a minority and had to stick together I appreciated that [. . .] I was of Jewish origin from Allentown, Pennsylvania, for God's sake. So I know what a minority is because I was highly criticized as a child for being Jewish. So I had a lot of empathy.*

In his notes for an unrealized autobiography, Bob Cato planned to emphasize the lasting effect that his friendships with his black schoolfriends had on his personal and intellectual development. Eliot Elisofon remembers that at a very young age his favorite musicians were black and his brother's white, but this was irrelevant, "We got the music [. . .] It didn't make a difference."

While these photographers had a close affinity with jazz and African American musicians there is little to suggest that they were partisans in the debates about the true meaning of jazz in the 1930s and 1940s; Leonard for one claimed to have had little knowledge of the various jazz wars. Whatever their leanings though it is clear that the photographers shared the broad assumptions of young middle-class enthusiasts and most jazz critics that the music offered a cultural touchstone for their own outlook and identity.

II. Framing authenticity and art

Provenance and place: Documenting authenticity

A key motivation for many among the interwar "new generation" of white photographers was to document the provenance of jazz and the authenticity of its practices. Whereas the African American photographers discussed in the preceding chapter expressed themselves *from within* the realities of personal, social, and communal activities, the documentary impulse was an enquiry *from without*. The photographers joined with other intellectuals, writers, and artists in the 1930s and 1940s—many, although by no means all, white—in a search for authenticity through the distinctive lineage of African American culture and folklore.[58]

It is this quest for authenticity that allows us to understand Berenice Abbott's portrait of Leadbelly as a rebuttal to the demeaning and racist fashion in which *Life* had described the blues singer in 1937.[59] Accompanying a photograph by Otto Hess that shows the singer seated on a pile of feed sacks, the short *Life* article linked Leadbelly to a primitive agricultural past and focused almost entirely on his taste for sex, criminality, and violence. Commissioned by Austin Wilder and James Gilvarry of the WGN Concert Bureau, Abbott's photography positioned Leadbelly in heroic mode as a symbol of the left, an endeavor that united her with Charles Williams and other "cultural workers" in lionizing Leadbelly. The image was in keeping with her belief in the pedagogical mission of photography as a strategy of "communicative action," stimulating the viewer's critical engagement rather than the objective portrayal of a subject, and is closely linked to the singer's relationships with leading cultural figures of the Popular Front. Closely associated with Abbott was Lucy Ashjian, the daughter of Armenian refugees and a committed communist. Ashjian shots in Harlem's Savoy Ballroom demonstrate a similar interest in black music, dance, and the "folk" roots of jazz.[60]

A quest for the authentic roots of vernacular music concerned the FSA photographers. With a perceptive eye for the authentic and the local, Jack Delano, Dorothea Lange, Russell Lee, Arthur Rothstein, Ben Shahn, Marion Post Wolcott depicted a range of everyday music in migrant work camps, farmers' homes, barn dances, on street corners and at church revivals, dance halls, and community festivals. Many, like Marion Post Wolcott's *Jitterbugging in Negro juke joint, Saturday evening, outside Clarksdale, Mississippi* (1939), consciously foregrounded the involvement of dancers and audiences in the performance of this music.[61] Several FSA photographers had a specific interest in the cultural roots and characteristic expressions of jazz. With his musical training and interest in composition Jack Delano was attracted to the subject, often framing the players in such a way as to include dancers and other audience members (Figure 108); and John Vachon's attraction to jazz was founded on what he described as the authenticity and "sensuous universality" of Sweatman, Spanier, Sophie Tucker, and the ODJB over Guy Lombardo's "wining."[62]

In 1941 Russell Lee undertook a two-week FSA project in Chicago's Southside with Edwin Rosskam. Lee was selected by Roy Stryker for the project primarily for his empathy with people; he was the most adept at indoor flash work and it was in his detailed interiors that he often moved beyond the general to capture the specifics of people's lives in unaffected images. Lee and Rosskam embodied the spirit of the age in their enthusiasm as white documentarians to explore the diversity and vibrancy of a black life about which they previously knew little: "I don't know if many white men had the opportunity to see it the way we saw it. Man, that was an experience," Rosskam recalled of this journey of discovery.[63]

Alongside churches, social activities, sports, and other aspects of black life Lee and Rosskam explored jazz taverns and clubs. In one photograph Lee captured a floorshow by light-skinned black dancers accompanied by Boyd Atkin's

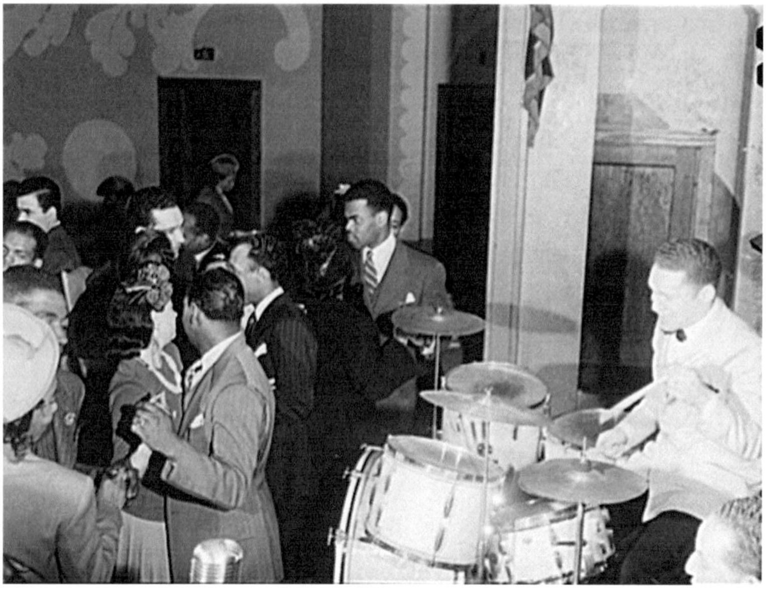

Figure 108: Jack Delano. *"Red" Saunders, drummer, and his band at the Club DeLisa.* Chicago, Illinois. 1942.
Library of Congress, Prints & Photographs Division, FSA/OWI Collection, LC-DIG-ds-09651.

all-black band in a "Negro cabaret" (Figure 109). The spectacle takes place in a designated performance space, a permanent stage with an elaborate backdrop separated by barriers from an all-white audience. The men are dressed in suits, the women wear showy hats, and couples sit nonchalantly at tables to watch the performance. Several black waiters can be seen and a few African American spectators are in the balcony. The image is a stark portrayal of the white gaze: the stage resembles nothing so much as a boxing ring and the posture and gestures of the white audience reinforce the "suggestive African American musical entertainment which helped customers create an atmosphere of inter-racial 'sensuality' characteristic of black-and-tan and other types of night spots."[64]

Contrasting photographs taken by Lee on April 6, 1941, in Tony's Tavern at 31st and Federal Streets in the heart of "Bronzeville" show the interior of a club patronized mainly by African Americans (Figures 110 and 111). This club was opened around 1900 by Tony Finkelstein, a white Jewish entrepreneur, who presented musicians such as Louis Armstrong, Cab Calloway, and Duke Ellington.[65] Lee's flash captured an all-black audience as well turned out as was the white audience in the cabaret, but the atmosphere could not be more different. The performance stage is a makeshift affair with painted backdrop showing cartoon characters. The photographs depicts a scene of jumbled informality with little to separate the performers and audience and evokes William Howland Kenney's description of the "powerfully concentrated, highly charged jazz experience of

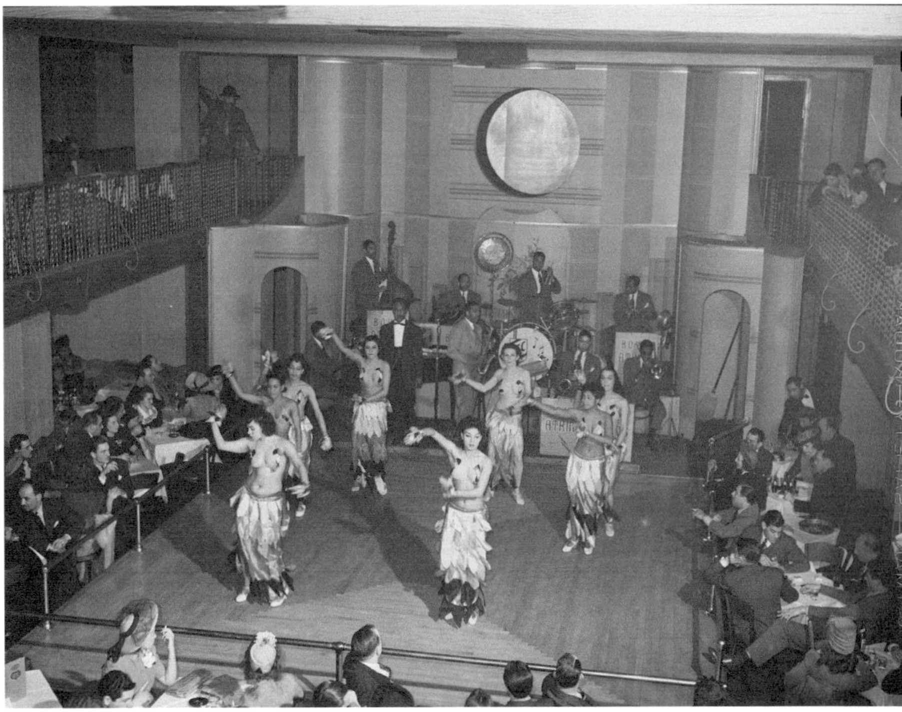

Figure 109: Russell Lee. *Negro Cabaret. Southside.* Chicago. 1941.
Library of Congress, Prints & Photographs Division, FSA/OWI Collection, 2017788740.

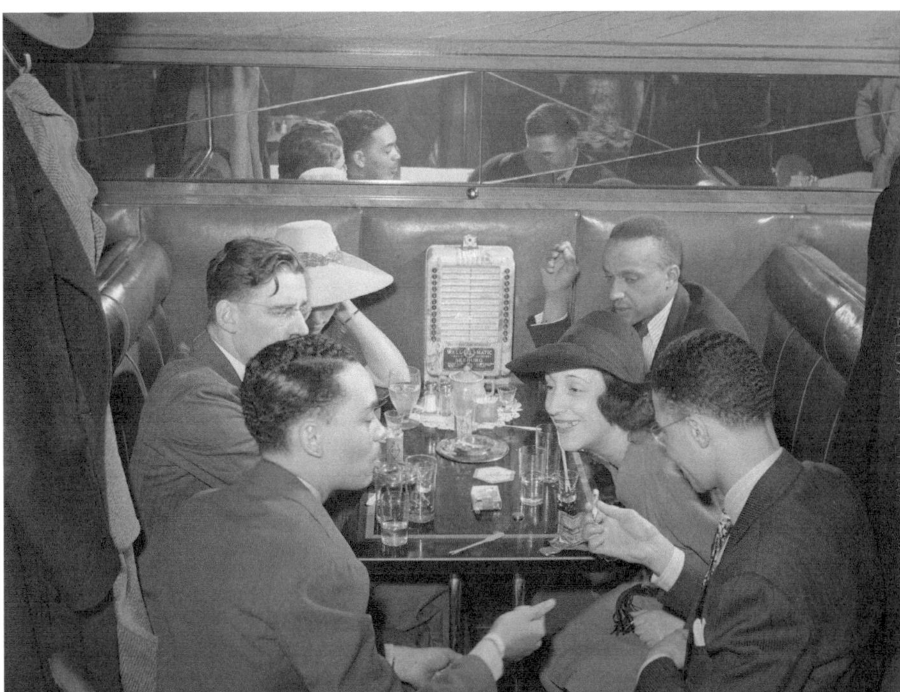

Figure 110: Russell Lee. *Booth in a Negro Tavern. Southside.* Chicago. 1941.
Library of Congress, Prints & Photographs Division, FSA/OWI Collection, 2017788778.

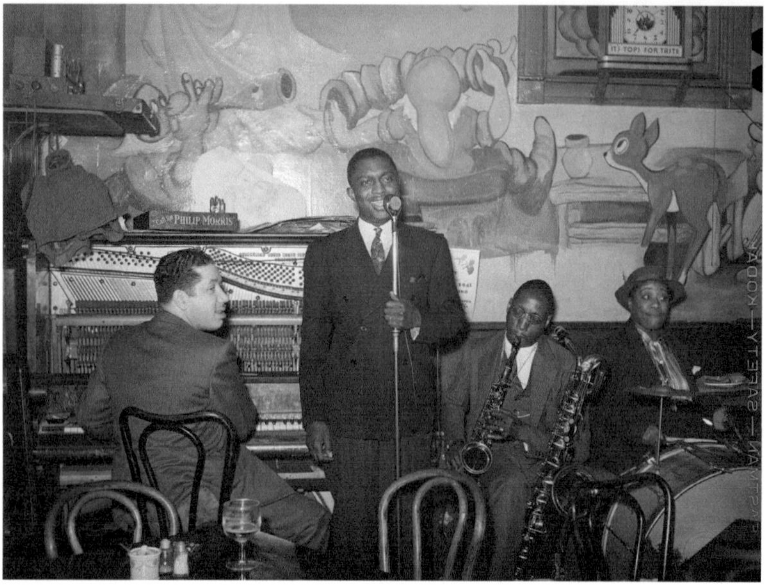

Figure 111: Russell Lee. *Entertainers at Negro Tavern*. Chicago, Illinois. 1941.
Library of Congress, Prints & Photographs Division, FSA/OWI Collection, 2017788785.

Chicago's clubs."[66] Lee represents Tony's Tavern as a scene of vibrant integrated social interactions and intense excitement, which is in distinct contrast to the spectral gaze of the cabaret. Commenting on Lee's Chicago archive, Nicholas Natanson observes: "To the extent that black migration *liberated* political energies, that liberation could be found in Lee and Rosskam's urban vision."[67]

The relationship between musical expression and place was nowhere more apparent than in New Orleans with all its ethnic, racial, and class complexities. The painter and photographer Ralston Crawford first visited New Orleans in 1938 and returned with his camera nearly every year for the rest of his life. Crawford was drawn to the city's parades and second lines, its bars, clubs, and musicians, many of whom he considered his closest friends. He began methodically documenting the musical culture of the city through photography. For Crawford the city was perceived in terms of its musical culture and inextricably linked with place and its characteristic social forms (Figures 112 and 113): "I have gone and shall continue to go, to bars, night clubs, dances, churches and parades, because the sounds coming from these places are fine. Here is part of my reaction in pictures."[68]

As he moved increasingly toward straight photographic representation, Crawford's paintings of grain elevators, bridges, boatyards, and factories rendered by precise lines in flat areas of color became even more abstract. Yet both practices were deeply rooted in the tangibility of place. For Crawford the signs of

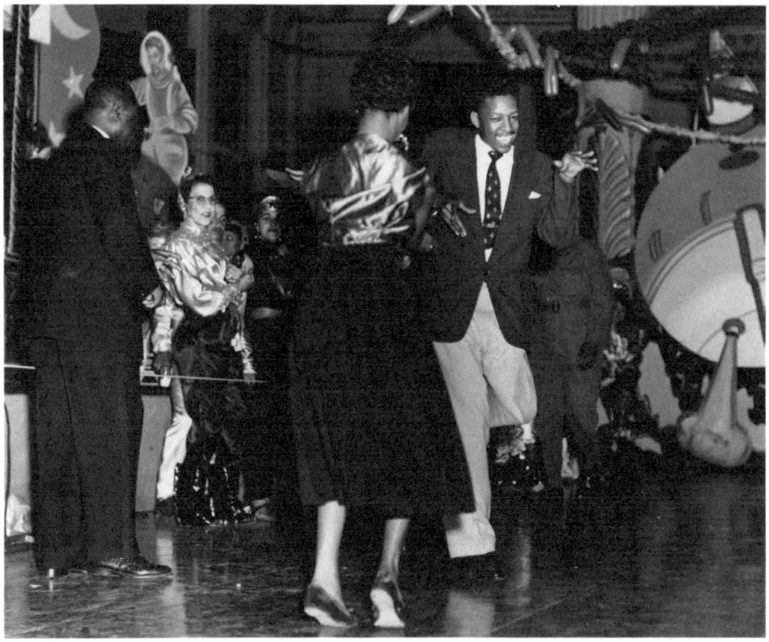

Figure 112: Ralston Crawford. *Saturday Night Function Dancers on floor; Bon Temps Carnival Ball at Decatur Street*. New Orleans. 1954.
Ralston Crawford Collection, William Ransom Hogan Jazz Archive, Howard-Tilton Memorial Library, Tulane University.

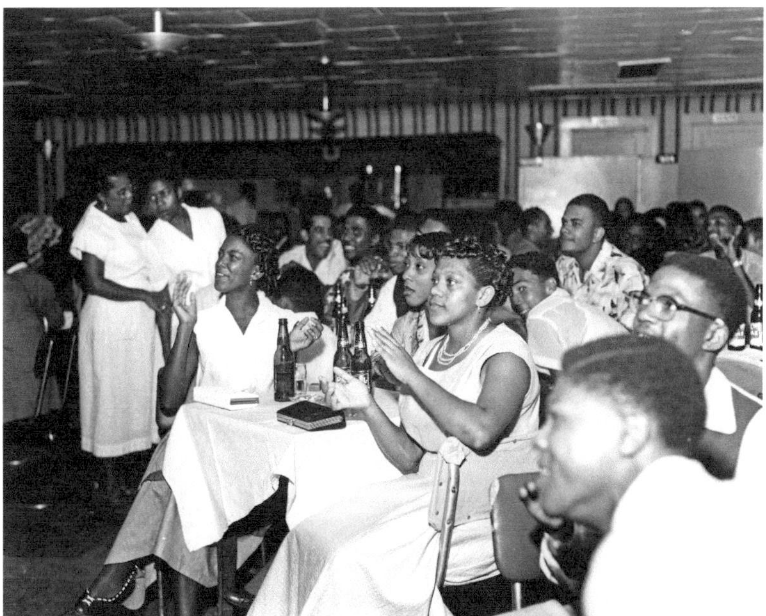

Figure 113: Ralston Crawford. *Audience at the Dew Drop Inn*. New Orleans. 1952.
Ralston Crawford Collection, William Ransom Hogan Jazz Archive, Howard-Tilton Memorial Library, Tulane University.

authenticity of musical and social practices in New Orleans that he captured with his camera were equivalent to the undecorated simplicity of line and form in his painted industrial landscapes, a search through geometrical shapes, patterns, and rhythms for a sense of order and permanence. In both media Crawford mirrored the concerns of many artists of the period for a "usable past"—in the jazz music of New Orleans as much as historical art, artifacts, and architecture which revealed the proportion, durability, and functional authenticity of an earlier time. Katherine Bourguinon is surely correct in noting that Crawford's photography and paintings both demonstrate the importance of place in the artist's "search for underlying structures" and as a personal "response to a changing world with self-control."[69]

William Claxton's *Jazz Life* discussed previously was also an exploration of place. African American jazz people appear in their homes, home towns, in cafes, hotels, restaurants, and bars, in marching bands and in performance, laughing, joking, relaxing, working. Many, like the toothless tub bassist in the Beale Street Jug Band and the "jazz postman" who played for poor kids on street corners in Washington, are ordinary people whose presence drew strength from their communities and families. A melancholy coda to the celebration of the Crescent City is Lee Friedlander's *Playing for the Benefit of the Band: New Orleans Music Culture*, also discussed previously. The title of this book anticipates the visual metaphors linking individual players and the ensemble with the forms of communal expression characteristic of New Orleans. Taken between 1958 and 1982 Friedlander's project was initiated just as the jazz revival movement was in full swing and many older musicians were enjoying renewed attention; a number of the enthusiasts promoting the revival of classic jazz guided Friedlander around New Orleans.[70] Whereas the revivalists could romanticize the life and achievements of the New Orleans pioneers, Friedlander images inscribe the toll which years of neglect and indifference have imposed.

In January 1955, W. Eugene Smith quit his well-paid job with *Life* magazine. He was 36, ambitious, quixotic, in search of greater artistic freedom. After four unfulfilling years on an assignment in Pittsburgh, Smith moved into a dilapidated, five-story loft building at 821 Sixth Avenue in New York's flower district. The space was a late-night haunt of musicians, including some of the biggest names in jazz, and countless avant-garde and underground characters including tobacco heiress and philanthropist Doris Duke, Norman Mailer, Diane Arbus, Robert Frank, Henri Cartier-Bresson, and Salvador Dalí as well as pimps, prostitutes, drug addicts, thieves, photography students, local cops, building inspectors, and marijuana dealers.[71] From 1959 to 1965 Smith made around 40,000 pictures in the loft, the largest body of work in his career, capturing more than 300 musicians including Roy Haynes, Sonny Rollins, Bill Evans, Roland Kirk, Alice Coltrane, Don Cherry, Paul Bley, Charles Mingus, Zoot Sims, Ronnie Free,

Bill Evans, Eddie Costa, Edgar Bateman, Henry Grimes and Thelonious Monk. He wired the building like a surreptitious recording studio, making 1,740 reels (some 4,000 hours) of stereo and mono audiotapes as well as capturing life on the streets of the flower district as seen from his fourth-floor window.

Favoring dark tones, his images of musicians seem to portray what Benjamin Cawthra has called the "dark room," the closed communal world of New York *avant-garde* insiders,[72] but the project has wider resonance in reclaiming ownership of what was once a uniquely jazz space. The general exclusion of the public from admission to late-night jam sessions in the 1930s in Kansas City, New York's Harlem and mid-town clubs and in other cities had created a form of professional self-enclosure: "Jazz players valued jam sessions as the antithesis of their professional work [. . .] as the ultimate locus of freedom, individuality, spontaneity and authenticity. A key condition for such freedom was liberation from the demands of the general public."[73] These unique forms of social interactions between musicians mutated as the jam session became commercialized and framed as a theatrical spectacle for paying audiences by Eddie Condon and jazz entrepreneurs such as Milt Gabler and Norman Granz.[74] Animated afresh by the creative energy that filled the loft, Smith returns a dilapidated physical space to that of an authentic and distinctively jazz space previously squeezed out by commercial pressures.

III. Authenticity and the "amateurs"

The quest for authenticity was nowhere stronger than among a subset of "amateurs" within the wider cohort of white new generation photographers. Working variously as writers, critics, journalists, historians, or critics, their photographs comprise a visual archive framed to convey the traditions and values of what they believed to be the true sounds of jazz.

The prevailing concern with authenticity led inevitably to a revival of interest in traditional jazz in the latter half of the 1930s. Although musicians like Eddie Condon and Mugsy Spanier in Chicago and New York and Lu Watters on the west coast had been performing traditional New Orleans jazz for a number of years, a revivalist movement gathered its forces around these players and others like Tommy Ladnier, Mezz Mezzrow, James P. Johnson, and perhaps most notably Bunk Johnson, who was rescued from obscurity. This movement developed its own visual aesthetic as could be seen in the photography and cover designs commissioned by Hughes Panassié for his RCA recordings in 1938–39 and William Russell's American Music label; and, as we have already seen from the work of Charles Peterson, these players cultivated an atmosphere that lent itself to visual interpretations as uninhibited, louche, and at odds with conventional 1930s America.

William Russell was one of the most energetic and influential advocates of traditional jazz. Born in 1905, Russell was a violinist and *avant-garde* composer, a skilled musical instrument craftsman, jazz record producer, archivist, writer, and, above all, a New Orleans jazz collector of quite extraordinary breadth.[75] Russell's contribution to *Jazzmen* was one of the first to note the importance of place: written with Stephen Smith, it interweaves vignettes describing the pioneers of the music from Congo Square to the fall of Storyville. In avocational photography as much as his writings (Figure 114), Russell did much to document and preserve memories of New Orleans as the authentic birthplace of jazz in images that supported the diffusionist arguments in *Jazzmen.* It was no coincidence that Russell choose "American Music" as the name of the company he formed in 1945 specifically to record Bunk Johnson and his record sleeve artwork occasionally featured images of vernacular New Orleans architecture where his recordings were made.

Russell's photographs—"straight" images firmly in the 1930s documentary tradition seemingly unconcerned with production values—present the old-timers he recorded as the personification of jazz authenticity. His photographs were mostly taken in performance in traditional settings although Russell's photographs of Mecca Flats, the apartment block at 3338–3360 South State Street in Chicago where many itinerant and musicians lodged, shows a wider interest in lives and living conditions of musicians.[76] Other "amateurs" approaching jazz with similar objectives

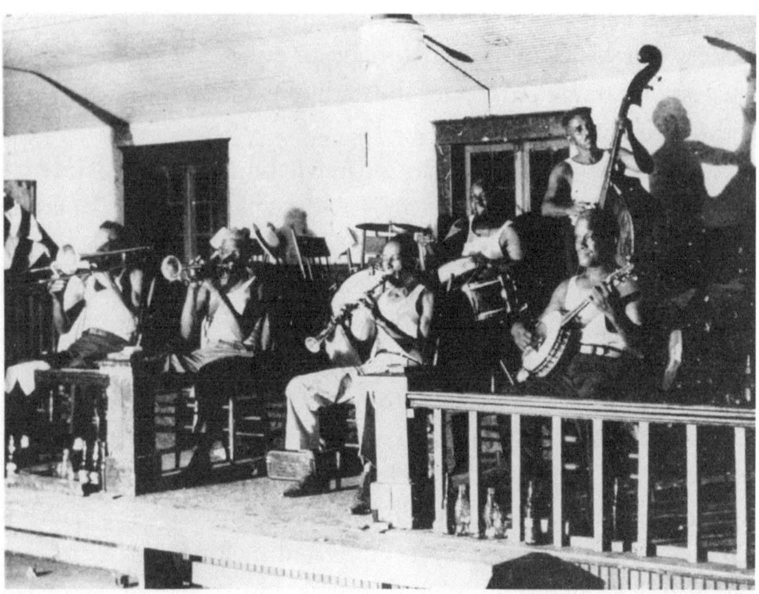

Figure 114: William Russell. *Bunk Johnson's Band.* San Jacinto Hall. New Orleans. 1944. *Peter Vacher Collection.*

include John Steiner, a Chicago producer, collector, and promoter who roomed with Russell in the 1930s, and Dr. Bernard ("Bernie") Meyer Steinau, who photographed numerous parades, funerals, and other events where jazz was played in the 1940s.[77] Grauman Marks's background was also typical of the enthusiasts. Born in Louisville, KY, Marks graduated from the University of Kentucky and received a law degree from Harvard University in 1926. During the late-1940s to 1960s he combined his passion as an amateur photographer of traditional New Orleans jazz with his job as the Hamilton County Assistant Prosecutor. His archive comprises photographs of jazz performances in Preservation Hall and other venues in New Orleans, often featuring the clarinetist George Lewis, and scenes of New Orleans street life.[78] His photograph of Ernest "Punch" Miller, taken to promote William

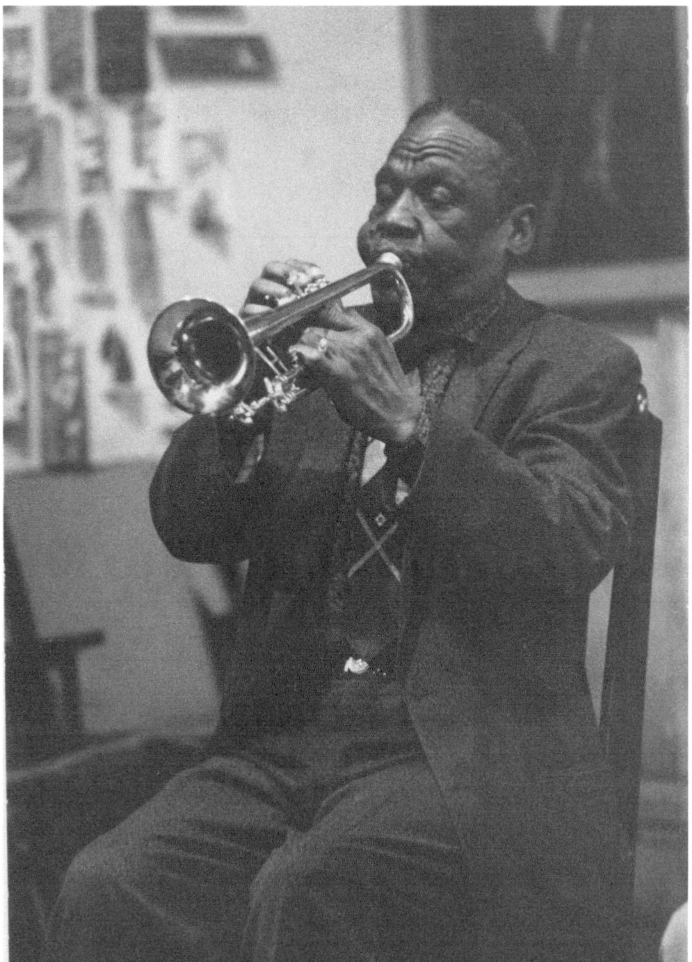

Figure 115: Grauman Marks. *Ernest "Punch" Miller.* New Orleans. *c.*1971. *Promotional photograph for New Orleans: 'Til the Butcher Cuts Him Down (dir. Philip Spalding, narrated by William Russell 1971). Peter Vacher Collection.*

Russel's 1971 documentary film (Figure 115), is typical of the reverence shown to the New Orleans linage by the traditionalists of this movement.

At least so far as photography goes, neither Stanley Kubrick nor John Kuhlman can be described as "amateurs," but their work is marked as much by a search for authenticity as those described above. Taken on assignment for *Look* magazine in 1950, Kubrick's photographs of the New Orleans jazzman George Lewis show an acute sensitivity for personalities and place, not least in his concerns to capture the response of ordinary people dancing to the music in the streets and backyard. John Kuhlman, a commercial photographer in New Orleans (Figures 116 and 117), devoted his weekends and spare time to his first love of music in the 1940s and 1950s. Deeply imbued with a sense of place, Kuhlman left thousands of images on his death in 2013.[79] A little later Michael P. Smith, a Tulane graduate and photographer, documented the African American music, culture, and folklife of New Orleans and Louisiana, from social club parades and jazz funerals, neighborhood Mardi Gras traditions, and spiritual church ceremonies to many of the city and state's renowned jazz, blues, R&B, and gospel musicians.[80]

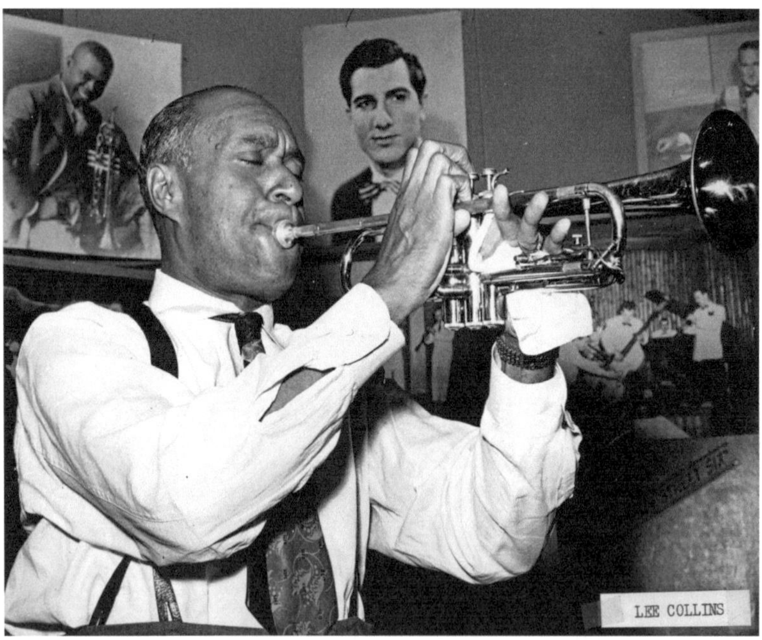

Figure 116: John E. Kuhlman. *Lee Collins. Southlands Records Recording Session*. New Orleans. 1953.
Peter Vacher collection/with permission of the New Orleans Jazz Club Collection of the Louisiana State Museum.

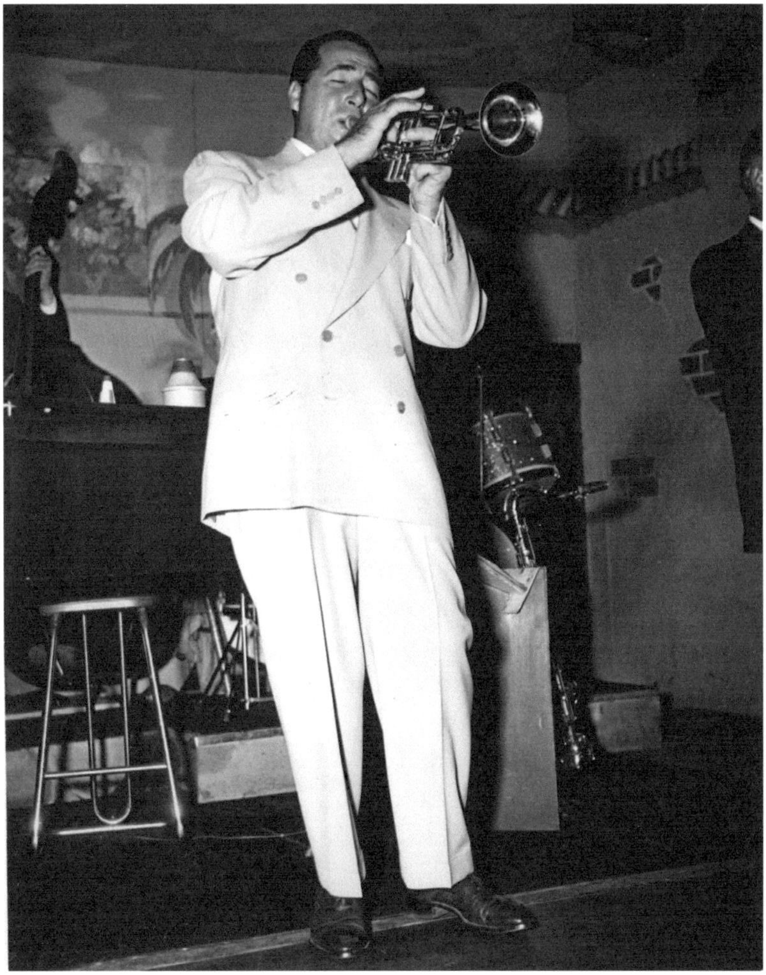

Figure 117: John E. Kuhlman. *Leon Prima*. New Orleans. 1953.
New Orleans Jazz Club Collection of the Louisiana State Museum.

Expressions of art

By the 1930s the artistry and accomplishments of individual musicians had become the defining feature of a music whose "extreme adherence to the trappings of romanticism" was the dominant paradigm. The arrival of the jazz musicians as "romantic outsiders" was, according to Amiri Baraka, nothing less than a mistaken valorization of Eurocentrism enforced on black musicians, but for many white photographers these players were exemplars of a new art form. This development in jazz shared a feature common to all previous romantic movements—the shift from a mimetic to an expressive aesthetic and increased prominence of the authorial voice.[81] Rather than looking backward as the white photographers discussed so far in this chapter tended to do, a number of key contributors among the new generation celebrated the art of jazz by elevating the skills and accomplishments of the current generation.

Equipped with modern lightweight cameras, portable and reliable lighting blocks, faster lenses, and film stock, these photographers asserted art directorial control in order to articulate their understanding of the meanings of jazz as it entered its own romantic phase. It is no coincidence that these photographers worked at the same time as critics such as Barry Ulanov were seeking to articulate the criteria of artistic criticism as it applied to jazz. For Ulanov, the critic's faculties needed to be disciplined, alert to the music, constantly aware of the intuitive power of the performer as expressed in the freshness, profundity, and skill of his output.[82] In similar fashion, photographers believed that only artistic criteria were adequate to the task of revealing the "genesis" (as Ulanov, quoting Stravinsky, termed it) of the music—that is, images which were themselves finished works of art. "My Dad was very serious about his work," Christopher Willoughby recalled of his father's work. "He felt that his photographs were art, he was an artist making art [. . .] he spent an enormous amount of time making his 400 'archival set' perfect."[83] An individualized and self-conscious representation of space, meaning, and light became the central content of the images of this group of photographers; and, as in most art photography, their images were permeated by a sensibility of abstracted *space*—the better to sign artistry—rather than the specificities of *place*.[84]

Capturing the artistry of the jazz musician

William Claxton observed of one of his photographs of Chet Baker, "Every note he blows seems to come from somewhere deep inside him [. . .] The sound is Chet, and Chet is the sound." As we saw in a previous chapter, many photographers believed the artistry of the jazz musician and deeper layers of artistic subjectivity were most forcefully expressed in performance.[85]

How did Claxton and other photographers of the period express this conception of jazz? One technique involved radical decontextualization and/or cropping in order to shift the visual point of emphasis decisively toward the individual artist. Whereas the African American photographers discussed in the previous chapter were primarily concerned to contextualize their subjects, Claxton was often inspired by revelatory detail: "By focusing on [Ornette] Coleman's luminescent eyes as they stare intensely, straight into the camera's lens, Claxton makes an instant connection with the intensity of Coleman's insistent vision of improvisational freedom,"[86] Another example must surely be Marvin Koner's extraordinary red-washed monochromatic image of Miles Davis on the cover of *'Round About Midnight*, an image removed of any trace of facial or environmental detail in order to focus on the musician's gestures in a statement of transcendent artistry. As one critic noted, the image of Davis "removed in thought behind dark glasses [. . .] is classic" and in which "careful packaging and exquisite artistry have created a legend."[87]

Decontextualization of this kind was central to what Benjamin Cawthra has called the "pure aesthetic space" of Herman Leonard's presentation of jazz musicians in his work from the late-1940s and early-1950s. Marked by their elegant styling, dramatic lighting, and shimmering points of light in black spaces, Leonard's "flagrantly artistic techniques" yielded a body of canonizing images in which attention is firmly directed toward the player and contextual intrusions radically downplayed.[88] The jazz work of the Florida-based photographer David G. Spitzer consistently employed similar techniques in his preference for closely cropped performance shots in which musicians emerge from black spaces largely devoid of environmental detailing (Figure 118). Explaining that jazz musicians seem appropriate subjects for the abstracted qualities of monochromatic film, Spitzer was unambiguous about his aesthetic objectives behind his work:[89]

> *My work attempts to freeze a moment that captures the wide range of emotions revealed by the performing musician. Body language, tactility and the shapes of instruments are all elements that I want to integrate meaningfully within the picture plane. The image, however, must stand on its own in its representation of the musician. I am especially grateful when someone is drawn to a photograph purely on aesthetics.*

Cropping images in this fashion was often carried out by magazine editors to suit newsprint and magazine layout. Photographers knew however that images impactfully composed to foreground the artist were more likely to be selected for publication particularly if combined with a low viewpoint designed to elevate the musician. Techniques such as these made photographs attractive to editors who knew well the effect they would have when set within the printed page.

As is so often the case in art photography, the most significant development in the visualization of jazz artistry came with innovative use of lighting and it is for this reason that Leonard is so often cited as the exemplar of the "jazz photographer." One of Leonard's major achievements was to adapt the portraiture lighting techniques used by Karsch and Mili to the cramped conditions of jazz clubs such as the Royal Roost: "[Mili's] way of lighting his subjects inspired me a great deal. For me he was one of the rare photographers with an artistic approach to music." Achieving the effects he wanted required Leonard to set up several hours before the performance, carefully positioning strobes and hiding trailing cables. Placing a light source behind the player meant that cigarette smoke could be captured and, although he explained that he had discovered this by accident during an early shoot while he was still in Ohio, it became a key feature of many of his images—at least in the minds of his many admirers.[90]

Leonard's apparent ownership of this space should not detract from the fact that other photographers were as consciously authorial in their use of lighting. Dennis Stock believed that the photographer's "ultimate goal is to retain on film an image

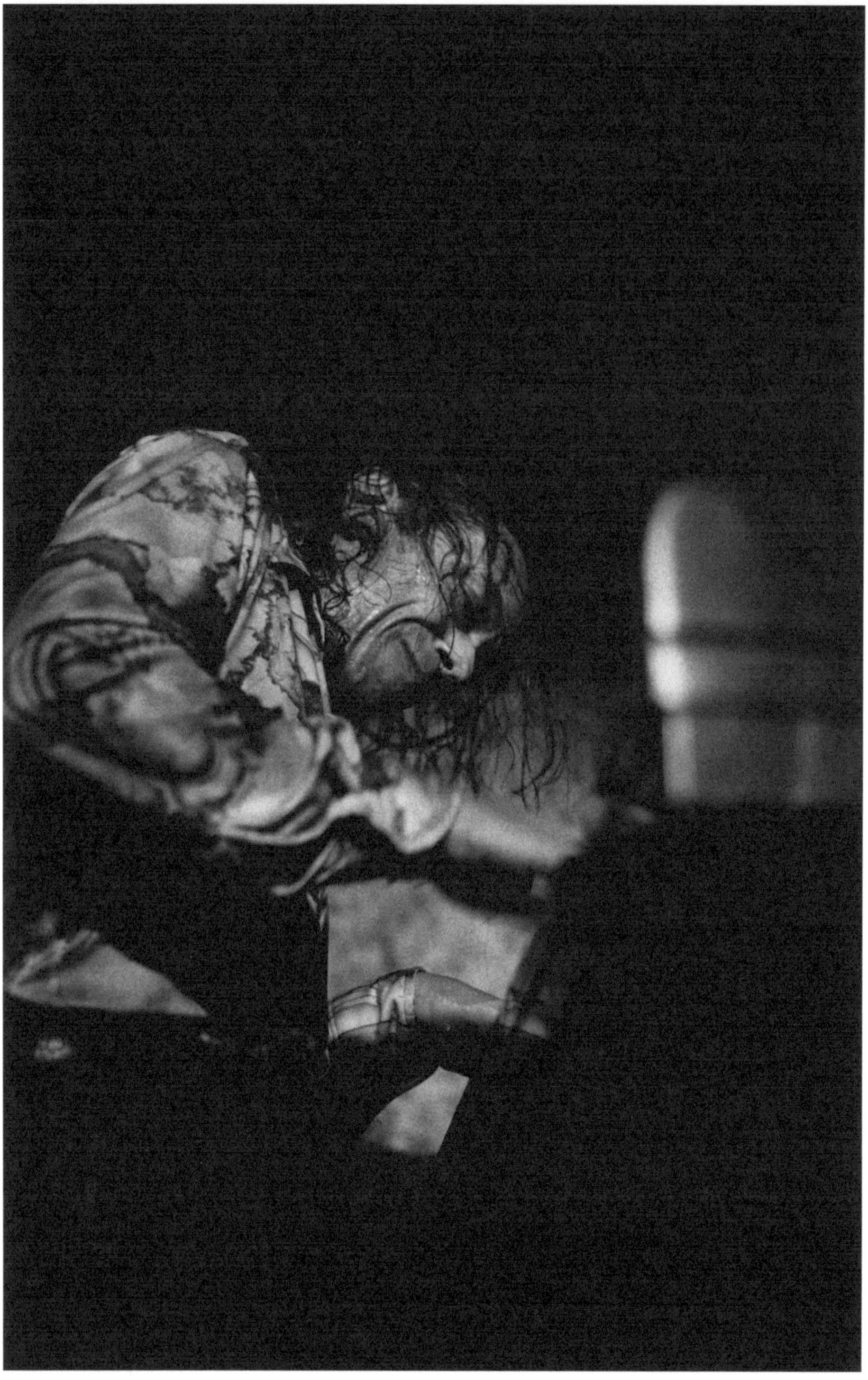

Figure 118: David Spitzer. *Horace Silver*. 1977.
David Spitzer Photography Collection, Miami Dade Public Library.

that will clearly state his appreciation (or at least his view)" of jazz players. To achieve this the photographer has at his disposal "a multitude" of equipment offering "many combinations of lenses, films, light sources, and darkroom manipulations" and he explained the artifice involved in elevating "the mood of the musicians":[91]

> *I often used the "Mighty Light", an electronic flash [which] was particularly helpful in jazz joints where existing light was insufficient and did nothing to support the mood of the musicians. Three to four lights positioned interpretatively often meant the difference between a dull and an exciting photograph. The rapid recharging of the units and the intrinsic fast speed of the lights made it possible to capture the gyrations—musical, emotional, and physical—of the more dynamic performers.*

Even with his bulky 4 × 5 Speed Graphic press camera, Frank Kuchirchuk aimed to achieve "theatricality, something extremely dramatic" in his performance shots. He experimented with different lighting techniques and effects: "I would sit at home with the lights down and listen to jazz records. The warmth that I felt in those performances when I was sitting in my darkened room was what I wanted to accomplish with my photographs." He noticed how the artists' moods changed with the lighting effects on stage. It is no coincidence that Kuchirchuk, like Leonard, had developed his lighting skills and techniques as a portrait photographer. Kuchirchuk's images demonstrate again how isolating the individual musician within the composition, tightening the crop, heroizing viewpoints, and careful deployment of lighting were employed by photographers to frame jazz musicians as artists (Figure 119).

As previously discussed, photographers also fixed on the kinesis of performance—gesture, facial expressions, stance, bodily positions, and instrumental address—to reinforce the message of their images. Capturing signs of this kind required the photographer to be sensitive to their fleeting emergence during the ebb and flow of improvisatory performance; a deep knowledge of the rhythms and cadences of the music, careful preparation, and speed of response were critical. William Claxton explained that he was intrigued by

> *the movements and body language of musicians while they play. I study them carefully before photographing them [. . .] I note how their faces and bodies reflect or catch the light; when and at what angles they look their best. I do all this, of course, while listening to their playing. I listen with my eyes.*

Writing in *Popular Photography* in 1946, Skippy Adelman made a similar point: "The face and expression are the thing and the picture emerges as portraits of music makers in the throes of their art."[92]

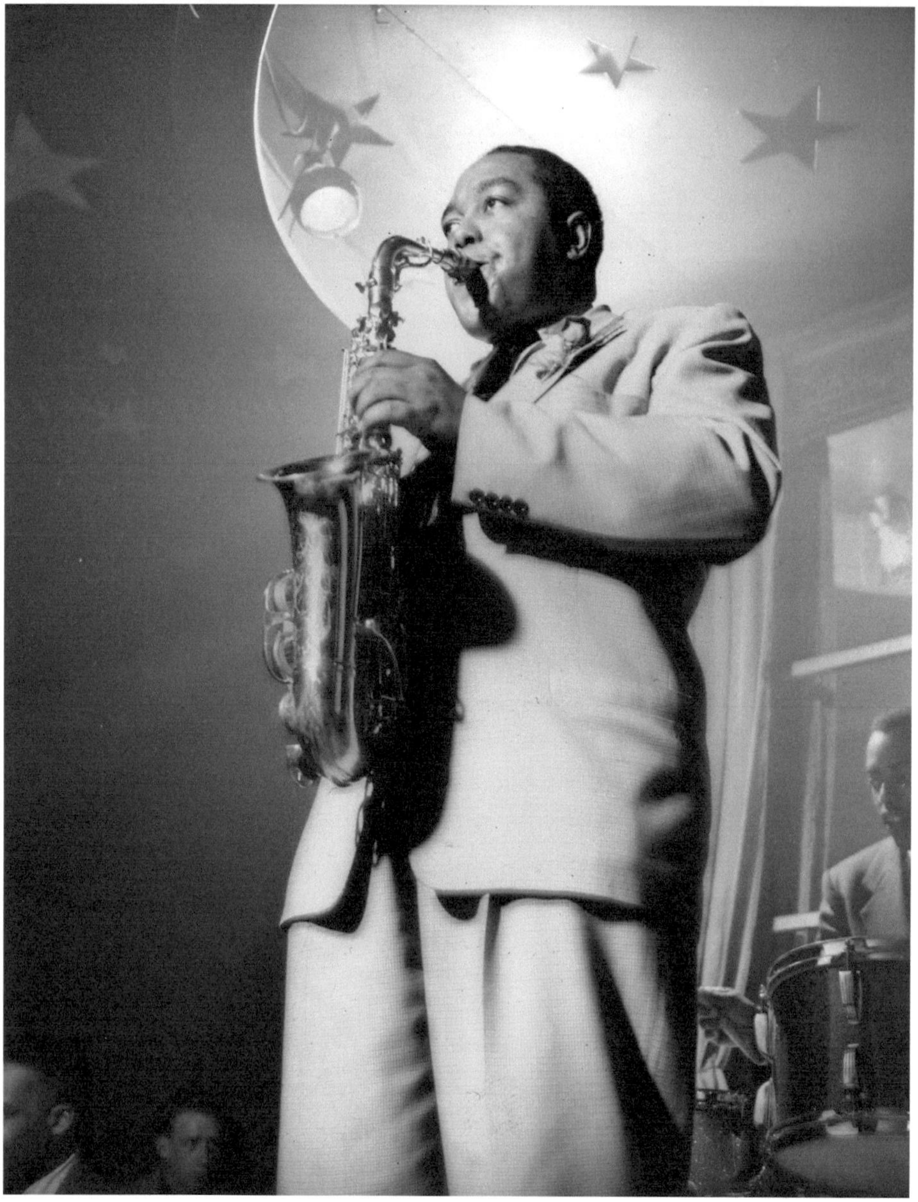

Figure 119: Frank Kuchirchuk. *Charlie Parker.* Cleveland. n.d.
The Frank Kuchirchuk Collection of Jazz Photography, Oberlin Conservatory Library (CSC_KJP_042).

The "look of jazz"

In a 1998 interview Herman Leonard spoke about the "look of jazz."[93] Leonard had in mind the way musicians of his era dressed in stylish up-to-the-minute fashion and he stressed the significance of this as both a personal and artistic statement. Always impressed by style, he referred to his photographs of Illinois Jacquet as "fashion shoots" and went on to critique the blurred informality of "modern jazz photography" in failing to show to full advantage musicians' carefully tailored presentation. "I would never submit a blurred shot," he said, explaining that his desire to convey the stylish look of jazz accurately required the sharply focused images that became his trademark:

> *I won't take a bad picture [. . .] I am dedicated to beauty [. . .] When I was apprenticing and studying photography and portraiture with [Yousuf] Karsh, he said to me, "Herman, always tell the truth in terms of beauty." In other words [. . .] do not exploit the unfavorable side. It isn't fair.*

Others among this group of photographers were equally enamored by the look of jazz. William Claxton showed in his jazz portraits the keen eye for material culture, pose, and gesture that would reappear in his later fashion and celebrity photography; as he expressed it:

> *Photographs of jazz musicians in hot, smoke-filled clubs and studios with perspiration running down their faces were, in my mind, too stereotypical and not even honest any more, certainly not on the west coast. So I began to shoot clean, distinguished, rather sedate portraits of stars.*[94]

Chet Baker's evolution toward film star idol owes much to Claxton's appreciation of his visual potential while Gerry Mulligan's racially integrated quartet, captured by Claxton in an overhead shot at Los Angeles' Haigh Club in 1952 for the cover of their band's first Pacific LP, did much to fix this visual aesthetic. Reviewing Claxton's West Coast Jazz, Whitney Balliett commented on the collective "taste" that the musicians displayed in their "genteel appearances"; the musicians, it seems, had hurriedly changed into their Brooks Brothers suit and hat.[95] Like Claxton, Bob Willoughby also caught west coast jazz's stylistic reaction to the gendered extroversion of the dominant east coast forms in an impressionistic style that framed leading lights of the west coast school like Chet Baker, Dave Brubeck, Gerry Mulligan, Shorty Rogers, and Shelly Manne as intensely romantic figures.[96] So pervasive were these images that the dichotomy between the musical east coast players and the arranged, "effete" music of the west coast was hyped up by eastern record companies and music publishers. Reinforced by appropriate album cover images, the strategy was effective in drawing in many new listeners.[97] Arthur Elgort often found himself shooting fashion and jazz in tandem: "I started as a ballet photographer, but there was no money in that. So I became a fashion photographer [. . .] [and] Whenever anybody needed jazz with their fashion, they called me," he explained. "*Vogue Italia* liked jazz, a lot."[98]

Peter Townsend has argued that this type of photography has done more than any other medium to deliver the myth of jazz:[99]

> *That is to say, the construct resulting from the ensemble of visual signs (among instruments saxophones and double bases typically signify jazz), iconic personalities and cool composition that comprise the myth of jazz, and which have come to assume, through use in album covers and magazine photography, the position of the very essence and identity of jazz.*

Important as material culture may be, Townsend is correct in widening the "look of jazz" to embrace the ensemble of signs that collectively have helped to sustain the myth of the jazz musician. So it is important to record that certain new generation photographers also strived to elevate the artistry of older jazz musicians, albeit in a rather different fashion from the traditionalists discussed earlier in the chapter.

Born around 1924, Skippy Adelman belonged chronologically to the new generation cohort but his life and work cautions against pigeonholing all these photographers as young, college-educated members of the middle class. Raised in a Jewish working-class background, Adelman combined his love of jazz with a street aesthetic and more pointed political stance that brought a grittier feel to his photography. Adelman has been described as one of the "old Speed Graphic boys," a hard-boiled New York photojournalist moving from story to story for *PM Picture News*, the left-leaning daily published by Ralph Ingersoll between 1940 and 1948. Driven to escape a poor childhood, he weighed against "bribe-taking cops, the self-loving pompous rich, the oppressor [. . .] [and] the silly, sassy café society."[100] Little is known of his later career other than that he had abandoned photography by 1950. When Stanley Kubrick made *Killer's Kiss*, a 1955 film that drew on the producer's immediate Jewish neighborhood, Adelman played the part of the owner of the mannequin factory and figured among a large number of extras recruited from Greenwich Village. Later, as Julius Adelman, he is credited with writing the script for a 1962 TV series called *The Rifleman.*[101]

Jazz for Adelman was more than passing interest for a journalist looking for a story. Adelman took a "thoroughgoing interest in the men who make this peculiarly American music" and his affinity to the musicians "inform his pictures, suffusing them with feeling and substance that go beyond mere recording."[102] He lived in Greenwich Village close to his friend Pee Wee Russell, frequented the West 10th Street saloon, and made press photographs in the Village Vanguard and other jazz haunts; and he authored a stunning series of portraits at Orson Welles and "Bunk" Johnson's New Orleans jazz band concert at New York's Town Hall in January 1947. His photography was used as cover artwork for records by Billie Holiday and Pee Wee Russell.

George S. Rosenthal and Frank Zachary's 1946 book *Jazzways* contained photographs by Charles Peterson, Sol Libsohn, Otto Hess, Sargent Marsh, Francis Wolff, and Berenice Abbott but with over 70 credits—including a special assignment with Eugene Williams to provide images to accompany Williams's essay on "New Orleans Today"—Adelman's contribution is by far the largest.[103] In this series Adelman presented musicians as accomplished, inspired, and committed artists, usually framed in a dark and apparently isolated setting. The portraits are notably closely cropped; faces dripping with perspiration, Adelman homes in on the expressive subjectivity of improvising musicians—Sidney Bechet, eyes half-closed caught in mid-breath, Mugsy Spanier struggling "to blow high notes," Lee Wiley, head thrown back, eyes closed in concentration, and a contemplative Bunk Johnson. In Adelman's portrait of Pee Wee Russell's face unbelievable grimaces of pain are dramatically captured. Set against backlighted smoke, Dizzy Gillespie's beret, thick-rimmed glasses, goatee, and cigarette holder cast the musician as the *avant-garde* artist (Figure 120), an image used the following year in the modernist-inclined *Metronome*. The musicians are almost always set against black backgrounds, obscuring any contextual detail that might impinge on Adelman's portrayal of individual artistry and the sense of cultural distinctiveness.[104]

IV. Conclusion

Born in New York City in 1934, Carol Reiff, the daughter of illustrator and photographer Hal Reiff, began photographing while still in her teens. She discovered jazz at about the same time, successfully gaining access to jazz clubs and concert halls as well as recording studios, rehearsal lofts, and all-night jam sessions. Her photograph of Thelonious Monk for the Riverside album *The Unique*, which *Metronome* magazine made their "Jazz Photograph of the Year, 1956," is characteristic of her work.[105] Deep black spaces isolate the musician from environmental distractions much as Leonard had done in his early work but the flared hot spot, motion blur, and use of grain make Reiff's images less declamatory than those of her predecessors. Even so, the single point of interest and simplicity of the composition is just as successful in elevating the artistry of the musician.[106] Using the twin-lens Rolleiflex camera her father had given her and relying only on mixed natural and house lighting, Reiff used faster film stocks and slow shutter speeds to make a striking photograph of Count Basie in Birdland in February 1955. The resulting blur and grain impress the surface of an image in which the band leader is almost entirely in silhouette; an overexposed house light spills flare over his right shoulder, obliterating any detail over the rear of the musician's head, but allows shadow details

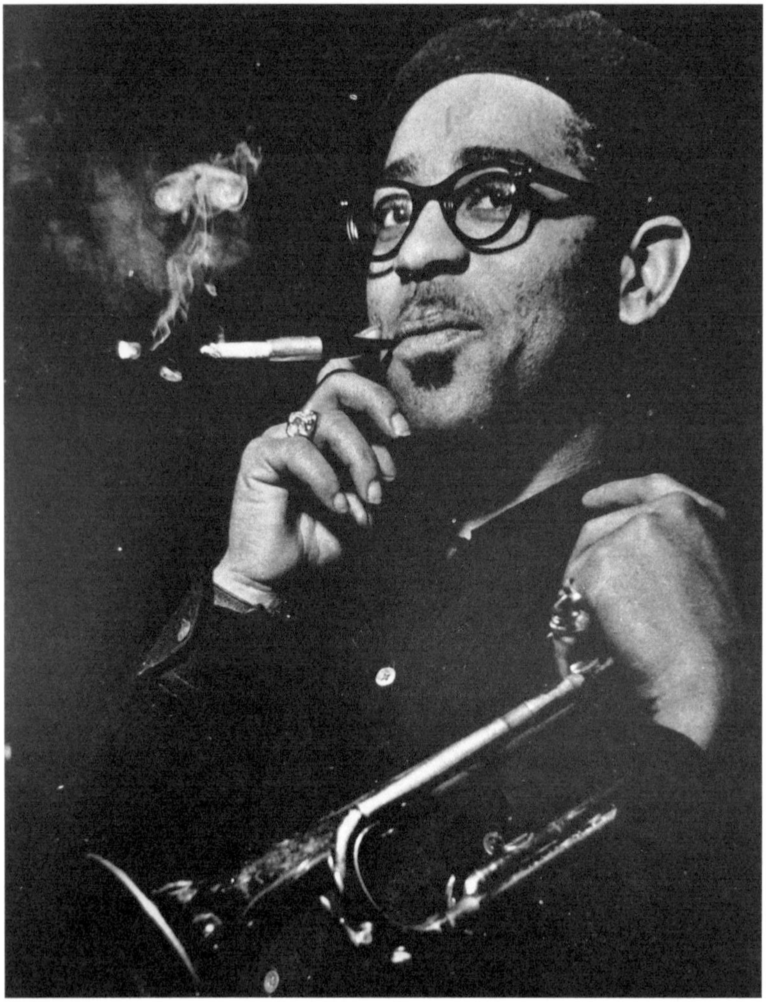

Figure 120: Skippy Adelman. *Dizzy Gillespie Is the Current Swing Favorite.* June 1946. *Author's collection.*

to emerge allowing us to identify the piano. Basie is isolated with deep blacks and overexposed whites, visually linked with nothing other than the piano.

Turning low light to advantage through the creative use of grain, blur and flare from house lights, Carol Reiff prefigured the more fluid, less mimetic explorations of metaphorical possibilities shown by jazz photographers after the 1960s. We shall return to this period in the final chapter. For the moment it is important to turn from the new generation photographers to the work of the photographic exiles of the 1930s and 1940s. Working at the same moment in time as the new generation photographers, the images made by these exiles evidence the distinctive stamp of displaced artists adapting to radically changed circumstances and suggest instructive points of comparison with the photographers discussed in this chapter.

Notes

1. Herman Leonard's handwritten dedication to William Gottlieb in the author's copy of Leonard's book *Jazz Memories*.
2. Barry Singer, "Eloquent Images of a Smoky, Sultry World," *New York Times*, 1997, https://www.nytimes.com/1997/04/27/books/eloquent-images-of-a-smoky-sultry-world.html; Krin Gabbard, "Images of Jazz," in *The Cambridge Companion to Jazz*, ed. Mervyn Cooke and David Horn (Cambridge: Cambridge University Press, 2002), 338–39; Cawthra, *Blue Notes in Black and White Photography and Jazz*, 89; Schaap quoted in "Biographies: Gottlieb's Life and Work," Library of Congress American Memory website, n.d., https://www.loc.gov/item/ihas.200185535/.
3. See "Biographies: Gottlieb's Life and Work"; William P. Gottlieb, "Preface," in *The Golden Age of Jazz* (San Francisco, CA: Pomegranate Art Books, 1995), viii–ix; Eric Brace, "Making the Scene with Bill Gottlieb," *Washington Post Weekend*, 1998; Oscar Halper, "Member Profile: William Gottlieb," *Imagist*, 1997, 4; Alan Nahigian, "Lifetime Achievement Award: Bill Gottlieb," *Down Beat*, no. 64 (1997): 30–34 and Terry Teachout, "Too Cool to Cash in, Favorite of the Few," *New York Times*, December 21, 1997.
4. Gottlieb, "Preface," viii; William Gottlierb, "Weird Wizard," *Down Beat*, nos. 14 and 19, September, 1947.
5. Cawthra, *Blue Notes in Black and White*, 85 repeats the story.
6. Steve Gottlieb, Interview with the Author: September 22, 2018. Washington DC. All quotations taken from this interview.
7. Robert H. Wiebe, *The Search for Order: 1877–1920* (New York: Hill and Wang, 1967), 129.
8. America's economic transformation is discussed by Hugh Brogan, *The Penguin History of the United States of America* (Penguin: Harmondsworth, 2001), 378–406; Gerald J. Goodwin, Richard N. Current, and Paula A. Franklin (eds.), *A History of the United States* (New York: Alfred A. Knopf, 1980), 462–76; Robert V. Remini, *A Short History of the United States* (New York: HarperCollins, 2008), 187–214; Philip Jenkins, *A History of the United States* (London: Palgrave Macmillan, 2012), 171–86 and Wiebe, *The Search for Order: 1877–1920*, esp. ch. 3. For the growth of the new middle class see C. Wright Mills, *White Collar: The American Middle Classes*, 2nd ed. (Oxford: Oxford University Press, n.d.); Alfred D. Chandler, *The Visible Hand: The Managerial Revolution in American Business* (Cambridge, MA: Harvard University Press, 1977), 143–44, 411–14; and Raymond H. Merritt, *Engineering in American Society 1850–1875* (Lexington: University Press of Kentucky, 1969), 9–11, who estimates that between 1900 and 1930 the number of engineers increased five-fold.
9. Wiebe, *The Search for Order: 1877–1920*, 113; William E. Leuchtenberg, *The Perils of Prosperity 1914–32* (Chicago: University of Chicago Press, 1958), 198–203; Susman, *Culture as History: The Transformation of American Society in the Twentieth Century*, 289–90; McGerr, *A Fierce Discontent: The Rise and Fall of the Progressive Movement in America, 1870–1920*, 43; Mills, *White Collar: The American Middle Classes*, 3–4; Lizabeth Cohen, *A Consumer's Republic: The Politics of Mass Consumption in Postwar America* (New York: Alfred A. Knopf, 2003), 22–23. Edwin Layton, "Veblen and the Engineers," *American Quarterly* 14, no. 1 (1962): 65–66, explains Veblen's belief that engineers were becoming *class*-conscious as they gained in ascendancy.
10. Mills, *White Collar: The American Middle Classes*, 142–43.
11. Amiri Baraka, *The Autobiography of LeRoi Jones* (Chicago: Lawrence Hill Books, 1997), 206.
12. Roy Emerson Stryker, "The FSA Collection of Photographs," in *Photography in Print: Writings from 1816 to The Present*, ed. Vicki Goldberg (Albuquerque: University of New Mexico Press, 1981), 350; John Raeburn, *A Staggering Revolution: A Cultural History of Thirties Photography* (Urbana: University of Illinois Press, 2006); Colin Osman and Jean-Claude Lemagny, "Photography Sure of Itself (1930–50)," in *A History of Photography: Social and Cultural Perspectives*, ed. Jean-Claude Lemagny and André Rouillé, trans. J. Lloyd (Cambridge: Cambridge University Press, 1987), 165–86; Stange, *Symbols of Ideal Life: Social Documentary Photography in America 1890–1950*, 89–131; Virgil Thompson, "The Cult of Jazz," *Vanity Fair*, 1925, 52–54, 118, recalled how *Vanity Fair* combined luxury product advertising with "far-out culture," a form of "highbrowism" that went along with the "cult of jazz." *Iron Age*, 90, no. 8 (1912): 393 cited by Robert Anthony, "Lenses of Industry: The Rise of Industrial Photography in the United States," *Access Master's Thesis, Technological University* (2015), digitalcommons.mtu.edu/etdr/4, 41.

13. Bill Crow, *From Birdland to Broadway: Scenes from a Jazz Life* (New York: Oxford University Press, 1992), 110.
14. Townsend, *Jazz in American Culture*, 163.
15. Randolf S. Bourne, *Youth and Life* (Boston, MA: Mifflin, 1913), 33–34, was an early statement of "youth culture." Wohl, *The Generation of 1914*. 204–7, provides an account of the factors leading to the growth of youth culture in the late nineteenth century.
16. Laura Browder, *Rousing the Nation: Radical Culture in Depression America* (Amherst: University of Massachusetts Press, 1998), 174.
17. Alfred Haworth Jones, "The Search for a Usable American Past in the New Deal Era," *American Quarterly* 23, no. 5 (1971): 715; Susman, *Culture as History: The Transformation of American Society in the Twentieth Century*, 157.
18. "Cows in Ballroom at Hotel Men's Fair," *New York Times*, May 24, 1935.
19. Jones, "The Search for a Usable American Past in the New Deal Era," 722; Stacy I. Morgan, *Frankie and Johnny: Race, Gender and the Work of African American Folklore in 1930s America* (Houston: University of Texas Press, 2017), 24; Michael C. Steiner, "Regionalism in the Great Depression," *Geographical Review* 73, no. 4 (1983): 431–43.
20. Michael Denning, *The Cultural Front: The Laboring of American Culture in the Twentieth Century* (London: Verso, 1996).
21. Jones, "The Search for a Usable American Past in the New Deal Era," 717; Alan Brinkley, *Culture and Politics in the Great Depression* (Waco, TX: Markham Press, 1999), 38; Susman, *Culture as History: The Transformation of American Society in the Twentieth Century*, 164.
22. Michael E. Parrish, *Anxious Decades: America in Prosperity and Depression, 1920–1941* (New York: W. W. Norton, 1992), 411, 424, 431.
23. David Eldridge, *American Culture in the 1930s* (Edinburgh: Edinburgh University Press, 2008), 30. Pells, *Radical Visions and American Dreams: Culture and Social Thought in the Depression Years*, 310–29; Eldridge, *American Culture in the 1930s*, 4–10, 16.
24. Browder cited by Erin P. Cohn, "Art Fronts: Visual Culture and Race Politics in Mid-Twentieth Century United States" (University of Pennsylvania, 2010), 12.
25. Richard Hofstadter, *The Age of Reform from Bryan to FDR* (London: Jonathan Cape, 1962), 300–301; Mark Whalen, *American Culture in the 1910s* (Edinburgh: Edinburgh University Press, 2010), 8; Richard H. Pells, *Radical Visions and American Dreams: Culture and Social Thought in the Depression Years* (New York: Harper & Rowe, 1973), 6. See further Michael McGerr, *A Fierce Discontent: The Rise and Fall of the Progressive Movement in America, 1870–1920* (New York: Free Press, 2003).
26. Herbert Croly's article, "The Progressive Voter" in the *New Republic* (July 25, 1928), is cited by Paul W. Glad, "Progressives and the Business Culture of the 1920s," *Journal of American History* 53, no. 1 (1966): 89; Michael E. Parrish, *Anxious Decades: America in Prosperity and Depression*, 209.
27. The moral as much as artistic legacy of the FAP is emphasized by Jonathan Harris, *Federal Art and National Culture: The Politics of Identity in New Deal America* (Cambridge: Cambridge University Press, 1995); and Steve Fraser and Gary Gerstle, "Introduction," in *The Rise and Fall of the New Deal Order 1930–1980*, ed. Steve Fraser and Gary Gerstle (Princeton, NJ: Princeton University Press, 1989).
28. A. Joan Saab, *For the Millions: American Art and Culture Between the Wars* (Philadelphia: University of Pennsylvania Press, 2004), 137–42.
29. Lauren Kroiz, " 'A Jolly Lark for Amateurs' John Steuart Curry's Pedagogy of Painting," *American Art*, 29, no. 1 (2015): 28–53.
30. "Chicago Active in Effort to Establish Community Arts Centre," *Chicago Defender*, May 20 1939, 24; Pollack cited by Cohn, "Art Fronts: Visual Culture and Race Politics in Mid-Twentieth Century United States," 114.
31. Cohn, "Art Fronts: Visual Culture and Race Politics in Mid-Twentieth Century United States," 77. Paul Moreno, "An Ambivalent Legacy: Black Americans and the Political Economy of the New Deal," *The Independent Review* 6, no. 4 (2002): 515, discusses the limits to FAP's "color blindness." Writers emphasizing the interconnections between politics and culture in the New Deal programs aimed in particular at African American include Lauren Rebecca Sklaroff, *Black Culture and the New Deal: The Quest for Civil Rights in the Roosevelt Era* (Chapel Hill: University of North Carolina Press, 2009) and Andrew Hemmingway, "Cultural Democracy by Default: The Politics of the New Deal Arts Programmes," *Oxford Art Journal* 30, no. 2 (20067): 272.
32. Saab, *For the Millions*, 80–81.
33. Jane De Hart Mathews, "Arts and the People: The New Deal Quest for a Cultural Democracy," *Journal of American History* 62, no. 2 (1975): 316; Harris, *Federal Art and National Culture: The Politics of Identity in New Deal America*, 21–22.
34. Saab, *For the Millions*, 11–12.

35. Barbara Rose, *American Art since 1900* (New York: Holt, Reinhart & Winston, 1967), 93–98.
36. Annelise K. Madsen, "Reviving the Old and Telling Tales: 1930s Modernism and the Uses of American History," in *America After the Fall: Painting in the 1930s* (Chicago: Art Institute of Chicago, 2017), 88–113.
37. Jean-Michel Rabaté, *1913: The Cradle of Modernism* (Oxford: Blackwell, 2007), 1–5; R. Roger Remmington, *American Modernism: Graphic Design 1920 to 1960* (London: Laurence King, 2003); and Jonathan M. Woodham, *Twentieth-Century Design* (Oxford: Oxford University Press, 1997), 65–76.
38. William Stott, *Documentary Expression and Thirties America* (Chicago: University of Chicago Press, 1986), 134; Joseph B. Entin, *Sensational Modernism: Experimental Fiction and Photography in Thirties America* (Chapel Hill: University of North Carolina Press, 2007).
39. Brian O'Doherty, *The Voice and the Myth: American Masters* (London: Thames & Hudson, 1988), 46–79; and Rudi Blesh, *Stuart Davis* (New York: Grove Press, 1960), assess Davis's art in relation to jazz.
40. Peter Martin, *Music and the Sociological Gaze: Art Worlds and Cultural Production* (Manchester: Manchester University Press, 2006), 65.
41. Gregory Clark, *Civic Jazz: American Music and Kenneth Burke on the Art of Getting Along* (Chicago: University of Chicago Press, 2005), 2.
42. Charles Edward Smith, "New Orleans Comes to New York," *Esquire*, March 1946, 93. Rudi Blesh, *Shining Trumpets: A History of Jazz* (London: Cassell & Company, 1946, 1954 ed.); and Sidney Walter Finkelstein, *Jazz, A People's Music (1988 Ed.)* (New York: International, 1948), expanded on the purist theme. Floyd Levin, *Classic Jazz: A Personal View of the Music and Musicians* (Berkeley: University of California Press, 2000), continued the tradition.
43. Gennari, *Blowin" Hot and Cool: Jazz and Its Critics*. 82–4; Meltzer (Ed.), *Reading Jazz*, 5; Court Carney, *Cuttin' Up: How Early Jazz Got America's Ear* (Lawrence, KS: University Press of Kansas, 2009), 129–31; and Kathy J. Ogren, *The Jazz Revolution: Twenties America and the Meaning of Jazz* (New York: Oxford University Press, 1989), 144–46. Stuart Nicholson, *Jazz and Culture in a Global Age* (Boston, MA: Northeastern University Press, 2014), 155–252, Mark S. Harvey, "Jazz and Modernism," in *Jazz in Mind: Essays on the History and Meaning of Jazz*, ed. Reginald T. Buckner and Steven Weiland (Detroit: Wayne State University Press, 1991), 128–47 and J. Rasula, "Jazz and American Modernism," in *The Cambridge Companion to American Modernism*, ed. W. Kalaidjian (Cambridge: Cambridge University Press, 2005), 157–76, are important critical surveys of the relationship between jazz and modernism. Joel Dinerstein, *Swinging the Machine: Modernity, Technology and African American Culture between the World Wars* (Amherst: University of Massachusetts Press, 2013) explores the relationship between the "machine aesthetic" and African American culture.
44. Michael Denning, *The Cultural Front: The Laboring of American Culture in the Twentieth Century*, 330. The son of a Russian-Jewish drug store owner, Mezzrow grew up in comfortable circumstances in Chicago. He identified so completely with New Orleans jazz and black musicians that he effectively classified himself as one, defying racial barriers to live in Harlem, marry a black woman, and officially elect to be black. See further Charles Hersch, "'Every Time I Try to Play Black, It Comes Out Sounding Jewish': Jewish Jazz Musicians and Racial Identity," *American Jewish History* 97, no. 3 (2013): 259–82.
45. Paul Bacon, "Jazz Fan," in *Black Beauty, White Heat: A Pictorial History of Jazz 1920–1950*, ed. F. Driggs and H. Lewine (New York: Willian Morrow and Company, 1982), 8–18, recalled the camaraderie and rivalries of the Hot Club of Newark in 1939:" a tightly knit band [. . .] a family: we were strangers and they took us in [. . .] It met on Monday nights in the Fuld Neighbourhood House, a Jewish community centre on the edge of the black section. We [. . .] had a communally-owner record player (the best we could get for $35), fierce loyalties and disagreements. We also had access to a gold mine [of records].

    See also Raeburn, *New Orleans Style and the Writing of American Jazz History*, 94–8, 154; Gennari, *Blowin' Hot and Cool: Jazz and Its Critics*, 62–76, 84 *et passim.*
46. Paul Lopes, *The Rise of a Jazz Art World* (Cambridge: Cambridge University Press, 2002), 169–70. Welburn, "Jazz Magazines of the 1930s: An Overview of Their Provocative Journalism" and Thomas Turner, "Being Bop: How the Press Shaped the Cult of Bebop," *Jazz Research Journal* 1, no. 2 (2007): 267, analyse the different ways in which jazz writing shaped perceptions of the music. DeVeaux, Scott. "Review: What Did We Do to Be so Black and Blue?" The Musical Quarterly 80, no. 3 (1996): 397.

47. Jim Goggin and Peter Clute, *The Great Jazz Revival* (San Rafael, CA: Donald Ewald, 1994), provides a pictorial account of "west coast" revivalism.
48. Bernard Gendron, " 'Moldy Figs' and Modernists: Jazz at War (1942–46)," in *Jazz Among the Discourses, ed. Krin Gabbard (Durham, NC and London: Duke University Press, 1995), 50.*
49. Amiri Baraka, "Jazz Criticism and Its Effects on the Music," in *Digging: The Afro-American Soul of American Classical Music* (Berkeley: University of California Press, 2009), 74–85, a restatement of his earlier critique "Jazz and the White Critic" originally published in *Down Beat*, August 15, 1963. See also Frank Kofsky, "The Jazz Tradition: Black Music and Its White Critics," *Journal of Black Studies* 1, no. 4 (1971): 403–33.
50. Rogers quoted by Addison Gayle, *The Black Aesthetic* (Garden City, NY: Doubleday, 1971), 107.
51. William H. Kenney, *Chicago Jazz: A Cultural History, 1904–1930* (New York: Oxford University Press, 1993), 116.
52. Leonard quoted by Lucinda Moore, "Herman Leonard's Eye for Jazz," *Smithsonian Magazine* (Washington, DC, 2010), https://www.smithsonianmag.com/arts-culture/herman-leonards-eye-for-jazz-131497921/.https://www.smithsonianmag.com/arts-culture/herman-leonards-eye-for-jazz-131497921/.
53. Jay Maisel, Interview with the Author (2018); Christopher Willoughby, Interview with the Author, 2018; William Claxton and Joachim E. Berendt, *Jazz Life* (Cologne: Taschen, 2003), 25.
54. Writers tackling the theme include Mark Gerber, *Jazz Jews* (Nottingham: Five Leaves, 2009); Michael Alexander, *Jazz Age Jews* (Princeton: Princeton University Press, 2001); Macdonald Smith Moore, *Yankee Blues: Musical Culture and American Identity* (Bloomington: Indiana University Press, 1985), 131–33; Bruce Boyd Raeburn, "Jewish Jazzmen in New Orleans 1890–1940: An Overview," *Jazz Archivist* 12, no. 1 (1997): 1–10; Charles B. Hersch, *Jews and Jazz: Improvising Ethnicity* (New York: Routledge, 2017).
55. Nathan Abrams, *Stanley Kubrick: New York Jewish Intellectual* (New Brunswick, Newark: Rutgers University Press, 2018), 4, 36; John Broven, *Record Makers and Breakers: Voices of the Independent Rock n' Roll Pioneers*, n.d., 188–89; Nadel's photographs can be viewed at "New York City's First Racially Integrated Nightclub," Ephemeral New York, 2012, https://ephemeralnewyork.wordpress.com/tag/segregation-new-york-city/. See further William Meyers, "Jews and Photography," *Commentary* 115, no. 1 (2003), 45, https://www.commentarymagazine.com/articles/jews-and-photography/. Dan Morgenstern, "Jazz-The Jewish Black Connection," in *Creators and Disturbers: Reminiscences by Jewish Intellectuals of New York*, ed. by Bernard Rosenberg and Ernest Goldstein (New York: Columbia University Press, 1982), 103, 107; and Nat Hentoff, "Jews in the Family of Jazz," *JazzTimes*, 2010.
56. Willoughby, Interview with the Author, 2018.
57. Leonard quoted by Lucinda Moore, "Herman Leonard's Eye for Jazz."
58. Stacy I. Morgan, *Frankie and Johnny: Race, Gender and the Work of African American Folklore in 1930s America* America, 24–26.
59. "Bad Nigger Makes Good Minstrel," *Life*, April 19, 1937. For the background to this article and the role of John Lomax in the presentation of Leadbelly, see Morgan, 70–71.
60. Terri Weissman, *The Realisms of Berenice Abbott: Documentary Photography and Political Action* (Berkeley: University of California Press, 2011), 19–22; Lucy Ashjian's photographs can be viewed at the Museum of the City of New York digital collection; Sean Corcoran, "Lucy Ashjian and the Photo League," Museum of the City of New York, 2015, https://blog.mcny.org/2015/12/01/lucy-ashjian-and-the-photo-league/.
61. Rich Remsburg, *Hard Luck Blues: Roots Music Photographs from the Great Depression* (Urbana: University of Illinois Press, 2010), reproduces around 200 FSA photographs of musicians and musical events during the Depression.
62. Hank O'Neal, *A Vision Shared: A Classic Portrait of America and Its People 1935–1943* (New York: St. Martin's Press, 1976), 267–69. Miles Orvell, "Introduction," in *John Vachon's America: Photographs and Letters from the Depression to World War II* (Berkeley: University of California Press, 2003), 10–11, 31, 236, 276.
63. Richard Doud, "Oral History Interview with Edwin and Louise Rosskam" (Washington, DC: Smithsonian Archives of American Art, 1965), 31. Whilst always sympathetic to the position of African Americans, Rosskam knew little of their life: Gary D. Saretzky, "Documenting Diversity: Edwin Rosskam and the Photo Book, 1941–41," Photo Review 23, no. 4 (2000): 10–25. For Lee's work in Chicago see Hank O'Neal, *A Vision Shared: A Classic Portrait of America and Its People*, 135–39, and Nicholas Natanson, *The Black Image in the New Deal: The Politics of FSA Photography* (Knoxville: University of Tennessee Press, 1992), 142–76.

John Szarkowski, *Looking at Photographs: 100 Pictures from the Collection of The Museum of Modern Art* (New York: Museum of Modern Art, 1973), 134, assess Lee's approach to photography.

64. Kenney, *Chicago Jazz: A Cultural History, 1904–1930*, 24.
65. Wilbert Jones, *Chicago Blues (Images of America)* (South Carolina: Arcadia Publishing, 2014), cover image and 2.
66. Kenney, *Chicago Jazz: A Cultural History, 1904–1930*, 147.
67. Natanson, *The Black Image in the New Deal: The Politics of FSA Photography*, 176.
68. J. Lee Anderson, "The Painter as Photographer," *Mississippi Rag*, 1990.1; Ralston Crawford, "Ralston Crawford's Photographs," *The Second Line*, 1953.1.
69. Katherine M. Bourguignon, "Cool Modernism in America, 1915–45," in *America's Cool Modernism: O'Keefe to Hopper* (Oxford: Ashmolian Museum, 2018), 34–35.
70. Whitney Balliett, "Mecca, LA," *New Yorker*, June 11, 1966, 128–166 (reproduced as an introduction to Friedlander's earlier book) describes the classic jazz revival going on at the time the photographer visited New Orleans.
71. Sam Stephenson, *The Jazz Loft Project: Photographs and Tapes of W. Eugene Smith from 821 Sixth Avenue 1957–65* (New York: Alfred A. Knopf, 2009). Smith's project is documented in a film directed and produced by Sara Fishko, *The Jazz Loft According to W. Eugene Smith*, 2016. I am grateful to Carl Fuldner of Yale University Art Museum for his observations on Smith's jazz loft project.
72. Cawthra, *Blue Notes in Black and White: Photography and Jazz*, 259–61.
73. Dana Gooley, "The Outside of 'Sitting In': Jam Sessions and the Politics of Participation," *Performance Research*, 16.3 (2011), 46. Ross Russell provides a brief account of the classic Kansas City jam sessions in Ross Russell, *Jazz Style in Kansas City and the Southwest* (Berkeley: University of California Press, 1971), 25–30.
74. On the later commercialization of jazz sessions and audience differentiation see Patrick Burke, *Come In and Hear the Truth: Jazz and Race on 52nd. Street* (Chicago: University of Chicago Press, 2008), 147–49. A photograph in Geoffrey C. Ward and Ken Burns, *Jazz: A History of America's Music* (London: Pimlico, 2001), 265, illustrates how the scene at Eddie Condon's 1939 staged jam session for *Life* magazine looked. Gjon Mili, *Gjon Mili: Photographs and Recollections* (Boston, MA: New York Graphic Society, 1980), 168–73, describes the jam session in his New York studio for *Life* magazine staged at the request of George Frazier in 1943. Tad Herschorn, *Norman Granz: The Man Who Used Jazz for Justice* (Berkeley: University of California Press, 2011), describes what was probably the most extravagant exercise in framing the jam session as a theatrical spectacle.
75. Bruce Boyd Raeburn, *New Orleans Style and the Writing of American Jazz History* (Ann Arbor: University of Michigan Press, 2009), 142, 291 n.38. For Russell's biography and recording activities see Mike Hazeldine, *Bill Russell's American Music* (New Orleans: Jazzology Press, 1993), ix-xi; Michael Slatter, "A Portrait of William Russell," *Jazz Journal* 12, no. 9 (1959): 28–29; Anon., "Obituary: Bill Russell," *New York Times*, August 11, 1992, 5.D, 19.
76. Many of Russell's Chicago photographs are reproduced in Demlinger and Steiner, *Destination Chicago Jazz*.
77. "Dr. Bernard "Bernie" Steinau Collection," Hogan Jazz Archive, n.d;
78. New Orleans Public Library, "Grauman Marks Photography Collection," n.d., https://cdm16880.contentdm.oclc.org/digital/collection/p16880coll20.
79. Tom Bethell, *George Lewis: Jazzman from New Orleans* (Berkeley: University of California Press, 1978), 229, reproduces Kubrick's photograph. For Kuhlman's see George Gurtner, "Music Through the Lens," MyNewOrleans.com, 2013, https://www.myneworleans.com/music-through-the-lens/.
80. Michael P. Smith, *In the Spirit: The Photography of Michael P. Smith* (New Orleans: Historic New Orleans Collection, 2009); Michael P. Smith and Alison Milner, *Jazz Fest Memories* (Gretna, LA: Pelican, 1997).
81. Ted Gioia, *The Imperfect Art: Reflections on Jazz and Modern Culture* (New York: Oxford University Press, 1990), 94; Neil Leonard, "Some Further Thoughts on Jazzmen as Romantic Outsiders," *Journal of Jazz Studies* 2, no. 2 (1975): 42–52; Amiri Baraka cited by William Walling, "The Politics of Jazz: Some Preliminary Notes," *Journal of Jazz Studies* 2, no. 1 (1974): 55; Tim Blanning, *The Romantic Revolution* (London: Weidenfeld & Nicholson, 2010) 15–42: Isaiah Berlin, *The Roots of Romanticism*, ed. Henry Hardy (London: Pimlico, 1999), 79.
82. Barry Ulanov, "Evaluation," in *A History of Jazz in America* (Viking Press, 1952), 338–41, 343.
83. Willoughby, Interview with the Author.
84. Barbara Rosenblum, "Style as Social Process," *American Sociological Review* 43, no. 3 (1978): 425.

85. Photo caption in William Claxton's *Jazz West Coast,* n.p. See further Robert Walser, "Deep Jazz: Notes of Interiority, Race, and Criticism," in *Inventing the Psychological: Toward a Cultural History of Emotional Life in America,* ed. Joel Pfister and Nancy Schnog (New Haven: Yale University Press, 1997), 272. Ingrid Monson, "The Problem with White Hipness: Race, Gender and Cultural Conceptions in Jazz Historical Discourse," *Journal of American Musicological Society,* 48, No. 3 (1995): 412.
86. Heckman, "Introduction," 13.
87. Bob Rusch of *Cadence* magazine cited by Christopher Laws, "Who Wore It Best," culturedarm, n.d., https://culturedarm.com/who-wore-it-best-round-about-midnight-miles-davis-blue-train-john-coltrane/.
88. Cawthra, *Blue Notes in Black and White: Photography and Jazz,* 103–23.
89. David G. Spitzer and Ira Gitler, *Jazz: Photographs by David G. Spitzer* (San Francisco, CA: Woodford Press, 1994), 6.
90. Cawthra, *Blue Notes in Black and White: Photography and Jazz,* 109 reports his 2006 discussions with Leonard in which the photographer explained how he set up his lighting; Herman Leonard, *The Eye of Jazz: The Jazz Photographs of Herman Leonard* (London: Viking, 1989), 15, recounts the accidental discovery of ways of lighting smoke.
91. Dennis Stock, *Jazz Street* (New York: Doubleday, 1960), 62.
92. 'Claxton, Jazz West Coast. n.p.; Editorial, "Jazz Pix: Skippy Adelman's Pictures Have the Spontaneity That Is the Very Soul of Jazz," *Popular Photography,* 1946, 54.
93. Herman Leonard, Interview with Tad Hershorn (Institute of Jazz Studies, Rutgers University, 1998). All quotations taken from the same interview.
94. William Claxton and Hitoshi Namekata, *Jazz West Coast: Artwork of Pacific Jazz Records* (Tokyo: Bijutsu Shuppan-Sha, 1992), 10.
95. Whitney Balliett, "The Gentlemen of Jazz," *Saturday Review,* March 1955, 50. Michael Thomas Spencer, "Pacific Standard Time: Modernism and the Making of West Coast Jazz" (Michigan State University, 2011), 353–8, points out Claxton and several other photographers cannot be excused from lapses into gendered, sexist, and sometimes ridiculous cover images.
96. Willoughby, Interview with the Author.
97. Mark C. Gridley, "Clarifying Labels: Cool Jazz, West Coast and Hard Bop," *Journal of Popular Music Studies* 2, no. 2 (1990): 8–9. Robert Leroy Hughes Jr., "Howard Rumsey's Lighthouse All-Stars: Modern Jazz in California 1952–1959" (Washington University, 2002), 2, suggests that "the so-called West Coast style was popular with critics, serious jazz fans, and the ranks of tweed-clad sophisticates whose opinions on music, fashion, and life were outlined for them in the pages of *Esquire* magazine. It also appealed to many casual listeners, some as attracted to the provocative album covers as they were to the music".
98. Elgort quoted by Neil Remsen, "Arthur Elgort: The King of Swing," *Financial Times,* September 21 2018, 18. Arthur Elgort's photographs can be viewed in his book *Arthur Elgort: Jazz,* ed. Marianne Houtenbos (New York: Damiani, 2018).
99. Townsend, *Jazz in American Culture,* 166.
100. Aron M. Mathieu, "The Hard-Boiled School of Photography: The Legend of Skippy Adelman," *Minicam Photography 8,* April 1945 cited by Patricia Vettel-Becker, *Shooting from the Hip: Photography, Masculinity and Postwar America* (Minneapolis: University of Minnesota Press, 2005), 63.
101. Nathan Abrams, *Stanley Kubrick: New York Jewish Intellectual* (New Brunswick, Newark: Rutgers University Press, 2018), 36.
102. Editorial, "Jazz Pix: Skippy Adelman's Pictures Have the Spontaneity That Is the Very Soul of Jazz."
103. Rosenthal and Zachary, *Jazzways,* (London: Musicians Press, 1946).
104. Nels Nelson, "Jazz: Some People Sweat Better Than Others," *Philadelphia Daily News,* 1985, argues that Adelman, as one of the very earliest white jazz photographers, paved the way for Otto Hess, Charles Peterson, "PoPsie" Randolph, Herman Leonard, Bob Parent, and many other better-known names.
105. Carol Reiff, *Nights in Birdland Jazz Photographs 1954–1960* (New York: Simon & Schuster, 1985), is the only anthology of her work.
106. Hal Reiff, "Faking a Magazine Cover," *Camera: A Practical Magazine for Photographers,* vol. 70, 1948, 38, suggests that Carol Reiff was influenced by her father's "keep it simple" message.

9

Interrogating Jazz
Exiles and Jewish Photography

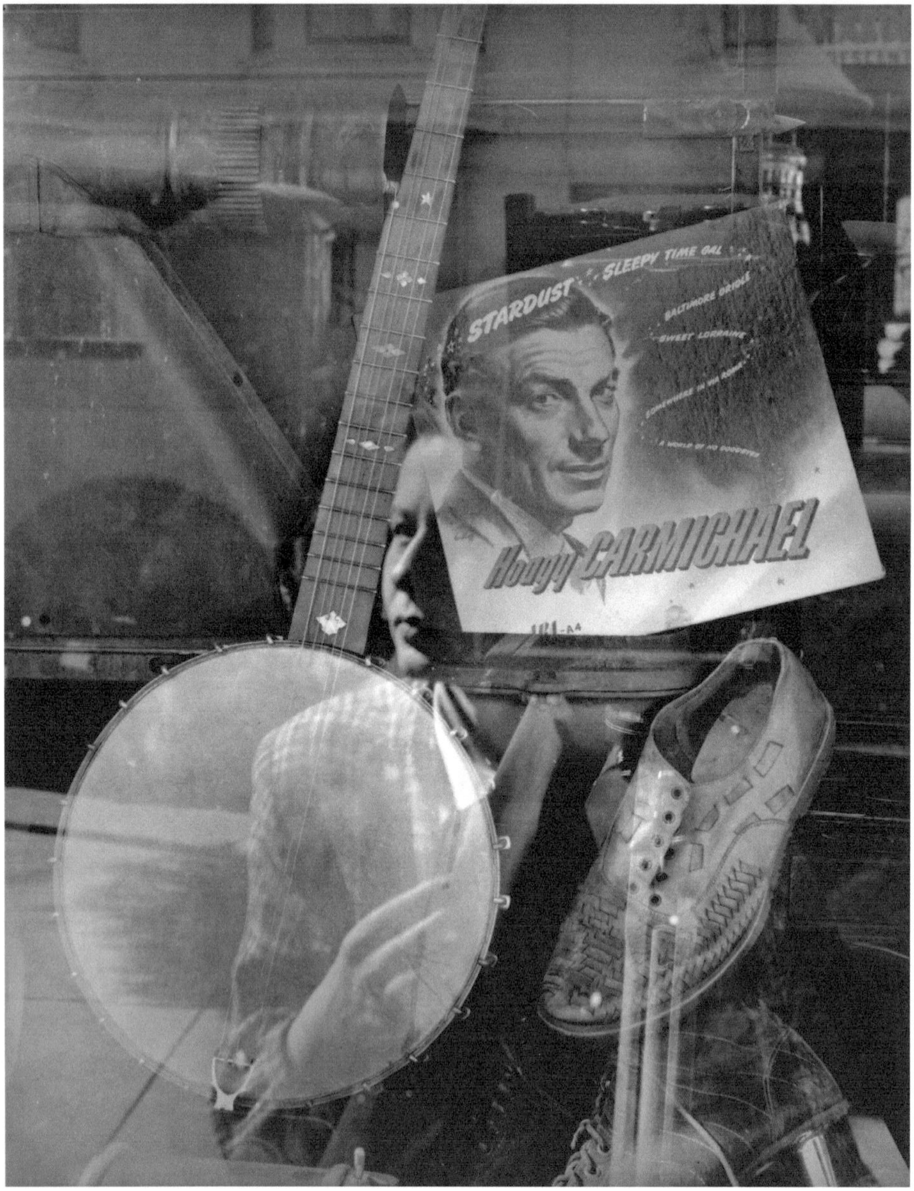

Figure 121: Rose Mandel. *On Walls and Behind Glass.* 1948.
Los Angeles County Museum of Art: The Marjorie and Leonard Vernon Collection.

Born into a Jewish Polish family in 1910, Rose Mandel arrived as an exile in New York with her husband in 1942. Her photograph *On Walls and Behind Glass* (Figure 121) offers a meditation on the position of the exile in which she drew among other sources on the iconography of jazz to interrogate and reflect (literally and metaphorically) her relationship with a new culture. Juxtaposing herself against a collage of cultural symbols from her new country, including a banjo and reference to Hoagy Carmichael, Mandel offers a visual representation of a relationship of affinity and difference expressed through reflection and its opposite. She is positioned in a space that is at once subjective and material, spatial and temporal, real and symbolic, "another place" through which she sought to define her relationships with others.[1]

Edward Said used musical terminology to describe the position of the exile: "Most people are principally aware of one culture, one setting, one home; exiles are aware of at least two, and this plurality of vision gives rise to an awareness of simultaneous dimensions, an awareness that—to borrow a phrase from music—is contrapuntal."[2] Arriving at Ellis Island in 1923, another photographer fleeing Nazi Europe, Alexander Alland asked himself "How would I make myself understood, understand others?"[3] Reveling in the diversity that made up America he answered his own question by photographing migrants, the poor and disadvantaged, and ethnic minorities. His work demonstrates how a photographer-in-exile could use his medium to make sense of his new life, not least between 1941 and 1943 as photo editor of *Common Ground*, a new publication of the Common Council of American Unity that emphasized issues of immigration and acculturation, social justice and equality. Alland made few images of jazz but his archive demonstrates that ethnic music was central to his sense of a democratic and multicultural society. It is significant that Alland's popular 1943 book documenting his photographic understanding of America was titled *American Counterpoint.*

Jazz pricked the imagination of a number of exiled photographers arriving in the United States during the second half of the 1930s and early-1940s. Many, like Mandel, Alland, and John Guttmann, photographed jazz subjects only occasionally while others made a specific study of the music, excited by its visual possibilities and its relevance to their new situation. Although these photographers approached the subject in different ways, the idea that jazz might be a subject of enquiry for displaced persons seeking to evolve a sense of understanding and identity during a period of dislocation was always present. The result is an enquiring and interrogative body of work reflecting the inevitably contrapuntal vision of the distanced observer.

I. Displaced identities

Exiled photographers of the 1930s and 1940s

Compared with the early émigrés discussed in Chapter 5 the character of immigrant photographers changed dramatically as more than 100,000 refugees arrived in the United States between 1933 and the end of 1941. Around 8,000 were academics; some 1,500 artists, sculptors, cultural journalists, designers, graphic designers; and nearly 400 were architects.[4] About 80 percent of German-speaking refugees were Jewish. Klaus Honnef and Frank Weyers have estimated that some 170 photographers emigrated from Germany in the 1930s, more than 40 of whom reached America, and Anna Auer has identified 53 Austrian émigrés to the United States. Sixteen of the 59 photographers presented in the Jewish Museum of New York's exhibition of urban photography in 2002 were first-generation Jewish immigrants and many of the others were born in the United States to immigrant parents.[5] In addition, many hundreds of immigrant photographers established local businesses that remain largely undocumented: the Russian immigrant Samuel "Sasha" Walters, for many years a celebrity portraitist in Seattle, and the pictorialist Elias Goldensky in Philadelphia both made important contributions although they remain largely unknown.[6]

Photographers in the 1930s diaspora included many illustrious names. Early to arrive were the composer and FSA photographer Jack Delano (arriving in 1923) and the Bauhaus-trained scientific photographer Hansel Mieth (1928). Otto Hess (1930), Fritz Goro, John Guttmann, and Martin Munkácsi (1933); Alfred Eisenstaedt and Lotte Jacobi (1935); Cornell Capa, Lisette Model, Henry Ries, and László Moholy-Nagy (1937); and Lisl Steiner (1938 via. Buenos Aires); Andreas Feiniger and David Seymour ("Chim") (1939); Roman Vishniac and Marion Palfi in 1940; Lucien Aigner (1941); and Rose Mandel and Clemens Kalischer (1942) all established international reputations in their chosen fields. Ellen Auerbach (1940), Fritz Neuglas (1941), and Walter Sanders (1945) found positions with *Life* or other illustrated magazines. Erwin Blumenfeld (1936), Horst P. Horst, and Serge Balkin (1939) forged successful careers in art and fashion photography and Erich Mendelsohn (1941) made striking photographic representations of American urban modernism. György Kepes (1937) experimented with abstraction, Otto Hagel (1928) documented the work of the Longshore Mens' Union while Nina Leen (1939) was known for her animal photography. Philippe Halsman arrived in the late-1930s while Josef Breitenbach, who arrived in 1941, was a noted photojournalist and educator. Bringing a particular interest in jazz subjects were Francis Wolff (1939), the cofounder with Alfred Lion of Blue Note Records, and Fred Plaut (1940), a German electrical engineer who became a sound engineer with Columbia as well as being an accomplished photographer. Henry Ries, Otto Hess, Roman Vishniac, Clemens Kalischer, John Guttmann, Gjon Mili, Lisl Steiner, and Lisette Model took a serious interest in jazz while Jacques Lowe and Philippe Halsman found time to capture jazz subjects in reportage and portraiture practices.

Adaptation and reflexivity

How well, and in what ways, did these exiles respond to life in America? There has been little systematic research into the experiences of exiled photographers who have tended to fall between two perspectives on the people movements of the 1930s—that of the artistic and intellectual exodus and Wolfgang Benz's *kleinen*

Leute.[7] We know from personal accounts however that the pervading problem for all exiles lay in dealing with ambiguities of self-conception and identity. Hannah Arendt's 1943 essay "We Refugees" evoked the endless anxiety and despair of the denial of Jewish heritage and Marion Berghahn's study of German Jewish exile is just one of many stressing that displacement inevitably requires profound reinterpretative shifts in personal and social identities.[8] Yet the sheer variety of personal strategies adopted by displaced artists and intellectuals of the 1930s has led many scholars to agree with Sybil Milton that "exile is a most heterogeneous and fragmented experience."[9]

The absence of "a figure in the carpet," to use Martin Jay's phrase, underlines the need to move beyond rigid definitions of "assimilation" conceived as absorption, and even the "co-constitution" of more recent scholarship, toward hybridity, mutuality, "and the agency of choosing and the awareness of self-fashioning [. . .] the creative imagination of an expanded self beyond the facts of natural kinship and a given place" in the relations between exiles and the host culture.[10] As migration scholars have come to understand, the heterogeneity of exilic response points to geographical dislocation as a particularly potent site of human reflexivity—the ability to reflect upon the relationship between biography and its concerns in a new context—and raises the possibilities that social theories stressing emergence, causal mechanisms, and the exercise of agency can round out migration theories significantly.[11] This is doubly important in the case of exiled Jews. Comprising a mixture of ethnic, religious, geographical, and cultural antecedents, fused with individual diasporic experience, the dynamic and multifaceted nature of Jewish identity is well-documented and calls into question the limits of assimilation conceived as absorption. According to Jay Geller, the overriding concern of displaced Jews was to engage in "different forms of contesting, negotiating and transforming the *Judentum* by which they were identified" while Michael Berkowitz argues that self-fashioning quite simply defines twentieth-century Jewishness.[12]

Forced exile creates its own conditions for reflexive reassessments, breaking down barriers and providing psychological and social space for an interrogative view detached from inherited customs and *mores,* a form of social deracination.[13] This is exactly what the Austrian exile photographer Lisette Model had in mind in describing herself as perpetually "*an den Rand,*" as always viewing society from its margins. Said's "detached and interrogative subjectivity" often finds itself expressed in new forms of art that provide opportunities—particularly, perhaps, for women—to move beyond inherited social and religious boundaries. Model was certainly clear that the "electrifying effect" of New York encouraged her to adopt the tilted angles and sometimes brutal exculpations of her photographs.[14] For Jewish exiles the city could be a liberating experience, which explains why so many Jewish photographers directed their attention outward toward their interactions with city living and newly emerging forms of Jewish culture rather than toward traditional Jewish communities and their iconography. The magnetic attraction for immigrant photographers of the louche environment at Sammy's Bar on the Bowery, where drag queens, prostitutes, and down-and-outs mingled with wealthy slummers, is a particularly vivid example.[15] Despite its implications of loss and abandonment then, artistic displacement proved to be an essential force for renewal and the modernization of American culture.

Photographers and the agency of adaptation

This was no less true in the case of the photographic diaspora. Exile studies have shown that an artist's identity is intimately related to the style, technique, materials, and subject matter of their practices, which may or may not find favor in the host country.[16] Artists themselves have often spoken of their routes to settled and fulfilling lives in a new country through practice. The Jewish Egyptian exile Edmond Jabès described his writing as the key to opening the doors of exile while V. S Naipaul, culturally dislocated between India, Trinidad and England, "sought to find his place in the world through words." Ruth Weisberg has pointed out that artistic practice allowed Jewish artists "to work through their ambivalence about being Jews."[17] If we are to understand the responses of photographers to emigration and exile it is important to trace the trajectory of their practices once in the host country.

The experience of photographers arriving in America was as varied as that of other artists and intellectuals. The year after relocating to America, André Kertész exhibited at the Levy and PM Galleries and was represented in *Photography 1839–1937* at MoMA but his subsequent relationships with American clients and publications were always strained. In 1941 Kertész and his wife were designated enemy aliens. Philippe Halsman's early days in America were also far from easy: "I spoke five languages, but I had almost no knowledge of English. I had no friends and almost no money. I spent the first three months trying to find work." Halsman was obliged to drop the second "n" of his last name to appear less foreign. Robert Capa famously changed his name to make it easier to sell himself as an American photographer and the other Hungarian photographers (Brassai, Munkácsi, Moholy-Nagy, Kertész, and Weegee) followed suit. With his facility for getting along with all sorts of different people Alfred Eisenstaedt, on the other hand, found the transition from Berlin to New York relatively painless and Josef Breitenbach, who left Germany in 1941, quickly found a deep affinity with his adopted city.[18]

It is, as Anne Swidler emphasizes, the "situational logic" that determines the efficacy of cultural tools in uncertain times and, from this point of view, émigré and exile photographers had a decided advantage.[19] Their arrival in the 1930s coincided with the rapid development of American visual culture, a transformative experience that created opportunities for newly arrived photographers to deploy their experience and skills to secure mutually beneficial points of entry into American culture. As photography expanded its reach during the decade it was the "émigré imaginations" of photographers such as Martin Munkácsi, Hansel Mieth, Alfred Eisenstaedt, Ellen Auerbach, Fritz Neuglas, and Walter Sanders that helped to create the distinctive look of the new illustrated publications such as *Life* and *Harper's Bazaar*. *Harper's* became the primary medium in which the startlingly innovative approach to fashion photography introduced by Munkácsi, Erwin Blumenfeld, and Horst P. Horst was widely noticed and admired and that led in the immediate postwar period to editors actively seeking out Jewish photographers. Fritz Goro recalled how he was able to apply his experiences of candid photography before leaving Germany to mainstream American-style reportage.[20] These were opportunities for immigrant photographers to make significant contributions to and shape the trajectory of this culture in a way that eluded many other displaced artists.

Rapidly finding mutually beneficial points of contact with the host culture, photographers had a further advantage in the transferability of the medium and adaptability of photographic language. Photography possessed a remarkable facility to cross borders due in part to the growing importance of photography agencies. From their initial establishment in London and Paris in the 1890s, agencies spread rapidly across the major cities of continental Europe facilitating the cross-border flow of images.[21] In parallel agencies were established in America to promote the work of immigrant photographers. Notable among these was the Black Star agency formed in 1935 by three German Jews—Kurt Safranski, previously a graphic designer and editor for the *Berliner Illustrirte Zeitung*; Ernest Mayer, who owned the publishing company and photo agency, *Mauritius*, in Berlin; and Kurt Kornfeld, a literary agent. Noted Black Star photographers included Robert Capa, Fritz Goro, Andreas Feiniger, Germaine Krull, Philippe Halsman, Martin Munkácsi, and Conrad Eiger. Henry Luce collaborated with Black Star and *Life* became the agency's most high-profile client, providing the publication with an invaluable link with developments in European photography.[22]

Just as significant was the mutable nature of photographic language itself. The mimetic relationship between observed reality and the photographic image means that photographers must respond directly rather than obliquely to new visual realities, freeing them from the need always to revert to the home culture and discursive modes as a point of reference. It is for this reason that displaced photographers were better equipped than other artists to come to terms with their new land and it helps explain why many exile photographers chose to couch their work in the vocabulary of modernism, with its inherent universalizing vision, stylistic shifts, and transformations. As Frank Weyers described the period, the photographer was always able to rely on the "*universales Auge*."[23]

The idea that the visual is more than capable of standing in for discourse was given intellectual rationale by the exiled Hungarian photographer György Kepes. Thus Martin Munkácsi, who spoke little English, became one of the highest-paid photographers in New York within 12 months of arriving and Alfred Eisenstaedt shunned words for "a world of sight, of endless sights, of sight and light." Robert Capa turned to photography to earn a living as it "was the nearest thing to journalism for those who found himself without a language." Indeed, the ability to communicate visually was of great importance to all the Hungarian photographers as few others spoke Magyar. It is noticeable that all the Hungarian writers—unlike the photographers—felt the need to return home to their native language as soon as it was safe to do so.[24]

Like many Jewish exiles, displaced photographers showed a profound affinity with the new and gravitated to the universalistic prescriptions of modernism, albeit tinged with a sense of ironic distance.[25] It was by drawing on the cultural inheritance of a European modernist photographic vocabulary therefore that immigrant photographers were able to forge visual rhetoric capable of expressing a new subjectivity; and, combining the celebratory and political modalities of modernism, photographers found ready acceptance in the rapidly expanding world of American visual culture. The result was that the photographic vocabulary of displaced photographers required neither the abandonment nor retreat back to cultural inheritance.

Jazz, Jews, and Jewish photography

The work of America's exiled photographers cannot be delimited by genre, style, or referential objects. True, exiled photographers trended to seek out people, events, and situations that both typified and exposed American cultural modernity—its consumerism; artifacts such as guns, storefronts, and automobiles; the signs of a multicultural society; music; and other forms of cultural expression. On the whole though their work offers a wide variety of styles and content and it is in a visual language that came naturally to cultural outsiders, a language expressing "the desire to melt in but the desire to embody an instructive difference,"[26] that we should look for commonalities. Exilic photographs presented as open-ended rather than assertive, anxious, enquiring, and full of nervous energy while penetrating the surface appearances of urban modernity. It is hardly surprising to find therefore that the restlessly questioning nature of exile photography struck a chord with other marginal intellectuals. Marion Palfi, the daughter of German theatre designer and Polish mother, was befriended after her arrival in 1940 by a number of prominent black intellectuals and writers including Langston Hughes, who became an ardent supporter: "A Palfi photograph brings us face to face with hidden realities that its surface only causes us to begin to explore," Hughes observed.[27]

It is the inquisitive and penetrating *relation* of subjectivity to its referential objects that defines exile photography: the distinctive vision of Ellen Auerbach's "third eye" and Ben Shahn's melding of European modernism with social realism in a photographic style that drew inspiration from a wide range of vernacular sources;[28] in Erich Mendelsohn's critique of architectural photography and urban modernism, Moholy-Nagy's "new experiences of space," Fred Stein's vertiginous urban photography, Andreas Feiniger's urban abstractions, and T. Lux Feiniger's cubist cityscapes. Otto Hagel, Hansel Mieth, and John Guttmann pushed the boundaries of the "documentary imagination" of the 1930s; Clemens Kalischer and Erika Stone brought a modernist sensibility to capture the culture of artistic gatherings; and Gjon Mili, Roman Visniac, and Fritz Goro revealed the "optical unconscious" through new types of scientific photography.[29] Just as influential was the adoption of modernism in photographic advertising pioneered by László Moholy-Nagy, Nikolas Murray, Xanti Schwansky, Anton Bruehl, Ruth Berhardt, and Herbert Beyer while Philippe Halsman turned to the vocabulary of surrealism. Jewish émigré photographers formed the core of the New York School that coalesced around American-born Jewish talent such as Sid Grossman, Helen Levitt, William Klein, Robert Frank, and Louis Faurer. In Harlem too, as Sara Blair has shown, a predominantly African American urban space became the testing ground for new aesthetic quite distinct from FSA documentary and modernist photography and in which Jewish photographers were well to the fore.[30]

The enormously varied nature of exilic Jewish photography has undermined attempts to identify a discernible "Jewish" aesthetic of the kind proposed by Max Kozloff and explains why A. D. Coleman believes that "there is no way of recognizing a 'Jewish photograph.' " Sara Blair emphasizes the point in an analysis of the complexly multifaceted nature of Jewish identity as reflected in contemporary photography while other critics have observed that it is almost impossible to distinguish Jewish from *goyish* photography.[31] Yet the absence of formal *stylistic* difference cannot hide the questioning subjectivity, the unavoidable voice of the photographer that speaks to the relationality of identities. It is in this respect that the evidence suggests that jazz played a particular role for exiled Jewish photographers.

The Jewish engagement with jazz was much more extensive than once thought to be the case.[32] Scholars have advanced various models to explain the Jewish presence in jazz including the idea of a natural affinity based on shared suffering between two disadvantaged marginal groups to which allusion was made in the preceding chapter. This explanation takes us only so far and several writers have highlighted the instrumental value of black identification as a means of upward Jewish assimilation or the exploitative nature of the relationship between white (particularly business) Jews and black musicians. In other approaches Charlie

Gerrard argues that urban proximity helped to break down barriers between Jews and jazz musicians although there is evidence that this proximity did not last long, particularly in Harlem, and was in any event mostly confined to economic transactions. Michael Alexander locates any mutual identification in the ongoing recreation of Jewish identity that focuses on black outsiders to compensate for feeling at home in America.[33]

Assessing this scholarship Charles Hersch has cautioned that the relationship between Jews and jazz was dynamic, shifting perceptibly between the early years of the twentieth century and the 1940s, and that monocausal explanations of any variety often fall short. His advice finds considerable support in recent scholarship that emphasizes historical contingency and shifting dynamics in the relationship between Jews and African Americans in general, one in which self-interest and periodic conflict have been as present as fellow feeling.[34]

Surprisingly in view of their unmistakable presence, there has however been little scholarly enquiry into the specific relationship between Jewish photographers and jazz.[35] The overwhelming majority of exiled photographers were Jewish and as previous chapters have shown there were many Jewish practitioners among early émigrés and new generation white photographers. While the explanations discussed above all provide valuable insights it is reasonable to ask whether they advance our understanding of the specific Jewish photographer/jazz nexus.

Photography provided a means by which the social, political, and economic distance between the two groups might be bridged. It provided a means for Jews to use their encounters with African Americans as a means of understanding their own minority immigrant position, provoking an internal conversation about race that helped them to apprehend their relationship to whiteness, to anti-Semitism, and to racial oppression.[36] The approach proposed here is to evaluate the relationship between Jewish photographers and jazz in terms of identification and reflexivity. Jazz and African American culture played a critical role in *anchoring* the construction of an identity appropriate to the new circumstances in which exiled photographers found themselves. Cultural anchoring is an approach that enquires into the role played by various cultural elements in the construction of identity and the ways in which cultural knowledge and skills are deployed in the quest for self-confirmation.[37] Central to the argument is that the ambiguous and dynamic nature of Jewish identity leads Jews to ask questions not just about the nature of Jewishness but "rather, to whom do they feel aligned with or marked off from"—a form of symbolic ethnicity beyond ties of physical and familial proximity. To borrow Jutta Vinzent's term, we can see the choice of jazz subjects by displaced photographers as a construction of "the Other of the Other."[38] Unavoidably confronted with questions of personal and artistic identities, displaced Jewish photographers could not but see in jazz a powerful, highly visual and concretely embodied form of cultural expression—an impressive template of what a marginalized people could achieve and the innovative forms in which that culture might be expressed.

Charlie Gerrard argues that "Jews considered African-American music emblematic of American culture, and Jews latched onto it as a way of discarding their old-world Jewish identities,"[39] but this is surely mistaken. The evidence suggests that many of these photographers did indeed feel a profound affinity with their African American subjects but not at the expense of Jewishness. When Edward Said famously observed that the process of identifying involves "establishing 'opposites' and 'others' whose actuality is always subject to the continuous interpretation and reinterpretation of their differences from 'us,'"[40] he had in mind the continually reflexive process of negotiation and reevaluation of identities, not a reversion to some form of "absorption highly visual and concretely embodied."

Emphasizing individual reflexivity as the mediating process between agency and situational forces means that there need be no contradictions between natural affinity, instrumentality, and contingency in the relationship between Jewish photographers and jazz. Jazz may well have been used by Jewish photographers as a "handy tool" or "stalking horse," to use Hasia Diner's descriptions,[41] but this does not necessarily remove a sense of natural affinity. The powerful expression of black cultural identity in jazz proved extremely attractive to Jewish exiles seeking grounding for their own evolving identity, a model of outsider cultural expression against which the shifting and unstable features of Jewish identity might be anchored and validated. This was a relationship of both affinity and difference, solidarity and distance, affectivity and instrumentality in which photography played a key role by offering the possibility of reimagining of self as other. Adopting a variety of photographic modernisms, which lifted their visual accounts beyond the particularities of Jewish experiences, Jewish photographers deployed their medium as a "cultural tool" through which they might come to know themselves in photographic practice.[42] It was here, in real-world engagement through photographic practice, that the "contrapuntal" vision was expressed; and it is at the level of individual expression, in the photographs they made, that the specifics of this vision are ultimately to be found.

II. Jazz and exilic vision

The exile as outsider

Arriving in America in 1909 at the age of 9, Weegee's work prefigures the deep interest in jazz that the forced exiles of the 1930s would exhibit. Fascinated by the gritty urban disorder of New York's underbelly, Weegee's voyeuristic photographs of street incidents, automobile crashes, cops, crime, murder, derelicts, and prostitution have been canonized as founding documents of the street photography tradition.[43] More recently however Daniel Morris has contextualized Weegee's work as part of the Jewish American experience and speaks of the continual search for identity of "an exiled wanderer who experienced an insecure cultural placement"; and Samantha Baskind recuperates the Jewish "cultural assertion of Weegee's less well known photographs of acculturation, social justice and anti-Semitism."[44] Weegee's images of African Americans are notable for the empathy and respect he accords his subjects, rarely accompanied by the acerbic commentaries and wisecracks with which he described his better known street work.

Many of Weegee's jazz images foreground audiences, locating the significance of the music in embodied interactions between players and listeners. His photographs of audience members at Bunk Johnson's performance at the Stuyvesant Casino and in other clubs offer acute observation through the isolation of individual detail: "At a Jazz Club" (1946) picks out three figures in the crowd, a man in the background with his drink, another young man staring at the players, and a well-dressed women who screams enthusiastically; "Listening to a jazz concert, Stuyvesant Casino" (c. 1946) shows a young woman responding ecstatically to the music while the arm of a trombone contextualizes the scene; and "Bunk Johnson and his Dixieland jazz band at the Stuyvesant Casino" (c.1946) shows part of the musician's figure but attention moves rapidly to the woman whose expression indicates her immersion in the music on offer. What strikes the viewer about these images is the outsider's interest in the passionate engagement of the crowd—including many women—in the performance event.

The picture editor of *PM* magazine, Ralph Steiner, could not believe his luck when, two years after arriving in America in 1940, Lisette Model showed him her coruscating images of elderly wealthy women on the promenade at Nice. She seemed to be a European version of Weegee, at that point his star photographer, and he published Model's portfolio under the title "Why France Fell." Model had been immediately fascinated by America, its customs and people.[45] She left her native Vienna in 1924 to pursue music and artistic studies in Paris eventually settling in New York in 1938. She had little good to say about her affluent bourgeois Austrian background but was energized by the sights and sounds of New York City, its skyscrapers, the speed of change, and atmosphere of frenetic energy. Her immersion in American culture provided the opportunity for a Jewish woman who described herself as having been a perennial outsider to her own upbringing to renew her own sense of self in her new country.

One aspect of Model's past she refused to disown was her musical training and it is perhaps not surprising that jazz quickly claimed her attention: "Ich war vom Jazz völlig überwältigt, den ich wusste, das ist Amerika—und das war es, was ich fotografieren wolte."[46] Her photographs of Louis Armstrong, Duke Ellington, Ella Fitzgerald, Joe Morello, Chico Hamilton, and Anita O'Day at the 1956 Newport Jazz Festival exhibit many of her stylistic trademarks—off-kilter compositions, unusual viewpoints—but lack the sarcasm of her portrayals of the aged dowagers of Nice. Like Weegee, it was the activities of audiences which fascinated her as much as the performers. Her photographs of the crowd listening to the music and taking in the sun at Newport recorded an informality almost completely absent from the Viennese middle-class life she was so quick to disown. In 1952 Model embarked on a jazz book project with poems by Langston Hughes and text by Rudi Blesh. She continued working on the project until 1956, when it was abandoned for lack of financial backing.

Clemens Kalischer

Throughout a long life as a German-born exile in America, Clemens Kalischer was "a silent observer" of people and places.[47] This was an exercise conducted strictly on his own terms: avoiding the constructed portrayals of the portrait photographer or the declamatory urge of the documentary photographer, he let his scenes unfold, always ready to be surprised. His photographs of refugees arriving in New York City taken in 1947–48 comprise his most recognizable body of work, but his wide-ranging interests included the longshore men of New York, the vernacular buildings of rural Vermont, train passengers, street vendors, children playing along Manhattan's West Side and sledding in Vermont, and pedestrians on the city streets. He was attracted to farming and nature and embarked on a cooperation with Norman Rockwell to photograph scenes of middle American life. In 1948 he traveled by train to Gatlinburg, TN, to photograph the folk artists at the annual Gatlinburg Craft Fair: "He didn't really focus so much on people's economic situations," his daughter Tanya recalls, "finding a richness of spirit or something interesting in the people he photographed, rather than observing people as poor or rich."[48] Journeying alone in the early-1950s to the segregated South, he visited out-of-the-way jazz clubs and blues joints. He traveled widely in western Europe and India and brought back memorable images but it was his exploration of the patchwork culture of his adopted homeland that most consistently engaged his attention.

Photography was Kalischer's way of understanding and understanding was the route to adapting to his new country. He had arrived in the United States in 1942 after fleeing the Nazis, penniless, exhausted, and speaking little English. But he was observant, resourceful, alert to his surroundings, and deeply empathetic. Less than six years after taking up photography, he was being shown at the Museum of Modern Art. Edward Steichen included his work in the landmark "Family of Man" exhibition and he rapidly acquired a roster of major American and international publications. He moved to Stockbridge, MA, in 1950, where he lived for the rest of his life raising a family and opening a gallery to display his own work and to encourage young artists.

If photography was the medium, the arts were central to Kalischer's search for meaning. His interest took him to photograph the Marlboro Music summer performances in Vermont, the South Mountain Music Festival, Tanglewood, black Mountain College, dance companies, the Flaherty Film Seminar, and the Berkshire Theater Group. Running through these images is his close observation of the ways in which creative people, communities, and spaces interacted. Kalischer was fascinated by jazz although he confessed to knowing little about the music. Starting in 1951 he created a substantial archive of photographs taken at Stephanie and Philip Barber's Music Inn and the Lenox School of Jazz; his daughter Tanya recalls her father speaking fondly about Ornette Coleman but he also came to know Marshall Stearns, John Lewis, Gunther Schuller, and many others involved with these summer activities.[49]

John Gennari encourages us to approach Kalischer's photographs taken at these gatherings as bridging ethnographic and documentary photography, a visual archive of the 1950s "mainstreaming" of jazz, that moment in which a series of key personalities and cultural trends converged in a quest to embed jazz at the center of American culture. It was in spaces defined as much by their cultural resonance as physical setting that Kalischer captured a community of the leading figures associated with the move of jazz toward the status and respectability of an art form. His photographs of performances, tutorials and, above all, the participants socializing in bucolic surroundings say little about the music but much about the musicians, their cultural aspirations, the community, and the rural spaces that both reflected and bounded this moment in the evolution of the music and provide an appropriate setting for the republican high-mindedness that appears to permeate activities at the Music Inn. Kalischer's photographs show him to be fascinated by the scene and its cultural richness in an outsider's view, which "demands attention not just for the iconic figures but because it presents a jazz narrative that moves us away from the photographs of the classic jazz tradition."[50]

Otto Hess and Henry Ries

A native of Berlin, Henry Ries was forced into exile in America in 1938. He served in the US Army Air Corps as an aerial photographer during the war and later worked as a photojournalist with the *New York Times Magazine* from 1947 to 1952. Ries produced several ground-breaking features on postwar Europe, particularly that on the Berlin blockade in which he juxtaposed symbols of the city's history with scenes of contemporary life and interviews with residents, visitors, and survivors of the Holocaust. Returning to New York in 1952, he turned to fashion photography and in 1955 he opened his own studio that handled major advertising agency and magazine accounts.[51]

People fascinated Ries and it was his incisive portraits that marked his photographic vision.[52] Soon after arriving, he set out on a photographic quest to understand America, his own "Suche nach einem neuen Affidavit." Spurning the skyscrapers and sights of Manhattan, Ries turned instead to capture scenes at the Festival of Swing held on Randall's Island Stadium in May 1938, a benefit sponsored by the American Federation of Musicians which attracted a crowd of around 23,000. Confessing he knew nothing about the island, its stadium, or the Festival before making the journey to the tiny island, the experience proved a revelation. The crowd went wild after the performance by the Ellington Orchestra; scheduled to play just two pieces, spectators demanded five pieces and three encores. Besides the music of Ellington, Basie and Woody Herman what seems to have impressed Ries most was a couple in the audience who suddenly launched into a wild dance on the grass between the stage and the audience. Quickly joined by more dancers of all races, the police watched on benevolently as the dancers became increasingly animated. Ries could not help drawing a contrast between these expressive outbursts from an integrated crowd and the lack of freedom in the Nazi Berlin he had left behind: "Faszinert und gebrannt beobachtete ich das ungewohnte Schauspiel." His book of reminiscences includes two photographs of Ellington on stage but twice as many of the spectators and dancers which so engaged his attention.[53]

Otto Hess also made the journey across the Triborough Bridge to Randall's Island Stadium in 1938 in his own quest to understand the culture of his adopted land. Born in Karlsruhe, Hess had emigrated to New York City in 1930 to join his brother Franz, an advertising photographer. By 1940 photography had become Hess's main activity. After a period in the army he started to exhibit his work at the Norlyst Gallery run by Elenor Lust and Jimmy Ernst. Archive material including contact sheets and notebooks in the Hess collection at the New York Public Library show clearly that the photographer was also as fascinated by the Randall Island crowd and their behavior as the musicians on stage (Figure 122). Like Ries, Hess found in the jazz audience forms of cultural expression distinctive to America, which "serve as indices pointing to Hess's immigrant identity."[54]

Other than Randall Island, Hess's photographs depict the cultural life of New York City between the 1930s and 1940s, especially the midtown jazz scene, as well as street scenes, nightclub and theatre interiors, and sporting events. Hess was a skilled photographer with a practiced eye for composition and exposure; there are few poorly exposed frames in his contact sheets in spite of the poor light with which he often had to contend. Working with both 35mm and 6 × 4 cameras, his jazz photography in New York City was mostly carried out in recording studios and performance spaces. Even so, his cultural interest is obvious. His photograph *Count Basie on the Coca-Cola Bottle* (Figure 15) shows his concern to

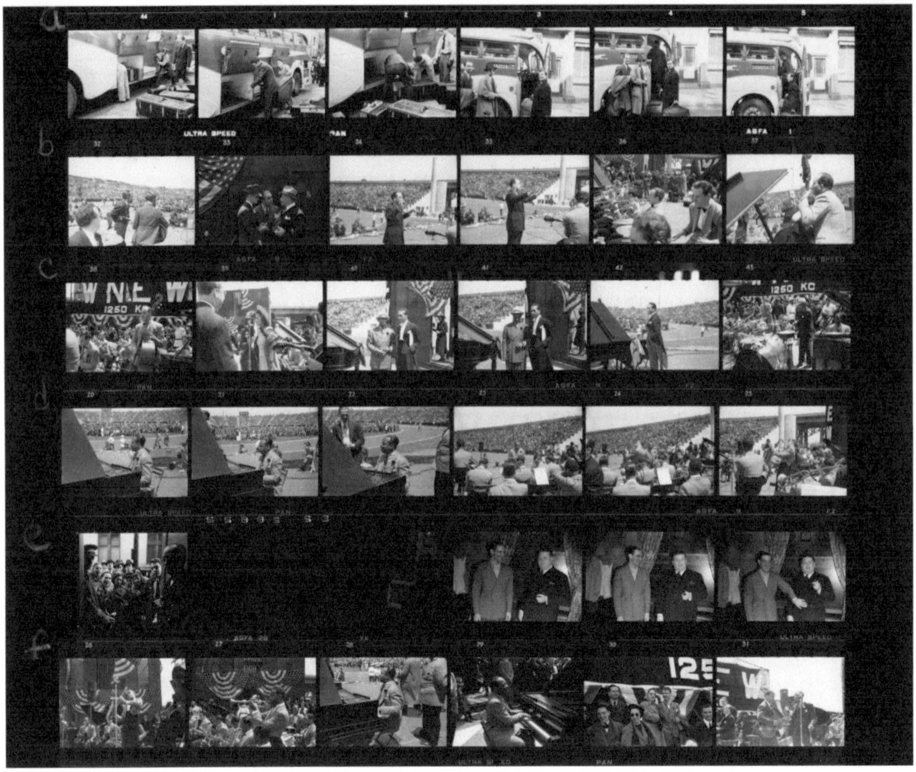

Figure 122: Otto Hess. Randall's Island contact sheets. 1938.
New York Public Library/Otto Hess Collection.

include iconic symbols of the American life in his framing choices. Hess's contact sheets from Louis Armstrong's Town Hall concert (almost certainly the concert of May 17, 1947, promoted by Ernie Anderson) show the photographer striving to convey a comprehensive sense of the moment. Moving between shots of the musician in his dressing room and from both front- and backstage, he made photographs of the building interior and audience members before, during, and after the performance (Figure 123). Like Ries, Hess's record of jazz events is in the nature of an immersive account through which the photographer strived to represent behaviors, spaces, and music as well as the personalities associated with the music.

The exile as portraitist

Gjon Mili

Gjon Mili was a portraitist of great sensitivity known for his photographs of celebrities, politicians, sportspeople, actors, and artists in *Life* magazine: "It seems that all my life I have done nothing but read faces," he recalled, adding "my basic intent is to establish character."[55] Most of the photographs Mili chose for a retrospective memoire are portraits in which he demonstrated the facility of the European exile to

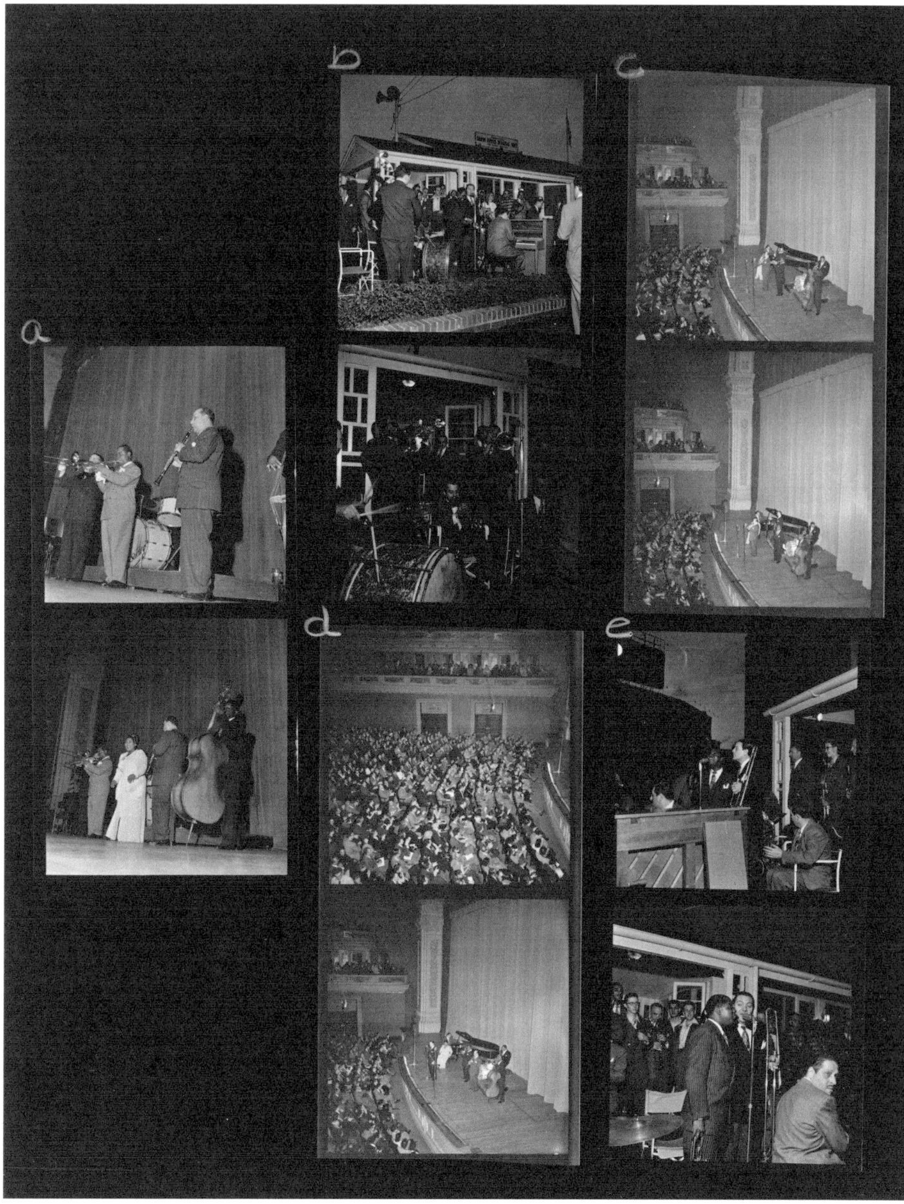

Figure 123: Otto Hess. Contact sheets from Louis Armstrong's Town Hall concert. n.d. *New York Public Library/Otto Hess Collection.*

enquire into the nature of artistry and the artistic personality. For Mili a shot of the artist's hands could say as much as a formal portrait and often did. Gently hinting at rather than imposing his views, photographs of artists such as Alexander Calder, the Budapest Quartet, Igor Stravinsky, Isaac Stern, Leopold Stokowski, Arthur Rubenstein, Ben Shahn, and popular singers like Frank Sinatra and Woody Guthrie tell us as much about the subjectivity of the exiled photographer as the sitter.

Mili is best known within the jazz community for the photographs he made at a staged jam session in 1943, stopped action shots of Lindy Hoppers and his film *Jammin' the Blues*. Born in 1904 in Korçë (present-day Albania), Mili had trained as an engineer and planned to follow a career in engineering once in America. After relocating in 1923 he was persuaded by fellow Albanian exile Faik Konitza to spend more time with film and photography and he added lighting and optics to his course in electrical engineering at MIT. He carried out research in lighting at Westinghouse for ten years, all the time continuing to explore new lighting ideas and equipment. In 1937 Mili became a freelance photographer and, after further experimentation with electronic flash, took the results to the newly founded *Life* magazine. *Life* editor and jazz enthusiast George Frazier suggested in 1943 that he set up and photograph a jazz jam session in Mili's two-story studio on East 23rd Street in New York City.

Mili had little interest in jazz but the session was a revelation, "not for the music itself—which sounded more like an outburst than a performance—but as a spectacle *non pareil*. It was a physical experience, compelling everyone's participation."[56] *Life's* connections assured a roster of big names, including Duke Ellington, Benny Goodman, James P. Johnson, Jess Stacey, Lee Wiley, Mary Lou Williams, Billie Holiday, and Cozy Cole, and the photographs from the session have often been reproduced as canonical to the jazz photography tradition. Benjamin Cawthra considers the session to have been a landmark event in foregrounding African American music and culture in what was otherwise a resolutely white publication, a "visual incursion of the cultural left into the pages of *Life* [. . .] an interracial art form at work" which "promoted African American artists as patriotic American nationalists."[57] For many jazz scholars the canonization of Mili as a jazz photographer was sealed the following year when he directed the short film *Jammin' the Blues* made by Warner Bros and featuring performances by Lester Young, Red Callender, Harry Edison, Sid Catlett, Illinois Jacquet, Barney Kessel, Jo Jones, and Marie Bryant. The film's style evokes Mili's multi-image still-frames of Lindy Hoppers and the imaginative use of the camera and lighting made this film a minor landmark in music film—and certainly the first to treat jazz seriously.

Framing the formerly closed practices of the jam session and "sitting in" as a spectacle for public gaze, Mili's images contributed an important—perhaps even defining—element to the construction of the myth of jazz. As Patrick Burke explains however, the commercialization and publicization of jam sessions, such as that represented by the *Life* session, was not without racial, artistic, and commercial tensions:[58]

> *Public jam sessions and their audiences represented the intensification of contradictory impulses that had pervaded 52nd. Street's jazz scene from its very beginning. These sessions ostensibly epitomized musical freedom and disregard for market concerns*

> *[. . .] supposedly sites of open-minded exchange among black and white musicians, they also exemplified the conflicts over race that affected 52nd. Street.*

Benjamin Cawthra highlights the significance of Mili's images of black artists in a mainstream publication, but the *Life* session photographs inevitably elided the tensions identified by Burke in an apparently untroubled portrayal of an integrated music with its associated tropes of night-time entertainment, drink, cigarette smoke, and elegant white spectators watching African American performers. The session also raises questions about Mili as a "jazz photographer" as it was something of an outlier within his *oeuvre*. Mili thought of the *Life* jam session more as a technical exercise, an opportunity to stretch his skills in creating atmospheric light conditions, and he devotes only six pages from a 250-page memoir to it.

On other occasions Gjon Mili made authentically evocative jazz imagery. With its off-kilter composition grabbed from a viewpoint deep in the audience, Mili's mid-1940s photograph in Café Society draws the viewer's eye toward the singer (occasionally identified as Billie Holiday) framed by affluent white patrons. Both as a document testifying to the audience and the nature of Barney Josephson's unique space and as an evocation of its atmosphere there are fewer more telling jazz photographs.

Francis Wolff

Almost all Francis Wolff's archive of over 30,000 photographs of jazz musicians were made in the context of Blue Note, the music label that Wolff ran with the founder and fellow German Jewish émigré Alfred Lion. With their distinctive lighting and compositional elegance, Wolff's presentations of jazz musicians embodied an aura of artistic transcendence that critics have linked with the label's artistic integrity and commitment to its artists.[59] It has been variously suggested that Wolff's style showed the influences of Yousuf Karsch's portraiture, European high culture, German 1920s expressionist cinema, and American film noir of the early-1930s.[60]

Wolff began photographing Blue Note sessions from the start of the company's operations, shooting almost every rehearsal between 1939 and 1967. Between 1953 and 1959 it was in the cramped conditions of Rudy Van Gelder's studio in Hackensack, New Jersey, that Wolff made many of his most notable photographs. With the advent of long-playing records in the mid-1950s his photography began to be used on Blue Note album covers designed by Paul Bacon, Gil Mellé, John Hermansader, and, a little later, Reid Miles, which have acquired the status of modern design classics.[61] As the demand for photography grew, Wolff used other locations, notably New York studios and streets as a backdrop for powerful portraits of players such as Thad Jones, Paul Chambers, Joe Henderson, Hank Mobley, and Grant Green and even captured Ornette Colman's trio in a snow-clad Scandinavian forest. On the whole, these location images lack the authorial focus of his studio work.

In the recording studio Wolff normally used a Rolleiflex twin-lens reflex loaded with Kodak Tri-X film. He would set the lens at f./8 or f./11 and use a flashgun held by hand off-camera.[62] Moving his flash around to create facial modeling and shadow effects, Wolff's aperture settings ensured that the ambient light of the studio surroundings hardly registered, the curtains, blinds, and lamps becoming indistinct compositional devices melting into a deep black background. Expressively lighted in this fashion, the musicians' skin tones were beautifully rendered and expressions of concentration perfectly captured. Turning cramped studio conditions to advantage, around half of Wolff's photographs employ a low camera angle, emphasizing the unique angle of view of the twin-lens Rolleiflex. Wolff, according to Michael Cuscuna, "was a fly on the wall. The musicians got used to his flash and it didn't disrupt anybody and he quickly became invisible. This allowed him to get pictures of the creative process without disturbing it. They were perfect portraits but they weren't posed portraits."[63] After arriving in America Wolff had abandoned darkroom work and his contact sheets and prints were processed by a specialist firm called Kennedy in Manhattan.

Wolff's photography has been extensively reproduced in books as well as a variety of different forms including calendars and postcards and is universally lauded by critics.[64] Less noticed has been the specific imprint of Jewish Weimar culture within which Wolff lived for nearly 30 years before his flight and the modalities of cultural exchange initiated by forced exile. Born in 1907, Jacob Franz ("Franny") Wolff's family were affluently bohemian and well-read; his father was a professor of mathematics, his mother had broad cultural interests and Wolff himself was "a softly-spoken, unobtrusive figure" with a penchant for modern suits and styling.[65] Always keen on jazz, Wolff was a member of the Berlin Melodie-Klub run by Hans Blüthner, a select group of around twenty young enthusiasts who met regularly at Café Hilbrich on the Kürstendamm to enjoy American recordings proscribed by the Nazis. The group was firmly middle class, with a smattering from the lower nobility such as Günther van Drenkmann, later West Berlin *Kammergerichtspräsident* and a victim of terrorism in 1974. For Jewish members the club offered the sustenance of belonging to German society rather than representing an act of rebellion against it, although members certainly took risks in making contact with black musicians like the trombonist Herb Fleming, whose International Rhythm Aces worked in Berlin at the time. The club eventually split into purist and more liberal factions, Wolff going along with Heinz Auerbach's faction which tended to favor only "black" jazz.[66]

Wolff became a commercial photographer in Berlin although we know little about his pre-America practice.[67] It is difficult to imagine that he was unaffected by "new vision" experimentation, and his appreciation of light and shade and the perceptual realignments of unusual viewpoints certainly hint at influences on Wolff of the Central European avant-garde. Wolff's style also bears comparison with the experimental advertising photography that began to appear from the 1920s onward in the German illustrated press. Here the boundaries between fashion, advertising, and avant-garde art were fluid as the modern in all its variety found common expression through photography. Wolff's concern with presentation and material culture paralleled the modernist chic deployed to sell expensive luxury products imported to America by Paul Outerbridge, Charles Sheeler, Clarence White, and Edward Steichen. His photographs offer little or no sense of performative context or the realities of the jazz life, and in effecting a visual shift toward the universal his images bear some of the hallmarks of the new vision.

The influence of Weimar culture on Wolff was however more than strictly photographic. Care is required when speaking of "Weimar culture" not to generalize from the political constructions attaching to the term.[68] Nevertheless it seems clear that jazz for Wolff was consistent with aspects of Weimar Berlin he found congenial. Berlin was a city with a hothouse identity of its own within the greater Germany: it was here that "un-German" Germans, liberals and Jews, *Aufklärer*, and the ironic and satiric outsiders of the Wilhelmian era promoted avant-garde art, opera, cinema, and literature. From the Expressionists, Bauhaus radicals, the *neue Sachlichkeit*, and Walter Gropius's Bauhaus prospectus to neo-Conservatives like Arthur Moeller and Oswald Spengler, there was a quest for cultural renewal, the cultivation of inner life, and articulation of religious and aesthetic sensibilities.[69] Conservatives and progressives fought over the meaning of culture, but most agreed on the importance of culture itself—not in the narrow sense of art and literature but as a national *Geist* in the "high" sense of everything noble. Adrift after the 1919 revolution, the German conception of *Kultur* and its companion idea of *Bildung* represented a sphere of freedom and pride. For many young people nothing seemed so attractive as the ragtime and syncopated music that echoed throughout the *Kabaretten* and dance halls, the raucous early jazz bands portrayed by Otto Dix, and the uninhibited jazz-inspired theatre of Paul Grunwald's *Variété* (1925) and scandalous new dances, but it could also be turned to conservative ends.[70]

Adherence to *Kultur* had been imbibed by Berlin's highly integrated Jewish population. Wolff's secularized bohemian family appears to have been typical of many Jewish families in which a deep allegiance to the central ideals of German culture, the liberal values of humanism, tolerance, and reason prevailed. While Russian Jews might deride the cultural tenacity of German-speaking *Yekke*, these were values and beliefs they took into exile.[71] The more the Nazi regime dismantled German culture, the more German refugees developed into a non-territorial "other Germany," which retained the main lines of pre-Nazi culture in a number of national contexts. As with so many other German-speaking Jewish exiles, Wolff took the cult of *Kultur* into exile; and it is precisely in this conjunction of "old world values" and American jazz as substitute for "Weimar modernism" that guided the construction of his identity in America and would so powerfully influence his photography. What Atina Grossmann has described as the "provincial cosmopolitanism" of those middle-class Germans refugees who clung provincially to German culture but which was combined with a cosmopolitan *Weltöffenichkeit* appears to describe Alfred Lion as much as his photographer partner, Francis Wolff.[72]

Like all émigrés and exiles, Wolff was forced to reconsider his own sense of selfhood once in America. That he carried over much of his cultural inheritance can be seen in the celebration of universal artistic achievement in photography. In these images we see Wolff holding firm to a deeply ingrained sense of *Kultur*, a German *Weltanscahauung* of wholeness and inner transcendence founded in an untouchable but communally rooted *Geist*. Clearly signed in the 1939 declaration of the new Blue Note label's plans was his and Lion's belief that such a communal rooting was to be found in jazz and its expressions of African American life:[73]

> *The uncompromising expression of hot jazz and swing [. . .] Any particular style of playing which represents an authentic way of musical feeling is genuine expression. By virtue of its significance in time, place and circumstance, it possesses its own tradition, artistic standards and audience that keeps it alive. Hot jazz, therefore, is expression and communication, a musical and social manifestation.*

Popular Front cultural policies, when jazz and leftist politics found common cause through the loose coalition of "white Patrician swing intellectuals, Jewish impresarios, and African American and white swing band leaders and musicians," facilitated the transition of this cultural inheritance into the American environment. Expressed in the shifting views of communists, socialists, and other radicals about the place of black culture, publications like the short-lived illustrated weekly *Friday*, the emergence of left-wing theatre, and what Michael Denning has called "Weimar on the Hudson" centered on Barney Josephson's integrated Café Society Downtown and Uptown, the period prompted a reappraisal of culture as a mixture of grassroots expression and a site of resistance.[74] Here, then, was an environment in which Wolff's ingrained sense of *Kultur* and youthful love of jazz might be recast as he sought identification with America. It was a supreme irony that Wolff should turn to the most mimetic of media to capture a longing for *geist*.

Fred Plaut

In his book *The Jazz Life* Nat Hentoff described the recording of Miles Davis's album "Sketches of Spain:"[75]

> *As more and more takes, most of them fragmentary, were tried, Miles' confidence in his own role grew markedly [. . .] He played as if all by himself, his tone becoming burningly dark in the somber passages and then cutting through with a sharper loneliness [. . .] At a few minutes past five, Fred Plaut began taking pictures during a playback. "This," said Plaut when the take was over, "is a life-time project."*

Exploring the souls of creative artists through photography was indeed a lifetime project for Fred Plaut. A German Jewish émigré who moved to America in 1940, Plaut worked for over 30 years at Columbia as a sound engineer where he was responsible for the majority of the Masterworks series, chamber performances, cast albums of Broadway shows, opera, and popular music. His many jazz sessions included landmark albums by Miles Davis, Dave Brubeck, and Charles Mingus. Plaut's thoughtful and informed approach to candid portraiture resulted in one of the most important photographic archives of the leading figures in American cultural life between 1940 and the early-1970s.

Plaut was born in Munich on May 12, 1907. He was educated at the City's Technical University and gained a degree in electrical engineering. Between 1933 and 1940 he lived in Paris, where he managed his own recording studio and worked as a consulting engineer for Polydor Records. He met Rose Kanter, a Polish-American soprano studying in France and the couple married in September 1938. Plaut spoke little about his early life in Germany and France, but there are indications that he might have been interned in Paris.[76] The couple moved to the United States in June 1940, securing a penthouse apartment in Manhattan that became the focus of their personal, social, and artistic life until Fred's retirement in early-1970s. After his retirement he joined the Yale School of Music as consultant and senior recording engineer and a few years later began teaching classes in recording methods.

Plaut made photographs throughout his life and rarely went anywhere without his camera; he was, as Gene Kimball recalled, "very relaxed with his camera." Eschewing posed shots, he made hundreds of candid portraits of artists such as Samuel Barber, Leonard Bernstein, Pablo Casals, Aaron Copeland, Glenn Gould, Dimitri Mitropoulos, Rudolf Serkin, Isaac Stern, Igor Stravinsky, Edgar Varese, and Bruno Walter. The Plauts entertained many guests from the world of arts, allowing Fred to take candid photographs of them in his apartment.[77] He recorded couple's frequent foreign travels during which he photographed Eleanor Roosevelt, Albert Schweizer, Francis Poulenc, Pierre Bernac, Alberto

Moravia, Pablo Picasso, Eugene Berman, and Janet Flanne, and made images of landscapes and people. Plaut's photograph of Stravinsky was seen by Edward Steichen who included him in at least five exhibitions staged by the Museum of Modern Art including *Music and Musicians* in 1947–47 and the 1955 *Family of Man* exhibition. "What Plaut has done," Steichen commented, was "to capture the emotions of musicians, using only his little camera and light as he found it."[78] Plaut's 1964 book, *The Unguarded Moment,* contained over 100 of his finest portraits, sensitively accompanied by carefully chosen quotations and brief text. His photographs have been exhibited at several important museums, appeared in magazines and as book illustrations and covers. Over 80 record album covers and concert programs have used his images.

Friends recall that Fred Plaut never lost his command of languages and his German accent was a reminder of the cultural inheritance on which he drew in making his "candid" portraits. Generally taken to mean those of unaware and unposed subjects, candid photography also takes on the meaning of directness, a frank exploration of inner subjectivity which forms the basis for the photographic portrait as an adventure in expressive narrative. It is with both senses of the term in mind that Plaut's photography should be approached. If the photograph was to be uniquely *his* probing of the subject, expressing as much his

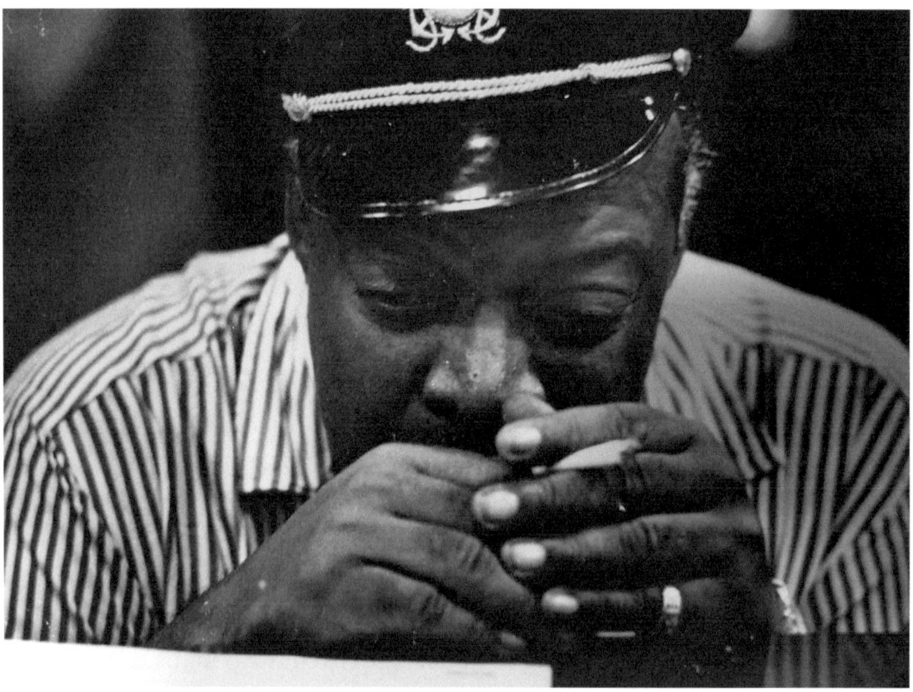

Figure 124: Fred Plaut. *Count Basie*. New York. n.d.
Fred Plaut Papers, Gilmore Music Library, Yale University.

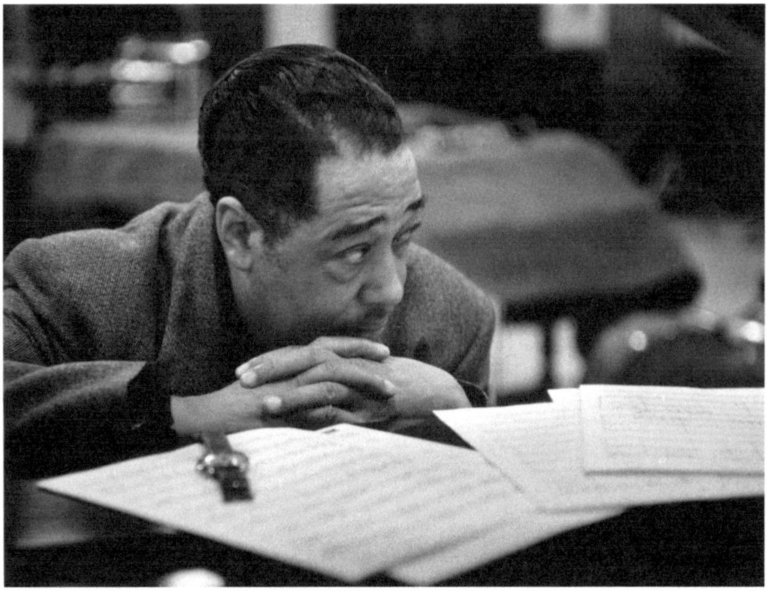

Figure 125: Fred Plaut. *Duke Ellington*. New York. n.d.
Fred Plaut Papers, Gilmore Music Library, Yale University.

own as the sitter's personality, it was crucial that it should be "candid." Gene Kimball stresses that Plaut would not accept money for his photography as a matter of principle; equally, "posing" would be equivalent to paying as ownership of the "unguarded moment" is transferred to the payer/sitter and away from the photographer.

In his jazz photographs Plaut strips away the public persona to reveal the inner strengths and vulnerabilities that accompany artistic intensity and accomplishment. The burdens of leadership appear momentarily to weigh heavily on Count Basie's shoulders, a leader whose success depended above all else on what most of the time appeared to band members to be his easy-going attitude (Figure 124). A rare moment of relaxed informality is conveyed in Plaut's image of Ella Fitzgerald, a side of the famously insecure and vulnerable singer rarely seen away from the performance stage. The craft and devotion to composition—much of it extemporized in the studio—which Ellington weaved around his individual players is signed in the photograph by the way in which Plaut has tellingly included the musical score and timepiece (Figure 125). There are certainly few photographs quite as expressive as Plaut's portrait of Louis Armstrong (Figure 126) taking a moment to reflect in the studio.

The "burning intensity" and "loneliness" which Nat Hentoff discerned in Miles Davis during the *Sketches of Spain* session were captured in Plaut's elegant portrait (Figure 127), an image that takes us to the heart of the photographer's

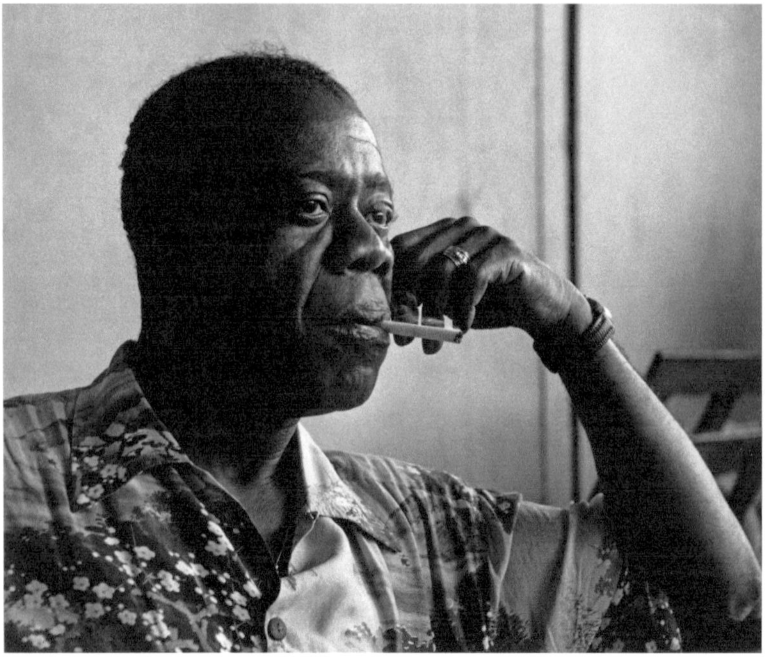

Figure 126: Fred Plaut. *Louis Armstrong*. New York. n.d.
Fred Plaut Papers, Gilmore Music Library, Yale University.

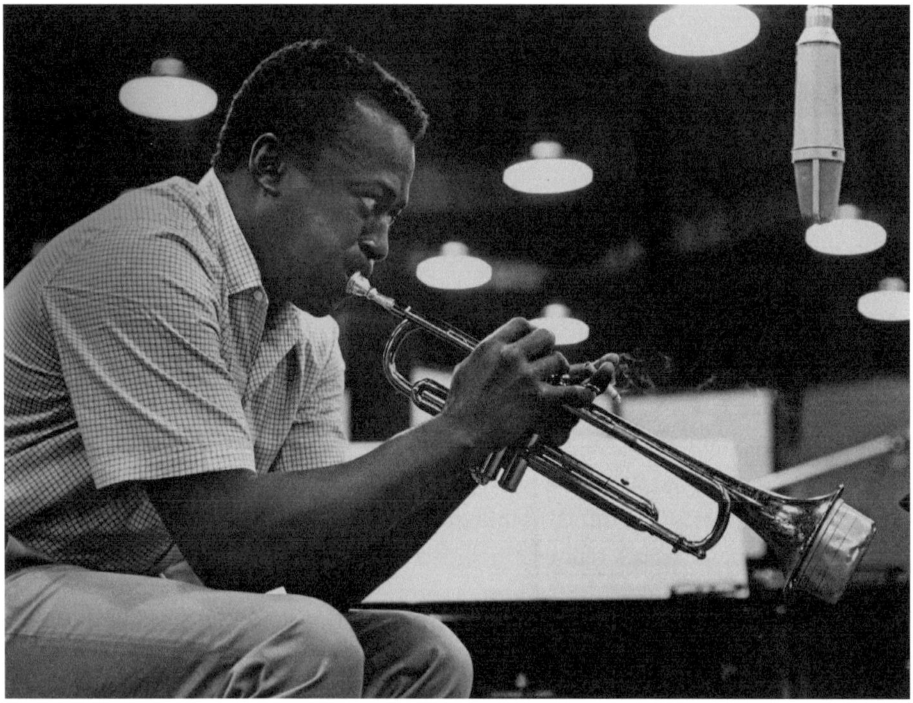

Figure 127: Fred Plaut. *Miles Davis' Sketches of Spain recording*. New York. n.d.
Fred Plaut Papers, Gilmore Music Library, Yale University.

own artistic philosophy. Speaking of Plaut's professional life as a sound engineer, Gene Kimball recalled his view that recording other artists' work was itself a work of art. Placing and balancing microphones for the session, he worked unobtrusively convinced that the best sound recording was that which brought out the finer qualities of the performance but was yet invisible to both the artist and the listener. There is a remarkable parallel with the photography in which Plaut sought to reveal the depths of the subject without declamatory stamp. Just as Plaut refused all offers by Columbia to move away from sound engineering into managerial positions because he would have had more direct influence on the nature of the session, he never wanted to define his subjects in photographs through the overt authorial presence. That definition would be self-revealed through the photograph so long as the "unguarded moment" was "candid." It was in the sense of both his absence and presence that the photograph became uniquely that of Fred Plaut.

Notes

1. Michel Foucault, "Of Other Spaces, Heterotopias," *Architecture, Mouvement, Continuité* 5 (1984): 46–49.
2. Edward Said, "Reflections on Exile," in *Out There: Marginalization and Contemporary Cultures*, ed. Russell Ferguson et al. (New York: MIT Press, 1990), 366.
3. Alland quoted in Codrescu and Pitts, *Reframing America*, 18. On Alland see further New York Historical Society, "Guide to the Alexander Alland Photograph Collection: Biographical Note," New York Historical Society Museum and Library, 2011 and Alexander Alland, *American Counterpoint*, ed. Pearl Buck (intro.) (New York: John Day, 1943), 147–58.
4. Laura Fermi, *Illustrious Immigrants: The Intellectual Migration from Europe 1930–41* (Chicago: University of Chicago Press, 1968), 233–47; R. Roger Remington, *American Modernism: Graphic Design 1920 to 1960* (London: Laurence King, 2003), 52–62; Martin Jay, "The German Migration: Is There a Figure in the Carpet?," in *Exiles and Émigrés: The Flight of European Artists from Hitler*, ed. Stephanie Barron (Los Angeles: Harry N. Abrams, 1997), 326–40.
5. Klaus Honnef and Frank Weyers, *Und Sie Haben Deutschland Verlassen ... Müssen. Fotografen Und Ihre Bilder 1928–1997* (Bonn: Rheinisches Landesmuseum, 1997), 496; Auer, *Ubersee: Flucht Und Emigration Osterreichischer Fotografen 1920–1940*; Max Kozloff, *New York: Capital of Photography* (New Haven: Yale University Press, 2002), 184–95.
6. Gary D. Saretzky, "Elias Goldensky: Wizard of Photography." *Philadelphia History* 64, no. 2 (1997): 206–72 .
7. Wolfgang Benz, *Das Exil Der Kleinen Leute: Alltagserfahrung Deutscher Juden in Der Emigration* (Frankfurt: Fischer, 1994); see also Andrea Hammel and Anthony Grenville, "Introduction," in *Exile and Everyday Life*, ed. Andrea Hammel and Anthony Grenville (Leiden: Brill Rodopi, 2015), xi–xv. André Kertész is the only full-time photographer to feature in Stephanie Barron's otherwise comprehensive survey of artists in exile *Exiles and Émigrés*. However, a number of important exhibitions have attempted to highlight the contribution made by immigrant photographers: Honnef and Weyers, *Und Sie Haben Deutschland Verlassen [. . .] Müssen. Fotografen Und Ihre Bilder, 1928–1997;* Barron, *Exiles and Émigrés; Übersee: Flucht Und Emigation Österreichenscher Fotografen 1920–40* (Kunsthalle Wien-Auer, Anna, 1998); Max Kozloff, *New York: Capital of Photography* (New Haven, CT: Yale University Press-Jewish Museum of New York, 2002); David Shneer and Lisa Tamiris Becker, *Through Soviet Jewish Eyes* (Boulder, CO: CU Art Museum, University of Colorado, 2011); Nissan N. Perez, *Displaced Visions: Émigré Photographers of the 20th Century* (Jerusalem: Israel Museum Jerusalem, 2013); Frauke V. Josenhans, *Artists in Exile: Expressions of Loss and Hope* (New Haven, CT: Yale University Press, 2017); and Codrescu and Pitts, *Reframing America*.
8. Hannah Arendt, "We Refugees," in *Altogether Elsewhere: Writers in Exile*, ed. Marc Robinson (Boston: Faber and Faber, 1994), 110–19; Marion Berghahn, "German Jews in England: Aspects of the Assimilation and Integration Process," in *Exile in Great Britain: Refugees from Hitler's Germany* (Atlantic Highlands, NJ: German Historical Institute, 1984), 288.
9. Sybil Milton, "Is There an Exile Art or Only Exile Artists?," in *Exil: Literatur Und Die Künst Nach 1933 (Studien Zur Literatur Der Moderne, No.17)* (Bonn: Bouvier, 1990), 83–89; Romy Golan, "On the Passage of a Few Persons through a Rather Brief Period of Time," in *Exiles and Émigrés* 144. See also John-Paul Stonnard, "Artists in Exile," *Burlington Magazine* 151, no. 1272 (2009): 185; Shulamith Behr and Sander L. Gilman, "Forced Journeys: An Introduction," in *Forced Journeys: Atists in Exile in Britain c.1933–45* (London: Jewish Museum of Art, 2009), 13; and Jay, "The German Migration: Is There a Figure in the Carpet?"
10. Asher D. Biemann, Richard I. Cohen, and Sarah E. Wobick-Segev, "Introduction," in *Spiritual Homelands: The Cultural Experience of Exile, Place and Displacement among Jews and Others*, ed. Asher D. Biemann, Richard I. Cohen, and Sarah E. Wobick-Segev (Berlin: DeGruyter, 2020), 2. Donald Peterson Kent provides an example of the older "absorptionist" approach when he described assimilation as "a process of absorption [. . .] It is he who elects to migrate, and it is he who must adapt to American culture:" Donald Peterson Kent, *The Refugee Intellectual: The Americanization of the Immigrants of 1933–41* (New York: Columbia University Press, 1953), 239.

11. For an example of the reassessment of migration theories in the light of emergentist theories see Oliver Bakewell, "Re-Launching Migration Systems," in *Second Workshop on Social Theory and Migration: What Post-Positivism, Critical Realism & Structuration Can Offer to Migration Studies* (Oxford: International Migration Institute/University of Oxford, 2012), 2–18.
12. Jay Geller, *The Other Jewish Question: Identifying the Jew and Making Sense of Modernity* (New York: Fordham University Press, 2011), 2; Michael Berkowitz, Susan L. Tannenbaum, and Sam W. Bloom, "Introduction: Anthologising Jews," in *Forging Modern Jewish Identities: Public Faces and Private Struggles*, ed. Michael Berkowitz, Susan L. Tannenbaum, and Sam W. Bloom (London: Vallentine Mitchell, 2003), 11. On the nature of Jewish identity see also Harvey E. Goldberg, "Dynamic Jewish Identities: Insights from a Comparative View," in *Dynamic Belonging: Contemporary Jewish Collective Identities*, ed. Harvey G. Goldbderg, Stephen M. Cohen, and Ezra Kopelowitz (New York: Berghahn Books, 2012), 1–27.
13. Said, "Reflections on Exile," 366. As a "stranger," "in but not of" the group, the exile can take a detached and interrogative view of the host culture. Georg Simmel, "The Stranger," in *The Sociology of Georg Simmel*, trans. and ed. Kurt Wolff (Glencoe: New York, 1950), 402–8; Edward A. Tiryakian, "Sociological Perspectives on the Stranger," *Soundings: An Interdisciplinary Journal* 56, no. 1 (1973): 46. Emily Bilski, "Introduction," in *Berlin Metropolis: Jews and the New Culture 1890–1918* (Berkeley: University of California Press, 1999), 4–5, notes that even before their flight German Jews had always been outsiders and this inherited mindset was reinforced after arriving in America. Julia Kristeva, "A New Type of Intellectual: The Dissident," in *The Kristeva Reader*, ed. Tori Moi (Oxford: Blackwell, 1986), 298–99, describes the position of the exile by posing the rhetorical question: "How can one avoid sinking into the more of common sense, if not by becoming a stranger to one's own country."
14. Eugenia Parry, *Lisette Model: A Narrative Biography* (Gottingen: Steidl, 2009), 49, 94–97.
15. Helen Roth, "The Bar Sammy's Bowery Follies as Microcosm and Photographic Milieu," in *Arrival Cities: Migrating Artists and New Metropolitan Topographies in the 20th Century*, ed. Burcu Dogramaci (Leuven: Leuven University Press, 2020), 293–313.
16. Frauke V. Josenhans, "(Re)Defining the 'I' in Exile," in *Artists in Exile*, 185.
17. Jabès cited by Tresa L. Grauer, "'The Changing Same': Narratives of Contemporary Jewish American Identity," in *Mapping Jewish Identities*, ed. Laurence J. Silberstein (New York: New York University Press, 2000), 37–64; Grauer takes Jabès as the starting point for an analysis of the way in which second-generation Jewish American writers have used writing "simultaneously as hermeneutic tools and as the subjects of interpretation" [37]; Ian Buruma, "V. S Naipaul (1932–2018)," *New York Review of Books* (2018): 16; Ruth Weisberg, "Between Exile and Irony: Modernism, Postmodernism, and Jewish Modes of Thought," in *You Should See Yourself: Jewish Identity in Postmodern American Culture*, ed. Vincent Brook (New Brunswick, NJ: Rutgers University Press, 2006), 166.
18. Peter Hamilton, "André Kertész," in *The Oxford Companion to the Photograph*, ed. Robin Lenman (Oxford: Oxford University Press, 2005), 340; see also Pierre Borhan, *André Kertész: A Lifetime in Photograpjy* (Boston: Bullfinch Press, 2000), 8–32. Philippe Halsman, "Autobiography," *Halsman Web Site*, 2015, http://philippe-halsman.com/halsman/autobiography/; Mary Panzer, "Introduction," in *Philippe Halsman: A Retrospective* (London: Pavillion Books, 1998), 7–11. Honnef and Weyers, *Und Sie Haben Deutschland Verlassen ... Müssen. Fotografen Und Ihre Bilder 1928–1997*, 86.
19. Ann Swidler, "Culture in Action: Symbols and Strategies," *American Sociological Review* 51, no. 2 (1986): 273–86.
20. Susan Morgan, *Martin Munkasci* (New York: Aperture, 1992), 46; Zoe C. Smith, "Fritz Goro on Tape: An Émigré Photojournalist's Professional Biography," paper presented at the Annual Meeting of the Association for Education in Journalism and Mass Communication (Memphis, TN, 1985); and Liz Ronk, "Photographer Spotlight: Fritz Goro," *Time-Life*, 2012. See further MacDonald Moore and Deborah Dash Moore, "Observant Jews and the Photographic Arena of Looks," in *You Should See Yourself: Jewish Identity in Postmodern American Culture*, ed. Vincent Brook (New Brunswick, NJ: Rutgers University Press, 2006), 183–84.
21. The importance of photo agencies has recently been highlighted by Anette Vowinkel, *Agenten Der Bilder. Fotografisches Handeln Im 20. Jahrhundert* (Göttingen: Wallstein, 2016). For a study of the founder of the Dephot agency, see

Nicholas Jacobs and Diethart Kerbs, "Wilhelm Simon Guttmann, 1891–1990: A Documentary Portrait," *German Life and Letters* 62, no. 2 (2009): 401–14.

22. Michael Torosian, *Black Star: The Ryerson University Historical Print Collection of the Black Star Publishing Company* (Toronto: Lumiere Press, 2013); Zoe C. Smith, "Black Star Picture Agency: Life's European Connection," *Journalism History* 13, no. 1 (1986): 19–25, https://files.eric.ed.gov/fulltext/ED244286.pdf.
23. Nissan N. Perez, "A Century of Migration," in *Displaced Visions: Émigré Photographers of the 20th Century*, 8–26; Frank Weyers, "Wendepunkte," in *Und Sie Haben Deutschland Verlassen ... Mussen: Fotografen Und Ihre Bilder 1928–1997*, 23.
24. György Kepes, *The Language of Vision* (Chicago: Paul Theobald, 1969), 13. John Berger, *Ways of Seeing* (Harmondsworth: Penguin Books, 1972), 7, might have had Kepes in mind when he suggested that "sight comes before words," that the visual impact is normally the first sensation to strike home and becomes the central orienting force for seeing. Julia Kristeva, "A New Type of Intellectual: The Dissident," in *The Kristeva Reader*, 293–94, argues that the shift from verbal to visual forms of dissent has been made possible by the condition of modernity. Henry R Luce, "Foreword," in *Eisenstaedt: Witness to Our Time* (London: Secker & Warburg, 1980), 7; Alex Kershaw, *Blood and Champagne: The Life and Times of Robert Capa* (London: Da Capa, 2020), 16, 258 fn.2; George Szirtes, "A Horse, a Circus and a Suit Case of Photographs," in *Eyewitness: Hungarian Photography in the Twentieth Century*, 34–41.
25. Norman L. Kleeblatt and Susan Chevlowe, "Painting a Place in America: Jewish Artists in New York, 1900–1945," in *Painting a Place in America: Jewish Artists in New York, 1900–1945: A Tribute to the Educational Alliance Art School*, ed. Norman L Kleeblatt and Susan Chevlowe (Bloomington: Indiana University Press, 1991), 101; Michael Kimmelman, "How Jewish Artists Found Their Place in New York," *New York Times* (1991): 73. Nachum T. Gidal, "Jews in Photography," in *Leo Baeck Institute Yearbook XXXII* (London: Secker & Warburg, 1987), 453; Goldberg, "Dynamic Jewish Identities: Insights from a Comparative View," 10.
26. Andrei Codrescu, "Notes on an Alien Son," in *Reframing America*, 13.
27. Hughes cited by Centre for Creative Photography, "Marion Palfi," https://ccp.arizona.edu/artists/marion-palfi; Arnold Rampersad, *The Life of Langston Hughes* (New York: Oxford University Press, 1988), 128.
28. Susanne Baumann, "The Essence of Things: An Interview with Ellen Auerbach," in *Ellen Auerbach: Berlin. Tel Aviv. Lond. New York* (Munich: Prestel, 1998), 9–14; Clara Sandler and Juan Mandelbaum, "Ellen Auerbach, 1906–2004," Jewish Women's Archive Encyclopedia https://jwa.org/encyclopedia/article/auerbach-ellen; Jenna Webster, "Ben Shahn and the Master Medium," in *Ben Shahn's New York: The Photography of Modern Times*, ed. Deborah Martin Kao, Laura Katzman, and Jenna Webster (Cambridge, MA: Harvard University Art Museum, 2000), 75–96.
29. Helmut Hess, "Mostly People: Erika Stone and New York Photography," in *Erika Stone: Mostly People: Photographs by a German Immigrant in New York*, ed. Erika Stone (Munich: Kehayoff); Beaumont Newhall, *The History of Photography from 1839 to the Present* (London: Secker & Warburg, 1982), 11 cites El Lizitzky's assessment of Mendelsohn's architectural photography as "America, not from the distance, but from the inside"; Lásló Moholy-Nagy, "A New Instrument of Vision," *Telehor* 1 (1936): 36.
30. Jane Livingstone, *The New York School: Photographs 1936–1963* (New York: Stewart, Tabori and Chang, 1992), 259–345. For the emergence of "The City as Subject," see Keith F. Davis, *An American Century of Photography: From Dry-Plate to Digital*, 2nd ed. (Kansas City, MO: Hallmark Cards, 1999), 64–66; Terence Pitts, "Reframing America," 15–17. Eli Lederhendler has described the "Great Urban Utopia" for Jewish immigrants in Eli Lederhendler, *New York Jews and the Decline of Urban Ethnicity 1950–1970* (Syracuse, NY: Syracuse University Press, 2001), 2–3, 1–9; Sarah Blair, *Harlem Crossroads: Black Writers and the Photograph in the Twentieth Century* (Princeton: Princeton University Press, 2007), esp. 14–15.
31. Max Kozloff, "Jewish Sensibility and the Photography of New York," in *New York: Capital of Photography*, 69–78; A. D. Coleman, "No Pictures: Some Thoughts on Jews in Photography," in *Übersee: Flucht Und Emigation Österreichenscher Fotografen*, 28–31. Gidal, "Jews in Photography," 437; Sarah Blair, "Jewish America through the Lens," *Michigan Quarterly Review* 42, no. 1 (2003): 95–132, stress the absence of any clear definition of "Jewish" photography and Richard B. Woodward, "Behind a Century of Photos, Was There a Jewish Eye?," *New York*

Times, July 7, 2002, 5.2, 1. asks why so many non-Jewish photographers appeared to speak the same language as Jews.

32. Mark Gerber, *Jazz Jews* (Nottingham: Five Leaves, 2009); and Michael Alexander, *Jazz Age Jews* (Princeton: Princeton University Press, 2001). Moore, *Yankee Blues: Musical Culture and American Identity*, 131–33, speaks of the "Jewish nexus" influencing the fusion of jazz and classical music that posed a challenge to Yankee leadership of musical culture. Bruce Boyd Raeburn, "Jewish Jazzmen in New Orleans 1890–1940: An Overview," *Jazz Archivist* 12, no. 1 (1997): 1–10, highlights the contribution of Jewish musicians such as the Korn brothers, Charlie Fischbein, Dave Winstein, Godfrey Hirsch, and Meyer Weinberg within the varied ethnic mix of New Orleans music making.
33. For the "affinity thesis" see Michael Goldfarb, "The Age of Reaction: Jews, Blacks and American Progress," *Jewish Quarterly* (2016): 20–25, and Nat Hentoff, who spoke of the warm embrace of "the family of Jazz" for Jewish "outsiders" like himself: "Jews in the Family of Jazz," *JazzTimes*, 2010, www.jazztimes.com. For the "exploitation" thesis see Michael Rogin, "Blackface, White Noise: The Jewish Jazz Singer Finds His Voice," *Critical Inquiry* 18, no. 3 (1992): 417–53; Jeffrey Melnick, *A Right to Sing the Blues: African Americans, Jews and American Popular Song* (Cambridge, MA: Harvard University Press, 1999) and the same author's "A Black Man in Jewface," in *Race and the Modern Artist*, ed. Heather Hathaway and Jeffrey Jar'ab, Josef-Melnick (New York: Oxford University Press, 2003), 126–39, focus on the exploitative aspects of the Jewish-Jazz relationship. Jeffrey S. Gurock, *Jews in Gotham: New York Jews in a Changing City, 1920–2010* (New York: New York University Press, 2012), 34–37, questions residential proximity as suggested by Charley Gerard, *Jazz in Black and White: Race, Culture, and Identity in the Jazz Community* (Westport, CT: Praeger, 1998), 103.
34. Charles B. Hersch, "Introduction," in *Jews and Jazz: Improvising Ethnicity* (New York: Routledge, 2017), n.pag. Cheryl Lynn Greenberg, "Introduction," in *Troubling the Waters: Black-Jewish Relations in the American Century* (Princeton: Princeton University Press, 2006), 5; Hasia R. Diner, "Drawn Together by Self-Interest: Jewish Representation of Race and Race Relations in the Early Twentieth Century," in *African Americans and Jews in the Twentieth Century: Studies in Convergence and Conflicy*, ed. V. P. Franklin, Nancy L. Grant, Harold M. Kletnick and Genna Rae McNeil (Columbia: University of Missouri Press, 1998), 27–39. Mark K. Bauman, "On German American and American Jewish History," *Journal of American Ethnic History* 29, no. 1 (2009): 70 fn.5, provides a useful summary of scholarly research into the problematic relationship between southern Jews, many of whom were slave-owners, and African Americans.
35. Larry Silver and Samantha Baskind, "Looking Jewish: The State of Research on Modern Jewish Art," *Jewish Quarterly Review* 101, no. 4 (2011): 631–52, argue that Jewish art generally has been underresearched until recently.
36. Jennifer Young, "Beyond the Color Line: Jews, Blacks and the American Racial Imagination," *In Geveb: A Journal of Yiddish Studies* (June 2016): 2.
37. Andrew Miles, "Addressing the Problem of Cultural Anchoring: An Identity-Based Model of Culture in Action," *Social Psychology Quarterly* 77, no. 2 (2014): 210–27.
38. Elan Ezrachi, "In Search of Roots and Routes: The Making and Remaking of the Diasporic Jewish Identity," in *Dynamic Belonging: Contemporary Jewish Collective Identities*, ed. Harvey G. Goldbderg, Stephen M. Cohen, and Ezra Kopelowitz (New York: Berghahn Books, 2012), 209; Julia Vinzent, "The Other as Other: Refugee Artists and Black Subjects," in *Forced Journeys: Artists in Exile in Britain c.1933–45*, ed. Shulamith Behr and Sander L. Gilman (London: Ben Uri Gallery, 2009), 80–85.
39. Gerard, *Jazz in Black and White: Race, Culture, and Identity in the Jazz Community*, 104.
40. Edward Said, "East Isn't East: The Impending End of the Age of Orientalism," *Times Literary Supplement* (February 3, 1995): 3.
41. Diner, "Drawn Together by Self-Interest: Jewish Representation of Race and Race Relations in the Early Twentieth Century," 36, 37.
42. Roland Barthes, *Camera Lucida: Reflections on Photography*, trans. Richard Howard (London: Vintage Books, 2000), 12–13; Jack Kugelmass, "Jewish Icons: Envisioning the Self in Images of the Other," in *Jews and Other Differences: The New Jewish Cultural Studies*, ed. Jonathan Boyarin and Daniel Boyarin (Minneapolis: University of Minnesota Press, 1997), 46–47. Maris Damon, "Jazz-Jews, Jive and Gender: The Ethnic Problems of Jazz Argot," in *Jews and Other Differences*, ed. Jonathan Boyarin and

Daniel Boyarin (Minneapolis: University of Minnesota Press, 1997), 150–75. Swidler, "Culture in Action: Symbols and Strategies," 277, speaks of culture as comprising a "tool-kit" or repertoire from which actors select differing pieces for the constructing lines of action.

43. Colin Westerbeck and Joel Meyerowitz, *Bystander: A History of Street Photography* (Boston, MA: Little Brown, 1994), 335–41. See also Miles Orvell, "Weegee's Voyeurism and the Mastery of Urban Disorder," *American Art* 6, no. 1 (1992): 18–41.
44. Daniel Morris, "Introduction," in *After Weegee: Essays on Contemporary Jewish American Photographers* (Syracuse, NY: Syracuse University Press, 2011), 10; Samantha Baskind, "Weegee's Jewishness," *History of Photography Journal* 34, no. 1 (2010): 60–78; Samatha Baskind, "Navigating the Worldly and the Divine: Jewish AmericaN Artists on Judaism and Their Art," *Shofar: An Interdisciplinary Journal of Jewish Studies* 32, no. 1 (2013): 30–35.
45. Steiner's encounter with Model and its consequences is described by Jason E. Hill, *Artist as Reporter: Weegee, Ad Reinhardt and the PM News Picture* (Oakland: University of California Press, 2018), 117–60. For Model's life and work see Parry, *Lisette Model: A Narrative Biography*; Ann Thomas, "Lisette Model," in *Lisette Model* (Ottawa: National Gallery of Canada, 1990), 26–174; Berenice Abbott, "Preface," in *Lisette Model* (New York: Aperture, 1979), n.pag; and David Chandler, "Lisette Model," in *Lisette Model*, ed. David Chandler (London: The Photographers' Gallery, 1991).
46. Lisette Model, "Before I Started to Be a Photographer, I Was a Musician," in *Lisette Model: Fotografen 1934–1960*, ed. Edek Bartz (Wien: Kunsthalle Wien, 2000), 71.
47. Kalischer's photographs have been published in a number of book: Marc Vausort and Xavier Canonne, *Clemens Kalischer: Le Flux Du Quotidien* (Charleroi: Musée de la Photographie, n.d.); Clemens Kalischer, *New York-Photographieren 1947–1959* (Brochiert, n.d.) and Clemens Kalischer, "A Photographic Selection (1948–1966)," *Ploughshares* 6, no. 2 (1980): 107–14. An account of Kalischer's life is provided by Scott Christian, "Photographer Clemens Kalischer Survived Holocaust but Struggles to Adapt," *Forward*, 2013.
48. Tanya Kalischer, Correspondence with the Author, 2020.
49. John Gennari recalls that Kalischer was indifferent toward jazz and his real love was classical music. Gennari estimates that Kalischer made some 500 images at Music Inn and the School of Jazz: John Gennari, "Photographing the Jazz Salon: Clemens Kalischer at Music Inn," unpublished paper presented at the *Documenting Jazz Conference, Dublin*, 2019 and correspondence with the author (September 2017). John Gennari, *Blowin' Hot and Cool: Jazz and Its Critics* (Chicago: University of Chicago Press, 2006), 210, describes the origins of these events.
50. Gennari, "Photographing the Jazz Salon." I am also extremely grateful to John Gennari for sharing draft text on Kalischer and the Music Inn from a forthcoming book. The observation about republican high-mindedness was developed in discussions of his text in correspondence.
51. See Henry Ries, *Ich War Ein Berliner: Erinnerungen Eines New Yorker Fotojournalisten* (Berlin: Parthas Verlag, 2001); Ellen Handy (ed.), *Reflections in a Glass Eye: Works from the International Centre of Photography Collections* (Boston, MA: Little Brown, 1999), 225–26.
52. In an interview in 1999, Ries told Sybil Milton that it was his Berlin people portraits that most interested him: Sybil Milton, "Henry Ries," *History of Photography* 23, no. 4 (1999): 359.
53. Ries, *Ich War Ein Berliner*, 32–35, reproduces these photographs. Ken Burns also reproduces several of Ries's photographs in Ward and Burns, *Jazz: A History of America's Music*, 260–61.
54. Jessica Wood, "Carnival of Swing: Uncovering an Historic Jazz Concert at Randall's Island Stadium, 1938," New York Public Library, 2018, https://www.nypl.org/blog/2018/09/25/carnival-swing-jazz-randalls-island-stadium-photos-1938; Isaac Maupin, "Photographing the Carnival of Swing: An Immigrant's Perspective on the First Jazz Festival," unpublished paper presented to the *Documenting Jazz Conference, Dublin*, 2019. I am grateful to Isaac Maupin for his suggestions at this point.
55. Mili, *Gjon Mili: Photographs and Recollections*, 140.
56. *Gjon Mili: Photographs and Recollections* (Boston, MA: New York Graphic Society, 1980), 168, describes the sessions and reproduces photographs between 168 and 171.
57. Cawthra, *Blue Notes in Black and White: Photography and Jazz*, 47.
58. Patrick Burke, *Come In and Hear the Truth: Jazz and Race on 52nd. Street* (Chicago: University of Chicago Press, 2008), 154.
59. Joe Maita, "Michael Cuscuna Announces the Release of Francis Wolff's Blue Note

Session Photographs," Jerry Jazz Musician, 2019, https://jerryjazzmusician.com/2019/08/michael-cuscuna-discusses-the-release-of-francis-wolffs-blue-note-session-photographs/ announced the release in a new website where some 3,500 of Wolff's Blue Note photographs can be viewed. Stan Britt, *Long Tall Dexter: A Critical Musical Bibliography of Dexter Gordon* (London: Quartet Books, 1989), 81, offers just one of many testimonies to Lion and Wolff's integrity and commitment to their artists; Paul Bacon, "The High Priest of Bebop: The Inimitable Mr. Monk," in *The Thelonious Monk Reader*, ed. Rob van der Bliek (Oxford: Oxford University Press, 2001), 61, recalls Blue Note as "a firm of almost suicidal integrity."

60. Cuscuna, "Alfred Lion, Francis Wolff and Blue Note Records," in *Blue Note Photos: Francis Wolff* (Paris: Flammarion, 2014), 14. Richard Cook, *Blue Note Records: The Biography* (London: Secker & Warburg, 2001), 13, stresses the influence of "European cultural values"; Cawthra, *Blue Notes in Black and White,* 204, 314, fn.134, speaks of German expressionism and film noir but acknowledges "the association between jazz and film noir is largely a recent nostalgic invention."
61. Tony Whyton, *Jazz Icons: Heroes, Myths and the Jazz Tradition* (Cambridge: Cambridge University Press, 2010), 7, interprets the "cultural borrowings" of Blue Note's artwork as "indicative of an attempt to establish a distinct experimental art aesthetic for jazz," but one should be wary of retrospective interpretation. The distinctive duo-tone album graphics and tinted photography were originally adopted because the label could not afford the four-color process. Similar financial constraints dictated Wolff's almost exclusive use of monochrome film stock and it wasn't until 1961 that Wolff shot his first color rolls at an Art Blakey session. On Reid Miles' Blue Notes cover designs, see further Shipton, *The Art of Jazz: A Visual History,* 152–59, and Graham Marsh and Glyn Callingham, *The Cover Art of Blue Note Records: The Collection* (London: Collins and Brown, 2010).
62. Michael Cuscuna, Charlie Lourie, and Oscar Schnider, *Blue Note Jazz Photography of Francis Wolff* (New York: Universe, 2000), 6 fns.136 and 137, 314, cite Rudy Van Gelder's account of Wolff's working methods.
63. Michael Cuscuna, Interview with the Author, 2018. Benjamin Cawthra, *Blue Notes in Black and White: Photography and Jazz,* fns.136 and 137, 314, quotes Herbie Hancock's comment that Wolff was "easy-going and didn't talk very much. He stayed pretty much in the background" while Sonny Rollins remembered him as "unobtrusive when he was taking photographs."
64. Cuscuna, *Blue Note Jazz,* 6–7 describes Wolff as a "master photographer [. . .] His ability to light, frame and capture a shot was astonishing [. . .] The majesty and power of the music and the personality of the musicians come alive through Francis Wolff's loving and caring eye"; Richard Cook, *Blue Note Records: The Biography* (London: Secker & Warburg, 2001), 81, says Wolff's photography, "catches the atmosphere as much as it memorializes the musicians. The players [. . .] seem to emerge from complete darkness [. . .] Beautiful faces and expressive eyes and mouths dominate the frame. Saxophones glint like polished weapons; trumpets and trombones muster a metallic shine." See also Krin Gabbard, "Images of Jazz," in *The Cambridge Companion to Jazz,* ed. Mervyn Cooke and David Horn (Cambridge: Cambridge University Press, 2002), 337; and Cuscuna, Lourie, and Schnider, *Blue Note Jazz Photography of Francis Wolff,* 6.
65. Michael Cuscuna, "Alfred Lion, Francis Wolff and Blue Note Records 3–14"; Cuscuna, Lourie, and Schnider, *Blue Note Jazz Photography of Francis Wolff,* 5–7; Cook, *Blue Note Records: The Biography,* 13.
66. Michael H. Kater, *Different Drummers: Jazz in the Culture of Nazi Germany* (New York: Oxford University Press, 1992), 75, 83–85, 98; Thomas Schmidt, "Das Erste Opfer Des Linksterrorismus," Welt Digital, 2010, https://www.welt.de/politik/deutschland/article10918644/Das-erste-Opfer-des-Linksterrorismus.html; Matthias Reichelt, "It Must Schwing-Blue Note," Zukunft braucht Erinnerung, 2010, https://www.zukunft-braucht-erinnerung.de/it-must-schwing-blue-note/. Jonathan O. Wipplinger, *The Jazz Republic: Music, Race and American Culture in Weimar Germany* (Ann Arbor: University of Michigan Press, 2017), 2–3, contextualizes black jazz in Weimar culture.
67. Michael Cuscuna, Interview with the Author, 2018, recalled that even Alfred Lion knew little about Wolff's professional work in Berlin.
68. See Jochen Hung and Godela Weiss-Sussex, eds., Beyond, *Glitter and Doom: The Contingency of the Weimar Republic* (Munich: Germanic Studies Institute, 2012), in which several contributors question the received "dancing on the volcano" view of the experiment in German

democracy as a mixture of modernist glitter and socioeconomic doom. I am grateful to Jochen Hung for his comments on this section and for drawing my attention to recent critical scholarship on "Weimar culture".

69. Golo Mann, *The History of Germany since 1789* (London: Penguin Books, 1990), 606; Richard J. Evans, *The Coming of the Third Reich* (London: Penguin Books, 2003), 118–53; Peter Gay, *Weimar Culture: The Outsider as Insider* (New York: Harper & Row, 1968), 128–31. Jochen Hung, "'Der Deutschen Jugend!' The Newspaper Tempo and the Generational Discourse of the Weimar Republic," in *Beyond Glitter and Doom; The Contingency of the Weimar Republic*, 105–18.
70. Wolf Lepenies, *The Seduction of Culture in German History* (Princeton, NJ: Princeton University Press, 2006), 9–26; Elias Norbert, *The Germans: Power Struggles and the Development of Habitus in the Nineteenth and Twentieth Centuries* (New York Columbia University Press, 1996), 126– 27.
71. Karl A. Schleunes, *The Twisted Road to Auschwitz: Nazi Policy Towards German Jews 1933–39* (London: André Deutsch, 1972), 38. Steven M. Lowenstein, *Frankfurt on the Hudson: The German-Jewish Community of Washington Heights, 1933–1983, Its Structure and Culture* (Detroit: Wayne State University Press, 1989), 185, recalls a strong commitment within the Jewish community of Washington Heights to German bourgeois high culture.
Marion Berghahn found a similar "highly developed sense for 'culture' and refinement" among German Jewish refugees in England, a passion for collecting objects of art and a lively interest in literature: Berghahn, "German Jews in England: Aspects of the Assimilation and Integration Process," 299.
72. Jacob Katz, *Out of the Ghetto: The Social Background of Jewish Emancipation, 1770–1870* (New York: Schocken Books, 1978), 6; Martin Jay, "Review of Lepenies," *Central European History* 40, no. 2 (2007): 343–45; Atina Grossman, "German Jews as Provincial Cosmopolitans: Reflections from the Upper West Side," *Leo Baeck Institute Year Book* 53, no. 1 (2008): 162.
73. Cook, *Blue Note Records: The Biography*, 12.
74. Lewis A. Erenberg, *Swingin' the Dream: Big Band Jazz and the Rebirth of American Culture* (Chicago: University of Chicago Press, 1998), 144–49; David W. Stowe, "The Politics of Cafe Society," *Journal of American History* 84, no. 4 (1988): 1391; David W. Stowe, *Swing Changes: Big-Band Jazz in New Deal America* (Cambridge, MA: Harvard University Press, 1998), 53–54: Mark Naison, *Communists in Harlem during the Depression* (Urbana: University of Illinois Press, 1983), 211–14; 298–301; Michael Denning, *The Cultural Front: The Laboring of American Culture in the Twentieth Century* (London: Verso, 1996), 156–57; Whitney Balliettt, "Night Clubs," *New Yorker* (October 8, 1971): 50–65.
75. Nat Hentoff, *The Jazz Life* (New York: Da Capo, 1975), 133, 136.
76. Gene Kimball, Interview with the Author, 2018, Dan Mortensen, Interview with the Author, 2018. Much of the biographical information in this section was kindly provided by Mr. Kimball while Dan Mortensen provided valuable information about the Columbia studio and recording techniques during Plaut's time.
77. Claudio Spies, "Two Apparently Disparate Paragraphs," *Music Theory Spectrum* 34, no. 1 (2012): 25, provides a brief account of the photographer's working methods: "we trooped on to the Plauts' apartment where we were offered delicious pastries and coffee [. . .] the assembled entourage began to maneuver so as to sit close to Stravinsky on a couch near which Mr. Plaut had set up his camera for an obviously expected picture-taking session [. . .] Milton and I, who disliked these goings on, withdrew without a further word".
78. Steichen cited by Barnett Bildersee, "Music and Musicians," *Bulletin of the Museum of Modern Art* 15, no. 2 (1948): 7.

10

Looking Back, Looking Forward

Jazz Photography after 1960

Bert Stern, a mercurial fashion and celebrity photographer; Bill Bernbach, a pioneering advertising executive who redefined the place of Madison Avenue in American commercial culture; and Louis Armstrong, a musician born in poverty in New Orleans and one of America's most successful and revered entertainers. There could not have been three more different personalities yet their paths coincided to remarkable effect in the unlikely setting of an advertising campaign launched by the Polaroid Corporation. This is a story of three cultural outsiders united around a single photograph and a turning point in the relationship between jazz and photography.

A little over ten years after William Gottlieb left the jazz scene, Bert Stern was commissioned in 1959 by Polaroid to make a photograph of Louis Armstrong as part of a series of portraits for a national advertising campaign. The image was subsequently used extensively in publicity material by Joe Glazer's American Booking Corporation (Figure 128). Known for his fashion and celebrity portraiture, Stern was born in Brooklyn in 1929 to a family of Jewish immigrants. He dropped out of school at 16 but was encouraged to pursue photography by Stanley Kubrick while working in the mailroom at *Life* in the late-1940s. Inspired, iconoclastic, and almost uncontrollably volatile, Stern's reputation quickly grew and it was not long before he became a mainstay for leading fashion magazines such as *Vogue*. He famously captured Marilyn Monroe in *The Last Sitting*, the actress's last group of portraits taken six weeks before her death.[1]

Looking back on his career, Stern confirmed the importance of photography in shaping the identity of a Jewish outsider:[2]

> *At that time I was a photographer and a pretty good one at that [. . .] I was getting a lot of work in advertising. I took audacious pictures that got people to want things [. . .] For a kid from a medium-poor Brooklyn family, I was on my way [. . .] I was beginning to realize that the American dream machine really existed. For me it took the shape of a camera. As long as I carried one around it was amazing what I could get, and who I could get. A lot of my wildest dreams were beginning to come true.*

Stern flourished during a period of cultural change, "a cultural provocateur who defined the creative revolution with his seminal Smirnoff-vodka ads [. . .] He was the first photographer superstar and his Manhattan studio became a crossroads of '60s pop culture."[3] From his earliest days Stern was always conscious of being a cultural pioneer: "I was the first juke-box photographer. It went right back to my beginnings at the soda fountain, where I used to make artistic ice cream sodas in six colors [. . .] to the accompaniment of the juke-box."[4] He brought an acute cultural awareness to his photography, which was revealed in campaigns for Martini, Revlon, and Smirnoff and which made him rich.

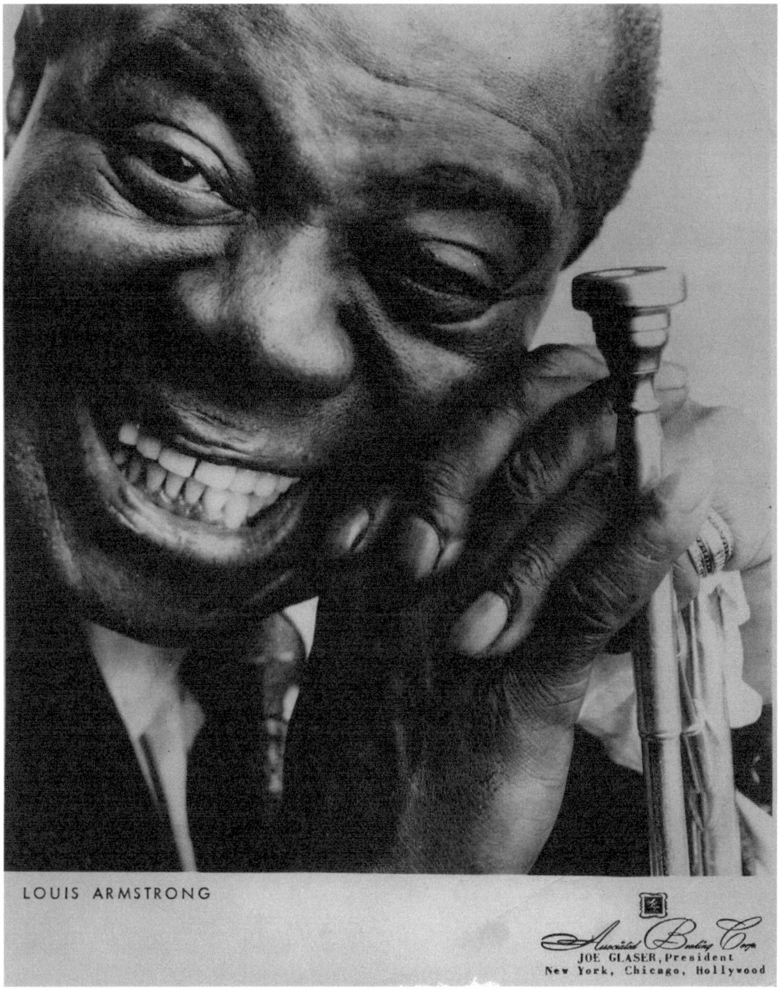

Figure 128: Bert Stern. *Louis Armstrong.* ABC promotional material using Polaroid advertisement photograph. 1959.
Louis Armstrong House Museum.

And it was precisely this cultural awareness that links Stern with jazz. Stern's best-known foray into the field is as a director of *Jazz on a Summer's Day*, the documentary film of the 1958 Newport Jazz Festival. It has been pointed out that Stern had little appreciation of jazz before making the film, but this perhaps misunderstands the broad affinity between artistic expression and cultural forces. What drew him to the subject was, as Nate Chinen puts it, "jazz's flirtation with Newport leisure and luxury [. . .] a popular perception of the music as something glamorous and modern [. . .] jazz's growing traction with the worlds of high fashion and Madison Avenue style."[5] This potent if broad cultural affinity led Stern to other points of contact with jazz. A little-known collection of contact sheets and prints in the New York Public Library's Schomberg Centre shows how the photographer melded contemporary fashion aesthetic with jazz. This collection includes portraits of Gerry Mulligan (posing with Monique Chevier for *Vogue* in 1962), Jack Teagarden, Dinah Washington, Sonny Stitt, George Shearing, Benny Goodman, and Art Farmer, all immaculately dressed and shown to best advantage in moody subtly lighted images printed on large format luster stock. Pride of place in this collection must go to the striking close-up image of Louis Armstrong shown above.

Stern's pioneering approach to advertising photography had impressed Bill Bernbach, a founder of the Madison Avenue firm Doyle Dane Bernbach. Like Stern, Bernbach was also an outsider. While the two men could hardly have been more different, both were born and raised in New York City into modest, but aspirational, Jewish immigrant families and both faced the challenge of accommodating to American culture in the New York public school system. Both were cultural iconoclasts.[6] Starting with the William Weintraub agency, Bernbach worked closely with art director Paul Rand. Steeped in the visual language of modern European graphic design and the German *Sachplakat* movement, Rand (born Peretz Rosenbaum) used collage techniques, dynamic composition, and modern-style typography. The combination of art and copy in dynamic new forms would emerge as the hallmark of Bernbach's advertising creed at DDB where he combined copywriters and art directors in the same team, redefining the role of the photograph and text.[7] Coming to WASP-dominated Madison Avenue as an outsider.[8]

> *Bill Bernbach used his exceptionality as both a Jew and a creative trendsetter to set new industry standards. Under the creative direction of Bernbach, DDB launched a legendary advertising revolution [. . .] Capitalizing on the rebellious mood of the sixties, thanks to disillusions over Vietnam and Civil Rights, Bernbach in turn created revolutionary ads.*

Stern's pioneering approach chimed with the changes then taking place among the advertising agencies of Madison Avenue and of which Bernbach was the leading representative. The Polaroid campaign built on DDB's work for Levy's Rye Bread, which used closely cropped photographs of ordinary people drawn from very different walks of life, their expressive faces characterizing the authentic America in all its diversity.[9] Bernbach's genius lay in harnessing people's skepticism of consumerism and mass conformity itself. He rejected the market research and algorithms of advertising convention and replaced them with aesthetic inspiration; in their simplicity and directness his advertisements enabled viewers to reject those values while at the same time enticing them to buy. Stern picked up on the idea producing a series of celebrity portraits featuring husband and wife actors Jessica Tandy and Hume Cronyn as well as Armstrong—personalities who

Bernbach and Stern saw as iconically representative of mainstream culture—to which Stern's Salvador Dali portrait brought his own brand of commercialized modernism. A remarkable image in its own right, the impact of Stern's portrait of Armstrong derives directly from the way it brilliantly leverages the musician's status at the very heart of American culture—a position consolidated just one year later when the musician embarked on the State Department tour of 1960. Its credibility rests on the widely perceived authenticity of the musician, the glowing humanity of his facial features, and the acceptance of commercialized jazz as a mainstream art form—a powerful statement of artistic universality achieved through an assertion of unabashed individuality.

Jazz, photography, and photographers after 1960

Americans hoped life would return to normal after 1945, but the war released social, economic, and cultural changes with their own unstoppable dynamic. The reconversion of the immediate postwar period was fraught but laid the basis for the affluent consumer society of the Eisenhower years and the rapidly growing autonomy of mass communications. The external threat of Cold War with an identifiable enemy fostered consensus around American values, albeit marked by an inward-looking and experiential frame of mind. Yet any consensus forged by the Cold War broke down in the social and racial conflicts in the 1960s and the civil rights movement. Youth culture emerged as a potent cultural and political force underpinned by the growing economic presence of the new generation; for the first time rebellious youth created their own musical identity in the form of rock 'n' roll instead of appropriating an existing form, as had been the case with jazz. The ease and frequency of travel and cross-border communications sealed the transition to a culture marked by cross-currents of opinion and social action.

The context encouraged jazz artists to reimagine the music and its future. Virtually all jazz histories describe the diversification of the music from the 1960s onward. Ted Gioia locates a fragmentation of jazz styles in the immediate post-bop era, Stephen B. Elworth speaks of the years between 1948 and 1958 as those of "crisis" for jazz, while Alyn Shipton prefers to focus on the "postmodern" jazz of the 1970s; and John F. Szwed takes the middle road in locating the "splintering of the jazz tradition" in the 1960s, drawing on changes in the previous decade and extending into the mid-1970s. Whatever the precise date, a new tone was clearly discernable in Whitney Balliett's first jazz review in the April 13, 1957, *New Yorker,* which predicted the potential influence of Cecil Taylor's album *Jazz Advance* ("Progress") in contrast to Gerry Mulligan's *Jazz Mainstream* ("Prudence").[10]

The next few years were transformative, sealing jazz's status as art music and redefining its relationship with mainstream culture. With Charles Mingus's *Mingus Ah Um,* Ornette Coleman's *The Shape of Jazz to Come,* and Dave Brubeck's *Time Out,* jazz struck out in radically new directions. The nuanced trumpet of

Miles Davis with *Kind of Blue* revolutionized jazz audiences and listening practices and redefined the presentation of the black male jazz musician. Although Davis and Mingus identified their music with a black aesthetic, musical crossovers shifted the understanding of jazz as a form of cultural production in what Richard Williams has called the "Blue Moment" turning point. Within two years Booker Little's experiments with the expressive range of the bebop idiom with Eric Dolphy amounted to nothing less than a "deconstruction" of the jazz ensemble; John Coltrane, Archie Shepp, Pharoah Sanders, and Cecil Taylor were powering "new thing" avant-garde jazz at the same time as the cultural and racial impetus of Chicago's Association for the Advancement of Creative Musicians found expression in the work of the Art Ensemble of Chicago.[11]

If mainstreaming took jazz in one direction, the civil rights movements took it in another. It is important not to impute direct correlations between music styles such as free or avant-garde jazz and sociopolitical movements. Nevertheless few would dissent from Ken Burn's assertion that by the 1960s some black musicians saw their mission not only radically to advance the music but to reclaim it for the black community. Black assertiveness found a voice with the work of Nina Simone, Max Roach, Sonny Rollins, Charles Mingus, and John Coltrane, among others. A wide range of African Americans became involved in benefits, fundraisers, and demonstrations in support of black causes.[12] The impetus continued as black advocacy permeated the work of many 1970s artists.

These changes were but a prelude to the process of hybridization of jazz, which has seen the music evolve multiple interethnic cross-conversations and fusions with rock, eastern, Indian and African music, folk traditions both in the United States and elsewhere, and classical music. Jazz mutated in conversation with local forms outside the United States only to return to the home shore in changed form—the flip side of the process dubbed "glocalization."[13] Yet, as Alyn Shipton is careful to explain, "postmodern jazz" did not float free from its heritage. Shipton encourages us to understand contemporary jazz through the work of musicians looking either backward toward the tradition or forward from it.[14] The diversity of later twentieth-century jazz styles and the increasing distancing of performative practices from the communal, racial, and social roots of the music had the contra effect of *simultaneously* enhancing the totemic status of the tradition. Since the 1960s musicians have increasingly felt it necessary to explain radical artistic departures by reference to the innovative spirit of the tradition while in other quarters decrying new directions in jazz as a betrayal of that same tradition. The practice of jazz criticism moreover was not immune from secular change: the passing of what Ted Gioia has called the "insider" generation of critics (Gunther Schuller, André Hodier, Martin Williams, Leonard Feather, among others) left a gap to be filled in exemplary fashion by Gary Giddins, whose *Village Voice* articles offered a younger, hipper take on the evolving scene, and Whitney Balliett who, as previously mentioned, in over 500 articles in the *New Yorker* from 1957 couched a preference for the "tradition" in elegant and poetic rhetoric. Both postures can be either radical or conservative and Steven Elworth is surely mistaken in characterizing those elements of postmodern jazz which look backward as inevitably negative.[15]

Similar trends sent a charge through American photography and prefigured the expanded field of postmodern contemporary practices. The 1950s has been described as a decade in which photography emerged as a tool for the construction of a new supranational subjectivity, a turn from mimesis to metaphor that would be canonized by John Szarkowski in MoMA's 1967 exhibition *New Documents* as a fundamentally new aesthetic. Edward Steichen's *Family of Man* exhibition in 1955 embodied the new subjectivity but it was in Robert Frank's photobook *The Americans*, the US edition of which appeared in 1959, that the transition from modernism to postmodernism was most impressively signaled. In 83 gritty, dark, and blurred images of flags, cars, jukeboxes, televisions, and segregated buses, the photographer cast himself—just as Whitney Balliett had cast Miles Davis in the same year—as a young Werther, an alienated and introspective outsider more concerned with symbolic material objects of American life than its people.[16]

Frank's work appears now as a turning point, the moment of reversal of the sense of self-confidence established between 1930 and 1950 when photography's dominant paradigm was, in Gretchen Garner's words, that of the "spontaneous witness" of humanistic documentary. Constantly alert to capture a found moment of which they were witnesses, photographers up to this point accepted implicitly the immanence of their relationship with reality.[17] As the surety of this mission dissolved, art photographers turned to personal subjectivity, exploring abstract and metaphorical possibilities of photographic expression (Callaghan, Steinert), mysticism (Minor White), consumer culture and mass media (Klein), art and fashion photography (Avedon, Penn), visceral street imagery (Winogrand, Klein), and marginal social groups (Davidson). Duane Michals, Jerry Uelsmann, and Lucas Samaras created new paradigms that focused on dreams, memories, and fantasies through staging, manipulation, and combination. By the late-1960s photography had become an expanded space for nontraditional artists to make subjective dreams and fantasies a reality.[18] The development of digital photography completed this trend, severing further the photographer from the "reality" that had once dominated its practice.

Looking forward, looking back

Varied and multilayered though the work of jazz photographers between 1900 and 1960 might have been, it has been argued throughout this book that subjective affinities with jazz found expression in their images. The profound changes unleased in the 1960s and beyond call for a recalibration of the affinity between photographers and jazz. Jazz photographers after around 1960 may have been living and working in radically changed circumstances but were also responding for the first time to an anterior tradition. How they looked back to that tradition, or forward from it, provides a starting point in mapping the changing representations of jazz from this point onward.

The growth of jazz festivals, the diversity of musical forms into and through which jazz mutated, and the range of publications carrying photographic imagery after 1960 created new opportunities for commercial photographers like Steve Banks and Jim Marshall. Marshall exemplifies the changing nature of jazz and its melding with other musical forms, particularly rock. While he ranged widely in his choices of musical subjects and personal style, Marshall remained as closely in touch with the jazz tradition. Other photographers in these years combined jazz with portraiture, reportage, documentary, and/or art practices. Larry Fink has commented on the seeming incongruity between his jazz work and the glossy world of Hollywood portraiture; Arthur Elgort continued to pursue his twin interests in fashion and jazz while John Abbott has established a secure position as a leading music photographer in contemporary color portraiture.

Carol Friedman's clean, uncluttered portrait style with their white backgrounds on the other hand brought a fresh eye to the jazz portrait: a former student of Philippe Halsman, Friedmann took Blue Note's art direction in a new direction while retaining certain aspects of the label's renowned aesthetic. Steve Shapiro made photographs for Riverside Record album covers within a practice that spanned reportage and celebrity portraiture; R. Andrew Lepley's work was largely directed toward the needs of specialist and general publications and Gene Martin has become known for his conceptual portraits of music personalities (especially jazz) and celebrities. John Loengard's photographs of Louis Armstrong deployed an experienced photo editor's eye when he captured the musician in the barbershop during one of his rare visits to his home district of Queens. Influenced by Roy DeCarava and Romare Bearden, Frank Stewart used his position as official photographer at Jazz at Lincoln Center Orchestra to capture innovative and compositionally dynamic environmental portraits. Much of Nancy Miller Elliott's work was candid portraits of the musicians around Buck Clayton and she combined this with street photography and documenting the homeless in New York City.

The tradition of the introspective art portrait continued with the work of Lida Moser. The daughter of Russian Jews, Moser had been assistant to Berenice Abbot in 1948 and an active member of the New York Photo League. Like Lisette Model and Diane Arbus, Moser evolved a fluid, open-ended, and interrogatory style able to reveal the innermost character of her subjects.[19] Her sensitive series of portraits of New York artists are quietly perceptive investigations into the creative mind. Setting Charles Mingus in his apartment, surrounded by his instruments and domestic objects, Moser managed to capture not only the personality but also the artistic climate of New York City in the 1960s. Her portraits are as experimental as the musician himself and depict Mingus as the sensitive and complex personality he was.[20] The archive of Sy Johnson, the jazz composer and pianist, mirrors his close association with Charles Mingus. Paul Slaughter and Enid Farber are also anxious to explore the expressive potentialities of their subjects. On the west coast, Kathy Sloane's portrayals of the Keystone Korner jazz club demonstrate the insights of a sustained documentary project from the inside. Subtitled "Portrait of a Community," Sloane's book combines photography and oral history to portray a diverse community of participants including club management and technicians, cooks, waitresses, artists, writers, and teachers as they revolve around and interact with the musicians.[21]

An important group of post-1960s photographers continues to be fascinated by the authenticity of place and its traditions. If Lee Friedlander's sensitive documentary portraying the personalities and lives of the New Orleans jazz pioneers was in the nature of an oblique gaze, the record of New Orleans' music culture, brass bands, jazz funerals, social clubs, and benevolent societies in the work of Jules Allen, Sydney Byrd, Keith Calhoun and Chandra McCormick, Michael P Smith, Leo Touchet, and Girard Mouton III is a conscious exercise in documenting and preservation. Smith, a commercial photographer who documented black music, culture, and folklife in New Orleans for over 30 years recorded every New Orleans Jazz Festival from the first in 1970 until 2004. "The camera is an extension of my knowledge of the inner working of the community that I have come to understand over a 25-year period," Smith recalled in 1993: "It's my art, my subjective view of the world I'm experiencing."[22] In *Rejoice When You Die,* photographer Leo Touchet also explored the fading years of the classic jazz funeral; his images from 1968 to 1970 capture the last journeys of old-timers such as George Lewis, Alcide Pavageau, Paul Barbarin, and Leon Shelly. Chuck Fishman's 1976 New Orleans project is particularly worthy of note: contemporaneously with Friedlander and Smith, Fishman immersed himself in a project as much ethnographic as aesthetic, recording interviews with many older musicians alongside making photographs of musicians and their environment—a combination of visual and textual material that is the hallmark of documentary practice (Figure 128).

Other photographers consciously positioned themselves as heirs to the tradition by elevating the art of jazz. Lee Tanner, who combined photography and curation with a life-long career as a scientist, Tom Marcello, Paul Hoeffler, Veryl Oakland, Leo Howard Lubow (Figure 130), Tad Herschorn, Ken Franckling, Patrick Hinley, Gerard Futrick, and Lauren Deutsch are exemplary proponents. Ed Berger, the noted archivist at the Institute of Jazz Studies, writer, researcher, educator, and jazz record producer, was also a superb photographer. Berger began taking photographs in the

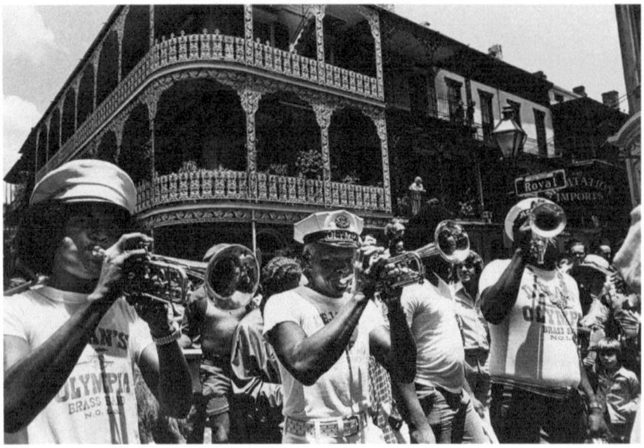

Figure 129: Chuck Fishman. *Street parade in the French Quarter. Wendell Brunious (tpt)*. 1976. © *Chuck Fishman.*

mid-1960s and captured many jazz greats mainly in New Jersey and New York right up until his death in 2017. He worked in a variety of settings—rehearsals, live performances, memorials and tributes, festivals, museum and gallery openings, lectures, seminars, and educational events—but it was in his elegant portraits that his feeling for the music came to the fore. His archive, notable for the collection of images of Benny Carter, has recently passed to Oberlin College.

Two high-profile photographers on the contemporary jazz photography scene are Michael Wilderman and Jimmy Katz. Katz is arguably the leading exponent of the artistic style pioneered by the "classic" tradition:[23]

> *I was very influenced by the "big four" photographers—Bill Gottlieb, William Claxton, Francis Wolff and the grand master Herman Leonard: they shot the major figures of the era, they have a large body of work and they have a distinctive sound in their work. Leonard's photo [of Dexter Gordon] is an image which almost singularly represents the history and totality of jazz. For me jazz is [. . .] the only art form of the level of the great European art forms. I also felt that jazz musicians were not represented as being on that very highest of levels and so I felt that I was going to shoot in a way that was going to give jazz musicians a heroic look when I did portraits rather than just documenting them. It's a very conscious thing that I did and I did it right from the beginning.*

An interest in the culture of jazz continued to inform the post-1960s cohort. For West coast photographer Jerry Stoll, capturing Kedneth Rexroth in a poetry and jazz reading at New York's Five Spot with the Pepper Adams Quintet was as important as his festival performance photography.[24] The mercurial career of the Greenwich village habitué Bob Campbell demonstrated an interest in jazz as part of the emerging counterculture of the decade.[25] While jazz was a small part of Joe Alper's output, he also added a particular dimension to our understanding by casting his subjects in the context of 1960s civil rights activism to which he was committed. Alper's portrait of Archie Shepp for his 1965 album *New Thing at Newport* creates an ironic contrast between the musician's conservative dress and the unconstrained music he played that year on stage.

Like Alper, the photographer and filmmaker George Pickow chronicled folk events and festivals but also captured jazz musicians. Bruce Davidson's jazz archive at the Schomberg Center 1958 comprises grainy monochromatic images from the late-1950s of artists like Ellington, Lester Young, Ella Fitzgerald, Joe Williams, and Billy Strayhorn, often taken backstage or chatting among themselves. Among a series of portraits taken at Newport, Davidson's evocative photo of Young captures a look that is intense yet vulnerable. These images should be read alongside his documentary photographs in the series *Brooklyn Gang, Subway* and *East 100th Street* and his images of the civil rights movement as forming an archive of cultural change. Jay Maisel and Ave Pildas likewise considered jazz integral to their practices as urban/street photographers.

Reflecting the growing awareness and validation of the black archive, significant changes in postwar jazz photography are to be found among African American photographers. Moneta Sleet, Jr., the staff photographer at *Ebony* magazine between 1955 until 1996, was the first African American to win a Pulitzer Prize for his photograph of Coretta Scott King at the funeral of Dr. Martin Luther King, Jr. in 1968. Sleet documented the Civil Rights Movement, black independence movements, and made a series of images of children among other reportage work. His portraits of jazz musicians need to be seen as part of a body of documentary work from the 1970s, which offers witness to the growing independence and freedom of people around the world. Esmond Edwards was for many years the first African American to hold positions of producer and photographer at a white-owned label, Prestige. Anthony Barboza, a close friend of Miles Davis and other musicians, has pursued an extremely successful commercial practice that has at times taken inspiration from jazz. The artist and photographer Adger Cowens has used jazz themes in his paintings.

On the west coast African American photojournalists following in the footsteps of Bob Douglas, Bob Moore, and Harry Adams saw jazz through a lens conditioned by the aftermath of the Watts disturbances: Guy Crowder, Joe Flowers, James Jeffries, and Maxie Floyd, whose portrait of Miles Davis among a sea of white faces at the 1962 Monterey Jazz Festival is as striking in its signification as it is in composition (Figure 131). JazzMobile, organized in 1964 by Billy Taylor to bring free musical programs to deprived cultural areas as Harlem,

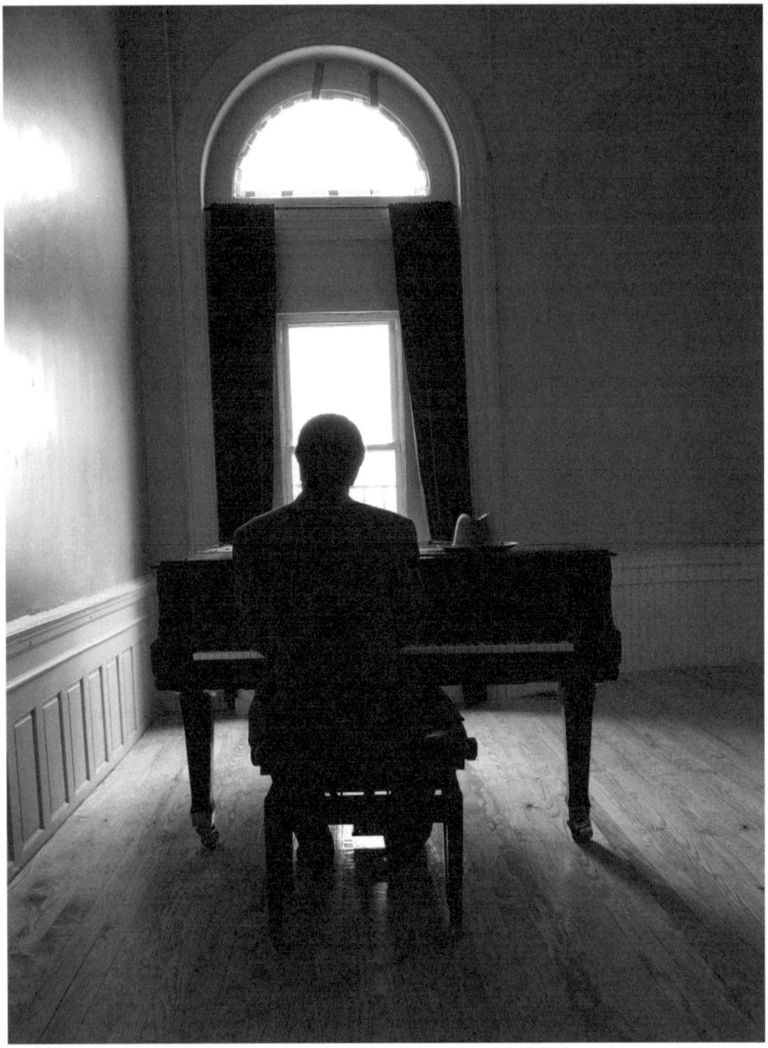

Figure 130: Leo Howard Lubow. *Lafeyette Gilchrist*. An die Music. Baltimore. July 2005. *© 2005 Leo Howard Lubow. All rights reserved.*

Bedford-Stuyvesant, and the south Bronx, was documented by local African American photographers such as Leroi Abramson and Sam Berkeley.

Much of the credit for the resurgence of black photography must be given to Roy DeCarava whose subtle representation of black subjectivity laid foundations that in time moved the debate beyond the "black aesthetic." DeCarava inspired a generation of black photographers through the Kamoigne Collective, whose members such as Ming Smith, Beuford Smith, Bruce Talamon, and Gerald Cyrus have shown particular interest in jazz. Gerald Cyrus was born in 1957 in Los Angeles. In 1990 he moved to New York City and obtained a Master of Fine Arts degree from the School of Visual Arts during which he interned at the Schomburg Center under the supervision of Deborah Willis. Cyrus photographed regularly on the streets of Manhattan, Harlem, and Brooklyn. In 1994 he began visiting the nightclubs in Harlem and photographed the vibrant music scene for over six years. The resulting body of work, published as *Stormy Monday: New York's Uptown Jazz Scene* in 2008, was a contemporary take on the tradition of African American photography that views music as a form of communal expression. Cyrus found the interactions between couples and the musicians and the rituals of socializing, dance, and physical movement to be a visual reaffirmation of black culture. Robert G. O'Meally speaks of the "intimacy" of Cyrus's images, pictures that "take you inside places [. . .] at once public and intensely private, places of entertainment [. . .] of personal as well as community transformation."[26] Cyrus draws parallels with Roy DeCarava's work and the characteristic use of wide angles and flash in family photography; and he speaks approvingly of Herman Leonard's lighting techniques although his photograph "Smoke" inverts Leonard's use of the cigarette smoke by shifting the emphasis toward the spectator whose immersion in the scene becomes the central point of focus (Figure 132).

Approaching jazz from a different angle was Roland Charles and the photographers he encouraged by providing exhibition space in the black Photographers of California Gallery in the Crenshaw district of Los Angeles. Charles established the Gallery in 1984 and kept it going for over twenty years. Many

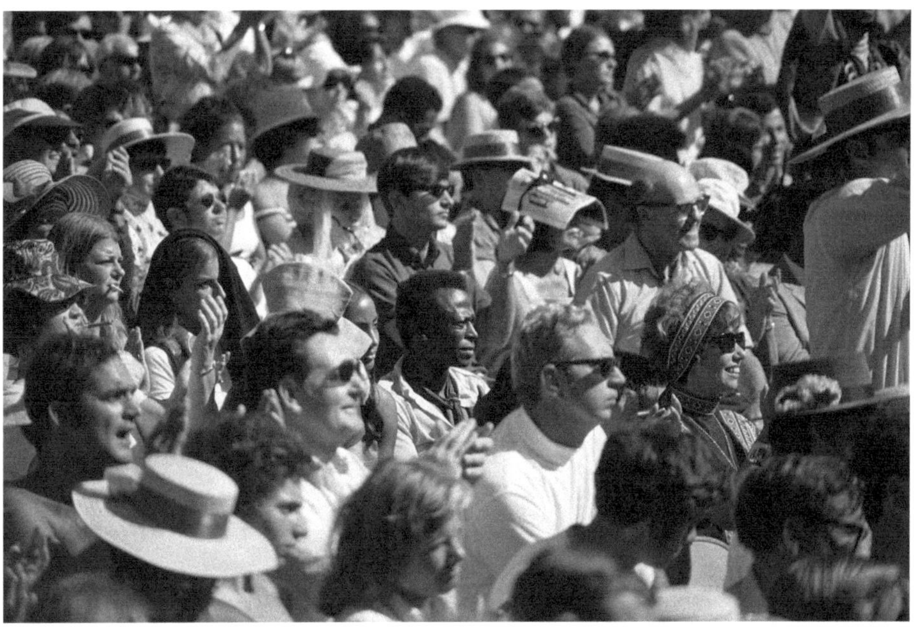

Figure 131: Maxie Floyd. *A Face in the Crowd-Miles Davis.* Monterey Jazz Festival. 1962. *Tom and Ethel Bradley Centre for African American Arts, California State University, Northridge.*

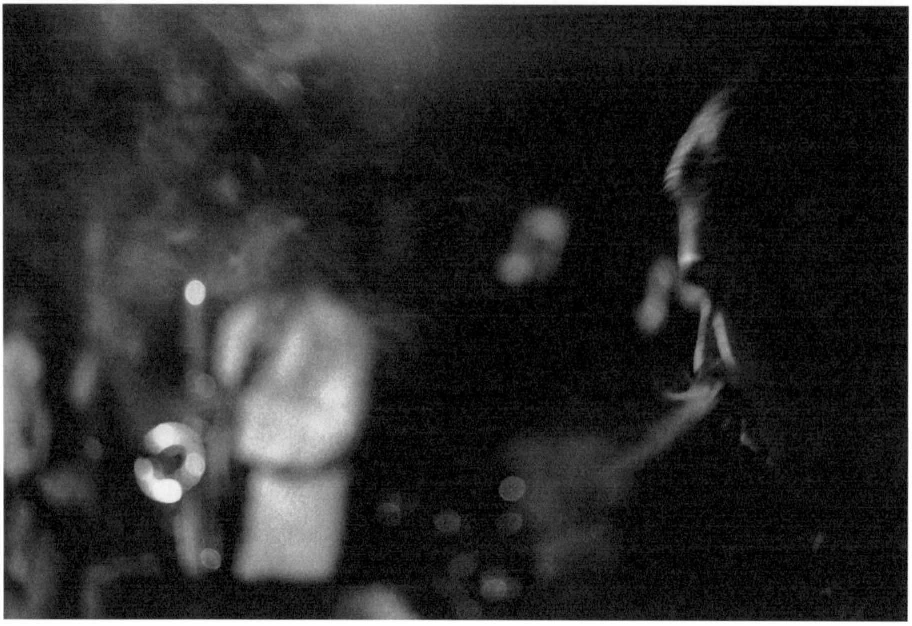

Figure 132: Gerald Cyrus. *Smoke, St. Nick's Pub.* New York. 1994.
Gerald Cyrus.

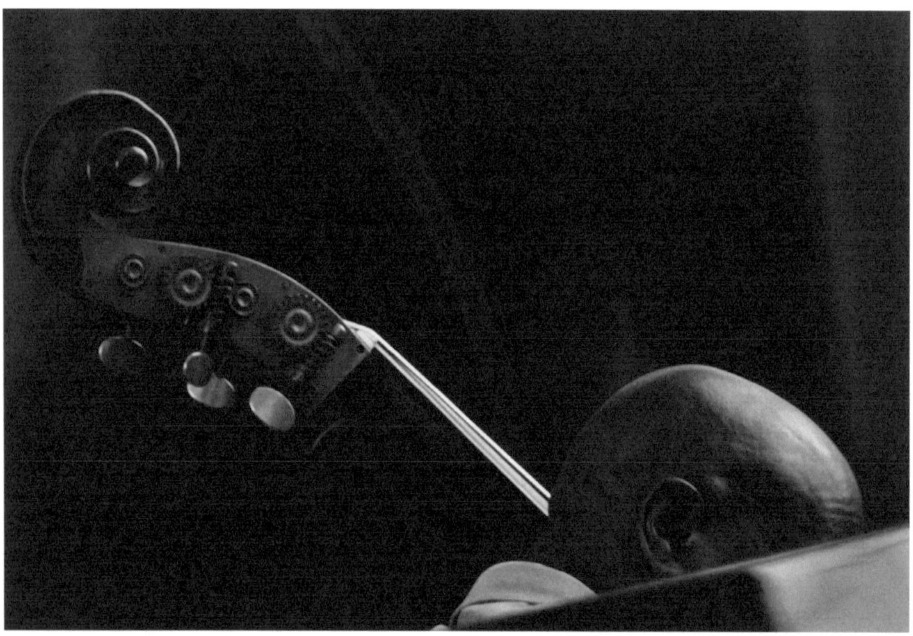

Figure 133: Roland Charles. *Bass.* n.d.
Tom and Ethel Bradley Centre for African American Arts, California State University, Northridge/ with permission of DeBorah Charles.

long-time African American jazz photographers, such as Bob Douglas and Bob Moore, benefited from the opportunities provided by Charles's venture and his role as a mentor. Reflecting on its legacy, Charles said later that bringing Douglas's work to light was one of the most important successes of the black Gallery.[27] As a young photographer Gerald Cyrus recalls how the black Gallery allowed him to make contacts, pick up creative ideas, and gain information about commercial opportunities. He met older photographers like Douglas, Howard Morehead, and Charles; younger photographers like Bruce Talamon; and black west coast artists Donald Bernard and Wille Middlebrook, all of whom were habitués of the black Gallery.

Charles was himself an extremely accomplished photographer for whom jazz was a central element of his practice—subtle, metaphorical, and often employing simple graphical compositions (Figure 133). He developed a unique voice that appears again to sit at a point of intersection: a heightened sense of black assertiveness spiked by the Watts riots and other expressions of racial inequalities coupled with a more nuanced sense of black identity in its relation to the wider society. He is a much underappreciated presence in west coast photography.

Notes

1. Robert A. Sobieszek, *The Art of Persuasion: A History of Advertising Photography* (New York: Harry N. Abrams, 1988), 98–99, 169, 198; Paul Vitello, "Bert Stern, Eilte Photographers Known for Images of Marlyn Monroe, Dies at 83," *New York Times*, June 26, 2013, B17; Chris Wiegland, "Bert Stern Obituary," *The Guardian*, June 30, 2013.
2. Bert Stern and Annie Gottlieb, *The Last Sitting* (New York: William Morrow, 1982), 12.
3. Jeffrey Podolsy, "Bert Offerings," *Vanity Fair*, April 5, 2013, 183.
4. Stern and Gottlieb, *The Last Sitting*, 31.
5. Nate Chinen, "Lensing the Newport Mob: 60 Years Later, A Deep Dive into 'Jazz on a Summer's Day,'" WGBO.org, 2018, https://www.wbgo.org/post/lensing-newport-mob-60-years-later-deep-dive-jazz-summers-day#stream/0, .
6. Doris Willens, *Nobody's Perfect: Bill Bernbach and the Golden Age of Advertising* (Seattle, WA: CreativeSpace, 2009), 21–23; Deborah Dash Moore, "At Home in America?: Revisiting the Second Generation," *Journal of American Ethnic History* 25, nos 2–3 (2006): 162, points out that "The presence of large numbers of second-generation Jewish teachers in the [New York public] schools made them interpretative purveyors of American education to second- and third-generation Jewish students."
7. Kerri P. Steinberg, *Jewish Mad Men: Advertising and the Design of the American Jewish Experience* (New Brunswick, NJ: Rutgers University Press, 2015), 10.
8. Steinberg, *Jewish Mad Men*, 3.
9. For Bernbach and the Polaroid campaign see Stephen Fox, *The Mirror Makers: A History of American Advertising and Its Creators* (London: William Heinemann, 1990), 239–59; Jackson Lears, *Fables Of Abundance: A Cultural History of Advertising In America* (New York: Basic Books, 1994), 342; Juliann Sivulka, *Soap, Sex, and Cigarettes: A Cultural History of American Advertising* (Belmont, CA: Wadsworth, 1998), 282–86; and Thomas Frank, *The Conquest of Cool: Business Culture, Counterculture and the Rise of Hip Consumerism* (Chicago: University of Chicago Press, 1997), 59–73.
10. Ted Gioia, *The History of Jazz* (New York: Oxford University Press, 1998), chapters 7 and 8; Steven B. Elworth, "Jazz in Crisis, 1948–1958: Ideology and Representation," in *Jazz Among the Discourses*, ed. Krin Gabbard (Durham, NC: Duke University Press, 1995), 57–75; Alyn Shipton, *A New History of Jazz* (London: Continuum, 2002), 873; John F. Szwed, *Jazz 101: A Complete Guide to Learning and Loving Jazz* (New York: Hyperion, 2000), 251; and Whitney Balliett, *The Sound of Surprise: 46 Pieces of Jazz* (Harmondsworth: Penguin Books, 1959), 33–36 reprints the *New Yorker* article.
11. Krin Gabbard, *Jammin' at the Margins: Jazz and the American Cinema* (Chicago: University of Chicago Press, 1996), 140–45; Richard Williams, *The Blue Moment: Miles Davis's Lind of Blue and the Remaking of Modern Music* (London: Faber & Faber, 2010); Tom Perchard interviewed by Alyn Shipton, "Jazz Library-Booker Little" (London: BBC, 2009).
12. Geoffrey C. Ward and Ken Burns, *Jazz: A History of America's Music* (London: Pimlico, 2001), 439. Mark Gridley, "Misconceptions in Linking Free Jazz with the Civil Rights Movement," *College Music Symposium* 47 (2007): 139–55, warns against simple correlations between jazz and sociopolitical movements; Ingrid Monson, "Miles, Politics and Image," in *Miles Davis and American Culture*, ed. Gerald Early (St. Louis: Missouri Historical Society Press, 2001), 86–97.
13. For the "glocalization" thesis see Stuart Nicholson, *Jazz and Culture in a Global Age* (Boston: Northeastern University Press, 2014).
14. Shipton, *A New History of Jazz*, 875.
15. Elworth, "Jazz in Crisis, 1948–1958: Ideology and Representation," 72. Ted Gioia, "The True Poet of Jazz," *City Journal*, Summer (2020) contrasts Giddins and Ballett, https://www.city-journal.org.
16. John Szarkowski, "New Documents, Press Release," New York: Museum of Modern Art, 1967, https://www.moma.org/momao-rg/%0Dshared/pdfs/docs/press_archives/3860/releases/MOMA_1967_Jan-June_0034_21.pdf; Jonathan Green, *American Photography: A Critical History 1945 to Present* (New York: Harry N. Abrams, 1984), 83; Whitney Balliett, *Dinosaurs in the Morning: 41 Pieces on Jazz* (Philadelphia: J. B. Lippincott, 1965), 142. See further on the 1950s as a pivot period Blake Stimson, *The Pivot of the World: Photography and Its Nation* (Minneapolis: University of Minnesota Press, 2005).
17. Gretchen Garner, *Disappearing Witness: Change in Twentieth Century American Photography*

(Baltimore, MD: John Hopkins University Press, 2003), 246.

18. George Baker, "Photography between Narrative and Stasis: August Sander, Degeneration and the Decay of the Portrait." *October* no. 76 (1966): 73–113.
19. Moser cited by Elizabeth Lee, "Looking for Lida Moser," in *A Lens without Limits: The Photography of Lida Moser*, ed. Jacqueline Hochheiser (Carlisle, PA: Trout Gallery, Dickinson College, 2018), 6, 8.
20. Moser's portraits of Mingus can be viewed in Monica Skelly, "Portraits of New York Artists," in *A Lens without Limits: The Photography of Lida Moser*, ed. Jacqueline Hochheiser (Carlisle, PA: Trout Gallery, Dickinson College, 2018), 17–18. Her artist portraits are available online at the National Gallery of Art, Lida Moser archive at https://library.nga.gov/.
21. Kathy Sloane, *Keystone Korner: Portrait of a Jazz Club*, ed. Sascha Feinstein (Bloomington: Indiana University Press, 2012).
22. Smith quoted by Garth Cartwright, "Michael P. Smith," *The Guardian*, 2008, https://www.theguardian.com/artanddesign/2008/dec/11/obituary-michael-smith-photographer.
23. Katz, Interview with the Author.
24. Jerry Stoll's photographs can be seen at https://stevenewmanwriter.medium.com/dinosaurs-in-the-morning-whitney-balliett-be412c3cd4e4.
25. Jessica Ferber, Interview with the Author, 2018, described Campbell as "an outsider. He had a very atypical childhood, moved quite a lot. He was reclusive but got out quite a lot. Bob established few personal relationships, never married and was forever a lone wolf throughout his life. He had few friends." See further Jessica Ferber, *Rebirth of the Cool: Robert James Campbell* (New York: Powerhouse Books, 2015).
26. Gerald Cyrus, Interview with the Author, 2018; Gerald Cyrus, *Stormy Monday: New York's Uptown Jazz Scene* (Philadelphia: Private Publication, 2018); and Robert G. O'Meally, "Gerald Cyrus, Jazz Photographer," in *Stormy Monday,* 111.
27. Deborah Charles, interview with the author, Los Angeles, September 15, 2018; Joe Rose, "Interview with Roland Charles" (CSU Oral History project recording 99.01.OH.01.01–02 Oral History Program, Tom & Ethel Bradley Center, Oral History Collection, Oviatt Library Special Collections, California State University, Northridge, 1999.

Conclusion
Herb Snitzer, *Pops* (1960)

In June 2016 I visited Herb Snitzer at his home in St. Petersburg, Florida. It was a humid summer afternoon, but a breeze cooled Herb's sitting room in which the walls were filled with his photography and paintings by his wife, Carol Dameron. We talked about his life and experiences for nearly three hours before he took me into another room to show me boxes of prints. Leafing through the prints we came across his famous portrait of Louis Armstrong, "Pops," which he made in 1960. I asked if I could buy the print. Herb was reluctant because the negative had vanished in a house move some years ago, but he eventually agreed (Figure 134).

Born in Philadelphia in 1932 to Ukrainian refugee parents, Herb Snitzer could not wait to leave the City: "Philadelphia was so dead and the very day after graduating art college I moved to New York to become a freelance photographer." In 1958 he secured an assignment with *Metronome* to photograph Lester Young at the Five Spot Café; as he remembers it, "I didn't know who he was, it was just a shooting opportunity but hearing Prez play took me to the stars, it was an amazing night."[1] In 1960 he obtained Joe Glaser's consent to accompany Louis Armstrong on his tour bus. It was here, on the way to Tanglewood and only moments after Armstrong was refused entry to a whites-only bathroom in Connecticut, that Snitzer made his well-known portrait of Armstrong (Figure 135):[2]

> *When he returned to the bus he was furious. I had not yet seen a look like that on his face. To make Pops furious was doing something, because he was usually so mellow. I will never forget the look on his face. The most famous entertainer in America, and he couldn't use the bathroom because he was black.*

Contrasting Armstrong's expression and pose in this photograph with the ubiquitous images of him in his tuxedo onstage, many have fixed on the Star of David that Armstrong wore in tribute to the New Orleans family who befriended him as a child. Snitzer himself stresses its symbolism of Armstrong's ethnic and racial tolerance.[3]

Although "Pops" was taken by Herb Snitzer just one year after Bert Stern's portrait for Polaroid discussed in the previous chapter, it shows a very different side of the musician. Stern's image gained its power from its portrayal of a unique personality at the heart of American entertainment, a figure of such resonance that his features alone were sufficient to evoke a cultural moment. Benjamin Cawthra, whose book *Blue Notes in Black and White* begins with a discussion of "Pops," suggests that Snitzer's image challenges the dominant representation of Armstrong by "slipping into a node where a very different Armstrong could be found." Even in 1960, at the peak of his fame and popularity, Armstrong still faced the "invisibility" of a black crowd-pleasing entertainer playing to mostly white audiences in a white-dominated society. Jazz photography, Cawthra suggests, has the capacity

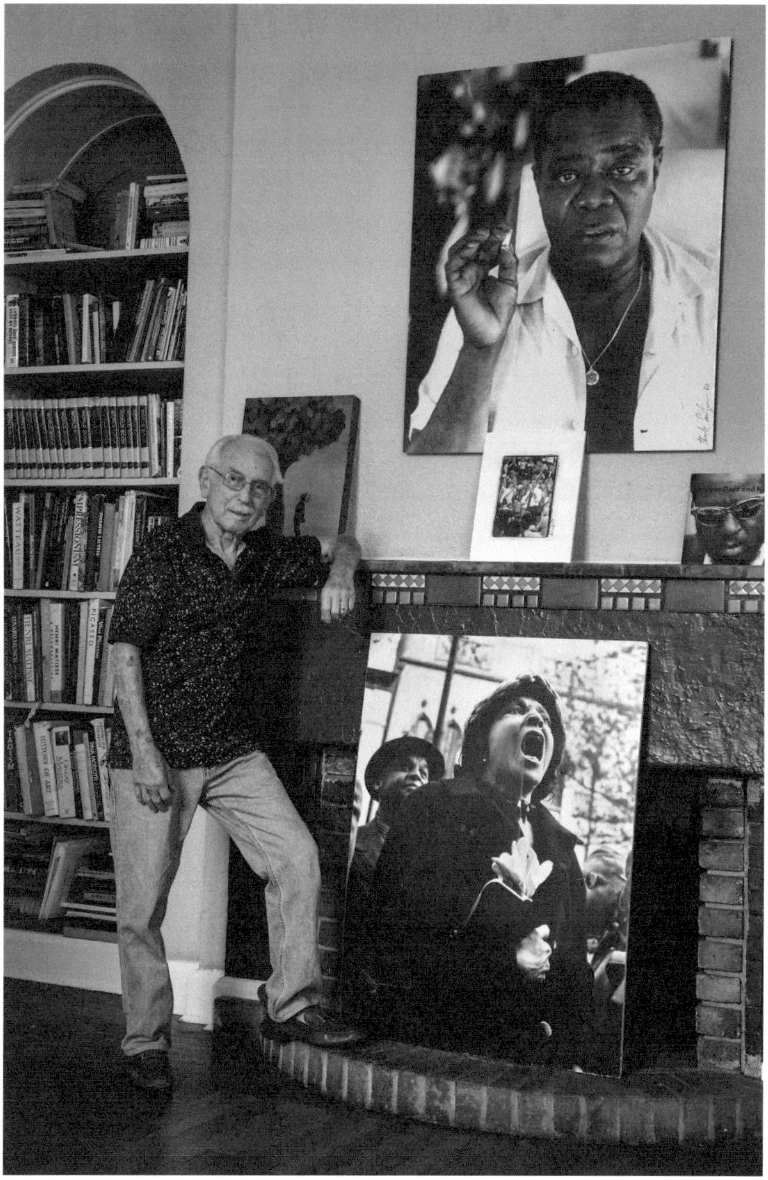

Figure 134: Tom Kramer. *Herb Snitzer and "Pops."* St. Petersburg, Florida. 2018. *Tom Kramer Photography (http://www.tkramerphoto.com/).*

to identify these nodes, the fleeting moments in which the veil might be torn away to reveal the features of a musician rendered invisible for years by race.[4]

It is significant that Cawthra should begin his book with this image and that this book ends with it. In *Blue Notes in Black and White* Cawthra moved on from "Pops" to explore how a number of key photographers, most of whom were white, worked with black jazz musicians to create validating images of artistic achievement. *Sight Readings* has taken a different approach, reaching back to the early years of the music through to around 1960 to show how during this period a wider range of photographers used the photographic medium to document and express a musical and cultural form with which they felt affinity. They did so taking full advantage of a medium through which they were able to express their own ideas about the music and its meanings to their own place in the world.

From this perspective, Snitzer's image confirms the transition in the relationship between photographers and jazz after 1960. Like Cawthra, I am also seized with the theme of invisibility. Snitzer's photograph shows Armstrong in a close physical space yet strikingly isolated within it. We know this space to be the tour bus, but its representation is indeterminate: the background is blurred, the headrests form an indistinct barrier, and the musician seems to be cut off from other band members, bounded in a world of subjectivity. Armstrong stares directly toward the camera with a look of weary defiance. The photograph has captured a moment in which a world-famous musician has retreated into a personal space forced on him by a racially motivated incident just minutes before. Snitzer recounts that Armstrong was soon back on stage at Tanglewood, radiating the *bonhomie* for which he was famous. On the bus, the racial slur seems momentarily to have turned Armstrong into a stranger in which distance and proximity coexist. This striking image returns us to Georg Simmel's account of the stranger and his assertion of the "importance of the gaze of the persons portrayed in interpreting and structuring the space in the picture itself." Here precisely is the disconcerting—even disruptive—effect of the *en face* pose. In spite of Armstrong's status as an entertainer and ambassador, the face of the stranger could not hide the fact of racism. When, just two years later, Armstrong sang the anti-racist lyrics of *The Real Ambassadors* penned by Dave Brubeck's wife, Iola, the pianist recalled that "Louis was making a political statement through our words. He had tears in his eyes as he sang . . . The lyrics expressed what Louis felt in his heart."[5]

It was a quest to exploit the expressive possibilities of the photograph that led Snitzer on several occasions to inveigh against the ubiquitous jazz performance shot, the worn trope of the "guy with the horn in his mouth."[6] Here, for instance, he speaks of his approach to making a portrait of Cecil Taylor:[7]

> *He was really out there. I have to say I didn't really understand his music [. . .] he was sitting in a diner and I photographed him through the window. So what you see is the reflections of buildings [. . .] and street life partially hiding his face. It's a very abstract photograph. Since I felt separated from his music, I tried to get the same feeling in my portrait [. . .] as if to say, "The window is a barrier between me and Cecil"*

Snitzer was swimming with the experiential tide of American photography after around 1960. The affinity he felt with jazz and the personal meaning of that affinity

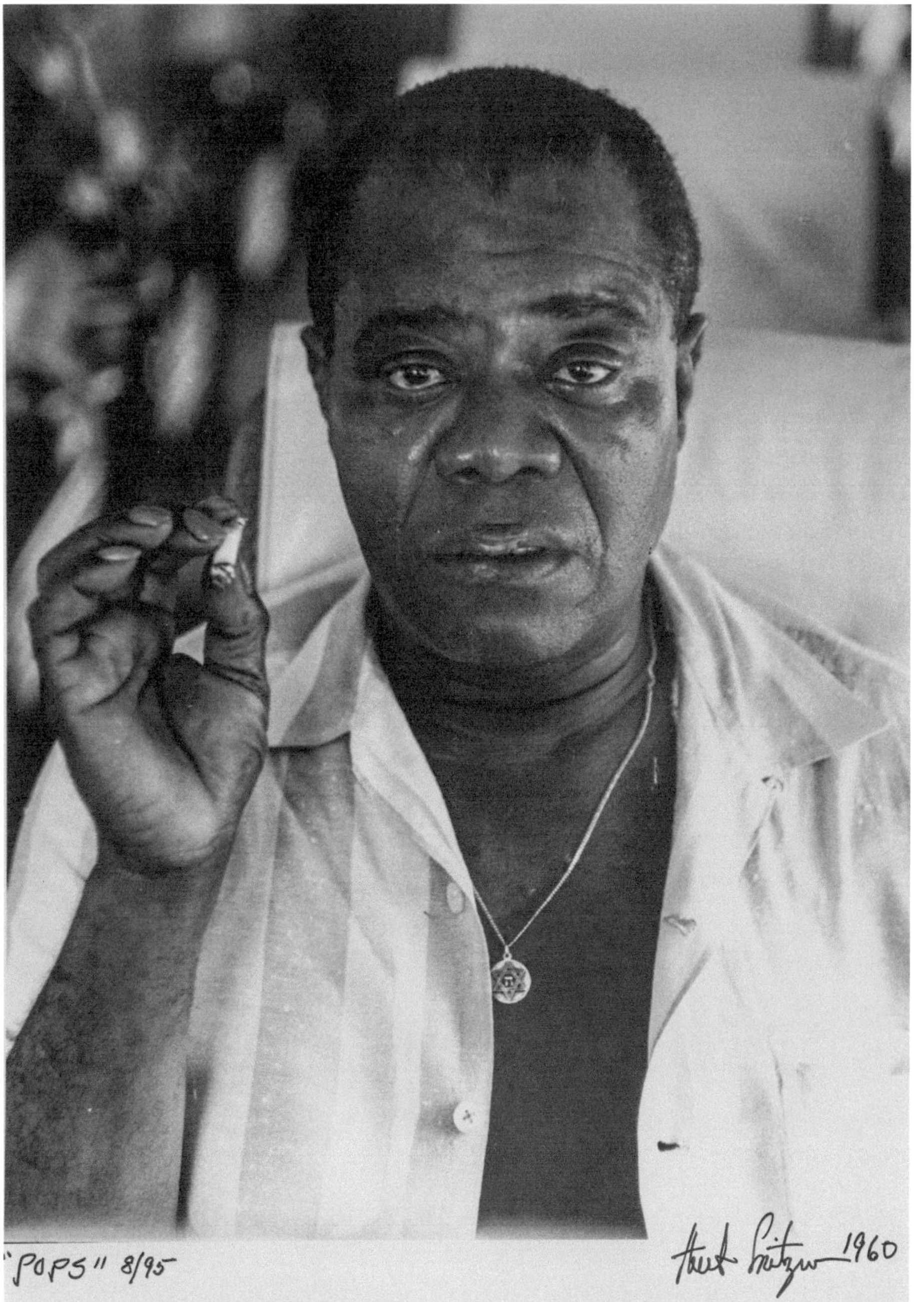

Figure 135: Herb Snitzer. *Pops*. 1960.
Author's Collection/Permission of Herb Snitzer.

was as deeply felt as that which we have seen in the photographers preceding him. Yet, while earlier photographers had responded to jazz as it was being created, photographers in the later decades of the twentieth century found their response to the music conditioned *both* by a tradition that contemporary jazz was increasingly leaving behind and an established tradition of the jazz photographer. Representing these musicians in a post-1960 world marked as much by a sense of possibilities as failed opportunities, Snitzer could not but look back to the tradition:

> *Very occasionally, for whatever reason, a group of people who change the world come together at a moment in time. I was thinking about jazz recently and the American founding fathers—George Washington, Adams, Jefferson, Madison, Franklin. These men left a legacy that has shaped the world. So did Pops, Ellington, Basie, Miles, Prez—all the players I got to know in the late-50s. They just came together at that moment. And I was there.*

The photographers who followed over the next few decades could not avoid looking back to a tradition; how they interpreted this tradition conditioned how they looked forward.

Herb was tired after we had finished talking and asked Carol to show me out, and we spoke for a few moments in the late-afternoon sun. I told her how much I had enjoyed the afternoon and how much I had learned about jazz in the 1960s and 1970s. "Herb remembers everything," she said; "After all, jazz and photography were his life."

Notes

1. Snitzer, Interview with the Author, 2016. All quotations are taken from this interview.
2. Herb Snitzer, *Glorious Days and Nights: A Jazz Memoire* (Jackson: University of Mississippi Press, n.d.), 26.
3. *Glorious Days and Nights,* 27. Herb Snitzer emphasized this point when I met with him.
4. Cawthra, *Blue Notes in Black and White,* 2–4.
5. Marc Myers, "Interview with Dave Brubeck," JazzWax, https://www.jazzwax.com/2010/02/interview-dave-brubeck-part-4.html, accessed October 23, 2020.
6. Gary Carner, "Jazz Photography: A Conversation with Herb Snitzer," *Black American Literature Forum* 25, no. 3 (1991): 563.
7. Snitzer, *Glorious Days and Nights,* 22.

Appendix
Agency in Jazz Photography

> *I have taken the photographer's underlying purpose to be the most important determinant of a work's historical meaning or at least the place to begin. Any photographic image—from news, medicine, or science, or any family picture—can easily migrate from one context to another [. . .] Nevertheless, one must begin to understand a work by developing a historical sense of its original purpose.*[1]

> *When I use the term "jazz photographer," I am referring to [photographers] who have earned their reputations not by how many times they have aimed a camera at various jazz subjects but by the way they have used their [. . .] equipment and professional sensibilities to produce the result that most closely and tangibly represents an aesthetic. It is the inner vision that fuels the outer view.*[2]

As photographs are disseminated, circulated, and consumed a range of mediating forces come into play: the institutional context of production, expectations associated with generical classification (photojournalism, documentary, portraiture, reportage, etc.), the spatial and material contexts of presentation, the rhetorical purpose in the service of which the image might be mobilized, and the language by which it is described and surrounded. The effect over time is that the metaphorical and expressive aspects of the photograph gain ever greater traction, subsuming the reality photographs are assumed indexically to represent. Removed from their contexts of production, many "iconic" jazz images pass through an "aesthetic-historical moment," when the original documentary purpose cedes to the formal qualities of the image hanging on museum walls, in photobooks, and as illustrations on album reissues accompanied by curators' text or explanatory essays and captions.[3] As images change their meanings an increasingly suffusing patina envelops their subjects with nostalgia: "All photographs are *memento mori*," Susan Sontag noticed, "Precisely by slicing out this moment and freezing it, all photographs testify to time's relentless melt."[4] The combination of aestheticization and nostalgia is nowhere more evident than in the case of classic jazz photography and its effects have conditioned the selection and understanding of these images by jazz scholars just as much as the music's general readership.

I. Photography and agency

The case for photographic agency

How, then, should we approach the jazz photograph—and at what point in its life cycle? As we saw in Chapter 2, jazz texts rarely move beyond "picture perception" or the higher level of "surface interpretation," in their use of visual material. Such readings fall short of "deep interpretation" which as Arthur Danto argued can only be considered adequate if it is founded on coherent bodies of ideas, concepts, and theories that accurately reflect the creator's own aims and intentions.[5] While less certain than Danto about the creator's consciousness of cultural symbols, Edwin Panofsky also proposed that iconographical interpretation requires "insight into the manner in which, under varying historical conditions, essential tendencies of the human mind were expressed." Both writers are clear that deep interpretation requires situational analysis to grasp (in Panofsky's words) "those basic principles which underlie the choice and presentation of *motifs,* as well as the production and interpretations of *images, stories* and *allegories* which give meaning to the formal arrangements and technical procedures employed.[6] E. D. Hirsch Jr. has also argued strongly for the primacy of the author's original meanings as the only "correct" interpretation of a work of art; he concedes that "we can never be certain that our interpretative guesses are correct" even though we "know they *can* be correct."[7]

Danto, Panofsky, and Hirsch insist on the impossibility of reaching any deeper understanding of art without at least some understanding of the objectives and motivations of the artist. Stated like this, the proposition seems uncontentious; and, to be sure, many contemporary critics would go along with Janet Wolff in seeking to "incorporate original meaning (and its construction)" as well as the "mediation of that meaning through, for example, a series of critics, and meanings attached to the work by any new reader, as well as the interrelations between them." The author may have been "de-centered" by cultural theorists in recent decades but in the process has been "re-focused" and so it is no longer necessary to "choose whether to give priority to 'action' or to 'structure,' [. . .] we have to operate with a model which posits the mutual interdependence of structure and agency, rather than the primacy of one or other."[8]

What is less clear however is whether art and photography critics have adequately described the empirical modalities through which the "mutual interdependence" of structure and agency operate. This is particularly the case with photography where several important arguments raise questions about the limits of agency—and even question its existence. Most of these ideas have been carried over to photography from challenges to the "authorial" art historical tradition which located the genesis of the artwork in the capacities and vision or, *pace* Susanne Langer, the emotions and feelings of the creator posed by Roland Barthes, who pronounced the death of the author in 1967, and Michel Foucault's deconstruction of the authorial function in favor of a model premised on the cultural construction of creative agency.[9] These arguments are summarized below.

The positivist image. The first of these arguments holds that the photograph is the product of a causal process making it little more than an image *of* something. For many Victorian observers the inherent referentiality of the photograph assured the new medium a glorious future in the fields of science, architecture, exotic scenes, and portraiture but hardly as art. Descending from this claim, the positivist view holds that nothing stands between the photograph and the reality it purports to record and so unlike painting photography cannot be said to be representational in any meaningful sense.[10]

Automatism and chance. The positivist argument is bolstered by propositions which pivot on the notions of automatism and chance. The photograph is the product of an automatic process which unlike painting inevitably captures unwilled, arbitrary, accidental, and random elements of chance and contingency. This is again a long-established view. André Bazin described the photograph as formed "without the creative intervention of man" and Walter Benjamin drew a distinction between the skilled hand of the painter and its absence in photography, a point of view which David Hockney and W. J. T. Mitchell appeared later to adopt. Rudolf Arnheim made a similar point when he wrote that photographs are visual accidents with little to do with the photographer; while conceding that "the photographer is a part of the situation he depicts ... the photographer must be present where the action is," Arnheim argued that this very feature enforces a "ceiling" on the stamp of the photographer.[11]

These arguments are not wholly convincing. Even as Bazin removes human agency from the photographic act he holds that a measure of proactivity is embedded in the mechanism, a technology with a will of its own. Photographers however point to the conscious role of intentionality and exploitation of chance, habit, and procedures in photographic seeing. "Photography as a creative expression [. . .] must be seeing plus." Edward Weston claimed: "Wisdom controlling the means—the camera—makes manifest this knowledge, this revelation." Ansel Adams countered charges of automatism and chance simultaneously with his notion of "pre-visualization," which insisted that the agency of the photographer *precedes* the operation of the mechanism. Other photographers have pointed out that awareness of contingency and chance can *enhance* photographic vision: as the photographer Guy Le Querrec observed: "I would always like to be available [. . .] to be surprised by what I didn't expect."[12] These testimonies challenge the notion that habit, tradition, or repetition somehow strip their actions of agency—a fallacy which Mustafa Emirbayer and Ann Mische convincingly establish overlooks the agential aspects of iteration.[13]

These counterarguments do not so much deny the automatism of the camera as assert its liberating function as photography structures the negotiation of senses through tropes of its construction. Early twentieth-century commentators like László Moholy-Nagy seized precisely on the liberating "*mechanical and technical*" construction of the apparatus while Harry Callaghan believed that the mechanism of the camera *intensified* his vision. Patrick Maynard has taken up and expanded this argument explaining how the central feature of photography as a technology lies precisely in its ability to amplify "our powers to imaging things and our powers to detect."[14] André Rouillé—who argued forcefully for the notion of human control in the photographic act—unreservedly charges Bazin with establishing a tradition (through Roland Barthes to Rosalind Krauss) which closes down photography's liberating capabilities.[15] Finally, although some critics have equated agency with intentionality, arguing that photographic intentionality and chance are in tension with each other, intention cannot be reduced to a reconstituted state of mind but is to be found in a relation between the object (photograph) and that purposefulness that happens in and within social actions and interactions.[16]

The "fallacy" of recontextualization. Several critics argue that bringing the photographers' intentions into the interpretation of their photographs must be futile since the very nature of the medium is its ability to generate new meanings. The photograph as image cannot be "recontextualised" as the product of individual consciousness according to Susan Buck-Morss, who puts the case as follows:[17]

> *... to bind [photographs] again to their source is not only impossible (as it actually produces a new meaning); it is to miss what is powerful about them, their capacity to generate meaning, and not merely to transmit it [. . .] Meaning will not stick to the image. It will depend on its deployment, not its source.*

To go back to the photographer's intentions may well be imperfect or partial but is no more nor less impossible than any other form of empirically founded historical enquiry; and that it may produce a new meaning is surely positive in offering another—and possibly more contextually sensitive—perspective on the image. It is hard to envisage how the historian seeking to make greater use of photographic evidence can do so without first recreating the social point of view through which *both* the makers and consumers of these images viewed the world.[18]

Hegemony and ideology. By the 1970s theorists were engaged in directing attention away from the formal properties of the photograph, the integrity and specificity of the medium, and the role of the author to focus on the institutional and discursive framing that asserts itself and fixes expressive meanings. The "new" photography studies of Allan Sekula, Victor Burgin, Abigail Solomon-Godeau, Douglas Crimp, Hal Foster, Martha Rosler, Benjamin Buchloh, and John Tagg challenged the dominant formalist interpretations of photography as ideological importations. Discourses, not universal essences, constitute the proper object of photographic enquiry; photography is always a space of cultural production articulated through the conflicting and intersecting operations of power. For John Tagg the photograph is an object to be understood through investigation of material history and usage; its meaning is revealed by the bias of interest and the institutional parameters, power structures, and relations of power which are vested in codes outside the photograph but within social structures. Neither chance nor artistic intention need be taken into account.[19]

The "hegemonic" vision of photography assumes a considerable degree of precision in the transmission powers of photographic messages in what is generally accepted as a notoriously ambiguous medium; and it allows little room for the view that works of art can engender those liberating forms of expression which Raymond Williams called new "structures of feeling."[20] Treating *all* photographs as the carriers of a well-formed ideologies, these theorists have imported a degree of determinism which precludes experimentation and diversity. Without adequate reference to the worldviews of photographers or their ability to transcend simplistic rendering of ideological positions, Lawrence Levine believes Tagg's analysis of the FSA file seriously overemphasizes ideological hegemony; and Geoffrey Batchen has similarily charged writers like Tagg as holding to a purely instrumental view of photography as little more than vehicles for the transfer of power from one place to another and in assuming that power preceeds representation.[21] From Alfred Stieglitz, Paul Strand, Edward Steichen, Ansel Adams, and Edward Weston through James Agee, Clement Greenberg, and John Szarkowski to documentarians like Dorothea Lange, Walker Evans, and the "new" school of Diane Arbus and Robert Frank, American photographers have cleaved to photography as a medium of subjective expression. Abigail Solomon-Godeau has accepted the continuity of authorship into the modernist age when "the locus of art was now placed squarely within the sensibility—be it eye or mind—of the photographers" and Patricia Vettle-Becker has shown the subsequent reemergence in the late-1950s of a return to subjectivity with the realism of the "aesthetic of existential man."[22]

Far from calling into question the validity of authorial purposes, the "hegemonic" approach to photography underlines the importance of the photographer as a baseline point of reference. The more the meanings of photographs change in distribution, use, and application and the more the image is subjected to ideological pressure, the greater is the importance of reasserting and restating the originating context of production. To super-contextualize photographs in usage is to excise from consideration the key modalities of production; and, by failing to take the photographer into account, these approaches in effect *weaken* the power of contextual analysis and obscure the plurality of photographic meaning.[23]

Each form of cultural expression has its own conditions of production and distinctive codes of representation. Like Miles Orvell, whose view is cited at the beginning of this chapter, I advocate the need to understand and establish photographic agency as the starting point in analyzing jazz photography. If the defining ontological feature of the photograph is the index—asserting as it must the presence of the photographer—there is a necessary relationship between that subjectivity and the image which remains encoded whatever the subsequent life cycle experience of the image. As André Rouillé reminds us, the relationship between things and their representation is as much that of contiguity as resemblance, of contact as visual similarity.[24] Secondly, the technology which underpins photography as a medium offers facilitation to the exercise of agency. These affordances are key to understanding the relationship between structure and agency. Finally, the recognition of agency provides a means of analyzing the *relationships* between the sites at which interpretation of a photography occur—the sites of production, the image, and audience. However much, and for what purposes, photographs might be deployed in circulation, identifying the agency at the point of production is essential if our understanding of that image is not to be reduced to a form of radical relativism or hegemonic co-option. Throughout this book therefore emphasis has been placed on both the biographical and broader context in which photographers approached jazz and the objectives which they set out to achieve in representing the music and its practitioners.

A technology of self

The case for photographic agency need not therefore involve denying that photographs become subject to subsequent competing choices and meanings, nor should it be interpreted as a plea for a return to authorial primacy, still less some new variant of Greenbergian formalism. Drawing on the reanimated concept of context as relational and dynamic, nuanced accounts of the emergent properties of structure and agency and the materiality of artistic practice proposed by writers such as Alfred Gell, Arthur C. Danto, Tia DeNora, Patrick Maynard, Margaret Archer, and Elizabeth Edwards, it becomes possible to conceptualize processes through which the subjectivity of the photographer might become encoded in the resulting image. It is in this sense that we can regard photography as a "technology of self," a term that Michel Foucault introduced in his later writings to describe the technologies of production, signs systems, power, and self-direction which permit individuals to transform themselves. These technologies facilitate the self-creation of human subjectivity enabling the individual to challenge, reject, and even escape the domination of structural or institutional powers through a form of critical self-awareness and styling he termed "self-care." These technologies rarely function in isolation and there is constant interaction between them; and each requires a certain mode of training.[25]

Through the opportunities it affords to achieve self-expression, the idea that photography functions as a technology of the self is a potent one which theorists are only now recognizing but which practitioners have long acknowledged. The nineteenth-century portraitist Nadar claimed the brain as the elemental force behind a photograph, the source of the originating idea infusing the image with creativity; and Saul Warkov expressed a similar view when he said "The camera is a wonderful mechanism. It will reproduce, exactly, what is going on inside of your head". Henri Cartier-Bresson emphasized the perpetually evaluating eye as mediating the brain and the apparatus; only at the decisive moment of affirmative selection, in which the mind guides the hand through the facilities of the eye, can a composition can be created from a scene in which the photographer cannot move the constituent elements.[26]

Edward Weston believed that photography had brought him closer to a realization of his own self while Anthony Barboza has also spoken of photography as a medium of self-expression:[27]

> *It explains to the photographer a lot about himself. That is the reason why visually it may be a subject in the frame, but it is also a biographical portrait of the photographer and his personality. It reveals to him what he is sensing and feeling. [. . .] photos explain what I have come to realize about myself and how much music, childhood, love, sex, death, and spirituality play an important part of how I feel about myself and the life I have been living.*

Few commentators have confirmed the inscription of the photographer in the photographic image as confidently as the novelist and photographer Hervé Guibert. For Guibert it is the photographer rather than the subject of the photograph who leaves a trace in the image through the choices he makes at point of capture. He goes so far as to claim that the subject is *assimilated* by the photographer through the act of photography: "Rarement le suject se retrouve dans sa propre histoire: il en est sorti de force par l'empreinte du photographe, se determinisme du cadre qui l'efface un peu comme individu." In Guibert's opinion photographs emerge as "Voices of the Self," deeply and directly expressive of subjectivity and which on more than one occasion he described as "attempts at biography."[28]

If photography is capable of facilitating agency in this way it is necessary to understand what Emirbayer and Mische have called the "practical-evaluative" components of human agency given license through the specific operational enablement of photographic technology. The choices engaged by the photographer direct us toward the acting subject and "photographic framing," a term used here to embrace the intentions and purposes of the photographer expressed through the choices made at point of capture. Conceived in this way, photographic framing comprises conceptual and visual modalities which together exploit photography's role as a technology of self (Figure 136).

Conceptual framing. For Clement Greenberg, "it is in choosing and accosting his story, or subject, that the artist-photographer makes the decisions crucial to his art. Everything else—the pictorial values and the plastic values, the composition and its accents—will more or less derive from these decisions."[29]

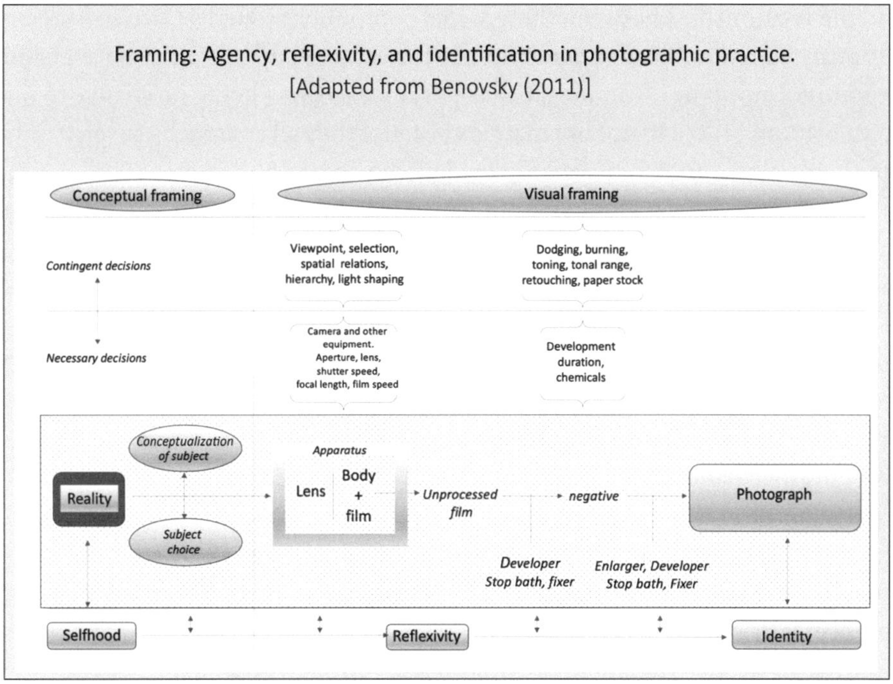

Figure 136: Framing: Agency, reflexivity, and identification in photographic practice.

It is not necessary to subscribe to Greenberg's formalism *tout court* to accept his point that it is in the intellectual prism which photographers bring to their subject that reflexive engagement in the real world is initiated. Of course, photographic framing is but one specific instance of that general framing process by which we make sense of the world and attribute meaning to it, albeit with the crucial difference that it has as its end product the material *re*-presentation of that which has been framed.[30] The first moments of agency for photographers therefore precede that of capture. Approaching jazz subjects photographers will be alert for visual embodiments of their ideas, beliefs, and ultimate concerns. The conceptualization of subject will inform vision and influence what photographers find interesting and worth capturing, even encouraging them to photograph what might otherwise be overlooked. In a self-referential process, the photographer builds more and more comprehensive models of concerns and will arrange the visual material into the patterns and sequences that are the visual analog of those concerns.

Visual framing. Photographs comprise fragmentary excerpts from reality. It is a way of seeing based on selection rather than synthesis, which creates the space to reflect on and even reconstruct former environments and totalities or to speculate beyond the frame.[31] Skilled photographers know the importance of judicious selection—who and what to include, partially include or exclude from the frame, and the relationships between these visual components. Henri Cartier-Bresson famously aimed for final composition in the camera and had a strong aversion to editorial cropping: "I attach great importance to there being no change to my compositions [. . .] Do not use margins because they all encroach—even if only infinitesimally—on the image projected by the negative."[32]

John Berger described the selection involved in visual framing as a "quotation from reality" and argued that ambiguity can be turned to advantage as the photographer has it within his grasp to control the "length" of that quotation. His account is premised on the initial selection, or decontextualization, and subsequent recontextualization, of visual elements in the photograph. Photographers control the constituent elements of the image and seek to hold these components in tension and/or harmony.[33] It is through visual framing that the photographer consciously balances the documentary and expressive elements of the photographic image and so understanding the photographer's selection is thus essential to any interpretation. This is not a question of photographic style nor confined to what is included in the frame. The photograph is a site of presence and absence: if by ontological necessity the photograph states "what is," it becomes an equally assertive statement of "what is not" through absence.[34]

Photographic agency in practice

Photographic agency—the imposition of an inner-directed personal vision and identity on the image—is thus engaged in the processes of conceptual and visual framing and given practical expression through a series of necessary and contingent decisions. As Dennis Stock explained in his introduction to *Jazz Street*, these decisions give form and content to the photographer's intentions, ideas, concerns, and beliefs:[35]

> *Amateur or professional, the photographer's ultimate goal is to retain on film an image that will clearly state his appreciation (or at least his view) of the subject he has selected to record. To facilitate his ideas and the retention of the image, there are a multitude of photographic implements [. . .] many different combinations of lenses, films, light sources, and darkroom manipulations [. . .] "Jazz Street" illustrates a variety of choices.*

The significance of these decisions is such that their outcome fundamentally shapes the nature of photographic of "reality" as Alan Trachtenberg has explained:[36]

> *Even the slightest adjustment in point of view, in lighting, in the type of film used, can produce a "reality" in a different register. Then there is the inescapable subjectivity of the photographer, differences in the vision, the quality of the eye, the instinctive sense of where to place the camera—all of which bear on what individual pictures give us to understand by "the real."*

Connotations are lodged not simply in the "content" of photographic-based media but also in the form in which a particular "reality" is constructed in the significations of the medium's very language—camera angles, conventions of representation, lighting, editing, "pace" —all techniques which are seen as "natural." It is the ability of the camera to create "reality" through its technological modalities that has prompted radical film-makers from Rodchenko onward to break the realist illusions of the medium by using lighting, the camera, angles of view, editing, selection, and so on in unconventional and disruptive ways.

The photographer's choice of equipment and its use are first-order necessary decisions (see again Figure 136). The camera body might be light enough to facilitate free-flowing shooting actions whereas heavier equipment will restrict movement and the choice of viewpoint. The New York Photo Leaguer Morris Engel described in 1936 how his Rolleiflex twin-lens reflex enabled him to shoot "completely candid pictures," changing the relationship between photographer, viewer, and subject.[37] A particular lens might resolve fine details or it may be inherently "soft," and flash or strobes and film speed will create an effect that is quite different from that of ambient light. The photographer's equipment can also determine shooting locations, access, and choice of viewpoints while a longer lens will compress spatial relationships.

At point of capture the photographer is required to make decisions about aperture, shutter speed, focal length, and film speed, all having regard to light values. These decisions crucially affect not just overall exposure, as is often assumed to be the case, but also the relative hierarchy of subjects by size, depth of field, distance, or illumination. Contingent decisions made at the same time include choice of viewpoint, elements to be included/excluded, spatial relationships between elements, and the shaping effects of light, all of which interact with each other to produce an infinity of possible effects. Post-capture, choices of chemicals, duration of and techniques such as dodging, burning, toning, retouching, and choice of paper stock can modify in various further directions the choices made at point of capture. The latitude the photographer has to impose a vision on the final image is enhanced by the complex network of interrelationships between these decisions.

The following examples illustrate the ways these decisions interact and some of their main effects in jazz photography:

- The moment the shutter is released has consequences which go well beyond quality of exposure. It is the point external to the event itself at which forces and patterns create harmony, clarity, and balance within the continuous flow of an ensemble performance or improvised solo. The choice of shutter speed can change the representation of motion, give greater prominence to certain elements over others, affect the relationship between tonal values, enhance or diminish light and shadow values, establish relationships between different elements within the frame, and decisively shift the point of focus.

- Light values create visual hierarchies by elevating one subject in importance over another. The effects can be exaggerated or minimized when combined with choices of viewpoint, focal length, and aperture determining who or what emerges from the surface with the power of illumination, spatial precedence, or focus. Light, shadow, and shadow-doubling can enhance these effects. Decisions around focus points will also create their own hierarchy and lens optics have an effect as subjects near the edge of the lens will be less distinct.

- The sensitivity of film stock used by jazz photographers is a vital consideration. Was sufficiently sensitive film available to capture everything in dim lighting or were darker values distorted or obscured? could movement be held? and what effect did film choices have on tonal vales? Back-lighted smoke as captured by films of different speeds can look quite different to that perceived by the human eye. What subtle shades of meaning are imparted when developing, toning and cropping and masking, dodging and burning when printing to compensate for or enhance film speed?

- Angles, graphic patterns of light and shade, abruptly arrested motion, amputations of form, extreme close-ups, off-kilter framing rhyming and doubling, conjunction of still and moving elements, juxtapositions, rectilinear and curvilinear line, mass and shapes, and light trails can be changed dramatically with only small shifts in position of body stance. Even tiny movements will subtly shift the center of focus and its relative importance within the frame, defamiliarize familiar objects/subjects, and disturb the orders of visual precedence.

- Viewpoint, focal length, and aperture combine to situate the viewer as well as elements within the frame. Paul Strand's portraits of peasants from all over the world convey an attitude of respect by habitually photographing his subjects at eye level, directly facing the camera, thus treating them as equals. Much the same applies in the jazz world where Tom Seymour observed that David Redfern:[38]

... knew where he needed to stand (seemingly close enough to the horn section to be rubbing shoulders with the trombone player); he had the eye, and patience, to frame the image dramatically; he had the sensitivity to know (and feel) when the moment was just right; and he had the craft and skill to ensure his exposure was exactly right [. . .] The resulting print sings [. . .] he has placed the viewer as a participant in that singularly intense moment of artistic creation.

In practice conceptual and visual framing form a single dynamic feedback loop. As the photographer develops and clarifies his ideas about his subject photographs are made which increasingly correspond to and amplify these concerns. The distinctive style which many photographers have been able to develop is the product of this process. As Carol Armstrong puts it, the ability of photographers to create and impose their own style on the world as seen through the frame argues for a distinctive form of photographic seeing "demanding a combination and intertwined relation between the aleatory and the authorial."[39]

Agency rests then in the ability of photographers to impose their will on the apparatus to give concrete form to their conceptions of the subject through the conscious management of multiple elements in visual framing. The scope for photographic agency is not unlimited, but it is *sui generis* in tying the photograph as material object back to the creator in both an aesthetic and biographical sense. This relationship binds the photograph into the general conception of art suggested by Alfred Gell when he argued that art objects should be regarded as material extensions of the agency of those who create and employ them. For Gell, art objects are capable of actively or passively "participating" in social relationships with people and each other. Arguing for an *indexical* relationship between an art work and its creator, Gell contends that art works reflect the social identity of the creator.[40]

It would of course be possible to accept that the photograph embodies the identity of the photographer while maintaining that any such inscriptions inevitably fade as the image is circulated and subjected to multiple interpretations; as Walter Benjamin famously maintained, reproduction and circulation inevitably strip art work of its original aura. Many argue however that Benjamin overemphasized the effects of reproduction. Gérard Genette's distinction between the two regimes to which a work of art might belong helps make the point. Genette argued that a work of art exists "autographically" in an object or event created by the artist, or "allographically" in versions or copies in which the results of some second-order creativity is evident when viewed or received.[41] Photographs can be considered examples of a "multiple autographic" work (which Genette also calls a "plurality of immanence") at the point of reception in that each manifestation of the work of art is identical although minor manipulations (e.g. a small crop) might lead us to think of the amended image as an example of "partial immanence." More far-reaching manipulations however might well transform a photograph in such a way as to render it allographical: a radical crop of the original image or its integration into other artistic creations by someone other than the photographer should be considered a second-order act of creativity. The essential point is that reproduction *in itself* need not necessarily remove autographic immanence in which photographic agency is embedded.

II. Tradition, affinity, and subjectivity

Having outlined the case for photographic agency we can now return to the discussion of jazz photography as set out in the preceding chapters of this book. Throughout this discussion differences between the many photographers attracted to the jazz subject and the nature of their output have been emphasized. The practices of studio photographers working with black talent as they negotiated their relationship with commercial entertainment, the rooting of early African American photography in communal relationships, and the expressive realism of mid-century black photographers were distinct from each other and also stand in contrast with the preoccupation with authenticity and art among white practitioners of the interwar years. Again, the interrogative and enquiring jazz images of mostly Jewish exiled photographers speak to specific concerns about displacement and identity. These differences cast doubt on the idea of a jazz photography tradition as a unified lineage although it is an assumption that has often been taken over in jazz literature.

Yet, whatever their differences, this book has demonstrated that photographers attracted to jazz were motivated by a common affinity with the music and jazz culture. This affinity often developed at an early stage—in many cases before adulthood—and remained with these photographers as their careers took them in other directions. Jazz became a meaningful activity for photographers in a way that was in certain respects removed from that of commercial assignments—even when the images were made as part of a commercial arrangement—and generally found expression in a belief in the cultural significance of the music and its intimate relationship with the politics of race. A relationship of this nature suggests the differences in photographers' approaches to jazz are to be found above all in the nature of that affinity between photographer and subject. Ira Gitler is surely correct when he asserts in the quotation which introduces this appendix that jazz photographers are defined not by the extent of their involvement but by "the inner vision that fuels the outer view."

According primacy to subjective affinity makes possible a pluralistic and inclusive approach to jazz photography that has allowed this book to take a wider and more embracing approach to its subject than anything attempted to date.

Conceptualized this way jazz photography need not be considered as subject or genre specific, finding expression in commercial, photojournalist, artistic, or other forms of professional photographic practices and spilling across boundaries in a way that conventional approaches to categorizing photographers often fail to recognize. Affinity forms a common bond between professional, semiprofessional, and amateur photographers and allows the contribution of vernacular and "non-artistic" photography to be recognized. This approach encourages consideration of images beyond the performance shots which figure so prominently in jazz texts and to embrace social, cultural, or other environmental images which are often overlooked.

Finally, it becomes possible to retain the notion of a jazz photography tradition but now characterized by shared affinities which grant recognition of differences within its broad ambit. If there is a model, it might be Henry Louis Gates's deprecation of the old canon of mainly white male Western culture not by abjuring canonical tradition as such but by proudly reasserting the existence of a *discrete* black literary canon, a *counter*-canon rooted in the black race and its experience. Invoking Gates among others, Charles Hersch argues that references to the "jazz tradition" while respecting multiple voices are perfectly possible if contingently and constantly reassessed: rather like an expanding dining room table, "there is a stable foundation, but it can be lengthened by adding more leaves."[42]

Reflexivity, identity, and photographic practice

A key theme underpinning the discussion in *Sight Readings* has therefore been that of a jazz photography tradition comprising multiple subjectivities. As we have seen, photography affords agential space to these subjectivities but we have yet to consider the practices through which subjectivity finds expression in the image. The question speaks to the nature of identity and its relationship to the creation of an art work. "Hard" conceptions of identity based on essentialist notions of class, race, ethnicity, or nationality are now generally replaced by "soft" constructions involving fluid, multivalent, and processual characteristics subject to the continuous play of history, culture, and power relations: as Stuart Hall has described it, identities "multiply constructed across different, often intersecting and antagonistic, discourses, practices and positions."[43] This shift toward a constructivist notion of identity recognizes the possibilities of hybridity and mutability but has arguably denuded the term of analytical precision. If identity is everywhere, it is, as Rogers Brubaker points out, nowhere: "If it is fluid, how can we understand the ways in which self-understandings may harden, congeal, and crystallize? If it is constructed, how can we understand the sometimes coercive force of external identifications?"[44] My concern throughout this book has been to understand the simultaneous layering of common affinities and different worlds as their figures are described by the interplay of subjectivity and agency, on the one hand, and sociocultural enablement and constraint on the other. These questions pivot around the relationship between agency and structure as we have already seen; and vision, the most acute and sensitive of our senses, is situated at the ever-shifting point at which nature and culture meet. How we visualize the world—and how that vision expresses the evolving sense of human identity—is an exemplary test case for the duality of subjective agency and objective determination.[45]

Accounting for the relationship between structure and agency was a central problematic of the classical social theory of Marx, Durkheim, Weber, and Georg Simmel. More recently, scholars such as Harold Garfinkel, Alfred Schutz, and Erving Goffman working with interpretative micro-sociologies, Pierre Bourdieu (with the concept of "habitus"), Bernard Lahire's emphasis on dispositional practices, and Anthony Giddens's notion of "structuration" have attempted to address this question in such a way as to avoid the extremes of voluntarism and determinism. Building on the critical realism of Ray Bhaksar and others, a persuasive approach accounting for agency and the emergence of identity which can be deployed in analysis of photographic practice is to be found in the theoretical work of Margaret Archer with its central organizing principle of "reflexivity."[46] Archer sets out to account for the relationship between structure and agency through a rigorous insistence on the ontologically *sui generis* nature of social properties. Human beings, social structures, and cultural entities have their own distinct existences and influences on social outcomes and cannot be reduced to each other. Their interaction over time gives rise to emergent properties, one of which is the development of a personal and social identity. These properties exert independent causal influence and so we must study the interplay between structure and agency, as well as that between culture and agency, as the interplay of different levels with their own temporal cycles without "conflating" the levels.

Crucially for Archer, human agency is not a contingent or determined force but is an expression of something fundamental to the human condition which emerges through practice in the real world. The certainty of self, as someone separate from others, emerges in human beings at a young age and precedes the effects of sociality. Our fundamental sense of self is never superseded; it continues to endow us with a "private/individual" sphere that is brought to subsequent social interactions as the self broadens into personal and social identity. It is our guarantee that we are never simply a product of society or culture. Identity then might better be described as "identification," the continuous and emergent process of becoming.

Identification is rooted in the permanent and continuous sense of selfhood but evolves through the primacy of practice. There is an indissoluble relationship between people and the orders of the real world in which individuals respond to and prioritize their concerns in different ways through "a process of conscious reflexive deliberations during internal conversations with ourselves about ourselves."[47]

> *Personal identity is an achievement [. . .] we are who we are because of what we care about: in delineating our ultimate concerns and accommodating our subordinate ones, we also define ourselves [. . .] Without this rich inner life of reflection upon reality, which is the generative mechanism of our most important emergent personal property, our unique identity and way of being in the world.*

Reflexivity, as an emergent personal property, mediates the impact of structure and conditions individual responses to social circumstances: this is "consciousness with a real history [. . .] firmly grounded in the natural praxis of humanity [. . .] the source not only of consciousness but of our distinctive self-reflexivity, whose origins are equally practical."[48] The mediation of human agency and structural forces "depends on reflexivity, namely our powers to deliberate internally upon what to do in situations that were not of our making."[49]

Archer's schema allows us to conceptualize photography as a form of embodied practice in which reflexivity unfolds and is expressed through agential processes of photographic framing described above and given subsequent material presence in the photograph. It is primarily the notion of reflexivity—which Archer also calls "the inner conversation"—that allows us to concretize agency in the person of the photographer, to recognize the role of subjectivity without lapsing into essentialism, or the fluidity of constructed identities. Reflexivity is an empirical process that unfolds through practical engagement in the different orders of the real world, an engagement initiated by the affinity which subsists between photographers and jazz. This is not simply an act of validation nor, as is often suggested, an aesthetic choice based on the visual potential of the subject, although it will in many cases reflect elements of both. It is ultimately the designation of a site of reflexivity and potential self-realization; and, as in other areas of social life, this designation flows toward areas of the real world in which a form of affinity subsists.

The idea of photography as a site of reflexive agential *praxis* and identification takes us beyond the reductive consequences of positivism or contextual determinism in photographic theory; and it addresses the conflation of structure and agency which Archer argues compromises understanding because reflexive deliberation requires a clear separation between subject and object precisely so that their interplay can be identified and analyzed. John Roberts for example has proposed a theory of "dialectical realism," "the negotiated and constraining relations between social agency and social structure," and, as we have already noticed, Janet Wolff's asserts "the mutual interdependence of structure and agency, rather than the primacy of one or other."[50] But what are the precise mechanics of this interdependence? Simply asserting the complexity and mutuality of contextual and agential forces, even their "dialectical" character, cannot be held to constitute a causal explanation. Both writers elide discussion of the ontological uniqueness of human agency and its workings through emergent properties.[51] Other writers have drawn on Mikhail Bhaktin to describe the dialogical relationship between subjectivity and photography. Erina Duganne's analysis is a refreshing escape from contextualism and welcome in its emphasis on photographic practice as an expression of self. In drawing on the structural linguistic analysis of Emile Benveniste however Duganne's account, like that of Roberts and Wolff, lacks the ontologically grounded conception of self and agency which finds expression in the emergent social and cultural features.[52]

III. Conclusion

The approach developed throughout this book conceives jazz photography as a site of human agency. Photographs are objects which embody and articulate the agency of the photographer by pointing the identity of the creator as well as their referents. Identity is inherently an agential process, an emergent property arising from the embodied engagement of photographers in the real world and mediated by the "inner conversation" of reflexivity. Encouraged to engage in the field by subjective affinity, the choices effected through photographic framing by photographers embody that subjectivity. It is at this point that the photographer makes selections from reality and chooses the content and form of its representation. Photographic agency exercised through the essentially human *praxis* of reflexivity is thus one element in the process of identification. Interpretations of jazz photographs will evolve over time, subtly shifting as the image moves away from the original point of production and enters new contexts of distribution and usage. Any critical evaluation of these various readings can only be accomplished by reference to the purposes and objectives of the photographer, in effect by "re-contextualizing" the image at the moment of production, reestablishing the creator's relationship with the object in order to penetrate the layers of subsequent mediation. Deep interpretation requires an understanding of the purposes of the photographer, as consciously inscribed in the image through the processes of photographic framing, as much as an analysis of their usage in circulation and understanding in reception.

In making the case for photographic agency it must not be assumed that the photographer's original intentions and aspirations will always be known, articulated, or applied: as Walker Evans said, "People often read things into my work, but I did not consciously put these things in the photographs."[53] Photographers will read a scene in different ways, some consciously seeking particular effects through specific technical and aesthetic choices while others might react instinctively, summing up a scene as a whole and drawing on experience to create a less declamatory but still conscious result. Yet, as Siegfried Kracauer reminds us, even Proust's "alienated" photographer, interested only in recording what appears before the camera,[54]

> *spontaneously structures the inflowing impressions; the simultaneous perceptions of his other senses, certain perceptual form categories inherent in his nervous system, and not least his general dispositions prompt him to organize the visual raw material in the act of seeing. And the activities in which he thus unconsciously engages are bound to condition the pictures he is taking.*

The historian seeking to interpret jazz images must rely on plausible reconstructions of the photographer's intentions by drawing on all available evidence, proceeding intertextually to resituate the photograph within the context of production and the trajectory of the photographer's practice as a whole.[55] Using a variety of images and textual material, including interviews and biographical information, institutional developments and processes, "latent structures of meaning" are revealed and which may differ from the representations of the subjects. Conclusions about the photographer's intentions cannot be deduced from a single image and are more profitably read across that practice or at least a series of photographs as each picture reinforces the other. Identifying, describing, and explaining the photographer's intentions is the starting point for deep interpretation without which the historian's reconstruction of the surface interpretation will never approach resolution. This, in summary, has been the central problematic of *Sight Readings.*

Notes

1. Miles Orvell, *American Photography* (Oxford: Oxford University Press, 2003), 16.
2. Ira Gitler, "Introduction," to David G. Spitzer and Ira Gitler, *Jazz: Photographs by David G. Spitzer* (San Francisco, CA: Woodford Press, 1994), 7.
3. Clive Scott, *The Spoken Image: Photography and Language* (London: Reaktion Books, 1999), 10, 34–6; Martha Rosler, "In, Around, and Afterthoughts (On Documentary Photography)," in *Decoys and Disruptions: Selected Writings 1975–2001* (Cambridge, MA: MIT Press, 2004), 185–86.
4. Susan Sontag, *On Photography* (London: Penguin Books, 1977), 15.
5. Arthur C. Danto, "The Artworld," *The Journal of Philosophy* 61, no. 19 (1964): 571–84. While Danto argues that surface interpretations must necessarily *agree* with the artists' aims and objects I follow Peg and Myles Brand who have shown that surface interpretations must be "accurate" rather than "correct:" "Surface and Deep Interpretation," in *Danto and His Cities*, Mark Rollins, ed., (Oxford: Blackwell, 2012), 72–74.
6. Erwin Panofsky, *Studies in Iconology: Humanistic Themes in the Art of the Renaissance* (New York: Harper & Row, 1972), 14, 15.
7. E. D. Hirsch Jr., *Validity in Interpretation* (London: University of Chicago Press, 1967), 207.
8. Janet Wolff, *The Social Production of Art* (London: MacMillan, 1993), 103, 136, 138, 146. Wolff concedes that the development of theory since her book was first published (1981) has continued radically to "de-center the subject and displace the artist as creator."
9. Roland Barthes, "The Death of the Author," in *Image Music Text*, ed. Stephen Heath (trans.) (London: Fontana, 1984), 142–48; Michel Foucault, "What Is an Author?," in *Language, Counter-Memory, Practice*, ed. Donald F. Bouchard (trans.) (Ithaca, NY, 1967), 113–38. See further William Wimsatt and Monroe C. Beardsley, "The Intentional Fallacy," *Swanee Review*, 54 (1946): 468–88, 468; and J. C. Carlier and C. T. Watts, "Roland Barthes's Resurrection of the Author and Redemption of Biography," *Cambridge Quarterly* 29, no. 4 (2000): 386–93.
10. Mary Warner Marien, *Photography: A Cultural History*, 3rd ed. (London: Laurence King Publishing, 2010), 28; Roger Scruton, "Photography and Representation," *Critical Inquiry*, 7, no. 3 (1981): 580; Clive Scott, *Street Photography: From Atget to Cartier-Bresson* (London: I. B. Tauris, 2007), 33, references Francois Soulages's argument that photographers cannot make any claims about the truth of the reality the camera indexically mirrors; their input cannot exceed the theatricality of creating a mise-en-scène in the act of framing.
11. Lady Elizabeth Eastlake, "Photography," *London Quarterly*, 101 (1857), reprinted in *Photography: Essays and Images*, ed. Beaumont Newhall (New York: New York Museum of Modern Art, 1980), 89, 91; A. Bazin, "The Ontology of the Photographic Image," in *Classic Essays on Photography*, ed. Alan Trachtenberg (New Haven, CT: Leet's Island Books, 1980), 241; Paul Joyce, *Hockney on Photography: Conversations with Paul Joyce*, ed. Wendy Brown (London: Jonathan Cape, 1988), 75; W. J. T. Mitchell, "There Are No Visual Media," *Journal of Visual Culture* 4, no. 2 (2005): 259; Rudolf Arnheim, "On the Nature of Photography," *Critical Inquiry* 1 (1974): 151.
12. Edward Weston, *The Daybooks of Edward Weston, Vol. 2*, ed. Nancy Newhall (New York: Aperture, 1973), 240–41; Ansel Adams, "A Personal Credo 1943," in *Photography in Print: Writings from 1816 to the Present*, ed. Vicki Goldberg (Albuquerque: University of New Mexico, 1981), 378; Guy Le Querrec quoted by Scott, *The Spoken Image: Photography and Language*, 18–19.
13. Mustafa Emirbayer and Ann Mische, "What Is Agency?," *American Journal of Sociology* 103, no. 4 (1998): 975–83.
14. Lásló Moholy-Nagy, "A New Instrument of Vision," in *The Photography Reader*, ed. Liz Wells (London: Routledge, 2003), 92–96; Harry Callaghan, "Statement 1964," in *Photography in Print: Writings from 1816 to the Present*, ed. Vicki Goldberg (Albuquerque: University of New Mexico Press, 1981), 421; Patrick Maynard, *The Engine of Visualization: Thinking through Photography* (Ithaca, NY: Cornell University Press, 1997), x. Walter Rosenblum and Naomi Rosenblum, "The Art Historian and the Photographic Image," *Art Journal* 36, no. 2 (n.d.): 139–42, located the authenticity of Hine's photographs through "his way of handling the physical means [. . .] In photography, these marks are equivalent to the fingerprint."
15. André Rouillé, *La Photographie: Entre document et art contemporain* (Paris: Gallimard, 2005), 207.

16. Margaret Iveson, "Analogue: Zoe Leonard and Tacita Dean," *Critical Inquiry* 38 (2012): 797–819; Robin Kelsey, "Of Fish, Birds, Cats, Mice, Spiders, Flies, Pigs, and Chimpanzees: How Chance Casts the Historic Action Photograph into Doubt," *History and Theory* 48, no. 4 (2009): 59–76; Michael Baxandall, *Patterns of Intention: On the Historical Explanation of Pictures* (New Haven, CT: Yale University Press, 1985), 41–42. See further Dominic McIver Lopes, "Afterword: Photography and the 'Picturesque Agent,'" *Critical Inquiry*, 38, no. 4 (2012): 862.
17. Susan Buck-Morss, "Visual Studies in Global Imagination," in *The Politics of Imagination*, ed. Chiara Bottici and Benoit Challand (Abingdon: Birkbeck Law Press, 2011), 228–29.
18. Martin A. Berger, "Photography, History and the Historian," *American Art* 29, no. 1 (2015): 3.
19. John Tagg, "Neither Fish nor Flesh," *History and Theory* 48, no. 4 (2009): 77–81. See further John Tagg, *The Burden of Representation: Eassys on Photographies and Histories* (London: MacMillan, 1988).
20. Raymond Williams, *Marxism and Literature* (Oxford: Oxford University Press, 1977), 123–27, 133, describes "new structures of feeling." Barnaby E. Haran, "The New Vision in American Photography: Ralph Steiner, Walker Evans, and 'Americanism.'" *Object*, no. 8 (2005): 26–42, analyses the "multi-accentual" nature of photographic signs and the ways in which subject matter can destabilize the signifier from the signified.
21. Lawrence W Levine, "The Historian and the Icon: Photography and the History of the American People in the 1930s and 1940s," in *Documenting America, 1935–1943*, ed. Carl Fleischhauer and Beverly W. Brannan (Berkeley: University of California Press, 1988), 15–42, 37; Geoffrey Batchen, *Burning with Desire: The Conception of Photography* (Cambridge, MA: MIT Press, 1997), 20–21 and 187–89. Jorge Ribalta, "Towards a New Documentalism," *Variant* 43 (Spring 2012), n. pag. argues that "Tagg's theoretical framework simply does not allow him to study anything but hegemonic practices and discourses [. . .] rather than deviations, ruptures and moments of indeterminacy or resistance." Ian Jeffrey, "Review of Some Sacred Sites: Thinking Photography' Edited by Victor Burgin," in *Creative Camera: Thirty Years of Writing*, ed. David Brittain (Manchester: Manchester University Press, 1999), 90, describes this trend in photographic theory as a form of contextual determinism "in which individuals scarcely appear, one in which credit is given to impersonal ideological determinants."
22. Abigail Solomon-Godeau, *Photography at the Dock: Essays on Photographic History, Institutions, and Practices* (Minneapolis: University of Minnesota Press, 1991), 113; Patricia Vettel-Becker, *Shooting from the Hip: Photography, Masculinity and Postwar America* (Minneapolis: University of Minnesota Press, 2005), 68.
23. Robert Hariman and John Louis Lucaites, *The Public Image: Photography and Civic Spectatorship* (Chicago: University of Chicago Press, 2016), 29.
24. Rosalind E. Krauss, "Notes on the Obtuse," in *Photography Theory*, ed. James Elkins (New York: Routledge, 2007), 339–42; Rouillé, *La Photographie*, 248.
25. Michel Foucault, "On the Genealogy of Ethics: An Overview of Work in Progress," in *The Foucault Reader*, ed. Luther H. Martin, Huck Gutman, and Patrick H. Hutton (London: Penguin Books, 1984), 350; Rux Martin, "Truth, Power, Self: An Interview with Michel Foucault, October 25 1982," in *Technologies of the Self: A Seminar with Michel Foucault*, 9; Michel Foucault, "Technologies of the Self," in *Technologies of the Self*, 18 For an application of the "technology of self" concept in music see Tia DeNora, *Music in Everyday Life* (Cambridge: Cambridge University Press, 2000).
26. On Nadar see Mary Price, *The Photograph: A Strange Confined Space* (Stanford, CA: University of Stanford Press, 1994), 9; Saul Warkov quoted by Howard S. Becker, "Visual Sociology, Documentary Photography, and Photojournalism: It's (Almost) All a Matter of Context," *Visual Studies* 10, no. 1 (1995): 5–6; Henri Cartier-Bresson, "The Decisive Moment," in *Photography in Print: Writings from 1816 to the Present*, ed. Vicki Goldberg (Albuquerque: University of New Mexico Press, 1981), 384–86, and Lincoln Kirstein cited by Assouline, *Cartier-Bresson: L'oeil Du Siecle* (Paris: Plon, 1999), 203. Even while describing the photograph as a message without a code, Roland Barthes spoke of the photographer's control over the image through the "connotative procedures" and "trick effects" that inscribed messages in advertising and press photographs: Roland Barthes, "The Photographic Message," in *Photography in Print*, ed. Vicki Goldberg (Albuquerque: University of New Mexico, 1961), 525–29.

27. Edward Weston, *The Daybooks of Edward Weston* 239; "Timeless: Photographs by Kamoinge," ed. Anthony Barboza, Herb Robinson, and Vincent Alabiso (Atglen, PA: Schiffer, 2015), 85.
28. Guibert cited by Akane Kawakami, *Photobiography: Photographic Self-Writing in Proust, Guibert, Ernaux, Mace* (Oxford: Legenda, 2013), 39–40, 55; Jean-Pierre Boulé, *Hervé Guibert: Voices of the Self* (Liverpool: Liverpool University Press, 1999), 62.
29. Clement Greenberg, "Four Photographers: Review," in *Clement Greenberg: The Collected Essays and Criticism*, ed. John O'Brian (Chicago: University of Chicago Press, 1993), 183.
30. Eviatar Zerubavel, *The Fine Line: Making Distinctions in Everyday Life* (Chicago: University of Chicago Press, 1991), esp. 5–20, for an account of the general processes of framing in social life.
31. Ian Jeffrey, "Fragment and Totality in Photography," *History of Photography* 16, no. 4 (1992): 351–57.
32. Cartier-Bresson quoted in Assouline, *Cartier-Bresson: L'oeil Du Siecle*, 129.
33. John Berger and Jean Mohr *Another Way of Telling*, (New York: Pantheon, 1982), 119–22. Martin Gayford, *Modernists and Mavericks: Bacon, Freud and the London Painters* (London: Thames & Hudson, 2018), 117–18, describes this process as it has informed painters seeking to achieve a representational *presence* without necessarily achieving mimetic likeness.
34. For an application of this idea see Jordan Bear, "The Silent Partner: Agency and Absence in Julia Margaret Cameron's Collaborations," *Grey Room*, no. 48 (2012): 78–101.
35. Dennis Stock, "How the Photographs Were Made," in *Jazz Street* (London: Andre Deutsch, 1960), 61–2.
36. Alan Trachtenberg, "Signifying the Real: Documentary Photography in the 1930s," in *The Social and the Real: Political Art of the 1930s in the Western Hemisphere*, ed. Alejandro Anreus, Diana L. Linden, and Jonathan Weinberg (University Park: Pennsylvania State University Press, 2006), 17; Carl Gardner, "Introduction," in *Media, Culture and Politics: A Socialist View* (London: Macmillan, 1979), 6–7, makes a similar point. Joel Snyder and Neil Walsh Allen, "Photography, Vision and Representation," *Critical Inquiry* 2, no. 1 (1975): 143–70, illustrate photographic decisions in an analysis of specific photographs including Dennis Stock's image of James Dean at his brother's grave side.
37. Engel quoted by Trachtenberg, "Photography and Social Knowledge," 5.
38. Tom Seymour, "Remembering David Redfern, the King of Jazz Photography," *British Journal of Photography*, 2014.
39. Carol Armstrong, "Automatism and Agency Intertwined: A Spectrum of Photographic Intentionality," *Critical Inquiry* 38, no. 4 (2012): 706.
40. Alfred Gell, *Art and Agency: An Anthropological Theory* (Oxford: Oxford University Press, 1998). Robert Layton, "Art and Agency: A Reassessment," *The Journal of the Royal Anthropological Institute* 9, no. 3 (2003), 458, notes "Agency derives from a position in a network of social relationships [. . .] Personal agency creates the distributed art objects that belong to the corpus; our mind becomes manifest in the objects, traces and leavings that we generate during our lifetime." Elizabeth Edwards has been especially influential in stressing the agency of photographs in human relations: see for example Elizabeth Edwards and Janice Hart, "Introduction: Photographs as Objects," in *Photographs Objects Histories: On the Materiality of Images*, ed. Elizabeth Edwards and Janice Hart (London: Routledge, 2004), 1–15. The relationship between photographer and the material image as discussed here is similar to the concept of double indexicality as proposed by Robin Kelsey and Blake Stimson, "Photography's Double Index (A Short History in Three Parts)," in *The Meaning of Photography*, ed. Robin Kelsey and Stimson (New Haven, CT: Yale University Press, 2008), xvi–xvii.
41. Gérard Genette, *The Work of Art: Immanence and Transcendence (Trans. G. M. Goshgarian)* (Ithaca, NY: Cornell University Press, 1997), 40–41.
42. Gates Jr., "The Master's Pieces," 39; Charles Hersch, "Reconstructing the Jazz Tradition," *Jazz Research Journal* 2, no. 1 (2008): 25.
43. Stuart Hall, "Who Needs Identity?," in *Questions of Cultural Identity*, ed. Stuart Hall and Paul Du Gray (Thousand Oaks, CA: Sage, 1996), 4.
44. Rogers Brubaker and Frederick Cooper, "Beyond 'Identity'," in *Ethnicity without Groups*, ed. Rogers Brubaker (Cambridge, MA: Harvard University Press, 2004), 29.
45. Martin Jay, "In the Realm of the Senses: An Introduction," *American Historical Review* 116, no. 2 (2011): 309.

46. Key texts include Margaret S. Archer: *Realist Social Theory: The Morphogenetic Approach* (Cambridge: Cambridge University Press, 1995); *Culture and Agency: The Place of Culture in Social Theory* (Cambridge: Cambridge University Press, 1996); *Being Human: The Problem of Agency* (Cambridge: Cambridge University Press, 2000); "Introduction: How Does Structure Influence Agency?," in *Structure, Agency and the Internal Conversation* (Cambridge: Cambridge University Press, 2003), 1–16; *Making Our Way Through the World: Human Reflexivity and Social Mobility* (Cambridge: Cambridge University Press, 2007); "Introduction: The Reflexive Re-Turn," in *Conversations about Reflexivity*, ed. Margaret S. Archer (Abingdon: Routledge, 2010), 1–13; "Routine, Reflexivity, and Realism," *Sociological Theory* 28, no. 3 (2010): 272–303; and *The Reflexive Imperative in Late Modernity* (Cambridge: Cambridge University Press, 2012).
47. Archer, *Structure, Agency and the Internal Conversation*, 25.
48. Archer, *Being Human: The Problem of Agency*, 22.
49. Archer, *Structure, Agency of the Internal Conversation*, 342.
50. John Roberts, *The Art of Interruption: Realism, Photography and the Everyday* (Manchester: Manchester University Press, 1998), 5–7; Wolff, *The Social Production of Art*, 138.
51. Christopher Smith, "Review of 'Jazz Cultures' and 'Going for Jazz'," *Journal of the American Musicological Society* 58, no. 2 (2005): 486, levels a similar criticism against Nicholas Gebhardt whose book theorizes the relationship between agency in the jazz act and structure: Nicholas Gebhardt, *Going for Jazz: Musical Practices and American Ideology* (Chicago: University of Chicago Press, 2001).
52. Erina Duganne, "Transcending the Fixity of Race: The Kamoigne Workshop and the Question of a 'Black Aesthetic' in Photography," in *New Thoughts on the Black Arts Movement*, ed. Lisa Gail Collins and Margo Natalie Crawford (New Brunswick, NJ: Rutgers University Press, 2006), 185–209; see also Erina Duganne, *The Self in Black and White: Race and Subjectivity in Postwar American Photography* (Hanover, NH: Dartmouth College Press, 2010).
53. Evans cited by Hank O'Neal, *A Vision Shared: A Classic Portrait of America and Its People 1935–1943* (New York: St. Martin's Press, 1976), 60; Herman Leonard, "Interview with Tad Hershorn" (Institute of Jazz Studies, Rutgers University, n.d.) made a similar point when he said "well you can glean things out of the photographs that I don't."
54. Kracauer, *Theory of Film: The Redemption of Physical Reality*. 16. Kracauer is quoting from Proust's book *The Guermantes Way*.
55. There are similarities between this approach and what has been termed "biographical sociology"—see Ines W. Jindra, "Why American Sociology Needs Biographical Sociology—European Style," *Journal for the Theory of Social Behaviour* 44, no. 4 (2014): 389–412, https://doi.org/10.1111/jtsb.12055.

Bibliography

Personal interviews and correspondence

Berger, David G. Telephone interview, October 8, 2018 and subsequent correspondence.

Blecha, Peter. Telephone interview, July 26, 2018 and subsequent correspondence.

Bultman, Janis. Telephone interview, July 18, 2018 and subsequent correspondence.

Cawthra, Benjamin. Personal interview, August 18, 2018, Long Beach, CA, and subsequent correspondence.

Charles, Debora. Personal interview, September 15, 2018, Los Angeles.

Crosland, Ben. Personal interview, January 20, 2019, London.

Cuscuna, Michael. Telephone interview, November 15, 2018.

Cyrus, Gerald. Personal interview, September 25, 2018, Germantown, PA.

Delgardo, Lourdes. Telephone interview, August 15, 2017.

Farber, Enid. Personal interview, August 26, 2018, New York.

Ferber, Jessica. Telephone interview with the author, May 21, 2018.

Fishman, Chuck. Zoom interview. July 22, 2020.

Galbraith, Steven. Personal interview, August 3, 2018, Rochester, NY, and subsequent correspondence.

Gottlieb, Steve. Personal interview, September 22, 2018, Washington, DC.

Hersch, Robin. Personal interview, August 23, 2018, New York.

Hershorn, Tad. Personal interviews, August 27, 2018, and subsequent occasions, Institute of Jazz Studies, NJ, and subsequent correspondence.

Katz, Jimmy. Personal interview, August 26, 2018, New York, and subsequent correspondence.

Kimball, Gene. Telephone interview with the author, July 30, 2018.

Kriegsmann Jr., James J. Telephone interview, October 18, 2018, and subsequent correspondence.

Lara, Diane. Correspondence with the author, October 9, 2020.

Loengard, John. Personal interview, August 23, 2018, New York, and subsequent correspondence.

Lubow, Leo. Personal interview, September 26, 2018, and subsequent correspondence.

Maisel, Jay. Personal interview, August 23, 2018, Brooklyn, NY, and subsequent correspondence.

Mortensen, Dan. Telephone interview, July 31, 2018.

Oakland, Veryl. Telephone interview, November 12, 2018.

O'Neal, Hank. Personal interviews, July 16, 2017 and August 24, 2018, New York, and subsequent correspondence.

Pinson, Heather. Telephone interview, January 23, 2019, and subsequent correspondence.

Snitzer, Herb. Personal interview, June 9, 2016, St. Petersburg, FL.
Vacher, Peter. Personal interviews, June 23, 2018, and subsequent occasions and correspondence with the author.
Willard, Patricia. Telephone interview, May 6, 2019, and subsequent correspondence.
Williams, Adrienne. Telephone interview, December 20, 2018.
Withers, Rosalind. Telephone interview, September 16, 2020.

Photographic archives consulted

Author's collection
Carnegie Museum of Art
Chuck Fishman Photography
Clyde Adams Collection
Department of Art, University of Memphis, Charles Church Collection
Down Beat
Don Peterson
Ed Gottlieb/Library of Congress, William P. Gottlieb Collection
Ernest Withers Collection
Fernando de Ortiz Urbina Collection
Fireball Entertainment Group/Kim Stewart
Gerald Cyrus
Gilmore Music Library, Yale University, New Haven,
Hogan Jazz Archive, Tulane University
Howard Morehead Photographs and Papers, UCLA Library Special Collections
Iconic Publishing, London
Institute of Jazz Studies, Rutgers University
Library of Congress, Prints and Photographic Division, Farm Security Administration/Office of War Information Collection
Los Angeles County Museum of Art
Louis Armstrong House Museum
Louisianna State Museum, New Orleans Jazz Club Collection
Maxine Gordon/Library of Congress, Dexter Gordon Collection
Miami Dade Public Library
Michael Randolph, Executive to the Estate of William "PoPsie" Randolph
Milt Hinton Photographic Collection
Museum of History and Industry, Seattle, Al Smith Collection
New York Public Library/Otto Hess Collection
Oberlin College Library, The Frank Kuchirchuk Collection of Jazz Photography
Peter Vacher Collection
Rochester Institute of Technology, Bob Cato Collection

Schomberg Centre, New York Public Library
Tom and Ethel Bradley Centre for African American Arts, California State University, Northridge
Tom Kramer Photography
UMKC University Library, LaBudde Special Collections
Vintage Guitar Magazine
Western Reserve Historical Society, Cleveland, Ohio

Other sources

Abbott, Berenice. "Preface." In *Lisette Model*. New York: Aperture, 1979, n.pag.

Abe, K. *Jazz Giants: A Visual Retrospective*. New York: Billboard, 1986.

Abrams, Nathan. *Stanley Kubrick: New York Jewish Intellectual*. New Brunswick, Newark: Rutgers University Press, 2018.

Adams, Ansel. "A Personal Credo 1943." In *Photography in Print: Writings from 1816 to The Present*, edited by Vicki Goldberg, 377–80. Alberqueque: University of New Mexico, 1981.

Adams, Clyde. "The One Big Name." Murray Korman Photography, 2017. https://www.murraykorman.com/bio.

Agovino, Michael J. "Ornette Coleman, the Saxophonist Who Transformed Jazz." *New Republic*, June 17, 2015. https://newrepublic.com/article/122051/ornette-coleman-saxophonist-who-transformed-jazz.

Ainsworth, Alan John. " 'A Private Passion': The Jazz Photography of Bob Douglas." *Southern California Quarterly* 101, no. 3 (2019): 317–38.

Ainsworth, Alan John. "Early New Orleans Band Photography." *Jazz Research Journal* 11, no. 1 (2017): 28–61. https://doi.org/10.1558/jazz.33607.

Ainsworth, Alan John. "Photographic Representations of Jazz: Testimonial Advertising in Down Beat, 1938–48." *Jazz Research Journal* 11, no. 2 (2018): 111–52.

Ake, David. *Jazz Cultures*. Berkeley: University of California Press, 2002.

Alexander, Michael. *Jazz Age Jews*. Princeton, NJ: Princeton University Press, 2001.

Alland, Alexander. *American Counterpoint*. Edited by Pearl Buck (intro.). New York: John Day, 1943.

Amram, David. "David Amram: Ringing the Bells of Freedom in 1950s East Village." The Local East Village, n.d. http://localeastvillage.com/2012/01/23/david-amram-ringing-the-bells-of-freedom-in-1950s-east-village/.

Anderson, J. Lee. "The Painter as Photographer." *Mississippi Rag*, 1990.

Anderson, Jervis. *Harlem: The Great Black Way, 1900–1950*. London: Orbis, 1982.

Anderson, Paul Allen. " 'My Foolish Heart:' Bill Evans and the Public Life of Feelings." *Jazz Perspectives* 7, no. 3 (2013): 205–49. https://doi.org/10.1080/17494060.2014.911404.

Anon. "Hooks Brothers Photography Studio–164 Beale Street, Memphis." Mississippi Blues Travellers. http://www.mississippibluestravellers.com/hooks-brothers-photography-beale-street-memphis-tennessee/.

Anon. "Lens on Gibson." Bentley Historical Library Magazine, 2019. https:// bentley.umich.edu/news- events/magazine/lens- on- gibson/.

Anon. "Obituary. Bill Russell." *New York Times*, August 11, 1992, s.D, 19.

Anon. "Obituary: James J. Kriegsmann; Theatrical Photographer, 85." *New York Times*, May 1, 1994. s.1, 54.

Anthony, Arthé A. "Florestine Perrault Collins and the Gendered Politics of Black Portraiture in 1920s New Orleans." *Louisiana History: The Journal of the Louisiana Historical Association* 43, no. 2 (2002): 167–88.

Anthony, Arthé A. *Picturing Black New Orleans: A Creole Photographer's View of the Early Twentieth Century*. Gainsville: University Press of Florida, 2012.

Anthony, Robert. "Lenses of Industry: The Rise of Industrial Photography in the United States." Access Master's Thesis, Technological University, 2015. digitalcommons.mtu.edu/etdr/4.

"Apollo Threater's Gordon 'Doc' Anderson and Billie Holiday, 1950s." Harlem World, 2014.

Appel, Alfred. *Jazz Modernism: From Ellington and Armstrong to Matisse and Joyce*. Vol. 11. New York: Alfred A Knopf, 2005. https://doi.org/10.1215/0961754X-11–3-500.

Applebaum, Larry. "Before & After: Sonny Rollins." https://larryappelbaum.wordpress.com/2011/09/07/before-after-sonny-rollins-2/.

Archer, Fred. *Fred Archer on Portraiture*. San Francisco, CA: Camera Craft Publishing, 1954.

Archer, Margaret. *Being Human: The Problem of Agency*. Cambridge: Cambridge University Press, 2000.

Archer, Margaret. *Culture and Agency: The Place of Culture in Social Theory*. Cambridge: Cambridge University Press, 1996.

Archer, Margaret. "Introduction: How Does Structure Influence Agency?" In *Structure, Agency and the Internal Conversation*, 1–16. Cambridge: Cambridge University Press, 2003.

Archer, Margaret. *Realist Social Theory: The Morphogenetic Approach*. Cambridge: Cambridge University Press, 1995.

Archer, Margaret S. "Introduction: The Reflexive Re-Turn." In *Conversations about Reflexivity*, edited by Margaret S. Archer, 1–13. Abingdon: Routledge, 2010.

Archer, Margaret S. *Making Our Way through the World: Human Reflexivity and Social Mobility*. Cambridge: Cambridge University Press, 2007.

Archer, Margaret S. *Structure, Agency and the Internal Conversation*. Cambridge: Cambridge University Press, 2003.

Archer, Margaret S. *The Reflexive Imperative in Late Modernity*. Cambridge: Cambridge University Press, 2012.

Archibald, Paul. "Construction of, and Performance on, the Early Drum Kit." Unpublished Ph.D. thesis, University of Edinburgh, 2017.

Arendt, Hannah. "We Refugees." In *Altogether Elsewhere: Writers in Exile*, edited by Marc Robinson, 110–19. Boston, MA: Faber and Faber, 1994.

Armstrong, Carol. "Automatism and Agency Intertwined: A Spectrum of Photographic Intenionality." *Critical Inquiry* 38, no. 4 (2012): 705–26.

Armstrong, Elizabeth. *Birth of the Cool: California Art, Design and Culture at Midcentury*. Newport Beach, CA: Orange County Museum of Art, Prestel Publishing, 2007.

Armstrong, Nancy. "Realism before and after Photography: The Fantastical Form of a Relation among Things." In *Adventures in Realism*, edited by Matthew Beaumont, 84–102. Malden, MA: Blackwell, 2007.

Arnheim, Rudolf. "On the Nature of Photography." *Critical Inquiry* 1 (1974), 149–61.

Assouline, Pierre. *Cartier-Bresson: L'oeil Du Siecle*. Paris: Plon, 1999.

Atkins, Jerry. "Magnificent Obsession: The Discographers," reprinted at JazzDiscography.com. https://jazzdiscography.com/magnificent-obsession-the-discographers/

Auer, Anna. (ed.). *Übersee: Flucht Und Emigation Österreichenscher Fotografen 1920–40*. Vienna: Kunsthalle WienAuer, Anna, 1998.

Auer, Anna. "Laszlo Willinger." In *Übersee: Flucht Und Emigation Österreichenscher Fotografen 1920–40*, edited by Anna Auer, 244–46. Vienna: Kunsthalle Wien, 1998.

Aviv, Caryn, and David Shneer. *New Jews: The End of the Jewish Diaspora*. New York: New York University Press, 2005.

Bacon Hales, Peter. *Silver Cities: Photographing American Urbanization, 1839–1939*. Alberqueque: University of New Mexico Press, 2005.

Bacon, Paul. "Jazz Fan." In *Black Beauty, White Heat: A Pictorial History of Jazz 1920–1950*, edited by F. Driggs and H. Lewine, 8–18. New York: William Morrow, 1982.

Bacon, Paul. "The High Priest of Bebop: The Inimitable Mr. Monk." In *The Thelonious Monk Reader*, edited by Rob van der Bliek, 56–62. Oxford: Oxford University Press, 2001.

Badger, Anthony J. *The New Deal: The Depression Years 1933–40*. London: Macmillan, 1989.

Badger, Gerry. "To Make the Present Time Come Alive: Magazine Photography 1891–1940." In *Photography: A New Vision of the World 1891–1940*, edited by W. Guadagnini, 162–79. Milan: Skira, 2011.

Bailey, Derek. *Improvisation: Its Nature and Practices in Music*. Ashbourne: Moorland, 1980.

Baker, George. "Photography between Narrative and Stasis: August Sander, Degeneration and the Decay of the Portrait." *October*, no. 76 (1966): 73–113.

Bakewell, Oliver. "Re-Launching Migration Systems." In *Second Workshop on Social Theory and Migration: What Post-Positivism, Critical Realism & Structuration Can Offer to Migration Studies*. Oxford: International Migration Institute/ University of Oxford, 2012, 2–18.

Baldwin, Davarian L. "Our Newcomers to the City: The Great Migration and the Making of Modern Mass Culture." In *Beyond Blackface: African Americans and the Creation of American Popular Culture 1890–1930*, edited by W. Fitzhugh Brundage, 159–89. Chapel Hill: University of North Carolina Press, 2011.

Balliett, Whitney. *Dinosaurs in the Morning: 41 Pieces on Jazz*. Philadelphia: J. B. Lippincott, 1965).

Balliett, Whitney. "The Gentlemen of Jazz." *Saturday Review*, March 1955.

Balliett, Whitney. "Mecca, LA." *The New Yorker*, 128–166 1966.

Balliettt, Whitney. "Night Clubs." *The New Yorker*, October 9, 1971.

Balliett, Whitney. *The Sound of Surprise: 46 Pieces of Jazz*. Harmondsworth: Penguin Books, 1959.

Baraka, Amiri. "Jazz Criticism and Its Effects on the Music." In *Digging: The Afro-American Soul of American Classical Music*, 74–85. Berkeley: University of California Press, 2009.

Barbeau, Arthur E., and Florette Henri. *The Unknown Soldiers: African American Troops in World War 1*. New York: Da Capo, 1996.

Barboza, Anthony, Herb Robinson, and Vincent Alabiso, eds. "Timeless: Photographs by Kamoinge." Atglen, PA: Schiffer, 2015.

Barker, Danny. *A Life in Jazz*. Edited by Alyn Shipton. Basingstoke: Macmillan, 1986.

Barlow, William. "Black Music on Radio during the Jazz Age." *African American Review* 29, no. 2 (1995): 325–28.

Baron, Stanley. *Benny King of Swing: A Pictorial Biography*. London: Thames & Hudson, 1979.

Barron, Stephanie, Sabine Eckmann, and Matthew Affron. "Exiles and émigrés." Los Angeles: Harry N. Abrams-Los Angeles County Museum of Art, 1997.

Barros, Paul De. *Jackson Street after Hours: The Roots of Jazz in Seattle*. Seattle, WA: Sasquatch Books, 1993.

Barthes, Roland. *Camera Lucida: Reflections on Photography*. Translated by Richard Howard. London: Vintage Books, 2000.

Barthes, Roland. "Droit Dans Les Yeux." In *L'obvie et l'obtus: Essais Critiques III*, 279–83. Paris: Editions du Seuil, 1982.

Barthes, Roland. "The Death of the Author." In *Image Music Text*, edited by Stephen Heath (trans.). London: Fontana, 1984. 142–148.
Barthes, Roland. "The Photographic Message." In *Photography in Print*, edited by Vicki Goldberg, 521–33. Alberqueque: University of New Mexico, 1961.
Barthes, Roland. "The Third Meaning: Research Notes on Some Eisenstein Stills." In *Image-Music-Text*, edited by S. Heath, 52–69. London: Fontana, 1977.
Bartz, Edek. "Before I Started to Be a Photographer, I Was a Musician." In *Lisette Model: Fotografen 1934–1960*, 71–85. Wien: Kunsthalle Wien, 2000.
Baskind, Samantha. "Weegee's Jewishness." *History of Photography Journal* 34, no. 1 (2010): 60–78.
Baskind, Samatha. "Navigating the Worldly and the Divine: Jewish American Artists on Judaism and Their Art." *Shofar: An Interdisciplinary Journal of Jewish Studies* 32, no. 1 (2013): 27–42.
Batchen, Geoffrey. "Vernacular Photographies: Responses to a Questionnaire." *History of Photography Journal* 24, no. 3 (2000): 229–31.
Bate, David. "The Memory of Photograph." *Photographies* 3, no. 2 (2010): 243–57.
Bauman, Mark K. "On German American and American Jewish History." *Journal of American Ethnic History* 29, no. 1 (2009): 67–71.
Baumann, Susanne. "The Essence of Things: An Interview with Ellen Auerbach." In *Ellen Auerbach: Berlin. Tel Aviv. Lond. New York*, 9–14. Munich: Prestel, 1998.
Baxandall, Michael. *Patterns of Intention: On the Historical Explanation of Pictures.* New Haven, CT: Yale University Press, 1985.
Bazin, A. "The Ontology of the Photographic Image." In *Classic Essays on Photography*, edited by Alan Trachtenberg, 237–44. New Haven, CT: Leet's Island Books, 1980.
Bear, Jordan. "The Silent Partner: Agency and Absence in Julia Margaret Cameron's Collaborations." *Grey Room*, no. 48 (2012): 78–101.
Bechet, Sidney. *Treat It Gentle.* New York: Hill and Wang, 1960.
Becker, Howard. "Jazz Places." In *Music Scenes: Local, Translocal, and Virtual*, edited by Andy Andy Bennett and Richard A. Peterson, 17–27. Nashville, TN: Vanderbilt University Press, 2004.
Becker, Howard S. "Visual Sociology, Documentary Photography, and Photojournalism: It's (Almost) All a Matter of Context." *Visual Studies* 10, no. 1 (1995): 5–14.
Behr, Shulamith, and Sander L. Gilman. "Forced Journeys: An Introduction." In *Forced Journeys: Artists in Exile in Britain c.1933–45*, edited by Shulamith Behr and Sander L. Gilman, 12–17. London: Ben Uri Gallery, 2009.
Belting, Hans. *Likeness and Presence: A History of the Image before the Era of Art.* Chicago: University of Chicago Press, 1994.

Benedict-Jones, Linda. "A Place in the Pantheon: Teenie Harris in the History of African-American Photography." In *Spirit of a Community: The Photographs of Charles 'Teenie' Harris*, 13–15. Greensburg, PA: Westmoreland Museum of American Art, 2001.

Bennet, Andy. "Music, Space and Place." In *Music, Space and Place: Popular Music and Cultural Identity*, edited by Sheila Whiteley, Andy Bennet, and Stan Hawkins, 2–8. Aldershot: Ashgate, 2004.

Bennett, Andy. *Popular Music and Youth Culture: Music, Identity and Place*. London: Palgrave, 2000.

Benovsky, Jiri. "Three Kinds of Realism about Photographs." *Journal of Speculative Philosophy* 25, no. 4 (2011): 375–95.

Benz, Wolfgang. *Das Exil Der Kleinen Leute: Alltagserfahrung Deutscher Juden in Der Emigration*. Frankfurt: Fischer, 1994.

Berardi, Gayle K., and Thomas W. Segady. "The Development of African-American Newspapers in the American West: A Sociohistorical Perspective." *Journal of Negro History* 75, nos. 3/4 (1990): 96–111.

Berendt, J.-E. *Jazz: A Photo History*. Translated by William Odom. London: Andre Deutsch, 1979.

Berger, David G. "Milt Hinton's Jazz Legacy." *USA Today*, March 13 (1998): 66–73.

Berger, Doris. "Illuminated Darkness: Exiles and Émigrés in the Golden Age of Hollywood." *Jewish Culture and History* 17, no. 1–2 (2016): 81–93.

Berger, John, and Jean Mohr. *Another Way of Telling*. New York: Pantheon, 1982.

Berger, Lynn, "Snapshots, or: Visual Culture's Clichés," Photographies 4, no. 2 (2011): 180.

Berger, Martin A. "Photography, History and the Historian." *American Art* 29, no. 1 (2015): 2–5.

Berger, Maurice. "Documenting the Dynamic Black Community of 1940s Seattle." *New York Times*, March 27. 2018.

Berghahn, Marion. "German Jews in England: Aspects of the Assimilation and Integration Process." In *Exile in Great Britain: Refugees from Hitler's Germany*, edited by Gerhard Hirschfeld, 285–306. Atlantic Highlands, NJ: Humanities Press, 1984.

Berkowitz, Michael. *Jews and Photography in Britain*. Austin: University of Texas Press, 2015.

Berkowitz, Michael, Susan L. Tannenbaum, and Sam W. Bloom. "Introduction: Anthologising Jews." In *Forging Modern Jewish Identities: Public Faces and Private Struggles*, edited by Michael Berkowitz, Susan L. Tannenbaum, and Sam W. Bloom, 1–15. London: Vallentine Mitchell, 2003.

Berlin, Isaiah. *The Roots of Romanticism*. Edited by Henry Hardy. London: Pimlico, 1999.

Berliner, Paul F. *Thinking in Jazz: The Infinite Art of Improvisation*. Chicago: University of Chicago Press, 1994.

Bernard, Susan. "Introduction." In *Bernard of Hollywood*, 7–14. Koln: Taschen, 2002.

Bethell, Tom. *George Lewis: Jazzman from New Orleans*. Berkeley: University of California Press, 1978.

Biemann, Asher D., Richard I. Cohen, and Sarah E. Wobick-Segev. "Introduction." In *Spiritual Homelands: The Cultural Experience of Exile, Place and Displacement among Jews and Others*, edited by Asher D. Biemann, Richard I. Cohen, and Sarah E. Wobick-Segev, 1–8. Berlin: DeGruyter, 2020.

Bieze, Michael. "Ruskin in the Black Belt: Booker T. Washington, Arts and Crafts and the New Negro." *Source: Notes in the History of Art* 24, no. 4 (2005): 24–34.

Bigard, Barney. *With Louis and the Duke: The Autobiography of a Jazz Clarinetist*. Edited by Barry Martyn. London: Macmillan Press, 1985.

Bildersee, Barnett. "Music and Musicians." *The Bulletin of the Museum of Modern Art* 15, no. 2 (1948): 3–8.

Billops, Camille, and Owen Dodson. *The Harlem Book of the Dead*. Dobbs Ferry, NY: Morgan & Morgan, 1978.

Bilski, Emily. "Introduction." In *Berlin Metropolis: Jews and the New Culture 1890–1918*. Berkeley: University of California Press, 1999.

"Biographies: Gottlieb's Life and Work." Library of Congress American Memory website, n.d. https://www.loc.gov/item/ihas.200185535/.

Birt, Rodger C. "A Life in American Photography." In *VanDerZee Photographer 1886–1983*, edited by Deborah Willis-Braithwaite and Rodger C. Birt, 26–74. New York: Harry N. Abrams, 1994.

Blair, Sarah. *Harlem Crossroads: Black Writers and the Photograph in the Twentieth Century*. Princeton, NJ: Princeton University Press, 2007.

Blair, Sarah. "Jewish America through the Lens." *Michigan Quarterly Review* 42, no. 1 (2003): 95–132.

Bland, Kalman. *The Artless Jew: Medieval and Modern Affirmations and Denials of the Visual*. Princeton, NJ: Princeton University Press, 2000.

Blanning, Tim. *The Romantic Revolution*. London: Wiedenfeld & Nicholson, 2010.

Blecha, Peter. *Music in Washington: Seattle and Beyond*. Charleston, SC: Arcadia, 2007.

Blecha, Peter. "Smith, Al (1916–2008)." HistoryLink. org, 2015.

Blesh, Rudi. *Combo USA: Eight Lives in Jazz*. New York: Chilton, 1971.

Blesh, Rudi. *Shining Trumpets: A History of Jazz*. London: Cassell, 1954.

Blesh, Rudi. *Stuart Davis*. New York: Grove Press, 1960.

Blesh, Rudi, "Old Photographs: They Document the Legendary Days of Jazz." In *Jazzways*, edited by George S. Rosenthal and Frank Zachary. London: Musicians Press, 1946.

Blum, Paul Von. *Resistance, Dignity and Pride: African American Artists in Los Angeles*. Los Angeles: CAAS Publications, University of California, 2004.

Boehm, Gottfried. "Es Zeight Sich: Geste-Deixis-Bild." In *Hold It!: Zur Pose Zwischen Bild Und Performance, Theater Der Zeit*, edited by John Hoberman, 22–40. Berlin: Theater der Zeit-Recherchen 89, 2012.

Bolton, Richard. "Introduction." In *The Contest of Meaning: Critical Histories of Photography*, edited by Richard Bolton, ix–xix. Cambridge, MA: MIT Press, 1989.

Bone, Robert, and Richard A. Courage. *The Muse in Bronzeville: African American Creative Expression in Chicago, 1932–1950*. New Brunswick, NJ: Rutgers University Press, 2011.

Bongiovanni, Domenica. "How a Quirky Indiana Studio Was the First to Record Many of America's Famous Musicians." *Indianapolis Star*, 2020. https://eu.indystar.com/story/entertainment/music/2020/07/27/richmonds-gennett-records-first-record-louis-armstrong/3215616001/.

Borhan, Pierre. *André Kertész: A Lifetime in Photography*. Boston, MA: Bullfinch Press, 2000.

Boulé, Jean-Pierre. *Hervé Guibert: Voices of the Self*. Liverpool: Liverpool University Press, 1999.

Bourdieu, Pierre. "Outline of a Theory of Art Perception." *International Social Science Journal* 20, no. 4 (1968): 589–612.

Bourguignon, Katherine M. "Cool Modernism in America, 1915–45." In *America's Cool Modernism: O'Keefe to Hopper*, 25–37. Oxford: Ashmolian Museum, 2018.

Bourne, Randolf S. *Youth and Life*. Boston, MA: Houghton Mifflin, 1913.

Boyd, Robert L. "The 'Black Metropolis' Revisited: A Comparative Analysis of Northern and Southern Cities in the United States in the Early 20th Century." *Urban Studies* 49, no. 4 (2012): 845–60.

Brace, Eric. "Making the Scene with Bill Gottlieb." *Washington Post Weekend*, August 14, 1998, 14.

Brand, Peg, and Myles Brand. "Surface and Deep Interpretation." In *Danto and His Critics*, edited by Mark Rollins, 69–83. Oxford: Blackwell, 2012.

Brinkley, Alan. *Culture and Politics in the Great Depression*. Waco, TX: Markham Press, 1999.

Britt, Stan. *Long Tall Dexter: A Critical Musical Bibliography of Dexter Gordon*. London: Quartet Books, 1989.

Brogan, Hugh. *The Penguin History of the USA*. 2nd ed. London: Penguin, 2001.

Brooks, Peter. *Realist Vision*. New Haven, CT: Yale University Press, 2005.

Brothers, Thomas. "'Swing a Lot of Type Writing' An Introduction to Louis Armstrong's Writings." In *Louis Armstrong in His Own Words: Selected Writings*, vii–xxiii. Oxford: Oxford University Press, 1999.

Broussard, Albert S. "In Search of the Promised Land: African American Migration to San Francisco, 1900–1945." In *Seeking El Dorado: African Americans in California*, edited by L. B. De Graaf, K. Mulroy, and Q. Taylor, 181–209. Los Angeles: Autry Museum of Western Heritage, 2001.

Broven, John. *Record Makers and Breakers: Voices of the Independent Rock 'n' Roll Pioneers.* Chicago: University of Illinois Press, 2010.

Browder, Laura. *Rousing the Nation: Radical Culture in Depression America.* Amherst: University of Massachusetts Press, 1998.

Brown, Charles E. "Al Smith Sr., Photographer, Historian." *Seattle Times*, 2008.

Brown, Joshua. "Historians and Photography." *American Art* 21, no. 3 (2007): 9–13.

Brubaker, Rogers, and Frederick Cooper. "Beyond 'Identity.'" In *Ethnicity without Groups*, edited by Rogers Brubaker, 28–63. Cambridge, MA: Harvard University Press, 2004.

Brundage, W. Fitzhugh, "Working in the 'Kingdon of Culture.'" In *Beyond Blackface: African Americans and the Creation of American Popular Culture, 1890–1930*, ed. W. Fitzhugh Brundage. Chapel Hill: University of North Carolina Press, 2011, 1–42.

Buck-Morss, Susan. "Visual Studies in Global Imagination." In *The Politics of Imagination*, edited by Chiara Bottici and Benoit Challand. Abingdon: Birkbeck Law Press, 2011.

Bultman, Janis. "James J. Kriegsmann: An Eye for Entertainers." In *Legacies: Interviews with Masters of Photography*. Coralville, IA: Quercus Agrifolia Press, Kindle ed., 2018.

Bunch, Lonnie G. "A Past Not Necessarily Prologue: The Afro-American in Los Angeles." In *20th Century Los Angeles: Power, Promotion and Social Conflict*, edited by Norman M. Klein and Martin J. Schiesl, 101–30. Claremont, CA: Regina Books, 1990.

Buni, Andrew. *Robert L. Vann of the Pittsburgh Courier: Politics and Black Journalism*. Pittsburgh: Universiuty of Pittsburgh Press, 1974.

Burke, Patrick. *Come In and Hear the Truth: Jazz and Race on 52nd. Street.* Chicago: University of Chicago Press, 2008.

Burke, Peter. *Eyewitnessing: The Uses of Images as Historical Evidence.* London: Reaktion Books, 2001.

Buruma, Ian. "V. S Naipaul (1932–2018)." *New York Review of Books* 55, no. 14 (2018): 16.

Richard Cahan and Michael Williams, *Revolution in Black and White: Photographs of the Civil Rights Era by Ernest Withers*. Chicago: CityFiles Press, 2019.

Callaghan, Harry. "Statement 1964." In *Photography in Print: Writings from 1816 to The Present,* edited by Vicki Goldberg, 420–21. Alberqueque: University of New Mexico Press, 1981.

Calo, Mary Ann. "African American Art and Critical Discourse between World Wars." *American Quarterly* 51, no. 3 (1999): 580–621.

Campbell, Marne L. *Making Black Los Angeles: Class, Gender and Community, 1850–1917*. Chapel Hill: University of North Carolina Press, 2016.

Campbell, Mary Schmidt. "Introduction." In *Harlem Renaissance: Art of Black America,* edited by Charles Miers, 11–56. New York: Abradale Press and Harry N. Abrams, 1994.

Caponi, Gena Dagel. "Introduction: The Case for an African American Aesthetic." In *Signifyin(g), Sanctifyin' and Slam Dunking: A Reader in African American Expressive Culture,* edited by Gena Dagel Caponi, 1–41. Amherst: University of Massachusetts Press, 1999.

Carlebach, Michael. *Photojournalism Comes of Age*. Washington, DC: Smithsonian Institution Press, 1997.

Carlebach, Michael. *Working Stiffs: Occupational Portraits in the Age of Tintypes.* Washington, DC: Smithsonian Institution Press, 2002.

Carlier, J. C., and C. T. Watts. "Roland Barthes's Resurrection of the Author and Redemption of Biography." *Cambridge Quarterly* 29, no. 4 (2000): 386–93.

Carner, Gary. *Jazz Performers: An Annotated Bibliography of Biographical Materials*. New York: Greenwood Press, 1990.

Carner, Gary. "Jazz Photography: A Conversation with Herb Snitzer." *Black American Literature Forum* 25, no. 3 (1991): 560–92.

Carner, Gary. "Literature of Jazz Issue: Introduction." *Black American Literature Forum* 25, no. 3 (1991): 442–48.

Carney, Court. *Cuttin' Up: How Early Jazz Got America's Ear*. Lawrence: University Press of Kansas, 2009.

Carr, Ian. *Miles Davis: The Definitive Biography*. London: HarperCollins, 1999.

Cartier-Bresson, Henri. "The Decisive Moment." In *Photography in Print: Writings from 1816 to The Present,* edited by Vicki Goldberg, 384–86. Alberqueque: University of New Mexico Press, 1981.

Cartier-Bresson, Henri. *The Mind's Eye: Writings on Photography and Photographers*. New York: Aperture, 1999.

Cartwright, Garth. "Michael P. Smith." *The Guardian,* 2008. https://www.theguardian.com/artanddesign/2008/dec/11/obituary-michael-smith-photographer.

Casetext. "White Studio, Inc. v Dreyfoos," 1913. https://casetext.com/case/white-studio-inc-v-dreyfoos.

Castaneda, Ramsey, and Amanda Quinlan. "Through the Lens: How Photography in Jazz History and Appreciation Textbooks Shapes Our Understanding of the Music." Unpublished paper presented to the *Documenting Jazz Conference*. Birmingham City University, 2020.

Cawthra, Benjamin. *Blue Notes in Black and White: Photography and Jazz*. Chicago: University of Chicago Press, 2011.

Centre for Creative Photography. "Marion Palfi." https://ccp.arizona.edu/artists/marion-palfi.

Chalfen, R. *Snapshot Versions of Life*. Bowling Green, OH: Bowling Green State University, 1987.

Chambers, Frank V. "James J. Kriegsmann." *Camera: A Practical Magazine for Photographers*, January 1944.

Chandler, Alfred D. *The Visible Hand: The Managerial Revolution in American Business*. Cambridge, MA: Harvard University Press, 1977.

Chandler, David. "Lisette Model." In *Lisette Model*, edited by David Chandler. London: The Photographers' Gallery, 1991.

Chapman, Con. *Rabbit's Blues: The Life and Music of Johnny Hodges*. Oxford: Oxford University Prss, 2019.

Charles, Roland. "Interview with Joe Rose." Oral History Interview 99.01. OH.01.01–02 Oral History Program, Tom & Ethel Bradley Center, California State University, Northridge, 1999.

Chéroux, Clément. "The Avant-Garde of Amateurs." In *Photography: A New Vision of the World 1891–1940*, edited by W. Guadagnini, 14–29. Milan: Skira, 2011.

Chilton, John. *Roy Eldridge: Little Jazz Giant*. London: Continuum, 2002.

Chinen, Nate. "Lensing the Newport Mob: 60 Years Later, A Deep Dive into 'Jazz on a Summer's Day.'" WGBO. org, 2018. https://www.wbgo.org/post/lensing-newport-mob-60-years-later-deep-dive-jazz-summers-day#stream.

"Chords and Dischords." *Down Beat*, March 7, 1940.

Christian, Scott. "Photographer Clemens Kalischer Survives Holocaust but Struggles to Adapt." Forward, 2013. https://forward.com/author/scott-christianson/.

Clark, Gregory. *Civic Jazz: American Music and Kenneth Burke on the Art of Getting Along*. Chicago: University of Chicago Press, 2005.

Claxton, William, and Joachim E. Berendt. *Jazz Life*. Cologne: Taschen, 2003.

Claxton, William, and Hitoshi Namekata. *Jazz West Coast: Artwork of Pacific Jazz Records*. Tokyo: Bijutsu Shuppan-Sha, 1992.

Clayton, Buck, and Nancy Miller Elliott. *Buck Clayton's Jazz World*. Oxford: Bayou Press, 1989.

Clifford, Marie J. "Helena Rubenstein's Beauty Salons, Fashion and Modernist Display." *Winterthur Portfolio* 38, nos. 2–3 (2003): 83–108.

Cock, Lilian De, and Reginald McGhee. *James Van Der Zee*. New York: Morgan & Morgan, 1973.

Codrescu, Andrei. "Notes on an Alien Son." In *Reframing America*, 9–14. Tucson, AZ: Centre for Creative Photography, 1995.

Cohen, Lizabeth. *A Consumer's Republic: The Politics of Mass Consumption in Postwar America*. New York: Alfred A. Knopf, 2003.

Cohen, Lizabeth. *Making a New Deal: Industrial Workers in Chicago 1919–1939*. Cambridge: Cambridge University Press, 1990.

Cohen, Richard I. "The Visual Revolution in Jewish Life." In *Visualizing and Exhibiting Jewish Space and History: Studies in Contemporary Jewry XXVI*, 3–24. Oxford: Oxford University Press, 2019.

Cohen, Sara. "Sounding Out the City: Music and the Sensuous Production of Place." *Transactions of the Institute of British Geographers* 20, no. 4 (1995): 434–46.

Cohn, Erin P. "Art Fronts: Visual Culture and Race Politics in Mid-Twentieth Century United States." unpublished Ph.D. thesis 2020, University of Pennsylvania Scholarly Commons, 2010.

Cohodas, Nadine. *Queen: The Life and Music of Dinah Washington*. New York: Knopf Doubleday, 2004.

Colberg, Joerg. "Spotlight: Photographs from the Memphis World 1949– 1964." November 19, 2008. http://jmcolberg.com/weblog/2008/11/spotlight_photographs_from_the_memphis_world_1949–1964/.

Coleman, A. D. "James Van Der Zee." In *Light Readings: A Photography Critic's Writings, 1968–1978*, 16–18. New York: Oxford University Press, 1979.

Coleman, A. D. "No Pictures: Some Thoughts on Jews in Photography." In *Übersee: Flucht Und Emigation Österreichenscher Fotografen 1920–40*, edited by Anna Auer, 28–31. Vienna: Kunsthalle Wien, 1997.

Coleman, A. D. "Roy DeCarava: 'Thru Black Eyes.' " In *Light Readings: A Photography Critics Writings 1968–1978*, 18–28. New York: Oxford University Press, 1979.

Collier, James Lincoln. *The Making of Jazz: A Comprehensive History*. London: Macmillan, 1978.

Collier Jr, John, and Malcolm Collier. *Visual Anthropology: Photography as a Research Method*. Alberqueque: University of New Mexico Press, 1986.

Collins, Mary. *Oh, Didn't He Ramble: The Life Story of Lee Collins*. Edited by Frank J. Gillis and John W. Miner. Oxford: Bayou Press, 1989.

Collins, R. *New Orleans Jazz: A Revised History*. New York: Vantage Press, 1996.

Congress, Library of. "The Faces of Jazz." Online Text. Retrieved from the Library of Congress. https://www.loc.gov/item/ihas.200185530/.

Cook, Richard. *Blue Note Records: The Biography*. London: Secker & Warburg, 2001.

Corcoran, Sean. "Lucy Ashjian and the Photo League." Museum of the City of New York, 2015. https://blog.mcny.org/2015/12/01/lucy-ashjian-and-the-photo-league/.

Cosgrove, Steve. "The Zoot Suit and Style Warfare." In *Zoot Suits and Second-Hand Dresses: An Anthology of Fashion and Music,* edited by Angela McRobbie, 3–22. Basingstoke: Macmillan, 1989.

Cottrell, Stephen. "Charlie Parker, Massey Hall and Grafton 10265: An Object Biography." Unpublished paper presented to the *Documenting Jazz Conference*. Birmingham City University, 2020.

"Cows in Ballroom at Hotel Men's Fair." *New York Times,* May 24, 1935.

"Courier Reporter Surveys Broadway." *Pittsburgh Courier*, 1928.

Crawford, Ralston. "Duncan Ralston Crawford's Photographs." *The Second Line*, 1953.

Cross, Karen, and Julia Pec. "Editorial: Special Issue on Photography, Archive and Memory." *Photographies* 3, no. 2 (2010): 127–38.

Crouch, Stanley. *One Shot Harris: The Photographs of Charles "Teenie" Harris*. New York: Abrams, 2002.

Crouch, Stanley. "Steel City Swing." In *One Shot Harris: The Photographs of Charles 'Teenie' Harris*, 8–27. New York: Abrams, 2002.

Crow, Bill. *From Birdland to Broadway: Scenes from a Jazz Life*. New York: Oxford University Press, 1992.

Csikszentmihalyi, Mihaly, and Eugene Rochberg-Halton. *The Meaning of Things: Domestic Symbols and the Self*. Cambridge: Cambridge University Press, 1981.

Curran, Geoffrey M. "From 'Swinging Hard' to 'Rocking Out': Classification of Style and the Creation of Identity in the World of Drumming" *Symbolic Interaction* 19, no. 1 (1996): 37–60.

Cuscuna, Michael. "Alfred Lion, Francis Wolff and Blue Note Records." In *Blue Note Photos: Francis Wolff*. Paris: Flammarion, 2014.

Cuscuna, Michael, Charlie Lourie, and Oscar Schnider. *Blue Note Jazz Photography of Francis Wolff*. New York: Universe, 2000.

Cyrus, Gerald. *Stormy Monday: New York's Uptown Jazz Scene*. Philadelphia: Private Publication, 2018.

D'Amato, Paul. "Race and the U.S. Socialist Tradition." *Socialist Worker,* November 18, 2010. https://socialistworker.org/2010/11/18/race-and-us-socialist-tradition.

Damon, Maris. "Jazz-Jews, Jive and Gender: The Ethnic Problems of Jazz Argot." In *Jews and Other Differences*, edited by Jonathan Boyarin and Daniel Boyarin, 150–75. Minneapolis: University of Minnesota Press, 1997.

Dance, Robert. "The Hollywood Studio Photographers." In *Glamour of the Gods: Photographs from the John Kobal Foundation*, edited by Robert Dance and John Taylor, 20–35. Göttingen: Steidl, 2008.

Dance, Robert, and Bruce Robertsdon. *Ruth Harriet Louise and Hollywood Glamour Photography*. Berkeley: University of California Press, 2002.

Daniels, Douglas Henry. *Pioneer Urbanites: A Social and Cultural History of Black San Francisco*. Philadelphia: Temple University Press, 1980.

Daniels, Douglas Henry. *Lester Leaps In: The Life and Times of Lester "Pres" Young*. Boston, MA: Beacon Press, 2002.

Daniels, Roger. *Coming to America: A History of Immigration and Ethnicity in American Life*. New York: HarperCollins, 1990.

Danto, Arthur C. "The Artworld." *Journal of Philosophy* 61, no. 19 (1964): 571–84.

Danto, Arthur C. *The Philosophical Disenfranchisement of Art*. New York: Colombia University Press, 1986.

Davis, Angela. "Photography and Afro-American History." In *A Century of Black Photographers: 1840–1960*, edited by V. H. Coar, 25–28. Rhode Island: Rhode Island School of Design, 1983.

Davis, Keith F. *An American Century of Photography: From Dry-Plate to Digital*. 2nd ed. Kansas City, MO: Hallmark Cards, 1999.

Dawson, Michael. "Photography: South of Point Lobos." In *LA's Early Moderns: Art/Architecture/Photography*, edited by Victoria Dailey, Natalie Shrivers, and Michael Dawson, 264–65. Los Angeles: Balcony Press, 2003.

DeCarava, Roy. *Photographs*. Edited by James Alinder. New York: Friends of Photography, 1981.

DeCarava, Roy. *Roy DeCarava: A Retrospective*. Edited by Peter Galassi and Sherry Turner DeCarava, n.d.

DeCarava, Roy. *The Sound I Saw: Improvisation on a Jazz Theme*. London: Phaidon, 2001.

Delgardo, Lourdes. "The Photography of Lourdes Delgardo." http://www.jazzhouse.org/jpg/delgado/.

DeMichael, Don. "Johnny Hodges." *Down Beat*, 1962.

Demlinger, Sandor, and John Steiner. *Destination Chicago Jazz*. Stroud: Tempus, 2003.

Denning, Michael. *The Cultural Front: The Laboring of American Culture in the Twentieth Century*. London: Verso, 1996.

DeNora, Tia. *Music in Everyday Life*. Cambridge: Cambridge University Press, 2000.

Derrida, Jacques. *Archive Fever: A Freudian Impression*. Chicago: University of Chicago Press, 1996.

DeVeaux, Scott. "Review: What Did We Do to Be so Black and Blue?" *The Musical Quarterly* 80, no. 3 (1996): 397.

DeVeaux, Scott. *BeBop: A Social and Musical History*. Berkeley: University of California Press, 1997.

DeVeaux, Scott. "The Emergence of the Jazz Concert 1935–1945." *American Music* 7, no. 1 (1989): 6–29.

DeVeaux, Scott. "Review: What Did We Do to Be so Black and Blue?" The Musical Quarterly 80, no. 3 (1996): 397.

Diner, Hasia R. "Drawn Together by Self-Interest: Jewish Representation of Race and Race Relations in the Early Twentieth Century." In *African Americans and Jews in the Twentieth Century*, edited by V. P. Franklin, Nacy L. Grant, Harold M. Kletnick, and Genna Rae McNeil, 27–39. Columbia: University of Missouri Press, 1998.

Dinerstein, Joel. "Lester Young and the Birth of the Cool." In *Signifyin(g), Sanctifyin' and Slam Dunking: A*, edited by Gena Dagekl Caponi, 239–76. Amherst: University of Massachusetts Press, 1999.

Dinerstein, Joel. *Swinging the Machine: Modernity, Technology and African American Culture between the World Wars*. Amherst: University of Massachusetts Press, 2013.

Dinerstein, Joel. *The Origins of Cool in Postwar America*. Chicago: University of Chicago Press, 2017.

Ditlea, Steve. "American Glamour." *Esquire*, July 1, 1980.

Dobbin, Len. "Legendary Jazz Photographer Paul Hoeffler Passed Away." AllAboutJazz.com, 2005. https://archive.is/20120722154154/http:/www.allaboutjazz.com/php/news.php?id=6823#selection-1057.0–1057.53.

Doi, Cristina, "Prentiss Taylor and George Biddle on the Scottsboro Trials," in *The Left Front: Radical Art in the "Red Decade", 1929–1940*, ed. Lisa Graziose Corrin (Evanston, IL, 2014), 15.

Domanska, Ewa. "The Material Presence of the Past." *History and Theory* 45, no. 3 (2006): 337–48.

Doud, Richard. "Oral History Interview with Edwin and Louise Rosskam." Washington, DC: Smithsonian Archives of American Art, 1965.

Doughty, Craig. "Black Elitism and Cultural Entrepreneurship in 1920s Boston." *European Journal of American Studies* 14, no. 2 (2019): 1–14.

Douglas, Ann. *Terrible Honesty: Mongrel Manhattan in the 1920s*. London: Picador, 1996.

Douglas, Bob. "Interview with Joe Rose." Oral History Interview 99.01.OH.03.01–04 Oral History Program, Tom & Ethel Bradley Center, California State University, Northridge, 1999.

"Dr. Bernard 'Bernie' Steinau Collection." Hogan Jazz Archive, n.d.

Driggs, Frank, and Harris Lewine. *Black Beauty, White Heat: A Pictorial History of Jazz 1920–1950*. New York: Da Capo, 1995.

Driskell, David C. *Two Centuries of Black American Art*. New York: Alfred A. Knopf, 1976.

Düchting, Hajo. *Paul Klee: Painting Music*. Munich: Prestel Verlag, 2004.

Dufour, Charles L. *The Past as Prelude: New Orleans 1718–1968*, 20–41. New Orleans: Tulane University Press, 1968.

Duganne, Erina. *The Self in Black and White: Race and Subjectivity in Postwar American Photography*. Hanover, NH: Dartmouth College Press, 2010.

Duganne, Erina. "Transcending the Fixity of Race: The Kamoigne Workshop and the Question of a 'Black Aesthetic' in Photography." In *New Thoughts on the Black Arts Movement*, edited by Lisa Gail Collins and Margo Natalie Crawford, 185–209. New Brunswick, NJ: Rutgers University Press, 2006.

Dyer, Geoff. *But Beautiful: A Book about Jazz*. London: Jonathan Cape, 1991.

Dyer, Geoff. "On Portraits." *Aperture*, no. 224 (2016): 23–24.

Eastlake, Lady Elizabeth. "Photography." *London Quarterly* 101 (1857): 442–68.

Editorial. "Jazz Pix: Skippy Adelman's Pictures Have the Spontaneity That Is the Very Soul of Jazz." *Popular Photography*, June, 1946: 54.

Edwards, Brent Hayes. *Epistrophies: Jazz and the Literary Imagination*. Cambridge, MA: Harvard University Press, 2017.

Eldridge, David. *American Culture in the 1930s*. Edinburgh: Edinburgh University Press, 2008.

Elgort, Arthur. *Arthurt Elgort: Jazz*. Edited by Marianne Houtenbos. New York: Damiani, 2018.

"Ella Fitzgerald Mobbeb by Crowd." *Down Beat*, 1940.

Ellington, Edward Kennedy. *Music Is My Mistress*. New York: Da Capo, 1973.

Elwood, Philip. "Introduction." In *Jazz*, 5–11. San Francisco, CA: Chronicle Books, 2005.

Elwood, Philip. "Introduction." In *Jim Marshall/Jazz*. San Francisco, CA: Chronicle Books, 2005.

Elworth, Steven B. "Jazz in Crisis, 1948–1958: Ideology and Representation." In *Jazz among the Discourses*, edited by Krin Gabbard, 57–75. Durham, NC: Duke University Press, 1995.

Emirbayer, Mustafa, and Ann Mische. "What Is Agency?" *American Journal of Sociology* 103, no. 4 (1998): 962–1023.

Engstead, John. *Star Shots: Fifty Years of Pictures and Stories by One of Hollywood's Greatest Photographers*. London: Columbus Books, 1978.

Entin, Joseph B. *Sensational Modernism: Experimental Fiction and Photography in Thirties America*. Chapel Hill: University of North Carolina Press, 2007.

Erenberg, Lewis A. *Swingin' the Dream: Big Band Jazz and the Rebirth of American Culture*. Chicago: University of Chicago Press, 1998.

Evans, Richard J. *The Coming of the Third Reich*. London: Penguin Books, 2003.

Eyerman, Ron. "Intellectuals and the Construction of African American Identity: Outline of a Generational Approach." In *Generational Consciousness, Narrative and Politics*, edited by June Edmunds and Bryan S. Turner, 51–74. Lanham, MD: Rowman & Littlefield, 2002.

Ezrachi, Elan. "In Search of Roots and Routes: The Making and Remaking of the Diasporic Jewish Identity." In *Dynamic Belonging: Contemporary Jewish Collective Identities*, edited by Harvey G. Goldbderg, Stephen M. Cohen, and Ezra Kopelowitz, 206–18. New York: Berghahn Books, 2012.

Facini, Peter. "Four Titans of Bebop, and 'the Greatest Photo in Jazz.'" *New York Times*, March 8, 2019: section MB: 5.

Fahey, David, and Linda Rich. *Masters of Starlight: Photographers in Hollywood*. London: Columbus Books, 1988.

Farmer, Patty. *Playboy Swings: How Hugh Hefner and Playboy Changed the Face of Music*. New York: Beaufort Books, 2015.

Fax, Elton C. "Roy DeCarava." In *Seventeen Black Artists*, 167–87. New York: Dodd Mead, 1971.

Feather, Leonard, and Gitler, Ira. *The Biographical Encyclopaedia of Jazz*. Oxford: Oxford University Press, 1999.

Feather, Leonard. "The Memories of Sweethearts." *Los Angeles Times*, April 13, 1980: 64.

Feather, Leonard. "The Sight of Jazz." In *Jazz*, edited by William Claxton and Terry Southern, 5–6. San Francisco, CA: Chronicle Books, 1966.

Ferber, Jessica. *Rebirth of the Cool: Robert James Campbell*. New York: Powerhouse Books, 2015.

Fermi, Laura. *Lllustrious Immigrants: The Intellectual Migration from Europe 1930–41*. Chicago: University of Chicago Press, 1968.

Ferris, John. "Dancer or Deb, Korman's Lens Pleases Them All." *Baltimore Sun*, June 1, 1941.

Finkelstein, Sidney Walter. *Jazz: A People's Music (1988 Ed.)*. New York: International, 1948.

Finler, Joel W. *Hollywood Movie Stills: Art and Technique in the Golden Age of the Studios*. London: Titan Books, 2.

Finley, Cheryl, Laurence Glasco, and Joe Trotter. *Teenie Harris Photographer: Image, Memory, History*. Pittsburgh: University of Pittsburgh Press, 2011.

Fishko, Sara. *The Jazz Loft According to W. Eugene Smith*, 2016.

Flamming, Douglas. *African Americans in the West*. Santa Barbara, CA: ABC-CLIO, 2009.

Folkart, Burt A. "Photographer Bruno Bernard Dies at 75." *Los Angeles Times*, June 9, 1987: 18.

Foner, Philip S. *American Socialism and Black Americans: From the Age of Jackson to World War II*. Westport, CT: Greenwood Press, 1977.

Ford, Colin. "Photography: Hungary's Greatest Export." In *Eyewitness: Hungarian Photography in the Twentieth Century*, edited by Peter Baki, Colin Ford, and George Szirtes, 10–23. London: Royal Academy of Arts, 2011.

Foucault, Michel. "Of Other Spaces, Heterotopias." *Architecture, Mouvement, Continuité* 5 (1984): 46–49. https://foucault.info/documents/heterotopia/foucault.heteroTopia.en/.

Foucault, Michel. "On the Genealogy of Ethics: An Overview of Work in Progress." In *The Foucault Reader*, 340–72. London: Penguin Books, 1984.

Foucault, Michel. "Technologies of the Self." In *Technologies of the Self: A Seminar with Michel Foucault*, edited by Luther H. Martin, Huck Gutman, and Patrick H. Hutton, 16–49. London: Tavistock Publications, 1988.

Foucault, Michel. "What Is an Author?" In *Language, Counter-Memory, Practice*, edited by Donald F. Bouchard (trans.), 113–38. Ithica, NY: Cornell University Press, 1967.

Fox, Stephen. *The Mirror Makers: A History of American Advertising and Its Creators*. London: William Heinemann, 1990.

Frank, Thomas. *The Conquest of Cool: Business Culture, Counterculture and the Rise of Hip Consumerism*. Chicago: University of Chicago Press, 1997.

Fraser, Gerald C. "For Ray DeCarava, 62, It's Time for Optimism." *New York Times*, June 6, 1982: S.1, 60.

Fraser, Steve, and Gary Gerstle. "Introduction." In *The Rise and Fall of the New Deal Order 1930–1980*, edited by Steve Fraser and Gary Gerstle, ix–xxv. Princeton, NJ: Princeton University Press, 1989.

Freeman, Alma Williams. "New Orleans Jazz Photography." *Jazz Archivist* 15 (2001): 17–22.

Freeman, Daniel. "Photography as a Business-National Negro Business League, Report of the Sixteenth Annual Convention of the National Negro Business League." Boston, MA: National Negro Business League, 1915.

Freer, Regina. "L.A. Race Woman: Charlotta Bass and the Complexities of Black Political Development in Los Angeles." *American Quarterly* 56, no. 3 (2004): 607–32.

Freulich, Roman, and Joan Abramson. *Forty Years in Hollywood: Portraits of a Golden Age*. South Brunswick, NJ: A.S. Barnes, 1971.

Friedlander, Lee. *Playing for the Benefit of the Band: New Orleans Music Culture*. New Haven: Yale University Press, 2013.

Friedlander, Lee. *The Jazz People of New Orleans*. London: Jonathan Cape, 1992.

Friedlander, Lee, and John Szarkowski, eds. *E. J. Bellocq: Storyville Portraits*. Museum of Modern ArtNew York, 1970.

Friedman, Carol. "Rembering Chuck Stewart." WGBO Livestream, 2017.

Frohlich, David, and Ella Tallyn. "Audiophotography: Practice and Prospects." In *Extended Abstracts of CHI '99, New York: ACM SIG-CHI*, 1999.

Fyfe, Gordon, and John Law. "On the Invisibility of the Visual." In *Picturing Power*, edited by Gordon Fyfe and John Law, 1–14. London: Routledge, 1988.

Gabbard, Krin. *Better Git It in Your Soul: An Interpretive Biography of Charles Mingus*. Oakland: University of California Press, 2016.

Gabbard, Krin. "Images of Jazz." In *The Cambridge Companion to Jazz*, edited by Mervyn Cooke and David Horn, 332–46. Cambridge: Cambridge University Press, 2002.

Gabbard, Krin. "Introduction: Writing the Other Jazz History." In *Representing Jazz*, edited by Krin Gabbard, 1–8. Durham, NC: Duke University Press, 1995.

Gabbard, Krin. *Jammin' at the Margins: Jazz and the American Cinema*. Chicago: University of Chicago Press, 1996.

Gabler, Neal. *An Empire of Their Own: How the Jews Invented Hollywood*. New York: Crown, 1988.

Galassi, Peter. "Introduction." In *Roy DeCarava: A Retrospective*, 11–39. New York: Museum of Modern Art, 1996.

Galassi, Peter. "Two Stories." In *American Photography 1890–1965: From The Museum of Modern Art*, 11–41. New York: MoMA, New York, 1995.

Gara, Larry. *The Baby Dodds Story*. Baton Rouge: Louisiana State University Press, 1992.

Gardner, Carl. "Introduction." In *Media, Culture and Politics: A Socialist View*, 1–13. Applebaum, Larry. London: Macmillan, 1979.

Garner, Gretchen. *Disappearing Witness: Change in Twentieth Century American Photography*. Baltimore, MD: John Hopkins University Press, 2003.

Gates Jr., Henry Louis. "New Negroes, Migration, and Cultural Exchange." In *Jacob Lawrence: The Migration Series*, edited by Elizabeth Hutton Turner, 17–21. Urbanna, VA: Rappahannock Press, 1993.

Gates Jr., Henry Louis. "The Master's Pieces: On Canon Formation and the African-American Tradition." In *Loose Canons: Notes on the Culture Wars*, 17–42. New York: Oxford University Press, 1992.

Gay, Peter. *Weimar Culture: The Outsider as Insider*. New York: Harper & Row, 1968.

Gayford, Martin. *Modernists and Mavericks: Bacon, Freud and the London Painters*. London: Thames & Hudson, 2018.

Gayle, Addison. *The Black Aesthetic*. Garden City, NY: Doubleday, 1971.

Gayle Jr., Addison. "The Harlem Renaissance: Towards a Black Aesthetic." In *The Addison Gayle Jr. Reader*, edited by Nathaniel Norment J., 71–80. Urbana: University of Illinois Press, 2009.

Gebhardt, Nicholas. *Going for Jazz: Musical Practices and American Ideology*. Chicago: University of Chicago Press, 2001.

Gelder, Ken. *Subcultures: Cultural Histories and Social Practice*. London: Routledge, 2007.

Gell, Alfred. *Art and Agency: An Anthropological Theory*. Oxford: Oxford University Press, 1998.

Geller, Jay. *The Other Jewish Question: Identifying the Jew and Making Sense of Modernity*. New York: Fordham University Press, 2011.

Gelly, Dave. *Being Prez: The Life and Music of Lester Young*. 2nd ed. London: Equinox, 2009.

Gendron, Bernard. *Between Montmartre and the Mudd Club: Popular Music and the Avant-Garde*. Chicago: University of Chicago Press, 2002.

Gendron, Bernard. " 'Moldy Figs' and Modernists: Jazz at War (1942–46)." In *Jazz Among the Discourses*, edited by Krin Gabbard, 31–56. Durham, NC: Duke University Press, 1995.

Genette, Gérard. *The Work of Art: Immanence and Transcendence (Trans. G. M. Goshgarian)*. Ithaca, NY: Cornell University Press, 1997.

Gennari, John. *Blowin' Hot and Cool: Jazz and Its Critics*. Chicago: University of Chicago Press, 2006.

Gennari, John. "Jazz Criticism: Its Development and Ideologies." *Black American Literature Forum* 25, no. 3 (1991): 447–523.

Gennari, John. "Photographing the Jazz Salon: Clemens Kalischer at Music Inn." Unpublished paper presented to the *Documenting Jazz Conference*. Dublin, 2019..

George, Nelson. *Elevating the Game:* New York: Fireside, 1992.

George, Nelson. "New Photos of John Coltrane Rediscovered 50 Years After They Were Shot." Smithsonian Magazine, 2014. https://www.smithsonianmag.com/smithsonian-institution/new-photos-john-coltrane-rediscovered-50-years-after-they-were-shot-180950260/.

Gerard, Charley. *Jazz in Black and White: Race, Culture, and Identity in the Jazz Community*. Westport, CT: Praeger, 1998.

Gerber, Mark. *Jazz Jews*. Nottingham: Five Leaves, 2009.

Gershenson, Olga, and David Shneer. "Soviet Jewishness and Cultural Studies." *Journal of Jewish Identities* 4, no. 1 (2011): 129–46.

Gibson, Ann. "Recasting the Canon: Norman Lewis and Jackson Pollock." *Artforum* March (1992): 66–73.

Gidal, Nachum T. "Jews in Photography." In *Leo Baeck Institute Yearbook XXXII*, 437–53. London: Secker & Warburg, 1987.

Giddins, Gary, and Scott DeVeaux. *Jazz*. New York: W. W. Norton, 2009.
Gillespie, Dizzy, 'Foreword.' In *Jazz People: Photographs by Ole Brask*, edited by Dan Morgenstern. New York: Da Capo, 1993.
Gilroy, Paul. "Black Music, Ethnicity, and the Challenge of a 'Changing' Same." *Black Music Research Journal* 11, no. 2 (1991): 111–36.
Gilroy, Paul. *The Black Atlantic: Modernity and Double Consciousness*. Cambridge, MA: Harvard University Press, 1993.
Gioia, Ted. *The History of Jazz*. New York: Oxford University Press, 1998.
Gioia, Ted. *The Imperfect Art: Reflections on Jazz and Modern Culture*. New York: Oxford University Press, 1990.
Gioia, Ted. "The True Poet of Jazz." *City Journal* Summer (2020). https://www.city-journal.org/jazz-whitney-balliett.
Gioia, Ted. *West Coast Jazz: Modern Jazz in California 1945–1960*. Berkeley: University of California Press, 1998.
Giske, Howard. "Meeting Al Smith." In *Seattle on the Spot: The Photographs of Al Smith*, edited by Jacqueline E. A. Lawson, 11–12. Seattle, WA: Museum of History and Industry, 2017.
Glad, Paul W. "Progressives and the Business Culture of the 1920s." *Journal of American History* 53, no. 1 (1966): 75–89.
Glinn, Burt. *The Beat Scene*. New York: Real Art Press, 2018.
Goggin, Jim, and Peter Clute. *The Great Jazz Revival*. San Rafael, CA: Donald Ewald, 1994.
Golan, Romy. "On the Passage of a Few Persons through a Rather Brief Period of Time." In *Exiles and Émigrés: The Flight of European Artists from Hitler*, edited by Stephanie Barron, 128–46. Los Angeles: Museum Associates, 1997.
Goldberg, Harvey E. "Dynamic Jewish Identities: Insights from a Comparative View." In *Dynamic Belonging: Contemporary Jewish Collective Identities*, edited by Harvey G. Goldbderg, Stephen M. Cohen, and Ezra Kopelowitz, 1–27. New York: Berghahn Books, 2012.
Goldblatt, Burt. *Newport Jazz Festival: The Illustrated History*. New York: The Dial Press, 1977.
Golden, Thelma. "James Van Der Zee's 'Christmas Morning' 1933." *Aperture*, no. 223 (2016): 152.
Goldfarb, Michael. "The Age of Reaction: Jews, Blacks and American Progress." *Jewish Quarterly* 63, no. 4 (2016): 20–25.
Gooley, Dana. "The Outside of 'Sitting In': Jam Sessions and the Politics of Participation." *Performance Research* 16, no. 3 (2011): 43–48.
Gordon, Maxine. "Sophisticated Giant: The Life and Legacy of Dexter Gordon." Unpublished paper presented at *Jazz Journeys*. Graz, 2019.
Gordon, Maxine. *Sophisticated Giant: The Life and Legacy of Dexter Gordon*. Oakland: University of California Press, 2018.

Gosnell, Harold F. *Negro Politicians: The Rise of Negro Politics in Chicago*. Chicago: University of Chicago Press, 1935.

Gottlieb, William. "Thelonious Monk-Genius of Bop." *Down Beat,* September 24, 1947.

Gottlieb, William P. "Preface." In *The Golden Age of Jazz,* viii–ix. San Francisco, CA: Pomegranate Art Books, 1995.

Govenar, Alan. *Portraits of Community: African American Photography in Texas*. Austin: Texas State Historical Association, 1996.

Govenar, Alan, and Benny Joseph. *The Early Years of Rhythm and Blues: Focus on Houston*. Houston, TX: Rice University Press, 1990.

Graaf, Lawrence B. De, Kevin Mulroy, and Quintard Taylor, eds. *Seeking El Dorado: African Americans in California*. Los Angeles: Autry Museum of Western Heritage, 2001.

Grauer, Tresa L. "'The Changing Same': Narratives of Contemporary Jewish American History." In *Mapping Jewish Identities,* edited by Laurence J. Silberstein, 37–64. New York: New York University Press, 2000.

Green, Jonathan. *American Photography: A Critical History 1945 to Present*. New York: Harry N. Abrams, 1984.

Greenberg, Cheryl Lynn. "Introduction." In *Troubling the Waters: Black-Jewish Relations in the American Century,* 1–14. Princeton, NJ: Princeton University Press, 2006.

Greenberg, Cheryl Lynn. *To Ask for an Equal Chance: African Americans in the Great Depression*. Lanham, MD: Rowman & Littlefield, 2010.

Greenberg, Clement. "Four Photographers: Review." In *Clement Greenberg: The Collected Essays and Criticism,* edited by John O'Brian, 183–87. Chicago: University of Chicago Press, 1993.

Gridley, Mark. "Misconceptions in Linking Free Jazz with the Civil Rights Movement." *College Music Symposium* 47 (2007): 139–55.

Gridley, Mark C. "Clarifying Labels: Cool Jazz, West Coast and Hard Bop." *Journal of Popular Music Studies* 2, no. 2 (1990): 8–16.

Grinberg, Emanuella. "Photography of Benny Joseph: 'The Early Years of Rhythm and Blues.'" CNN Photos, 2015.

Grossman, James R. *Land of Hope: Chicago, Black Southerners and the Great Migration*. Chicago: University of Chicago Press, 1989.

Gurtner, George. "Music through the Lens." MyNewOrleans.com, 2013. https://www.myneworleans.com/music-through-the-lens/.

Haas, Joseph. "The Saga behind the Signature, 'Maurice Seymour, Chicago.'" *Chicago Daily News,* May 11, 1968.

Hadley, Mona. "Jazz and the New York School." In *Representing Jazz,* edited by Krin Gabbard, 247–59. Durham, NC: Duke University Press, 1995.

Hadley, Mona. "Jazz and the Visual Arts." *Arts Magazine,* 1983, 91–101.

Hajdu, David. *Lush Life: A Biography of Billy Strayhorn*. London: Granta Books, 1996.

Hall, Stuart. "Who Needs Identity?" In *Questions of Cultural Identity*, edited by Stuart Hall and Paul Du Gray, 1–17. Thousand Oaks, CA: Sage, 1996.

Halper, Oscar. "Member Profile: William Gottlieb." *The Imagist*, 1997, 4.

Halsman, Philippe. "Autobiography." Halsman website, 2015. http://philippe-halsman.com/halsman/autobiography/.

Hamilton, Peter. "André Kertész." Edited by Robin Lenman. *The Oxford Companion to the Photograph*. Oxford: Oxford University Press, 2005, 340.

Hammel, Andrea, and Anthony Grenville. "Introduction." In *Exile and Everyday Life*, edited by Andrea Hammel and Anthony Grenville, xi–xv. Leiden: Brill Rodopi, 2015.

Handy, Antoinette D., *The International Sweethearts of Rhythm: Ladies' Jazz Band from Piney Woods Country Life School*. Lanham MD: Scarecrow Press, 1998.

Handy, Ellen. *Reflections in a Glass Eye: Works from the International Centre of Photography Collections*. Boston, MA: Little, Brown, 1999.

Haran, Barnaby. "Homeless Houses: Classifying Walker Evans's Photographs of Victorian Architecture." *Oxford Art Journal* 33, no. 2 (2010): 189–210.

Haran, Barnaby. " 'We Cover New York': Protest, Neighborhood, and Street Photography in the (Workers Film and) Photo League." *Arts*, 2019. Creative Commons open access article.

Haran, Barnaby E. "The New Vision in American Photography: Ralph Steiner, Walker Evans, and 'Americanism.'" *Object*, no. 8 (2005): 26–42.

Hariman, Robert, and John Louis Lucaites. *The Public Image: Photography and Civic Spectatorship*. Chicago: University of Chicago Press, 2016.

Harper, Colter. " 'The Crossroads of the World': A Social and Cultural History of Jazz in Pittsburgh's Hill District, 1920–1970." University of Pittsburgh, 2011.

Harris, Charles A., Henry J Simonds, Kenneth Love, and Linda Benedict-Jones. *Spirit of a Community: The Photographs of Charles "Teenie" Harris*. Greensburg, PA: Westmoreland Museum of American Art, 2001.

Harris, Jonathan. *Federal Art and National Culture: The Politics of Identity in New Deal America*. Cambridge: Cambridge University Press, 1995.

Harrison, Paul Carter, and Chuck Stewart. "Vampin.'" In *Chuck Stewart's Jazz Files*, 9–19. London: Quartet, 1986.

Harvey, Mark S. "Jazz and Modernism." In *Jazz in Mind: Essays on the History and Meaning of Jazz*, edited by Reginald T. Buckner and Steven Weiland, 128–47. Detroit, MI: Wayne State University Press, 1991.

Haskins, Jim. *James Van Der Zee: The Picture Takin' Man*. Trenton, NJ: Africa World Press, 1991.

Hasse, John Edward. *Beyond Category: The Life and Genius of Duke Ellington*. New York: Simon & Schuster, 1993.

Hassner, Rune. "Amateur Photography." In *A History of Photography: Social and Cultural Perspectives*, edited by Jean-Claud Lamagy and André Rouillé, translated by Janet Lloyd, 80–81. Cambridge: Cambridge University Press, 1987.

Hazeldine, Mike. *Bill Russell's American Music*. New Orleans: Jazzology Press, 1993.

Hebdige, Dick. *Subculture: The Meaning of Style*. London: Methuen, 1979.

Heckman, Don. "Introduction." In *Jazz Seen by William Claxton*. Cologne: Taschen, 1999.

Hemmingway, Andrew. "Cultural Democracy by Default: The Politics of the New Deal Arts Programmes." *Oxford Art Journal* 30, no. 2 (20067): 271–87.

Henderson, Stephen. "Saturation: Progress Report on a Theory of Black Poetry." In *African American Literary Theory: A Reader*, edited by Winston Napier, 102–12. New York: New York University Press, 2000.

Hennessey, Thomas J. *From Jazz to Swing: African-American Jazz Musicians and Their Music 1890–1935*. Detroit, MI: Wayne State University Press, 1994.

Hentoff, Nat. *Boston Boy: Growing Up with Jazz and Other Rebellious Passions*. Boston, MA: Faber & Faber, 1986.

Hentoff, Nat. "Introduction." In *Jazz Street: Photographs by Dennis Stock*, 12–15. London: Andre Deutsch, 1960.

Hentoff, Nat. "Introduction." In *The Jazz Image: Masters of Jazz Photography*, edited by Lee Tanner, 6-7. New York: Abrams, 2006.

Hentoff, Nat. "Jews in the Family of Jazz." *JazzTimes*, May 1, 2010. www.jazztimes.com.

Hentoff, Nat. *The Jazz Life*. New York: Da Capo, 1975.

Hentoff, Nat, "Introduction." In *Jazz: A Visual Retrospective Compiled by K. Abé*, edited by K. Abé. New York: Billboard, 1986.

Hersch, Charles. " 'Every Time I Try to Play Black, It Comes Out Sounding Jewish': Jewish Jazz Musicians and Racial Identity." *American Jewish History* 97, no. 3 (2013): 259–82.

Hersch, Charles. "Reconstructing the Jazz Tradition." *Jazz Research Journal* 2, no. 1 (2008): 7–28.

Hersch, Charles B. *Jews and Jazz: Improvising Etnicity*. New York: Routledge, 2017.

Hershorn, Tad. *Norman Granz: The Man Who Used Jazz for Justice*. Berkeley: University of California Press, 2011.

Hess, Helmut. "Mostly People: Erika Stone and New York Photography." In *Erika Stone: Mostly People: Photographs by a German Immigrant in New York*, edited by Erika Stone, 4–15. Munich: Kehayoff, n.d.

Hickey, Dave. "Cool on Cool: William Claxton and the Way Music Looked." In *Birth of the Cool: California Art, Design and Culture at Mid-Century*, edited by Elizabeth Armstrong, 134–49. Newport Beach, CA: Orange County Museum of Art, Prestel Publishing, 2007.

Higham, John. *Strangers in the Land: Patterns of American Nativism 1860–1925.* Brunswick, NJ: Rutgers University Press, 2002.

Hill, Ginger. "'Rightly Viewed': Theorisations of Self in Frederick Douglass's Lectures on Pictures." In *Pictures and Progress: Early Photography and the Making of African American Identity,* edited by Maurice O. Wallace and Shawn Michelle Smith, 41–82. Durham, NC: Duke University Press, 2012.

Hill, Jason E. *Artist as Reporter: Weegee, Ad Reinhardt and the PM News Picture.* Oakland: University of California Press, 2018.

Hill, Robert A. "Making Noises: Marcus Garvey Dada, August 1922." In *Picturing Us: African American Identity in Photography,* 181–205. New York: New Press, 1994.

Hills, Patricia. *Cultural Legacies and the Transformation of the Cubist Collage Aesthetic.* Washington, DC: National Gallery of Art, 2011.

Hine, Darlene Clark, and John McCluskey. *The Black Chicago Renaissance.* Urbana: University of Illinois Press, 2012.

Hinton, Milt. "Milt on Photography." Unpublished paper courtesy David Berger, 2008.

Hinton, Milt, and David G. Berger. *Bass Line: The Stories and Photographs of Milt Hinton.* Philadelphia: Temple University Press, 1988.

Hinton, Milt, David G. Berger, and Holly Maxson. *Overtime: The Jazz Photography of Milt Hinton.* San Francisco, CA: Pomegranate Art Books, 1991.

Hirsch Jr., E. D. *Validity in Interpretation.* Chicago: University of Chicago Press, 1967.

Hirsch, Marianne. *Family Frames: Photography, Narrative and Postmemory.* Cambridge, MA: Harvard University Press, 1997.

Hofstadter, Richard. *The Age of Reform from Bryan to FDR.* London: Jonathan Cape, 1962.

Holland, Patricia. "Introduction: Memory and the Family Album." In *Family Snaps: The Meanings of Domestic Photography,* edited by Jo Spence and Patricia Holland, 1–14. London: Virago Press, 1991.

Hollins Coar, V. *A Century of Black Photographers: 1840–1960.* Rhode Island: Rhode Island School of Design, 1983.

Holschbach, Susanne. "The Pose: Its Troubles and Pleasures." In *Street & Studio: An Urban History of Photography,* edited by U. Eskildsen, F. Ebner, and B. Kaufmann, 171–77. London: Tate Modern, 2008.

Honnef, Klaus, and Frank Weyers. *Und Sie Haben Deutschland Verlassen ... Müssen. Fotografen Und Ihre Bilder 1928–1997.* Bonn: Rheinisches Landesmuseum, 1997.

hooks, bell. "In Our Glory: Photography and Black Life." In *Picturing Us: African American Identity in Photography,* 43–54. New York: New Press, 1994.

hooks, bell. *Outlaw Culture: Resisting Representations.* London: Routledge, 1994.

"Hooks Brothers Photography-Where the Only Known Studio Portrait of Robert Johnson Was Taken." Mississippi Blues Travellers, 2016. http://www.mississippibluestravellers.com/blues-history/hooks-brothers-photography-where-the-only-known-studio-portrait-of-robert-johnson-was-taken/.

Hope Franklin, John. *Reconstruction after the Civil War*. 3rd ed. Chicago: University of Chicago Press, 2013.

Hoskins, Janet. *Biographical Objects: How Things Tell the Stories of Peoples' Lives*. New York: Routledge, 1998.

Howe, Irving. *World of Our Fathers: The Journey of East European Jews to America*. London: Phoenix Press, 1976.

Hoy, Anne H. " 'I'm Ready for My Close-Up': Hollywood's Glamour Photographs." In *Silver Screen Silver Prints: Hollywood Glamour Portraits from the Robert Dance Collection*, 11–24. New York: Grolier Club, 2011.

Hung, Jochen. " 'Der Deutschen Jugend!' The Newspaper Tempo and the Generational Discourse of the Weimar Republic." In *Beyond Glitter and Doom; The Contingency of the Weimar Republic*, edited by Jochen Hung and Godela Weiss-Sussex, 105–18. Munich: IUDICIUM Verlag, 2012.

Hurley, F. J. *Portrait of a Decade: Roy Stryker and the Devleopment of Documentary Photography in the Thirties*. New York: Da Capo, 1977.

Ings, Richard. " 'And You Slip into the Breaks and Look Around': Jazz and Everyday Life in the Photographs of Roy DeCarava." In *The Hearing Eye: Jazz and Blues Influences in African American Visual Art*, 303–30. Oxford: Oxford University Press, 2009.

Ings, Richard. "Making Harlem Visible: Race, Photography and the American City, 1915–1955." Unpublished Ph.D. thesis, University of Nottingham, 2004.

Irwin, Michael. "Roy DeCarava in New York: A Jazz Photographer in Subject and Technique." Ocula, 2019. https://ocula.com/magazine/insights/roy-decarava-in-new-york/.

"IS THIS WHAT CHARLIE PARKER ACTUALLY LOOKED LIKE?!?!" *Jazz Guitar Online*, 2018. https://www.jazzguitar.be/forum/players/66492-what-charlie-parker-actually-looked-like-print.html.

Iveson, Margaret. "Analogue: Zoe Leonard and Tacita Dean." *Critical Inquiry* 38 (2012): 797–819.

J.C.L.H. "The Photographer-Arthur Bedou (1880–1966)." *Creolegen*, 2013. www.creolegen.org.

Jacobs, Nicholas, and Diethart Kerbs. "Wilhelm Simon Guttmann, 1891–1990: A Documentary Portrait." *German Life and Letters* 62, no. 2 (2009): 401–14.

Jäger, Jens. "Elective Affinities? History and Photography." In *Global Photographies: Memory–History–Archives*, edited by Sissy Helf and Stephanie Michels, 39–56. Bielefeld: Transcript-Verlag, 2018.

James, Stephanie. "Extraordinary Shades of Gray: The Photographs of Roy De-Carava." *Bulletin of the Detroit Institute of Arts* 80, nos. 1–2 (2006): 58–67.

Jarrett, Michael. "The Tenor's Vehicle: Reading Way Out West." In *Representing Jazz*, edited by Krin Gabbard, 260–82. Durham, NC: Duke University Press, 1995.

Jay, Martin. "In the Realm of the Senses: An Introduction." *American Historical Review* 116, no. 2 (2011): 307–15.

Jay, Martin. "Review of Lepenies." *Central European History* 40, no. 2 (2007): 343–45.

Jay, Martin. "The German Migration: Is There a Figure in the Carpet?" In *Exiles and Émigrés: The Flight of European Artists from Hitler*, edited by Stephanie Barron, 326–40. Los Angeles: Harry N. Abrams, 1997.

Jeffrey, Ian. "Fragment and Totality in Photography." *History of Photography* 16, no. 4 (1992): 351–57.

Jeffrey, Ian. "Review of Some Sacred Sites: 'Thinking Photography' Edited by Victor Burgin." In *Creative Camera: Thirty Years of Writing*, edited by David Brittain, 88–92. Manchester: Manchester University Press, 1999.

Jenkins, Earnestine Lovelle. *Race, Representation and Photography in 19th-Century Memphis*. London: Routledge, 2016.

Jenkins, Ernestine. "Hooks Brothers Photography Documented Black Memphis." Choose 901, 2019. https://choose901.com/hooks-brothers-photography-documented-black-memphis/.

Jenkins, Ernestine. "The Hooks Brothers Photographers." Choose 901. https://choose901.com/hooks-brothers-photography-documented-black-memphis/#:~:text=It has been said that,photograph.&text=Robert and Henry Hooks opened,sons%2C Charles and Henry Hooks.

Jindra, Ines W. "Why American Sociology Needs Biographical Sociology—European Style." *Journal for the Theory of Social Behaviour* 44, no. 4 (2014): 389–412. https://doi.org/10.1111/jtsb.12055.

Johnson, Deborah J. "Black Photography: Contexts for Evolution." In *A Century of Black Photographers: 1840–1960*, edited by V. H. Coar, 15–20. Rhode Island: Rhode Island School of Design, 1983.

Jones, Alfred Haworth. "The Search for a Usable American Past in the New Deal Era." *American Quarterly* 23, no. 5 (1971): 710–24.

Jones, Wilbert. *Chicago Blues (Images of America)*. South Carolina: Arcadia, 2014.

Josenhans, Frauke V. "(Re)Defining the 'I' in Exile." In *Artists in Exile: Exptressions of Loss and Hope*, 185–207. New Haven, CT: Yale University Press, 2017.

Jost, Ekkhard. "Jazz in Deutschland: Von Der Weimar Republik Zur Adanauer-Ära." In *Jazz: Der Sound Des 20. Jahrhunderts*, edited by Klaus Wolbert. Franfurt am Main: Verlag Erwin Bochinsky, 1988.

Joyce, Paul. *Hockney on Photography: Conversations with Paul Joyce*. Edited by Wendy Brown. London: Jonathan Cape, 1988.

Julius, Anthony. *Idolizing Pictures: Idolatry, Iconoclasm and Jewish Art (Walter Neurath Memorial Lectures)*. London: Thames & Hudson, 2001.

Kahn, Ashley. *A Love Supreme: The Creation of John Coltrane's Classic Album*. London: Granta Books, 2002.

Kahn, Ashley. *Kind of Blue: The Making of the Miles Davis Masterpiece*. 2nd ed. London: Granta Books, 2002.

Kalischer, Clemens. "A Photographic Selection (1948–1966)." *Ploughshares* 6, no. 2 (1980): 107–14.

Kalischer, Clemens. *New York-Photographieren 1947–1959*. Aachen: Brochiert, n.d.

Kaplan, Louis. *American Exposures: Photography and Community in the Twentieth Century*. Minneapolis: University of Minnesota Press, 2005.

Kasher, Steven. *America and the Tintype*. Gottingen: ICP/ Stedl, 2008.

Kater, Michael H. *Different Drummers: Jazz in the Culture of Nazi Germany*. New York: Oxford University Press, 1992.

Katz, Jacob. *Out of the Ghetto: The Social Background of Jewish Emancipation, 1770–1870*. New York: Schocken Books, 1978.

Katz, Mark. *Capturing Sound: How Technology Has Changed Music*. Berkeley: University of California Press, 2004.

Kawakami, A. Kane. *Photobiography: Photographic Self-Writing in Proust, Guibert, Ernaux, Mace*. London: Legenda, 2013.

Keepnews, Orin, and Bill Grauer Jr. *A Pictorial History of Jazz: People and Places from New Orleans to Modern Jazz*. Feltham, Middlesex: Spring Books, 1968.

Keepnews, Peter. "Milt Hinton, Dean of Jazz Bassists, Is Dead at 90." *New York Times*, 2000. https://www.nytimes.com/2000/12/21/nyregion/milt-hinton-dean-of-jazz-bassists-is-dead-at-90.html.

Keightley, Emily, and Michael Pickering. "Echoes and Reverberations: Photography and Phonography as Historical Forms." *Media History* 13, nos. 2–3 (2007): 273–88.

Keightley, Emily, and Michael Pickering. "For the Record: Popular Music and Photography as Technologies of Memory." *European Journal of Cultural Studies* 9, no. 2 (2006): 149–65.

Keightley, Emily, and Michael Pickering. *Photography, Music and Memory: Pieces of the Past in Everyday Life*. London: Palgrave Macmillan, 2015.

Kelley, Robin D. G. "New Monastery: Monk and the Jazz Avant-Garde." *Black Music Research Journal* 19, no. 2 (1999): 135–69.

Kelley, Robin D. G. *Race Rebels: Culture, Politics and the Black Working Class*. New York: Free Press, 1996.

Kelley, Robin D. G. *Thelonious Monk: The Life and Times of an American Original*. London: JR Books, 2009.

Kelsey, Robin. "Of Fish, Birds, Cats, Mice, Spiders, Flies, Pigs, and Chimpanzees: How Chance Casts the Historic Action Photograph into Doubt." *History and Theory* 48, no. 4 (2009): 59–76.

Kenney, William. *Recorded Music in American Life: The Phonograph and Popular Memory 1890–1945*. New York: Oxford University Press, 1999.

Kenney, William H. *Chicago Jazz: A Cultural History, 1904–1930*. New York: Oxford University Press, 1993.

Kenney, William H. "Negotiating the Color Line: Louis Armstrong's Autobiographies." In *Jazz in Mind: Essays on the History and Meanings of Jazz*, edited by Reginald T. Buckner and Steven Weiland, 38–59. Detroit, MI: Wayne State University Press, 1991.

Kent, Donald Peterson. *The Refugee Intellectual: The Americanization of The Immigrants of 1933–41*. New York: Columbia University Press, 1953.

Kepes, György. *The Language of Vision*. Chicago: Paul Theobald, 1969.

Kernfeld, Barry, ed. *The New Grove Dictionary of Jazz*. London: Macmillan, 1988.

Kerouac, Jack. "Essentials of Spontaneous Prose." In *A Casebook on the Beat*, edited by Thomas Parkinson, 65–68. New York: Thomas Y. Crowell, 1961.

Kershaw, Alex. *Blood and Champagne: The Life and TImes of Robert Capa*. London: Da Capo, 2002.

Kimmelman, Michael. "How Jewish Artists Found Their Place in New York." *New York Times*, May 17, 1991: Section C, 25.

Kinzer, Stephen. "News Photographer's Quick Eye Revealed an Artist at Heart." *New York Times*, February 7, 2001.

Kirk, Andy. *Twenty Years on Wheels*. Oxford: Bayou Press, 1989.

Kirkeby, Ed, Duncan P. Schiedt, and Sinclair Traill. *Ain't Misbehavin': The Story of Fats Waller*. New York: Da Capo, 1975.

Kirkton, Kent, ed. *Camera and Community: Photographs from the Collection of the Institute for Arts and Media*. Los Angeles: California State University Northridge, 2008.

Kirkton, Kent, ed. *Identity and Affirmation: Post-War African American Photography*. Los Angeles: California State University Northridge, 2011.

Kirkton, Kent. *Harry Adams: Camera and Community*. Northridge: California State University Northridge, 1997.

Kittler, Friedrich A. *Discourse Networks 1800/1900*. Edited by Michael Meteer and Chris Cullens. Cambridge, MA: MIT Press, 1990.

Kleeblatt, Norman L, and Susan Chevlowe. "Painting a Place in America: Jewish Artists in New York, 1900–1945." In *Painting a Place in America: Jewish Artists in New York, 1900–1945: A Tribute to the Educational Alliance Art School*, edited by Norman L Kleeblatt and Susan Chevlowe, 101. Bloomington: Indiana University Press, 1991.

Knight, Arthur. "'Jammin the Blues, or the Sight of Jazz." In *Representing Jazz,* edited by Krin Gabbard, 11–53. Durham, NC: Duke University Press, 1995.

Kobal, John, ed. *Hollywood Glamour Portraits: 145 Photos of Stars 1926–1949.* New York: Dover, 1976.

Kobal, John. *The Art of the Great Hollywood Portrait Photographers 1925–1940.* London: Allen Lane, 1980.

De Koenigswarter, Pannonica. *Three Wishes: An Intimate Look at Jazz Greats.* New York: Abrams Image, 2008.

Kofsky, Frank. "Elvin Jones Part I: Rhythmic Innovator." *Journal of Jazz Studies* 4, no. 1 (1976): 3–24.

Kofsky, Frank. "The Jazz Tradition: Black Music and Its White Critics." *Journal of Black Studies* 1, no. 4 (1971): 403–33.

Kolb, Carolyn. "Developing Images." My New Orleans.com, 2008. https://www.myneworleans.com/developing-images/.

Kozloff, Max. "Jewish Sensibilty and the Photography of New York." In *New York: Capital of Photography,* edited by Max Kozloff, 69–78. New York: Jewish Museum New York, 2002.

Kozloff, Max. "New York: Capital of Photography." In *New York: Capital of Photography,* 9–77. New Haven, CT: Yale University Press, 2002.

Kozloff, Max. "New York: Capital of Photography." Yale University Press-Jewish Museum of New York, 2002.

Kracauer, Siegfried. "Photography." In *The Mass Ornament: Weimar Essays,* edited by Thomas Y. Levin (trans.), 47–64. Cambridge, MA: Harvard University Press, 1995.

Kracauer, Siegfried. *Theory of Film: The Redemption of Physical Reality.* New York: Oxford University Press, 1965.

Kraft, James P. *Stage to Studio: Musicians and the Sound Revolution, 1890–1950.* Baltimore, MD: John Hopkins University Press, 1996.

Krasner, David, "The Real Thing." In *Beyond Blackface: African Americans and the Creation of American Popular Culture 1890–1930,* ed. W. Fitzhugh Brundage, 99–123. Chapel Hill: University of North Carolina Press (2011).

Krauss, Rosalind E. "Notes on the Obtuse." In *Photography Theory,* edited by James Elkins, 339–42. New York: Routledge, 2007.

Krauss, Rosalind, "Sculpture in the Expanded Field." *October* 8 (1979): 30–44.

Kristeva, Julia. "A New Type of Intellectual: The Dissident." In *The Kristeva Reader,* edited by Tori Moi, 292–300. Oxford: Basil Blackwell, 1986.

Kroiz, Lauren, " 'A Jolly Lark for Amateurs' John Steuart Curry's Pedagogy of Painting." *American Art* 29, no. 1 (2015): n. pag.

Kubik, Gerhardt, Justin Winston, and Clive Wilson. "The Buddy Bolden Band Photograph." *The Jazz Archivist* 22 (2009): 1–24.

Kugelmass, Jack. "Jewish Icons: Envisioning the Self in Images of the Other." In *Jews and Other Differences: The New Jewish Cultural Studies*, edited by Jonathan Boyarin and Daniel Boyarin, 30–53. Minneapolis: University of Minnesota Press, 1997.

Latour, Bruno. "Why Has Critique Run Out of Steam? From Matters of Fact to Matters of Concern." *Critical Inquiry* 30, no. 2 (2004): 225–48.

Lauterbach, Preston. *Bluff City: The Secret Life of Photographer Ernest Withers.* New York: W.W. Norton & Co, 2019.

Laver, Mark. *Jazz Sells: Music Marketing and Meaning*. New York: Routledge, 2015.

Laws, Christopher. "Who Wore It Best." culturedarm, n.d. https://culturedarm.com/who-wore-it-best-round-about-midnight-miles-davis-blue-train-john-coltrane/.

Layton, Edwin. "Veblen and the Engineers." *American Quarterly* 14, no. 1 (1962): 64–72.

Layton, Robert. "Art and Agency: A Reassessment." *The Journal of the Royal Anthropological Institute* 9, no. 3 (2003): 447–64.

Lears, Jackson. *Fables Of Abundance: A Cultural History Of Advertising In America*. New York: Basic Books, 1994.

Lederhendler, Eli. *New York Jews and the Decline of Urban Ethnicity, 1950–1970.* Syracuse, NY: Syracuse University Press, 2001.

Lee, Elizabeth. "Looking for Lida Moser." In *A Lens without Limits: The Photography of Lida Moser*, edited by Jacqueline Hochheiser, 6–9. Carlisle, PA: Trout Gallery, Dickinson College, 2018.

Lees, Gene. "A Cool Appraisal." In *The Iconic Images of Ted Williams*, edited by Ted Williams,8. London: ACC Editions, 2016.

Leland, John. "Hearing Music in Photos of Jazz Giants." *Lens*, August 16, 2016. https://lens.blogs.nytimes.com/2016/08/16/hearing-music-in-photos-of-jazz-giants/.

Lemagny, J.-C., and A. Rouillé, eds. *A History of Photography: Social and Cultural Perspectives*. Cambridge: Cambridge University Press, 1987.

Leonard, Herman. "Interview with Tad Hershorn." Institute of Jazz Studies, Rutgers University, n.d.

Leonard, Herman. *Jazz Memories*. Paris: Filipacchi, 1995.

Leonard, Herman. *The Eye of Jazz: The Jazz Photographs of Herman Leonard.* London: Viking, 1989.

Leonard, Herman. "William Claxton." *Jazz Times*, 2008. https://jazztimes.com/archives/william-claxton/.

Leonard, Neil. "Some Further Thoughts on Jazzmen as Romantic Outsiders." *Journal of Jazz Studies* 2, no. 2 (1975): 42–52.

Leppert, Richard. "Cinematic Iconographies of Artistic Desire." In *Music, Body and Stage: The Iconography of Music, Theater and Opera*. New York: Research Centre for Music Iconography, 2008.

Leuchtenberg, William E. *The Perils of Prosperity 1914–32*. Chicago: University of Chicago Press, 1958.

Levin, Floyd. *Classic Jazz: A Personal View of the Music and Musicians*. Berkeley: University of California Press, 2000.

Levine, Lawrence W. *Black Culture and Black Consciousness: Afro-American Folk Thought from Slavery to Freedom*. Oxford: Oxford University Press, 1978.

Levine, Lawrence W. "The Historian and the Icon: Photography and the History of the American People in the 1930s and 1940s." In *Documenting America, 1935–1943*, edited by Carl Fleischhauer and Beverly W. Brannan, 15–42. Berkeley: University of California Press, 1988.

Lewis, George E. *A Power Stronger Than Itself: The AACM and American Experimental Music*. Chicago: University of Chicago Press, 2008.

Lindstrom, Bo. "Charles Peterson and the Life Magazine Photo Story on Panassie," n.d. http://www.jazzresearch.se/upl/website/charles-peterson/PhotographerCharlesPeterson.pdf.

Lisle, Andria. "Black and White: Three Photo Exhibits Bring the Long-Hidden World of Segregated Memphis to Life." *Memphis Flyer* 1, no. 886 (2006): 20–22. https://www.memphisflyer.com/memphis/black-and-white/Content?oid=1124496.

Livingstone, Jane. *The New York School: Photographs 1936–1963*. New York: Stewart, Tabori and Chang, 1992.

Locke, Alain. "The New Negro." In *The Portable Harlem Renaissance Reader*, edited by David Levering Lewis, 46–51. New York: Viking, 1994.

Logan, Rayford W. *The Betrayal of the Negro from Rutherford B. Hayes to Woodrow Wilson*. New York: Da Capo, 1997.

Lopes, Dominic McIver. "Afterword: Photography and the 'Picturesque Agent.' " *Critical Inquiry* 38, no. 4 (2012): 855–69.

Lopes, Paul. *The Rise of a Jazz Art World*. Cambridge: Cambridge University Press, 2002.

Lovelle Jenkins, Earnestine. *African Americans in Memphis*. Charleston, SC: Arcadia, 2009.

Lovelle Jenkins, Earnestine. "The Hooks Brothers of Memphis: Artist-Photographers of the 'New Negro' Movement in the Urban South." In *Memphis: 200 Years Together*, edited by Karen B. Golightly and Jonathan Judaken, 84–99. Memphis, TN: Susan Schadt Press, 2019.

Lowe, Jacques, Bob Blumenthal, and Cliff Preiss. *Jazz: Photographs of the Masters*. New York: Artisan, 1995.

Lubow, Leo Howard. *Blue Note Moments and Other Points in Time*. Baltimore, MD: Private Publication, 2009.

Luce, Henry R. "Foreword." In *Eisenstaedt: Witness to Our Time*, 7–9. London: Secker & Warburg, 1980.

Macchiarella, Lindsey. "Early French Modernism Across Modalities: Erik Satie and Eugène Atget." *Music in Art* 42, nos. 1–2 (2017): 309–28.

Maeder, Edward, ed. *Hollywood and History: Costume Design in Film*. Los Angeles: Thames & Hudson/LA County Museum of Art, 1987.

Magee, Jeffrey. *Fletcher Henderson: The Uncrowned King of Swing*. Oxford: Oxford University Press, 2005.

Maita, Joe. "Michael Cuscuna Announces the Release of Francis Wolff's Blue Note Session Photographs." Jerry Jazz Musician, 2019. https://jerryjazzmusician.com/2019/08/michael-cuscuna-discusses-the-release-of-francis-wolffs-blue-note-session-photographs/.

Maita, Joe. "The Jazz Photography Issue." Jerry Jazz Musician, 2019. https://jerryjazzmusician.com/2019/08/the-jazz-photography-issue/.

Mallozzi, Vincent M. "Behind the Lens, Continuing a Legacy." *New York Times*, January 11, 2010. https://www.nytimes.com/2010/01/11/nyregion/11photog.html.

Mann, Golo. *The History of Germany since 1789*. London: Penguin Books, 1990.

March, John. "Gerty Simon's Berlin Years, c.1919–1933." In *Berlin-London: The Lost Photographs of Gerty Simon*, edited by Barbara Warnock and John March, 11–18. London: Wiener Library, 2019.

Margolick, David. *Strange Fruit: Billie Holiday, Café Society and an Early Cry for Civil Rights*. Philadelphia: Running Press Books, 2000.

Marien, Mary Warner. *Photography: A Cultural History*. 3rd ed. London: Laurence King, 2010.

Marmorstein, Gary. "Central Avenue Jazz: Los Angeles Black Music of the Forties." *Southern California Quarterly* 70, no. 4 (1988): 415–26.

Martin Jr, Waldo E. *No Coward Soldiers: Black Cultural Politics in Postwar America*. Cambridge, MA: Harvard University Press, 1988.

Marquis, Donald M. *In Search of Buddy Bolden: First Man of Jazz*. New York: Da Capo, 1978.

Marsh, Graham, and Glyn Callingham. *The Cover Art of Blue Note Records: The Collection*. London: Collins and Brown, 2010.

Marsh, Graham, and Simon Whittle. *Ronnie Scott's 1959–69: Photographs by Freddy Warren*. London: Reel Art Press, 2019.

Marshall, Jim. *Jazz*. San Francisco, CA: Chroncile Books, 2005.

Martin, Peter. *Music and the Sociological Gaze: Art Worlds and Cultural Production*. Manchester: Manchester University Press, 2006.

Martin, Rosy. "Family History and Photography." In *Oxford Companion to the Photograph,* edited by Robin Lenman, 212–13. Oxford: Oxford University Press, 2005.

Martin, Rux. "Truth, Power, Self: An Interview with Michel Foucault, October 25 1982." In *Technologies of the Self: A Seminar with Michel Foucault,* edited by Luther H. Martin, Huck Gutman, and Patrick H. Hutton, 9–15. London: Tavistock, 1988.

Masters, Ann V. "Behind the Star-Studded Camera: Bruno of Hollywood." *Bridgeport Sunday Post,* September 21, 1969: 96.

Mathews, Jane De Hart. "Arts and the People: The New Deal Quest for a Cultural Democracy." *Journal of American History* 62, no. 2 (1975): 316–39.

Mathieu, Aron M. "The Hard-Boiled School of Photography: The Legend of Skippy Adelman." *Minicam Photography,* 1945.

Maupin, Isaac. "Photographing the Carnival of Swing: An Immigrant's Perspective on the First Jazz Festival." Unpublished paper presented to the *Documenting Jazz Conference*. Dublin, 2019.

Maynard, Patrick. *The Engine of Visualization: Thinking Through Photography*. Ithaca, NY: Cornell University Press, 1997.

McCandless, Barbara. "The Portrait Studio and the Celebrity." In *Photography in Nineteenth Century America,* edited by Martha A. Sandsweiss, 48–75. Fort Worth: Harry N. Abrams, 1991.

McCausland, Elizabeth. "Documentary Photography." *Photo Notes,* January 1939: 1–2.

McClendon, Alphonso D. *Fashion and Jazz: Dress, Identity and Subcultural Improvisation*. London: Bloomsbury, 2015.

McDowell, Winston C. "Keeping Them 'In the Same Boat Together.' " In *African Americans and Jews in the Twentieth Century,* edited by V. P. Franklin, Nacy L. Grant, Harold M. Kletnick, and Genna Rae McNeil, 208–36. Columbia: University of Missouri Press, 1998.

McEvilley, Thomas. *Art and Otherness: Crisis in Cultural Identity*. Kingston, NY: McPherson, 1992.

McGerr, Michael. *A Fierce Discontent: The Rise and Fall of the Progressive Movement in America, 1870–1920*. New York: Free Press, 2003.

McKay, Claude. *Harlem: Negro Metropolis*. New York: E. P. Dutton, 1940.

McLuhan, Marshall. *Understanding Media*. Cambridge, MA: MIT Press, 1994.

Meadows, Eddie S. *Jazz Scholarship and Pedagogy: A Research and Information Guide*. New York: Routledge, 2006.

Melnick, Jeffrey. "A Black Man in Jewface." In *Race and the Modern Artist,* edited by Heather Hathaway and Jeffrey Jar'ab, Josef Melnick, 126–39. New York: Oxford University Press, 2003.

Melnick, Jeffrey. *A Right to Sing the Blues: African Americans, Jews and American Popular Song*. Cambridge, MA: Harvard University Press, 1999.

Meltzer (ed.), David. *Reading Jazz*. San Francisco, CA: Mercury House, 1993.

Mercer, Kobena. *James Van Der Zee*. London: Phaidon Press, 2003.

Merriam, Alan P., and Raymond W. Mack. "A Theory of Jazz Community." *Social Forces* 7, no. 2 (1960): 211–22.

Merritt, Raymond H. *Engineering in American Society 1850–1875*. Lexington: University Press of Kentucky, 1969.

Mestrich, Qiana. "RIP Photographer Hugh Bell." *Dodge and Burn: Decolonizing Photography*, 2012. https://dodgeburnphoto.com/2012/11/rip-photographer-hugh-bell/.

Meyers, William. "Jews and Photography." *Commentary* 115, no. 1 (2003). https://www.commentarymagazine.com/articles/jews-and-photography/.

Miles, Andrew. "Addressing the Problem of Cultural Anchoring: An Identity–Based Model of Culture in Action." *Social Psychology Quarterly* 77, no. 2 (2014): 210–27.

Mili, Gjon. *Gjon Mili: Photographs and Recollections*. Boston, MA: New York Graphic Society, 1980.

Miller, Daniel. "Why Some Things Matter." In *Material Cultures: Why Some Things Matter*, edited by Daniel Miller, 3–21. London: UCL Press, 1998.

Miller, Jared T. "Through Chuck Stewart's Lens, A History of Jazz." *Newsweek*, March 1, 2015, https://www.newsweek.com/through-chuck-stewarts-lens-history-jazz-310085.

Mills, C. Wright. *White Collar: The American Middle Classes*. Oxford: Oxford University Press, 2002.

Milton, Sybil. "Henry Ries." *History of Photography* 23, no. 4 (1999): 359–60.

Milton, Sybil. "Is There an Exile Art or Only Exile Artists?" In *Exil: Literatur Und Die Künst Nach 1933 (Studien Zur Literatur Der Moderne, No.17)*, 83–89. Bonn: Bouvier, 1990.

Mitchell, W. J. T. "There Are No Visual Media." *Journal of Visual Culture* 4, no. 2 (2005): 257–66.

Modica, Lou and Max. "Discovering the Historic Jazz Photography of Ted Williams." Kickstarter, 2012. https://www.kickstarter.com/projects/342833186/discovering-the-historic-jazz-photography-of-ted-w.

Moholy-Nagy, Làszló. "A New Instrument of Vision." In *The Photography Reader*, edited by Liz Wells, 92–96. London: Routledge, 2003.

Moller, Horst. *Die Weimarer Republik: Demokratie in Der Krise*. Berlin: Piper Verlag, 2018.

Monson, Ingrid, "The Problem with White Hipness: Race, Gender and Cultural Conceptions in Jazz Historical Discourse," *Journal of American Musicological Society*, 48, No. 3 (1995): 396–422.

Monson, Ingrid. *Freedom Sounds: Civil Rights Call Out to Jazz and Africa*. Oxford: Oxford University Press, 2007.

Monson, Ingrid. "Miles, Politics and Image." In *Miles Davis and American Culture*, edited by Gerald Early, 86–97. St. Louis: Missouri Historical Society Press, 2001.

Mooney, Amy. "'Visions of Great Usefulness and Progress': A Chicago Photographer's Studio and Black Modern Subjectivity." Courtauld Institute of Art, 2019. https://courtauld.ac.uk/event/visions-of-great-usefulness-and-progress-modern-black-subjectivity-through-a-mid-twentieth-century-chicago-photographers-studio.

Mooney, Amy M. "Photos of Style and Dignity: Woodard's Studios and the Delivery of Black Modern Subjectivity." In *Beyond the Face: New Perspectives on Portraiture*, edited by Wendy Wick Reaves, 212–31. Washington, DC: National Portrait Gallery, 2018.

Moore, Bob. "The Role of the Picture Editor: Interview with John Loengard." ScottKelby website, 2010. https://scottkelby.com/its-guest-blog-wednesday-featuring-john-loengard/.

Moore, Deborah Dash. *At Home in America: Second Generation New York Jews*. New York: Columbia University Press, 1981.

Moore, Deborah Dash. "At Home in America?: Revisiting the Second Generation." *Journal of American Ethnic History*, 25, nos 2–3 (2006): 156–68.

Moore, Deborah Dash. "The Urban Vision of East European Jewish Immigrants to New York." In *Proceedings of the World Congress of Jewish Studies*, 31–38. World Union of Jewish Studies, 1981.

Moore, Deborah Dash. *Young Jewish Women with Cameras*. Bloomington: Indiana University Press, 2011.

Moore, Lucinda. "Herman Leonard's Eye for Jazz." *Smithsonian Magazine*. Washington, DC, 2010. https://www.smithsonianmag.com/arts-culture/herman-leonards-eye-for-jazz-131497921/.

Moore, MacDonald, and Deborah Dash Moore. "Observant Jews and the Photographic Arena of Looks." In *You Should See Yourself: Jewish Identity in Postmodern American Culture*, edited by Vincent Brook, 176–204. New Brunswick, NJ: Rutgers University Press, 2006.

Moore, Macdonald Smith. *Yankee Blues: Musical Culture and American Identity*. Bloomington: Indiana University Press, 1985.

Morgan, Alun, and Raymond Horricks. *Modern Jazz: A Survey of Developments since 1939*. London: Victor Gollancz, 1956.

Morgan, Stacy I. *Frankie and Johnny: Race, Gender and the Work of African American Folklore in 1930s America*. Houston: University of Texas Press, 2017.

Morgan, Susan. *Martin Munkácsi*. New York: Aperture, 1992.

Morgenstern, Dan. "Jazz-The Jewish Black Connection." In *Creators and Disturbers: Reminescences by Jewish Intellectuals of New York*, edited by Bernard Rosenberg and Ernest Goldstein, 95–112. New York: Columbia University Press, 1982,. –

Morin, Violette. "L'Object Biographique." *Communications* 13 (1969): 131–39.

Morris, Daniel. "Introduction." In *After Weegee: Essays on Contemporary Jewish American Photographers*, xv–xxxi. Syracuse, NY: Syracuse University Press, 2011.

Morris, John G. *Get the Picture: A Personal History of Photojournalism*. Chicago: University of Chicago Press, 1998.

Mosbrook, Joe. "Evelyn Freeman Remembers Her Swing Band." *Jazzed in Cleveland*, 2001. http://207.170.138.18/wmv_news/jazz67.htm.

Motion, Tim. *Jazz Portraits: An Eye for the Sound: Images of Jazz and Jazz Musicians*. New York: Salamander, 1995.

Mouton, Girard P. III, and Alma D. Williams. "The Eyes of Jazz." *Jazz Archivist* 6, no. 1 (1991): 10–11.

Moutoussamy-Ashe, Jeanne. *Viewfinders: Black Women Photographers*. New York: Readers and Writers, 1993.

Muchnic, Suzanne. "Bernard: He Wanted Out, Is Now In." *Los Angeles Times-Calendar*, January 8, 1984: 312.

Murray, Albert. *Good Morning Blues: The Autobiography of Count Basie*. New York: Da Capo, 1995.

Murray, Albert. *Murray Talks Music: Albert Murray on Jazz and Blues*. Edited by Paul Devlin. Minneapolis: University of Minnesota Press, 2016.

Myers, Marc. "The Photographer Who Never Was But Now Is." In *Rebirth of the Cool: Discovering the Art of Robert James Campbell*, edited by Jessica Ferber, 7–9. Brooklyn, NY: Powerhouse Books, 2015.

Marc Myers, "Interview with Dave Brubeck," JazzWax. https://www.jazzwax.com/2010/02/interview-dave-brubeck-part-4.html.

Myers, William J. "Jews and Photography." *Commentary*, 2003. https://www.commentarymagazine.com/articles/jews-and-photography/.

Nahigian, Alan. "Jazz Photo as Art Form: Capturing Soul on Film." *International Herald Tribune*, May 3–4, 1997.

Nahigian, Alan. "Lifetime Achievement Award: Bill Gottlieb." *Down Beat*, no. 64 (1997): 30–34.

Naison, Mark. *Communists in Harlem during the Depression*. Urbana: University of Illinois Press, 1983.

Natanson, Nicholas. *The Black Image in the New Deal: The Politics of FSA Photography*. Knoxville: University of Tennessee Press, 1992.

Neal, Larry. "The Black Arts Movement." In *Visions of a Liberated Future: Black Arts Movement Writings*, edited by Michael Schwartz, 62–78. New York: Thunder's Mouth Press, 1989.

Nelson, Nels. "Jazz: Some People Sweat Better Than Others." *Philadelphia Daily News*, November 22, 1985: 70.

Nesbit, Molly. *Atget's Seven Albums*. New Haven, CT: Yale University Press, 1992.

"New York City's First Racially Integrated Nightclub." Ephemeral New York, 2012. https://ephemeralnewyork.wordpress.com/tag/segregation-new-york-city/.

Newhall, Beaumont, ed. *Photography: Essays and Images*. New York: New York Museum of Modern Art, 1980.

Newhall, Beaumont. *The History of Photography from 1839 to the Present*. London: Secker & Warburg, 1982.

Newhart, Sally. *The Original Tuxedo Jazz Band: More Than a Century of a New Orleans Icon*. Charleston, SC: History Press, 2013.

New Orleans Public Library. "Grauman Marks Photography Collection," n.d. https://cdm16880.contentdm.oclc.org/digital/collection/p16880coll20.

Nicholson, Stuart. *Ella Fitzgerald: A Biography of the First Lady of Jazz*. London: Indigo, 1996.

Nicholson, Stuart. *Jazz and Culture in a Global Age*. Boston, MA: Northeastern University Press, 2014.

Nicosia, Gerald. *Memory Babe: A Critical Biography of Jack Kerouac*. Berkeley: University of California Press, 1994.

Nora, Pierre, "Between Memory and History: *Les Lieux de Mémoire*." *Representations*, no. 26 (1989): 7–24.

Norbert, Elias. *The Germans: Power Struggles and the Development of Habitus in the Nineteenth and Twentieth Centuries*. New York: Columbia University Press, 1996.

O'Doherty, Brian. *The Voice and the Myth: American Masters*. London: Thames & Hudson, 1988.

O'Meally, Robert G. "Gerald Cyrus, Jazz Photographer." In *Stormy Monday: New York's Uptown Jazz Scene*, 111–14. Philadelphia: Private Publication, 2008.

O'Meally, Robert G. "The Flat Plane, the Jagged Edge: Aaron Douglas's Musical Art." *American Studies* 49, nos. 1/2 (2008): 21–35.

O'Neal, Hank. *A Vision Shared: A Classic Portrait of America and Its People 1935–1943*. New York: St. Martin's Press, 1976.

O'Neal, Hank. "Introduction." In *Charlie Parker*. Filipacchi, 1995.

O'Neil, Paul, "The Only Rebellion Around," *Life*, November 30, 1959.

Oakland, Veryl. *Jazz in Available Light: Illuminating the Jazz Greats from the 1960s, '70s and '80s*. Atglen, PA: Schiffer, 2018.

Obituary. "Maurice Seymour: Photographed Stars." *Chicago Tribune,* October 9, 1993. https://www.chicagotribune.com/news/ct-xpm-1993-10-09-9310090166-story.html.

Ochs, Michael. *Rock Archives: A Photographic Journey through the First Two Decades of Rock & Roll.* Poole, Dorset: Blandford Press, 1985.

Ogren, Kathy. "'Jazz Isn't Just Me': Jazz Autobiographies as Public Personas." In *Jazz in Mind: Essays on the History and Meaning of Jazz,* edited by Reginald T. Buckner and Steven Weiland, 112–27. Detroit, MI: Wayne State University Press, 1991.

Ogren, Kathy J. *The Jazz Revolution: Twenties America and the Meaning of Jazz.* New York: Oxford University Press, 1989.

Ohlin, Margaret. "Putting Down Photographic Roots in Harlem." In *Touching Photography,* 131–60. Chicago: University of Chicago Press, 2012.

Oliver, Myrna. "Howard Morehead, 79; Photographer of Jazz Musicians Broke Color Barrier." *Los Angeles Times,* 2003. http://articles.latimes.com/2003/jul/24/local/me-morehead24.

Ortiz de Urbina, Fernando. "Electric Guitar-Who's on First?" The Sounds of Surprise, 2016. http://jazzontherecord.blogspot.com/2016/09/electric-guitarwhos-on-first.html.

Orvell, Miles. *American Photography*. Oxford: Oxford University Press, 2003.

Orvell, Miles. "Introduction." In *John Vachon's America: Photographs and Letters from the Depression to World War II,* 1–36. Berkeley: University of California Press, 2003.

Orvell, Miles. "Weegee's Voyeurism and the Mastery of Urban Disorder." *American Art* 6, no. 1 (1992): 18–41.

Osman, Colin, and Jean-Claude Lemagny. "Photography Sure of Itself (1930–50)." In *A History of Photography: Social and Cultural Perspectives,* edited by Jean-Claude Lemagny and André Rouillé, translated by J. Lloyd, 165–86. Cambridge: Cambridge University Press, 1987.

Osofsky, Gilbert. *Harlem: The Making of a Ghetto, Negro New York 1890–1930.* 2nd ed. New York: Harper & Row, 1971.

Painter, Nell. "Black Journalism, The First Hundred Years." *Harvard Journal of Afro-American Affairs* 2, no. 2 (1971): 30–42.

Painter, Nell Irvin. *Creating Black Americans: African-American History and Its Meanings, 1619 to the Present.* New York: Oxford University Press, 2007.

Panichas, George E. "Somewhere There's Music." In *Larry Fink: Somewhere There's Music*. Bologna: Damiani Editore, 2006.

Panish, Jon. "The Subterraneans: A Study of 'Romantic Primitivism.'" *Melus* 19, no. 3 (1994): 107–23.

Panofsky, Erwin. *Studies in Iconology: Humanistic Themes in the Art of the Renaissance.* New York: Harper & Row, 1972.

Panzer, Mary. "Introduction." In *Philippe Halsman: A Retrospective*, 7–11. London: Pavillion Books, 1998.
Parks, Gordon. "Foreword." In *Harlem: The Vision of Morgan and Marvin Smith*, edited by James A. Miller, ix. Lexington: University Press of Kentucky, 1998.
Parks, Gordon. "Foreword." In *Carol Friedman, the Jazz Pictures*, 9. Santa Fe, NM: Arena Editions, 2001.
Parrish, Michael E. *Anxious Decades: America in Prosperity and Depression, 1920–1941*. New York: W. W. Norton, 1992.
Parry, Eugenia. *Lisette Model: A Narrative Biography*. Gottingen: Steidl, 2009.
Paudras, Francis. "Introduction." In *Herman Leonard: The Eye of Jazz*, 15–17. London: Viking, 1985.
Pells, Richard H. *Radical Visions and American Dreams: Culture and Social Thought in the Depression Years*. New York: Harper & Row, 1973.
Pepper, Terence, and John Kobal. *The Man Who Shot Garbo: The Hollywood Photographs of Clarence Sinclair Bull*. London: National Portrait Gallery Publications, 1989.
Perchard, Tom. "Mid-Century Modern Jazz: Music and Design in the Postwar Home." *Popular Music* 36, no. 1 (2017): 55–74.
Perchard, Tom interviewed by Alyn Shipton. "Jazz Library-Booker Little," 2009.
Peretti, Burton W. *Jazz in American Culture*. Chicago: Ivan R. Dee, 1997.
Peretti, Burton W. "Oral Histories of Jazz Musicians: The NEA Transcripts as Texts in Context." In *Jazz among the Discourses*, edited by Krin Gabbard, 117–33. Durham, NC: Duke University Press, 1995.
Peretti, Burton W. "Speaking in the Groove: Oral History and Jazz." *The Journal of American History* 88, no. 2 (2001): 582–95.
Peretti, Burton W. *The Creation of Jazz: Music, Race and Culture in Urban America*. Urbana: University of Illinois Press, 1994.
Perez, Nissan N. "A Century of Migration." In *Displaced Visions: Émigré Photographers of the 20th Century*, edited by Nissan N. Perez, 8–26. Jerusalem: The Israel Museum and Lund Humphries, 2013.
Perez, Nissan N. *Displaced Visions: Émigré Photographers of the 20th Century*. Jerusalem: Isreal Museum Jerusalem, 2013.
Perry, Regina. *James Van Der Zee*. Dobbs Ferry, NY: Morgan & Morgan, 1973.
Perry, Regina A. "Introduction." In *James Van Der Zee*, edited by Liliane De Cock and Reginald McGhee, np. Dobbs Ferry, NY: Morgan & Morgan, 1973.
Peyton, Strauss. "Strauss Peyton: Exceptional Portraiture." Strauss Peyton website, n.d. http://www.strausspeytonkc.com/blog/history-strauss-peyton/.
Phillips, Christopher. "The United States: American Society." In *A History of Photography: Social and Cultural Perspectives*, edited by Jean-Claude Lemagny and A. Rouillé, translated by J. Lloyd, 158–64. Cambridge: Cambridge University Press, 1987.

Photographer, Staff. "Elcha's Work Known from Coast to Coast." *Pittsburgh Courier*, June 7, 1924: 1.

Pinson, K. Heather. *The Jazz Image: Seeing Music through Herman Leonard's Photography*. Jackson: University of Mississippi Press, 2010.

Piper, William Brian, "Cameras at Work: African American Studio Photographers and the Business of Everyday Life, 1900–1970." Dissertation presented to the Graduate Faculty of the University of Virginia, Charlottesville, 2016.

Pitts, Terence. "Reframing America." In *Reframing America*, 15–17. Tucson: Centre for Creastive Photography, 1995.

Placksin, Sally. *American Women in Jazz 1900 to the Present: Their Worlds, Lives and Music*. New York: Wideview Books, 1982.

Podolsy, Jeffrey. "Bert Offerings." *Vanity Fair*, May 2013. https://archive.vanityfair.com/article/2013/5/bert-offerings.

Porter, Eric. "Incorporation and Distinction in Jazz History and Jazz Historiography." In *Jazz/Not Jazz: The Music and Its Boundaries*, edited by David Ake, Charles Hiroshi Garrett, and Daniel Goldmark, 13–30. Berkeley: University of California Press, 2012.

Porter, Roy. "Seeing the Past." *Past & Present* 118 (1988): 186–205.

Pratt Guterl, Matthew. *The Color of Race in America, 1900–1940*. Cambridge, MA: Harvard University Press, 2001.

Prendeville, Brendan. *Realism in 20th Century Painting*. London: Thames & Hudson, 2000.

Press releases from Bronze Beauty Enterprises. " '1993 Bronze Beauty Calendar Hits Market' and 'Bronze Beauty Calendar Acclaimed Worldwide,' " 1993.

Price, Mary. *The Photograph: A Strange Confined Space*. Stanford, CA: University of Stanford Press, 1994.

Prouty, Ken. "The Problem with Community." In *Knowing Jazz: Community, Pedagogy, and Canon in the Information Age*, 13–45. Jackson: University Press of Mississippi, 2012.

Prouty, Kenneth E. "Toward Jazz's 'Official' History: The Debates and Discourses of Jazz History Textbooks." *Journal of Music History Pedagogy* 1, no. 1 (2010): 19–43.

Rabatè, Jean-Michel. *1913: The Cradle of Modernism*. Oxford: Blackwell, 2007.

Rachleff, M. "Photojournalism in Harlem: Morgan and Marvin Smith and the Construction of Power, 1934–1943." In *Visual Journal: Harlem and D.C. in the Thirties and Forties*, edited by D. Willis and J. Lusaka, 15–33. Washington, DC: Smithsonian Institution Press, 1996.

Raeburn, Bruce Boyd. "Appreciating Jazz Discography." *Jazz Archivist* 3, nos. 1–2 (1988): 3–8.

Raeburn, Bruce Boyd. "Jazz and the Italian Connection." *Jazz Archivist* 6, no. 1 (1991): 1–6.

Raeburn, Bruce Boyd. "Jewish Jazzmen in New Orleans 1890–1940: An Overview." *Jazz Archivist* 12, no. 1 (1997): 1–10.
Raeburn, Bruce Boyd. *New Orleans Style and the Writing of American Jazz History*. Ann Arbor: University of Michigan Press, 2009.
Raeburn, Bruce Boyd. " 'That Ain't No Creole': Masquerade, Marketing and Transgression against the Color Line in New Orleans." Unpublished paper, 2017.
Raeburn, John. *A Staggering Revolution: A Cultural History of Thirties Photography*. Urbana: University of Illinois Press, 2006.
Raether, Scott W. *Wisconsin Family Albums & Photographer's Imprints and Biographies 1800s to Early 1900s*. Xlibris, 2013.
Raiford, Leigh. "Photography and the Practices of Critical Black Memory." *History and Theory* 48, no. 4 (2009): 112–29.
Rampersad, Arnold. *The Life of Langston Hughes*. New York: Oxford University Press, 1988.
Ramsey Jr., Frederic, and Charles Edward Smith. *Jazzmen*. London: Jazz Book Club, Sidgwick & Jackson, 1958.
Rasula, Jed. "The Media of Memory: The Seductive Menace of Records in Jazz History." In *Jazz among the Discourses,* edited by Krin Gabbard, 134–62. Durham, NC: Duke University Press, 1995.
Raynor, Vivien. "Art; From the Famous to the Nameless." *New York Times,* June 14, 1998. https://www.nytimes.com/1998/06/14/nyregion/art-from-the-famous-to-the-nameless.html.
Reardon, Ed. "Passing By: Murray Korman." *Herald-News Passaic N.J.,* 1937.
Reed, Christopher Robert. *Knock at the Door of Opportunity: Black Migration to Chicago, 1900–1919*. Carbondale: Southern Illinois University Press, 2014.
Reed, Christopher Robert. *The Chicago NAACP and the Rise of Black Professional Leadership, 1910–1966*. Bloomington: Indiana University Press, 1997.
Reed, Christopher Robert. *The Rise of Chicago's Black Metropolis, 1920–1929*. Edited by Darlene Clark Hine and Dwight A. McBride. Urbana: University of Illinois Press, 2011.
Reichelt, Matthias. "It Must Schwing-Blue Note." Zukunft braucht Erinnerung, 2010. https://www.zukunft-braucht-erinnerung.de/it-must-schwing-blue-note/.
Reiff, Carol. *Nights in Birdland: Jazz Photographs 1954–1960*. New York: Simon & Schuster, 1985.
Reiff, Hal. "Faking a Magazine Cover." *Camera: A Practical Magazine for Photographers, Vol. 70*, 1948: 56.
Reisner, Robert George. *Bird: The Legend of Charlie Parker*. London: McGibbon and Kee, 1962.

Remmington, R. Roger. *American Modernism: Graphic Design 1920 to 1960*. London: Laurence King, 2003.
Remsburg, Rich. *Hard Luck Blues: Roots Music Photographs from the Great Depression*. Urbana: University of Illinois Press, 2010.
Remsen, Neil. "Arthur Elgort: The King of Swing." *Financial Times,* September 20, 2018: 18.
Ries, Henry. *Ich War Ein Berliner: Erinnerungen Eines New Yorker Fotojournalisten*. Berlin: Parthas Verlag, 2001.
Robb, Frances Osborn. *Shot in Alabama: A History of Photography 1839–1941*. Birmingham: University of Albama Press, 2016.
Roberts, John. "Realism, Modernism, and Photography: 'At Last, at Last the Mask Has Been Torn Away.'" In *Adventures in Realism,* edited by Matthew Beaumont, 158–76. Malden, MA: Blackwell, 2007.
Roberts, John. *The Art of Interruption: Realism, Photography and the Everyday*. Manchester: Manchester University Press, 1998.
Rogin, Michael. "Blackface, White Noise: The Jewish Jazz Singer Finds His Voice." *Critical Inquiry* 18, no. 3 (1992): 417–53.
Rose, Al, and Edmond Souchon. *New Orleans Jazz: A Family Album*. Baton Rouge: Louisiana State University Press, 1978.
Rose, Barbara. *American Art since 1900*. New York: Holt, Reinhart & Winston, 1967.
Rose, Gillian. "Family Photographs and Domestic Spacings: A Case Study." *Transactions of the Institute of British Geographers* 28, no. 1 (2003): 5–18.
Rose, Gillian. *Visual Methodologies: An Introduction to the Interpretation of Visual Materials*. Los Angeles: Sage, 2007.
Rosenblum, Barbara. "Style as Social Process." *American Sociological Review* 43, no. 3 (1978): 422–38.
Rosenblum, Walter, and Naomi Rosenblum. "The Art Historian and the Photographic Image." *Art Journal* 36, no. 2 (n.d.): 139–42.
Rosenthal, George S., and Frank Zachary. *Jazzways*. Musicians Press, 1946.
Rosler, Martha. "In, Around, and Afterthoughts (On Documentary Photography)." In *Decoys and Disruptions: Selected Writings 1975–2001*, 151–206. Cambridge, MA: MIT Press, 2004.
Ross, George, "Showgirls' Favorite Photographer Turns Lens on Debs," *Wausau Daily Record-Herald,* March 14, 1939, 6.
Roth, Helen, "The Bar Sammy's Bowery Follies as Microcosm and Photographic Milieu." In *Arrival Cities: Migrating Artists and New Metropolitan Topographies in the 20th Century,* edited by Burcu Dogramaci, 293–313. Leuven: Leuven University Press, 2020.

Rouillé, André. *La Photographie: Entre document et art contemporain.* Paris: Gallimard, 2005.

Russell, Ross. *Jazz Style in Kansas City and the Southwest.* Berkeley: University of California Press, 1971.

Rust, Brian. *Jazz and Ragtime Records, 1897–1942.* 6th ed. Littleton, CO: Mainspring Press, 2002.

Saab, A. Joan. *For the Millions: American Art and Culture between the Wars.* Philadelphia: University of Pennsylvania Press, 2004.

Said, Edward. "East Isn't East: The Impending End of the Age of Orientalism." *Times Literary Supplement,* February 3, 1995: 3–4.

Said, Edward. "Reflections on Exile." In *Out There: Marginalization and Contemporary Cultures,* edited by Russell Ferguson, T Martha Gever, Trihn Minh-ha, and Cornel West, 357–66. New York: MIT Press, 1990.

Salaam, Kaluma Ya. "Herman Leonard: Making Music with Light." *African American Review* 29, no. 2 (1995): 241–46.

Sandler, Clara, and Juan Mandelbaum. "Ellen Auerbach, 1906–2004." *Jewish Women's Archive Encyclopedia,* 2019. https://jwa.org/encyclopedia/article/auerbach-ellen.

Sandomir, Richard. "Chuck Stewart, Jazz Photographer, Dies at 89." *New York Times,* January 27, 2017. https://www.nytimes.com/2017/01/27/arts/design/chuck-stewart-jazz-photographer-dies-at-89-youve-seen-his-album-covers.html.

Sandweiss, Martha A. "Photography in Nineteenth Century America." In *Photography in Nineteenth Century America,* edited by Martha A. Sandweiss, xiii–xv. Fort Worth: Harry N. Abrams, 1991.

Saretzky, Gary D., "Documenting Diversity: Edwin Rosskam and the Photo Book, 1941–41," *Photo Review* 23, no. 4: 10–16.

Saul, Scott. "Jazz as a Religion of Work: Roy DeCarava's John Coltrane." In *Freedom Is, Freedom Ain't: Jazz and the Making of the Sixties,* 248–53. Cambridge, MA: Harvard University Press, 2003.

Sayej, Nadja. "Hidden Portraits: Rare Photos of African American Life Get a Spotlight." *The Guardian,* 2018. https://www.theguardian.com/artanddesign/2018/jun/21/metropolitan-museum-art-african-american-portraits-exhibition.

Saretzky, Gary D., "Documenting Diversity: Edwin Rosskam and the Photo Book, 1941-41," *Photo Review* 23, no. 4: 10-16.

Schiedt, Duncan. *Twelve Lives in Jazz.* Parma, Italy: Delta, 1996.

Schimmelman, Janice G. "The Tintype in America 1856–1880." *Transactions of the American Philosophical Society* 97, no. 2 (2007): 1–270.

Schleunes, Karl A. *The Twisted Road to Auschwitz: Nazi Policy Towards German Jews 1933– 39.* London: André Deutsch, 1972.

Schmidt, Thomas. "Das Erste Opfer Des Linksterrorismus." Welt Digital, 2010. https://www.welt.de/politik/deutschland/article10918644/Das-erste-Opfer-des-Linksterrorismus.html.

Schuller, Gunther. *Early Jazz: Its Roots and Musical Development*. New York: Oxford University Press, 1968.

Schulz, Constance B. "African American Photography to c.1960." In *The Oxford Companion to the Photograph*, edited by Robin Lenman, 13–17. Oxford: Oxford University Press, 2005.

Scott, Clive. *Street Photography: From Atget to Cartier-Bresson*. London: I. B. Tauris, 2007.

Scott, Clive. *The Spoken Image: Photography and Language*. London: Reaktion Books, 1999.

Scott, James C. *Domination and the Arts of Resistance: Hidden Transcripts*. New Haven, CT: Yale University Press, 1990.

Scruton, Roger. "Photography and Representation." *Critical Inquiry* 7, no. 3 (1981): 577–603.

Seebass, Tilman. "Iconography." In *Grove Music Online*, 2001. https://doi-org.nls.idm.oclc.org/10.1093/gmo/9781561592630.article.13698.

Seeger, Charles. "On the Principles of Musicology." *Musical Quarterly* 10, no. 2 (1924): 244–50.

Sekula, Allan. "Reading An Archive: Photography Between Labor and Capital." In *The Photography Reader*, edited by Liz Wells, 443–52. London: Routledge, 2003.

Sekula, Allan. "The Body and The Archive." In *The Contest of Meaning: Critical Histories of Photography*, edited by Richard Bolton, 342–89. Cambridge, MA: MIT Press, 1989.

Sengstock Jr., Charles A. *That Toodlin' Town: Chicago's White Dance Bands and Orchestras 1900–1950*. Chicago: University of Chicago Press, 2004.

Serlin, David, and Jesse Lerner. "Weegee and the Jewish Question." *Wide Angle* 19, no. 4 (1997): 1–9.

Seymour, Ron. "Photographer to the Celebrities," n.d. https://ronseymour.com/the-maurice-seymour-gallery/.

Seymour, Tom. "Remembering David Redfern, the King of Jazz Photography." *British Journal of Photography*, October 21, 2014: 18.

Shanklin, Eugenia. "Two Meanings and Uses of Tradition." *Journal of Anthropological Research* 37, no. 1 (1981): 71–89.

Shapiro, Nat, and Nat Hentoff. *Hear Me Talkin' to Ya*. New York: Dover Books, 1955.

Sharpe, Jennifer. "Dumpster of Forgotten Musicians Launches Quest." NPR, November 2, 2007. https://www.npr.org/templates/story/story.php?storyId=15772871.

Shields, David. "George Maillard Kesslère." Broadway Photographs, n.d. https://www.broadway.cas.sc.edu/content/g-maillard-kesslere.

Shields, David. "Maurice Seymour." Broadway Photographs, 2019. https://www.broadway.cas.sc.edu/content/maurice-seymour.

Shields, David. "Murray Korman." Broadway Photographs. https://broadway.cas.sc.edu/content/murray-korman.

Shields, David S. "Kansas City Style: The Artist's Hand and the Vaudeville Portrait 1912–1930." Broadway Photographs, 2019. https://www.broadway.cas.sc.edu/content/kansas-city-style-artists-hand-and-vaudeville-portrait-1912–1930.

Shields, David S. "Photography & the American Stage." Broadway Photographs, 2019. https://broadway.cas.sc.edu/.

Shields, David S. *Still: American Silent Motion Picture Photography*. Chicago: University of Chicago Press, 2013.

Shipton, Alyn. *A New History of Jazz*. London: Continuum, 2002.

Shipton, Alyn. *Hi-De-Ho: The Life of Cab Calloway*. Oxford: Oxford University Press, 2010.

Shipton, Alyn. *The Art of Jazz: A Visual History*. Watertown, MA: Imagine Publishing, 2020.

Shneer, David. *Through Soviet Jewish Eyes: Photography, War and the Holocaust*. New Brunswick, NJ: Rutgers University Press, 2011.

Shneer, David, and Lisa Tamiris Becker. *Through Soviet Jewish Eyes*. Boulder, CO: CU Art Museum, University of Colarado, 2011.

Siddons, Louise. "African Past or American Present? The Visual Eloquence of James Van Der Zee's 'Identical Twins.'" *African American Review* 46, nos. 2–3 (2013): 439–59.

Sidran, Ben. *Black Talk*. New York: Da Capo, 1981.

Siegel, Adrian. "Photographs of Musicians." *The Image* 2, no. 9 (1953), 24.

Silver, Larry, and Samantha Baskind. "Looking Jewish: The State of Research on Modern Jewish Art." *Jewish Quarterly Review* 101, no. 4 (2011): 631–52.

Simmel, Georg. "The Stranger." In *The Sociology of Georg Simmel,* trans. and ed. Kurt Wolff, 402–8. Glencoe, IL: The Free Press, 1950.

Simmons, Charles A. *The African American Press: A History of News Coverage During National Crises*. Jefferson, NC: McFarland, 1998.

Sinclair Bull, Clarence, and Raymond Lee. *The Faces of Hollywood*. South Brunswick, NJ: A.S. Barnes, 1968.

Singer, Barry. "Eloquent Images of a Smoky, Sultry World." *New York Times,* 1997. https://www.nytimes.com/1997/04/27/books/eloquent-images-of-a-smoky-sultry-world.html.

Sivulka, Juliann. *Soap, Sex, and Cigarettes: A Cultural History of American Advertising*. Belmont, CA: Wadsworth, 1998.

Skelly, Monica. "Portraits of New York Artists." In *A Lens without Limits: The Photography of Lida Moser*, edited by Jacqueline Hochheiser, 10–15. Carlisle, PA: The Trout Gallery, Dickinson College, 2018.

Sklaroff, Lauren Rebecca. *Black Culture and the New Deal: The Quest for Civil Rights in the Roosevelt Era*. Chapel Hill: University of North Carolina Press, 2009.

Slatter, Michael. "A Portrait of William Russell." *Jazz Journal* 12, no. 9 (1959): 28–29.

Sloane, Kathy. *Keystone Korner: Portrait of a Jazz Club*. Edited by Sascha Feinstein. Bloomington: Indiana University Press, 2012.

Small, Christopher. *Music of the Common Tongue: Survival and Celebration in Afro-American Music*. New Haven, CT: John Calder, 1987.

Smalls, James. "African-American Self-Portraiture: Repair, Reclamation, Redemption." *Third Text* 15, no. 54 (n.d.): 47–62.

Smith, Charles Edward. "New Orleans Comes to New York." *Esquire*, March 1, 1939: 93–102.

Smith, Christopher. "Review of 'Jazz Cultures' by David Ake and 'Going for Jazz: Musical Practices and American Ideology' by Nicholas Gebhardt." *Journal of the American Musicological Society* 58, no. 2 (2005): 476–88.

Smith, Jason Scott. "The Strange History of the Decade: Modernity, Nostalgia, and the Perils of Periodization." *Journal of Social History* 32, no. 2 (1998): 263–85.

Smith Jr., Al "Butch." "My Father and His Camera." In *Seattle on the Spot: The Photographs of Al Smith*, Seattle, WA: Museum of History & Industry, 2017.

Smith, Margaret Denton, and Mary Louise Tucker. *Photography in New Orleans: The Early Years, 1840–1865*. Baton Rouge: Louisiana State University Press, 1982.

Smith, Melissa. "The Photos That Lifted Up the Black Is Beautiful Movement." *New York Times*, 2018. https://www.nytimes.com/2018/11/27/lens/kwame-brathwaite-black-is-beautiful.html.

Smith, Michael P. *In the Spirit: The Photography of Michael P. Smith*. New Orleans: Historic New Orleans Collection, 2009.

Smith, Michael P., and Alison Milner. *Jazz Fest Memories*. Gretna, LA: Pelican, 1997.

Smith, Ryan P. "Jazz Has Never Looked Cooler Than It Does in This New Exhibition." Smithsonian.com, 2016. www.smithsonianmag.com/smithsonian-institution/jazz-has-never-looked-cooler-than-it-does-new-exhibition-180960191/.

Smith, Shawn Michelle. "'Looking at One's Self through the Eyes of Others': W. E. B. Du Bois's Photographs for the 1900 Paris Exposition." *African American Review* 34, no. 4 (2000): 581–600.

Smith, Shawn Michelle. *Photography on the Color Line: W. E. B. DuBois, Race and Visual Culture*. Durham, NC: Duke University Press, 2004.

Smith, Shawn Michelle. "Unfixing the Frame(-up): A. P. Bedou." In *Pictures and Progress: Early Photography and the Making of African American Identity*, edited by Maurice O. Wallace and Shawn Michelle Smith, 267–73. Durham, NC: Duke University Press, 2012.

Smith, Susan J. "Performing the (Sound) World." *Environment and Planning D: Society and Space* 18 (2000): 615–37.

Smith, Zoe C. "Black Star Picture Agency: Life's European Connection." *Journalism History* 13, no. 1 (1986): 19–25. https://files.eric.ed.gov/fulltext/ED244286.pdf.

Smith, Zoe C. "Fritz Goro on Tape: An Émigré Photojournalist's Professional Biography," paper presented at the Annual Meeting of the Association for Education in Journalism and Mass Communication. Memphis, TN, 1985.

Snelson, Floyd. "Don Albert Tries for 'Comeback.'" *Pitsburgh Courier*, October 20, 1937: 30.

Snitzer, Herb. *Glorious Days and Nights: A Jazz Memoire*. Jackson: University of Mississippi Press, 1988.

Snyder, Joel, and Neil Walsh Allen. "Photography, Vision and Representation." *Critical Inquiry* 2, no. 1 (1975): 143–70.

Sobieszek, Robert A. *The Art of Persuasion: A History of Advertising Photography*. New York: Harry N. Abrams, 1988.

Society, Minnesota Historical. "Directory of Minnesota Photographers." https://www.mnhs.org/people/photographers/S.php.

Society, New York Historical. "Guide to the Alexander Alland Photograph Collection: Biographical Note." New York Historical Society Museum and Library, 2011.

Solomon-Godeau, Abigail. *Photography at the Dock: Essays on Photographic History, Institutions, and Practices*. Minneapolis: University of Minnesota Press, 1991.

Spady, James G. "Gardiner, Leon (1892–1945)." In *Dictionary of African Negro Biography*, edited by Rayford W. Logan and Michael R. Winston. New York: W. W. Norton, 1982.

Sparti, Davide. "Images of a Sound: Portraits and Pictures of Jazz." *Imaginations: Journal of Cross-Cultural Image Studies* 1, no. 1 (2014): n.pag.

Spear, Allan H. *The Making of a Negro Ghetto, 1890–1920*. Chicago: University of Chicago Press, 1967.

Spence, Charles, Nancy M. Puccinelli, Dhruv Grewal, and Anne L. Roggeveen. "Store Atmospherics: A Multisensory Perspective." *Psychology and Marketing* 31, no. 7 (2014): 472–88. https://doi.org/NCE ET AL. Psychology and Marketing DOI: 10.1002/mar.

Spence, Charles, and Massimillano Zampini. "The Role of Auditory Clues in Modulating the Perceived Crispness and Staleness of Potato Chips." *Journal of Sensory Studies* 19, no. 5 (2005): 347–63.

Spencer, Michael Thomas. "Pacific Standard Time: Modernism and the Making of West Coast Jazz." Unpublished Ph.D. Thesis, Michigan State University, 2011.

Spies, Claudio. "Two Apparently Disparate Paragraphs." *Music Theory Spectrum* 34, no. 1 (2012): 25.

Spitzer, David G., and Ira Gitler. *Jazz: Photographs by David G. Spitzer*. San Francisco, CA: Woodford Press, 1994.

Squiers, Carol. "Introduction." In *The Critical Image: Essays on Contemporary Photography*, edited by Carol Squiers, 7–14. Seattle: Bay Press, 1990.

Stange, Maren. "Illusion Complete within Itself: Roy DeCarava's Photography." In *A Modern Mosaic: Art and Modernism in the United States*, edited by Townsend Ludington, 279–305. Chapel Hill: University of North Carolina Press, 2000.

Stange, Maren. *Symbols of Ideal Life: Social Documentary Photography in America 1890–1950*. Cambridge: Cambridge University Press, 1989.

Stein, B. E. and M. A. Meredith, *The Merging of the Senses*. Cambridge, MA: MIT Press, 1993.

Stein, Daniel. *Music Is My Life: Louis Armstrong, Autobiography and American Jazz*. Ann Arbor: University of Michigan Press, 2012.

Steinberg, Kerri P. *Jewish Mad Men: Advertising and the Design of the American Jewish Experience*. New Brunswick, NJ: Rutgers University Press, 2015.

Steiner, Michael C. "Regionalism in the Great Depression." *Geographical Review* 73, no. 4 (1983): 430–46.

Stephenson, Sam. *The Jazz Loft Project: Photographs and Tapes of W. Eugene Smith from 821 Sixth Avenue 1957–65*. New York: Alfred A. Knopf, 2009.

Stern, Bert, and Annie Gottlieb. *The Last Sitting*. New York: William Morrow, 1982.

Stewart, Charles, and Paul Carter Harrison. *Chuch Stewart's Jazz Files*. London: Quartet Books, 1986.

Stewart, Rex, and Claire P. Gordon. *Boy Meets Horn*. Oxford: Bayou Press, 1991.

Stieglitz, Alfred. "Pictorial Photography." In *Classic Essays on Photography*, edited by Alan Trachtenberg, 115–24. New Haven, CT: Leete's Island Books, 1980.

Stimson, Blake. *The Pivot of the World: Photography and Its Nation*. Minneapolis: University of Minnesota Press, 2005.

Stock, Dennis. *Jazz Street*. New York: Doubleday, 1960.

Stoddard, T., ed. *Pops Foster: The Autobiography of a New Orleans Jazzman*. Berkeley: University of California Press, 1971.

Stokes, W. Royal. *Swing Era New York: The Jazz Photographs of Charles Peterson*. Philadelphia: Temple University Press, 1994.

Stonnard, John-Paul. "Artists in Exile." *Burlington Magazine* 151, no. 1272 (2009): 185.

Stott, William. *Documentary Expression and Thirties America*. Chicago: University of Chicago Press, 1986.

Stowe, David W. "The Politics of Cafe Society." *Journal of American History* 84, no. 4 (1988): 1384–1406.

Stryker, Roy Emerson. "The FSA Collection of Photographs." In *Photography in Print: Writings from 1816 to The Present*, edited by Vicki Goldberg, 349–54. Alberqueque: University of New Mexico Press, 1981.

Sudhalter, Richard M., Philip R. Evans, and William Dean-Myatt. *Bix: Man & Legend*. London: Quartet Books, 1974.

Sudnow, David. *Ways of the Hand: A Rewritten Account*. Cambridge, MA: MIT Press, 2001.

Sullivan, George. *Black Artists in Photography 1840–1940*. Dutton: Cobblehill Books, 1996.

Susman, Warren. *Culture as History: The Transformation of American Society in the Twentieth Century*. New York: Pantheon Books, 1984.

Sutton, Mathew. "Bitter Crop: The Aftermath of' Lady Sings the Blues'." *a/b: Auto/Biography Studies*, 27, no. 2 (2012): 294–315.

Swidler, Ann. "Culture in Action: Symbols and Strategies." *American Sociological Review* 51, no. 2 (1986): 273–86.

Sylvester, Robert. *No Cover Charge: A Backwards Look at the Night Clubs of New York*. London: Peter Davis, 1936.

Szarkowski, John. *Looking at Photographs: 100 Pictures from the Collection of The Museum of Modern Art*. New York: The Museum of Modern Art, 1973.

Szarkowski, John. "New Documents, Press Release." New York: Museum of Modern Art, 1967. https://www.moma.org/momaorg/%0Dshared/pdfs/docs/press_archives/3860/releases/MOMA_1967_Jan-June_0034_21.pdf.

Szirtes, George. "A Horse, a Circus and a Suit Case of Photographs." In *Eyewitness: Hungarian Photography in the Twentieth Century*, edited by Peter Baki, Colin Ford, and George Szirtes, 34–41. London: Royal Academy of Arts, 2011.

Szwed, John F. *So What: The Life of Miles Davis*. London: Arrow Books, 2003.

Szwed, John F. *Jazz 101: A Complete Guide to Learning and Loving Jazz*. New York: Hyperion, 2000.

Tackley, Catherine. "Recording as Social Text." In *Recorded Music: Performance, Culture and Technology*, edited by Amanda Bayley, 167–86. Cambridge: Cambridge University Press, 2010.

Tagg, John. "Neither Fish nor Flesh." *History and Theory* 48, no. 4 (2009): 77–81.

Tagg, John. *The Burden of Representation: Eassys on Photographies and Histories.* London: Macmillan, 1988.

Tanner, Lee. *The Jazz Image: Masters of Jazz Photography*. New York: Abrams, 2006.

Tawney, Raj. "The Dave Brubeck Quartet's 'Time Out' at 60: Inside Jazz's First Million-Selling LP." Billboard.com, 2019. https://www.billboard.com/articles/news/8545907/dave-brubeck-quartet-time-out.

Taylor, Billy. "Foreword." In *Chuck Stewart's Jazz Files*, 7. London: Quartet Books, 1986.

Taylor, Joshua C. *Learning to Look: A Handbook for the Visual Arts*. Chicago: University of Chicago Press, 1957.

Taylor, Quintard. *The Forging of a Black Community: Seattle's Central District from 1870 through the Civil Rights Era*. Seattle, WA: University of Washington Press, 1999.

Teachout, Terry. "Too Cool to Cash in, Favorite of the Few." *New York Times*, December 31, 1997: S.2, 34.

"The American Photographic Exchange Club." *Image: Journal of Photography of the Geaorge Eastman House* 1, no. 2 (1952): 4.

"The Black Press: Soldiers without Swords: Press Release." PBS, 2019. https://www.pbs.org/blackpress/film/pressrelease.html.

The Camerads. Blue Book of Amateur Photographers, the New Photographic Club Directory, American Societies, Boston, MA, 1893.

Thomas, Julia Adeney. "The Evidence of Sight." *History and Theory* 48, no. 4 (2009): 151–68.

Thomas, Kevin. "When Sex Was Innocent, Sweet and Seductive." *Los Angeles Times-Book Review*, 2002.

Thompson, Shirley. " 'Ah Toucoutou, Ye Conin Vous': History and Memory in Creole New Orleans." *American Quarterly* 53, no. 2 (2001): 232–66.

Tiryakian, Edward A. "Sociological Perspectives on the Stranger." *Soundings: An Interdisciplinary Journal* 56, no. 1 (1973): 45–58.

Torosian, Michael. *Black Star: The Ryerson University Historical Print Collection of the Black Star Publishing Company*. Toronto: Lumiere Press, 2013.

Townsend, Peter. *Jazz in American Culture*. Edinburgh: Edinburgh University Press, 2000.

Trachtenberg, Alan. "Photography and Social Knowledge." *American Art* 29, no. 1 (2015): 5–8.

Trachtenberg, Alan. "Signifying the Real: Documentary Photography in the 1930s." In *The Social and the Real: Political Art of the 1930s in the Western Hemisphere*, edited by Alejandro Anreus, Diana L. Linden, and Jonathan Weinberg, 3–20. University Park: Pennsylvania State University Press, 2006.

Tucker, Jennifer. "Entwined Practices: Engagements with Photography in Historical Inquiry." *History and Theory* 48, no. 4 (2009): 1–8.

Tucker, Sherrie. "A Feminist Perspective on New Orleans Jazz Women." Lawrence, KS: University of Kansas, 2004.

Tucker, Sherrie. "Bordering on Community: Improving Women, Improvising Women in Jazz." In *The Other Side of Nowhere: Jazz Improvistion and Comunities in Dialogue*, edited by Daniel Fischlin and Ajay Heble, 244–67. Connecticut: Wesleyan University Press, 2004.

Tucker, Sherrie. "Deconstructing the Jazz Tradition: The 'Subjectless Subject' of New Jazz Studies." In *Jazz/Not Jazz: The Music and Its Boundaries*, edited by David Ake, Charles Hiroshi Garrett, and Daniel Goldmark, 264–84. Berkeley: University of California Press, 2012.

Tucker, Sherrie. *Swing Shift: "All-Girl" Bands of the 1940s*. Durham, NC: Duke University Press, 2000.

Tucker, Sherrie. "Telling Performances: Jazz History Remembered and Remade by the Women in the Band."*Oral History Review* 26, no. 1 (1999): 67–84.

Tulloch, Carol, *The Birth of Cool: Style Narratives of the African Diaspora*. London: Bloomsbury, 2016.

Turezky, Bertram. "Introduction." In *Pops Foster: The Autobiography of a New Orleans Jazzman*, edited by Tom Stoddard, xi–xxii. Berkeley: University of California Press, 1971.

Turner DeCarava, Sherry. "Celebration." In *Roy DeCarava Photographs*, edited by James Alinder, 7–20. Carmel, CA: Friends of Photography, 1981.

Turner DeCarava, Sherry. "Roy DeCarava." *Massachusetts Review* 29, no. 3 (1988): 477–92.

Turner, Thomas. "Being Bop: How the Press Shaped the Cult of Bebop." *Jazz Research Journal* 1, no. 2 (2007): 205–24.

Tuttle, William M. *Race Riot: Chicago in the Red Summer of 1919*. New York: Atheneum, 1970.

Ulanov, Barry. "Evaluation." In *A History of Jazz in America*, 336–48. Viking Press, 1952.

Ullrich, Sebastien. *Der Weimar-Komplex: Das Scheitern Der Ersten Deutschen Demokratie Und Die Politische Kultur Der Frühen Bundesrepublik 1945–1959*. Berlin: Wallstein Verlag, 2009.

Vacher, Peter. *Swingin' on Central Avenue: African American Jazz in Los Angeles*. Lanham, MD: Rowman & Littlefield, 2015.

Vail, Ken. *Swing Era Scrapbook: The Teenage Diaries and Radio Logs of Bob Inman 1936–38*. Lanham, MD: Scarecrow Press, 2005.

Vaillant, Derek W. "Sounds of Whiteness: Local Radio, Racial Formation, and Public Culture in Chicago, 1921–1935." *American Quarterly* 54, no. 1 (2002): 25–66.

Vausort, Marc, and Xavier Canonne. *Clemens Kalischer: Le Flux Du Quotidien*. Charleroi: Musée de la Photographie, n.d.

Vettel-Becker, Patricia. *Shooting from the Hip: Photography, Masculinity and Postwar America*. Minneapolis: University of Minnesota Press, 2005.

Vinzent, Julia. "The Other as Other: Refugee Artists and Black Subjects." In *Forced Journeys: Artists in Exile in Britain c.1933–45*, edited by Shulamith Behr and Sander L. Gilman, 80–85. London: Ben Uri Gallery, 2009.

Vishochil, Larry. "Photography." Encyclopedia of Chicago, n.d. http://www.encyclopedia.chicagohistory.org/pages/967.html.

Viskochil, Larry A. "The Elephant That Never Forgets." In *Chicago at the Turn of the Century in Photographs*, edited by Larry A. Viskochil, ix–xv. New York: Dover Publications, 1984.

Vitello, Paul. "Bert Stern, Eilte Photographers Known for Images of Marlyn Monroe, Dies at 83." *New York Times,* June 27, 2013: S.B, 17.

Vowinkel, Anette. *Agenten Der Bilder: Fotografisches Handeln Im 20. Jahrhundert*. Göttingen: Wallstein, 2016.

Wajda, Shirley Teresa. "History Writing, With Light." *Reviews in American History* 26, no. 3 (1998): 565–74.

Wald, Gayle F. *Shout, Sister, Shout!: The Untold Story of Rock-and-Roll Trailblazer Sister Rosetta Tharpe*. Boston, MA: Beacon Press, 2007.

Wallace, Maurice O., and Shawn Michelle Smith. "Introduction." In *Pictures and Progress: Early Photography and the Making of African American Identity*, edited by Maurice O. Wallace and Shawn Michelle Smith, 1–17. Chapel Hill: Duke University Press, 2012.

Walling, William. "The Politics of Jazz: Some Preliminary Notes." *Journal of Jazz Studies* 2, no. 1 (1974): 46–60.

Walsah, Colleen. "The Soul of a Jazz Man." *Harvard Gazette*, 2019. https://news.harvard.edu/gazette/story/2019/10/the-sound-of-my-soul-brings-frank-stewarts-photos-into-focus-at-cooper-gallery/.

Walser, Robert. "Deep Jazz: Notes of Interiority, Race, and Criticism." In *Inventing the Psychological: Toward a Cultural History of Emotional Life in America*, edited by Joel Pfister and Nancy Schnog, 271–96. New Haven, CT: Yale University Press, 1997.

Walser, Robert. "Valuing Jazz." In *The Cambridge Companion to Jazz,* edited by Mervyn Cooke and David Horn, 301–20. Cambridge: Cambridge University Press, 2002.

Wang, Richard. "Researching the New Orleans-Chicago Jazz Connection: Tools and Methods." *Black Music Research Journal* 8, no. 1 (1988): 101–12.

Ward, Geoffrey C., and Ken Burns. *Jazz: A History of America's Music.* London: Pimlico, 2001.

Washburn, Partick S. *The African American Newspaper: Voice of Freedom.* Evanston, IL: Northwestern University Press, 2006.

Watkins, Holly. "Musical Ecologies of Place and Placelessness." *Journal of the American Musicological Society* 64, no. 2 (2011): 404–8.

Webster, Jenna. "Ben Shahn and the Master Medium." In *Ben Shahn's New York: The Photography of Modern Times,* edited by Deborah Martin Kao, Laura Katzman, and Jenna Webster, 75–96. Cambridge, MA: Harvard University Art Museum, 2000.

Weinreich, Regina. *The Spontaneous Poetics of Jack Kerouac: A Study of the Fiction.* New York: Paragon House, 1990.

Weisberg, Ruth. "Between Exile and Irony: Modernism, Postmodernism, and Jewish Modes of Thought." In *You Should See Yourself: Jewish Identity in Postmodern American Culture,* edited by Vincent Brook, 157–75. New Brunswick, NJ: Rutgers University Press, 2006.

Weissman, Terri. *The Realisms of Berenice Abbott: Documentary Photography and Political Action.* Berkeley: University of California Press, 2011.

Welburn, Ron. "Jazz Magazines of the 1930s: An Overview of Their Provocative Journalism." *American Music* 5, no. 3 (1987): 255–70.

Wells, Christopher J., "You Can't Dance to It," Daedalus, 148, No. 2: 36–51.

Wertheim, Arthur Frank. *Vaudeville Wars: How the Keith-Albee and the Orpheum Circuits Controlled the Big-Time and Its Performers.* New York: Palgrave Macmillan, 2006.

Westerbeck, Colin, and Joel Meyerowitz. *Bystander: A History of Street Photography.* Boston, MA: Little, Brown, 1994.

Weston, Edward. *The Daybooks of Edward Weston, Vol. 2.* Edited by Nancy Newhall. New York: Aperture, 1973.

Weyers, Frank. "Wendepunkte." In *Und Sie Haben Deutschland Verlassen...Mussen: Fotografen Und Ihre Bilder 1928–1997,* edited by Klaus Honnef and Frank Weyers, 23–28. Bonn: Rheinisches Landesmuseum Bonn, 1997.

Whalen, Mark. *American Culture in the 1910s.* Edinburgh: Edinburgh University Press, 2010.

Whyton, Tony. *Jazz Icons: Heroes, Myths and the Jazz Tradition.* Cambridge: Cambridge University Press, 2010.

Wiebe, Robert H. *The Search for Order: 1877–1920*. New York: Hill and Wang, 1967.
Wilber, Bob. "The Mysterious Rabbit." *Blue Light: The Journal of the Duke Ellington Society UK* 26, no. 4 (2019): 6–12.
Wilder, Kelley E. "Disdéri, André-Adolphe-Eugène." *Oxford Companion to the Photograph*. Oxford: Oxford University Press, 2005.
Wilkinson, Helen. "'The New Heraldry': Stock Photography, Visual Literacy and Advertising in 1930s Britain." *Journal of Design History* 10, no. 1 (1997): 23–38.
Willens, Doris. *Nobody's Perfect: Bill Bernbach and the Golden Age of Advertising*. Seattle, WA: CreativeSpace, 2009.
Williams, Cecil J. *Freedom and Justice: Four Decades of the Civil Rights Struggle as Seen by a Photographer of the Deep South*. Orangeburg, SC: Mercer University Press, 1995.
Williams, Charles. *African American Life and Culture in Orange Mound: Case Study of a Black Community in Memphis, Tennesse 1890–1980*. Lanham, MD: Lexington Books, 2013.
Williams, Lisa R. "The Furious Battleground: World War 1 and the Development of Jazz in American Popular Culture." *Jazz Perspectives* 8, no. 2 (2014): 153–84.
Williams, Martin. *Jazz Masters of New Orleans*. New York: Macmillan, 1967.
Williams, Martin. *The Art of Jazz: Ragtime to BeBop*. New York: Da Capo, 1981.
Williams, Martin, *Jazz Heritage*. New York: Oxford University Press, 1985.
Williams, Raymond. *Keywords*. Croon Helm: Fontana, 1976.
Williams, Raymond. *Marxism and Literature*. Oxford: Oxford University Press, 1977.
Williams, Raymond. "Metropolitan Perceptions and the Emergence of Modernism." In *The Politics of Modernism: Against the New Conformists*, edited by Tony Pinkney, 37–48. London: Verso, 1989.
Williams, Richard. *Miles Davis: The Man in the Green Shirt*. London: Bloomsbury, 1993.
Williams, Richard. *The Blue Moment: Miles Davis's Kind of Blue and the Remaking of Modern Music*. London: Faber & Faber, 2010.
Williams, Ted. *Jazz: The Iconic Images of Ted Williams*. London: Iconic Images, 2016.
Willis-Braithwaite, Deborah. "They Knew Their Names." In *Van Der Zee Photographer 1886–1983*, edited by Deborah Willis-Braithwaite and C. Birt, Ridger, 8–25. New York: Harry N. Abrams, 1994.
Willis-Thomas, D. *An Illustrated Bio-Bibliography of Black Photographers: 1940–1988*. New York: Garland, 1989.
Willis-Thomas, Deborah. *Black Photographers, 1840–1940: An Illustrated Bio-Bibliography*. New York: Garland, 1985.

Willis, Deborah. "Imagining Themselves: Photography, Race and Representation, 1945–1980." In *Identity and Affirmation: Post War African American Photography*, edited by R. Kent Kirkton, 6–11. California State University, 2011.
Willis, Deborah. "Introduction." In *Teenie Harris Photographer: Image, Memory, History*, edited by Cheryl Finley, Laurence Glasco, and Joe Trotter, xi–xiv. Pittsburgh: University of Pittsburgh Press, 2011.
Willis, Deborah. "Photographing Memphis: The Memphis World." In *Photographs from the Memphis World 1949–1964*, edited by M. Pacini, 11–15. Memphis, TN: Memphis Brooks Museum of Art and University Press of Mississippi, 2008.
Willis, Deborah, ed. *Picturing Us: African American Identity in Photography*. New York: New Press, 1994.
Willis, Deborah. *Posing Beauty: African American Images from the 1890s to the Present*. New York: W. W. Norton, 2000.
Willis, Deborah. *Reflections in Black: A History of Black Photographers 1840 to the Present*. New York: W. W. Norton, 2000.
Wilmer, Val. *As Serious as Your Life: John Coltrane and Beyond*. London: Allison & Busby, 1992.
Wilson, Elizabeth. *Adorned in Dreams: Fashion and Modernity*. Berkeley: University of California Press, 1987.
Wilson, Olly. "The Heterogeneous Sound Ideal in African American Music." In *Signifyin(g), Sanctifyin' and Slam Dunking: A Reader in African American Expressive Culture*, edited by Gena Dagel Caponi, 157–71. Amherst: University of Massachusetts Press, 1999.
Wimsatt, William, and Monroe C. Beardsley. "The Intentional Fallacy." *Swanee Review* 54 (1946): 468–88.
Winklbauer, Andrea. *Vienna's Shooting Girls - Jüdische Fotografinnen Aus Wien*. Judisches Museum Wien, 2012.
Winston, Brian. "A Whole Technology of Dyeing: A Note on Ideology and the Apparatus of the Chromatic Moving Image." *Daedalus* 114, no. 4 (1985): 105–23.
Wipplinger, Jonathan O. *The Jazz Republic: Music, Race and American Culture in Weimar Germany*. Ann Arbor: University of Michigan Press, 2017.
Wohl, Richard. *The Generation of 1914*. Cambridge, MA: Harvard University Press, 1980.
Wolff, Daniel J., and Ernest C. Withers. *The Memphis Blues Again: Six Decades of Memphis Music Photographs*. New York: Viking Studio, 2001.
Wolff, Janet. *The Social Production of Art*. London: MacMillan, 1993.
Wolseley, Roland E. *The Black Press, U.S.A.* Ames: Iowa State University Press, 1980.

Wood, Brian. *The Song For Me: A Glossary of New Orleans Musicians (And Others of That Ilk)*. Walmer, Kent: Brian Wood, 1999.
Wood, Jessica. "Carnival of Swing: Uncovering an Historic Jazz Concert at Randall's Island Stadium, 1938." New York Public Library, 2018. https://www.nypl.org/blog/2018/09/25/carnival-swing-jazz-randalls-island-stadium-photos-1938.
Woodham, Jonathan M. *Twentieth-Century Design*. Oxford: Oxford University Press, 1997.
Woodward, Richard B. "Behind a Century of Photos, Was There a Jewish Eye?" *New York Times*, July 7, 2002.
Young, Jennifer. "Beyond the Color Line: Jews, Blacks and the American Racial Imagination." *In Geveb: A Journal of Yiddish Studies*, 2016, 1–7.
Zerubavel, Eviatar. *The Fine Line: Making Distinctions in Everyday Life*. Chicago: University of Chicago Press, 1993.
Zuromskis, Catherine. *Snapshot Photography: The Lives of Images*. Cambridge, MA: MIT Press, 2013.

Index

Note: Page numbers in *italic* indicate a figure on the corresponding page.

K

L

Z